ST PETERSBURG DIALOGUES

St Petersburg Dialogues

Or Conversations on the Temporal Government of Providence

JOSEPH DE MAISTRE

Translated and edited by
RICHARD A. LEBRUN

McGill-Queen's University Press
Montreal & Kingston • London • Buffalo

© McGill-Queen's University Press 1993
ISBN 0-7735-0982-8

Legal deposit 1st quarter 1993
Bibliothèque nationale du Québec

Printed in Canada on acid-free paper

This book has been published with the help of a grant from the Canadian Federation for the Humanities, using funds provided by the Social Sciences and Humanities Research Council of Canada.

Canadian Cataloguing in Publication Data

Maistre, Joseph, comte de, 1753-1821
  St Petersburg Dialogues: Or Conversations on the temporal government of Providence

  Translation of: Les soirées de Saint-Pétersbourg.
  Includes bibliographical references and index.
  ISBN 0-7735-0982-8

  1. Providence and government of God. 2. Good and evil. 3. Sacrifice. I. Lebrun, Richard A. (Richard Allen), 1931- . II. Title. III. Title: Conversations on the temporal government of Providence.
  BT96.M34 1993   844 .6   C92-090681.8

Contents

ELUCIDATION ON SACRIFICES

Preface

I owe a great debt to all who have assisted me in preparing this translation. In the first instance, I want to thank Dr William R. Everdell of Saint Ann's School in Brooklyn, New York, who read the entire manuscript. I gratefully acknowledge his encouragement, and his many corrections, suggestions, and translations. I must also thank my colleagues at the University of Manitoba who provided assistance with translations from languages other than French. In particular, Dr Edmund G. Berry, Professor Emeritus of the Department of Classics, provided translations of a large number of Greek and Latin citations. Dr Timothy E. Anna of the Department of History helped with Spanish passages, and Mrs C. Povoledo of the Department of French and Spanish assisted with some Italian passages. Where published translations have been used, these have been acknowledged in the notes. I would also like to thank Dr E.T. Annandale of the Department of French and Spanish for identifying a number of Maistre's citations from eighteenth-century French authors. Lastly, I want to acknowledge the support and assistance of my fellow "maistrian," Professor Jean-Louis Darcel of the Université de Savoie in Chambéry; in particular, I am most grateful to him for sending me a photocopy of the page proofs of his new critical edition of the *Soirées de Saint-Pétersbourg*. His kindness made it possible for me to make a considerable number of corrections and additions to my text.

Introduction

The *St Petersburg Dialogues*, Joseph de Maistre's startling and enigmatic masterpiece, has challenged strong minds ever since its publication in 1821. Maistre himself was quite aware of the greatness of his achievement, even though he never lived to see the work in print. In private correspondence he described it as his "great work," and said that "this book is all that I can do, and all that I can know."[1] Although its importance was not recognized immediately, the work has been acknowledged as a classic of French literature for well over a century. We might have expected that the festive celebration of the bicentenary of the French Revolution would finally elbow the paladin of throne and altar into oblivion. However, just the opposite appears to be happening; interest in his writings and appreciation of his importance continues to grow. Indeed, Sir Isaiah Berlin argues that it is only the horrors of the totalitarian regimes of the twentieth century that have "vindicated the depth and brilliance of a remarkable, and terrifying, prophet of our day."[2] The distinguished literary scholar George Steiner, writing in the context of the bicentenary, identifies Maistre as a "writer of genius" who "represents the counter-revolution in essence," and characterizes his *Dialogues* as being, "together with Galileo's *Dialogo*, the most powerful philosophic-dramatic dialogues written in the West after Plato."[3]

Recognition of Maistre's genius has not, however, inhibited questions about his sanity. Norman Hampson, for example, feels that Maistre's "insistence on the importance of punishment and sacrifice seems to have been an unconscious pretext for indulging his obsession with the infliction of pain, and especially with bloodshed." In the context of a short quotation from the *Dialogues*, Hampson avers that he "cannot help suspecting that he was mentally ill."[4] Similarly, Stephen Holmes, who acknowledges that Maistre was "the most fascinating figure on the European right," and that his "description of violence and cruelty in human history is accurate enough," nevertheless finds Maistre's "account of the origins of gratuitous bloodshed, his whole theory of sacrifice ... obscure to the point of insanity."[5]

How, then, should we interpret the *Dialogues*? Should we dismiss the work as no more than the record of nightmares on the banks of the Neva, or should we agree with George Steiner in acknowledging it as "the principal feat of precise foresight in the history of modern political thought and theory?"[6]

Given the importance and controversial nature of the work, what is astonishing is that the *St Petersburg Dialogues* has never before been made available in a full English translation. It is the only one of Maistre's major works to be so neglected.[7] Reasons for this disregard are not hard to find. The length of the work, the subtle evocation of the ambassador's salon and the unique "white nights" of St Petersburg in the midst of the Napoleonic era, the suppleness with which Maistre handles the cut and thrust of argument, the profundity and breadth of subject matter, the lingering ambiguity of differing points of view vigorously propounded by three engaging personalities, and the abundance of notes in a half-dozen languages, are formidable obstacles to a satisfactory rendering of Maistre's text. Perhaps because they may have appeared more pertinent to immediate political and religious concerns, or because they may have been thought to be more easily understood examples of his thought, or simply because they were shorter, it was other works that caught the attention of translators seeking to make Maistre better known in English.[8] In the *Dialogues*, however, Maistre treated a number of topics that he either did not write about – or touched on only lightly – in the other works already available in English translation. These include a well-developed apologetic for traditional Christian beliefs about Providence, a stinging critique of John Locke's sensationalist psychology, scandalous reflections on the social role of the public executioner and the "divinity" of war, sombre meditations on prayer and sacrifice, and a minicourse on "illuminism."

Moreover, this work is important for literary history as well as for the history of ideas. The literary form is that of the "philosophical conversation," a genre that goes back at least as far as Plato, but that in Maistre's hands reproduces the ambience of an eighteenth-century salon. Just as the French philosophes had used their access to the Paris salons to undermine traditional beliefs, Maistre took advantage of his access to the drawing rooms of Lausanne and St Petersburg for his own apologetic purposes. In the *Dialogues* Maistre captures the charm of salon repartee and puts its appeal at the service of traditional doctrines. The form allowed Maistre to be deliberately provocative and to indulge his taste for paradox, a "methodical extravagance" he judged particularly appropriate for the salon.

In short, there appears ample warrant for attempting an English version of Joseph de Maistre's greatest work. While no translation can ever be completely successful in capturing the nuances of Maistre's marvellous French style, it still seems a worthwhile endeavour to provide as complete and accurate a rendering as possible so that those who are unable to read him in his original language can come to a better understanding and appreciation of his contributions to French and European thought.

With the goal of enhancing understanding and appreciation of Maistre's *Dialogues*, what I will attempt to do in this introduction is situate the work in the context of the author's life, identify and characterize the three speakers in the dialogues, discuss the literary form Maistre chose as a vehicle for his ideas, highlight the topics treated in their conversations, point out how the work exemplifies the author's broad culture and linguistic skills, assess the charge that it was somehow the product of a warped mind, and say something about the book's reception and influence.

At first glance, Joseph de Maistre's professional career in law and diplomacy appears an unlikely milieu to nurture the rich philosophical, religious, and theological flowering of the *St Petersburg Dialogues*.[9] Remarkable as well is that fact that this great French stylist was never French by citizenship. Our author was born in 1753 in the sub-Alpine city of Chambéry in Savoy. Although French in language and culture, Savoy was then a province of the largely Italian kingdom of Piedmont-Sardinia, and Maistre, despite his later emotional and literary identification with the cause of counter-revolution in France, always remained a subject of the House of Savoy.

Joseph de Maistre's father, a life-long official of the Piedmontese monarchy, concluded his career as Second President of the Senate of Savoy, a judicial body similar to a French parlement. In 1778, in recognition of his contribution to the codification of the laws of the realm, he was granted hereditary nobility with the title of count. In origins, however, the Maistre family should be classed among the upper bourgeoisie. Joseph's paternal grandfather had been a cloth merchant in Nice.

As the eldest surviving son, Joseph was expected to follow his father in the legal profession, and after early training with the Jesuits and at the local college, he was sent to study law at Turin. On his return to Chambéry in 1772, he entered the magistrature. A hard-working and competent jurist, he advanced at a normal pace in his profession, being named a Senator in 1788, just on the eve of the great upheaval in France. He married in 1786, and on the death of his father in 1789 inherited a modest fortune. If the French Revolution had not intervened, Maistre might well have devoted his life to routine legal affairs and published nothing of importance.

There was little in these pre-revolutionary years to forecast the later publicist of reaction. From 1774 to 1790 he belonged to Masonic lodges in Chambéry and associated with a more esoteric and "illuminist" brand of Scottish Rite Masons in neighbouring Lyon. This link may appear odd for a future Catholic apologist, but at the time these clubs were often frequented by priests and bishops as well as Catholic noblemen. The lodges were opportune places for an ambitious young man to make friends useful for advancement and to discuss political reforms. In addition, the mystical doctrines popular in the Masonic circles Maistre frequented appeared to him a providential counter-force to the rationalism and irreligion of the time. In an unpublished memoir he wrote in 1781, he suggested that the fraternity act as a kind of power behind the throne to enlighten and guide monarchs, and he proposed that one of the goals of Masonry should be the reunion of the Christian churches. Even after he dissociated himself from the lodges in about 1790, he retained an interest in the doctrines he had encountered in this milieu. Maistre's treatment of illuminism in the *Dialogues* was informed by a lifetime familiarity.

In addition to his legal work and his Masonic activities, the young magistrate also devoted long hours to scholarly and literary activities. He polished his linguistic skills and read extensively in classical and contemporary authors, including those of the Enlightenment. He would become a bitter opponent of the philosophes and their ideas, but he never doubted their importance. Maistre's earliest writings were the kind of set pieces expected of young magistrates, orations for opening sessions of the Senate. However, we know from surviving notebooks and correspondence that he was consciously honing his literary style, and his papers include an untitled "dialogue" in his hand that must have been written between 1786 and 1789.[10] This dialogue involves a lively exchange between a Mr Dennis, who uses contemporary natural law arguments to defend freedom of the press, and a court "President," who argues, from the unitary nature of sovereignty, that magistrates must enforce existing laws (no matter what their private beliefs about the justice of the laws). It seems a pity that Maistre did not use the dialogue format again until the *St Petersburg Dialogues*, since it is a literary form well-suited to his genius. He was always a very complex man – curious, extremely intelligent, and able to see various facets of issues. His response to the intellectual currents of his time, such as the Enlightenment and the "illuminist" ideas he encountered in Masonic circles, was often simultaneous attraction and repulsion. These tensions, his sense of irony, and his rich intellectual gifts could all find expression in the dialogue. Perhaps one of the ironies of Maistre's relationship to the French Revolution is that it distracted him from a genre that might have won him literary renown at an earlier date.

A close and sympathetic observer of developments in France in the years immediately preceding the Revolution, Maistre looked to the magistrates of the French parlements as the natural leaders of moderate reform, and approved their efforts to force the king to call the Estates-General. Initially enthusiastic about reform possibilities, he may even have considered seeking election to the Estates-General himself; he owned property across the frontier in France and could probably have met the eligibility requirements. In any case, Maistre was soon disillusioned by the news from Versailles. He opposed the joining together of the three orders, and by mid-June 1789 he was predicting that a "deluge of evils" would follow such "levelling."[11] It was the revolutionary legislation of the night of 4 August 1789 that appears to have been decisive in turning Maistre against the Revolution. By September he was thinking of taking up his pen to oppose the current of events. He read Edmund Burke's *Reflections on the Revolution in France* soon after it appeared in 1790 and found that it reinforced his own "anti-democratic and anti-gallican ideas."[12] Alarmed by the spread of revolutionary ideas in Savoy, he offered unsolicited advice to the government in Turin on how to meet the threat. Ironically, because of his earlier involvement with Masonry, Maistre was regarded as a dangerous innovator and his suggestions spurned.

By the time a French army invaded Savoy in September of 1792, Maistre's intellectual opposition to the Revolution and all its works was firmly fixed. He immediately fled to Piedmont with his wife and children, the only native Savoyard senator to do so. Maistre did return to Chambéry briefly in January 1793, in part to protect his property, in part because Turin appeared reluctant to reward his loyalty by offering him a suitable position. However, he soon found he could not support the new French-sponsored regime, and he emigrated again, this time to Switzerland, where he settled in Lausanne and began a new career as a counter-revolutionary publicist.

Maistre's first effort, four *Lettres d'un royaliste savoisien*, published in 1793 for clandestine circulation in French-occupied Savoy, revealed the dilemma of a purely political royalism in an age of democratic revolution. While he complained that political loyalty was becoming a matter of calculation rather than an instinct as it had once been, his own appeal was precisely to enlightened self-interest. He asked his readers to judge the rule of the House of Savoy on its record, and told his fellow Savoyards: "Love your sovereign as you love *order* with all the strength of your intelligence."[13] This was the very rationalism that had repudiated the old order.

Maistre quickly abandoned a purely political analysis in favour of a providential interpretation of events. Although there is good evidence that he had arrived at a thoroughly theological explanation of the French Revolution by the summer of 1794, it was not until early 1797 that the publication of his *Considérations sur la France* announced his new interpretation to the world. Maistre gave cosmic significance to the French Revolution by proclaiming that never had the role of Providence in human affairs been more palpable. Maistre was not the first, of course, to advance a providential interpretation of the Revolution. The Judeo-Christian tradition provided ample precedent for regarding such a catastrophe as the work of Providence and a number of royalist writers had used the theme. Joseph de Maistre, however, presented the theory with distinctive sophistication, force, and clarity. Construing what was happening as both a divine punishment and as a providentially ordained means for the regeneration of France, Maistre was able to condemn the Revolution and the ideas it embodied, and, at the same time, treat it as a necessary prelude to the restoration of the Bourbon monarchy. The political dilemma of the Savoyard royalist had found its resolution in a religious vision of redemption.

Though *Considérations sur la France* was prohibited in France, Maistre's essentially religious interpretation of the Revolution proved popular in émigré circles, and the work, which had been published anonymously, soon went through a number of editions. While it would establish his reputation as a major apologist of throne and altar, the book's immediate effect on Maistre's personal fortunes was disastrous. Called to Turin in early 1797 with the prospect of being named a minister under King Charles-Emmanuel IV, he lost his chance when the French government of the Directory published an intercepted letter from the exiled French pretender's court to Maistre. This correspondence exposed Maistre publicly as the author of the *Considérations* and made it impossible for the Piedmontese king, who was bound by a close alliance with the French, to favour him in any way.

There followed two years of unemployment and grave financial hardship for Maistre and his family in Turin and Venice before he was finally named to the top judicial position on the island of Sardinia. Maistre continued to read broadly during this period, but published practically nothing. Among his papers, however, there is an "Essai sur les Planètes," dated "Venice, 1799," which reveals that Maistre was mediating on some of the problems he would one day explore in the *St Petersburg Dialogues*. Although the manuscript was entitled "Essay on the planets," it deals with philosophical and religious issues, not astronomy. Maistre's concern was to protest the way the philosophes had exploited astronomy "to diminish man" by stressing the immense distances of space and by ridiculing the idea that this vast universe could have been made for humanity. He based his case on a couple of statements he put forward as incontestable metaphysical axioms. Since "everything has been created *by* and *for* intelligence," and since the universe is only "a system of invisible things visibly manifested" (Hebrews 11:5), for Maistre it followed that the whole universe had to be related to created intelligence and to humanity in particular. The argument led Maistre to theorize about the possibility that the other planets might be inhabited, and to speculate about the nature of intelligence, which he argued had to be something "absolute," essentially the same in the deity, angels, and men.[14] In short, the piece displays a hint of the imagination and verve that will characterize the *Dialogues*.

Maistre's tenure as Regent of Sardinia, from January 1800 to February 1803, meant unrewarding efforts to bring some measure of orderly civilian justice to a rebellious population, misunderstanding and quarrels with a viceroy who preferred vigorous military methods, the complete lack of the sophisticated salon milieu Maistre had come to enjoy in Lausanne, and almost no time for reading or composition. It is no wonder he welcomed his appointment as ambassador to St Petersburg as a stroke of good fortune, even though he had to leave his family behind.

The fourteen years (1803–17) Joseph de Maistre spent in the Russian capital were the most productive years of his life. His official position as the envoy of the Sardinian monarchy at the court of the tsar gave him opportunities to play a number of roles. In addition to representing Sardinia, Maistre was consulted by the exiled Louis XVIII of France and involved himself in Russian politics (becoming at one point a secret adviser to Tsar Alexander). He became a familiar figure in the salons of St Petersburg, where he won friends and influenced people in the French émigré community, the diplomatic community, and elite Russian families. He was also a close associate of the Jesuit community, using his influence at the Russian court on their behalf, and with them, proselytising for Catholicism. Finally, amidst all these activities, he found time to continue serious studies and to write his most important works, including the *St Petersburg Dialogues*.

Using methods analogous to those used by Benjamin Franklin in Paris as representative of the rebellious American colonies, Joseph de Maistre did not hesitate to capitalize on his literary reputation and skills to influence people, or to exploit his own personality to advance his chosen cause. The most effective approach open to the impecunious representative of a powerless monarch was to win the friendship of influential people in the diplomatic community and in court circles. Although some who opposed his views spoke slightingly of him as a "salon orator," Maistre did win genuine renown in the drawing rooms of the Russian capital. One Russian observer, years later, still remembered him with awe and affection:

Monsieur de Maistre was, without contradiction, the outstanding personage of the time and place where we lived, I mean to say the court of the Emperor Alexander and the time between 1807 and 1820 ... We were all ears when, seated in an armchair, his head high ... Count de Maistre abandoned himself to the limpid course of his eloquence, laughing whole-heartedly, arguing with grace, animating and governing the conversation.[15]

The Count of the *Dialogues* is quite clearly a self-portrait of Maistre himself playing the role of the witty philosopher of reaction.

Attendance at the capital's lively salons was a necessary part of Maistre's duties as a diplomat, but he also enjoyed these social activities for their own sake. These occasions stimulated him to develop his ideas and served as forums where his views could be exposed and tested. The opening paragraphs of the *Dialogues* give us a charming description of many of the things Maistre found so attractive in St Petersburg. The depiction of his study, his books and notebooks, and his relationship with good friends in whose conversation he found enjoyment and stimulation, confirms that Count de Maistre had at hand all he needed for a rich life of the mind.

Considering all his other activities, Maistre's literary productivity during his years in St Petersburg is quite remarkable. In addition to voluminous diplomatic correspondence (which included memoirs that were in themselves minor works) and private letters, Maistre wrote five major works and more than a dozen minor works during his fourteen years in Russia. Only two of these works were published before his return to Italy in 1817, and others were not published until after death in 1821, so it took some time for the full stature of these literary activities to become known.

The first hint that Maistre was thinking of something like the *St Petersburg Dialogues* appears in a private letter written in 1806. Writing to an old acquaintance, he remarked: "For a long time, Monseigneur, I have been thinking of certain dialogues on Providence where I would make it be seen clearly enough, I think, that all these hackneyed complaints about the impunity of crime are only sophisms and manifestations of ignorance."[16] Providentialism, of course, had been a feature of Maistre's thinking since at least 1794, but this is the first indication that he was considering the dialogue as an appropriate literary form for treating the theme. What Maistre himself identified as the "first thought" of his *Dialogues* occurs in an 1808 notebook entry added to the first page of copied excerpts from Seneca and Plutarch on the theme of Providence.[17] Since the opening scene of the *Dialogues* is set on a summer evening in 1809, we can assume that at least the first dialogues date from that year. In April 1813, Maistre described his "great work" as "far advanced."[18] We know that Xavier de Maistre, the author's brother who was himself also an author, provided suggestions for revision on most of the work before Joseph left Russia.[19] Others there may also have been allowed to read the manuscript.[20] Occasional references to the work in his correspondence in the later years of his life, and the dates of publication of works cited in the notes, suggest that Maistre kept polishing his masterpiece as long as he lived. Although he died before he had the opportunity to complete the final dialogue to his satisfaction, it seems that about all that remained unfinished was an appropriate closing scene. The very short "sketch of a final piece," first published in 1851, consists of farewell remarks by the Count to his interlocutors, the Chevalier and the Senator.

If the real-life identity of the Count of the *Dialogues* was undoubtedly the ambassador himself, the identification of the other participants in the dialogues is not so certain. While the characters are in part literary creations of Maistre's imagination, commentators have not failed to find their models among the author's friends and acquaintances in St Petersburg.[21] The Russian Senator, introduced by Maistre in the *Dialogues* as "Privy Councillor T***," is most likely based on a certain Tamara, former Russian ambassador to Constantinople and a brother-in-law of Kotochoubei, a well-known minister of the tsar. Tamara is known to have been an enthusiastic admirer of German mysticism, Swedenborg, and Jung-Stilling, as well as Labzine, who introduced German theosophy to Russia. In the *Dialogues* Maistre also makes the Senator a representative of Russian Orthodoxy.[22]

The third figure of the dialogues, introduced as "Chevalier de B***, a young Frenchman," has been linked with three different émigrés Maistre knew in St Petersburg in these years. The first, the Marquis de Romance-Mesmon, was a close friend of Maistre; but the initial is wrong, and what is more important, so is his age, since he was eight years older than Maistre himself. The second candidate is the Count de Blacas, who was the unofficial representative of the French pretender in St Petersburg from 1804 to 1808, and with whom Maistre later carried on a long correspondence.[23] Blacas was seventeen years younger than Maistre, but he was no longer in St Petersburg in July 1809, the date the author gives for the first dialogue. So the more likely real-life model was the Chevalier François Gabriel de Bray, who was the Bavarian ambassador to St Petersburg from 1809 to 1812.

From an old Norman family, Bray had begun his varied career by entering the Order of Malta as a very young man. Then he had turned to diplomacy, and in 1789 was serving with a French delegation at the Diet of Ratisbon. Following the overthrow of the monarchy in August 1792, he abandoned French service, and after extensive travels in Germany, Switzerland, Holland, England, and Austria, he served as a counsellor for the Order of Malta at the Congress of Rastadt in 1797. In 1799 the order sent him to St Petersburg on an important mission. After a similar mission to London, he served as the Bavarian ambassador in Berlin from 1801 to 1808, where he married the daughter of a Livonian count. Bray then obtained the same post in St Petersburg, where he met Joseph de Maistre. Bray's sympathies for Napoleon did not prevent their friendship, and Maistre was a frequent guest at Bray's salons. Something of an intellectual, Bray would later publish books on the history of Livonia. He loved Germany, and was well read in learned works on German medieval history as well as philosophy. Portrait or not, the Chevalier of the *Dialogues* does resemble what is known of the Chevalier de Bray.

The full French title of Maistre's *St Petersburg Dialogues* is *Les Soirées de Saint-Pétersbourg ou Entretiens sur le Gouvernement Temporel de la Providence*. A recent commentator on the *Dialogues* thinks that the term *entretien* was "undoubtedly" suggested to Maistre by Malebranche's *Entretien sur la métaphysique et la religion*.[24] This seems unlikely, however, since there is no evidence Maistre knew any of Malebranche's works beyond the *Recherche de la vérité*.[25] On the other hand, Maistre owned Fontenelle's *Entretiens sur la pluralité des mondes* as well as the same author's *Dialogues des morts*.[26] Moreover there is a reference in the *Dialogues* to *Les Entretiens et colloques spirituelles* of St Francis de Sales.[27] Whatever the case, Maistre very consciously chose the term "*entretien*" for his work. He has the Chevalier, in the discussion that opens the Eighth Dialogue, distinguish among the three terms: "*conversation*," "*dialogue*," and "*entretien*." The first two of these words have about the same meaning in English as in French, but there is no good English equivalent to the third French word, at least as Maistre defines and uses it.[28] According to Maistre's Chevalier, mere conversation is characterized by random disorganized talk among any number of speakers, while a "dialogue" is clearly a work of fiction. An "*entretien*" is more serious. It supposes a subject, and if the subject is important, it must follow the rules of dramatic art, which means the *entretien* will not admit a fourth speaker. Moreover, unlike the case with a (fictional) "dialogue," where an author may designate his characters with capital letters, an *entretien* involves "very real, very palpable human beings" who "are talking to instruct and console each other." At least part of Maistre's artistic intention, then, seems to have been to depict personalities and their discussions as realistically as possible. However, the *Dialogues* are no mere verbatim record. This a work of art, a work of imagination and invention, and it would be a mistake to think that Maistre's own personal points of view are mouthed only by the Count of the *entretiens*. Using the personae of the Senator and the Chevalier allowed the author to air opinions that were more hazardous or heterodox than those for which he was willing to take full responsibility in his public role as the defender of orthodox Catholicism. Moreover, the affirmations of the interlocutors are further nuanced by many, at times lengthy, footnotes and endnotes. Even among the notes there are further subtleties in that some are identified as "Editor's notes" and others are not. In fact, we know from the author's correspondence with Guy-Marie de Place, the scholar who edited Maistre's *Du Pape*, that most, if not all, of these "Editor's notes" in the *Dialogues* were also concocted by Maistre himself.[29]

The announced subject of Maistre's *entretiens*, the "temporal government of Providence," was scarcely original. A long line of Christian apologists, preceded in turn by pagan authors such as Plutarch and Seneca, had developed the classic arguments. Maistre borrows freely from this rich tradition, and usually acknowledges his debts in footnotes or endnotes. Moreover, the discussion of serious philosophical and religious issues was common enough in certain salons of Lausanne and St Petersburg in the years of the French Revolution and Napoleon. What seems more daring and original was Maistre's decision to attempt a literary reproduction of this milieu for apologetic purposes.

The theme of theodicy, justifying the ways of God to men, provides the focus of the *Dialogues*, but Maistre also allows himself the freedom to bring in a host of other topics as well. The amazing diversity of subject matter is one of the characteristics that lends great interest to the *St Petersburg Dialogues*. On the pretext of dealing with challenges to traditional Christian beliefs about Providence, Maistre offers his views on such diverse topics as prayer, prophecy, bloodshed, sacrifice, capital punishment, and war. Other specifically philosophical excursions include speculation on the origin and nature of language, a hard-hitting attack on the epistemological theories of John Locke, and the elaboration of Maistre's own theory of innate ideas. Along the way there are criticisms of particular philosophes, with special attention to Voltaire, Jean-Jacques Rousseau, and David Hume. In addition there is a trenchant critique of scientism, dealing in particular with Francis Bacon, Descartes, and Newton. All this is in the context of general hostility to Protestantism, the Enlightenment, and the French Revolution. Finally, the unfinished Eleventh Dialogue includes a minicourse in "illuminism."

In dealing with all these diverse and interesting topics, Maistre displays his remarkably broad reading and his impressive linguistic skills. Numerous citations and references reveal his familiarity with the Scriptures, his intimate knowledge of Greek and Latin classical authors, and Greek and Latin Church Fathers. He also cites German, Italian, and Spanish authors, illuminist and mystical writings, and Anglican divines. The *Dialogues* show Maistre's broad interests and his knowledge of such topics as the geography and ethnography of the Americas, China, and India, as well as his familiarity with things English and Russian.

The *Dialogues* are also a showcase for Maistre's forensic and polemic proficiency. We should remember that the author was trained as a lawyer and served as a diplomat; he was willing and able to use every trick of argument to make his case.[30] He believed that "it is persuasion that persuades and persuasion never hesitates."[31] If logic and evidence were insufficient, he was quite ready to appeal to authority and emotion. There are passages, such as the famous (or infamous) pieces on the executioner in the First Dialogue and on the "divinity of war" in the Seventh Dialogue, where the reader can easily feel overwhelmed by Maistre's rhetoric. The brilliance of these pages has, in fact, worked against a balanced understanding of the author's position, since they have often been cited or interpreted out of context. The passage on the divinity of war, for example, occurs in an extended argument on the utility of prayer in a world ruled by Providence.[32] One of the advantages of reading these celebrated passages in the context of a complete translation is that the reader will be less tempted to mistake Maistre's occasional literary extravagances as the essence of his position, or as symptoms of mental illness.

In the first place, there is ample evidence that Maistre quite consciously used literary artifice to challenge the assumptions of his age. To a friend who questioned provocative passages in one of his works he replied: "In all these questions, I have two ambitions. The first, would you believe it? *It is not be be right,* it is to force the kind reader to know what he believes."[33] In the second place, it is very significant that the passages cited by those who question Maistre's mental health all occur in his carefully crafted literary works. There is nothing in his private correspondence and diaries, or even in his diplomatic correspondence, to suggest that Maistre was any more obsessed with war and bloodshed than any other witness of the violence of the Revolutionary and Napoleonic era. There are, to be sure, a couple of passages from notebooks dating from his youth in which Maistre fantasized about keeping his father's embalmed corpse near him as an encouragement to virtue – but I would read these as evidence of youthful romanticism rather than hard evidence of mental disorder.[34]

The power and importance of the *St Petersburg Dialogues* does not rest on mere oratorical cleverness. One quickly senses that Maistre's passion is genuine. His religious, philosophical, and political positions are very deeply held. If he sometimes exaggerates to defend the ramparts, it is because it is his profound conviction that the essentials of the doctrines he defends are of the utmost importance for the survival and well-being of European civilization. Clearly, Maistre sees himself as reiterating the foundational truths of the Judeo-Christian tradition. These include the doctrines of God as the creator of all, and the utter dependence of all things, humanity included, on the creating and sustaining will of the deity. Maistre believes that humans have been created in the image and likeness of God, and condemns philosophies that would degrade human beings by denying them this ontological dignity. However, it is the existence of evil in the world, and of human wickedness in particular, that provides the crux of the subject matter of the *Dialogues*.

Though clothed in ironic and paradoxical rhetoric, Maistre's explanation of the mystery of evil and human malevolence is the classic Christian doctrine of original sin. As he puts it, it is "original sin that explains everything and without which nothing is explained."[35] The meaning of history and human social institutions can only be understood by acknowledging some primordial guilt in human nature. History's never-ending parade of injustice, public and private misery, suffering, and war is the direct result of man's fallen state. From this fallen condition there can be no secular escape. Attempts to create "kingdoms of justice," to legislate secular utopias, defy the realities of original sin and divine Providence. Humanity's only real hope for amelioration lies in religious redemption.

As George Steiner emphasizes, this is the essence of the counter-revolutionary position. It postulates, literally and metaphorically, the fact of original sin. "Being theological and prophetic, it is not debatable or negotiable on positivist and ideological terms ... "[36] Maistre's stance embodies a politics of transcendence in the tradition of Plato's *Republic*, Dante, and Shakespeare. Steiner suggests that "it is Maistre's eminence to have applied these archetypal intimations to the modern circumstance, that of 1789, and to have opened his clairvoyance to the proof of ensuing events."[37] We can well ask whether the blood-stained history of the world since Maistre's time has refuted his case.

Apart from instances that had occurred without his authorization, this was the first of Maistre's works to be published with his name (and all his titles) on the title-page. Although it received generally favourable reviews when it appeared,[38] it did not really become popular until after 1850.[39] We can note that some theologically conservative Catholics were scandalized by the speculative spirit of the work, and that it eventually provoked an industrious French abbé to produce three volumes of reflections on its "excesses."[40] While none of Maistre's works were ever officially censured by the Church, this has not deterred some critics from accusing him of having wandered "far outside of orthodox Christianity."[41]

It is noteworthy that for the most part charges of heterodoxy have come, not from Catholic scholars, but from commentators writing from outside the Catholic tradition.[42] Elsewhere I have argued that Maistre's political theory owed more to the assumptions of eighteenth-century theorists than to the scholastic natural law tradition, but I saw no reason to question either the sincerity or essential orthodoxy of his religious beliefs.[43] More recently, Dom Jean-Louis Soltner of the Abbey of Solemnes scrutinized Maistre's Christianity and concluded that it consisted "in a living faith based on the teaching of the supernatural Revelation confided to the Catholic Church."[44] Soltner's most serious reservation about Maistre's orthodoxy concerned the Savoyard's theory of war and sacrifice, which he criticized for its confusion of the natural and the supernatural realms. Where Maistre erred, according to Soltner, was to take the theological doctrine of substitution, by which God is understood to accept Christ's sacrifice (and the sufferings of those who voluntarily accept suffering in Christ's name) for the salvation of other members of the Communion of Saints, and to apply the concept universally as a "law of the world."[45] In strictly orthodox Christian teaching, human suffering *in itself* has no supernatural value, the shedding of blood *in itself* has no sacrificial value. Maistre pushed to extremes his great apologetic idea that Catholic "dogmas are only divinized laws of the world."[46] Soltner excused Maistre's failure to make a clear distinction between the natural order and the supernatural order as a failing common to ninteenth-century Catholics writing before the renewal of the realistic philosophy of Thomas Aquinas.

However, even if Maistre's basic orthodoxy be accepted, it should be noted that much of his argumentation for the existence and justification of Providence suffered from the same ambiguity that had characterized the efforts of most leading Christian apologists in the seventeenth and eighteenth centuries. As Michael J. Buckley has demonstrated, beginning with Lessius (Leanard Leys) in 1613, the major efforts of the defenders of the Christian concept of God against a perceived rising tide of atheism had focused almost exclusively on philosophical argumentation.[47] For various historical reasons, apologists had debated the issues on philosophical grounds (borrowing both their characterization of the problem and their arguments from classical pagan authors). The defence of theism of the major thinkers of the period, such as René Descartes and Isaac Newton, as well as that of their major disciples who tried to use their philosophical and scientific insights for explicitly apologetic purposes, such as Nicolas Malebranche and Samuel Clarke, followed this distinctive pattern. In turn, the atheism of the most radical thinkers of the Enlightenment, men such as Denis Diderot and Baron d'Holbach, was developed and argued against this essentially philosophical exposition of theism. On neither side did the person and teaching of Jesus enter the discussion in any serious way.

Maistre failed to perceive this paradox. He admired the leading exemplars of this peculiar current of apologetics – Lessius, Descartes, Malebranche, Leibniz, Newton, Clarke, Nicolas Bergier, and company – and he borrowed many of his arguments from them. If some of Maistre's critics have complained that his was a religion without Christ, this may well be because he followed these predecessors too closely. On the other hand, Maistre does seem to have sensed the weakness of an exclusively philosophical approach. He argued for the uniqueness and indispensability of the Christian revelation, and he admitted that those who lack a "religious sense" might well remain untouched by his best efforts.[48] Perhaps doubts about Maistre's Christian orthodoxy should be directed towards defects in the apologetic tradition upon which he relied rather than towards deficiencies in his personal religious belief and commitment.

Given its diffuse subject matter, the influence of the *St Petersburg Dialogues* is difficult to estimate. It is easier to trace the impact of particular themes than that of the work as a whole. The powerful pages on the "divinity of war" from the Seventh Dialogue, for example, were picked up in various ways by such diverse writers as Leo Tolstoy, Pierre Joseph Proudhon, and Louis Veuillot, and have been reprinted separately in times of war.[49] However as Saint-Beuve, the great French literary critic, pointed out early on, Maistre was not the sort of writer who left a school or coterie of disciples:

M. de Maistre appears to me, of all writers, the least made for the servile disciple who would take him literally: he misleads him. But he is especially for the intelligent and sincere adversary: he provokes him, he straightens him out ... the disciple who attaches himself to Maistre's very terms and follows him to the letter is *stupid*.[50]

Perhaps George Steiner comes closest to the mark when he suggests that the Maistre's influence has been "subterranean," something more in the nature of a "constant legacy."[51] When one looks closely at those writers who are commonly cited as having been most influenced by Maistre, one finds the relationship to be quite problematic. It is said that Baudelaire's approach to the issues of evil and human guilt owed much to Joseph de Maistre,[52] but if Baudelaire was attracted to some aspects of Maistre's writings he surely owed more to Edgar Allen Poe and to his own dissolute lifestyle (as different as can be from Maistre's). Similarly, Charles Maurras is described as exemplifying "Maistre's bracing pessimism and lucid sense of the infernal in history and politics,"[53] but it seems clear that Maistre himself would have been repelled if not horrified by the atheistic political Catholicism of the Action Française. More surprising still is the attempt to associate Maistre's vision with the "apocalyptic nihilism" of the more recent French writer E.M. Cioran.[54] Perhaps Cioran has in fact modelled his prose on that of Maistre, yet surely this author's cynical and atheistic nihilism is precisely the kind of philosophic stance that Joseph de Maistre would have been the first to repudiate and attack.

The fact is that estimates of the nature of Maistre's importance and influence still vary dramatically. In reading the *St Petersburg Dialogues* in translation, readers will have the opportunity to make their own assessment. Some, with Steiner, may find Maistre's vision as relevant as that of the contemporary prophet, Alexander Solzhenitsyn.[55] Others may agree with the nineteenth-century French liberal critic Charles de Rémusat, who insisted that he had "never read ten pages of Count de Maistre without feeling a profound joy at not thinking like him."[56] What is most unlikely is that the reader will remain indifferent.

NOTES TO THE INTRODUCTION

1 Maistre to Guy-Marie de Place, 9 July 1818, Camille Latrielle, "Lettres inédites de Joseph de Maistre," *Revue bleue* 50 (1912): 293.

2 See Berlin's extended essay, "Joseph de Maistre and the Origins of Fascism," newly edited and published in a volume entitled *The Crooked Timber of Humanity*, edited by Henry Hardy (London: John Murray 1990), 174.

3 See "Aspects of Counter-revolution," in *The Permanent Revolution: The French Revolution and Its Legacy 1789–1989*, ed. Geoffrey Best (Chicago: University of Chicago Press 1988), 144, and "Darkness Visible," *London Review of Books* 10 (24 November 1988).

4 Norman Hampson, *A Cultural History of the Enlightenment* (New York: Pantheon 1968), 264–65.

5 Stephen Holmes, "The Lion of Illiberalism," *New Republic5* 30 October 1990, 33 and 36.

6 Steiner, "Darkness Visible."

7 *The Works of Joseph de Maistre*, ed. and trans. Jack Lively (New York: Macmillan 1965), does contain excerpts from all eleven dialogues, but with almost all Maistre's notes omitted.

8 In chronological order, the works translated into English include: *Letters on the Spanish Inquisition* (London 1843), *Essay on the Generative Principle of Political Constitutions* (London 1847), *The Pope* (London 1850), and *Considerations on France* (London and Montreal 1974).

9 For details on Maistre's life, see Richard A. Lebrun, *Joseph de Maistre: An Intellectual Militant* (Kingston and Montreal: McGill-Queen's University Press 1988).

10 For the text of this piece, see the "Annexe" to Richard Lebrun, "Joseph de Maistre et la loi naturelle," *Revue des études maistriennes* no. 8 (1983): 136–44.

11 See Costa de Beauregard, *Un Homme d'autrefois* (Paris 1878), 83.

12 Maistre to Henry de Costa, January 1791, *Oeuvres complètes de Joseph de Maistre* (Lyons: Vitte 1884–93), 9:11.

13 *Oeuvres*, 7:82–230.

14 This essay is in a notebook labelled "Philosophie D," 653–72. Maistre family archives.

15 Alexander Stourdza, *Oeuvres posthumes* (Paris 1859), 3:170–1.

16 Maistre to Monsignor de la Fare, 25 May 1806. *Oeuvres*, 10:112.

17 In a register entitled "Manuscrits," 455. Maistre family archives.

18 Maistre to Abbé Nicole, 17 April 1813. Cited in Z. Frappez, *Vie de l'abbé Nicole* (Paris: Lecoffre 1857), 97.

19 For a detailed treatment of Xavier's comments and Joseph's replies, see Alfred Berthier, *Xavier de Maistre* (Paris: Vitte 1918), 236–48, 353–56.

20 Alexander Stourdza claimed to have read it under the title "Principes des institutions humaines" (*Oeuvres posthumes*, 3:192), but one wonders if his reference is not to Maistre's *Essai sur le principe générateur*.

21 See Robert Triomphe, *Joseph de Maistre* (Geneva: Droz 1968), 577–82.

22 Confirmation of Tamara's identity as the Senator exists in the form of a note in a jewellery box still treasured in the Maistre family. This note, written by Françoise de Villequier (Countess Charles de Maistre) mentions that she was given this souvenir by her mother-in-law, Azelie de Sieyes (Countess Rodolphe de Maistre), who was herself given it by "Countess de Tamara, wife of the Senator of the Soirées de Saint-Pétersbourg." Communication from Jacques de Maistre.

23 See *Joseph de Maistre et Blacas*, ed. Ernest Daudet (Paris: Plan-Nourit 1908).

24 Pierre Vallin, "Les 'Soirées' de Joseph de Maistre: Une création théologique originale," *Revue des Sciences Religieuses* 73/3 (1986): 345.

25 See Richard Lebrun, "Joseph de Maistre et Malebranche," *Revue des études maistriennes* no. 11 (1990): 127–37.

26 See Jean-Louis Darcel, "Les Bibliothèques de Joseph de Maistre 1768–1821," *Revue des études maistriennes* no. 9 (1985): 64.

27 See endnote ii to the Sixth Dialogue.

28 In the absence of a precise English equivilent to *entretien*, the English word "dialogue" is the word that is usually used in this translation for both *entretien* and *dialogue*.

29 Discussing possible publication of his *Soirées* with De Place, Maistre mentions points that could be "cast into the notes of an imaginary editor." Maistre to De Place, 9 July 1818, Camille Latrielle, "Lettres inédites de Joseph de Maistre," *Revue bleue* 50 (1912): 293. See the notes to Jean-Louis Darcel's critical edition of the *Soirées* for evidence on particular notes identified as "Editor's notes" in the 1821 edition.

30 For detailed studies of Maistre's mastery of the classical techniques of rhetoric, see Margrit Finger, *Studien sur literarischen Technik Joseph de Maistres* (Marburg 1972) and Margrit Zopel-Finger, "Quod semper, quod ubique, quod ob omnibus ou L'art de fermer la bouche au novateurs," in *Joseph de Maistre tra Illuminismo et Restaurazione* (Turin 1975).

31 Maistre to Guy-Marie de Place, 9 February 1819, "Lettres inédites," 326.

32 See Richard A. Lebrun, "Joseph de Maistre's 'Philosophic' View of War," *Proceedings of the Annual Meeting of the Western Society for French History* 7 (1979): 43–52.

33 As cited by Saint-Beuve, *Revue des Deux Mondes* 3 (13th year, new series) (1 August 1843): 371.

34 See Lebrun, *Joseph de Maistre*, 17–19.

35 See p. 33 below.

36 Steiner, *Aspects*, 148–9.

37 Ibid.

38 *Le Défenseur*, for example, welcomed it as the work of "one of those powerful geniuses who, rescuing peoples from the edge of an abyss, reinstall them forever in the conservative paths from which they have been diverted by pride and miserable perversity" 5 (1821): 423. However the Abbé Féletz published a much more critical review in the *Journal des Débats* (issues of 18 July, 1 and 2 August 1821).

39 The 1821 edition was followed by a second edition in 1822, but then only four further editions up to 1850. The thirty years from 1850 to 1880, however, saw some twenty-two editions or reprints.

40 J.-B.-M. Nolhac, *Soirées de Rothaval ... ou Réflexions sur les intempérances philosophiques de M. de Comte Joseph de Maistre dans ses Soirées de Saint-Pétersbourg*, 2 vols. (Lyons 1843), and as volume 3, *Nouvelles Soirées de Rothaval, ou Réflexions sur les intempérances théologiques de Joseph de Maistre* (Lyons 1844).

41 Holmes, "The Lion of Illiberalism," 36.

42 Those who have challenged the authenticity of Maistre's Catholicism include: Edmund Scherer, *Mélanges de critique religieuse* (Paris 1860), 293; Adolfo Omodeo, "Cattolicismo e civiltà moderna nel secolo XIX: Un reazianario, Il conte Joseph de Maistre," *La Critica* 34 (March 1936): 118; Aubain Vidalot, *L'Autorité d'après Joseph de Maistre* (Paris 1898), 61; and Bernard Fay, *Revolution and Freemasonry, 1680–1800* (Boston 1935), 293–95.

43 Richard Allen Lebrun, *Throne and Altar: The Political and Religious Thought of Joseph de Maistre* (Ottawa: University of Ottawa Press 1965).

44 "Le Christianisme de Joseph de Maistre," *Revue des études maistriennes* no. 5–6 (1980): 110.

45 Maistre was aware that the doctrine of substitution involved *voluntary* acceptance of suffering; a passing remark in the Tenth Dialogue on the sufferings of humanity notes that "these sufferings are not only useful for the just but ... they can by religious acceptance be turned to the profit of the guilty ..." (See p. 493). It is also true, however, that Maistre very often seems to have neglected this important qualification in the traditional doctrine.

46 *Du Pape, Oeuvres*, 2:x.

47 See Michael J. Buckley, *At the Origins of Modern Atheism* (New Haven and London: Yale University Press 1987).

48 See p. 270 [Ninth Dialogue] below.

49 See Lebrun, "Maistre's 'Philosophic' View of War," 50–52.

50 Charles Augustin Saint-Beuve, *Les Grands Ecrivains français: XIXᵉ siècle, philosophes et essayistes*, ed. Maurice Allem (Paris 1930), 1:89.

51 *Aspects*, 147.

52 See François-Xavier Eygen, "Influence de Joseph de Maistre sur les Fleurs du Mal de Baudelaire," *Revue des études maistriennes* no. 11 (1990): 139–47.

53 Steiner, *Aspects*, 147.

54 Ibid.

55 Ibid., 148.

56 "Du Traditionalisme," *Revue des Deux Mondes* 9 (27th year, 2nd period, 15 May 1857): 245.

Chronology

1753 Joseph de Maistre born at Chambéry, Savoy.

1769 Sent to Turin for his legal education.

1772 Begins legal career in the Senate of Savoy in Chambéry.

1773–92 Membership in Masonic lodges in Chambéry.

1775 Publishes *Eloge de Victor-Amédée III*.

1777 Delivers a "Discours sur la vertu" to the Senate (unpublished until 1896).

1782 Writes "Mémoire au Duc de Brunswick" on Freemasonry (unpublished until 1925).

1784 Delivers a "Discours sur le caractère extérieur du magistrate" to the Senate (unpublished until 1884).

1786 Marriage to Françoise-Margerite de Morand.

1787? Writes an untitled manuscript dialogue that critiques natural law arguments for freedom of the press (unpublished until 1983).

1787 Birth of daughter Adèle.

1788 Writes memoirs on venality of office and the French parlements (unpublished until 1895). Named a senator.

1789	Death of Maistre's father. Birth of son, Rodolphe.
1792	French invasion of Savoy. Maistre flees to Piedmont.
1793	Maistre returns to Chambéry (Jan.–Feb). Following birth of daughter Constance, Maistre departs for Switzerland, where he settles in Lausanne.
	Publishes "Adress de quelques parents des militaires savoisiens" and *Lettres d'un royaliste savoisien à ses compatriotes* (counter-revolutionary pamphlets).
	Named Sardinian "Correspondant" in Lausanne.
1794	Publishes "Discours à la marquise de Costa" (first exposition of Maistre's providential interpretation of the French Revolution).
1794–95	Writes manuscripts entitled "De la Souveraineté du Peuple" and "De l'état de nature," refutations of Rousseau (unpublished until 1870).
1795	Publishes "Jean-Claude Têtu (Adresse du maire de Montagnole à ses conpatriotes)," another counter-revolutionary pamphlet. Writes "Cinq paradoxes à Madame la marquiese de Nav..." (unpublished until 1851). Writes a "Mémoire sur la réunion de la Savoie au corps helvétique" (unpublished until 1961).
1796	Publishes "Mémoire sur les prétendus émigrés savoisiens." Writes *Considérations sur la France*.
1797	*Considérations sur la France* published anonymously. Recalled to Turin, but denied any official post after his authorship of the *Considérations* becomes public knowledge.
1798	Writes "Réflections sur le protestantisme et la souveraineté" (unpublished until 1870).
1799	Takes refuge in Venice. Writes "Discours du citoyen Cherchemot" (a burlesque on revolutionary cant, unpublished until 1884) and an "Essai sur les planètes" (never published).

1800–1803	Serves as regent (chief judicial officer) of the island of Sardinia.
1803-17	Serves as Sardinian ambassador to the court of Tsar Alexander in St Petersburg.
1809	Writes *Essai sur le principe générateur des constitutions politiques et des autres institutions humaines.* Begins composition of the *Soirées de Saint-Pétersbourg.*
1810	Writes "Cinq lettres sur l'éducation publique en Russie" (unpublished until 1851).
1811	Writes "Mémoire sur la liberté de l'enseignement public" (unpublished until 1884) and "Quatre chapitres sur la Russie" (unpublished until 1859).
1814	Publishes *Essai sur le principe générateur* ....
1814–16	Writes *Examen de la philosophie de Bacon* (unpublished until 1836).
1815	Writes *Lettres sur l'inquisition espagnole* (unpublished until 1822).
1816	Publishes a translation of an essay from Plutarch's *Moralia* under the title *Sur les Delais de la justice divine.*
1817	Recalled to Turin.
1819	Publishes *Du Pape.*
1821	Dies on 26 February. Later in the year, publication of the *Soirées de Saint-Pétersbourg* and *De l'église gallicane.*

Critical Bibliography

PRINCIPAL FRENCH EDITIONS OF MAISTRE'S
WORKS AND CORRESPONDENCE

Mémoires politiques et correspondance diplomatique. Ed. A. Blanc. Paris: Librairie Novelle 1858.

Correspondance diplomatique, 1811–1817. Ed. A. Blanc. Paris: Librarie Nouvelle 1860.

Oeuvres complètes, 14 vols. Lyon: Vitte 1884–93.

Joseph de Maistre et Blacas: leur correspondance inédite et l'histoire de leur amitié, 1804–1820. Introduction, notes, and commentary by E. Daudet. Paris: Plan-Nourit 1908.

Les Carnets du Compte Joseph de Maistre: Livre Journal 1790–1817. Published by X. de Maistre. Lyon: Vitte 1923.

Du Pape. Critical edition with an introduction by Jacques Lovie and Joannès Chetail. Geneva: Droz 1966.

Considérations sur la France. Critical edition by Jean-Louis Darcel. Geneva: Slatkine 1980.

Ecrits maçoniques de Joseph de Maistre et de quelques-uns de ses amis franc-maçons. Critical edition by Jean Rebetton. Geneva: Slatkine 1983.

De la souveraineté du peuple. Critical edition by Jean-Louis Darcel. Paris: Presses Universitaire de France 1992. This work was first published in 1870 under the title *Etude sur la souveraineté.*

Les Soirées de Saint-Pétersbourg. Critical edition under the direction of Jean-Louis Darcel. Geneva: Slatkine 1992.

PRINCIPAL ENGLISH TRANSLATIONS OF
MAISTRE'S WORKS

Considerations on France. Trans. Richard A. Lebrun. Montreal: Mc-Gill Queen's University Press 1974.

Essay on the Generative Principle of Political Constitutions. Reprint of 1847 edition. Delmas, NY: Scholars' Facsimiles and Reprints 1977.

Letters on the Spanish Inquisition. Reprint of 1843 edition. Delmas, NY: Scholars' Facsimiles and Reprints 1977.

On God and Society: Essay on the Generative Principle of Political Constitutions and Other Human Institutions. Ed. Elisha Greifer and trans. with the assistance of Lawrence M. Porter. Chicago: Regnery 1959.

The Pope. Trans. Aeneas McD. Dawson. Reprint of 1850 edition with an introduction by Richard A. Lebrun. New York: Howard Fertig 1975.

The Works of Joseph de Maistre. Ed. and trans. Jack Lively. New York: Macmillan 1965. Excerpts from Maistre's most important works, but without critical notes.

SELECTED STUDIES OF JOSEPH DE MAISTRE

Beik, Paul. *The French Revolution Seen from the Right: Social Theories in Motion, 1789–1799.* Philadelphia: American Philosophical Society 1956. The best general introduction to French counter-revolutionary writers.

Berlin, Isaiah, "Joseph de Maistre and the Origins of Fascism," in *The Crooked Timber of Humanity.* Ed. Henry Hardy. London: John Murray 1990. A provocative interpretation of Maistre's significance for the contemporary world.

Dermenghem, Emile. *Joseph de Maistre mystique: ses rapports avec le martinimse, l'illuminisme et la franc-maçonnerie, l'influence du doctrines mystiques et occultes sur sa pensée religieuse.* Paris: La Colombe 1946. Most detailed study of the origins of the mystical side of Maistre's thought.

Descostes, François. *Joseph de Maistre avant la Révolution: souvenirs de la société d'autrefois.* 2 vols. Paris: Picard 1893.

— *Joseph de Maistre pendant la Révolution: ses débuts diplomatiques, le marquis de Sales et les émigrés, 1789–1797.* Tours: A. Mame et fils 1895.

— *Joseph de Maistre orateur.* Chambéry: Perrin 1896.

— *Joseph de Maistre inconnu: Venice–Cagliari–Rome (1797–1803).* Paris: Champion 1904. Descostes made systematic use of private archives that have since disappeared. Consequently his volumes remain extremely useful for many details of Maistre's life.

Gignoux, G.-J. *Joseph de Maistre: prophète du passé, historien de l'avenir.* Paris: Nouvelles Editions Latines 1963. One of the most reliable of the many popular biographies of Maistre in French.

Godchot, Jacques. *The Counter-Revolution: Doctrine and Action, 1789–1804.* New York: Howard Fertig 1971. Includes English and German writers, but the treatment of French writers adds nothing to Beik.

Goyau, Georges. *La Pensée religieuse de Joseph de Maistre d'après des documents inédites.* Paris: Perrin 1921. Dated but useful introduction to the topic.

Greifer, Elisha. "Joseph de Maistre and the Reaction against the Eighteenth Century." *American Political Science Review* 15 (1961): 591–98. Brief introduction putting Maistre in context.

Holdsworth, Frederick. *Joseph de Maistre et Angleterre*. Paris: Campion 1935. Balanced and useful treatment of Maistre's knowledge of and debt to English writers.

Lebrun, Richard. *Throne and Altar: The Political and Religious Thought of Joseph de Maistre*. Ottawa: University of Ottawa Press 1965. Systematic analysis of the relationship between Maistre's religious and political thought.

— "Joseph de Maistre, Cassandra of Science." *French Historical Studies* 6 (1969): 214–31. Analysis of Maistre's critique of eighteenth-century scientism.

— "Joseph de Maistre's 'Philosophic' View of War." *Proceedings of the Annual Meeting of the Western Society for French History* 7 (1981): 43–52. Exploration of the context of Maistre's scandalous views on the divinity of war.

— *Joseph de Maistre: An Intellectual Militant*. Kingston and Montreal: McGill-Queen's University Press 1988. First full biography in English and the first to have benefited from access to the family archives.

— *Maistre Studies*. Lanham, New York, London: University Press of America 1988. Thirteen articles from the *Revue des études maistriennes*, edited and translated by Richard Lebrun.

Lombard, Charles M. *Joseph de Maistre*. New York: Twayne 1976. A helpful introduction from Twayne's World Authors series. A brief treatment based entirely on printed sources and concerned primarily with Maistre's place in literary history.

Maistre, Henri de. *Joseph de Maistre*. Paris: Perrin 1990. Especially stimulating on Joseph de Maistre's psychological development. Henri de Maistre is a direct descendant of Joseph de Maistre; his work benefited from access to the family archives.

Margerie, Amédée de. *Le Comte Joseph de Maistre: sa view, ses écrits, ses doctrines, avec des documents inédits*. Paris: Librairie de la Société Bibliographique 1882. Few unpublished documents, but useful as the first scholarly biography.

Montmasson, J.M. *L'Idée de Providence d'après Joseph de Maistre*. Lyon: Vitte 1928. Only systematic treatment of the central idea of the *Soirées*.

Murray, John Courtney. "Political Thought of Joseph de Maistre." *Review of Politics* 11 (1949): 63–86. Still useful despite the date. Murray, who is credited with authoring the Vatican II document on religious freedom, sketched a remarkably well balanced approach to Maistre.

Revue des études maistriennes. Thirteen numbers published between 1975 and 1990 contain many very useful articles based on access to new primary sources in the Maistre family archives.

Rials, Stéphane. "Lecture de Joseph de Maistre." *Mémoire* 1 (1984): 21–48. Offers a fresh reading of Joseph de Maistre.

Sainte-Beuve, Charles A. *Les Grands Ecrivains français: XIXe siècle; philosophes et essayistes*. Ed. Maurice Allem. Paris: Garnier 1930. Collects all of Saint-Beuve's writings on Maistre. The first to write of Maistre at any length, the great nineteenth-century French critic created what still remains the most enduring characterization of the Savoyard author.

Triomphe, Robert. *Joseph de Maistre: Etude sur la vie et sur la doctrine d'un matérialiste mystique*. Geneva: Droz 1968. Although systematically hostile to its subject, Triomphe's extended study does provide a valuable listing of all Maistre's writings as well as an annotated bibliography of earlier secondary literature in French, English, German, Italian, and Russian.

Vallin, Pierre. "Les 'Soirées' de Joseph de Maistre: Une création théologique originale." *Recherches des Sciences Religieuses* 74 (1986): 341–62. Written as the introduction to the new critical edition of the *Soirées*.

Watt, E.D. "The English Image of Joseph de Maistre." *European Studies Review* 4 (1979): 239–59. A good review of English-language literature on Maistre.

A Note on the Text

This translation of the *Soirées de Saint-Pétersbourg* is made from the edition appearing in Volumes IV and V of the *Oeuvres complètes de Joseph de Maistre* (Lyons: Vitte et Perrussel 1884); I have also consulted the original 1821 edition (Paris: Librairie Grecque, Latine et Française). Moreover, just prior to publishing this translation I had the opportunity to consult the page proofs of Jean-Louis Darcel's new critical edition of the *Soirées* (Geneva: Slatkine 1992); matters of fact (such as the identification of some of Maistre's citations) borrowed from this edition are identified by the notation "(Darcel ed.)."

All Maistre's footnotes and endnotes have been reproduced, but citations in the notes from various other languages have usually been given in English translation only – unless questions relating to etymology, literary style, or the accuracy of Maistre's translation of the particular passage were involved. In such cases the original languages are also cited. The titles of works by classical authors have usually been cited in English language versions.

The original edition of 1821 and subsequent editions of the *Soirées* include footnotes and endnotes identified with the notation "*Note de l'Editeur*." In fact, we know from the author's correspondence that many of these special notes were also concocted by Joseph de Maistre. But since the work was not published until after Maistre's death, it is also likely that others really were by an unidentified editor. In any case, I have identified all these notes with the indication: "Editor's note." All my own explanatory material (whether in the text, in additions to Maistre's notes, or in separate notes) has been placed in square brackets [ ].

Scripture passages proved a special problem. Since Joseph de Maistre habitually used the Latin Vulgate, the Douay-Rheims English translation (usually acknowledged as being closest to the Vulgate) was consulted first. If this version seemed to embody the sense that Maistre appeared to be trying to make in French, a modernized version of this translation is what is provided. If not, various other translations were also consulted. In many instances, however, to retain the point that it appeared Maistre was trying to make, I ended up making my own English translation from his French (checking a number of standard translations to ensure that the sense was retained). Instances where Maistre's versions appear idiosyncratic (or even in error) have been noted.

It was clearly Joseph de Maistre's intention that "The Elucidation on Sacrifices" should appear as an appendix to his *Dialogues*. The piece is bound with the *Dialogues* in the manuscript that survives in the Maistre family archives. In the Ninth Dialogue Maistre has a footnote reference to the piece. Moreover, the piece has been appended to most editions of the *Dialogues*, including the original 1821 edition. For the sake of completeness, and because the piece expands Maistre's ideas on one of the major themes of the *Dialogues*, I have included it in this translation.

ST PETERSBURG DIALOGUES

First Dialogue

At the end of a very warm day in the month of July 1809, I was returning up the Neva in a launch with Privy Councillor T***, a member of the Senate of St Petersburg, and Chevalier de B***, a young Frenchman who had been driven to this capital by the storms of the revolution in his country and by a series of bizarre events. Reciprocal esteem, a congruence of tastes, and some valuable relationships of service and hospitality had formed an intimate connection between us. Both of them were accompanying me that day to the country house where I was passing the summer. Although situated within the walls of the city, it was nevertheless far enough from the centre to be called *country* and to offer *solitude*; for much remains to be done before all the area within the city walls of St Petersburg is built up. Even though the open spaces to be found in the inhabited part are being filled in, it is still impossible to foresee whether the inhabitants will ever be able to advance to the limits traced by Peter the Great's bold finger.

It was a little after nine in the evening; the sun was setting, the weather superb. The soft breeze that was pushing us died in the sail we had seen *flapping*. The flag on the imperial palace, which announced the presence of the sovereign, soon fell limply along its supporting staff, heralding the stillness of the air. Our sailors took up their oars; we asked them to row slowly.

Nothing is rarer, nothing is more enchanting than a beautiful summer evening in St Petersburg. Whether the length of the winter and the rarity of these nights, which gives them a particular charm, renders them more desirable, or whether they really are so, as I believe, they are softer and calmer than evenings in more pleasant climates.

The sun, which in more temperate zones sinks quickly in the west leaving behind it only a brief twilight, here slowly brushes an earth it seems regretful to leave. Its disk surrounded with reddish haze rolls like a fiery chariot over the dark forests that crown the horizon, and its rays reflected in the windows of the palaces give the spectator the impression of a vast conflagration.

Great rivers usually have deep beds and steep banks that give them a wild appearance. The Neva flows full to its banks through the heart of a magnificent city. Its limpid waters skirt the grass of the islands it embraces, and through the entire extent of the city the river is contained by two granite embankments aligned as far as the eye can see, a kind of magnificence repeated along the three canals that go through the capital, and of which neither model nor imitation is to be found anywhere else.

A thousand boats cross and furrow the water in every direction. In the distance foreign vessels are furling their sails and dropping their anchors. They bring tropical fruit and the products of the whole world to this northern city. Brilliant American birds sail the Neva with orange groves; on arriving they find coconuts, pineapples, lemons, and all the fruits of their native land. Opulent Russians soon lay hands on the riches that have been presented to them, and, without counting, they throw their money to the avid merchants.

From time to time we meet elegant boats that have put up their oars and let themselves be carried quietly along the peaceful current of these beautiful waters. The rowers sing a folk song, while their masters enjoy in silence the beauty of the spectacle and the calm of the night.

Near us a small boat goes by rapidly with a wedding party of rich merchants. A crimson canopy decorated with a gold fringe covers a young couple and their parents. Squeezed between two lines of rowers a Russian band sends afar the sound of its noisy horns. This kind of music is peculiarly Russian[1] and is perhaps the only thing particular to this people, whose culture is not old. Many people still alive know the inventor, whose name in this country constantly recalls the idea of old-fashioned hospitality, elegant luxury, and noble pleasures. Singular music! A ringing emblem fit to occupy the mind more than the ear. What does it matter to the piece that the instruments know what they are doing; twenty or thirty automatons acting together produce something alien to each. The individual is a blind mechanism; the ingenious calculation, the imposing harmony, is in the whole.

---

[1] [The "horn band" that Maistre is describing was a peculiar Russian phenomenon of the second half of the eighteenth century. It consisted of a band of serf musicians, each of whom played a horn that produced only a single note. The horns varied in size from about three inches to over eight feet. The music was written with a special kind of notation. See Gerald Seaman, "An Outline of Eighteenth-Century Russian Music," in *Man and Nature/L' homme et la Nature* 5 (1986): 173.]

An equestrian statue of Peter I stands on the banks of the Neva at one end of the immense Isaac Square. His severe visage looks over the river and seems still to animate the navigation created by the genius of its founder. All that the ear can hear, all that the eye can see in this superb theatre, exists only because the thought of this powerful mind brought so many imposing monuments out of a swamp. Between these desolate rivers, where nature seemed to have exiled life, Peter placed his capital and created his subjects. His terrible arm is still extended over their posterity, who press around his august effigy. Looking at him, one does not know whether this bronze hand protects or threatens.

As our launch moves away, the song of the boatmen and the confused noise of the city fade away insensibly. The sun having descended below the horizon, the brilliant clouds shed a soft clarity, a golden half-light impossible to paint and that I have never seen elsewhere. The light and the shadows seem to mingle and conspire together to form a transparent veil covering the countryside.

If heaven in its goodness reserved for me one of those moments so rare in life where the heart is flooded with joy by some extraordinary and unexpected happiness, if a wife, children, and brothers separated from me for a long time without hope of reunion were suddenly to tumble into my arms, I would want it to happen here. Yes, I would want it to be on one of these beautiful nights on the banks of the Neva among these hospitable Russians.

Without openly sharing our feelings, we were enjoying the pleasures of the beautiful spectacle that surrounded us, when abruptly Chevalier de B*** broke the silence, exclaiming: "I would like to have here in this boat with us one of those perverse men born for society's misfortune, one of those monsters that weary the earth ..."

And what would you do if he accommodated you? This was the question the two friends asked, speaking at the same time. "I would ask him," the Chevalier replied, "if the night appeared as beautiful to him as it does to us."

The Chevalier's exclamation pulled us out of our reverie. Soon his original idea engaged us in the following conversation, of which we were far from foreseeing the interesting consequences.

The Count

My dear Chevalier, perverse hearts never have beautiful nights or beautiful days. They can amuse themselves, or rather divert themselves, but they never know real enjoyment. I do not believe them capable of experiencing the same sensations that we experience. In any case, God keep them away from our boat.

The Chevalier

So you believe the wicked are not happy? I too would like to believe this; however every day I hear how they succeed in everything. If this were really the case, I would be a bit angry that Providence should have reserved the punishment of the wicked and the reward of the just entirely for the other world. It seems to me that a little on account for one and the other, even in this life, would not hurt anything. This is what makes me wish, as you have just seen, that the wicked were not susceptible to the sensations that delight us. I admit to you that I do not see this question very clearly. Surely you must tell me what you think, you, sirs, who are so learned in this kind of philosophy.

> As for me, raised in camps since in my childhood,
> I always leave the task of vengeance to heaven.

I admit to you again that I am not too well informed as to the way it pleases God to exercise his justice. To tell you the truth, though, it seems to me, on reflecting about what happens in the world, that if he punishes in this life, he at least does not press the matter.

The Count

Since you so desire, we might well devote the evening to the examination of this question, which is not so difficult in itself, but which has been muddled by the sophisms of Pride and her eldest daughter Irreligion. I greatly regret those *symposia*,[2] of which antiquity has left us some valuable monuments. The ladies are undoubtedly lovable; we must live with them if we are not to become savages. Large gatherings have their place; it is even necessary to know how to participate in them with good grace. But when one has satisfied all the duties imposed by good manners, I find it very good that men sometimes assemble to reason, even at the table. I don't know why we do not imitate the ancients more on this point. Do you not think that the examination of an interesting question would occupy the after-dinner hour more usefully and more agreeably than the light or reprehensible conversations that animate ours? It seems to me it would be quite a good idea to sit Bacchus and Minerva down at the same table, one to defend the libertine, the other to be the pedant. We no longer have Bacchus; moreover our little *symposium* expressly rejects him. However we

---

2 [Convivial meetings of ancient Greece and Rome, devoted to drinking and intellectual conversation, were called symposia; one of Plato's dialogues is called the *Symposium*.]

have a much better Minerva than the ancients; let us invite her to have tea with us. She is sociable and dislikes noise; I do hope she will come.

You already see before you, above the entrance of my house, a small terrace supported by four Chinese columns. My study opens directly onto that kind of belvedere, what you might call a large balcony. It is there, seated in an old armchair, that I peacefully await the arrival of sleep. Struck twice by lightning,[3] as you know, I no longer have the right to what is vulgarly called *happiness*: I even confess to you it has too often happened that I have asked myself, *What is left for me?* But my conscience, forcing me to answer ME, made me blush at my weakness, and it's been a long time since I have even been tempted to complain. It is there in my observatory, especially, that I find delectable moments. Sometimes I surrender myself to sublime meditations and enter into a state that leads by degrees towards rapture. Sometimes, like an innocent magician, I evoke the venerable shades that once were for me terrestrial divinities and that today I evoke as tutelary geniuses.[4] Often they seem to signal to me. But when I hurry towards them, charming memories remind me of what I still have, and life appears to me as beautiful as if I were still in the age of hope.

When my oppressed heart demands repose, reading comes to my assistance. My books are all there under my hand: I require but few, for I have long been convinced of the perfect uselessness of very many works that still enjoy a great reputation ...

The three friends having disembarked and taken their places around the tea table, the conversation resumed its course.

The Senator

I am delighted our Chevalier's sally made you think of the idea of a philosophical *symposium*. The subject we are going to treat could not be more interesting: *the happiness of the wicked and the misfortune of the just!* This is the great scandal to human reason. Could we employ an evening any better than in consecrating it to an examination of this mystery of divine metaphysics? We will be led to probe, at least as far as it permitted to human weakness, *the totality of the ways of Providence in the government of the moral world.* But I must warn you, Count, that it could well happen to you, as to the sultana *Scheherazade*, that you will not be able to

---

[3] [Maistre's personal fortunes were battered by the French Revolution, which cost him his profession and his property, and by his posting to St Petersburg, which meant separation from his wife and daughters.]

[4] [Probably a reference to Maistre's parents; his mother had died in 1774, his father in 1789.]

quit after one evening. I am not saying that we will go on for a *thousand and one*; that would be an indiscretion. But at least we will meet more often than you imagine.

The Count

I accept what you are telling me as a polite warning and not a threat. In any case, gentlemen, when you put questions to me, I can direct you to each other. I do not ask for or even accept the principal part in our conversations; if you are agreed, we will do our thinking in common. Only on that condition will I begin.

For a long time, gentlemen, there have been complaints against Providence in its distribution of good and evil. I must tell you that these difficulties have never been able to make the least impression on my mind. I see with the certitude of intuition, and I humbly thank Providence for this, that on this point man DECEIVES HIMSELF, in the full meaning of the phrase and in its natural sense.

I would like to be able to say like Montaigne: *man fools himself*; for this is exactly right. Yes, man no doubt *fools himself*; he is his own dupe. He takes the sophisms of his naturally rebellious heart (alas, nothing is more certain) for real doubts born in his understanding. If sometimes superstition *believes in belief*, as it has been reproached for doing, *pride believes in disbelief*. It is always man who *fools himself*, but the second case is much worse than the first.

Finally, gentlemen, there is no subject on which I feel more strongly than on the temporal government of Providence. So it is with complete conviction and lively satisfaction that I will disclose to two men whom I love tenderly some useful thoughts that I have collected along the already long route of a life entirely dedicated to serious studies.

The Chevalier

I will listen to you with the greatest pleasure, and I have no doubt that our common friend will accord you the same attention. But permit me, I beg you, to start by quibbling with you before you begin. And do not accuse me of *replying to your silence*, for it is as if you have already spoken and I know very well what you are going to tell me. You are, without the least doubt, on the point of beginning where preachers end, *with eternal life*. "The wicked are happy in this world; but they will be chastised in the next; the just, on the other hand, suffer in this world, but will be happy in the next." That is what we always hear. And why should I hide from you the fact that this trenchant reply does not satisfy me completely. I hope you will not suspect me of wishing to destroy or weaken this great proof, but it seems to me that it would not be harmed a bit by association with others.

The Senator

If the Chevalier is indiscreet or too precipitate, I confess that like him I have been wrong and just as wrong. For I was also on the point of quarrelling with you even before you had broached the question – or, if you wish me to speak more seriously, I would like to ask you to leave the beaten path. I have read many of your first-rate ascetic writers, whom I venerate immeasurably. However even giving them all the praise they merit, I am pained to see that on this great question of the ways of divine justice in this world they almost all seem to accept criticisms of the fact, and to admit that there is no way of justifying divine Providence in this life. If this proposition is not false, it at least appears to me extremely dangerous. There is great danger in allowing men to believe that virtue will be recompensed and vice punished only in the other life. Unbelievers, for whom this world is everything, ask for nothing better, and the masses themselves necessarily follow the same line. Man is so distracted, so dependent on the objects that strike him, so dominated by his passions, that every day we see the most submissive believer risk the torments of the future life for the most wretched pleasure. What will happen to those who do not believe or whose belief is weak? So let us rely as much as you like on the future life, which responds to every objection. However if a truly moral government exists in this world, and if, even in this life, crime must tremble, why relieve it of this fear?

The Count

Pascal observes somewhere that *the last thing that one discovers in writing a book is to know what to put at the beginning.* I am not writing a book, my friends, but I am beginning what will perhaps be a long discourse, and I would have had to think about where to begin. Happily, you have dispensed me from the labour of deliberation; you yourselves have shown me where I must start.

The familiar expression that one should address only to a child or to a subordinate, *You do not know what you are saying*, is nevertheless the comment that a sensible man has the right to make to the crowd that gets mixed up in discussing thorny questions of philosophy. Gentlemen, have you ever heard a soldier complain that in war musket balls hit only honest men, and that it suffices to be a scoundrel to be invulnerable? I am sure the answer is no, because in fact everyone knows that the balls make no distinction between persons. I would certainly have the right to establish at least a perfect equivalence between the evils of war in relation to soldiers and the evils of life in relation to all men. This equivalence, presumed to be exact, suffices by itself to eliminate a difficulty founded on a manifest falsehood. For it is not only false, but obviously FALSE *that it is generally the case that crime is happy and virtue unhappy in this world.* On the contrary, there is the greatest evidence that the distribution of blessings and misfortunes is a kind of lottery where each, without distinction, can draw a winning or a losing ticket. So we must change the question, and ask *why, in the temporal order, the just are not exempt from the evils that can afflict the guilty. We must ask why the wicked are not deprived of the good things that the just can enjoy.* But this question is altogether different from the first. I would even be quite astonished if its simple enunciation would not demonstrate its absurdity to you. It is one of my favourite ideas that the upright man is commonly enough warned by an interior feeling of the falsehood or truth of certain propositions before any analysis, often even without having the necessary studies to examine them with a complete knowledge of the case.

The Senator

I agree so strongly with you, and I like this doctrine so much, that I have perhaps exaggerated it by applying it to the natural sciences. Moreover I can, at least up to a certain point, invoke experience in this regard. More than once, with respect to physics or natural history, I have been shocked, without being able to say quite why, by certain accredited opinions. Then, afterwards, I have had the pleasure (for such it is) of seeing these opinions attacked and even ridiculed by men profoundly versed in these sciences, in which I am poorly versed as you know. Do you think that one need be the equal of Descartes to have the right to mock his vortices [*tourbillons*]? If someone comes to tell me that this planet on which we live is only a fragment of the sun torn off millions of years ago by a fantastic comet racing through space, or that animals are constructed like houses by putting this beside that, or that all the strata of our globe are only the fortuitous result of chemical precipitation, or a hundred other beautiful theories of this kind that have been produced in our century, is it necessary to have read a lot or to have reflected deeply, or to have been a member of four or five academies, to sense their absurdity? I go even farther. I believe that in those very questions that belong to the exact sciences, or which would appear to rest entirely on experiments, this rule of intellectual conscience is not entirely worthless for those not initiated in these kinds of knowledge. This is what has led me to doubt several things that usually pass for certain. I admit this to you in confidence. The explanation of tides by lunar and solar attraction, the decomposition and recomposition of water,[5] and still other theories that I could cite for you and that are held as dogmas today,

---

[5] [An experiment on the decomposition and recomposition of water was carried out by Lavoisier in 1785.]

absolutely refuse to enter my mind. I feel myself inescapably led to believe that some honest scholar will come along someday to teach us that we were in error on certain of these great questions or that we did not understand them. Perhaps you will tell me (friendship has the right to do so) that *this is pure ignorance on my part*. I have said this to myself a thousand times. But tell me in your turn why I am not equally intractable to other truths. I believe them on the word of my teachers, and there has never arisen in my mind a single idea *against the faith*.

So where does this interior feeling come from, this feeling that revolts against certain theories? These theories are based on arguments that I do not know how to overturn, and yet this conscience we are discussing nevertheless tells us: *Quodcumque ostendis mihi sic, incredulus odi.*[6]

The Count

You are speaking Latin, Senator, although we are not living in a Latin country. It is all very well for you to make excursions to foreign lands; but according to the rules of etiquette you should have added, *with the permission of our Chevalier*.

The Chevalier

You are joking, Count. Please be aware that I am not as incompetent as you might think in the language of ancient Rome. It is true that I passed part of my youth in military camps, where Cicero is seldom cited, but I started out in a country where education itself usually began with Latin. I understand very well the passage that you have just cited, without however knowing where it comes from. In any case, I have no pretensions, on this point nor on so many others, to be the equal of the Senator, whose great and solid knowledge I honour most highly. He certainly has a right to say to me, even with a certain emphasis:

. . . . Go tell your fatherland,
That there is *knowledge* on the borders of Scythia.

But please permit the youngest among you, gentlemen, to lead us back to the road from which we have strangely digressed. I do not know how we have drifted from Providence to Latin.

---

[6] [Whatever you then show me, I discredit and abhor. Horace *The Art of Poetry* 188. Trans. H. Rushton Fairclough, Loeb Classical Library, 1955.]

The Count

Whatever subject we treat, my dear friend, we are still talking about Providence. Moreover, a conversation is not a book; perhaps it is even better than a book precisely because it permits us to ramble a bit. However let us return to our subject at the point where we left it. For the moment I will not examine to what degree we can rely on this interior feeling that the Senator so very justly calls *intellectual conscience.*

Even less will I permit myself to dispute the particular examples to which he has applied it; these details would carry us too far from our subject. I will say only that righteousness of heart and habitual purity of intention can have hidden influences and results that extend much farther than is commonly imagined. So I am very disposed to believe that among men such as those who now hear me, this secret instinct we have been talking about will often enough be right, even in the natural sciences. I am led to believe it nearly infallible in questions of rational philosophy, morality, metaphysics, and natural theology. It is infinitely worthy of the divine wisdom, which has created and regulated all things, to have dispensed man from science in everything that really matters to him. Therefore I was right to affirm that once the question occupying us was well posed, the interior agreement of every right-thinking mind would necessarily precede discussion.

The Chevalier

It seems to me that the Senator approves, since he does not object. As for me, I have always held to the maxim, *never contest useful opinions.* That the mind has a conscience like the heart, that an interior feeling leads man towards the good and puts him on guard against error, even in those things that seem to require preliminary preparation of study and reflection, is an opinion very worthy of divine wisdom and very honourable for man. Never to deny what is useful, never to support what can be harmful, this for me is a sacred rule that must always guide men like myself whose profession precludes profound studies. So do not expect any objection on my part. Nevertheless, without denying that my feelings have already taken sides, I would ask the Count to please address my reason.

The Count

I tell you again: I have never understood this eternal argument against Providence drawn from the misfortune of the just and the prosperity of the wicked. If the good man suffered because he is good and the wicked prospered precisely because he is wicked, the argument would be incontrovertible. It falls to the ground once one assumes that good and evil are distributed indifferently to all men. But false opinions resemble counterfeit money, which is struck by great scoundrels and then circulated by honest people who perpetuate the crime without knowing what they are doing. It was impiety that first made much ado with this objection, and though frivolity and flippancy have repeated it, there is, in truth, nothing to it. I come back to my first comparison: a good man is killed in war. Is this an injustice? No, it is a misfortune. If a man has gout or kidney stones, if his friend betrays him, if he is wiped out by the collapse of a building, etc., these again are misfortunes, but nothing more, since all men without distinction are subject to these sorts of accidents. Never lose sight of this great truth: *That a general law, if it is not unjust for all, cannot be so for the individual.* You do not have a particular illness, but you could have it; you have it, but you could have been exempt. The one who perished in a battle could have escaped; the one who returned could have fallen there. All are not dead, but all went there to die. So no more injustice: the just law is not that which affects everyone, but that which is made for everyone.[i] The effect on such and such an individual is no more than an accident. To find difficulties in this order of things, we must love difficulties for their own sake. Unfortunately we do love them and look for them. The human heart, continually in revolt against the authority that constrains it, tells tales to the mind, which believes them. We accuse Providence to be dispensed from accusing ourselves. We raise against Providence difficulties that we would blush to raise against a sovereign or a simple administrator whose wisdom we can appreciate. How strange! It is easier for us to be just to men than to God.[7]

It seems to me, gentlemen, that I would abuse your patience if I went any further in proving to you that the question is usually poorly posed. They really *do not know what they are saying* when they complain that vice is happy and virtue unhappy in this world. Even on the supposition most favourable to the grumblers, it is manifestly proved that evils of all kinds fall on the human race, like musket balls on an army, with no distinction of persons. Moreover, if the good man does not suffer *because he is good*, and if the wicked man does not prosper *because he is wicked*, the objection disappears, and good sense has triumphed.

The Chevalier

I admit that if only the distribution of physical or external misfortunes is considered, there is evidently inattention or bad faith in the objection

---

[7] *I have noticed many who deal fairly with their fellow-men, but none who deals fairly with the gods.* (Seneca *Epistle 93* [Trans. Richard M. Gummere, Loeb Classical Library, 1962].)

against Providence drawn from this argument. But it seems to me that it is the impunity of crimes that is more insisted upon. This is the great scandal, and this is the issue about which I am most curious to hear what you have to say.

The Count

My friend, it is not yet time. You have let me win a little too quickly with respect to the evils that you call *external*. If I have always supposed, as you have seen, that these evils are equally distributed among all men, I have done so only for the sake of argument, for in truth this is not the case. But before going any further, let us take heed, if you please, not to leave our route. There are questions that touch each other, so to speak, so that it is easy to slip from one to another without noticing it. So, for example, the question *Why do the just suffer?*, leads imperceptibly to another: *Why do men suffer?* The second however is quite a different question; it is that of the origin of evil. Let us therefore begin by avoiding all equivocation. *Evil is on the earth*; alas, this is a truth that need not be proved. But there is more: *it is there very justly, and God could not have been its author.* This is another truth that I hope neither of us doubt, and that I can dispense myself from proving, since I know to whom I am speaking.

The Senator

I profess this very truth with all my heart and without any qualification; but this profession of faith, precisely because of its latitude, requires an explanation. Your St Thomas said with the logical laconism that distinguished him: *God is the author of evil that punishes, but not of the evil that defiles.*[8] He is certainly right in one sense; but it is necessary to understand him correctly. God is the author of the evil *that punishes*, that is to say physical evil or suffering, as the sovereign is the author of the punishments that are inflicted by his laws. In a remote sense, it is certainly the sovereign himself who hangs men and breaks them on the wheel, since all authority and every legal execution derive from him. But in the direct or immediate sense, it is the thief, it is the forger, it is the assassin, etc., who are the real authors of the *evils that punish them*. They are the ones who build the prisons, who erect the gallows and the scaffolds. In all this the sovereign acts like Homer's Juno, *with his own will, yet with soul unwilling.*[9]

It is the same with God (always excluding any rigorous comparison, which would be insolent). Not only can he not be, in any sense, the author

---

[8]   *Summa Theologiae*, Part I, Q. 49, Art. 2.

[9]   *Iliad* IV.43 [Trans. A.T. Murray, Loeb Classical Library, 1924].

of moral evil, or *sin*, but he cannot even be understand to be the original author of physical evil, which would not exist if intelligent creatures had not rendered it necessary by abusing their freedom. Plato said it, and nothing is more obvious in itself: *the good being cannot wish to harm anyone.*[10] But since we would never maintain that a good man ceased to be such because he justly chastised his son, or because he killed an enemy on the battlefield, or because he sent a scoundrel to punishment, let us take care, as you said a little while ago, Count, not to be less equitable towards God than towards men. Every right-thinking mind is convinced by intuition that evil cannot come from an all-powerful being. It was this infallible feeling that formerly taught Roman good sense to unite as if by a necessary bond the two august titles of MOST GOOD and MOST POWERFUL. This magnificent expression, though born under the sign of paganism, appeared so just that it has passed into your religious language, so delicate and so exclusive. I will even tell you in passing that it has occurred to me more than once to think that the antique inscription, IOVI OPTIMO MAXIMO, could be put in full on the pediments of your Latin temples, for what is IOV-I if not IOV-AH?[ii]

The Count

You know very well that I do not wish to dispute anything you have just said. Undoubtedly *physical evil could only have come into the world through the fault of free creatures. It can only be there as a remedy or an expiation, and in consequence it cannot have God as its direct author.* For us these are incontestable dogmas. Now I come back to you, Chevalier. You admitted just now that one can scarcely quibble with Providence over the distribution of good and evil, but that the scandal lies above all in the impunity of scoundrels. I doubt, however, if you could renounce the first objection without abandoning the second. If there is no injustice in the distribution of ills, on what will you base the complaints of virtue? The world is governed by general laws. So if the foundations of the terrace on which we are speaking were suddenly thrown into the air by some subterranean disturbance, I do not believe that you would claim that God would be obliged to suspend the laws of gravity in our favour because at the moment this terrace holds three men who have never murdered or stolen. We would certainly fall and be crushed. The same would happen if we had been members of the Illuminati lodge of Bavaria or of the Committee of Public Safety. Would you want things arranged so that when it hails the fields of the just man are spared? That would be a miracle. But if, by chance, this just man were to commit a crime after the harvest, then

---

[10] *Probus invidet nemini* [The good (man) envies no one]. In the *Timaeus.*

it would have to rot in his granary. That would be another miracle. Each moment would require another miracle, and miracles would become the ordinary state of the world. This is to say that there would no longer be any miracles, since exceptions would become the rule, and disorder order. To set forth such ideas is to refute them sufficiently.

What still deceives us often enough on this point is that, without our perceiving it, we cannot prevent ourselves from ascribing to God our own ideas about the dignity and importance of persons. In relation to ourselves these ideas are quite just, since we are all subject to the order established in society. But when we carry them into the general order, we resemble the queen who said: *When it is question of damning people like us, you can well believe that God will think more than once.* Elizabeth of France[11] mounted the scaffold; Robespierre followed a bit later. By coming into the world, the angel and the monster both subjected themselves to all the general laws that rule here. No words can describe the crime of these scoundrels who caused the purest and most august blood in the world to flow. Yet in relation to the general order, there is no injustice; this is still a misfortune attached to the human condition, and nothing more. *Every man as man is subject to all the misfortunes of humanity*: the law is general, so it is not unjust. To claim that a man's rank or virtues should exempt him from the action of an iniquitous or misguided tribunal, is precisely the same as wanting such honours to exempt him from apoplexy, for example, or even death.

Observe, however, that, in spite of these general and necessary laws, this supposed equality, on which I have insisted up to now, is far from being the actual case. I have assumed it, as I have told you, *for the sake of my argument*; but nothing is more false, as you will see.

First, let us begin by taking no account of the individual. The general law, the visible and visibly just law, is *that the greatest amount of happiness, even temporal, belongs, not to the virtuous man, but to virtue.* If it were to be otherwise, there would no longer be vice, nor virtue, nor merit, nor demerit, and in consequence, no more moral order. Suppose that each moral action were *paid*, so to speak, by some temporal advantage; the act, having nothing more of the supernatural, would no longer merit a recompense of this kind. Suppose, on the other hand, that in virtue of some divine law the thief's hand should fall off the moment he committed a theft. People would refrain from theft as they refrain from putting their hands under the butcher's cleaver. The moral order would disappear entirely. Therefore to reconcile this order (the sole order possible for intelligent

---

[11] [Madame Elisabeth, who was executed in 1794, was a younger sister of King Louis XVI.]

beings, and that which is, moreover, proved by the facts) with the laws of justice, it is necessary that virtue be recompensed and vice punished, even in this world – but not always, nor immediately. It is necessary that the incomparably greater portion of temporal happiness be attributed to virtue, and the proportional amount of unhappiness fall to vice, but that the individual never be sure of anything. In fact, this is the case. Imagine any other hypothesis; it will lead you directly to the destruction of the moral order, or to the creation of another world.

To come now to particulars, let us begin, please, with human justice. God, wanting to govern men by men, at least exteriorly, has handed over to sovereigns the eminent prerogative of punishing crimes, and it is in this matter especially that they are his representatives. I found an admirable piece on this subject in the laws of Manu. Permit me to read it to you from the third volume of *The Works of Sir William Jones*, which is there on my table.

The Chevalier

Read if you wish; but after having the goodness to tell me about this king Manu, for I have never heard of him.

The Count

Manu, Chevalier, was the great legislator of India. Some say he was the son of the Sun, others that he was the son of Brahma, the first person of the Indian trinity.[12] Between these two opinions, equally probable, I remain suspended without hope of deciding. Unfortunately, it is equally impossible for me to tell you in what period one or the other of these two fathers might have engendered Manu. Sir William Jones, of learned memory, believed that this legislator's code was perhaps anterior to the Pentateuch, and *certainly* at the very least anterior to all the lawgivers of Greece.[13] But Mr Pinkerton, who also has a good claim on our confidence, has taken the liberty of mocking the brahmins. He believes himself able to prove that Manu could well have been an honest jurist of the thirteenth century.[14] My custom is not to dispute such slight differences. So, gentlemen, I am going

---

[12] [Thomas] Maurice, *History of Indostan*, 2 vols. (London [1795–98]), 1:53–4; 2:57.

[13] *The Works of Sir William Jones*, 6 vols. [London 1799], 3:__[sic]. [Sir William Jones (1746–94), also known as "Oriental Jones," was a brilliant linguist, Orientalist, and jurist. He was one of the first Europeans to master Sanskrit, and his translation of the "laws of Manu" (also called Menu) was a major achievement.]

[14] John Pinkerton, *Géographie moderne*, [6 vols. (Paris 1804)], 6:260–61.

to read to you the piece in question, whose date we are going to leave blank. Listen well.

"For his use Brahma formed in the beginning of time the genius of punishment, with a body of pure light, his own son, even abstract criminal justice, the protector of all created things. Through fear of that genius, all sentient beings, whether fixed or locomotive, are fitted for natural enjoyments and swerve not from duty. When the king, therefore, has fully considered place and time, and his own strength, and the divine ordinance, let him justly inflict punishment on all those who act unjustly. Punishment is an active ruler; he is the true manager of public affairs; he is the dispenser of laws; and wise men call him the *sponsor* of all the four orders for the discharge of their several duties. Punishment governs all mankind; punishment alone preserves them; punishment wakes, while their guards are asleep; the wise consider punishment as the perfection of justice. If the king were not, without indolence, to punish the guilty, the stronger would roast the weaker. The whole race of men is kept in order by punishment; for a guiltless man is hard to find: through fear of punishment, indeed, this universe is enabled to enjoy its blessings. All classes would become corrupt; all barriers would be destroyed; there would be total confusion among men, if punishment either were not inflicted, or were inflicted unduly. But where punishment, with a black hue and a red eye, advances to destroy sin, there if the judge discern well, the people are undisturbed."[15]

The Senator

Admirable! Magnificent! You are an excellent man for having unearthed for us this piece of Indian philosophy. In truth, the date does not matter.

The Count

It made the same impression on me. I find there European reason with a just measure of that Oriental emphasis that pleases everyone when it is not exaggerated. I do not believe it possible to express with more nobility and energy this divine and terrible prerogative of sovereigns: *the punishment of the guilty.*

But having forewarned you with these sombre thoughts, allow me to direct your attention for a moment to a subject that is undoubtedly shocking. It is nevertheless very worthy of occupying our reflections.

This formidable prerogative of which I have just spoken results in the necessary existence of a man destined to administer the punishments

---

[15] Jones, *Works*, 3:223–4.

adjudged for crimes by human justice. This man is, in effect, found everywhere, without there being any means of explaining how; for reason cannot discover in human nature any motive capable of explaining this choice of profession. I believe you too accustomed to reflection, gentlemen, not to have thought often about the executioner. So who is this inexplicable being who, when there are so many pleasant, lucrative, honest, and even honourable professions in which he could exercise his strength or dexterity to choose among, has chosen that of torturing and putting to death his own kind? Are this head and this heart made like our own? Do they contain anything that is peculiar and alien to our nature? For myself, I have no doubt about this. In outward appearance he is made like us; he is born like us. But he is an extraordinary being, and for him to be brought into existence as a member of the human family a particular decree was required, a FIAT of creative power. He is created as a law on to himself.

Consider how he is viewed by public opinion, and try to conceive, if you can, how he could ignore this opinion or confront it! Scarcely have the authorities assigned his dwelling, scarcely has he taken possession of it, when other men move their houses elsewhere so they no longer have to see his. In the midst of this seclusion and in this kind of vacuum formed around him, he lives alone with his female and his offspring, who acquaint him with the human voice. Without them he would hear nothing but groans. ... A dismal signal is given. An abject minister of justice knocks on his door to warn him that he is needed. He sets out. He arrives at a public square packed with a pressing and panting crowd. He is thrown a poisoner, a parricide, a blasphemer. He seizes him, stretches him out, ties him to a horizontal cross, and raises his arms. Then there is a horrible silence; there is no sound but the crack of bones breaking under the crossbar and the howls of the victim. He unties him and carries him to a wheel. The broken limbs are bound to the spokes, the head hangs down, the hair stands on end, and the mouth, gaping like a furnace, occasionally emits a few bloody words begging for death. He has finished; his heart is pounding, but it is with joy. He congratulates himself. He says in his heart, *No one can break men on the wheel better than I.* He steps down; he holds out his blood-stained hand, and justice throws him from afar a few gold coins, which he carries away through a double row of men drawing back in horror. He sits down to table and eats; then he goes to bed and sleeps. Awakening on the morrow, he thinks of something quite different from what he did the day before. Is this a man? Yes. God receives him in his shrines and allows him to pray. He is not a criminal, and yet no tongue would consent to say, for example, *that he is virtuous, that he is an honest man, that he is admirable,* etc. No moral praise seems appropriate for him, since this supposes relationships with human beings, and he has none.

And yet all greatness, all power, all subordination rests on the executioner; he is both the horror and the bond of human association. Remove this incomprehensible agent from the world, and in a moment order gives way to chaos, thrones fall, and society disappears. God, who is the author of sovereignty, is therefore also the author of punishment. He has suspended our earth on these two poles; *For the pillars of the earth are the Lord's, and he has set the world upon them.*[16]

There is then in the temporal sphere a divine and visible law for the punishment of crime. This law, as stable as the society it upholds, has been executed invariably since the beginning of time. Evil exists on the earth and acts constantly, and by a necessary consequence it must constantly be repressed by punishment. All over the globe what we see is the constant action of all governments stopping or punishing criminal outrages. The sword of justice has no sheath; it must always be threatening or striking. For whom are there knouts, gallows, wheels, and stakes? For criminals, obviously. Judicial errors are exceptions that do not upset the rule; moreover I have a number of reflections to propose to you on this point. In the first place, these fatal errors are far less frequent than is imagined. Public opinion is always opposed to authority whenever there is the least room for doubt. So it avidly welcomes the least rumours of purported judicial murder. A thousand individual passions can add to this general trend. But from long experience I swear to you, Senator, that it is an excessively rare thing for a court to put someone to death through passion or error. You are laughing, Chevalier!

The Chevalier

I was just thinking of the *Calas family*; and the Calas made me think *of the horse and the whole stable.*[17] That is how ideas are connected and how the imagination is always interrupting reason.

The Count

Do not apologize, for you have been of service to me in making me think of this famous decision, which furnishes me with another proof of what I have just been telling you. Nothing is less well proved, gentlemen, than the innocence of Calas. There are a thousand reasons to doubt it, and even to

---

[16] Canticle of Hannah, 1 Samuel 2:8.

[17] At the time when the memory of Calas was being rehabilitated, Duke d'A.....
asked a resident of Toulouse *how it could happen that one of their courts had been
so cruelly deceived*; to which the second replied by citing the common proverb:
There is no good horse who has never shied. To which the Duke quickly responded,
but a whole stable!

believe the contrary. But nothing struck me more than an original letter from Voltaire to the celebrated Tronchin of Geneva, a letter I was able to read some years ago.[18] In the midst of a very animated public discussion, where Voltaire is showing off and giving himself the title of the tutor of innocence and avenger of humanity, he clowns as if he were speaking about comic opera. I especially recall this phrase, which struck me: *You were right in finding my memoir too heated, but I am preparing another for you in a hotter bath* [*au bain marie*]. It is in this grave and sentimental style that this worthy man was speaking in the ear of his confidant at the same time Europe was resounding to his fanatical *Lamentations*.

But let Calas be. That an innocent perishes is a misfortune like any other. That a guilty man escapes is another exception of the same kind. But it always remains true, generally speaking, *that there is on the earth a universal and visible order for the temporal punishment of crimes*. I must also have you notice that the guilty do not deceive the eye of justice as often as one might suppose given the infinite precautions they take to hide themselves. In the circumstances that unmask the most cunning scoundrels there are often things so unexpected, so surprising, so *unpredictable*, that men who are led by their profession or by their reflections to follow affairs of this sort find themselves inclined to believe that human justice is not left entirely denuded of a certain extraordinary assistance in seeking out the guilty.

Allow me to add another consideration to conclude this chapter on punishments. Just as it is possible that we are in error when we accuse human justice of sparing a guilty man, because the one we regard as such is not really guilty, on the other side, it is equally possible that a man tortured for a crime he did not commit really merited punishment for an absolutely unknown crime. Happily and unfortunately, there are several examples of this kind proved by the confession of criminals. And there are, I believe, an even greater number of which we are ignorant. This last supposition merits especially close attention. Although in this case the judges are extremely blameworthy or unfortunate, Providence, for whom all things, even obstacles, are means, is no less served by crime or ignorance in executing the temporal justice that we demand. It is sure that these two suppositions notably restrain the number of exceptions. So you see how this assumed equality, which I first supposed, is already disrupted by the consideration of human justice alone.

Turning from the corporal punishments inflicted by justice, let us consider illnesses. You have already anticipated me. If every kind of

---

[18] [Dr Théodore Tronchin was Voltaire's friend and doctor. Joseph de Maistre became acquainted with the Tronchin family during his years in Lausanne.]

intemperance were removed from the world, most maladies would be driven out as well, and it is even possible that we could say that all of them would disappear. This is something that everyone can see in a general and confused way, but it is good to examine the matter more closely. If there were no moral evil on the earth, there would be no physical illness. And since an infinity of illnesses is the immediate product of certain moral disorders, is it not true that the analogy would lead us to generalize the observation? Have you by chance read Seneca's vigorous and sometimes a bit distasteful tirade on the illnesses of his time? It is interesting to see that Nero's time was marked by a deluge of diseases unknown to the preceding period. Seneca exclaims agreeably: "Are you astonished by this innumerable quantity of illnesses? Count the cooks."[19] He is especially angry with the women: "Hippocrates, the illustrious founder of the guild and profession of medicine, remarked that women never lost their hair or suffered from pain in their feet; and yet nowadays they run short of hair and are afflicted with gout. They have put off their womanly nature and are therefore condemned to suffer the diseases of men. *May heaven curse them for the infamous usurpation that these miserable creatures have dared to perpetrate on our sex!*"[20] Undoubtedly there are illnesses that are only the accidental results of a general law, as will never be said often enough: the most moral man must die. Of two men who run a forced race, the one to save his fellow man, the other to assassinate him, one or the other can die of pleurisy. But what a frightening number of illness in general and accidents in particular are due only to our vices. I recall that Bossuet, preaching before Louis XIV and his whole court, called on medicine to testify to the deadly consequences of sensual pleasure.[21] He was largely correct to cite what is most obvious and most striking, but it would have been right to generalize the observation. For my part, I cannot disagree with the opinion of a recent apologist who held that all illnesses have their origin in some vice proscribed by Scripture, and that this holy law contains true medicine for the body as well as the soul, so that if a society of just men

---

[19] Seneca *Epistle 95*. [Loeb]

[20] This is what he says, more or less. However one would do well to consult the text. The dreadful picture that Seneca presents here merits attention equally from the doctor and from the moralist.

[21] "Have tyrants ever invented tortures more unbearable than those that pleasures bring upon those who abandon themselves to them? They bring into this world misfortunes previously unknown to humanity, and doctors are agreed in teaching that these deadly complications of symptoms and illnesses that disconcert their art, confound their experience, and so often belie their old aphorisms, have their source in pleasures." (*Sermon contre l'amour des plaisirs*, I, point)

This man said what he wanted to say; nothing was above or below him.

made use of it, death would be no more than the inevitable term of a sane and robust old age. This opinion was, I believe, that of Origen.[iii] What deceives us on this point is that when the effect is not immediate we no longer perceive it; but it is no less real. Sicknesses, once established, propagate themselves, grow, and amalgamate with deadly affinity, so that we can suffer today the physical penalty of an excess committed a century ago. However, despite the confusion resulting from these horrible mixtures, the comparison between crimes and illnesses is plain to every attentive observer. As with sins, there are illnesses that are *actual and original, accidental and habitual, mortal and venial*. There are diseases of laziness, of anger, of gluttony, of incontinence, etc. Moreover observe that there are crimes that have distinctive characteristics, and consequently distinctive names in every language, such as murder, sacrilege, incest, etc., and others that can only be identified by general terms, such as fraud, injustice, violence, corruption, etc. In the same way there are distinctive diseases such as dropsy, consumption, and apoplexy, etc., and others that can only be identified by the general terms of malaise, discomfort, aches, and *nameless* fevers, etc. Now the more virtuous the man, the more immune he is from illnesses *that have names.*[iv]

Bacon, although a Protestant, as a good observer could not help noticing the great number of saints (monks especially and hermits) whom God had favoured with a long life,[v] nor help making the contrary no less striking observation that there is not a vice, not a crime, not a disordered passion that does not produce in the physical order a more or less fatal, more or less long term, effect. A beautiful analogy between illnesses and crimes can be drawn from the action of the divine author of our religion. Since he was the master certainly, he could have confirmed his mission in men's eyes by enkindling volcanoes or bringing down lightning, but he never derogated from the laws of nature except to do good things for men. Before healing the sick who were presented to him, this divine master never failed to remit their sins or to render public testimony to the faith that had reconciled the sinner.[22] What is even more striking is what he said to the lepers: "You see that I have healed you; take care now to sin no more, for fear that something worse happens to you."

It even seems that we are somehow led to penetrate to a great secret if we reflect on a truth whose very enunciation is a demonstration for any man who knows something of philosophy: we can know "that no illness is known to have a physical cause."[vi] However, although reason, revelation,

---

[22] Bourdaloue made just about the same observation in his sermon on predestination. VIS SANUS FIERI [Do you want to become healthy]? This work is a masterpiece of wholesome and consoling logic.

and experience unite to convince us of the deadly connection that exists between moral evil and physical evil, not only do we refuse to perceive the material consequences of those passions that reside only in the soul, but we do not examine enough or closely enough those that have their roots in physical organs or whose visible consequences must frighten us even more. For example, we have repeated a thousand times the old adage, *that the table kills more men than war*, but there are very few men who reflect enough on the deep truth of this axiom. If everyone examines themselves severely, they will remain convinced that they eat perhaps half again more than they should. For excesses of quantity let us pass to excesses of quality. Examine in all its details this perfidious art of exciting a deceptive appetite that kills us. Think of all the innumerable caprices of intemperance, of those seductive *compositions* that are to our body precisely what bad books are to our mind, which is at the same time overloaded and corrupted. You will see clearly how nature, continually attacked by these vile excesses, struggles vainly against our endless attacks. You will see how the body must, despite its marvellous resources, finally succumb, and how it accepts the germs of a thousand illnesses. Philosophy alone discovered long ago that all human wisdom is to be found in two words: SUSTINE ET ABSTINE.[23] And although philosophy is a feeble legislator whose best laws may even be ridiculed because it lacks the power to make itself obeyed, nevertheless we must be fair and give it credit for the truths that it has published. It has understood very well that man's strongest inclinations are vicious to the point of obviously tending towards the destruction of society, that man has no greater enemy than himself, and that when he has learned to vanquish himself, he knows everything.[24] But the Christian law, which is nothing but the revealed will of him who knows everything and can do everything, does not limit itself to vain counsels. It has made of abstinence, of habitual victory over our desires, a capital precept that must regulate man's entire life. Moreover, it has made the more or less severe, more or less frequent, privation of the permitted pleasures of the table a fundamental law that can be modified according to the circumstances, but that always remains invariable in its essence. If we would like to think about this privation called *fasting*, considering it from a spiritual point of view, it suffices for us to discover and understand the Church when she says to God, with an infallibility that she has received from him: *You use bodily*

---

[23] *Suffer and abstain.* This is the famous ANEKOU KAI APEXOU of the Stoics.

[24] The most simple, the most pious, the most humble, and for all these reasons the most penetrating of ascetic writers, has said "this ought to be our endeavour ... daily to wax stronger than ourselves" (Thomas à Kempis, *The Imitation of Christ*, Chap. 3), a maxim worthy of this Christian Epictetus.

fasting to raise our spirits to you, to repress our vices, and to give us virtues you can reward.[25] But I do not want to leave the temporal sphere just yet. Often I think with admiration and even gratitude of this salutary law that opposes legal and periodic abstinences to the destructive action that intemperance continually exercises on our organs, and that at least prevents this force from accelerating by obliging it to keep beginning anew. Nothing wiser can be imagined, even under the heading of simple hygiene; never has there been better agreement between man's temporal advantage and his interests and needs of a superior order.

The Senator

You have just indicated one of the great sources of physical evil, which alone justifies in great part the ways of Providence in its temporal governance, when we dare judge it in this way. But the most unrestrained passion and the one that is the dearest to human nature is also one that must attract our attention, since from it alone flows more temporal evils than all the other vices together. We have a horror of murder. But what are all murders put together, or war even, compared to the vice that is like the evil principle, *murderer from the beginning,*[26] that acts on potential life, that kills what does not yet exist, and that does not cease to stop up the very sources of life by weakening them and defiling them? Since there is in the world in its present state an immense conspiracy to justify, to embellish, and – I almost said – to consecrate this vice, there is no other vice on which the pages of Scripture have accumulated more temporal anathemas. The sage denounces for us with redoubled wisdom the deadly consequences of these *guilty nights.*[vii] If we look around us with pure and well-directed eyes, nothing can prevent us from observing the incontestable accomplishment of these anathemas. Human reproduction, which from one point of view approaches that of brutes, is from another point of view elevated as high as pure intelligence by the law that surrounds this great mystery of nature, and by the sublime participation accorded to those who make themselves worthy of it. But these laws have a terrible sanction! If we could clearly perceive all the evils that result from disordered procreation and from innumerable profanations of the first law of the world, we would recoil in horror. This is why the only true religion is also the only one that, without the power to say all things to man, nevertheless lays hold

---

[25]   (Preface of the Mass during Lent.) Plato said that if nature did not have the physical means to prevent at least some of the consequences of intemperance, this brutal vice alone would suffice to cost the inept man *all the gifts of genius, grace, and virtue, and to extinguish the divine spirit in him.* (*Timaeus.*)

[26]   John 8:44.

of marriage and submits it to its holy ordinances.[viii] I even believe that its legislation on this question must be placed high among the most tangible proofs of its divinity. The sages of antiquity, although denied the revelation that we possess, were nevertheless nearer to the origin of things and some remnants of primitive traditions had come down to them. We see that they were very much occupied with this important subject, for not only did they believe that moral and physical vices were transmitted from fathers to their children, but by a natural consequence of this belief they warned men to examine carefully the state of their souls when they seemed to be obeying only material laws.[ix] What would they not have said if they had known what man has become and what he can desire! So men have brought upon themselves most of the evils that afflict them; they suffer justly what they make others suffer in turn. Our children will carry the penalty of our faults; our fathers are avenged in them in advance.

The Chevalier

You know very well, my respectable friend, that if you were heard by certain men of my acquaintance, they could very well accuse you of being an illuminist.[27]

The Senator

If these men of whom you speak were to address this compliment (literally) to me, I would thank them sincerely, since there would be nothing more honourable than to really be *illuminated*. But that is not what you intended. In any case, if I am an *illuminist*, at least I am not one of those of whom we were speaking earlier.[28] My *enlightenment* surely does not come from them. For the rest, if the nature of our studies sometimes leads us to thumb through the works of some extraordinary men, you yourself have furnished me with a sure rule to keep us from being led astray, a rule to which you constantly submit your conduct, as you told us just a moment ago. This rule is one of general utility. When an opinion shocks no known truth, and when moreover it tends to elevate man, to perfect him, to make him master of his passions, I do not see why we would reject it. Can man be too convinced of his spiritual dignity? He would certainly not be deceiving himself in

---

[27] [Maistre uses the French term *illuminé*. This is frequently translated as illuminatus (illuminati), but in his time the term "illuminati" was usually understood to refer particularly to the secret society founded by Weishaupt in Bavaria in 1776 and characterized by deistic and republican ideas. Since Maistre's references are usually to the more moderate French *illuminés*, the blander and more neutral term "illuminist" seems a more appropriate translation.]

[28] See p. 15 above.

believing that it is of the highest importance for him never to act like a blind instrument of Providence in those things that are given over to his power, but to act like an intelligent, free, and obedient minister, with the anterior and determined will to obey the plans of the one who sent him. If he is mistaken on the extent of the effects he attributes to his own will, it must be admitted that he is innocently mistaken, and I dare add quite happily mistaken.

The Count

With all my heart I accept this rule of utility, which is common to all men; but we have another, you and I, Chevalier, which protects us from all error – it is that of authority. They can say or write what they wish; our fathers have thrown out an anchor, and holding on to it, we no more fear the illuminists than the impious. So leaving aside from this discussion everything that could be seen as hypothetical, I am still entitled to pose this incontestable principle: *Moral vices can augment the number and intensity of diseases to a degree that is impossible to determine. Reciprocally, this hideous empire of physical evil can be restrained by virtue to limits that are also impossible to fix.*[x] As there is not the least doubt on the truth of this proposition, there is no need to go further to justify the ways of Providence in the temporal order, especially if one adds to this consideration that of human justice, since it has been demonstrated that from this double point of view the privileges of virtue are incalculable, independently of any appeal to reason and even of any religious consideration. Would you now like to leave the temporal order?

The Chevalier

I am beginning to get a little bored by all these earthly considerations, so I would not be upset if you had the goodness to transport me to something a little higher. So therefore ...

The Senator

I am opposed to that voyage this evening. The pleasure of our conversation has seduced us and the length of the day has deceived us, for the clock has just sounded midnight. So with faith in our watches, let us go to bed, and tomorrow we will be faithful to our appointment.

The Count

You are right. Men of our age, in this season, must prescribe for themselves a conventional night of peaceful sleep, just as in winter they must create an artificial day for themselves for the sake of work. As for our Chevalier, nothing prevents him from amusing himself in fashionable society after quitting his grave friends. Undoubtedly he will find more than one house where they are still at table.

The Chevalier

I will profit from your counsel, on the condition however that you will do me the favour of believing that I am not sure, with great differences, of amusing myself *in fashionable society* as much as here. But tell me, before we part, if good and evil are not, by chance, distributed in the world like day and night. Today we light candles only for form; in six months we will scarcely extinguish them. In Quito they light them and extinguish them at the same hour every day. Between these two extremes, day and night lengthen from the equator to the pole, and in a contrary sense in invariable order. But at the end of the year, each has his own account, and each man has received his four thousand three hundred and eighty hours of day and as much of night. Count, what do you think of this?

The Count

We will talk about it tomorrow.

NOTES TO THE FIRST DIALOGUE

i "We should not manifest surprise at any sort of condition into which we are born, and which should be lamented by no one, simply because it is equally ordained for all ... for a man might have experienced even that which he has escaped. And an equal law consists, not of that which all have experienced, but of that which is laid down for all." (Seneca *Epistle 107*) "Into such a world have we entered, and under such laws do we live. If you like it, obey; if not, depart whithersoever you wish. Cry out in anger if any unfair measures are taken with reference to you individually ... These things of which you complain are the same for all. I cannot give anything easier to man." (Seneca *Epistle 91*) [Loeb]

ii There would not have been any less difficulty if the word had been written in Hebrew characters, for if each letter of IOVI is adorned with the proper diacritical marks, the result is exactly the same as the sacred name of the Hebrews. Omitting the word *Jupiter*, which is an anomaly, it is certain that the comparison of other formations of this name given to the supreme God with the *Tetragrammaton* is something remarkable enough.

iii I have not come across this observation in the works of Origen. But in his book *On First Principles* he maintains that, *if someone had the time to look up all the Scripture passages where it is a question of the diseases suffered by the guilty, one would find that these diseases are only of the kind that typify vices or spiritual punishments.* (*On First Principles* II.ii.) This is obscure probably through the fault of the Latin translator.

The apologist cited by the speaker appears to be the Spanish author [Pablo Antonio José de Olavides] of *Triomphe de l'Evangile* [Lyon 1805].

iv But there are fewer than commonly believed of these diseases that can be characterized and clearly distinguished from every other disease. First-class doctors admit that there are scarcely three or four diseases in all that have their own exclusive pathognomonic sign that makes it possible to distinguish them from all others. (Giovanni Battista Morgagni, *De sedibus et causis morborum*, [Venice 1761], Lib. V. in epist. ad Joh. Fried. Mechel.)

One would be tempted to say, why not three precisely, since the whole hideous family of vices is going to end in three desires? (See 1 John 2:16.)

v I believe I must cite here Bacon's words taken from his *History of Life and Death*. "For though the life of man is only a mass and accumulation of sins and sorrows, and they who aspire to eternity put little value on life; yet even we Christians should not despise the continuance of works of charity. *Besides, the beloved disciple survived the rest, and many of the Fathers, especially holy monks and hermits, were long-lived*; so that this blessing (so often repeated in the old law) appears to have been less withdrawn after the time of our Saviour than other earthly blessings." (*The Works of Sir Francis Bacon*, [10 vols.] (London 1803), 8:358.)

vi In support of this assertion I can cite the most ancient and perhaps the best of observers. *It is impossible*, said Hippocrates, to know the nature of diseases, if one does not know them in the INDIVISIBLE *from which* they emanate. *"In the indivisible (element) from which in the beginning it was separated out."* Hippocrates. *Opera omnia graece et latine*, Van der Linden Edition. 4 vols. (Leyden 1665), *De virginum morbis*. 2:355.

It is too bad that he did not give more development to this thought, but I find a perfect commentary on it in a work by a modern physiologist ([Paul-Joseph] Barthez, *Nouveaux éléments de la science de l'homme*. 2 vols. (Paris 1806), in which it is expressly recognized that the vital principle is one being, that this principle is one, that no mechanical cause or law is admissible as the explanation of the phenomena of living bodies, that an illness (excepting the cases of organic lesions) is only a disease of this vital principle *which is independent of the body*, according to ALL APPEARANCES (he is afraid), *and that this disease is determined by the influence that some cause can exert on this same principle.*

The errors that defile this book are only an offering to our century; they mar these great admissions without weakening them.

vii "For children begotten of unlawful intercourse, etc." (Wisdom 4:6) And human wisdom cries out from Athens:

O bride-bed of grievous pain,
How many ills you have already wrought for mortal men.

> Euripides *Medea* 1290.93

viii "The spouse must think only of having children, and less of having them than of giving them to God." (Fénelon, *Oeuvres spirituelles*, [4 vols., (Paris 1740)], Vol. III. Du mariage, n° XXVI.) *The rest is from man!* After having cited this law it is necessary to cite another dazzling stroke from this same Fénelon. *Ah!* he said, *if men had made religion, they would have made it very differently.*

ix These mysterious ideas have been grasped by several celebrated minds. Origen, whom I will let speak in his own language, for fear of embarrassing him, said in his work on prayer: *Unless the action of the mysteries of marriage, which deserve to be kept in silence, becomes more revered, stately, and more serious . . . (On Prayer* n° 2.)

Elsewhere again he says, in speaking of the Mosaic institution: *Among the Jews, women do not sell their youthful bloom to every man who wants to insult the nature of man's seed. (Against Celsus* I.V.)

Milton could not form a high enough idea of these *mysterious laws* (See *Paradise Lost*, IV, 743; VIII, 598). And *Newton*, commenting on him, warned that what Milton designated by these words *mysterious laws* was something that it would not be good to divulge, that it would be necessary to cover with a religious silence and to revere *as a mystery*.

But the elegant theosophist of our own time has taken a much higher tone: "Order permits that fathers and mothers are virgins in their procreation, so that disorder finds there its punishment; it is in this way that Your work advances, supreme God ... *Oh the profundity of knowledge attached to the generation of beings! (Physis tōn anthrōpinōn spermatōn* [the nature of human procreation].) Without reserve I leave this matter to the supreme agent: it is enough that He deigns to accord us here below an inferior image of the laws of His emanation. Virtuous spouses, look upon yourselves as angels in exile, etc." ([Louis-Claude de] Saint-Martin, *Homme de désir*, [Lyon 1790], § 81)

x Let us believe with all our strength, with this excellent Hebrew philosopher who united the wisdom of Athens and Memphis with that of Jerusalem, that *He who sins in the sight of his Maker, shall fall into the hands of the physician.* (Ecclesiasticus 38:15) Let us listen to him with religious attention when he adds: *they [the doctors] in turn will beseech the Lord to grant them the grace* to relieve and to heal, that life may be saved. (Ibid., 14) Let us observe that in the divine law, where everything is for the sake of spirit, there is however a *sacrament*, that is to say a spiritual means directly established for the healing of bodily diseases, in such a way that the spiritual effect is placed, in this circumstance, in second place. (See James 5:14–15) Let us conceive, if we can, the *operative* strength of the prayer of the just

(Ibid., 16), especially *of this apostolic prayer that, by a kind of divine charm, suspends the most violent pains* and lets death be forgotten. I HAVE OFTEN SEEN this among those who listen with faith. ([Jacques-Bénigne] Bossuet, *Oraison funèbre de la duchesse d'Orléans.)*

And we will have no difficulty understanding the opinion of those who believe that the leading quality of a doctor is piety. As for myself, I confess that I would much prefer to an impious doctor some highway murderer against which one is at least allowed to defend oneself, and who moreover can be hanged from time to time.

Second Dialogue

The Count

You are turning your cup over, Chevalier. Don't you want any more tea?

The Chevalier

No, thank you. This evening I will take only one cup. Raised in a southern province of France, as you know, where tea was drunk only as a cold remedy, I have since lived among people who use this beverage habitually. So I take it to do like the others, but without ever finding it pleasurable enough to find I need it. On principle, moreover, I am not a great partisan of new drinks; who knows if they may not bring us new illnesses.

The Senator

That could well be, although without increasing the total of diseases in the world, for in supposing that the cause you have indicated has produced some new illnesses or discomforts, which would seem to me difficult to prove, one would also have to take account of diseases that have been considerably weakened or even almost totally disappeared, such as leprosy, elephantiasis, and gangrene. In any case, nothing leads me to think that tea, coffee, and sugar, which have become so prodigiously popular in Europe, were given to us as punishments; I am rather inclined to see them as gifts. But one way or the other, I will never regard them as indifferent. Nothing happens by chance in the world, and I have long suspected that the exchange of food and beverages among men belongs in some way to a secret purpose operating in the world without our knowledge. For every man with a keen eye who wants to see, there is nothing so apparent as the link between the two worlds; or to put it better, there is only one world, rigorously speaking, since matter is nothing. Try, if you will, to imagine matter existing alone without intelligence – you will never be able to do it.

The Count

I also think that no one can deny the relationship between the visible and invisible worlds. The denials come from a double way of looking at the two worlds, for one or the other can be considered, or one in itself or in its relation to the other. It was in following this natural division that I first examined the question that occupies us. I considered only the temporal order, and I had just asked your permission to ascend higher when I was very appropriately interrupted by the Senator. Today I will continue.

Since every evil is a punishment, it follows that no evil should be considered necessary; and since no evil is necessary, it follows that all evil can be prevented, either by suppression of the crime that made it necessary, or by prayer, which has the power of preventing or mitigating it. The empire of physical evil can therefore be restrained indefinitely by this supernatural means, as you see ...

The Chevalier

Allow me to interrupt you and even to be a little impolite, if necessary, to force you to be clearer. You are touching here on a subject that has more than once disturbed me deeply; but for the moment I will defer my questions on this point. I should just like to point out to you that, unless I am mistaken, you are confusing the evils directly due to the faults of those who suffer them with those that are transmitted to us by an unfortunate heritage. You said *that we perhaps suffer today from excesses committed more than a century ago*; now it seems to me that we should not have to answer for these crimes as well as for that of our first parents. I do not believe that faith extends as far as that; and, if I am not mistaken, original sin is quite enough, since this sin alone has subjected us to all the miseries of this life. So it seems to me that the physical evils that come to us by inheritance have nothing in common with the temporal government of Providence.

The Count

Please note, I ask you, that I did not insist on this sad heredity, and that I did not cite it as a direct proof of the justice Providence exercises in this world. I spoke of it in passing as of an observation found along my way; but I thank you with all my heart, my dear Chevalier, for having brought it back to our attention, since it is well worth our consideration. If I have not made any distinction between illnesses, it is because they are all punishments. Original sin, which explains everything and without which nothing is explained, unfortunately repeats itself at every moment in time, although in a secondary way. I do not believe that this idea, when it is developed accurately for you, contains anything shocking to your intelligence as a Christian. Original sin is undoubtedly a mystery; however, if a man examines it closely he finds that this mystery, like others, has its plausible sides, even for our limited intelligence.

Let us leave to one side for the moment the theological question of *imputation*, which remains intact, and limit ourselves to the common observation, which accords so well with our most natural ideas, *that all beings with the faculty of reproduction will produce beings similar to themselves*. The rule suffers no exception; it is written everywhere in the universe. If such a being is degraded, its offspring will never resemble that being's primitive condition, but the state to which it has declined through some cause. This is very plain, and the rule holds in the physical as well as in the moral order. But it must be noted that there is the same difference between a *crippled man* and a *sick man* as there is between a *vicious* man and a *guilty* man. Acute illness is not transmissible, but that which vitiates the humours becomes an *original illness* capable of tainting a whole race.

It is the same with moral illnesses. Some belong to the ordinary state of human imperfection, but there are certain transgressions or certain consequences of transgressions that can degrade man absolutely. These are *original sins* of the second order, but which evoke the first for us, however imperfectly. From this origin come savages, about whom so many extravagant things have been said, and who served as the eternal text for J.-J. Rousseau, one of the most dangerous sophists of our century, and yet the one who was the most deprived of true knowledge, wisdom, and especially of profundity, with only an apparent depth that was all a matter of words.[i] He constantly mistook the savage for the primitive man, although the savage is and can only be the descendant of a man detached from the great tree of civilization by some transgression, but of a genre that can no longer be repeated, so far as we can judge, for I doubt new savages will be formed.

As a consequence of the same error, the languages of these savages have been taken for primitive languages, whereas they are and could only be the debris of ancient languages, *ruined*, if I may put it that way, and degraded, like the men who speak them. In effect, every individual or national degradation is immediately heralded by a rigorously proportional degradation in language.[ii] How could man lose an idea or merely the correctness of an idea without losing the word or the accuracy of the word that expresses it? And how, on the contrary, could he extend or sharpen his thinking without this advance being displayed immediately in his language?

So there is an *original illness* just as there is an original sin; which is to say that in virtue of this primitive degradation, we are all subject to all sorts of physical sufferings in *general*; just as in virtue of this degradation we are all subject to all sorts of vices in *general*. This original illness has no other name. It is only the capacity to suffer all kinds of illnesses, just as original sin (abstraction made of imputation) is only the capacity to commit all kinds of crimes, which completes the comparison.

But there are, moreover, original illnesses of the second order, just as there are *original* transgressions of the second order. Which is to say that certain transgressions committed by certain men can degrade them anew *more or less*, and thus be perpetuated more or less like illnesses in the vices of their descendants. It may be that these great transgressions are no longer possible, but it is nonetheless true that the general principle subsists, and that the Christian religion showed itself in possession of great secrets when it turned its whole attention and all the force of its legislative and teaching power to the legitimate reproduction of men to prevent every deadly transmission from fathers to children. If I did not distinguish the illnesses that we owe immediately to personal crimes from those that we owe to the sins of our fathers, the fault is slight, since as I told you a little while ago, they are all in truth punishments for crime. This heredity shocks human reason at first, but until we can talk of the matter at greater length, let us content ourselves with the general rule that I pointed out at the beginning: *all beings that reproduce will only produce what resembles themselves.*

Here, Senator, I invoke your *intellectual conscience*. If a man indulges in such crimes or such a series of crimes that they were capable of altering the moral principle within him, you understand that this degradation is transmissible, just as you understand the transmission of scrofulous or syphilitic vice. For the rest, I have no need of these hereditary evils. Look at all that I have said on this subject as a conversational parenthesis; all the rest remains unshakeable. In summing up all the considerations that I have put before you, there remains, I hope, no doubt *that the innocent man, when he suffers, suffers only in his quality as a man; and that the immense majority of evils fall on crime.* This is all I need for the moment. Now ...

The Chevalier

For me at least, it would be quite useless for you to go any further; for since you spoke of savages I have not been listening to you. In speaking about this kind of men, you mentioned, in passing, something that has kept me completely occupied. Are you really able to prove to me that the languages of savages are the *remnants* and not the *rudiments* of languages?

The Count

If I wanted to undertake this proof seriously, Chevalier, I would first have to prove to you that it would be up to you to prove the contrary; but I fear that this would involve me in a dissertation that would be much too long. If, however, the importance of the subject appears to you to merit my exposing my *faith* to you, I will do this willingly and without details for your future reflections. Here is what I believe on the principal points of which a simple consequence has caught your attention.

The essence of all intelligence is to know and to love. The limits of its knowledge are those of its nature. The immortal being learns nothing; he knows by nature all he must know. On the other hand, no intelligent being can love evil naturally or in virtue of its essence; for that God would have to have created it evil, which is impossible. If therefore man is subject to ignorance or evil, this can only be in virtue of an accidental degradation, which can only be the consequence of a crime. This need, this hunger for knowledge, which agitates man, is only the natural tendency of his being, which carries him towards his original state and alerts him to what he is. He *gravitates*, if I may so express myself, towards the regions of light. No beaver, no swallow, no bee wants to know more than its predecessors. All these beings are happy in the place they occupy. All are degraded, but are ignorant of it; man alone senses his degradation, and this feeling is at once the proof of his greatness and of his misery, of his sublime prerogatives, and of his incredible degradation. In the state to which he is reduced he has not even the sad happiness of being unaware of himself; he must ceaselessly contemplate himself, and he cannot contemplate himself without blushing; his very greatness humiliates him, since the enlightenment that raises him as high as angels only serves to show him the abominable tendencies within himself degrading him to the level of the brutes. He searches in the depth of his being for some healthy part without being able to find it: evil has soiled everything, *and the whole of man is only a disease*.[1] An inconceivable combination of two different and incompatible powers, a monstrous centaur, he feels that he is the result of some unknown crime, some detestable mixture that has vitiated man even in his deepest essence.

Every intellect is by its very nature the result, single yet in three parts, of a *perception* that apprehends, a *reason* that affirms, and a *will* that acts. The first two powers are only weakened in man, but the third *is broken*,[2] and like Tasso's serpent, *it drags itself behind itself*,[3] completely ashamed of its painful impotence. It is in the third power that man senses himself

---

[1] Hippocrates, *Letter to Demagates*, *Opera*, Van der Linden Edition, 2:925. That is true in every sense.

[2] *Fracta et debilitata* [maimed and emasculated]. This expression of Cicero is so accurate that the fathers of the Council of Trent found nothing better to express the state of the will under the rule of sin. *Liberum arbitrium fractum atque debilitatum* [free choice is maimed and emasculated]. (Council of Trent, Sixth Session. Cicero *Letters to his friends* 1.9 [Both these references are faulty.])

[3] *E sè dopo sè tira*. [Torquata] Tasso, [*La Gerusalemme liberata*] XV.48.

fatally wounded. He does not know what he wants; he wants what he does not want; he does not want what he wants; he *would want to want*. He sees in himself something that is not himself and that is stronger than himself. The wise man resists and cries out: *Who will deliver me?*[4] The fool obeys, and calls his cowardice *happiness*; but he cannot get rid of this other incorruptible will in his nature, although it has lost its power; and remorse, piercing his heart, never ceases to cry out to him: *By doing what you do not want, you acknowledge the law.*[5] Who could believe that such a being could have left the hands of the Creator in such a state? This idea is so revolting, that philosophy alone, I mean pagan philosophy, hit on original sin. Did not old Timon of Locris already say, after his master Pythagoras surely, *that our vices come less from ourselves than from our fathers and the elements of which we are made*? Did not Plato even say *that what one must take into account is the generator rather than the generated*? And in another place did he not add that *the Lord, God of Gods,*[6] *seeing that all beings subject to generation have lost* (or had destroyed in them) *the inestimable gift, had decided to subject them to a treatment suited at the same time to punish them and regenerate them.*[iii] Cicero did not distance himself from the feeling of these philosophers and of those initiates who had thought *that we are in this world to expiate certain crimes committed in another*. He even cited and adopted part of Aristotle's comparison, in which the contemplation of human nature reminded him of the dreadful punishment of a wretch tied to a cadaver and condemned to rot with it. Elsewhere he said expressly *that nature had treated us like a step-mother rather than as a mother, and that the divine spirit in us is as if stifled by the tendency we have within us for all the vices;*[7] and is it not a singular fact that Ovid spoke of man in precisely the same terms as St Paul? The erotic poet said: *I see what is good, I love it, and evil seduces me;*[8] and the apostle so elegantly translated by Racine said:

---

[4]   Romans 7:24

[5]   Romans 7:16.

[6]   DEUS DEORUM. Exodus 18:11, Deut. 10:17, Esther 14:12, Psalm 49:1, Daniel 2:47, 3:90.

[7]   See St Augustine, *Against Pelagius*, Bk. IV, and the fragments of Cicero, Elzevir ed. (1661), pp. 1314, 1342. [Maistre cites a passage from Book III of Cicero's lost treatise, *De Republica*, reproduced by St Augustine in Book VI of his *Contra Julianum haeresis pelagianae defensorem*. (Darcel ed.)]

[8]   *... I see the better and approve it,*
      but I follow the worse.
      (Ovid *Metamorphoses* VII.17)

I do not the good that I love,
And I do the evil that I hate.[9]

Moreover, when the philosophers whom I have just cited assure us that the vices of human nature pertain more *to the fathers than to the children*, clearly they are not speaking of any generation in particular. If the proposition remains vague, it makes no sense, so that the very nature of things relates it to a corruption that is original and in consequence universal. Plato tells us *that in contemplating himself, he does not know if he sees a monster more duplicitous and more evil than Typhon, or rather a moral, gentle, and benevolent being who partakes in the nature of the divinity.*[10] He adds that man, so torn in opposite directions, cannot act well or live happily *without reducing to servitude that power of the soul in which evil resides, and without setting free* that which is the home and *the agent of virtue.*[iv] This is precisely the Christian doctrine, and one could not confess more clearly the doctrine of original sin.

What do words matter? Man is evil, horribly evil. Did God create him this way? No, undoubtedly, and Plato himself hastens to reply *that the good being neither wishes nor does evil to anyone.* So we are degraded – but how? This corruption that Plato saw in himself does not appear to have been something particular to his person, and surely he did not believe himself worse than his fellow men. So he was saying essentially what David had said: *My mother conceived me in iniquity,* and if these words had occurred to him he would have adopted them without difficulty. Moreover, since all degradation can only be a punishment, and all punishment presupposes a crime, reason alone finds itself led forcefully to original sin. Since our deadly inclination towards evil is a truth of feeling and experience proclaimed in every century, and since this inclination is always more or less victorious over conscience, and since the laws have never ceased to produce transgressions of all kinds on this earth, man can never recognize and deplore this sad state without confessing at the same time the lamentable dogma that I have been expounding to you, for man cannot be *wicked* without being *evil*, nor evil without being degraded, nor degraded without being punished, nor punished without being guilty.

---

[9] [Romans, 7:18–19] Voltaire said it much less well:
One flees the good that one loves; one hates the evil one does.
(*Loi naturel*, II)
and then immediately after he adds:
Man, about whom so much has been said, is an obscure enigma;
But in what way is he more so than the whole of nature?
Scatterbrain! You have just said it.
[10] He sees the one and the other.

In short, gentlemen, there is nothing so well attested, nothing so universally believed in one form or other, nothing, finally, so intrinsically plausible as the theory of original sin.

Let me add one more thing. I hope you will have no difficulty in appreciating that an originally degraded intelligence is and remains incapable (barring a substantial regeneration) of that ineffable contemplation that our old teachers very appropriately called the *beatific vision*, since it produces, and even is, eternal happiness, just as you can understand that a material eye that is seriously injured can remain incapable in this state of enduring the light of the sun. Now this incapacity of enjoying the SUN, is, if I am not mistaken, the only consequence of original sin that we should regard as natural and independent of any actual transgression.[11] It seems to me that reason can reach this far, and I believe it has a right to applaud itself for this, without ceasing to be docile.

Such is man studied in himself; let us pass on to his history.

All of humanity is descended from one couple.ᵛ This truth, like every other, has been denied. So what are we to make of this?

We know very little about the time before the Flood, and according to some plausible conjectures, it will never be granted us to know more. Only one consideration is of interest to us and we should never lose sight of it: this is that punishments are always proportional to crimes, and crimes are always proportional to the knowledge of the guilty – so that the Flood presupposes unheard of crimes and these crimes assume knowledge infinitely higher than that which we possess today. This is what is certain and what must be more deeply studied. In the righteous family, this knowledge, freed from the evil that rendered it so deadly, survived the destruction of humanity. With respect to the nature and direction of science, we are blinded by a glaring sophism that has fascinated everyone: this sophism lies in judging the age in which men saw effects in causes by that in which they rise painfully from effects to causes, in which they even concern themselves only with effects, in which they say it is useless to concern oneself with causes, and in which they do not even know what a cause is. They never cease to repeat: *Think of the time that it took to know such and such a thing!* What inconceivable blindness! It only took a moment. If man could understand the cause of a single physical phenomenon, he could probably understand all the others. We do not want to see

---

[11] The loss of the vision of God, assuming that they (infants dying without baptism) are aware of it, cannot help causing them a sensible sorrow, which prevents them from being happy. ([Guillaume-Hyacinthe] Bougeant, *Exposition de la doctrine chrétien*, 4 vols. (Paris 1746), chap. II, art. 2, 2:150, and sect. iv, chap. III, 3:343.)

that the most difficult to discover truths are easy to understand. The solution of the problem of the *annulus* once brought a thrill of joy to the best geometer of antiquity, but this solution is found in every elementary mathematics textbook, and does not surpass the intellectual capacity of a fifteen-year old.

Plato, speaking somewhere of what is most important for man to know, suddenly adds with the penetrating simplicity natural to him: *These things are learned easily and perfectly IF SOMEONE TEACHES THEM TO US.*[12] This is exactly the case. It is, moreover, obviously apparent that the first men who repeopled the world after the great catastrophe would have needed extraordinary assistance to succeed against the difficulties of all kinds that faced them.[13] And see, gentlemen, the beautiful character of the truth! Is it a question of proving it? Witnesses come and present themselves from every side; they have never been silent and they have never contradicted themselves, whereas the witnesses of error contradict themselves, even when they are lying. Listen to what wise antiquity has to say about the first men: it will tell you that they were marvellous men, and that beings of a superior order deigned to favour them with the most precious communications.[vi] On this point there is no discord: initiates, philosophers, poets, history, fable, Asia and Europe, speak with one voice. Such agreement of reason, revelation, and every human tradition forms a demonstration that cannot be contradicted. So not only did men begin with science, but with a science different from our own, and superior to our own because it had a higher origin, which is what made it more dangerous. And this explains why science was always considered mysterious in principle, and why is was always confined to the temples, where the flame finally burned out when it could serve no purpose but to burn.

Not counting the first outlines of science, no one knows how far back to date certain great institutions, profound knowledge, and some magnificent monuments to human industry and human power. Near the site of St Peter's in Rome we find the great sewer of the Tarquins and certain Cyclopean constructions. This epoch goes back to the Etruscans, whose arts and

---

[12] *If one should teach us.* What follows is no less valuable: *but,* he says, *no one would teach us unless God showed him the way.* (*Epinomis* 989d)

[13] *I do not doubt,* says Hippocrates, *that the arts were originally graces (theōn charitas) accorded to men by the gods.* (Hippocrates, *Epistles, Opera,* Foesio ed. (Frankfort 1621), p. 1274). Voltaire did not agree: *To forge iron or to work it up, would have required so many happy ACCIDENTS, so much industry, so many centuries!* (*Essai sur les moeurs et l'esprit des nations,* intro. p. 45) The contrast is sharp, but I believe that a good mind reflecting attentively on the origins of the arts and sciences will not hesitate for long between *grace* and *chance.*

sciences are lost in antiquity,[14] whom Hesiod called *great and illustrious* nine centuries before Jesus Christ,[15] who established colonies in Greece and on numerous islands several centuries before the Trojan War. Pythagoras, travelling in Greece six centuries before the Christian era, learned there the cause of all the phenomena of Venus.[vii] It is from him, too, that we learn something even more curious, since all antiquity knew *that Mercury, to save a goddess from great embarrassment, played dice with the moon, and won from her the seventy-second part of the day.*[16] I even admit to you that in reading the *Banquet of the Seven Sages* in the *Moralia* of Plutarch, I could not help suspecting that the Egyptians knew the true form of planetary orbits.[viii] You can, when you like, give yourself the pleasure of verifying this text. Julian [the Apostate], in one of his tasteless discourses (I don't know which one) calls the sun *the god of the seven rays.*[ix] Where did he find this singular epithet? Certainly it could only have come to him from the ancient Asiatic traditions that he would have collected in his theurgic studies; and the sacred books of India give a good commentary on this text, since one reads there that seven virgins assembled to celebrate the coming of *Krishna*, who is the Indian Apollo, the god appearing all at once in the middle of them and proposing to them that they dance; but the virgins excusing themselves for lack of dancers, the god provided for them by dividing himself, so that each girl had her *Krishna.*[x] Add that the true system of the world was perfectly known in the most remote antiquity.[xi] Think of the pyramids of Egypt, rigorously oriented, preceding all the known epochs of history; that the arts are brothers that live and shine together; that the nation that was able to create colours capable of resisting the free action of the air for thirty centuries, raised to a height of six hundred feet weights that would defy all our mechanics,[17]

---

[14] *For a long time before the Roman state.* Livy.

[15] *Theogony* v.114. On the subject of the Etruscans, consult [Giovanni-Rinaldo] Carli-Rubbi, *Letteres américaines*, p. III, letter 2, pp. 94–104 of the Milan edition [18 vols., 1784–94] and [Luigi Antonio] Lanzi, *Saggio di lingua etrusca, etc.*, 3 vols. (Rome 1789). [Maistre's reference to Hesiod's *Theogony* appears to be in error. In v.1016 Hesiod speaks of "the country of the *glorious* Tyrrhenes." (Darcel ed.)]

[16] One can read this story in Plutarch's *On Isis and Osiris,* chap. XII. – It must be noticed that the seventy-second part of a day multiplied by 360 gives the five days that they added in antiquity to form a solar year; and that 360 multiplied by the same number gives 25,920, which measures the great revolution resulting from the precession of the equinoxes.

[17] See [Anne-Claude-P.] de Caylus, *Recueil d'antiquités égyptiennes, étrusques, grecques et romaines,* [7 vols. (Paris 1752–67)], Vol. V, preface.

sculpted in granite birds whose species the modern traveller can recognize;[18] this nation, I say, was *necessarily* also as eminent in the other arts, and even knew *necessarily* a host of things that we do not know. If I cast my eyes on Asia, I see the walls of Nemrod raised on an earth still wet from the flood, and astronomical observatories as old as the city. So where will we place the so-called times of barbarism and ignorance? Amusing philosophers tell us: *We lack centuries.* They are very much lacking for you, since the epoch of the Flood is there to smother all the romances of the imagination; and the geological observations that demonstrate the fact of the Flood also demonstrate its date with a limited uncertainty in time as insignificant as that which remains with respect to the distance to the moon in space. Even Lucretius could not prevent himself from rendering a striking testimony to the newness of the human family. And physics, which can pass for history in this case, draws from this a new support, since we see that historical certitude ends for all nations at the same time, this is to say towards the eighth century before our era. Let those people who believe everything except the Bible cite for us Chinese observations made four or five thousand years ago, on an earth that did not yet exist, by a people for whom the Jesuits had to make almanacs at the end of the sixteenth century.[xii]

All this merits no more discussion; let them talk.[xiii] I only want to present you with one observation that perhaps you have not made: this is that the whole system of Indian antiquities has been overthrown from top to bottom by the useful labours of the Calcutta Academy, and the simple inspection of a geographical map demonstrating that China could not have been inhabited before India, the same blow that strikes Indian antiquities has tumbled those of China, on which Voltaire especially never ceased to bore us.

For the rest, since Asia has been the theatre of the greatest marvels, it is not surprising that its peoples have kept a liking for the marvellous that is stronger than that which is natural for men in general, and which each can recognize in himself. It is because of this that they have always shown so little taste and talent for the *conclusions* of our sciences. One could say that they still recall that primitive science was an era of *intuitions.* Does a bound eagle ask for a *mongolfière*[19] to ascend into the sky. No, it only asks that its bonds be loosened. And who knows if these people are not yet

---

[18]   See the voyages of Bruce and Hasselquist, cited by Jacob Bryant, *New System, or An Analysis of Ancient Mythology, etc.*, [3 vols. (London, 1774–76)], 3:301.

[19]   [Hot air balloon, invented by the Montgolfière brothers.]

destined to contemplate spectacles that are refused to the quibbling genius of Europe?

Whatever happens, notice, I beg you, that it is impossible to think of modern science without seeing it constantly surrounded by all the machines of the mind and all the methods of its art. Under skimpy northern dress, his head lost in the curls of deceptive locks, his arms loaded with books and instruments of all kinds, pale from long nights and work, the modern scientist drags himself along the road to truth, soiled with ink and panting, always bending his algebra-furrowed brow towards the earth. There was nothing like this in high antiquity. In so far as it possible to perceive the science of early times at such a distance, one always sees it free and isolated, soaring rather than walking, and presenting in its whole being something airy and supernatural. Exposing to the winds the hair that escapes from an oriental *mitre*, an *ephod* covering a breast uplifted with inspiration, it looked only to the heavens, and its disdainful foot seemed to touch the earth only to leave it. However, although it demanded nothing of anyone and seemed to know no human support, it is no less proven that it possessed the rarest knowledge.[xiv] This is the great proof, if you really think about it, that antique science was dispensed from the labour imposed on ours, and that nothing could be more mistaken than all the calculations on which we base our modern experiments.

The Chevalier

You have just proved to us, good friend, that one speaks willingly of what one loves. You promised me a dry symbol, but your profession of faith has become a kind of dissertation. What is good in it, is that you have not said a word about those savages who started us off.

The Count

I confess to you that on this point I am like Job, *full of speeches*.[20] I willingly pour them out before you; but I cannot, though it cost me my life, be understood by all men or make them believe me. In any case, I don't know why you bring me back to savages. Really, it seems to me that I have never stopped speaking to you of them, even for a moment. If all humanity is descended from the three couples who repopulated the world, and if humanity began with science, the savage can only be, as I have told you, a detached branch of the social tree. Although it is incontestable, I could even abandon the argument from science, and restrict myself to religion, which alone suffices, though only very imperfectly, to exclude the state of

---

[20] Job 32:18–20.

savagery. Wherever you find an altar, there civilization is to be found. *The poor man in his cabin, covered with straw*[21] is undoubtedly less learned than we are, but more truly social if he learns his catechism and profits from it. The most shameful errors and the most detestable cruelties soil the annals of Memphis, Athens, and Rome, but all the virtues together honour the cabins of Paraguay.[22] Moreover, if the religion of Noah's family must necessarily have been the most enlightened and the most vital that it is possible to imagine, and if it is in this very reality that the causes of its corruption must be sought, this second demonstration added to the first surpasses it. Thus we must recognize that the state of civilization and knowledge is in a certain sense the natural and primitive state of man. As well, all oriental traditions begin with a state of perfection and enlightenment, what I again call *supernatural enlightenment*; and even Greece, deceitful Greece, *which dared everything in history*, rendered homage to this truth by placing its age of gold at the beginnings of things. It is no less remarkable that it did not attribute the savage state to the following ages, even to the age of iron. So that all that they have told us about the first men living in the woods, feeding themselves on acorns, and passing finally to the social state, puts them in contradiction with themselves, and can only be supported with respect to particular cases, this is to say some tribes that have been degraded and then painfully returned to *the state of nature*, that is to say, to civilization. Did not Voltaire, and that says everything, admit that the motto of every nation has always been: THE AGE OF GOLD WAS THE FIRST TO BE SEEN ON THE EARTH.[xv] So then, all nations have protested in concert against the hypothesis of an original state of barbarism, and surely this protest counts for something.

Now what does it matter to me to date the point at which such and such a branch was separated from the tree? That it did suffices for me. There is no doubt about the degradation, and I dare to say as well, no doubt about the cause of the degradation, which can only have been a crime. Some leader having altered a people's moral principle by some of those transgressions, which following appearances are no longer possible in the present state of things because happily we no longer know enough to become so guilty, this leader, I say, transmitted the anathema to his posterity; and since every constant force accelerates by its very nature since it is always acting on itself, this degradation bearing on his descendants

---

[21] [François de Malherbe, *Consolation á Monsieur Du Périer, gentilhomme d'Aix-en-Provence, sur la mort de sa fille*, v.77. (Darcel ed.)]

[22] [Maistre greatly admired the missionary work of the Jesuits in Paraguay. See his tribute to them in his *Essai sur le principe générateur des constitutions politiques*, chap. XXXV (*Oeuvres*, I:271–72)].

without interruption has finally made them into what we call savages. It is this final degree of brutalization that Rousseau and his like call *the state of nature*.

Two extremely different causes have thrown a deceptive cloud around the frightful state of the savages; the one is ancient, the other belongs to our own century. In the first place, the immense charity of the Catholic priesthood in speaking to us of these men has often placed its desires in place of reality. There was only too much truth in the first reaction of Europeans, in the time of Columbus, to refuse to recognize as equals the degraded men who peopled the new world. The priests used all their influence to contradict this opinion, which was too favourable to the barbarous despotism of the new masters. They cried out to the Spaniards: "No violence, the Gospel forbids it; if you do not know how to overthrow the idols in the hearts of these unfortunate beings, what good is it to overthrow their miserable altars? To make them know and love God requires other tactics and other weapons."[23] From deserts watered with their own sweat and blood, they made their way to Madrid and Rome to ask for edicts and bulls against the pitiless greed that wanted to enslave the Indians. The merciful priest exalted them to make them precious; he played down the evil, he exaggerated the good, he promised what he hoped would be. Finally Robertson, who is not suspect, warns us, in his history of America,[24] *that on this subject it is necessary to distrust all those writers belonging to the clergy, since, in general, they are too favourable to the natives.*

Another source of false judgements with respect to the Indians can be found in contemporary philosophy, which has used these savages to prop up its vain and culpable declamations against the social order. But the slightest attention is sufficient to keep us on guard against the errors of

---

[23] Perhaps the speaker had in mind the fine admonitions that Father Bartolomé de Olmedo addressed to Cortez, which the elegant Solis preserved for us. *Violence and the Gospel accord poorly with each other; therefore in substance, you err to overthrow altars and leave idols in the heart*, etc., etc. ([Antonio de Solis y Ribadeneyra], *Conquista de México* [Madrid 1648], III, 3). I have read a lot on America, and I am not aware of a single act of violence for which priests were responsible, except the celebrated adventure of *Valverde*, which would prove, if it were true, *that there was a fool in Spain in the sixteenth century*; but the story has all the characteristics of being false. I have not even been able to discover its origin; an extremely well-informed Spaniard told me: *I believe that it is a tale by the imbecile Garcilaso.* [Garcilaso de la Vega was the sixteenth-century Spanish author of works on Peru and the Incas, the most famous being *Royal Commentaries on the Incas*].

[24] [See note 25 below.]

both charity and bad faith. One cannot glance at the savage without reading the curse that is written not only on his soul but even on the exterior form of his body. This is a deformed child, robust and ferocious, on whom the light of intelligence casts no more than a pale and flickering beam. A formidable hand weighing on these benighted races effaces in them the two distinctive characters of our greatness, foresight and perfectibility. The savage cuts down the tree to gather its fruit, he unharnesses the ox that missionaries have just given him, and cooks it with the wood of the plough. He has known us for three centuries without having wanted anything from us, except gunpowder to kill his fellows and brandy to kill himself. Yet he has never learned to make these things; he relies on our greed, which will never fail him.

Just as the most abject and revolting substances are nevertheless still capable of a certain degradation, so are the natural vices of humanity even more vicious in the savage. He is a thief, he is cruel, he is dissolute; but he is these things in a different way than we are. To become criminals we must overcome our nature; the savage follows his. He has an appetite for crime, and no remorse at all. While the son kills his father to spare him the inconvenience of old age, his woman destroys in her womb the fruit of their brutal lust to escape the fatigue of nursing it. He rips off the bleeding scalp of his living enemy; he tears him to pieces, roasts him, and devours him while singing. If he comes upon strong liquor, he drinks to intoxication, to fever, to death, deprived equally of the reason that would command a man to fear it and of the instinct that warns the animal by distaste. He is visibly perverted; he has been stricken in the deepest layers of his moral being. He makes the observer who knows how to see tremble. But do we want to tremble for ourselves and in a very salutary way? Let us reflect that with our intelligence, our morals, our sciences, and our arts, we are to the primitive man precisely what the savage is to us.

I cannot abandon this subject without suggesting to you yet another important observation. The barbarian, who is a kind of proportional mean between the civilized man and the savage, has been and can still be civilized by any religion, but the savage properly speaking has never been civilized except by Christianity. This is a prodigy of the highest order, a kind of redemption, reserved exclusively to the true priesthood. So how could a criminal condemned to civil death recover his rights without letters of grace from the sovereign? And what letters of this kind are not countersigned?[25] The more you reflect on it, the more you will be

---

[25] I applaud all these great truths with all my heart. All savage peoples call themselves LO-HAMMI; and it is to them that it has been said: *You are my people*, and never could they say: *You are my God*! (Hosea, 2:24)

convinced that there is no other way of explaining the great phenomenon of savage peoples, which true philosophers have not occupied themselves with enough.

In any case, the *savage* must not be confused with the *barbarian*. In the one the germ of life is extinct or deadened; in the other it has been fertilized, but has not yet had time or circumstances to develop. At this point his language, which had been degraded with the man, is reborn with him, and perfects and enriches itself. If one wants to call this a *new language*, I would agree. The expression is right in one sense, but this sense is very different from that adopted by modern sophists when they speak of *new* or *invented* languages.

No language could be invented, either by one man who would be unable to make himself obeyed, or by the many who would be unable to understand themselves. What could be better said of the word, than what has been said of the one who calls himself WORD? *His going forth is from the beginning, from the days of eternity. ... Who will explain his descent?*[26] Already, despite the sad prejudices of our century, a physicist (yes, in truth, a physicist) has taken it upon himself to admit with intrepid timidity *that man first spoke because* SOMEONE *spoke to him.* God bless the word *someone*, which is so useful in difficult situations! In rendering to this first effort all the justice it merits, it must be agreed, however, that all the philosophers of this last century, without excepting even the best, are cowards who are afraid of ghosts.

Rousseau, in one of his sonorous rhapsodies, also showed some desire to speak reasonably. He admitted that languages appeared to him to be something beautiful enough. The word, that *hand of the mind*, as Charron puts it,[27] aroused a certain admiration in him, and all things considered, he could not clearly understand how it could have been invented. But the great Condillac pitied this modesty. He was astonished *that a man of intelligence like Monsieur Rousseau* had looked for difficulties where there were none, that he had not seen that languages form themselves insensibly,

---

One can read a very good piece on the savages in the *Journal du Nord*, September 1907, n° XXXV, p. 704 ff. [William] Robertson (*Histoire de l'Amérique* [4 vols. (Paris 1778)], Vol. II, Bk. 4) has perfectly described the brutalization of the savage. This is a portrait that is equally true and hideous.

[26]   Micah 5:2 and Isaiah 53:8. [Maistre's translation of the verse from Isaiah is from the Latin Vulgate – *generationem ejus quis enarrabit?* The Jerusalem Bible translates the verse as *would anyone plead his cause?* and adds this note: "The 'who will explain his descent' of the Greek and Lat. has been taken by Christian tradition to refer to the mysterious origin of Christ; the Hebr. *dor* (a generation) cannot however bear this sense."]

[27]   [Pierre Charron, *De la sagesse* (1601) I, 13.]

and that each man makes his contribution. So there is the whole mystery, gentlemen: one generation said BA, and the other BE. The Assyrians invented the nominative, and the Medes the genitive:

> ... *Quis inepti*
> *Tam patiens capitis, tam ferreus ut teneat se.*[28]

But before finishing with this subject, I would like to recommend to your attention one observation that has always struck me. How is it that we find in the primitive languages of all the ancient peoples words that necessarily suppose knowledge foreign to these peoples? For example, from where did the Greeks, at least three thousand years ago, take the epithet *Physizòos* (giving or possessing life), which Homer sometimes gives to the earth? Or that of *Pheresbios*, very nearly synonymous, which he attributes to Hesiod?[29] From where did they take the still more singular epithet of *Philimate (amorous or thirsty for blood)* given to the earth in a tragedy?[30] Who would have taught them to call sulphur, which is the cipher of fire, *the divine*?[31] I am no less struck by the name *Cosmos* given to the world.[xvi] The Greeks named it *beauty*, because *all order is beauty*, as the

----

[28] [*Nam quis iniquae / Tam patiens urbis, tam ferreus ut teneat se* ... ("For who can be so tolerant of this montrous city ... as to contain himself?" Trans. C.G. Ramsay, Loeb Classical Library 1965) Juvenal, *Satires* I.v.31–32. Note the corrections: "iniquae" for "inepti" and "urbis" for "capitis." (Darcel ed.)]

[29] *Iliad* III.243; XXI.63. *Odyssey* XI.300. Hesiod *Works and Days* V.694. This work had been in my possession for a long time when I ran across the following observation by a man accustomed to see and born to see well: *Several idioms, which today belong only to barbarous peoples, seem to be the debris of rich flexible languages announcing an advanced culture.* ([*Vues de Cordillères et*] *Monuments des peuples indigènes de l'Amerique*, by [Alexander von] Humboldt. 2 vols. (Paris 1816) Intro. p. 29.) [The reference to *Works and Days* is erroneous; the epithet is from Hesiod's *Theogony*, v.693. (Darcel ed.)]

[30] *And slaughter for it, streaming on the bloodthirsty earth.* (Euripides *Phoenician Women* V.179). Aeschylus had said earlier:
> *Of two rival brothers, the one slaughtered by the other,*
> *The earth DRINKS the blood, etc.*
> (*Seven Against Thebes*, u. 820-21)
This recalls an expression of Holy Scripture: *the ground that has opened its mouth to receive your brother's blood.* (Genesis 4:11)
Racine, who had such a high degree of feeling for antiquity, transported this expression (somewhat weakened by a useless epithet) into his tragedy *Phèdre*, II, 1.
> *And the moistened earth,*
> *DRANK with regret the blood of the nephew of Erechtheus.*

[31] *To Theion* [The divine].

good Eustathius said somewhere, and supreme order is in the world. The Latins encountered the same idea and expressed it by their word *Mundus*, which we have adopted by merely giving it a French ending, except however that one of these words excludes disorder and the other excludes defilement. Nevertheless it is the same idea, and the two words are equally correct and equally false. But again tell me, I ask you, how these ancient Latins, when they still knew only war and ploughing, thought to express by the same word ideas of prayer and torture?[xvii] And who taught them to call fever the *purifier*, or the *expiator*?[xviii] We would not say that there is here a real knowledge of cause by which a people affirmed the correctness of a name. But do you believe that these sorts of judgements could have belonged to a time when they scarcely knew how to write, when the dictator spaded his own garden, when they wrote verses that Varro and Cicero no longer understood? These words and still others that could be cited, and that belong completely to oriental metaphysics, are the evident debris of more ancient languages destroyed or forgotten. The Greek conserved some obscure traditions on this matter; and who knows if Homer did not attest to the same truth, perhaps without knowing it, when he speaks to us of certain men and certain things *that the Gods named in one way and men in another.*[xix]

Reading modern metaphysicians, you will encounter great chains of reasoning on the importance of symbols and on the advantages of what they call a philosophical language that should be created *a priori* or perfected by philosophers. I do not want to take up the question of the origins of language (the same, it must be noted in passing, as that of innate ideas), but what I can assure you of, for nothing is clearer, is the prodigious talent of infant peoples in forming words and of the absolute incapacity of philosophers to do the same thing. I recall that Plato, in the most refined of centuries, drew attention to this talent in nascent peoples.[xx] What is remarkable about this is that it has been said they proceeded by way of deliberation, in virtue of a determined system of agreement, although such a thing would have been rigorously impossible in every respect. Each language has its genius, and this genius is ONE, in a way that excludes all idea of composition, or arbitrary formation, or anterior convention. The general laws that constitute the genius of each language are what present the most striking characteristic of each. In Greek, for example, the rule is that words can be joined by a kind of partial fusion that unites them to produce a second meaning without making the two unrecognizable; this is a general rule from which the language never deviates. Latin, more refractory, lets one, so to speak, *break* words and chose and rejoin the fragments by a kind of unknown and totally singular *agglutination* that gives birth to new words of surprising beauty and of which the elements can scarcely be recognized even by an experienced eye. From these three words, for example, CA*ro*, DA*ta*, VER*mibus*, they made CADAVER, *flesh abandoned to the worms*. From the words MA*gis* and *vo*LO, NON and *vo*LO, they made MALO and NOLO, two excellent verbs that every language, even Greek, might envy Latin. From CÆC*us*, UT IRE (*to walk or grope like a blind man*) they made their CÆCUTIRE, another very successful verb that we lack.[32] MA*gis* and *au*CTE produced MACTE, a word completely peculiar to the Latins, and which they used with much eloquence. The same system produced their word UTERQUE, so happily formed from U*nus al*TERQUE,[33] an expression I very much envy them, for we can only express this idea with a phrase, *the one and the other*. And what can I say to you about the word NEGOTIOR, admirably formed from N*e* EGO *o*TIOR (I am busy, I cannot waste my time), from where they took *negotium, etc.*? But it seems to me that the Latin genius surpassed itself in the word ORATIO, from O*s* and RATIO, *mouth and reason*, which is to say *spoken reason*.

The French are not absolutely unacquainted with this system. Those who were our ancestors, for example, knew very well how to name theirs by a partial union of the word ANC*ien* with ÉTRE, just as they made *beffroi* from B*el* EFFROI. See how they worked with the two Latin words DU*o* and IRE, from which they made DUIRE, *going two together*, and by a very natural extension, *mener, conduire.*[xxi] From the personal pronoun SE, from the relative adverb of place HORS, and the verbal ending TIR, they made S-OR-TIR, that is to say SEHORSTIR, *or to put one's person outside the place where it was,*[xxii] which appears marvellous to me. Are you curious to know how they united words in the Greek way? I will cite for you the word COURAGE, from COR and RAGE, which is to say *rage du coeur,*[xxiii] or better said, *exaltation, enthusiasm of the heart* (in the English sense of RAGE). This word was in its principle a very happy translation of the Greek *thymos*, which no longer has a synonym in French. Trace the anatomy of the word INCONTESTABLE: you will find in it the negation IN, the sign of the means and of simultaneity CUM, the antique root TEST, common, if I am not mistaken, to the Latins and the Celts,[xxiv] and the sign of capacity ABLE, from the Latin *habilis*, if both do not come from yet another common and anterior root.[xxv] Thus the word INCONTESTABLE means precisely *a thing so clear that it does not admit of contrary proof.*

---

[32] The Chinese have made for the ear precisely what the Latins made for the eyes. (*Mémoires concernant l'histoire, les sciences, les arts, les mœurs, les usages, etc., des Chinois*, par des missionaires de Pékin, 15 vols. [Paris 1776–91], 8:121.)

[33] Since plurality was so to say hidden in the word, the Latins constructed it with the plural of verbs. *Utraque nupserunt* [either (woman) was married]. [Since "either" implies more than one, Latin uses a plural verb.] (Ovid *Fasti* VI.281.)

Admire, I beg you, the metaphysical subtlety that, from the Latin QUARE, *parcé detorto* [slightly deformed], made our CAR,[xxvi] and that knew how to draw from UN*us* the particle ON which plays such a great role in our language.[xxvii] I cannot keep from citing our word RIEN, which the French formed from the Latin REM, taken for some thing or for the absolute being. This is why, outside the case where RIEN, responding to an interrogation contains or supposes an ellipsis, we can only employ this word with a negation, since it is not negative,[34] which is different from the Latin NIHIL, which is formed from N*e* et HIL*um*, just as *nemo* is formed from NE and *ho*MO (*not an atom, not a man*).

It is a pleasure to be present, so to speak, at the work of this hidden principle that forms languages. Sometimes you see it struggling against some difficulty that impedes its development; it searches a form that it lacks; its materials resist it; then it will extricate itself from its embarrassment with a happy solecism, and it will say very effectively: *Rue passante, couleur voyante, place marchande, métal cassant, etc.* Sometimes you will see it evidently mistaken and making a formal blunder, as in the French word *incrédule*, which denies a lack instead of denying a virtue. Sometimes it will be possible to recognize at the same time the error and the cause of the error: for example, the French ear having required that the letter *s* not be pronounced in the monosyllable EST, third person singular of the substantive verb, it became indispensable, to avoid ridiculous equivocation, to exempt the little conjunction ET from the general rule that orders the liaison of every consonant with the vowel that follows it.[35] But nothing was more unfortunately established, since this conjunction, unique already, and in consequence insufficient, and thus refusing, *iratis musis* [to the displeasure of the muses], to be joined with following vowels, has become excessively embarrassing for the poet, and even for the prose writer who has a good ear.

But to come back to the primordial talent (and it is you, Senator, whom I address in particular): contemplate your nation, and ask it about the words with which it has enriched its language since the Enlightenment? Alas, this nation is made like all the others. Since it has got involved in reasoning it

---

[34] *Rien* is from *rem*, like *bien* from *bene*. Joinville, without referring to others, leads us to the creation of this word by telling us often enough, *que pour nulle* RIEN *au monde il n'eût voulu, etc.* In a canton of Provence I have heard, *tu non vales* REM, which is purely Latin.

[35] In effect, if the conjunction followed the general rule, the two phrases: *un homme* ET *une femme*, un honnête homme ET *un fripon* [a man and a woman, an honest man and a rogue], would be pronounced precisely the same as we pronounce: *un homme* EST *une femme, un honnête homme* EST *un fripon* [a man is a woman, an honest man is a rogue], etc.

has borrowed words and no longer creates them. No people can escape from this general law. Everywhere, in this genre, the epoch of civilization and philosophy is that of sterility. I read on your visiting cards: *Minister, Général, Kammerherr, Fraülen, Général-*ENCHEF, *Général-*DEJOURNEI, *Joustizii-Politzii Minister,* etc., etc. Business makes me read on its signs: *magazei, fabrica, meubel,* etc., etc. I hear military exercises: *directii na prava, no leva; deployade en échiquier, en échelon, contre-marche,* etc. The military administration says *haupt-wacht, exercice-hause, ordonnance-hause; commissariat, cazarma, canzellari,* etc. But all these words and thousands of others I could cite count for nothing beside all those words, so beautiful, so elegant, so expressive, that abound in your original language – for example, *souproug* (spouse), which means exactly *that one who is attached with another under the same yoke;*[xxviii] nothing more exact and more ingenious. In truth, gentlemen, it must be admitted that the savages or the barbarians, who formerly *deliberated* to form similar names, were not at all lacking in tact.

And what can we say of the surprising analogies that can be noticed between languages separated by time and space to the point of never having been able to influence each other? I could show you in one of the manuscript volumes that you see on my table, several pages covered with my fly specks, which I have entitled *Parallelisms of the Greek and French languages.* I know that I have been preceded on this point by a great master, *Henri Étienne;* but I have never come across his book,[36] and nothing is more amusing than to make for oneself these sorts of collections as one reads and as the examples present themselves. Please notice that I am not to be understood to be speaking of simple conformities of words acquired simply by way of contact or communication; I speak only of conformities of ideas proved by synonyms of sense, totally different in form, which excludes all idea of borrowing.[xxix] I will only have you notice one very singular thing, which is that when it is a question of rendering some of those ideas whose natural expression would in some way offend delicacy, the French often chanced upon the same turns of phrase formerly employed by the Greeks to save these shocking naïvetés,[xxx] that must appear quite extraordinary since in this regard we acted on our own without asking anything of our intermediaries, the Latins. These examples suffice to put us on the trail of this force that presides at the formation of languages, and to make us sense the nullity of all modern speculations. Each language, taken separately, mirrors the spiritual phenomena that took place at its birth; and

---

[36] [Henri Étienne (or Estienne)(1531–98) was a Genevan printer, writer, and Hellenist; Maistre's reference is probably to Estienne's *Traicté de la conformité du language françois avec le grec* (Geneva 1565).]

the more ancient the language, the more perceptible are these phenomena. Above all, you will find no exception to the observation on which I have insisted so often, which is that in proportion that one goes back to the times of ignorance and barbarism that saw the birth of languages, you will always find more logic and profundity in the formation of words, and that this talent disappears by a contrary gradation in proportion as one comes down towards the epochs of civilization and science. A thousand years before our era, Homer expressed in a single evident and harmonious word: *they will respond with a favourable acclamation to what they have just heard.*[37] In reading this poet, one sometimes hears oneself surrounded by the crackling of the generating fire that gave life to life,[38] and one sometimes feels oneself dampened by the dew that distilled his enchanting verses on the poetic couch of the immortals.[39] He knew how *to pour out* the divine voice around the human ear, like a sonorous atmosphere still resonating after the god has ceased to speak.[40] He could evoke Andromache, and we are shown her as her spouse saw her for the first time, quivering with tenderness and *laughing tears.*[41]

From where does this language come, which seems to have been born like Minerva, and whose first production is a hopeless masterpiece, without which it would never have been possible to prove that it had mumbled? We could exclaim like modern scholars: *How many centuries were required to form such a language!* In effect, it would have required many if it had been formed as they imagine. From the Oath of Louis the German in 842[xxxi] to Corneille's *Menteur* and the *Menteuses* of Pascal,[42] eight centuries passed: following the rule of proportion, it would not take more than two thousand years to form the Greek language. But Homer lived in a barbarous century, and for the little one might like to go back before his epoch, one finds

---

[37] It is a question here, undoubtedly, of the *EPEYPHÊMÊSAN* (*Epeuphemesan*) of the *Iliad* I.25. One could perhaps produce the shadow of this word in a barbarous form in French by saying *ils lui* SURBIENACCLAMÈRENT [(they) assented with a shout of applause].

[38] "Flaming life." *Iliad* XXI.465. [Loeb]

[39] "Fell drops of glistening dew," Ibid., XIV.352. [Loeb]

[40] "The divine voice was ringing in his ears," Ibid., II.41. *He who wishes to turn this speech into another will finally perceive what is the force and power of these words.* (Samuel Clarke, Note to his edition of the *Iliad* [2 vols. (London 1732)]) He rightly adds: *Madame Dacier puts it not badly*: "It seemed to him that the voice spilling out around him still rang in his ears."

[41] "Smiling through her tears," Ibid., VI.485. [Loeb]

[42] These *Menteuses* [liars] are the *[Lettres] Provinciales*. See the notes placed at the end of this dialogue. (Editor's note.)

oneself in the midst of Pelasgian vagabonds[43] and the first rudiments of society. Where will we find the centuries needed for the formation of this marvellous language? If, on this point of the origin of language, as on so many others, our century has missed the truth, it is because it has a mortal fear of meeting it.

Languages began, but *the word* never, and not even with man. The one has necessarily preceded the other, since *the word* is possible only through the VERB [i.e., the Word of God]. Every particular language comes into being like an animal, by birth and development, so that man never passed from a state of *voicelessness* to the use of the word. He has always spoken, and it is with sublime reason that the Hebrews called him a TALKING SOUL.[xxxii] When a new language takes form, it is born in the midst of a society that is in the full possession of language; and the action or the principle that presides at this formation cannot arbitrarily invent one word. It uses those it finds around it or that it calls from farther away; *it nourishes itself on them*, it chews them, it digests them, and it never adopts them without modifying them to some degree. In a century passionate for every gross expression excluding order and intelligence, they have talked a lot about arbitrary symbols; but there are no arbitrary symbols, every word having its reason. You lived for some time, Chevalier, in a beautiful country at the foot of the Alps, and, if I am not mistaken, you even killed some men ...

The Chevalier

On my honour, I killed no one. Moreover I could say like Madame de Sévigné's young man: *I did no harm there.*

The Count

Whatever the case, perhaps you will remember that in that country *son* (furfur) is called *Bren*. On the other side of the Alps, an owl is called *Sava*. If someone were to ask you why these two peoples have chosen these two arrangements of sound to express these two ideas, you would have been tempted to reply: *Because they judged it appropriate; things of this sort are arbitrary.* However you would have been in error; for the first of these two words is English and the second is Slavic; and from Ragusa to Kamchatka the word is used to signify in the beautiful Russian language what it

---

[43]   [The Pelasgians were an ancient people inhabiting the coasts and islands of the Eastern Mediteranean and Aegean Seas.]

signifies eight hundred leagues from here in a purely local dialect.[44] You will not be tempted, I hope, to tell me that men deliberating on the Thames, on the Rhone, on the Obi, or on the Po would by chance come across the same sounds to express the same ideas. Therefore the two words preexisted in the two languages that presented them to the two dialects. Would you like to think that the four peoples received them from some previous people? I know nothing of it, but I admit it: in the first place it is the consequence of that fact that these two immense families, Teutonic and Slavic, did not arbitrarily invent these two words, but that they received them. Then the question begins again with respect to earlier nations. Where did they get them? One must answer in the same way, *they received them and so one goes back to the origin of things*. The candles that are being carried in at the moment remind me of their name: at one time the French carried on a great commerce with the city of *Botzia* in the Kingdom of Fez; they brought from there a great quantity of wax candles that they took to naming *botzies*. Soon the national genius shaped this word and made *bougies* of it. The English retained the old expression *wax-candle*, and the Germans prefer to say *wachslicht* (light of wax); but everywhere you see the cause that determined the word. Even if I had not run across the etymology of *bougie* in the preface of Thomassin's Hebrew dictionary, where I certainly would never have looked for it, would I have been less sure of some such etymology? To be in doubt on such a matter, one would have to extinguish the flame of analogy, which is to say one would have to renounce reasoning. Notice, if you will, that the very word *etymology* is already a great proof of the prodigious talent of antiquity to run across or adopt the most perfect words, for it presupposes that each word is *true*, which is to say that it is not imagined arbitrarily – which is enough to lead a good mind a long way. Because of induction, what one knows in this genre demonstrates a great deal about other cases. What one does not know, on the contrary, proves nothing except the ignorance of the one who is looking. An arbitrary sound never expresses and can never express an idea. As thought necessarily exists prior to words, which are only the physical symbols of thought, words, in their turn, exist prior to the formation of every new language, which receives them ready-made and then modifies them to its own taste.[45] Like an animal, the genius of each

---

[44] Dialects, patois, and the proper names of men and places seem to me to be almost intact mines from which it is possible to draw great historical and philosophic riches.

[45] Without even excepting proper names, which by their nature would seem invariable. The nation that was most ITSELF in letters, Greece, is the one that in domesticating words altered them the most. Historians will no doubt be impatient

language hunts every source to find what suits it. In our language, for example, *maison* is Celtic, *palais* is Latin, *basilique* is Greek, *honnir* is Teutonic, *rabot* is Slavic,[46] *almanach* is Arab, and *sopha* is Hebrew.[47] Where does all this take us? It matters little to me, at least at the moment: it suffices for me to prove to you that languages are only formed from other languages, which they usually kill to nourish themselves, in the manner of carnivorous animals. So let us never speak of *chance* or of arbitrary symbols, *Gallis hœc Philodemus ait* [Says Philodemus to the Gauls].[48] One is already well advanced in this genre when one has reflected sufficiently on this first observation that I made to you, which is that the formation of the most perfect, the most meaningful, the most philosophic words, in the full force of the term, invariably belongs to the time of ignorance or simplicity. One must add, to complete this great theory, that similarly the *name-making* talent invariably disappears in the measure that one descends to the epochs of civilization and science.

In all the writings of our time on this interesting question, there has been a continuously expressed wish for *a philosophic language*, but without anyone knowing or even suspecting that the most philosophic language is that in which philosophy is least involved. Two little things are lacking to philosophy to create words: the intelligence to invent them and the power to get them adopted. If it sees a new object, it pages through its dictionaries to find an antique or foreign word, and almost always it turns out badly. The word *mongolfière*, for example, which is national, is correct, at least

---

about this, but such is the rule. A nation receives nothing without modifying it. *Shakespeare* is perhaps the only proper name that has taken its place in the French language with its national pronunciation of *Chekspire*; it was Voltaire who passed this on, but this was because the genius that was going to withdraw let it happen.

[46]   In effect, the word *rabot* signifies *work* in the Russian language; thus, when the French adopted the word, the most active instrument of carpentry [i.e., the plane] was named the *worker* par excellence. [In this case, at least, Maistre's etymology is faulty. *Petite Robert* gives two different derivations: one from the dialectical *rabotte* meaning "rabbit," and the other from the middle Dutch *robbe*.]

[47]   SOPHAN, *to elevate*, from whence *Sophetim*, the *Judges* (which is the title of one of the books of Scripture), *elevated men, those who sit higher than the others*. From whence also *suffetes* (or *soffetes*), the two great magistrates of Carthage. This is an example of the identity of the two languages, Hebrew and Punic.

[48]   This citation, to be correct, must be dated. Why would we not say: *Non si malè nunc et* OLIM *sic erit* [Horace], and why again would we not add, in profiting from the double meaning which belongs to the word OLIM: *Non si malè nunc et olim sic fuit?* [The Latin *olim* means "at that time" or "hereafter, one day." "Les Olim" also refers to a register recording enactments (1254–1318) of the Parlement of Paris, named for its first word.]

in one sense, and I prefer it to *aérostat*, which is the scientific term and which says nothing. One might as well call a ship a *hydrostat*. See this crowd of new words borrowed from the Greek these past twenty years, as crime or folly has found the need: almost all have been taken or formed in a way that is contrary to their literal meaning. The word *théophilanthrope*, for example, is more foolish than the thing, which is to say a lot: an English or German schoolboy would have known how to say *théanthrophile*. You tell me that this word was invented by wretches in a wretched period; but chemical nomenclature, which was certainly the work of very enlightened men, begins with a solecism of the worst sort, *oxigène* instead of *oxigone*. Moreover, although I am not a chemist, I have excellent reasons to think that this whole dictionary will be effaced; but merely looking at the matter from the philological and grammatical point of view, it would be perhaps the most unfortunate thing imaginable if the recently disputed metric nomenclature did not win the all-time award for barbarism. The superb ear of the seventeenth century would have rejected it with an unhappy shudder. That was a time when genius alone had the right to persuade the French ear, when Corneille himself was more than once quickly rebuffed; but in our time it is surrendered to everyone.

When a language is being made (as it can be made), it is in the hands of great writers who use it without thought of creating new words. Was there in the song of Athalie [Jean Racine], in the description of hell that one reads in *Télémaque* [Fénelon], or in the peroration of the funeral oration of Condé [Bossuet], a single word taken by itself that was not commonly used? If, however, the right of creating new expressions belongs to anyone, it belongs to great writers, and not to philosophers, who display a rare ineptitude in this matter. Yet writers use this privilege with excessive reserve – never in their inspired pieces and only for nouns and adjectives. As for *words*, they scarcely dream of offering new ones. Finally, we must abandon this idea of *new languages*, except in the sense that I have just explained. Or, if you would like me to employ another turn of phrase, the word is eternal, and every language is as old as the people who speak it. Some, without reflection, might object that there is no nation that can understand its ancient language – but what, I ask you, does it matter? Do alterations that do not touch principle exclude identity? Would someone who had seen me in my cradle recognize me today? However I think I have the right to say that I am *the same*. It is no different with language: it is the same as long as the people is the same.[xxxiv] The poverty of languages in their beginnings is another assumption made with *the full power and authority* of philosophy. New words prove nothing, since in the measure that they are acquired others are lost, in who knows what proportions. What is sure is that people have always spoken and they have spoken precisely as they have thought and as well as they have thought, for it is equal foolishness to believe that there is a symbol for a thought that does not exist as to imagine that a thought exists without a symbol to express it. The Huron does not say *garde-tems* [watch], for example; this is a word that is missing from his vocabulary. But *tomahawk* is happily missing from ours, and this word counts like any other. It would certainly be something to be desired to have a profound knowledge of *native* languages. The zeal and untiring work of missionaries would have prepared an immense work on this subject: the destructive fanaticism of the eighteenth century made it disappear forever.[49] If we had, I do not say the monuments, since there cannot have been any, but only the dictionaries of these languages, I do not doubt that we could have found there the words that I was just telling you about, evident remains of a previous language spoken by an enlightened people. And even if we could not find them, it would only be the result of degradation having proceeded to the point of effacing these last remains: *Etiam periere ruinæ*.[50] But in whatever state they are found, these *ruined* languages remain as terrible monuments to divine justice; and if we really knew them well, we would probably be more frightened by the words that they possess than by those they lack. Among the natives of New Holland there is no word to express the idea of God, but they have one for the operation that destroys an infant in its mother's womb to dispense her from the pains of nursing it – they call this the MI-BRA.[51]

The Chevalier

By treating with a certain extension a question that we found along our route, Count, you have interested me a great deal. But often remarks escape you that distract me, and which I always promise myself to ask you about. You said, for example, while discoursing about your subject, *that the question of the origin of speech* was the same as that of the origin of ideas. I would be curious to hear your reasons for saying this, for I have often heard different writings on the origin of ideas talked about and I have even read some of them, but the busy life I have led for so long, and perhaps also the lack of a good *aplanisseur* [planer?] (this word, as you see, does not belong to a primitive language) has always prevented me from seeing the thing clearly. This problem has always appeared to me to be surrounded by a kind of cloud that it has never been possible for me to dissipate, and

---

[49]   See the Italian work entitled *Memorie cattoliche* (3 vols.); although intentionally poorly written, it is curious and has become extremely rare.

[50]   [Even the ruins have perished. Lucan 9.969].

[51]   I do not know what traveller told the anecdote of the *Mi-bra*, but probably it would only have been cited by a reputable authority.

I have often been tempted to believe that bad faith and misunderstanding have also played a marked role here.

The Count

Your suspicion is perfectly well founded, my dear Chevalier, and I dare to think that I have reflected enough on this subject to be able to spare you some fatigue.

But first I would like to suggest to you that authority should be the fundamental ground for decision.[52] Human reason is manifestly convicted of impotence for guiding men, for few are capable of reasoning well, and no one can reason well on every subject; so that, in general, it is well to begin with authority, whatever people say. So balance the voices on both sides, and against the sensible origin of ideas you will see Pythagoras, Plato, Cicero, Origen, St Augustine, Descartes, Cudworth, Lamy, Polignac, Pascal, Nicole, Bossuet, Fénelon, Leibniz, and that illustrious Malebranche who sometimes erred in the pursuit of truth but never abandoned it. I will not give you the champions on the other side, since their names would offend my tongue. If I did not know anything about the question, I would decide without any other motive than my taste for good company and my aversion for bad.[53]

I would propose to you another preliminary argument that also counts: this is what I take to be the detestable results of this absurd system that would want, so to speak, to materialize the origin of our ideas. I believe there is nothing more degrading or more deadly for the human spirit. Because of it, reason has lost its wings and crawls like a slimy reptile; because of it, the divine source of poetry and eloquence has been dried up; because of it, all the moral sciences have perished.[54]

---

[52] *Naturæ ordo sic se habet ut quùm aliquid discimus, rationem præcedat auctoritas*, that is to say, the natural order requires that, when we learn something, authority precedes reason. (St Augustine *The Catholic Way of Life* C.II)

[53] This was Cicero's advice: "It seems to me," he said, "that one should call PLEBEIAN all those philosophers who do not adhere to Plato, Socrates, and all their family.""[Maistre has somewhat modified the text, which reads: "All the common crowd of philosophers – for such a title seems appropriate to those who disagree with Plato and Socrates and their school." (*Tusculan Disputations* I.23. Trans. J.E. King, Loeb Classical Library, 1927)]

[54] "The *sublime* theory that relates everything to sensations can only have been designed to open the way to materialism. We now see why Locke's philosophy has been so eagerly welcomed, and the effect that has been its result. It has been rightly censured (by the Sorbonne) as false, poorly reasoned, and leading to the most pernicious consequences." ([Nicolas] Bergier, *Traité historique et dogmatique de la vraie religion* [12 vols. (Paris 1780)], Chap. v, art. iv. § 14, 3:518)

The Chevalier

Perhaps it is not up to me to dispute the consequences of the system, but as to its defenders it seems to me, my dear friend, that it is possible to cite some respectable names besides these other names that *wound your tongue*.

The Count

Many fewer, I can assure you, than is commonly believed. In the first place it must be observed that a crowd of great men, made authorities by the last century, will soon cease to be so or to appear to be so. The great cabal had need of their great renown: they created their fame just as one makes a box or a shoe. But this great bogus reputation is at bay, and soon the dreadful mediocrity of these *great men* will be an inexhaustible European laughing-stock.

Moreover it is necessary to remove from the list of *these respectable names* those of the really illustrious philosophers that the philosophic sect inappropriately enrolled among the defenders of the sensory origin of ideas. Perhaps, Senator, you have not forgotten the day we were reading together Cabinis's book on *The Relations of the Physical and Ethical in Man*,[55] where he offhandedly places Hippocrates and Aristotle among the ranks of the defenders of the materialist system. I remarked to you on the double and invariable character of modern philosophism – its ignorance and its effrontery. How can people who are entirely ignorant of learned languages and especially of Greek take it upon themselves to cite or to judge the Greek philosophers? If Cabinis in particular had opened a good edition of Hippocrates, instead of citing on hearsay or carelessly reading some poor translation, he would have seen that the work that he cites as belonging to

---

Nothing is more accurate than this observation. With his crude system, Locke unleashed materialism. Condillac has since made this system fashionable in the country of fashion, by his so-called clarity, which at bottom is only the simplicity of a mere nothing; and vice has drawn from it maxims that it knew how to put at the very bounds of extreme futility. One can see in the letters of Madame du Deffant [Du Deffand] all the things that this *blind* woman draws from the ridiculously false maxim *that all our ideas come to us from our senses*, and what kind of an edifice she raises on this airy foundation! [*Lettres de la marquise Du Deffand á Horace Walpole, depuis Comte d'Oxford, écrites dans les années 1766–1780, auxquelles sont jointes les lettres de Mme du Deffand á Voltaire écrites dans les années 1759–1775, publieés d'après les originaux,* 4 vols. (Paris 1812)], l.XLI 4:339.

[55] [Pierre-Jean-Georges Cabinis, *Rapports du physique et du moral de l'homme*], 2 vols. (Paris: Crapelet 1805)

Hippocrates is a supposed fragment.[56] It would require no other proof than the style of the author, as bad a writer as Hippocrates is clear and elegant. Moreover this writer, whoever he was, speaks neither for nor against the question, which I pointed out to you at the time. He limited himself to treating the question of experience and to treating the medical theory that *sensitivity* is synonymous with *experience* and not with *sensation*.[57] I also showed you clearly why Hippocrates has a better title to be ranged among the defenders of innate ideas, since he was the teacher of Plato, who borrowed from him his principal metaphysical dogmas.[xxxv]

With respect to Aristotle, although it was not possible for me to give you immediately all the explanations you would have liked, you nevertheless had the goodness to agree when, on the basis of a memory that seldom fails me, I cited for you this fundamental maxim of Greek philosophy, *that man can learn nothing except on the basis of what he already knows*;[xxxvi] this alone necessarily presupposes something similar to the theory of innate ideas.

Moreover if you examine what he wrote with such strength of mind and truly admirable fineness of expression on the essence of the mind, which he placed in thought itself,[xxxvii] you will not remain in the least doubt on the error that, right down to Locke and Condillac, has claimed to disparage this philosopher.

As for the scholastics, who have been greatly denigrated in our time, what has especially deceived the crowd of superficial thinkers who have taken it upon themselves to treat this great question without understanding it, is the famous axiom of the schools: *Nothing can enter into the mind*

---

[56] This work is the *Avertissemens* (*Paraggeliai*). On this point one can consult the two principal editions of Hippocrates; that of Foëz, 2 vols. in folio (Geneva 1657), and that of Van der Linden, 2 vols. in-8vo (Leyden 1665); but especially the work of the celebrated [Albrecht von] Haller, *Artis medicae principes*, etc, [11 vols.] (Lausanne 1786), 4:86. In his Preface to this work, Haller comments: *Spurius liber, non ineptus tamen* [A spurious book, but still not stupid].

[57] Among the innumerable characteristics of bad faith that distinguish the modern sect, one can distinguish the one that confuses common or mechanical experiments – such as are carried out in our physics laboratories – with experience in a more lofty sense – i.e., with the impressions that we receive from external objects by means of our senses; and because the Spiritualist rightly maintains that ideas cannot have their origin in this completely secondary source, these honest philosophes make him say *that in the study of physical sciences one must prefer abstract theories to experience*. This gross imposture is repeated in I do not know how many books written about the question under discussion here; and a number of *inexperienced* people let themselves be taken in by this.

except by the senses.[58] Through lack of intelligence or good faith, they
have believed or have said that this famous axiom excludes innate ideas,
which is quite false. I know, Senator, that you have no fear of folios.
Someday I would like to have you read the doctrine of St Thomas on ideas;
you will sense at what point ...

The Chevalier

Good friends, you force me to meet some strange personages. I believed
that St Thomas was cited on the benches and sometimes in church, but I
little suspected that he might be relevant among us.

The Count

St Thomas, my dear Chevalier, flourished in the thirteenth century. He
could not occupy himself with sciences that did not exist in his time, and
with which no one then embarrassed themselves. His style, admirable with
respect to clarity, precision, strength, and brevity, cannot however be
compared to that of Bembo, Muret, or Maffei.[59] Nevertheless he had one
of the greatest minds that has ever existed in the world. Not even poetic
genius was a stranger to him. The Church has preserved some sparkling
examples that have since excited the admiration and envy of Santeuil.[60]
Since you know Latin, Chevalier, I would not want to exclude the
possibility that, at age fifty and retired to your old manor, God willing, you
might borrow St Thomas from your pastor to judge this great man for
yourself. But I return to the question. Since St Thomas was called the *angel
of the schools,* it is he especially who must be cited to absolve the school;
and in waiting for the Chevalier to turn fifty, it is to you, Senator, that I
will make known the doctrine of St Thomas on ideas. First, he does not
hesitate about deciding *that our intelligence, in our present state of
degradation, understands nothing without an image.*[61] Now listen to him

---

[58] *Nihil est in intellectu quòd priùs non fuerit sub sensu.* [Literally, "Nothing
is in the mind that was not previously present to the senses."]

[59] [Bembo, Muret (or Muretus), and Maffai were sixteenth-century Italian
humanists.]

[60] Santeuil said that he preferred to his own most beautiful composition, the
hymn, or as one says, the *prose* of St Thomas, for the feast of the Blessed
Sacrament: *Lauda, Sion, Salvatorum, etc.* [Jean de Santeuil was a seventeenth-
century French hymnographer.]

[61] *Intellectus noster, secundum statum praesentem, nihil intelligit siné
phantasmate* [that our intellect, according to its present state, understands nothing
without a phantasm]. St Thomas, *Summa Contra Gentiles,* Bk. III, chap. 41. [Trans.
Anton C. Pegis, *Basic Writings of Saint Thomas Aquinas,* 2 vols. (New York 1945),

speak on the mind and on ideas. He carefully distinguishes "*the passive intellect*, or this power that receives impressions, from the *active intellect* (which he also names *possible*), or from the intelligence properly speaking that reasons about impressions. The senses know only individuals; intelligence alone rises to the universal. Your eyes perceive a triangle; but this apprehension, which you have in common with the animal, only constitutes you as a simple animal; you will only be *man* or intelligence by elevating the *triangle* to *triangularity*. It is this power to generalize that *specializes* man and makes him what he is; for the senses count for nothing in this operation; they receive the impressions and transmit them to the intelligence. It is only the latter that can render impressions *intelligible*. The senses are unacquainted with all spiritual ideas, and are even ignorant of their own operation, since vision is neither able to see itself nor see that it sees."[62]

I would still like to have you read the superb definition of the truth that St Thomas has given us. *The truth,* he said, *is an equation between the affirmation and its object.*[xxxviii] What precision and what depth! This is a flash of the truth that defines itself, and it has the advantage of warning us that it is not a question of an *equation* between *what is said of the thing and what is in the thing*; "but with respect to the spiritual operation that affirms, it admits no *equation*," because it is above everything and resembles nothing, so that can be no relation, no analogy, no *equation* between the thing understood and the operation that understands it.[xxxix and xl]

Now, whether ideas are innate in us, or whether we see them in God,[63] or whatever you like, does not matter; this is not what I want to examine at the moment. The negative side of the question is undoubtedly what is most important; let us first establish that the greatest, the most noble, the most virtuous geniuses in the world are agreed in rejecting the origin of ideas in sensory perception. This is the holiest, most unanimous, most stirring protest of the human mind against the grossest and vilest of errors; for the rest, we can postpone the question.

You see, gentlemen, that I am able to reduce somewhat the number of these *respectable names* that you spoke to me about, Chevalier. As for the rest, I do not refuse to recognize that some among them are defenders of

---

2:66]

[62]   [This citation appears to be a constructed "quotation" in which Maistre has paraphrased his own understanding of what he takes Aquinas to have written on these issues.]

[63]   [Malebranche held that we see everything in God. Maistre had his doubts about Malebranche's view, but still counted the Oratorian as an ally against Locke and his French disciples. See Richard Lebrun, "Joseph de Maistre et Malebranche."]

sensibilism (this word, or any other that you might find better, has become necessary). But tell me, have you never found yourself, by misfortune or by weakness, in bad company? In this case, as you know, there is only one word to be said: LEAVE; as long as you are there, they have a right to mock you, to say nothing more.

After this short preliminary, Chevalier, since you have done me the honour of choosing me to introduce you to this kind of philosophy, I would first like to point out to you that any discussion of the origin of ideas is a ridiculous blunder so long as the question of the nature of the soul remains undecided. In the courts, would you be permitted to claim an inheritance as a relative, so long as there was any doubt that you were one? Well, gentlemen, it is the same in philosophical discussions, where there are questions that lawyers would call *pre-judicial*, and that simply must be decided before one can be permitted to pass on to others. If the estimable Thomas was right in the beautiful verse: *Man lives by his soul, and the soul is thought,*[64] everything has been said; for if thought is the essence of man, to ask what is the origin of ideas is to ask what is the origin of the origin.

Here is what Condillac has to say: *I will concern myself with the human mind, not to know its nature, which would be foolhardy, but only to examine its operations.* Let us not be the dupe of this modest hypocrite; every time you see a philosopher of this past century bowing respectfully before some problem and telling us *that the question exceeds the powers of the human mind; that he will not try to resolve it, etc.,* you can be sure that on the contrary he fears the problem as too clear, and that he is hurrying to pass it by in order to reserve the right *to muddy the waters.* I do not know one of these gentlemen to whom the sacred title of *honest man* would be perfectly fitting. You see an example of it here. Why lie? Why say that one does not want to pronounce on the nature of the soul while one is pronouncing very expressly on the essential point by supporting the thesis that ideas come to us through the senses, which obviously excludes thought from the category of essences.

I do not see, moreover, that the question of the essence of thought is any more difficult than that of its origin, which they tackle so courageously. *Can one think of thought as an accident of a substance that does not think? Or can one think of accident-thought knowing itself, as thinking and meditating on its essence as a non-thinking subject?* Here is the problem posed under two different forms, and for my part I admit to you that I have

---

[64]   [In 1782 Maistre had in his library the *Oeuvres diverses de M. Thomas de l'Académie française* (Lyons 1763). See Jean-Louis Darcel, "Les Bibliothèques de Joseph de Maistre. 1768–1821," *Revue des études maistriennes* no. 9 (1985): 83.]

never seen any so hopeless. Yet one is perfectly free to pass over it in silence, provided one agrees or even warns at the head of any book on the origin of ideas that it is being offered as a simple *jeu d'esprit*, or a completely airy hypothesis, since the question is not seriously admissible so long as the preceding one is not resolved. But such a declaration made in the preface would scarcely credit the book, and any one who knows this class of philosophers will scarcely wait for this kind of probity.

Then, Chevalier, I would point out that there is something equivocal in the very title of all the books written in the *modern* sense on the origin of ideas, since this word *origin* can apply equally to the cause simply occasioning or instigating ideas and to the cause producing ideas. In the first sense, there is no dispute since the ideas are assumed to pre-exist; in the second, it is precisely the same as maintaining that the substance of an electrical discharge is produced by the device that sparks it off.

Next, we will look into why these writers always speak of the origin of *ideas*, and never of the origin of *thoughts*. There must have been a secret reason for the preference constantly given to one of these expressions rather than the other: this point can be cleared up quickly. I would simply tell you, using the very words of Plato, whom I always cite willingly: *Do you and I understand the same thing by this word thought?* For me, thought is THE DISCOURSE THAT THE MIND HOLDS WITH ITSELF.[65]

And this sublime definition alone will prove to you the truth of what I just told you: *that the question of the origin of ideas is the same as that of the origin of speech*; for thought and speech are simply two superb synonyms; the intelligence not being able to think without knowing that it thinks, nor to know what it thinks without speaking, since it must say: *I know*.

So if some initiate of modern doctrines comes to say to you that *you speak* because someone has spoken to you, ask him (but will he understand you?) if, in his opinion, *understanding* is the same thing as *audition*, and if he believes that, to *understand* speech it suffices to hear the noise that strikes the ear?

In any case, we can, if you wish, leave this question aside. If we wanted to go into it more deeply, I would hasten to direct you to a very essential preliminary, that of convincing you that even after so many disputes the

---

[65] *(Do you know) what I call thought? It is the speech which the soul has with itself.* (Plato, *Theaetetus* 189e.)

Verb, word, and *reason,* are the same thing (Bossuet, *VIe et Avertissement aux protestants,* [Paris 1689], N° 48) and this *verb,* this *word,* this *reason,* is a being, a real *hypostasis,* in the image as in the original. This is why it is written *dic verbo* and not *dic verbum.*

definition of *innate ideas* is still not well understood. Would you believe that Locke never took the trouble to tell us what he understood by this phrase? Yet nothing is more true. Bacon's French translator says, while scoffing at *innate ideas*, that he confesses *that he does not remember knowing about the square of the hypotenuse while in his mother's womb*. So here is a man of intelligence (for Locke was that) who attributes to spiritualist philosophers the belief that a foetus in its mother's womb knows mathematics, that we can know without learning, which is to say, in other words, to learn without learning; and this is what these philosophers call *innate ideas*.

A very different writer with quite a different authority, who honours France today by his superior talents and by the noble use he knows how to make of them,[66] believed that he was arguing decisively against *innate ideas* by asking: "*how*, if God had engraved a certain idea in our minds, *man* could have succeeded in effacing it? How, for example, can the idolatrous child, born just like the Christian with the *distinct notion* of a single God, nevertheless be driven to the point of believing in a multitude of gods?"

I could tell you things about this *distinct notion* and the dreadful power that man, only too really, possesses of *more or less effacing* his innate ideas and of *transmitting his degradation!* I will limit myself here to pointing out to you the evident confusion between *idea* or simple *notion* and affirmation – two entirely different things. It is the first that is *innate*, and not the second, for no one, I believe, wants to say that there are innate *reasonings*. The theist says: *there is only one God*, and he is right; the idolater says: *there are several of them*, and he is wrong, but he is mistaken like a man who makes a mistake in a process of calculation. Does it by any chance follow that the latter has no idea of number? On the contrary, it is proof that he possesses it; for, without this idea he could not even be mistaken. In effect, to be mistaken, he must affirm, which he cannot do without using some form of the verb *to be*, which is the soul of all speech,[67] and every affirmation presupposes a pre-existing idea. Therefore, without the prior idea of a god, there would be neither theists nor polytheists, and in so far as one can say neither *yes* nor *no* to what one does not know about, it is impossible to be mistaken about God without having an idea of God. So it is the *notion* or pure *idea* that is innate and necessarily alien to the senses. If it is subject to the law of development, this is the universal law of

---

[66] [The reference is to Louis de Bonald. See footnote 68 below.]

[67] So long as the verb does not appear in the phrase, man does not speak, he makes NOISE. (Plutarch, *Platonic Questions*, chap. IX; Amyot translation. [Chap. IX does not appear to include this sentence. (Darcel ed.)])

thought and of life in all spheres of the earthly creation. For the rest, every notion is true.[68]

You see, gentlemen, that on this great question (and I could cite several other examples for you), we still do not know precisely *what the question is*.

And finally, one last no less essential preliminary would be for you to take note of this secret action, which, in all the sciences ...

The Senator

Believe me, my dear friend, you will not play any more on the edge of the question; for your foot will slip, and we will be obliged to spend the night here.

The Count

God keep you from that, my good friends, for you would be very poorly lodged. I would have pity only on you, my dear Senator, and none at all on this amiable soldier who could arrange himself very well on a couch.

The Chevalier

You call to mind my bivouacs. However, although you are not military men, you could also tell us about terrible nights. Courage, my dear friend! Certain misfortunes can have a certain sweetness; I at least have experienced this feeling, and I would like to believe that I share it with you.

The Count

I suffer no pain in resigning myself; I even admit it to you: if I were isolated, and if the blows that fallen upon me had wounded only myself, I could only look on all that is going on in the world as a great and magnificent spectacle that I could simply indulge in admiring. Nevertheless the entrance ticket has cost me dearly! ... However I am not murmuring against the adorable power that has so sharply narrowed my world. You see

---

[68] The one who was carrying on this discourse, more than ten years ago [which dates this footnote to about 1820], had little inkling then that he was on the eve of becoming the correspondent and soon the friend of the illustrious philosopher of which France has so many reasons to be proud; and that in receiving from the very hand of the Viscount [Louis] de Bonald the precious collection of his works, he would have the pleasure of finding there the proof that the celebrated author of *Législation primitive* [Paris 1802] was finally ranged among the most respectable defenders of *innate ideas*. Beyond that, we are speaking here only of the negative proposition that denies the immaterial origin of ideas; the rest is a question between us, a *family* matter in which the materialists must not meddle.

how it has already begun indemnifying me, since I am here, since it has so liberally given me friends such as you. Moreover it is necessary to know how to get out of oneself and to raise oneself high enough to see the whole world instead of seeing only one point. Never without admiration do I consider this political waterspout that has come to snatch from their places great numbers of men destined never to know one another, to swirl them together like the dust of the fields. We three are here, for example, who were born never to know each other; however we have come together, we converse; and even though our cradles were so far apart, perhaps our graves will touch.

If the mixture of language is remarkable, the communication of languages is no less so. One day in the library of the academy of science of this city, I ran across Bayer's *Museum sinicum,* a book that has become rare enough and that pertains most particularly to Russia, since the author, fixed in this capital, had his book printed here some eighty years ago. I was struck by a reflection of this learned and pious writer.

We do not yet see the use of our works on languages, but soon they will be seen. It is not without a great design of Providence that languages absolutely ignored in Europe two centuries ago are in our time made known to the whole world. It is already permitted to suspect the design; and it is a sacred duty for us to concur in it with all our strength.[xli]

What would Bayer say if he lived in our time? The march of Providence would appear to him as having been greatly accelerated. Let us reflect first on the *universal language.* Never has this title better fitted the French language; and what is strange is that its power seems to grow with its sterility. Its best days have past; however all the world understands it, all the world speaks it, and I do not believe that there is a city anywhere in Europe that does not contain some men able to write it purely. The just and honourable confidence accorded to French clergymen exiled in England has permitted the French language to sink deep roots there. This is a second conquest perhaps, which has not made much noise, for God did not want any,[69] but which can have more fortunate consequences than the first. Think of the singular destiny of these two peoples, who cannot cease either seeking each other or hating each other! God has put them in place like two great magnets that attract each other on one side and repel each other on

---

[69] *Non in commotione Dominus.* ["The Lord is not in the earthquake." 3 Kings 19:11.

the other, for they are at the same time enemies and relations.[70] This England has carried our language to Asia; it has had Newton translated into the language of Mohommed,[71] and young Englishmen defend theses in Calcutta in Arabic, Persian, and Bengali. For its part, France, which thirty years ago never doubted that there was more than one living language in Europe, learned them all while forcing other nations to learn its own. Add that the longest voyages have ceased to frighten the imagination; that all the great navigators are Europeans;[72] that the whole Orient is manifestly ceding to European ascendancy; that the crescent, pressed on its two points, at Constantinople and at Delhi, must necessarily break in the middle; that events have given England fifteen hundred leagues of frontiers with Tibet and China, and you have an idea of what is in preparation. Man, in his ignorance, is often mistaken on the ends and the means, on the instruments and the obstacles. Sometimes he wants to cut an oak with a penknife, and sometimes he throws a bomb to break a reed, but Providence never fumbles, and it is not in vain that it agitates the world. Everything announces that we are marching towards a great unity that we must *salute from afar*, to use a religious turn of phrase. We are sorrowfully and very justly ground. But if such miserable eyes as mine are worthy of catching a glimpse of divine secrets, we are *ground* to be *mixed*.

The Senator

O mihi tam longæ maneat pars ultima vitæ![73]

The Chevalier

I hope you will willingly allow the *soldier* to take the floor in French:

---

[70] "You seem to me to be – *gentis incunabula nostræ* [the cradle of our nation]. *France has always more or less influenced manners in England; and when your fountain is choked up and polluted, the stream will not run long, or not run clear with us*, or perhaps with any nation [Maistre's italics]. This gives all Europe, in my opinion, but too close and connected a concern in what is done in France." (Burke, *Reflections on the Revolution in France*, (London: Dodley 1793), pp. 118–19). "Paris is the centre of Europe." (Burke, *Lettres à un membre de la chambre des communes*, (1797), p. 18).

[71] The translator, who wrote almost under the dictation of an English astronomer, was named Tuffuzul-Hussein Khan. Boerhave received the same honour. (Jones, *Works*, 5:570. *Supplemental volumes to The Works of Sir. W. Jones*, [2 vols. (London 1801)], 1:278, 2:922.)

[72] See *Essays by the Students of Fort William in Bengal, etc.*, (Calcutta 1802). [Louis-Claude de] Saint-Martin remarked *that all the great navigators are Christians*. This is the same thing.

[73] [Oh may there remain for me so long a part of life!]

Run, steal, too slow hours,
That delay this happy day.

NOTES TO THE SECOND DIALOGUE

i   The merit of style must not be accorded to Rousseau without restriction. It
    must be noted that he wrote philosophical language very poorly, that he
    defined nothing, that he used abstract terms poorly, and that sometimes he
    used them in a poetic sense and sometimes in a conversational sense. As for
    his intrinsic merit, [Jean-François de] La Harpe captured it nicely: *Every-*
    thing, even the truth, is deceptive in his writings.

ii "Whenever you notice that a degenerate style pleases the critics, you may be
    sure that character also has deviated from the right standard." (Seneca,
    Epistle 114) [Loeb]. One can turn this thought around and say with as much
    truth: "Whenever you notice that character has deviated from the right
    standard, you may be sure that a degenerate style will please the critics." In
    France, the century that has just ended has given a very great and sad proof
    of this truth. However, some very good minds have recognized the evil and
    are defending the language with all their strength; it is not yet known what
    will happen. *Style takes refuge,* as they used to say, based on the same
    theory. By one of those false notions that is always being introduced into the
    domain of science, this style has been attributed to contact with foreign
    nations; and this is how the human mind wastes its time playing with mis-
    leading surface phenomena, where it even amuses itself by foolishly
    mirroring itself, instead of breaking through them to arrive at the truth.
    Persecuted French Protestantism, freed or protected, never produced and
    never will produce any work capable of honouring the language or the
    nation. At the moment there is nothing to contradict me. *Macte animo!* [*Take*
    courage!]

iii In general, these citations are accurate. They can be verified in the work of
    Timon of Locris, printed with the works of Plato (Bipontina ed. [*Platonis*
    philosophi quae existant, (by H. Stephanus and M. Ficino), ed. F.C. Extar
    and J.V. Embur, 11 vols. (Zweibrücken 1781–7). This appears to be the
    edition of Plato that Maistre owned and used.] X:26. See, as well, Plato's
    Timaeus, ibid., 426, and the *Critias,* Ibid., 65–66.) I will observe only that
    in the *Critias* Plato does not say *inestimable gift,* but *the most* beautiful
    things among the most precious: *Ta kallista apo tōn timiōtatōn apollyntes*
    [For they had lost the fairest of their goods from the most precious of their
    parts. Trans. R.G. Bury, Loeb Classical Editions 1929]. (*Critias* 121b) The
    Abbé Le Batteux in his translation of Timon of Locris, and the Abbé
    [François-Xavier] Feller (*Dictionnaire historique,* [Augsburg 1781–83], art.
    "Timon," and *Catéchisme philosophique,* [Liège 1788], Vol. III, n° 465)
    make this philosopher speak in a more specific way; but as the second part

of the cited passage is obscure, because Marsilio Ficino appears to me to have made a simple guess, I imitate the reserve of the speaker, who has restricted himself to what is certain.

iv In effect, all these ideas will be found in Plato's *Phaedrus* (*Opera*, [Bipont. ed.], X:286 and 341). This singular dialogue very much resembles *the man*. The most respectable truths are very poorly accompanied there, and *Typhon* is shown too close to *Osiris*. [Typhon was the name used by the Greeks for the Egyptian Set, the god of evil, who killed his brother (or father) Osiris. This myth is recounted in Plutarch's *Isis and Osiris*.]

v Newton, who perhaps could rightly have been called, to use Dante's phrase, MASTER OF THEM THAT KNOW, decided that in philosophy *more* should not be permitted when *less* sufficed to explain phenomena, and that therefore one couple sufficed to explain the population of the world and that one had no right to assume others. Linnaeus, who had no equal in the science he cultivated, even considered it an axiom *that living beings possessing sexuality come from one couple created by God in the beginning*; and Sir W[illiam] Jones, who meditated so much on languages and the different human families, declared that he embraced this doctrine *without reservation*. (*Asiatic Researches*, 3:480.)[1] Voltaire, basing himself on the miserable excuse of the diversity of species, hotly supported the contrary opinion, and he could be excused (if his intentions had not been bad) since he was speaking of something he did not understand. But what should we say of the physiologist cited above (Barthez; see note vi to the First Dialogue) who, after expressly acknowledging the omnipotence of the interior principle in the animal economy and its decaying action when it has itself been vitiated in some way, nonetheless adopts Voltaire's crude reasoning, and basing himself on the stature of the Patagonian, the woolly hair of the Negro, the nose of the Cossack, etc. told us gravely that, *following the most reliable opinion*, NATURE (who in world is this woman [*la nature*]?) has been *induced by primordial laws whose causes are unknown* TO CREATE *the diverse races of men*.

So that is how an otherwise very able man can finally find himself led by the anti-Mosaic fanaticism of his century to ignore what he knows and to deny what he affirms.

---

[1] [The original edition of *Asiatick Researches*, edited by William Jones, was published in Calcutta (1788–94) in 4 volumes; there were also at least a half dozen London pirated editions published in the years following 1796 (some versions up to 20 volumes). A French partial translation, *Recherches asiatiques*, was published in Paris in 1803, with two more volumes in 1805. Maistre appears to have used an English version as well as the French version; both versions are cited in the *St Petersburg Dialogues*.]

vi *Antiquitas proximè accedit ad deos* (Cicero *The Laws* II.11); "Still, I would
not deny that they were men of lofty spirit and – if I may use the phrase –
FRESH FROM THE GODS. *For there is no doubt that the world produced a
better progeny before it was yet worn out.*" (Seneca *Epistle 90* [Loeb])
Origen said very sensibly to Celsus: "The world having been created by
Providence, it was necessary that humanity, in its beginnings, be placed
under the tutelage of certain superior beings, and that then God had already
shown himself to men. This is also what Holy Scripture attests, etc. (Genesis
18)," and he held that "the human species, in the beginning, received
extraordinary assistance until the invention of the arts put men in a state
where they could defend themselves and no longer needed divine intervention, etc." Origen called on profane poetry as an aid to reason and revelation;
he cited from Hesiod the very well known passage that was so well
paraphrased by Milton (*Paradise Lost*, IX, 2, etc.). See Origen *Against
Celsus* IV.28.

vii *Pythagoras mistook the nature of the star Venus. Olymp. XLII, which were
the years of the city CXLII*. Pliny *Natural History* II.8. Macrobius *Saturnalia*
1.12. – Maurice, *History of Indostan*, 1:167.

viii *"Eit'" ephē, "sy dedias," k, t, l.* [And then ... you fear, etc.] *Sept. Sap. conv.
Edit. Steph in-fol*, 2:149. Amyot translated: – "The Egyptians say that the
stars, in making their ordinary revolutions, are high at one time and then
low, and according to whether they were high or low become worse or better
than they were, etc." (Plutarch *Banquet of the Seven Sages* c.XI.) [Loeb
trans.: "'So then,' said Thales, 'as the Egyptians say of the stars, when they
gain or lose altitude in their courses, that they are growing better or worse
than they were before, do you fear that the obscuration and degradation
affecting you because of your place at table will be brought about in a
similar way.'" The correct reference is III.149a.]

ix It is in the Fifth Discourse that he employs this remarkable expression; and
in it he in effect honours the Chaldeans. It is true that Petau, in the margin
of his edition (p. 323) cites a manuscript that reads *epaktina theon* [imported
god] instead of *heptantina* [seven-rayed (god)]; but the first lesson is
obviously the work of a copyist who, understanding nothing of the *seven
rays*, must have greatly congratulated himself for having thought of this
correction. This only proves how in correcting manuscripts one must guard
against making changes that are not based on other written authorities.

x This was not precisely the case. The Indian fable does not say that the
number of virgins was seven; but in the work that reproduced the fable and
of which a copy was sent to Europe, one sees, in effect, seven girls.
(Maurice, *History of Indostan*, 1:108); which nevertheless seems to come
back to the same thing, all the more so in that the Brahmins expressly state
that the sun had seven original rays. (*Sup. vols. to the Works of Sir W. Jones*,
2:116). (Editor's note)

Pindar said (*Olympian Odes* VII.131–5) "that after the gods had divided up the earth, and the sun, forgotten in the division, had recovered for himself the island of Rhodes, which had just come out of the depths of the sea, he had there a nymph who gave her name to the island, *seven sons of a marvellous spirit*"; and one can also see in the great work by P. [Bernard] de Montfaucon that all the figures that represent Apollo or the sun have the head adorned with seven luminous rays or a diadem with seven points, which again is the same thing. In one way or other, one constantly sees the number *seven* attached to the sun, and this has always appeared remarkable to me. (*Antiquité expliquée et représentée en figures*. [10 vols.] (Paris 1722), chap. VI, 3:119) [The diadem with seven points adorns the head of the Statue of Liberty in New York harbour.]

xi On this point one can see the numerous testimonies of antiquity collected in the fine preface that Copernicus placed at the head of his famous *De Revolutionibus Orbium Coelestium*, dedicated to Pope Paul III, the great protector of the sciences and especially of astronomy. With respect to this book, one can observe that the sovereign pontiffs powerfully favoured the discovery of the true system of the universe through the protection they accorded at different times to the defenders of this system. It has become completely useless to speak of the condemnation of Galileo, whose wrongs are no longer unkown except by the ignorant. (See the Memoir read to the Academy of Mantua by the Abbé [Girolamo] Tiraboschi. *Storia della letteratura italiana*, 8 vols. (Venice 1796), 8:313.)

xii Seneca said: *Philosophi credula gens* [The credulous tribe of philosophers.]. (*Investigations in Natural Philosophy* V.26.) So how could they not be credulous, those who believe all they want to believe. Examples are not lacking. Some are remarkable. Have we not seen them, for half a century, showing us that the Biblical Flood was impossible because the water necessary for the great submersion was lacking. But just as soon as they needed more water than the Flood to form the mountains through precipitation, they did not hesitate to cover the globe to depth of the Cordilleras. Say that the gigantic blocks that form certain monuments in Peru could well have been imitation stones and you will immediately find one of the these gentlemen who will tell you: *I see nothing improbable in that* ([Carli-Rubbi], *Lettres américaines*, Letter VI, 1:93, translator's note). Show them the Siberian rock that is in the Academy of Sciences of St Petersburg, and which weighs 2,000 pounds. They say: *This is an aerolith; it fell from the skies and was formed in an instant.* But if it is a question of terrestrial *strata*, that is something else. A Peruvian could very well have made impromptu granite, just as it is often formed in the air; but for limestone, God will have needed at least sixty thousand years. So they must be found.

xiii Bailli [Jean Sylvain Bailly] *demonstrated* that the famous tablets of Trivalore in India go back to the greatly celebrated time of *Cali-Yug*, that is to 2,000 years before our era. But now these tablets are found to have been *written*, and even by chance *dated* from towards the end of the thirteenth century. (*De l'antiquité du Surya-Sidhanta*, by M. Bentley, in *Recherches asiatiques*, 6:538.) What a misfortune for science if the French had dominated India during the irreligious fever that has affected this great people, and that does not yet appear weakened because it has weakened the illness! These detestable scholars of the last century would have allied with the brahmins to stifle the truth, and we would not have known how to get at it. Europe owes much to the English society of Calcutta, whose honourable works have broken this arm in the hands of the ill-intentioned.

xiv The celebrated work by [Jacob] Bryant, *A New System, [or an Analysis of ancient mythology* (London 1774–76)], etc. can be considered a wise commentary on this proposition. A work of this kind necessarily contains a hypothetical part, but the work as a whole, and the third volume especially, seems to me a veritable demonstration of primitive science, and even of the powerful physical means that were put at the disposition of the first men, since their material creations surpass human strength, *qualia nun hominum producit corpora tellus* [the earth does not produce such strong men]. Caylus dared all of Europe, with all its mechanical skill, to construct one Egyptian pyramid. (*Recueil d'antiquités*, etc., Vol. 5, preface).

xv In effect, he [Voltaire] said it in his *Essai sur les moeurs, etc., aurea prima sata est ætus.* Chap. IV, *Oeuvres de Voltaire,* (1785), 16:289. It is quite remarkable that similar traditions are to be found in America. *The reign of Quetzalcoatl was the age of the gold of the peoples of Anahnac; then the animals, and even men, lived in peace; the earth produced the richest harvests without cultivation. ... But this reign ... and the happiness of the world did not last long, etc.* (Humboldt, *Vues des Cordillères*, Plate VII, 1:3)

xvi See Eustathius [*Commentarii ad Homerii Iliadem*, 3 vols. (Florence 1730–35)] on verse 16 of the first book of the *Iliad*. For the rest, without wanting to contest the general observation, *that there is to be found in ancient languages, back to the epochs of a more or less profound barbarism, words that assume knowledge foreign to those epochs,* I nevertheless confess that the word COSMOS does not seem to me to be appropriately cited in support of the proposition, since it is obviously new in the sense of *world*. Homer only uses it in its primitive sense of *order, decency,* ornament, etc. *Iliad* II.214; V.759; VIII.179, 364, 489, 492; XIV.622, etc. *Odyssey* VIII.179, 364, 489, 492; XIV.363, etc. Hesiod makes almost no use of this word (even in the sense of *ornament*) nor of any of its so numerous and elegant derivatives. What is singular is that COSMOS is to be found only once in his *Theogony* (V.588), and COSMEO in V.572. Pindar almost always employed this word COSMOS in the sense of *ornament*, and sometimes in the sense of *convenience*, never in the sense of *world*. Even Euripides never uses it in the latter sense, which must appear very surprising. In truth, one finds it in the latter sense in the hymns attributed to Orpheus (*to the earth*, V, 4; *to the sun*, V, 16, etc.). But this is only a proof that these hymns were fabricated or interpolated at a time very much later than that to which they are attributed.

xvii   Sallust, who loved archaisms, said: *And so the Senate, because of these successful actions, decreed a "supplication" to the immortal gods.* [Ancient form of thanksgiving; *supplica* in the Latin of Sallust's time meant "punishment."] (*The War with Jurgurtha* LV.2.) And more than a century later, Apuleius, mimicking the same style, said again: *Plena aromatis et* SUPPLICIIS [full of fragrances and offerings] (*Metamorphoses* XI.16.9). Moreover, *supplicatio, supplicari, etc., etc.* come from the same word, and the same analogy is found in our language, where one finds *supplice* [torture] and *supplication* [entreaty], *supplier* [to entreat] and *supplicier* [put to the torture].

xviii   In fact, there does not appear to be the least doubt on the etymology of *febris*, which obviously comes from the ancient word *februare*. From which comes *Februarius*, the month of expiations.

     Among the ranks of singular words, I would place *Rhumb*, which for a long time has belonged to a number of the maritime languages of Europe. *Rhumbos* in Greek generally meaning *rotation*, and *rhumbon* a *spiral convolution*, could one not, without being a *Mathanasius*,[2] see in the word *rhumb* an ancient knowledge of *loxodromics* [the technique of navigating according to loxodromes or rhumb lines].

xix   One may observe, with respect to this expression, that it is never encountered in the *Odyssey*; and this observation could be joined to others that permit a guess that these two poems, the *Iliad* and *Odyssey,* are not from the same hand, since the author of the *Iliad* is very consistent in his use of names, surnames, epithets, turns of phrase, etc.

xx   In fact, he said that *many of the names bestowed in ancient times are deserving of notice and praise for their excellence and descriptiveness.* (*Laws* VII.816b [Trans. R.G. Bury, Loeb Classical Library, 1926])
Seneca admires the same talent of antiquity in designating objects *efficacissimis notis* [by means of striking notations]. (Seneca *Epistle 81.*) He himself is admirable in this expression, which is completely *efficacious* in making us understand what he wants to say.

     Plato did not keep himself from recognizing this talent in antiquity, and he drew from it the unquestionable consequence; he said: *For myself, I consider it an obvious truth that words could only have been imposed on things originally by a power above man,* AND THIS IS WHY THEY ARE SO ACCURATE. (*Cratylus* 438c)

---

[2] [Dr Chrisostyme Mathanasius was the pseudonym of Hyacinthe Cordelier, an eighteenth-century author who published a number of works in Belgium.]

xxi [Pierre] Charron also said: *Celui que je vuex DUIRE et instruire á la sagesse, etc.* [The one that I want to lead [or conduct] and instruct in wisdom, etc.] (*De la sagesse*, [1601], Bk. II, ch. v, n° 13). This word was born at a time in our language when the meaning of the two words *duo* and *ire* were generally known. When the idea of simultaneity grew dim in men's minds, *onomatopoeic* action joined there the particle destined to express the same idea in French, that is to say the CUM of the Latins, and so one says *conduire* [conduct, guide]. When we say today, in familiar style: *Cela ne me* DUIT *pas*, the original meaning still subsists, for it is as if we said: *Cela ne peut* aller *avec moi; m'accompagner, subsister à côté de moi*, and again it is in a wholly similar sense that we say: *Cela ne vous* VA *pas*. [*Petit Robert* derives *conduire* from the Latin *conducere*.]

xxii Roubaud, in the preliminary discourse of his new dictionary of French synonyms,[3] sees in *sortir* HORS and IRE. He does not understand this word because he has neglected the consonants, to which a real etymologist must give almost exclusive attention. The vowels represent the pipes of the organ, which is the animal power that can only sound; but the consonants are the *keys*, that is to say the sign of the intelligence that articulates the sound.

xxiii *Je disois en mon* COURAGE : *Si le Roi s'en alloit, etc.* (Joinville, in his collection of memoirs, etc., Vol I) This phrase is completely Greek: *Egō de eō tō THYMŌ moy elegon, etc.* [And I said this is my heart (courage), etc.]

   To the middle of the sixteenth century, this word COURAGE still retained its original meaning. *Le vouloir de Dieu tout-puissant lui changea le courage.* (See the safe conduct given by the Sultan to a subject of the very Christian king, at the end of the book entitled *Promptuaire des Conciles, etc.*, (Lyon: de Tournes 1546), p. 208). Moreover, *cor* made *coeur*, in virtue of the same analogy by which *bos* made *boeuf* [beef], flos, fleur [flower], *cos*, queux [tails], *votum, voeu [vow], ovum*, oeuf [egg], *nodus*, noeud, [knot], etc.

xxiv From whence the word TEST*is* in Latin, the word TE*moin* (formerly TES*moing*) in our language, TEST in English – as in TEST oath, etc.

xxv CAP*ut h*ABILE; CAPABLE: *powerful head that possesses a great capacity.* The first root having disappeared, we have attributed to this word *capable* the unique sense of the second, *habile* [clever, skilful]. The English have preserved it pure and simple: *an* ABLE *man (un homme capable).*

xxvi *Quare* made *car*, as *quasi* made *casi; quartus, cart; querela, kérelle; quicumque, kiconsque; quamquam, cancan* (this one is celebrated), and so many other words that retained or rejected the Latin orthography. *Car* preserved it for quite a long time; one reads *car* in an ordinance of Philip the

---

   [3] [Pierre Joseph André Roubaud, *Nouveaux synonymes français* (1785, 4 vols., and later editions).]

Long, of 28 October 1318: QUAR *se nous souffrions, etc.* (*Mémoires du sire de Joinville*, in the *Collection complète des mémoires relatifs à l'histoire de France*, etc., (Paris 1819), preface, p. 88). And at the beginning of the sixteenth century, a poet still said:

QUAR mon mari est, je vos di
Bon mire, je le vos affi.

(Verse cited in Lebret's notice on Molière's *Le Médicin malgré lui*.)

xxvii   The numerical expression ONE, converted into an indefinite pronoun to express the vague unity of something, is so necessary or so natural that the Latins sometimes used it almost without noticing that it went against some of the spirit and some of the most certain rules of their language. A passage from Terence is often cited: *fortè* UNAM *vidi adolescentulam* [*The Lady of Andros* 118. The text reads *aspicio* rather than *vidi*. (Darcel ed.) John Sargent translates as "I caught sight of one girl who figure was ..." (Loeb Classical Editions 1912).] Others could also be cited: Cornelius Nepos *Life of Hannibal* XII.3, Cicero *On the Nature of the Gods* II.7, *Letters to his Friends* XV.16, *Philippics* II.3, Tacitus *Annals* II.30, etc., etc. This indefinite pronoun being one of the primordial elements of the French language, our fathers, employing a very natural and very convenient ellipse, separated it from the substantive *homme*, kept in order to repeat every time it was a question of expressing what an abstract man said or did, and they said UN *a dit, c'est* UN *qui passe*, as is said in our time in some of the neighbourhood dialects of France. La Fontaine still said:

Vous rappelez en moi la souvenance
D'UN qui s'est vu mon unique souci.

But soon UN was changed to ON by the general analogy which always changed the initial Latin U to the French O, as in *onde, ombre, once, onction, onguent etc.* instead of *unda, umbra, etc.* This analogy is so strong that it has often made us pronounce O even in words where the orthography has retained the U, as in *nuncupatif, fungus, duumvir, triumvir, nundinal, etc.* which we pronounce *noncupatif, fongus, etc.* From whence still comes the Latin pronunciation of the French that so amuses the Italians – *gonom, malom, Dominus vobiscom, etc.* So I willingly agree with the opinion of the speaker on the origin of our particles CAR and ON. The Port-Royal folks, however, have claimed that our *car* comes from the Greek GAR, and that ON comes from HOMME. But it appears certain to me that, in these two cases, these gentlemen have lacked the *grace* of etymology: God is the master. (See *La Grammaire générale et raisonnée de Port-Royal*, chap. XIX)

xxviii   Who would not be struck by the perfect analogy of this word *souproug* with the *conjux* of the Latins, a purely intellectual analogy since it has nothing in common with the senses. This word *conjux*, moreover, is a syncope of CONJUG*atus*, the "G" and the remainder being hidden in the "X."

The fraternity of Latin and Slavonic, which positively presupposes a common origin, is a known thing. Less known in the relationship of Slavonic to Sanskrit, which I learned for the first time in reading Paulin de Saint-Barthélemi's dissertation, *De latini sermonis origine de cum orientalibis linguis connexione*, (Rome 1802,).

I especially recommend to philologists the names of numbers, which are essential for research of this kind.

xxix I know that the indicated collection once existed, but I do not know if it still exists, and even in this case I would have little hope of obtaining it today. I will try to supplement it to a certain degree by some remarkable examples that I have noted myself.

Anakephalaiōsis, récapitulation [recapitulation]. *Sygkatábasis, condescendance* [condescension]. *Diasyrmos, persiflage* [irony], *Diasyrein, persifler* [ridicule]. *Eparisterotēs, gaucherie* [awkwardness]. *Dēmou (t') andra, homme du peuple* [man of the people]. (Homer *Iliad* II.II.198.) *Makra philē, grande amie* [great friend]. (Theocrites II.42.) *Kálamas aulon, flûte de canne* [stick flute]. (Ibid.) *Heortēn poieitn, faire une fête* [celebrate]. *Orthōsai hymnon, dresser un contrat, un plan*, etc. [draw up a contract, a plan, etc.] (Pindar *Olympian Odes* III.5). *Myrian (echō) charin, mille grâces* [a thousand thanks]. (Euripides *Alcestis* v.544). *'Ep amphō katheudein, dormir sur les deux oreilles* [sleep soundly]. *Ophra IDE Menélaon*, voir *un malade (en parlant d'un médecin)* [to see a sick person {in speaking of a doctor}]. (Homer *Iliad* IV.v.205). *Haimatos eis agathoio, vous êtes d'un bon sang* [you are of good stock]. (Homer *Odyssey* IV.v.611) *Oikias megalēs ēn, il étoit d'un grande maison* [he was from a great house]. (Plato, *Meno*). *Thatton ē badēn, plus vite que le pas* [faster than the step]. (Xenophon *Hellenica* V.4.53). *Ēn autois eidenai, c'étoit à eux de savoir* [it was for them to know]. (Demosthenes *On the Embassy* 20) *Poi son pod' (epi synnoia) kykleis, tournez-vous vos pas, etc., etc.* [turn your steps, etc.]. (Euripides *Orestes* v.632).

From *misère* [destitution] and from *malheur* [bad luck, misfortune] we have taken *misérable* [miserable] and *malheureux* [unlucky], which belong equally to destitution and to vice, the one leading only too often to the other: the Greeks proceeded the same way with their two words *Pónos* [toil] and *Mochthos* [troubles].

But all these analogies disappear before that of *Nostimos (nostimos)* [returning] and *revenant* [said of someone one has not seen for a long time and that one never expected to see again]. As there is nothing so sweet as the return of a cherished person long separated from us, and reciprocally, nothing so sweet for the *revenant*, for the warrior especially the day that fortune returns him safe and sound to his country and his family (*Nostimon ēmar* [day of return]). The Greeks used the same word for *plaisir* [pleasure] and *revenir* [to return]. Now the French have followed precisely the same idea. They have said comely [*avenant*] *homme*, comely *femme*; *figure, physionomie*. *Cet homme me* REVIENT; which is to say, *it is as agreeable to me as a friend who comes back to me.*

I see nothing so surprising.

xxx Such, for example, are the words *Eumaria* (*Eumaria*) [easy things], and *Nōi aphrodisiō* [we two will make love] – Theocrites, id. VI.26. Eustathius, *Commentarii ad Homerii Iliadem* [Florence 1730–35], I, v. 113)

   Ta moria, ek temnein (hippon). Dromas, etc. etc.

   [To cut out the parts of a (running) horse. Dromas, etc.]

   It is quite essential to observe, with respect to these words and the previous ones, that these marvellous coincidences of ideas did not come to us by the way of Latin intermediaries, not even when we have taken from them the words that represent the ideas. We received from the Latins, for example, the word *advenant (adveniens* [arriving]), but the Latins never used this word to mean *that which is agreeable*. For this word, as for so many others, there is no link between us and the Greeks, no visible communication. What a subject for meditation, *his quibus datum est* [for those to whom it was given]!

xxxi This oath, which passes for the oldest written example of our language, has often been printed. It can be found at the head of one of the volumes of [Antoine] Court de Gébelin's *Le Monde primitif [analysé et comparé avec le monde moderne*, 9 vols. (Paris, 1771–82)]; in the Roman, Wallon, Celtic, and German, etc. dictionary, (1777) and in the *Journal historique et littéraire*, July 1777, p. 324, etc. The full maturity of this language is rightly dated from Corneille's *Menteur* and the *Lettres provinciales* [of Pascal]. This latter work especially is grammatically irreproachable; one never finds there a shadow of the kind of dross that one still finds floating on Corneille's best pieces.

xxxii HHAIME-DABER. This is Homer's *articulating man.* The solemn Voltaire tells us: "Man has always been what he is. This is not to say that he has always had beautiful cities, twenty-four pound cannon, comic operas and convents of religious." (Tacitus in person!) "But ... the foundations of society always existing, there has therefore always been some society ... Do we not see that all the animals, as well as all other beings, invariably execute the law that their *nature* has given them. The bird makes his nest as the stars follow their course by a principle that never changes. How could man change it? etc. etc." But the following page, he will nevertheless ask, *by what law, by what hidden bounds, by what instinct is it that man has* ALWAYS *lived in families, without yet having formed a language.* (Introduction to the *Essai sur l'histoire universel, Oeuvres,* 6:31–3.

   Romani tollent equites peditesque cachinnum!

   [Let the Romans, cavalry and infantry alike, raise a loud guffaw. Horace *Art of Poetry* v.113.]

xxxiii And even so they use this right only very soberly and with a marked timidity. *I would like to be permitted to use the term* DEMAGOGUE (Bossuet, *Histoire des variations* [*des églises protestantes* (Paris 1700)], 5:18). SAGACITE, if I dare use this term (Bourdaloue, *Serm. sur la parf. observ. de la loi*, II* part). *Esprit* LUMINEUX [luminous spirit], *as our friends* [of Port-Royal] *say* (Madame de Sévigné, 27 September 1671). – L'ÉCLAT [outburst] *of thoughts* (Nicole, cited by Madame de Sévigné, 4 November 1671). She underlines BAVARDAGE [gossip] (11 December 1695) and AIMABILITÉ [kindness] (proof that *aimabilité* had not existed) (7 October 1676). – RIVALITÉ [rivalry], word invented by Molière (Le Bret's commentary on the *Dépit amoureux*, Act I, Scene IV). EFFERVESCENCE: *how do you like that one, my dear? That is a word that I have never heard spoken* (Madame de Sévigné, 2 August 1689). OBSCENITY: *What do you say to that, Madame?* (Molière, *Critique de l'Ecole des femmes*).

In general, great writers fear neologisms; a secret feeling warns them that it is not permitted to interline the writings *of our superiors.*

xxxiv It is quite remarkable that while a language is gradually approaching the point of perfection that belongs to it, the characters that paint it vary in the same proportion, and are only fixed when the language itself is fixed. Everywhere where the true principles of the language are altered, one will perceive at the same time an alteration in its writing. This happens because each nation *writes its language.* There is a great exception in the heart of Asia, where the Chinese, on the contrary, seem *to speak their writing*; but I do not doubt that there the least alteration in the system of writing must immediately produce another in the language. These considerations destroy the least idea of prior or arbitrary reasoning in languages. In any case, since it is a question of writing, whatever Bryant and the others say, I agree with Pliny's view: *apparet æternum litterarum usum* [It seems the use of letters has been eternal]. (*Natural History* VII.56.)

xxxv Galen seems to leave no doubt on this matter: "Hippocrates admitted two sources for our knowledge: the sensible principle and intelligence. He believed that through the first power, we know sensible things, and by the second, spiritual." (*In lib. de offic. Med.* 1, 4) "The first among the Greeks of whom we have knowledge, he recognized that all error and all disorder come from matter, but that all idea of order, of beauty, and of artifice comes to us from above." (Id., *De dieb. decret.*) From this it follows "that Plato was the greatest partisan of Hippocrates, and that he borrowed from him the most important of his teachings." (Id. *De usu part.*, 1. VIII). These texts can be found cited at the end of good editions of Hippocrates, *inter testimonia veterum.* The reader who wants to verify them in the Van der Linden edition (2:1017) must observe with respect to the first text, of which I give only the substance, that the Latin translator *Vidus Vidius*, is mistaken in making

Hippocrates himself speak, instead of Galen who has taken the floor. *Which things you know I also did, etc.* Ibid.

xxxvi This decisive axiom in favour of innate ideas is found, in effect, in Aristotle's *Metaphysics. All knowledge (comes) from things known before.* Bk. I, chap. vii. Elsewhere, he repeats *that all teaching and learning that involves the use of reason proceeds from pre-existent knowledge. ... logical arguments, whether syllogistic or inductive, both effect instruction by means of facts already recognized, the former making assumptions as though granted by an intelligent audience, and the latter proving the universal from the self-evident nature of the particular (Posterior Analytics,* Bk. I, chap. 1, "Of demonstration.")

xxxvii I find in Aristotle's *Metaphysics* (Bk. VII, chap. ix) some ideas that relate beautifully with what the speaker says here. "As there is nothing above thought, if it were not substance, but simple act, it would follow that the act would have the superiority of excellence or perfection – *To eu to semnon* [the good is the holy] – on the very principle that produces it, which is revolting. – *Hōst'(ei) pheukton touto* [so that this is to be avoided] – One is too accustomed to envisaging thought as it is applied to external objects, as science, or sensation, or opinion, or knowledge; while the apprehension of the intelligence that understands itself appears to be a kind of masterpiece. *Autēs de (hē noēsis) en parergō.* [And this (intelligence) is secondary] – This knowledge of the mind is nevertheless *itself*; the intelligence can only be intelligence by intelligence. *Kai estin hē noēsis noēseōs noēsis.* – The understood and the understanding are one. – *Ouch heteron oun ontos tou nooymenou kai tou nou, etc,* [The perceived is not other than the perceived]." I am inclined to believe that this chapter of Aristotle's *Metaphysics* was present in at least a vague way in the mind of the speaker as he refuted the popular prejudice that so unjustly ranked Aristotle among the defenders of a system no less false than vile and dangerous. (Editor's note)

xxxviii In effect, I find this definition in St Thomas, under a little less laconic form. *The truth of the intellect is the adequation of intellect and thing, inasmuch as the intellect says that what is and what is not is not. (Summa Contra Gentiles,* Bk. I, chap. XLIX, no. 2.) – *What the intellect in understanding says and knows* (for it can not know and judge without SAYING) *must be adequated to the thing, so that, namely, the thing be such as the intellect says it to be.* (Ibid.) [Trans. Anton C. Pegis]

xxxix *That is true about what the intellect speaks, but (not about) the operation by which it speaks.* (Ibid.)

xl *The possible* [or active] *intellect is part of a man ... and it is the most noble and most formal thing in him. – The possible intellect, moreover, is demonstrably not an act of the body, because it is cognizant of all sensible forms universally. Therefore, no power whose operation can extend to the universals of all sensible forms can be the act of a body.* St Thomas Ibid.,

Bk. II, chap. LX, n° 4, 5. *Now universal species cannot be in the passive intellect, since it is a power using an organ, but only in the possible intellect.* Ibid., n° 12. – *The potential perception ... is attained by intelligible appearances and immaterial apparitions.* Ibid., n° 15 [or 24]. *Sense is cognizant only of singulars ... through individual species [received] through bodily organs ... the intellect is cognizant of universals.* Ibid., Bk. II, chap. LXVI, N° 3. – *Sense cognition is limited to corporeal things ... a sense knows neither itself nor its operation ... sight neither sees itself nor sees that it sees.* Ibid., n° 4, 5.

This small number of citations suffices, I think, to justify the speaker's assertions on the subject of St Thomas. In passing, one can read there the condemnation of Condillac, so ridiculous with his *transformed sensations*, so obstinately confused about the truth that when he encounters it by chance he cries out: *This is not it.* (Editor's note)

xli Although the general meaning of the indicated passage has been given, it is still worth the trouble of citing the original, especially seeing the extreme rarity of the book from which it has been taken.

I would like, moreover, that everyone would by himself so perceive what rewards both literature and Christianity may obtain from these remarks of ours, that he would not need our admonition; and although it perhaps will not be clear immediately to each one what gains we have brought in the first place to religion, still the time will come when it will not be so difficult. I for my part reckon it to be a singular benefaction of the heavenly Deity that all the languages of all the races, which for the last two hundred years have been completely unknown, have either been brought to light by the efforts of good men or are still being brought forth. For if reason cannot search out the purpose of the eternal mystery and the plans of the divine mind for the future, still there exist today many evidences of that Providence. From these we may perceive that some greater thing is being planned, something that it is right and good to ask for in prayer. It is extraordinarily glorious to offer the work of our hands according to the capacity of man and to bring together even the smallest amount of material.

(Theophile Sigefridi Bayeri, *Museum sinicum* [*in quo sinicae linguae et litterarae ratio explicatur*], [2 vols.] (St Petersburg 1730), preface, 2:143–4).

Third Dialogue

The Senator

Tonight, my dear Count, I will begin our discussion, Bible in hand, by proposing a difficulty for you; this is serious, as you will see. When the disciples of the Man-God asked him if the man born blind, whom they encountered along the way, was in this state because of his own crimes or for those of his parents, the divine teacher gave them this answer: *It is not that he has sinned nor those who brought him into the world* (that is to say, it was not that either his parents or himself had committed some crime, of which his state was the immediate consequence), *but that God's power be made manifest in him.* Father de Ligny, whose excellent work you no doubt know,[1] has taken the reply that I have just cited for you as a proof that illnesses are not the result of crime. How, if you please, do you understand this text?

The Count

In the most natural way. In the first place, I would ask you to notice that the disciples believed that one or the other of these two propositions was sure; *that the blind man suffered the consequences of his own faults or that of his parents*, which accords marvellously with the ideas that I have just exposed to you on this point. In the second place, I observe that the divine answer only presents the idea of a single exception that confirms the law instead of overturning it. I can understand wonderfully that this blindness could have had no other cause than that of the solemn manifestation of the power that had come to change the world. The celebrated Bonnet of Geneva took the miracle worked on the man born blind as the subject of

---

[1] [François Ligny, *Histoire de la vie de Notre Seigneur Jésus-Christ, depuis son incarnation jusqu'à son ascension* (Avignon 1774).]

an interesting chapter in his book on the truth of the Christian religion,[2] because, in effect, it would be difficult to find in all history, I would say even in all sacred history, any fact where the truth was clothed in such striking characteristics so appropriate to compel conviction. Finally, if you want to speak rigorously, one could say that, in a more remote sense, this blindness was yet another consequence of original sin, without which the Redemption, like the works that accompanied and proved it, would never have taken place. I know Father de Ligny's precious book very well, and I even remember, and this perhaps escaped you, that, to confirm his thought, he asked about the origin of the physical evils suffered by children baptised before they reached the age when they could have sinned. But, without gainsaying the respect due a man of this merit, it seems to me that one can recognize here one of those distractions to which we are all somewhat subject when we write. The physical state of the world, which is the result of the fall and degradation of man, will not vary until some future epoch to come, which must be as general as that of which it is the result. The spiritual generation of the individual man has and can have no influence on these laws. The infant suffers even as he dies, because he belongs to a mass that must suffer and die, because he has been degraded in his principle, and in virtue of a sad law that proceeds from this, every man, because he is a man, is subject to all the evils that can afflict man. Everything leads us back to this great truth that every evil, or to speak more clearly, all *suffering*, is a punishment imposed for some actual or original crime.[3] If this heredity of pain embarrasses you, forget, if you will, all that I have said on this point, since I have no need of this consideration to establish my first assertion, which is that we do not know what we are saying when we complain *that the wicked are happy in this world and the just unhappy*, since nothing is so true as the contrary proposition. To justify the ways of Providence, even in the temporal order, it is not at all necessary that crime be punished *always* and without delay. For one last time, it is singular that man cannot find it in himself to be as just towards God as towards his own kind. Who has ever thought to maintain that there is no order or justice in a state because two or three criminals escape

---

[2] [Charles Bonnet, *Recherches philosophiques sur les preuves de christianisme* (Geneva 1770).]

[3] One can add that every punishment [*supplice*] is punishment in both senses of the Latin word *supplicum*, from which our own word comes, for EVERY punishment punishes [*tout supplice supplie*]. Catastrophe, therefore, awaits any nation that would abolish punishments! For the debts of the guilty would continue to fall on the nation, which would be forced to pay without mercy, and which could in the end see itself treated as *insolvent* according to all the rigour of the laws.

justice? The only difference between the two kinds of justice is that ours lets the guilty escape through powerlessness or corruption while if the other sometimes *appears* not to perceive crimes, it only suspends its blows for adorable motives that are not very much beyond the scope of our intelligence.

The Chevalier

For my part, I would not want to quibble any more on this point, the more so in that I am not in my element here, for I have read very few books of metaphysics in my life. But permit me to point out to you a contradiction that has never ceased to strike me since I entered into this great whirlwind of the world, which is also a book, as you know. On one side, the whole world celebrates the happiness, even temporal, of virtue. The first verses that I memorized were those of Louis Racine, from his poem on religion: *Adorable virtue, which your divinities attract*,[4] and so forth. You know them. My mother taught them to me when I did not yet know how to read; and I still see myself on her knees repeating this beautiful declamation, which I will never forget. In truth, I find the sentiments it expresses very reasonable, and sometimes I am tempted to believe that all mankind must be in agreement on this point, since, on this side there is a kind of concerted effort to exalt the happiness of virtue: the books are full of it, the theatres resound with it; there is not a poet who does not outdo himself to express this truth in a vivid and touching way. Racine has embedded in the conscience of princes his words so sweet and so encouraging: *Everywhere they bless me, they love me*; and there is not a man to whom this happiness cannot belong more or less, according to the extent of the sphere of which it occupies the centre. In our familiar conversation, we commonly say, for example: *that the fortune of this merchant is not surprising, that it is due to his probity, his punctuality, and his economy, which have gained him esteem and universal confidence.* Who among us has not heard the good sense of the people say a thousand times: *God blesses this family; they are good people who take pity on the poor; is it surprising that everything succeeds for them?* In society, even the most frivolous society, there is not a subject that is treated more willingly than that of the advantages of the isolated honest man over the more fortunate scoundrel. There is no empire more universal, more irresistible, than that of virtue. It must be admitted, if even temporal happiness is not found there, where will it be found?

But on the other side, a no less universal voice shows us, from one end of the world to the other, *Innocence on its knees baring its throat to crime.*

---

4 [Louis Racine, *De la religion: poème* (Paris 1742).]

One could say that virtue is only in this world to suffer, to be martyred by vice, shameless and always unpunished. They speak only of the success of audacity, fraud, and bad faith; they never exhaust the eternal disappointment of simple-hearted uprightness. Everything is given to intrigue, ruse, corruption, etc. I cannot without laughing recall the letter that a witty man wrote to his friend, in speaking to him of a certain personage of their acquaintance who had just obtained a distinguished position: M. *** well merited this position in every way, NEVERTHELESS *he obtained it.*

In effect, one is sometimes tempted, on looking at the matter closely, to believe that in most cases vice has a decided advantage over uprightness. So explain this contradiction to me, I beg you. It has struck my mind a thousand times: most men seem persuaded of two contrary propositions. Weary of occupying myself with this tiresome problem, I end up not thinking of it any more.

The Count

Before giving you my opinion, Chevalier, permit me, if you will, to congratulate you on having read Louis Racine before Voltaire. His muse, heiress (but not universal) of another more illustrious muse, must be cherished by all teachers, for it is a *family muse*, which sings only of reason and virtue. If the voice of this poet is not ringing, it is at least sweet and always correct. His *Poésies sacrées* are full of thoughts, feelings, and healing. [Jean-Baptiste] Rousseau leads him in the world and the academies, but in the Church I would hold for Racine. I have congratulated you for having begun with him; I must congratulate you again for having learned him on the knees of your excellent mother, whom I have venerated profoundly all her life, and whom today I am sometimes tempted to invoke. It is for our sex, undoubtedly, to form geometers, tacticians, chemists, etc.; but what is called *the man*, that is to say the *moral* man, is perhaps formed by the age of ten; and if it has not been done *on the knees of his mother*, it will always be a great misfortune. Nothing can replace this education. If the mother especially has made it a duty to imprint the divine character deeply on the brow of her son, one can be quite sure that the hand of vice will never efface it. The young man can go astray, undoubtedly, but he will experience, if you will permit me this expression, a *returning curve* that will lead him back to the point where he began.

The Chevalier (laughing)

Would you believe, my good friend, that the curve, with me, begins to *turn back*.

The Count

I don't doubt it, and I can even give you speedy proof, *which is that you are here*. What charm snatches you from society and its pleasures to lead you each night to these two old men, whose conversation promises nothing amusing? Why, at the moment, are you listening to me with pleasure? It is that you carry on your brow the sign that I have just been speaking to you about. Sometimes when I see you arriving from afar, I think I also see your mother by your side, clothed in a luminous robe, who points you straight to this terrace where we are waiting for you. Your mind, I know, still seems to refuse certain knowledge, but this is only because every truth needs preparation. Someday, never doubt, you will have a taste for it, and today I even congratulate you on the wisdom with which you have perceived and brought to light a great human contradiction, with which I have not yet dealt, even though it is really striking. Yes, Chevalier, you are no doubt right: humankind never stops talking about either the happiness or the calamities of virtue. But, in the first place, men can be told: *Since loss and profit seem evenly balanced, in cases of doubt you must decide in favour of virtue, which is so lovable,* all the more so in that we are not reduced to this ambivalence. In effect, you will find this contradiction of which you have just spoken everywhere, since the whole world obeys two forces.[5]

In turn, I am going to cite an example for you: you go to the theatre more often than we do. The beautiful speeches of Lusignan,[6] Polyeucte,[7] Mérope,[8] etc. – do they ever fail to excite the most lively enthusiasm? Do you recall a single sublime character of filial piety, or conjugal love, of piety even, that has not been deeply felt and loudly applauded? Return the next night, and you will hear the same noise[9] for Figaro's couplets.[10] This is the same contradiction that we have been talking about all the time; but in fact there is no contradiction properly speaking, since it is not the same subject who holds these opposing views. Like us, have you not read?

---

[5] *Feels the double force.* Ovid *Metamorphoses* VIII.472.

[6] [Lusignan, a prince of the blood of the kings of Jerusalem, appears in Voltaire's *Zaïre*.]

[7] [*Polyeucte* is a tragedy by Corneille, with a hero of the same name.]

[8] [*Mérope* is the name of another of Voltaire's plays, with a heroine of the same name.]

[9] *As much noise perhaps*; which suffices for the justice of the observation, but not *the same noise*. Conscience does nothing like vice, and even its applause has its own accent.

[10] [Beaumarchais, *Le Mariage de Figaro*.]

My God, what a cruel war!
I find two men within me.[11]   '

The Chevalier

Undoubtedly, and I even believe that each is obliged in conscience to cry out like Louis XIV: *Ah! How well I know these two men!*

The Count

Well! Here is the solution to your problem and to so many others, which are only the same problem in different forms. It is *one man* who very justly praises the advantages, even in this world, of virtue, and it is *another man* within the same man who will argue, a minute later, that virtue exists on earth only to be persecuted, despised, and slaughtered by crime. So what have you heard in the world? Two men who do not agree. In truth, there is nothing astonishing in this; but it would require a lot for the two men to be equal. It is right reason, it is conscience, which tells us what the evidence shows: that in every profession, in every enterprise, in every business, the advantage, all other things being equal, always lies on the side of virtue; that health, the first of all temporal goods without which all the others are useless, is in part its result; and that, finally, it fills us with an interior contentment a thousand times more precious than all the treasures in the world.

On the other hand, it is rebellious or resentful pride, it is envy, avarice, and impiety that complains about the temporal disadvantages of virtue. So this is no longer the *man* who speaks, or rather it is *another man*.

In his discourses even more than in his actions, man is too often determined by the passion of the moment, and especially what is called *humour*. I want to cite for you on this matter an ancient, even antique, author, whose works I very much regret, because of the power and good sense that shine in the fragments that remain to us. This is the grave Ennius, who once had these strange maxims sung on the Roman stage:

> I said it was of the gods; I will say it unceasingly:
> But I say it again, their profound wisdom
> Was never mixed with the things of here below.
> If I was in error, would we not see them
> Rewarding the just and punishing the guilty?
> Alas! There is none of this ...[i]

And Cicero lets us know, I don't remember where, that this piece was met with applause.[ii]

---

[11] [Louis Racine, *Cantiques spirituels*, Cantique III, v. 1–2. (Darcel ed.)]

But in the same century and in the same theatre, Plautus was surely no less applauded when he said:

> From the height of his holy abode,
> An always wakeful God watches us walk;
> He see us, hears us, observes us at every hour,
> And the darkest night knows not how to hide us.[iii]

Here, I think, is a good enough example of this great human contradiction. Here it is the wise philosopher-poet who reasons badly and the amiable humbug who preaches well.

But it you agree to follow me, let us leave Rome and go to Jerusalem for a moment. A quite short psalm says everything on the subject we are discussing. Ready to confess some doubts that had formerly arisen in his soul, the King-Prophet, author of this beautiful canticle, believes himself obliged to condemn them in advance; in beginning his outburst of love, he cries out: *How good God is to the upright!*

After this fine sentiment, he can then painlessly confess his old doubts:

> But, as for me, I almost lost my balance;
> My feet all but slipped,
> Because I was envious of the arrogant
>   when I saw them prosper though they were wicked.
> And they say, "How does God know?"
> Is it but in vain that I have kept my heart clean?
> Though I tried to understand this
>   it seemed to me too difficult ...

These are doubts that present themselves rather vividly to all minds; these are what are called, in ascetic literature, *temptations*; and he hastens to tell us that the truth did not hesitate to impose silence on them.

> Till I entered the sanctuary of God
>   and considered their final destiny.
> You set them, indeed, on a slippery road;
>   you hurl them down to ruin.
> How suddenly they are made desolate!
>   They are completely wasted away amid horrors.
> As though they were the dream of one who had awakened, O Lord,
>   so will you, when you arise, set at naught these phantoms.[iv]

Having thus abjured all the sophisms of the mind, he only knows how to love. He cries out:

> Whom else have I in heaven?
> And when I am with you, the earth delights me not.

Though my flesh and my heart waste away,
  God is the rock of my heart and my portion forever.
For indeed, they who withdraw from you perish;
  you destroy everyone who is unfaithful to you.
But for me, to be near God is my good;
  to make the Lord God my refuge.
I shall declare all your works
  in the gates of the daughter of Sion.^v

Here is our master and our model; one must never begin, in these sorts of questions, with a contentious pride that is a crime because it argues against God, which leads straight to blindness. Before all else, one must cry out: *How good you are!* And assume that there is in our mind some error that it is simply a question of unravelling. With these dispositions, we will not delay in finding peace, which will only be denied us so long as we do not demand it of its author. I concede to reason all that I owe it. Man received it only in order that it serve him; and we have proved well enough, I think, that it is not greatly embarrassed by the difficulties that are raised against Providence. Nevertheless let us not count exclusively on a too subjective light that finds itself eclipsed by the *shadows of the heart*, always ready to arise between the truth and ourselves. *Let us enter into the sanctuary!* It is there that all the scruples and all the scandals will disappear. Doubt resembles a troublesome fly that one chases away and that always returns. It no doubt takes off with the first wave of reason; but religion kills it, and frankly, this is a bit better.

The Senator

I have followed your excursion to Jerusalem with much pleasure; but allow me to add to your ideas by observing that it is not always simply impiety, ignorance, or levity that lets itself be dazzled by the sophism that you have attacked with such good reasons. The mistake is such in this matter, and the error so deeply rooted, that the wisest writers, seduced or stunned by foolish complaints, end up by expressing themselves just like the crowd and seem to deserve condemnation on this issue. A little while ago you cited Louis Racine; recall this verse of the declamation you were looking at: *Wealth, it is true, escapes you.*[12]

Nothing is more false; not only do riches not flee virtue, there are, on the contrary, no more honourable and permanent riches than those acquired and possessed by virtue. The others are contemptible and only passing. But here is a wise man, a profoundly religious man who comes to repeat to us

---

[12] [*Cantiques spirituels.*]

like a thousand others: *that riches and virtue are at odds*. Like a thousand others he has no doubt repeated many times in his life the old universal infallible adage: *goods badly acquired scarcely profit*.[13] We would, therefore, be obliged to believe that riches flee equally both vice and virtue. So, for pity's sake, where are we? If we had moral observations like meteorological observations, if tireless observers kept a penetrating eye on the history of families, we would see that badly acquired goods are so many anathemas, whose accomplishment is inevitable on the individuals or on the families.

But even among writers of the good party who have exercised themselves on this subject there is a secret error that appears to me to merit being exposed. They see in the prosperity of the wicked and the sufferings of virtue a strong proof of the immortality of the soul, or what comes back to the same thing, of the punishments and rewards of the other life. So they are carried along, perhaps without noticing it, to closing their eyes to those of this world, for fear of weakening the proofs of a truth of the first order on which rests the whole edifice of religion. But I dare to believe that they are wrong about this. I do not think it is necessary or even permitted to disarm, so to speak, one truth to arm another. Each truth can be defended by itself. Why make unnecessary admissions?

Read, I beg you, the first time you have time, the critical reflections of the illustrious Leibniz on the principles of Pufendorf; you will read there in his own words that the chastisements of the other life are demonstrated by the simple fact that it has pleased the sovereign master of all things to leave *the majority of crimes unpunished in this life and the majority of virtues without reward*.

But do not believe that he leaves us the trouble of refuting this statement. He hastens, in the same work, to refute it himself with the superiority that characterizes him; he recognizes expressly: *that even in making abstraction* of the other punishments that God awards in this world in the manner of human legislators, he shows himself no less legislator directly in this life, since in virtue of the very laws of nature, which he has established with so much wisdom, every wicked man is a HEAUTONTIMORU-MENOS.[14]

---

[13]   *Malè parta malè dilabuntur*. This proverb in found in all languages and all styles. Plato put it this way: *It is virtue that produces riches, just as it produces all other goods, public as well as private*. (*Apologia*) This is the same truth which is thus expressed.

[14]   *The Self-Tormentor*; this is the well known title of a comedy by Terence [and, after Maistre's time, of a poem by Baudelaire]. The venerable author of *L'Evangile expliqué* said with as much wit and more authority: *A guilty heart*

It could not be said any better. But tell me yourselves how it is possible that, God *having imposed punishments in this life in the manner of legislators, and every wicked person being moreover, in virtue of natural laws, AN EXECUTIONER OF HIMSELF, the majority of crimes remain unpunished?*[15] The illusion of which I have just spoken and the force of prejudice show themselves to be discovered. I will not uselessly try to make the matter any clearer, but I want to cite for you still another man, Father Berthier, a man superior in his genre and whose ascetic works are incontestably one of most beautiful presents that talent has made to piety. I recall that on these words of a psalm: *Yet another moment and the impious will exist no more; you will seek his place and you will find nothing*, he observes that if the prophet did not have eternal happiness in mind his proposition would be false, *for*, he says, *good men have perished, and the place on the earth where they lived is no longer known; they possessed no riches during their lives, and no one could see that they were more tranquil than the wicked, who, despite the excesses of their passions, seemed to have had the privilege of* HEALTH AND A VERY LONG LIFE.[16]

One can scarcely understand how a thinker of this power could have let himself be blinded by popular prejudice to the point of misunderstanding the most palpable truths. *Good men have perished*, he says. But no one, I think, would still maintain that good men have the privilege of not dying. *The place on the earth where they lived is no longer known.* – In the first place, what does that matter? Moreover, are the sepulchres of the wicked better known than those of good men, all things being equal with respect to birth, position, and style of life. Were Louis XI or Peter the Cruel more celebrated or richer than St Louis or Charlemagne? Did Suger and Ximénès live less tranquilly or were they less celebrated after their deaths than Sejanus or Pombal?[17] What follows with respect to *the privilege of health*

---

always takes against itself the part of divine justice. (Vol. 13, 120, med. 3rd point.)

[15] *Leibnizii monita quaedam ad Puffendorfii principia*, Opp. Tom IV, part III, p. 227. The most important thoughts of this great man have been made available to everyone in a book that has been equally well conceived and well executed: *Pensées de Leibniz* [2 vols., Paris 1803], 2:296 and 375.

[16] [Guillaume-François Berthier, *Les Psaumes traduits en français avec des notes et des réflexions* (Paris 1785), or, perhaps, his *Réflexions spirituelles* (Paris 1750).]

[17] [Suger was a twelfth-century French abbot who served as regent for King Louis VII while the latter went on Crusade; Ximines was a reforming Spanish churchman who served Queen Isabella and King Ferdinand. Sejanus was a favourite and minister of the Emperor Tiberius; his ambition and misdeeds led to his arrest and execution. Pombal was a reforming first minister in eighteenth-century Portugal; his role in the suppression of the Jesuits attracted Maistre's condemnation.]

and very long life is perhaps an even more terrible proof of the power of a general prejudice on minds best made to escape it.

But what happened to Father Berthier is what happened to Leibniz, and what will always happen to men of their kind. This is to refute themselves with a power and a clarity worthy of them; and moreover, as for Father Berthier, he does it with an unction worthy of a master who compares with Fénelon in the annals of spiritual science. In several places in his works, he recognizes that even on earth there is happiness only in virtue, that our passions are our executioners, *that the abyss of happiness is to be found in the abyss of charity*, that if an *evangelical* city existed, it would be a place worthy of the admiration of the angels, and that it would be necessary to leave everything to go and contemplate these happy mortals from up close.[vi] Full of these ideas, he at one point addresses God himself, and says to him: *So is it true that beyond the happiness that awaits me in the other life, I can still be happy in this one?* Read, I beg you, the spiritual works of this wise and holy personage; you will easily find the different passages that I have seen, and I am sure that you will thank me for having gotten to know these books.

The Chevalier

My dear Senator, why don't you admit frankly that you want to seduce me and get me involved in your favourite reading? Surely your proposition is not addressed to your *accomplice*, who is smiling. In any case, I promise you that if I begin, I will begin with Father Berthier.

The Senator

With all my heart, I exhort you not to delay. While waiting, I am happy to have shown you both science and holiness first being deceived, and reasoning like the crowd, gone astray by a noble motive while seeking the truth, but soon letting themselves be led back by the evidence and contradicting themselves in the most solemn way. So there we have, if I am not mistaken, two errors clearly elucidated: the error of pride that refuses evidence to justify its own guilty objections; and the error of virtue, which lets itself be seduced by the desire to reinforce one truth, even at the expense of another. But there is yet a third error that must not be passed over in silence – it is that this crowd of men who never stop talking about the *successes* of crime, without knowing what happiness and misfortune really are. Listen to the misanthrope, whom I will have speak for them:

And that contemptible boor notoriously
Has made his way in the world by dirty means.
So that his splendid situation
Makes merit grumble and makes virtue blush.

...

And yet his fawning face is widely welcomed,
He crawls in everywhere, he is accepted;
And if intrigue can gain some precedence,
You will see him win, over the worthiest man.[18]

The theatre pleases us so much because it is the eternal accomplice of all our vice and all our errors.[19] An honest man must not contest a rank *through intrigue*, and much less contest boorishness. They never cease to cry out: *all positions, all ranks, all distinctions are for men who do not merit them.* In the first place, nothing is more fallacious; moreover, by what right do we call all these things *goods.* A little while ago, Chevalier, you cited for us a charming epigram: *he merited this position in every way;* NEVERTHELESS *he obtained it.* Wonderful, if it is only a question of a laugh, but if one must reason, it is something else. I would like to share with you a reflection that occurred to me one day while reading a sermon by your wonderful Bourdaloue – but I am afraid that you will again treat me as an *illuminist.*

The Chevalier

Come now, I never said that. I only said, and this is something quite different, *that certain people hearing you, could well take you for an illuminist.* Moreover, these *certain people* are not here, and even if they were, even if we had to print what we are saying, we would not have to be embarrassed. What one believes to be true must be said and said boldly; *even though it cost me a great deal I would want to* discover a truth made to shock all of humanity: I would say it point-blank.

The Senator

If you are ever enrolled in the army that Providence is raising in Europe at this time, you will be placed among the grenadiers; but here is what I want to tell you. One day I read a passage, in I don't remember which of Bourdaloue's sermons, where he argued without the least qualification: *that it is not permissible to request a position.*[20] To tell you the truth, I first

---

[18] [Molière, *Le Misanthrope*, 1.1, 129–40.]

[19] *... Dramatists find few plays such as this which make good men better.* (Plautus *The Captives* Epilogue.) [Trans. Paul Nixon, Loeb Classical Library, 1919] One can believe him, I hope.

[20] Following all appearances, the speaker had in mind the passage where this great orator said with a severity that appears excessive: "But what, you tell me, that it is therefore never permitted to a man of the world to want to be greater than he

took this for a simple counsel, or one of those ideas of perfection, useless in practice, and I passed on. But soon reflection led me back, and I did not delay finding in this text the subject of a long and serious meditation. Certainly a great part of the evils of society come from the agents of authority, poorly chosen by the prince; but the majority of these bad choices are the work of ambition, which has deceived him. If everyone awaited the choice instead of striving to determine it by every means possible, I am inclined to believe that the world would change for the better. By what right dare one say: *I am better than anyone else for this position*; for this is what one says when one requests it. What an enormous responsibility one takes on oneself! One is exposed to disturbing a hidden order. I will go even further: I say that every man, if he examines himself with care, and examines the others and all the circumstances, will know how to distinguish quite clearly between the case where one is called and the case where one has forced the passage. This comes from an idea that will perhaps appear paradoxical to you; but make of it what you will. It seems to me that the existence and operation of governments cannot be explained by human means, any more than the movements of bodies can be explained by mechanical means. *Mens agitat molem.*[21] There is in each state a *directing spirit* (allow me to steal a word from chemistry by denaturing it), which animates it as the soul animates the body, and which produces death when it withdraws.

The Count

You have given a new name, a happy enough one it seems to me, to a very simple thing, which is the necessary intervention of a supernatural power. This is recognized in the physical world without excluding the action of secondary causes. Why not recognize it in the same way in the political world, where it is no less indispensable. Without its direct intervention, one cannot, as you very rightly say, explain either the creation or duration of governments. It is manifested in the national unity that constitutes them, in the multiplicity of wills that concur in the same goal without knowing what they are doing, which shows that they are simply *used*; it is there especially in the wonderful action that uses all the circumstances we call *accidental*, even our follies and our crimes, to maintain and often to establish order.

---

is? No, my dear listener, you will never be permitted to desire it: it will be permitted to you when God wills it, when your king destines you for it, when the public voice calls you to it, etc." (*Sermon sur l'état de vie*, or rather *against ambition*, first part). (Editor's note)

[21] [The mind moves the mass of the world. Vergil *Aeneid* VI.727. (Darcel ed.)]

The Senator

I don't know if you have understood my ideas perfectly – but for the moment, it doesn't matter. Once the supernatural power is recognized, in whatever manner it may be understood, one can rely on it; but it can never be repeated often enough, we will deceive ourselves less often on this subject if we have clearer ideas on what we call *goods* and *happiness*. We speak of the success of vice, but we do not know what *success* is. What appears to us to be happiness is often a terrible punishment.

The Count

You are certainly right, sir, man doesn't know what is good for him; and even philosophy has caught a glimpse of this truth, since it has discovered that man, of himself, does not know how to pray, and that he needs some divine instructor, who comes to teach him what he must ask.[22] If virtue sometimes appears to be less talented than vice in obtaining wealth, positions, etc., if it is awkward in all kinds of intrigues, so much the better for it, even in this world. There is no error more common than that of mistaking a blessing for a disgrace. Envy crime nothing, let it have its sad successes; virtue has others, it has all those one is permitted to desire, and were it to have less, still nothing would be lacking to the just man, since he would remain at peace. Peace of heart, what an inestimable treasure! Health of soul, the charm of life, which replaces everything else and which nothing can replace! By what inconceivable blindness do we often fail to notice to this? On the one side is peace and even glory: a good reputation at least is an inseparable companion of virtue, and this is one of the most delicious joys of life. On the other side one finds remorse, and, often, infamy. The whole world agrees with these truths; thousands of writers have explained them clearly, and yet some argue as if they were not known. However, can one prevent oneself from contemplating with delight the happy man who can say each day before going to sleep: *I have not lost the day*, who sees in his heart no hateful passions, no guilty desires, who sleeps with the certitude of having done what is good, and who awakens with new strength to become better still? Deprive him, if you will, of all the goods that men covet so passionately, and compare him to the happy powerful Tiberius on the island of Capri writing his famous letter to the

---

[22] It is no longer necessary to cite this passage from Plato, which, from this great man's book, has passed into a thousand others.

Roman Senate.[23] It will not, I think, be difficult to decide between these two situations. Around the wicked I believe I always see all the hell of the poets, TERRIBILES VISU FORMÆ [shapes terrible to behold]: *devouring cares, pale illnesses, base and precocious old age; fear, indigence (a sad adviser), false joys of the mind, civil war, vengeful furies, black melancholy, and the sleep of conscience and death.*[vii] The greatest writers have exercised themselves to describe the inevitable torture of remorse; but Persius strikes me especially, when his energetic pen makes us understand how, *during the horror of the deepest night*, the guilty man, troubled by frightful dreams, led by his conscience to the slippery edge of a bottomless precipice, cries out to himself: *I am lost! I am lost!* And to complete the picture, the poet shows us the innocent man sleeping in peace beside the tormented scoundrel.[viii]

The Chevalier

In truth, you would frighten a *grenadier*. But look, here is one of those contradictions you mentioned a little while ago. Everyone speaks of the happiness attached to virtue, and everyone speaks too of the terrible torture of remorse, but it seems to me that these truths are pure theories, and that when it is a question of reasoning about Providence they are forgotten as if they were null in practice. Here we have both error and ingratitude. When I think about it now, it seems ridiculous to complain about the misfortunes of innocence. It is precisely as if one complained that God is pleased to render happiness unhappy.

The Count

You know very well, Chevalier, that the Senator could not have put it better. In effect, God has given everything to men he has protected or delivered from vices.[24] Thus, to say that crime is happy in this world and innocence unhappy, is a veritable contradiction in terms; it is to say precisely that poverty is rich and opulence poor. However man is made this way. He will always complain, he will always argue against his father. It is not enough that God has attached ineffable happiness to the practice of virtue; it is not enough that in the general division of the goods of this world he has promised it the greatest portion without comparison; these

---

[23] "If I knew what to write to you, Conscript Fathers, or how to write it, or what not to write at all at this time, may gods and goddesses destroy me more wretchedly than I feel myself to be perishing every day!" (Tacitus *Annals* VI.6)

[24] *Evil of every sort he [God] keeps from them – sin and crime, evil counsel and schemes for greed, blind lust and avarice intent upon another's goods.* (Seneca *On Providence* VI.1) [Trans. John W. Basone, Loeb Classical Library, 1963.]

foolish heads *from which reasoning has banished reason* will not be satisfied. They make an absolute demand that their imaginary justice be impassive, that nothing bad happen to the JUST MAN: that the rain not soak him, that the insects stop respectfully at the limits of his field, and that, if by chance he forgets to lock his door, God must send an angel to his door with a flaming sword, for fear a *happy* thief might come and steal his gold and jewels.[25]

The Chevalier

I also get your joke, Mr Philosopher, but I take care not to quarrel with you, for I fear the reprisals; I agree willingly, moreover, that, in this case, a joke can be introduced into a serious discussion. One could imagine nothing more unreasonable than the deaf pretence that would want every just man dunked in the Styx and made inaccessible to every blow of this sort.

The Count

I don't know what *this sort* might be, but I confess to you, that for my part, I see something still more unreasonable in what you see as the excess of nonsense: this is the inconceivable folly that dares to base arguments against Providence on the misfortunes of the innocent, *who do not exist.* Where are the innocent, I ask you? Where are the just? Are they here, around this table? Good God! So who could believe in such an excess of delirium, if we did not always witness it? I reflect often on the place in the Bible where it says: *I will search Jerusalem with lamps.*[26] Do we have the courage to search our own hearts *with lamps*? Let us begin by looking for the evil that is within us, and let us blanch in taking a courageous look at this abyss; for it is impossible to know the number of our transgressions, and it is no less so to know at what point such and such guilty act wounded the general order and opposed the plans of the eternal legislator. Let us think too of the frightful criminal relationships that exist among men: *complicity, counsel, example,* and *approbation* are terrible words that we must meditate upon unceasingly. What sensible man can think unflinchingly of the disordered influence he has exercised on his fellow human beings,

---

[25]   *Does any require of God that he also guard the good man's luggage?* (Seneca, Ibid.) Yes, undoubtedly, this is what we ask every day, without noticing it. What is called *an honest man* being fleeced by thieves was something that drew an approving laugh according to this passage from Seneca, who says immediately: *Such a misfortune would not happen to a rich rascal; these things only happen to honest people.* [Loeb]

[26]   Zephaniah 1:12.

and of the possible consequences of this deadly influence? Rarely does a man make himself guilty alone; rarely does one crime not produce another. Where are the limits of responsibility? For this reason this luminous passage sparkles among a thousand others in the book of Psalms: *What man can know the extent of his offences? Oh God, purify me from those that I am unaware of, and forgive me even for those of others.*[27]

After having meditated on our crimes in this way, there is still another examination that is even sadder for us, which is to meditate on our virtues; what a frightening search, which would have for its object the minuscule number, the falsity, and the inconstancy of these virtues! Above all we would have to probe their bases. Alas! They are more often determined by prejudice than by considerations of the general order founded on the divine will. An action revolts us less because it is *bad* than because it is *shameful*. When two common people fight armed with knives, they are two *scoundrels*; but simply lengthen their weapons and attach to the crime the ideas of nobility and independence, and this will be the action of gentlemen, and the sovereign, vanquished by prejudice, *for honour of himself* will be unable to prevent the crime committed against *himself*, that is to say, rebellion added to murder. The criminal spouse speaks tranquilly of the *infamy* of a wretch that misery led to visible weakness. From the height of a gilded balcony the adroit squanderer of the public treasury sees the unfortunate servant who stole an *écu* from his master marched off to the gibbet. There is a very profound remark in a work of pure charm; I read it, forty years ago to be precise, and the impression it made on me has never been effaced. A peasant, whose daughter had been dishonoured by a great seigneur, said to this brilliant corrupter: *You are very lucky, sir, not to have loved gold as much as women: you would have been a Cartouche* [a famous French robber].[28] What do we ordinarily do during our whole life? *What pleases us.* If we deign to abstain from stealing and killing, it is that we have no wish to do so, *for that is just not done:*

---

[27] *Delicta quis intelligit? Ab occultis meis munda me, et ab alienis parce servo tuo.* (Psalm 18(19):13–14) [Maistre appears to have mistranslated the last phrase; most translations do not construe it as referring to others. The *Revised English Bible*, for example, reads: "Who is aware of his unwitting sins? Cleanse me of any secret fault. Hold back your servant also from wilful sins."]

[28] [This anecdote is from a tale entitled "Laurette," in Marmontel's *Contes moraux*. Maistre's first library included an edition of this work. (Darcel ed.)]

Sed si
Candida vicini subrisit molle puella,
Cor tibi rite salit ... ?[29]

It is not crime that we fear, it is dishonour. Provided that opinion rules out shame, we boldly commit the crime, and the man who is so disposed freely calls himself *just*, or at least an *honest man*, and who knows if he does not thank God *for not being like other men*? The least reflection should make us blush at such delirium. It was no doubt profound wisdom that led the Romans to call *strength* and *virtue* by the same name. In fact, there is no virtue properly speaking without victory over ourselves, and anything that costs us nothing is worth nothing. Take away from our miserable virtues what we owe to temperament, to honour, to opinion, to pride, to powerlessness, and to circumstances, and what is left to us? Alas! Very very little. I'm not afraid to confess to you that never have I meditated on this frightful subject without being tempted to throw myself on the ground like a guilty wretch asking pardon, and without accepting in advance all the evils that could fall upon my head as a light compensation for the immense debt I have contracted towards eternal justice. Nevertheless, you would not believe how many people in my life have told me that I was *a very honest man*.

The Chevalier

I assure you that I think like all these people, and I am ready to bet you money on it, without witnesses and without a ticket, without even seeing if you care to pay me or not. However, tell me, I beg you, have you not unconsciously hurt your cause by showing us this public thief who sees, from the height *of a gilded balcony*, the preparations for a punishment more suited for himself than for the unfortunate victim who is going to perish? Without your noticing it, have you not led us back *to the triumph of vice and the misfortunes of innocence*?

The Count

In truth, no, my dear Chevalier, I am not in contradiction with myself; it is you, with your permission, who are distracted in speaking to us of the misfortunes of innocence. It is only necessary to speak of the *triumph of vice*, for the servant who is hanged for having stolen an *écu* from his master is not the least *innocent*. If the law of the country prescribes the

---

[29] But if the fair daughter of your neighbour flashes you a voluptuous smile, will your heart continue to beat wisely? (Persius *Satires* III.110–11).

death penalty for all domestic theft, every servant knows that if he steals from his master, he exposes himself to death. If other more considerable crimes are neither known nor punished, that is another question. As for him, he has no right to complain. He is guilty according to the law; he is judged according to law, he is put to death according to the law; no wrong has been done to him. And as to the public thief, of whom we were just speaking, you have not grasped my thought very well. I did not say that he was happy; I did not say that his corruption would never be known nor punished. I said only that this guilty one had the skill, *up to that point*, of hiding his crimes, and that he passed for what is called *an honest man*. He is not so, however, for the eye that sees all. If therefore gout, or stone, or some other terrible supplement of human justice, comes to make him pay on the *gilded balcony*, do you see some injustice? Moreover, the assumption that I am now making is being realized at every moment in all parts of the world. If there are truths that are certain for us, they are that man has no means of judging hearts, that the conscience that we are lead to judge most favourably may be horribly tarnished in the eyes of God, that there is not an innocent man in the world, that all evil is a punishment, and that the judge who condemns us is infinitely just and good. This is enough, it seems to me, to teach us that we should at least keep silent.

However before finishing, permit me to share with you a reflection that has always struck me forcibly; perhaps it will make no less an impression on your minds.

There is no just man upon the earth.[30] The one who said this became himself a great and sad proof of the astonishing contradictions of man. In thought I can well imagine this just man, and I can overwhelm him with all possible evils. I ask you, who has a right to complain in this case? It is the just man apparently, it is the just man who is suffering. However this is precisely what will never happen. At the moment I cannot stop thinking of this young girl who became famous in this great city among the charitable persons who make it a sacred duty to seek out the unfortunate to assist them. She is eighteen years old, and for five of these years she has suffered from a horrible cancer that is eating into her head. Already her eyes and nose have disappeared, and the evil thing is advancing on her virginal flesh like a fire devouring a palace. A prey to the most acute suffering, a tender and almost celestial piety completely detaches her from the earth and seems to render her inaccessible or indifferent to pain. She does not say like the pompous stoic: *Oh pain! You have acted in vain, you will never make me*

---

[30] Ecclesiastes 7:21. It was said a long time ago: *What is man that he should be without spot, and he that is born of a woman that he should appear just? Behold among his saints none is unchangeable.* (Job 15:14–15.)

agree that you are an evil. She does much better; she never speaks of it at all. Nothing leaves her lips but words of love, submission, and gratitude. This girl's unalterable resignation has become a kind of spectacle, and as in the first centuries of Christianity when they went to the amphitheatre through simple curiosity to see *Blandine, Agatha, and Perpetua* delivered to the lions or savage bulls, and more than one spectator returned surprised to be Christian, in our noisy city the curious come also to see this young martyr *suffering from cancer.* As she loses her life, they can approach her without troubling her, and several have reported better thoughts from this. One day when someone showed her particular compassion for her long and cruel sleeplessness, she said: *I am not as unfortunate as you think; God gives me the grace to think only of him.* When one good man, whom you know Senator, said to her one day: *What is the first grace that you will ask of God, my dear child, when you come before him?* She replied with an angelic naivety: *I would ask for my benefactors the grace to love him as much as I love him.*

Certainly, gentlemen, if innocence exists anywhere in the world, it is found on the bed of pain to which the course of this conversation has just led us; and if reasonable complaints could be addressed to Providence, they could justly come from this pure victim, who however knows only how to bless and love. Moreover, what we see here has always been seen, and will always be seen until the end of time. The more someone approaches that state of justice whose perfection does not belong to our weak nature, the more you will find this person loving and resigned, even in the most cruel situations of life. What a strange thing! It is crime that complains of the sufferings of virtue! It is always the guilty person, and often the culprit, *happy* as he would be, plunged in delights, and abounding in the only goods that he esteems, who dares quarrel with Providence when it judges it appropriate to refuse these goods to virtue! So who gives these rash people the right to speak in the name of the virtue that disavows them with horror, and to interrupt with insolent blasphemies the prayers, offerings, and voluntary sacrifices of love?

The Chevalier

Ah, my dear friend! I thank you! I don't know how to tell you how touched I have been by this reflection, which would never have occurred to me. I will keep it in my heart, since we must separate. It is not yet night, but it is no longer day, and already the burnished waters of the Neva announce the hour of sleep. I don't know, in any case, if I will find it. I think that I will certainly dream of that young girl, and not later than tomorrow I will search out her home.

The Senator

I will take it upon myself to take you there.

NOTES TO THE THIRD DIALOGUE

i   *I have always said and will say that there is a race of gods in the heavens; but I do not think that they care what the race of men does. For if they cared for men, good men would prosper, and bad men come to grief, but this is not so.*

   (Ennius, in Cicero *On Divination* II.50. For the integrity of the text, see Olivet's note on this passage.) [Maistre's citation is faulty; the passage is from Cicero *The Nature of the Gods* III.32.79. (Darcel ed.) The last sentence is from Ennius's *Telamon*. Maistre owned an edition of Cicero (*M.T. Ciceronis opera cum delectu Commentariorum*, 9 vols. (Geneva 1788)) edited by the Abbé Olivet.]

ii   *He speaks to great applause, as the people give their agreement.* (Cicero, *On Divination* II.50, citing Ennius.)

iii   *THERE SURELY IS A GOD who hears and sees what we do; and according to your treatment of me here, so will he look after your son there. He will reward the deserving and requite the undeserving.* (Plautus *The Captives* II.ii.63–65) [Loeb]. See, in the works of [Louis] Racine, his translation of the Roman breviary, the hymn for Lauds: *Lux ecce surgit aurea, etc.* One could scarcely doubt that he has translated Plautus in this passage.

iv   Psalm 72:2,3,13,17,18,20.

   Diderot, in the moral principles that he composed in the style of Shaftesbury's *Characteristics*, cites this passage from David, *I almost lost my balance,* as a fixed doubt in the mind of the prophet, and without saying a word of what precedes it and of what follows it. Rash youth! When you come across some book by these perverted men, remember the first quality that they lack – which is always honesty.

v   Psalm 72:25–28.

vi   See Berthier, *Les Psaumes traduits ... avec ... des réflexions*, Ps. 36:2, 2:77–8,85, and *Réflexions spirituelles*, 2:438, etc. If I did not fear exceeding the limits of a note, I would cite a crowd of passages that bear on what one of the speakers is saying here. I will limit myself to some striking comments on the kind of prayer he points out here in a general way: "So is it true that beyond the happiness that awaits me in the celestial realm, I can also flatter myself with being happy in this mortal life? ... Happiness is not to be found in any of the goods of this world. ... Those who enjoy them all complain of the situation in which they are. They desire something that they do not have or something other than they have. On the other side, all the evils that inundate the face of the earth *are the work of vices, ... which presents us with the image of hell unchained to render men unhappy.* ... Were they at the high point of glory or in the very lap of pleasures, men who do not understand the true doctrine are unhappy, because goods are incapable of satisfying them. Those, on the contrary, who have received the word of life, ... always walk in the way of happiness, *even when they are delivered to all kinds of temporal calamities.* ... In reviewing the annals of the world ... I find happiness only among those who carry the lovable and light yoke of the Gospel. *The precepts of the Lord are right, delighting the heart* (Psalm 18(19):9) ... It provides a state of rest, of contentment, of delight even, ... and which even subsists in the midst of tribulations ... On the contrary, says the Sage (Ecclesiasticus 41:11-12) *Woe to you, ungodly men ... malediction shall be your portion.* ... Trouble, perplexity, even despair, will be, *in this life*, the torment of the enemies of your law." (Berthier, *Réflexions spirituels,* 4th meditation, 3rd reflection, pp. 1:438 ff). (Editor's note.)

vii *Just before the Entrance, even within the very jaws of Hell, Grief and avenging Cares have made their bed; their pale Diseases dwell, and sad Age, and Fear, and ill-counselling Famine, and loathing Want, shapes terrible to man; and Death and Distress; next Death's own brother Sleep,* AND THE SOUL'S GUILTY JOYS, *and, on the threshold opposite, the Death-bearer War, and the Furies' iron cells, and savage Strife, her snaky locks entwined with bloody fillets.*

Vergil *Aeneid* VI.273–81. [Trans. H. Rushton Fairclough, Loeb Classical Library, 1918)

There is a moral treatise in the words: *And the soul's guilty Joys.*

viii *Did ever sword hanging from gilded ceiling strike more terror into the purple necks below, than for a man to say to himself, "I am falling, falling to ruin," and to turn pale, poor wretch, for a misdeed which the wife of his bosom may not know.* (A. Persius *Satires* III.40,44. [Trans. G.G. Ramsay, Loeb Classical Library 1918])

Fourth Dialogue

The Count

I recall that our Chevalier had a scruple; for a long time he has had to let on that he was no longer thinking of it, for there are in conversations such as ours veritable *currents* that carry us along despite ourselves. However, it is time to return.

The Chevalier

I knew very well that we were off course, but since the sea was perfectly peaceful and without reefs, and since we had nothing else to do (which appears to me to be the essential point), there remained to me the pleasure of seeing the country. In any case, since you want to *return*, I have not forgotten that in our second conversation you said something about prayer that caused me a certain amount of pain by bringing to mind ideas that have more than once obsessed me. Recall your ideas for me, I beg you.

The Count

Here is how I came to talk to you about prayer. Since every evil is a punishment, it follows that no evil can be regarded as necessary, because it could have been prevented. On this point, as on so many others, the temporal order is the image of a higher order. Punishments being made necessary only by crimes, and every crime being the act of a free will, it follows that every punishment could have been prevented, since the crime need not have been committed. I would add that after it has been committed, the punishment can still be prevented in two ways; first, the merits of the guilty person, or even those of his ancestors, can balance out his fault; and second, his fervent supplications, or those *of his friends*, can disarm the sovereign.

One of the things that philosophy never ceases to repeat to us is that we must take care not to imagine God to be like us. I accept this warning, provided that philosophy in its turn accepts that of religion, *which makes us like unto God.*[i] Divine justice can be contemplated and studied in ours more than we usually believe. Do we not know that we have been created *in the image of God*, and have we not been ordered to work to *make ourselves perfect like him?* I understand very well that these words are not meant to be taken literally, but they always show us what we are since the least resemblance to the sovereign being is a title of glory that no one can imagine. Resemblance having nothing in common with equality,[ii] we are only using our rights in glorifying ourselves with this resemblance. He himself has declared himself our father and the *friend of our souls.*[1] The God-Man called us his *friends*, his *children*, and even his *brothers*;[2] and his apostles never ceased repeating to us the precept *to be like unto him.* So there is not the least doubt on this august resemblance. Man deceives himself twice with respect to God: sometimes he makes him similar to man by lending him our passions; sometimes, on the contrary, he is deceived in a way more humiliating for his own nature by refusing to recognize there the divine characteristics of his model. If man knew how to discover and contemplate these characteristics, he would not mistakenly judge God after his cherished creation. It is sufficient to judge him according to all our virtues, that is to say, according to all the perfections that are contrary to our passions, perfections of which every man feels himself susceptible, and which we are forced to admire in the depths of our heart, even when they are foreign to us.[3]

Moreover do not let yourself be seduced by what modern theologians say about the immensity of God, our littleness, and the foolishness that we commit in wanting to judge him according to ourselves, fine phrases that tend not to exalt God but to degrade man. Intelligences can only differ between themselves in perfection, just as similar figures can only differ in dimensions. The path that Uranus describes in space and the figure enclosing the shell of a tiny seed undoubtedly differ immensely. Reduce the one to the size of an atom, enlarge the other towards infinity, they will always be two ellipses and you can represent them with the same formula. If there were no relation and no real resemblance between divine intelli-

---

[1] Wisdom 11:27

[2] But only after his resurrection; as to the title of *brother*, this is Bourdaloue's remark in a fragment on the resurrection.

[3] The Psalms present a good lesson against the contrary error, and this lesson proves the truth: "You make friends with a thief as soon as you see one, you feel at home with adulterers, your mouth is given freely to evil and your tongue to inventing lies. You sit there, slandering your brother, you malign your own mother's son. You do this, and expect me to say nothing? *Do you really think I am like you?*" (Psalm 49(50):18–22.) One must argue otherwise and believe the same.

gence and our own, how could man, even after his degradation, exercise such a striking empire over the creatures that surround him. When in the beginning God said: *Let us make man in our likeness*, he subsequently added: *And let him have dominion over every creature.* Here is the original title of divine investiture, since man reigns over the earth only because he resembles God.[iii] Let us never fear to elevate ourselves too high or to weaken the ideas that we have of the divine immensity. To put an infinity between two terms, it is not necessary to lower the one; it suffices to raise the other without limits. Images of God on earth, all the good in us resembles him. You would not believe how awareness of this sublime resemblance helps resolve a score of questions. So do not be surprised if I really insist on this point. Let us not, for example, have any repugnance about believing or saying that one prays to God as one prays to a sovereign, and that prayer has, in the higher order as in the lower, the power of obtaining graces and preventing evils – so that it can constrict the rule of evil to equally unassignable limits.

The Chevalier

I must tell you frankly: the point of view that you have just offered is one of those where, without envisaging a formal denial (for I have made it a point on these sorts of matters to have a general theory to guard against positive error), I nevertheless see the question in a confused way. I never mocked my pastor when he threatened his parishioners with hail or crop failure because they had not paid their tithes, yet I see such an invariable order in physical phenomena that I do not understand how the prayers of these poor little men could have any influence on these phenomena. Lightning, for example, is as necessary to the world as fire and light, so how could it occur without thunder? The lightning bolt comes down like the dew; the first is terrible for us, but what does it matter to nature, which fears nothing? When a meteorologist assures himself by a series of exact observations that so many inches of rainfall per year must fall on a certain country, he would laugh at attending public prayers for rain. I am not approving of him, but why should I hide from you the fact that the jeers of the physicist cause me a certain interior distress, which I distrust all the less as I would like to dismiss it? Again, I do not want to argue against received ideas, but how can we pray that lightning bolts act civilized, that tigers tame themselves, and that volcanoes provide only illumination? Does the Siberian ask Heaven for olive trees or the native of Provence for *klukwas*?[4]

---

[4] Small red berries from which the Russians make jams and a pleasant and healthy drink.

And what can we say about war, an eternal subject of our prayers or our demands for favours? Everywhere everyone asks for victory, without being able to overturn the rule that grants it *to the big battalions*. Injustice under its laurels dragging the good side in its wake defeated and denuded, does this sight not stun us every day with its insupportable *Te Deum*? Good God, what does divine protection have in common with all these horrors that I have seen too close up? Every time that I have heard these canticles of victory, every time I have even thought of it, I have never ceased to see all these

> ... thieves of the night
> Who, in an empty street, quietly and noiselessly,
> Discreetly armed with sabres and ladders,
> First assassinate five or six watchmen;
> Then, climb nimbly over the walls of the city,
> Where the poor townsmen sleep in safety,
> Carry flaming irons into their homes,
> Stabbing the men, dishonouring the women,
> Crushing the children, and, weary with so much effort
> Drink the wine of others on the piles of the dead.
> The next morning they are taken to church
> To thank God for their noble enterprise,
> Singing to him in Latin that he is their worthy support
> That in the burned city they could have done nothing without him;
> That they could neither steal nor massacre his world,
> Nor burn cities if God did not help us.[5]

The Count

Ah! I have got you there, my dear Chevalier, you are citing Voltaire. I am not so severe as to deprive you of the pleasure of recalling in passing some happy lines fallen from that sparkling pen, but you cite him as an authority, and that is not permissible in my house.

The Chevalier

Oh! My dear friend, you are much too rancorous towards *François-Marie Arouet*; since he is no longer alive, how can you keep up so much rancour towards the dead?

---

[5] [Voltaire, "La Tactique" (1773), *Oeuvres*, ed. Molund, 10:189–90.]

The Count

However his works are not dead. They are alive, and they are killing us. It seems to me that my hate is sufficiently justified.

The Chevalier

Perhaps, but permit me to tell you that we should not allow this sentiment, although well founded in principle, to make us unjust towards such a wonderful genius and to close our eyes to this universal talent, which must be regarded as a brilliant French possession.

The Count

As great a genius as you wish, Chevalier, but it is no less true that in praising Voltaire, one must praise him with a certain restraint, I almost said grudgingly. The uncontrolled admiration with which too many people surround him is an infallible sign of a corrupt soul. Let us not be under any illusion: if someone, in looking over his library, feels himself attracted to the *works of Ferney*, God does not love him. Ecclesiastical authority is often mocked for having condemned books *in odium auctoris*;[6] in truth, nothing is more just. *Refuse to honour the genius who has abused his gifts.* If this law were severely observed, we would soon see poisonous books disappear. Since it is not up to us to promulgate such a law, let us at least be careful not to allow ourselves the excess, much more reprehensible than one might have thought, of exalting guilty authors beyond measure, and especially this one. He pronounced a terrible sentence upon himself, without noticing it, for he is the one who said: *A corrupt mind is never sublime.* Nothing is more true, and this is why Voltaire, with his hundred volumes, was never anything more than *pretty*. I except tragedy, where the nature of the work forced him to express noble feelings alien to his character, and even in this genre, which was his greatest, he does not deceive experienced eyes. In his best pieces he resembles his great rivals as the most able hypocrite resembles a saint. However I should not be understood as contesting his dramatic merit. I restrict myself to my first observation, which is that when Voltaire is speaking in his own name, he is only *pretty*. Nothing can excite him, not even the battle of Fontenoy. They say, *He is charming*; I say it too, but I take this as a criticism. Moreover I cannot stand the exaggeration that calls him *universal*. I certainly see fine exceptions to this universality. He is nothing in the ode – and why should

---

6 [The Index of Prohibited Books, in effect from the Council of Trent until after the Second Vatican Council, condemned all the works of certain named authors. The cited phrase was used to indicate this class of books.]

we be astonished by this? Considered impiety killed in him the divine flame of enthusiasm. He was also nothing – to the point of ridicule – in lyric drama, his ear being absolutely deaf to harmonic beauties, just as his eyes were closed to those of art. In the genres that appear more analogous to his natural talent, he got along: so he was mediocre, cold, often heavy and gross in comedy (who would believe it), for the wicked are never funny. For the same reason, he never knew how to write an epigram; the least vomiting of his bile required at least a hundred verses. If he tried satire, he slipped into libel; he was insupportable in history, despite his art, his elegance, and the graces of his style. No quality can replace those he lacked and which are the life of history – seriousness, good faith, and dignity. As for his *epic* poem, I have no right to talk about it, for to judge a book one must have read it, and to read it one must stay awake. A stupefying monotony weighs on most of his writings, which were on only two subjects, the Bible and his enemies. He blasphemed or he insulted. His highly vaunted humour was however far from being irreproachable; the laugh that he excites is not legitimate – it is a grimace. Have you ever noticed that the divine anathema was written on his face? After so many years there is still time to have the experience. Go contemplate his figure in the Hermitage Palace.[iv] I never look at it without congratulating myself that it was not done for us by some chisel imitative of the Greeks, which would perhaps have known how to render a certain idealized image. Here everything is natural. There is as much truth in this head as if it had been taken from a cadaver and placed on a plate. Look at this abject brow that never blushed from modesty, these two extinct craters where lust and hate still seem to boil. This mouth – I say it badly perhaps, but it is not my fault – this horrible *rictus* running from ear to ear, and these lips pinched by cruel malice like a spring ready to spout forth blasphemy or sarcasm. Do not speak to me of this man; I cannot stand the idea. Ah! The harm he has done us. Like an insect, the scourge of gardens, who only attacks the roots of the most valuable plants, Voltaire, with his *sting*, never ceased to attack the two roots of society, women and young people. He injected them with his poisons, which he thus transmits from one generation to the other. It is in vain that to cloak his inexpressible offence, his stupid admirers bore us with sonorous tirades where he spoke superlatively of the most venerated things. These willingly blind people do not see that they thus accomplish the condemnation of this guilty writer. If Fénelon, with the same pen that painted the joys of Elysium had written the book *The Prince*, he would have been a thousand times more guilty than Machiavelli. Voltaire's great crime was the abuse of talent and the considered prostitution of a genius created to celebrate God and virtue. He could not, like so many others, claim youth, rashness, the heat of passion, or, finally, the sad weakness of our nature. Nothing absolves him. His corruption is of a kind that belonged only to him; it was rooted in the deepest fibres of his heart and fortified with all the strength of this intelligence. Always allied to sacrilege, it braved God while losing men. With a fury that is without example, this insolent blasphemer went so far as to declare himself the personal enemy of the Saviour of mankind. He dared, from the depths of his nothingness, to give him a ridiculous name, and this adorable law that the Man-God brought down to earth, he called INFAMOUS. Abandoned by God, who punished him by withdrawing from him, he lacked all restraint. Other cynics astonished virtue, Voltaire astonished vice. He plunged into the mire; if he rolled in it, it was to slake his thirst. He surrendered his imagination to the enthusiasm of hell, which lent him all its forces to lead him to the limits of evil. He invented prodigies, monsters that make us blanch. Paris crowned him; Sodom would have banished him. Shameless profaner of the universal language and its greatest names, the last of men after those who love him! How can I tell you how he makes me feel? When I see what he could have done and what he did, his inimitable talents inspire in me no more than a kind of nameless holy rage. Suspended between admiration and horror, sometimes I would like to raise a statue to him – by the hand of the executioner.

The Chevalier

Citizen, remember your grey hair.

The Count

Ah! You quote to me another of my *friends*;[7] but I will answer like him: *See rather winter on my head.*[8] These grey hairs tell you clearly enough that for me the time of fanaticism or even simple exaggerations has passed. There is, moreover, a certain *rational anger* that accords very well with wisdom; the Holy Spirit himself formally declared it exempt from sin.[9]

The Senator

After our friend's *rational sally,* what could I add about *the universal man*? Believe me, my dear Chevalier, in basing yourself on Voltaire, you have, unfortunately, just shown us the most perfidious temptation that can present itself to the human mind – that of believing in invariable laws of nature. This system offers seductive appearances, yet it leads directly to the decline of prayer, that is to say, to the death of the spiritual life, for prayer is the

---

7 J.-J. Rousseau.
8 See the preface to the *Nouvelle Héloise.*
9 *Tremble, and sin no more.* (Psalm 4:5.)

respiration of the soul, as was said, I believe, by M. de Saint-Martin. He who no longer prays no longer lives. *No religion without prayer*, said Voltaire, whom you have just cited.[10] Nothing is more obvious, and it necessarily follows, *No prayer, no religion*. This is just about the state to which we are reduced. Since men have never prayed except by virtue of a revealed religion (or one recognized as such), in the measure that they have approached deism, which is and can do nothing, they have ceased to pray, and now you see them bent towards the earth, uniquely occupied with physical laws and studies, and no longer having the least inkling of their natural dignity. Such is the misfortune of these men that they can no longer even desire their own regeneration, not only because of the recognized reason *that what is not known cannot be desired*, but because they find in their moral brutalization some curious but frightful charm, which is an appalling punishment. It is in vain that one speaks to them of what they are and must be. Plunged in the divine atmosphere, they refuse to breathe, *whereas if they only opened their mouths, they would imbibe the spirit*.[11] Such is the man who no longer prays; and if the public cult did not offer some little opposition to the universal degradation (we need no other proof of its indispensable necessity), I honestly believe that we would finally be reduced to veritable brutes. Consequently, nothing equals the antipathy of the men of whom I have just been speaking for this cult and for its ministers.

Sad confidences have taught me that there are those for whom the air of a church is a kind of cape that literally oppresses them and forces them to leave; whereas healthy souls feel themselves penetrated there by some kind of spiritual dew, which has no name but needs none since no one could mistake it.ᵛ Your Vincent de Lérins set forth a famous rule in matters of religion: he said that it was necessary to believe what has been believed ALWAYS, EVERYWHERE, AND BY ALL.[12] There is nothing so true and so universally true. Despite his fatal degradation, man always carries the obvious marks of his divine origin, so that every universal belief is always more or less true. Which is to say that man may well have covered over and so to say *encrusted* the truth with the errors he has loaded onto it; but these errors are local, and the universal truth will always show itself. Moreover, men have prayed always and everywhere. Undoubtedly, they could have prayed badly; they could have asked for what they did not need,

---

[10] He said it in his *Essai sur les mœurs et l'esprit, etc.*, Vol. 1, on the *Koran*, *Oeuvres*, 16:332.

[11] Psalm 118 (119):131.

[12] QUOD SEMPER, QUOD UBIQUE, QUOD AB OMNIBUS.

or not asked for what they needed, which is human; but they have always prayed, and this is of God.

The fashionable system of invariable laws would lead us straight to fatalism and make a statue of man. I protest, as our friend did yesterday, that I do not mean to insult reason. I respect it very much despite all the harm it has done us; but what is really sure is that every time we find it opposed to *common sense*, we must repress it as a poisoner. It is reason that has said: *Nothing can happen except what happens, and nothing happens except what must happen.*[vi] But good sense has said: *If you pray, something that was to happen will not happen.* In this case, common sense has reasoned very well, whereas reason has lacked common sense. For the rest, it matters little to proven truths that certain subtle arguments can be raised that reasoning does not know how to answer immediately, for there is no source of error more gross or more dangerous than that of rejecting such and such a dogma simply because it suffers from an objection that we do not know how to resolve.

The Count

You are perfectly right, my dear Senator: no objection can be admitted against the truth, otherwise it would no longer be the truth. As soon as its character is recognized, the insolubility of the objection demonstrates no more than a lack of knowledge on the part of the one who cannot resolve it. History, chronology, astronomy, geology, etc., have been called in testimony against Moses. The objections disappeared in the face of true science; but the wisest people were those who scorned these objections without examination, or who only examined them to find a response, but without ever doubting that there was one. Even the mathematical objection must be scorned: for while it will undoubtedly be a demonstrated truth, they will never be able to demonstrate that it contradicts a previously demonstrated truth. Suppose it a fact that agreement among a sufficient number of historical witnesses (which I am only assuming) proved absolutely that Archimedes burned Marcellus's fleet with a burning mirror; then all the objections of geometry would disappear. It would be useless to tell me: but are you not aware that every burning mirror unites the rays *to the quarter of the diameter of its sphericity; that you cannot lengthen the focus without diminishing the heat, so that you cannot enlarge the mirror in sufficient proportion, and that assuming the least possible size to burn the Roman fleet it would have had to have been at least as large as the city of Syracuse? What have you to say to that?* I would say to him: *I have to reply to you that Archimedes burned the Roman fleet with a mirror.*

Afterwards Kircher[13] came to explain Archimedes' mirror to me (*tulit alter honores [another brought the honours]*), and writers buried in the dust of libraries emerged to render homage to the genius of this modern scholar. I will admire Kircher very much, I will even thank him, but I did not need him to believe.

They once said to the celebrated Copernicus: *If your system were true, Venus would have phases like the moon; however it does not, therefore the whole new system disappears.* This was certainly a mathematical objection in the full sense of the term. According to an old tradition, whose origin I can no longer find in my memory, he responded: *I admit that I have nothing to reply to you; but God will give the grace to find an answer.* In effect, *God gave the grace* (but after the death of the great man) when Galileo discovered the telescope with which he saw the phases [of Venus]; so that the *insoluble objection* became a complement to the demonstration.[14] This example furnishes an argument that appears to me to be particularly strong in religious discussions, and more than once I have used it to advantage on some good minds.

The Chevalier

You remind me an anecdote from my earliest youth. There lived near me an old Abbé *Poulet*, a real fixture around the chateau, who had drubbed my father and my uncles as children, and who would have been hung for the whole family; a little morose and always grumbling, he nevertheless remained the best of humans. I went into his study one day, and the conversation having fallen, I don't know how, on the arrows of the

---

[13] [On the history of Archimedes' famous mirror, see J. Baltrusaitis, *Essai sur une légende scientifique. Le Miroir* (Paris 1978), pp. 91–141. Athanasisus Kircher's *Ars magna lucis et umbrae* (Rome 1646) marked a turning point in the dispute over the authenticity of the story; Kircher followed twelfth-century Byzantine authors in proposing that the device used flat mirrors instead of a parabolic mirror. (Darcel ed.) Kircher (1601–80) was a learned German Jesuit, Egyptologist, scientist, and Hermeticist, whose *China illustrata* (1667) Maistre owned.]

[14] I know nothing of this fact. But the English astronomer [John] Keill (*Astronomical Lectures* [London 1721], XV), cited by the author of an interesting historical eulogy of Copernicus (Warsaw, 1803, p. 35, note G), attributes to this great man the glory of having predicted that one could recognize on Venus the same phases the moon presents to us. Whatever supposition one makes, the argument remains the same. It suffices that one could object to Copernicus that his theory was in contradiction with a mathematical truth, and that Copernicus, in this case, would have been obliged to reply, which is incontestable, E PUR SI MUOVE. ["And yet it moves" – Galileo's reputed reply to the Inquisition when required to abjure his "error" about the movement of the planets.]

ancients, he said to me: *Do you know, Chevalier, that there was only one antique arrow, and do you know its speed? It was such that the piece of lead used as ballast on the arrow sometimes was heated by the friction of the air to the point of melting.* I began to laugh. *Go on, my dear Abbé, you are talking nonsense. Do you believe that an antique arrow went faster than a modern ball fired from a rifled canon? You know, however, that this ball does not do that.* He looked at me with a certain grimacing laugh that would have shown all his teeth if he had had any, and which said clearly enough, you are only a *young smart aleck.* Then he went to a worm-eaten pedestal table, picked up an old Aristotle he had been using to press his collars, and carried the volume to the table. He leafed through it for a few minutes, then slapping his hand on the place he had found, said, *I am not talking nonsense; here is a text the most splendid cannon in the world will never efface*, and he marked the margin with his thumbnail. I often think of the lead of these ancient arrows, which you have just recalled for me. If what Aristotle said is true,[vii] here is another truth that must be admitted despite an insoluble objection taken from physics.

The Count

Undoubtedly, if the fact is proved, which is something I cannot look into at the moment. It suffices for me to take a general theory from the mass of these facts, a kind of *formula* that serves to resolve all the particular cases. I would say that "every time a proposition is proved by the kind of proof relevant to it, no objection whatsoever, *even an unanswerable one, should be countenanced.*" The very inability to reply shows only that the two propositions taken to be true are not really contradictory, which can always happen when the contradiction is not, as they say, *in the terms.*

The Chevalier

I would like to understand this better.

The Count

No authority in the word, for example, has the right to reveal that *three and one are the same*; for I know the meaning of *one* and *three*, and as the meanings assigned to the terms have not changed in the two propositions, to want to make me believe that *three* and *one* are and are not the same thing, is to order me to believe in God's name that God does not exist. But if I am told that *three persons have only one nature*; I am ready to believe it, provided that revelation provides me with sufficient proof, especially, although not necessarily, if revelation accords with the most solid speculations of psychology and even with the more or less obscure beliefs of every nation; and it matters little to me that *three is not one*, since this is not the question here, which is to know if *three persons* can have a *single nature*, which is quite another question.

The Senator

Indeed, where is the contradiction in this case, when it cannot be supported either by the facts, since we do not know them, nor in the terms, since they have changed? So let us allow the Stoics to tell us that the proposition *it will rain tomorrow* is as certain and immutable in the ordained order of things as the proposition *it rained yesterday*; and allow them, if they can, to embarrass us with the most dazzling sophisms. Let them tell us what they will, since even the unanswerable objection (which I am very far from admitting in this case), must not be admitted against the demonstration that results from the innate belief of all men. So if you believe me, Chevalier, you will continue to say your Rogation prayers[viii] when you get home. It would even be well, while waiting, to pray to God with all your strength to grant you the grace of returning there, while letting the same objectors tell you that it is decided in advance whether you will ever see your beloved homeland.

The Count

Although I am, as you have seen, completely persuaded that the general feelings of all men form so to speak, verities of intuition before which all the sophisms of reasoning disappear, still I believe like you, Senator, that on the present question we are by no means reduced to feelings, since, first of all, if you look at it closely you will sense the sophism without being able to explain it clearly. Undoubtedly, the proposition, *it rained yesterday*, is no more sure than the other, *it will rain tomorrow*; but only *if it must rain*. However this is precisely the issue, and so the question begins again.

In the second place, and this is the principal point, I see no immutable rules nor this inflexible chain of events about which so much has been said. On the contrary, I see in nature only flexible forces, such as must necessarily be the case if the action of free beings, combining frequently with the laws of nature, is to be accommodated. Look at how many ways and to what extent we influence the reproduction of animals and plants. Grafting, for example, is or is not a law of nature, depending on whether men exist. You were telling us, Chevalier, of a certain precise quantity of rains due to each country every year. As I have never occupied myself with meteorology, I do not know what has been said on this issue; but to tell you the truth, it seems to me impossible to prove, at least with even approximate certainty. Whatever the case, it can only be a question of an average year, and on what period are we to base this average? Ten years perhaps, or perhaps a hundred? I want to continue the discussion with these people who reason this way. I will admit that each year exactly the same quantity of water must fall in each country: let this be an invariable law; but the distribution of this water will be, if one may express it this way, the *flexible part* of the law. So you see that even with your *invariable* laws we can still very well have floods and droughts: *general* rains for the world at large, and *exceptional* rains for those who know how to ask for them.[15] Of course we do not pray for olives to grow in Siberia or the *klukwa* in Provence; but we pray that the olives do not freeze in the countryside of Aix and that it does not get too hot for the *klukwa* during your short summer.

Certainly all the philosophes of our time speak only of invariable laws; for them it is simply a question of preventing men from praying and this is the infallible means of success. This is the reason these unbelievers are angry when preachers or moralist writers take it upon themselves to tell us that the physical scourges of this world, such as volcanic eruptions, earthquakes, etc., are divine punishments. They tell us that it was strictly necessary that Lisbon should have been destroyed on 1 November 1755, as it was necessary that the sun should have risen that day; in truth a fine theory quite suited to the perfection of man. I recall how indignant I was one day while reading the sermon that *Herder* addressed to *Voltaire* on the subject of his poem about the Lisbon disaster. He addressed him seriously, "You dare to complain to Providence about the destruction of this city. You are not thinking! This is a formal blasphemy against the *eternal wisdom*. Do you not know that man, like his beams and tiles, is a *debtor for his existence*, and that all things in existence must pay their debts? Elements combine, elements disassemble; *this is a necessary law of nature*. What then is astonishing about this that should motivate a complaint?"[ix]

Gentlemen, is this not a fine consolation and quite worthy of this honest comedian who preached the Gospel in the pulpit and pantheism in his writings?[16] But philosophy does not know any better. From Epictetus to the *Bishop of Weimar*,[17] and to the end of time, this will be its invariable way and *its necessary law*. It does not know the oil of consolation. It withers and hardens the heart, and when it has made a man callous, it

---

[15] *God, you will rain a downpour of blessings.* Psalm 67(68):10. This is precisely the *kekrimenon ouron* [choice rain] of Homer. (*Iliad* XIV.19). Rain or wind, it does not matter, provided that they are *kekrimenon* [choice].

[16] [In a letter to Serge Ouvarov, 8 December 1810, Maistre described Herder as "one of the most dangerous enemies of Christianity, a subtle and guilty comedian who preached the Gospel from the pulpit, and Spinozism in his writings." S. Ouvarov, *Etudes de philosophie et de critique* (Paris 1847).]

[17] [Maistre is indulging in a bit of irony; Herder was the court preacher in Weimar, but never a bishop.]

believes it has made him a sage.[18] Voltaire, moreover, had replied in advance to this criticism in this same poem on the Lisbon disaster:

> No, do not present to my distressed heart
> Any more of these immutable laws of nature,
> This chain of bodies, minds, and worlds:
> Dreams of scholars, profound illusions!
> God holds the chain in his hand and is not enchained:
> By his beneficent choice all is determined;
> He is free, he is just, he is not implacable.[19]

Up to this point, this could not be better put, but as if repenting of having talked sense, he adds immediately:

> So why do we suffer under a just master?
> This is the fatal knot that must be untangled.[20]

Here the rash questions begin. *Why do we suffer under a just master?* The catechism and common sense reply in concert: BECAUSE WE DESERVE IT. *This is the fatal knot wisely untangled*, and never do we move away from this solution without talking nonsense. In vain does Voltaire exclaim:

> On seeing this pile of victims, do you say:
> God is avenged; their death is the price of their crimes?
> What crime, what fault have these children committed
> Crushed and bloody on their mother's breast?[21]

This is bad reasoning, lacking attention and analysis! Undoubtedly there were children in *Lisbon* just as there were in *Herculanum* in the year

---

[18] There is as much difference between true morality and theirs (that of Stoic philosophers and epicureans) as there is between joy and patience, for their tranquillity is based only on necessity. (Leibniz, *Essais de Théodicée* [Amsterdam 1710], 2:215, n° 251.)

Jean-Jacques has justified this observation when in the course of his vain pathos on morals and virtue he finishes by telling us: "The wise man, the one who is superior to all reverses, is the one who sees in all these misfortunes the blows of blind necessity." (*Eighth Promenade, Oeuvres*, [33 vols.] (Geneva 1782), p. 25.). Always the *hardened* man in place of the *resigned* man! This is all that these preceptors of humanity can preach to us. Emile, remember well this lesson of your master: do not think of God before age twenty, and at this age you will be a charming creature!

[19] [Voltaire, "Poëme sur le désastre de Lisbonne," *Oeuvres*, ed. Molund, 9:472–73.]

[20] [Ibid.]

[21] [Ibid., 9:470.]

seventy-nine of our era, and just as there were in Lyon a long time previously,[22] or as there were, if you like, at the time of the Flood. When God punishes any society for the crimes it has committed, he exacts justice as we do ourselves in this sort of case, without anyone thinking of complaining. A city revolts: it massacres the representatives of the sovereign; it closes its gates to him; it defends itself against him; it is taken. The prince dismantles it and deprives it of all its privileges; no one will blame him for this judgement on the pretext that some in the city were innocent. We should never treat two questions at once. *The city was punished because of its crime, and without this crime it would not have suffered.* Here is a proposition that is true, independent of all others. Will you then ask me *why the innocents have been caught up in the same punishment?* This is a different question to which I am not obliged to reply. I could admit that I have no idea of the reason without weakening the argument for the first proposition. I could also reply that it was impossible for the sovereign to act otherwise, and I would not lack good grounds for proving this.

The Chevalier

Allow me to ask you this: what would have prevented this good king from taking under his protection all the inhabitants in the city who remained loyal to him and transporting them to some other more fortunate province where they could have enjoyed, I won't say the same privileges, but greater privileges, more fitting to their loyalty?

The Count

This is precisely what God does when innocent people perish in a general catastrophe. However let us return to the argument. I flatter myself that I feel a pity no less sincere than Voltaire for these unfortunate *children crushed and bloody on* their mother's breast; but it is delirium to cite them to contradict the preacher who cries out: *God is avenged; these evils are the price of our crimes*; for nothing is more generally true. The only question is that of explaining why the innocent are caught up in the

---

[22] *Lyon, the pride of Gaul is missing. ... only a single night elapsed between the city as the greatest and the city non-existent.* (Seneca *Epistle 91* [Loeb]). One used to be able to read these two passages from Seneca beneath two great paintings representing the destruction of Lyon on the great stairway of the town hall. I do not know if the new catastrophe has spared them. [Attributed to the seventeenth-century painter Thomas Blanchet, the paintings depict the great Fire of Lyons in Nero's time. Maistre could have seen them on one of his visits to Lyon (in 1776 and 1779). The paintings survive today, having recently been restored. (Darcel ed.)]

punishment carried out against the guilty: but as I just said to you, this is only an objection, and if we abandoned truths because of difficulties, there would be no more philosophy. Moreover, I doubt whether Voltaire, who wrote so fast, noticed, that instead of treating a particular question relating to an event that concerned him on that occasion, he treated a general one, and that he asked, without being aware of it, *why infants, who could not yet merit punishment or rewards, are in the whole world subject to the same evils that can afflict grown men?* For if it is agreed that a certain number of infants must perish, I do not see how it matters to them whether they die in one way rather than another. Whether a dagger pierces a man's heart or a little blood accumulates in his brain, he is equally dead; but in the first case we say that he ended his days *by a violent death.* For God, however, there is no such thing as violent death. A steel blade in the heart is an illness, just like a simple lump that we call a *polyp.*

So we must go on to a more difficult question and ask *by virtue of what cause has it become necessary for so many infants to be stillborn, for fully half those who are born to die before two years of age, and for a very large number of those remaining to die before reaching the age of reason?* Posed in a spirit of pride and contention all these questions are quite worthy of *Mathieu Garo;*[23] but posed with respectful curiosity they can exercise our minds without danger. Plato occupied himself with them, since I recall that in his treatise on the Republic he brought onto the scene, I don't know how, a certain Levantine (an Armenian, if I'm not mistaken),[24] who told many things about the punishments of the other life, for he distinguished them very carefully. Concerning children dying before reaching the age of reason, Plato says: *as to their condition in the other life, this stranger told things that must not be repeated.*[25]

Why are these children born, or rather why do they die? What will happen to them one day? These are perhaps unapproachable mysteries; but one would have to lose all common sense to argue what is not understood against what is very well understood.

Would you like to hear another sophism on the same subject? Again it is Voltaire who offers it, and always in the same work:

---

[23]   [A pretentious ignoramus, Garo was the hero of La Fontaine's fable *Le Gland et la Citrouille.*]

[24]   This appears to be an error, and that instead of reading *Her the Armenian,* one must read *Heris, son of Harmonius.* ([Pierre-Daniel] Huet, *Demonstratio evangelica* [Paris 1679], Vol. I, Prop. 9, chap. 142, N° 11.) (Editor's note.)

[25]   Here the speaker's memory is a bit defective; Plato said only: "That with respect to children, Er told things that were *not worth remembering.*" (*Republic* X) Without disputing the expression, it must be admitted that Plato certainly knocked on all the doors. (Editor's note.)

Lisbon, which is no more, did it have more vices
Than London, than Paris plunged in its delights?
Lisbon is destroyed, and they dance in Paris.[26]

Good God! Does this man want the Almighty to convert the sites of all large cities into places of execution? Or does he really mean that God should never punish because he does not always punish everywhere and at the same time?

So had Voltaire been given a divine balance in which to weigh the crimes of kings and private persons, and to assign the appropriate time for their punishments? What would this bold writer have said, if at the moment he wrote these foolish lines in the middle of the city *plunged in its delights*, he could suddenly have seen in the not so distant future the Committee of Public Safety, the Revolutionary Tribunal, and the long pages of the *Moniteur* quite red with human blood?

For the rest, pity is undoubtedly one of the most noble feelings that honour man, and we must be careful not to extinguish it or even to weaken it in our hearts; however when we treat philosophical subjects we must carefully avoid any kind of poetry and see things as they are. Voltaire, for example, in the poem that I have just cited for you, shows us *a hundred thousand unfortunates that the earth has devoured*. But first, why a *hundred thousand*? He was all the more wrong in that he could have told the truth without exaggeration, for in fact only about twenty thousand men perished in this horrible catastrophe, in fact many fewer than in quite a few battles I could name for you.

Then we must notice that very many of the circumstances in these great calamities are only superficially shocking. That an unfortunate child, for example, is *crushed by a stone* is a dreadful spectacle for us. For the child it is much better than dying of smallpox or a painful dental operation. For our reason it is undoubtedly the same if three or four thousand men perish spread out over a large area or if they die all at once in a single catastrophe, in an earthquake or a flood, but for our imagination the difference is enormous. So it can very well happen that one of these terrible events that we rank among the world's greatest scourges is in fact of no account at all, not just for humanity, but for a single country.

You see here a new example of these laws, at the same time flexible and invariable, that rule the universe. Let us take it, if you wish, as a proven fact that in a given period a certain number of men must die in a given country; this is what is invariable. The distribution of life among individuals as well as the times and places of their deaths, constitutes what I have

---

[26] [Voltaire, "Poëme sur Lisbonne," *Oeuvres*, ed. Molund, 9:470.]

called the flexible part of the law – so that an entire city can be destroyed without an overall increase in mortality. The scourge can even be just, in two ways, by reason of the guilty who are punished and the innocent who in compensation acquire a longer and happier life. The omnipotent wisdom ruling all things has means so numerous, so diversified, so admirable, that the part accessible to our observation should certainly teach us to revere the other. A good many years ago I encountered certain mortality tables for a very small province prepared with great care and all possible accuracy. I was not very surprised to learn from these tables that two furious smallpox epidemics had not augmented the mortality for the years when this sickness had raged. So true is it that this hidden force we call *nature* has means of compensation that we can scarcely doubt.

The Senator

A sacred adage says that *pride is the beginning of all sin;*[27] I think that one could well add: *and of all our errors*. It misleads us by inspiring in us an unfortunate spirit of contention that makes us seek difficulties to have the pleasure of arguing instead of referring them to a proven principle. However I would be very surprised if the disputants themselves did not feel deep down that it is all in vain. How many disputes would end if every man were forced to say what he thought.

The Count

I agree with you completely; but before going any further, allow me to point out to you a particular character of Christianity that strikes me with respect to these calamities that we have been speaking about. If Christianity were a human creation, its teaching would vary with human opinions; but since it emanates from the immutable Being it is as immutable as he is. Certainly this religion, which is the mother of all good and true science that exists in the world, and whose greatest interest is the advancement of science, takes good care not to forbid it to us or to impede its march. For example, it very much approves our study of the nature of all the physical agents that play a role in the great convulsions of nature. As for itself, finding itself in direct relations with the sovereign, it scarcely occupies itself with the agents executing his orders. It knows that it was created to pray and not to argue, since it knows with certainty all that it needs to know. Whether one approves it or condemns it, whether one admires it or ridicules it, it remains unmoved, and on the ruins of a city destroyed by an

---

[27] Ecclesiasticus X:15.

earthquake, it exclaims to the eighteenth century what it would have said to the twelfth:

We beseech you, Lord, to deign to protect us; restore by your supreme grace this earth ruined by our iniquities, so that the hearts of all men will know that this is your anger that sends us these punishments, just as it is your mercy that delivers us from them.[x]

There are no invariable laws, as you can see. Now it is for the legislator to know, even apart from all discussion of the truth of these beliefs, if a particular nation really gains when it is penetrated with these feelings that lead it to surrender itself exclusively to research on physical causes, with respect to which I am nevertheless far from refusing a very great merit of the second order.

The Senator

I strongly approve the fact that your church, which claims to teach the whole world, does not allow itself to be taught by anyone, and it must undoubtedly be gifted with a great confidence in itself, since opinion has absolutely no effect on it. In your quality as a Latin ...

The Count

So whom do you call *Latin*? Be aware, I beg you, that in the matter of religion I am quite as Greek as you.

The Senator

Let us go on then, my good friend, let us forget the joke, if you please.

The Count

I am not joking a bit, I must assure you; was not the Apostle's creed written in Greek before it was written in Latin? Do not the *Greek creeds of Nicea and Constantinople*, and that of Athanasius contain my faith? Must I not die for them to defend the truth? I hope that I am of the religion of St Paul and St Luke, who were *Greeks*. I am of the religion of Saints Ignatius, Justin, Athanasius, Gregory of Nyssa, Cyril, Basil, and Gregory of Nazianzus, in a word of all the saints who are on your altars and whose names you bear, and namely of St [John] Chrysostom, whose liturgy you have retained. I accept all that these great and holy persons accepted; I reject everything that they rejected; I moreover receive as gospel all the ecumenical councils convoked in the *Greece of Asia* or in the *Greece of Europe*. I ask you how it would be possible to be more Greek?

The Senator

What you have just said gives me an idea that I believe just. If it were ever a question of a peace treaty between us, one could propose the *statu quo ante bellum.*

The Count

As for myself, I would sign it immediately and even without instructions, *sub spe rati* [with the hope that it is true]. But then what did you want to say about my *Latin* quality?

The Senator

I want to say that in your quality as a *Latin* you are always returning to authority. I am often amused to see you go to sleep on that ear. In any case, even if I were a Protestant, we would not be arguing today. For in my opinion, the statement *that every scourge of heaven is a punishment* is very well, very justly, and even, if you will, very philosophically, suited to be established as a national dogma. What human society has not believed this? What nation, ancient or modern, civilized or barbarian, with every possible system of religion, has not looked on these calamities as the work of a superior power that it was possible to appease? However I must praise our Chevalier if he has never mocked his curé when he heard him advise payment of the tithe *on pain of hail or lightning*, since no one has the right to claim that such a misfortune is the consequence of such a fault (especially such a minor one). One can and in general one must certify that every physical evil is a punishment, and that consequently what we call the *scourges of Heaven* are necessarily the result of a great national crime or the accumulation of individual crimes, so that each one of these scourges could be prevented, first by a better life, and second, by prayer. So we can let these sophists talk of their *eternal and immutable laws*, which exist only in their imaginations, and which tend to nothing less than the extinction of all morality and the absolute brutalization of the human species.[28] We must have electricity, you would say, Chevalier; therefore we must have thunder and lightning, just as we must have the dew. You could also add: as we must have wolves, tigers, and rattlesnakes, etc., etc. – In truth, I don't know. Man being in a state of degradation as visible as it is

---

[28] Not only care and work, but prayers too, are useful, God having these prayers in view when he rules things, and not only those who claim, under the vain pretext of the necessity of events, that one can neglect the care that business demands, but even more those who reason against prayers, falling into what the ancients already called the *lazy sophism.* (Leibniz, *Essais de Théodicée,* 2:416.)

deplorable, I don't know enough to decide whether such a being and such phenomena are due entirely to this state. Moreover, even in the state where we are, they have about dispensed with wolves in England. Why, I ask you, can't we dispense with them elsewhere? I don't know at all if it is necessary for the tiger to be what he is; I don't even know if it is necessary that there be tigers, or, to speak frankly, whether I am sure of the opposite view. Who can forget the divine prerogative of man: *that wherever he is found established in sufficient numbers, the animals that surround him must serve him or amuse him, or disappear?* However let us take leave, if you will, of this foolish hypothesis of optimism. Supposing that tigers must exist and be what they are, do we say: *That is necessary that one of these animals enter such and such dwelling today and that it there devours ten persons?* It is necessary that the earth contain, in its depths, diverse substances that in certain given circumstances be ignited or vaporized and produce an earthquake? Very well, do we add: *therefore it was necessary that on 1 November 1755 Lisbon be entirely destroyed by one of these catastrophes? Moreover the explosion could not have taken place elsewhere, in a desert, for example, or under the bottom of the sea, or a hundred leagues from the city. The inhabitants could not have been warned by preliminary light shocks so that they could have taken shelter by flight.* The most unsophisticated human reason would be revolted by such consequences.

The Count

Undoubtedly, and I believe that universal good sense is incontestably right when it holds to the etymology of which it is itself the author. *Scourges* are destined to *buffet* us, and we are *struck* because we deserve it. We could, undoubtedly, avoid meriting punishment, and even after meriting it, we could obtain pardon. This, it seems to me, is the sum of all that can be sensibly said on this point; and this is again one of the numerous enough cases where philosophy, after long and painful detours, comes at last to agree with universal belief. So, my dear Chevalier, you see clearly enough how opposed I am to your comparison *of nights and days.*[29] The course of the stars is not an evil; it is, on the contrary, a constant rule and good that belongs to the whole human race. But how could the evil that is a punishment be necessary? Innocence could have prevented it; prayer could have held it off. I always return to this great principle. Notice with respect to this subject a strange sophism of impiety, or, if you will, of ignorance, for I ask nothing more than to see the one in place of the other. Because the all powerful goodness knows how to use one evil to exterminate

---

[29] See p. 28.

another, it is believed that the evil is an integral part of the whole. Let us recall what the sage of antiquity said: *that Mercury* (which is reason) *has the power to pluck the nerves of Typhon*[30] *to make them the strings of the divine lyre.*[31] However if Typhon did not exist, this marvellous feat would be useless. Our prayers being only the effort of an intelligent being against the action of *Typhon*, their utility, and even their necessity, has been philosophically demonstrated.

The Senator

This word *Typhon*, which in antiquity was the emblem of every evil and especially of every temporal scourge, reminds me of an idea that has often struck me and that I would like to share with you. However I will spare you my metaphysics for the moment, since I must leave you to go and see the great fireworks display being put on this evening on Peterhoff road, and which will represent an explosion of Vesuvius. This is a *typhonic* display, if you will, but quite innocent.

The Count

I would not want to answer for the flies and for the numerous birds that nest in the neighbouring woods, or even for some bold humans who could well risk their lives or some limbs, all the while saying *Niebosse!*[32] I don't know how it happens that men never come together without exposing themselves to risks. However, my dear friend, go, and do not fail to come back tomorrow with a head full of *volcanic* ideas.

NOTES TO THE FOURTH DIALOGUE

i   It must even be observed that antique philosophy had foreshadowed this principle. Pythagoras said: IMITATE GOD. Plato, who owed so many things to this ancient sage, said: *the just man is the one who has made himself like God in so far as our nature permits.* (*Politicus* X [In fact, *Republic*

---

[30]   [In French the spelling of the name of the mythological monster born of the union of Gaia (Earth) and Tartarus is the same as the spelling for "typhoon." The etymology appears to be debated. Some trace "typhoon" back to the legend of Typhon, others suggest it derives from the Chinese "t'ai-fung" (great wind). Maistre's point obviously depends on the first derivation.]

[31]   This sublime allegory comes from the Egyptians. (Plutarch *On Isis and Osiris* 53.373 c–d.).

[32]   *Never fear!* A common expression of the Russians, the most hardy and enterprising of men, who never fail to use it when they are confronted with the most terrible and most evident dangers.

X.613.a–b (Darcel ed.)]), and reciprocally, *nothing resembles God more than the just man*. (*Theaetetus*) Plutarch added that man can not play God in a more delightful way than in making himself, as much as he can, similar to him by the imitation of divine perfections. *On the Delays of Divine Vengeance, Moralia,* C.IV.)

ii The resemblance that exists between man and his creator is that of the image to the model. *As it were, from a model, though this likeness does not amount to equality.* (St Thomas, *Summa Theologiae,* part. I, Q. 93, art. I.) On this resemblance, see as well Noël Alexandre, *Historia ecclessiastica Veteris Novique Testamenti,* [9 vols. (Luca 1734)], I, art. 7, Prop. ii.) If someone tells us that *a man resembles his portrait,* the absurdity is all his, since the contrary is what we say.

iii An evident axiom and truly divine! *For the supremacy of man can have no other foundation than his resemblance to God.* ([Francis] Bacon, *in Dialogum de bello sacro. Works,* 10:311.) He attributes this magnificent idea to a Spanish theologian, *Francisco de Vitoria,* who died in 1532 [1546], and to some others. In fact, Philo, and some Greek fathers and theologians, had made the point a long time ago, as can be seen in [Denis] Petau's fine work. (*De VI dier. opif.* [a commentary on Philo's *De Opificio Mundi (On the Creation)*], lib. II, cap. 2,3. *Theologicorum Dogmatum,* (Paris 1644), 3:296.)

iv Voltaire's library, as we know, was bought after his death by the court of Russia. Today it is deposited in the Hermitage Palace, the magnificent addition to the Winter Palace built by the Empress Catherine II. The statue of Voltaire, executed in white marble by the sculptor François Houdon, is placed in the library and seems to inspect it. This library leads me to important observations that have not been made before, if I am not mistaken. I remember, as well as one can recall something that one read fifty years ago, what Lovelace, in the novel on Clarissa, wrote to his friend: *If you would like to know a young person, begin by knowing the books that she reads.* There is nothing so incontestable; but this truth is of a more general order than that which occurred to Richardson. It is related to knowledge as well as to character, and it is certain that in looking over the books a man has collected one soon knows what he knew and what he loved. It is from this point of view that Voltaire's library is particularly curious. One will not get over one's astonishment in considering the extreme mediocrity of the works that sufficed for the former *patriarch* of Ferney. One searches there in vain for what are called the *great* books and especially for learned editions of the classics. The whole collection gives the idea of a library put together for the evening amusement of an old soldier. One must also notice there a bookcase full of odd books whose margins are laden with notes written in Voltaire's hand, and almost all marked by mediocrity and poor taste. The entire collection is a demonstration that Voltaire was a stranger to every kind of serious knowledge, but especially of classical literature. If

something is missing from this demonstration, it will be completed by the
traces of unexampled ignorance that escape Voltaire in a hundred places in
his works, despite all sorts of precautions. Perhaps one day, to be finally
finished with this man, it would be a good thing to offer a choice collection
of these examples.

v Pythagoras, almost twenty-five centuries ago, said that a man who puts his
foot in a temple feels another spirit born within him. (Seneca, *Epistle 94*
[Loeb]). Kant, in our modern times, was an example of the contrary feeling.
Public prayer and religious chants shocked him. (*Lautes beten und singen
war ihm zuwider.* See the notice on Kant, taken from the *Freymüthig*, in the
Correspondant de Hambourg of 7 March 1804, n° 38.) This was a sign of
reprobation of which the Germans can think what they will.

vi ... *that nothing has been which did not have to be, and (that) whatever can
be, that either is not or is going to be.* "Scipio was slain" *is no more immune
from change from true to false than* "Scipio will be slain." (Cicero *De fato*
IX)

vii There is nothing so well known as this text from Aristotle, which one can
read in the book *On the Heavens*, chap. VII, where he in effect says that this
missile that we could call a *leaden ball* is heated in the air *so that it is
melted.* Latin authors attributed the same phenomenon to the ball of lead
hurled from the catapult.
*It bursts into flame just as a Balearic sling hurls lead missiles. It flies and
by its flight turns with fire. And the flames which it did not have it discovers
beneath the clouds.* (Ovid *Metamorphoses* [II.727–29])
The leaden missile rolling in its long flight, melts.
(Lucretius [*The Nature of the Gods* VI.179])
*The missile, struck by the sling and by the wearing down of the air, sends
fire trickling down.* (Seneca *Investigations in Natural Philosophy* II.57)
And he split open his adversary's forehead with the melted lead.
Vergil *Aeneid* IX.588.)
M. Hehne said about these verses: *It is not as if they thought that the lead
hurled from the slings melted in the air, which would have been ominous [a
portent] but it was struck and ground by hard bones,* etc. There would have
been little difficulty if this text had been unique, or even if Aristotle, Seneca,
Lucretius, and Ovid had not spoken as physicists.

viii I would observe that one finds among the ancient Romans veritable
Rogations, of which this formula has been preserved for us:
*Father Mars, I beg and pray you that ... you keep off diseases seen and
unseen, dearth, destruction, disaster, and excess; that you increase crops,
grains, vines, trees, and allow them to turn out well; that you keep safe
shepherds and flocks.* (Cato *On Agriculture* 141.2–3)

ix One can find a little caricature in this citation from memory, but the sense
is presented exactly. Here are Herder's own words. – This is a complaint as

little philosophic as that of Voltaire with respect to the *destruction* of Lisbon, *of which he complains to the divinity in a way that is almost a blasphemy.* (What a good Christian!) *Are we not, we and all that belongs to us, and even our dwelling,* the debtors of the earth and its elements? *And if, in virtue* of the laws of nature, *it again demands from us* what belongs to it ... *will anything happen other than what must happen* in virtue of the eternal laws *of wisdom and of order?* ([Johann Gottfried von] Herder, *Ideen für die Philosophie der Geschichte der Menschheit* [Riga and Leipzig 1784–91], Vol. I, Bk. II, chap. 3.)

x   *Guard us, Lord, we pray ... and strengthen by power from above the earth that we have seen rocked by our evils; so that the hearts of mortals may learn, when you are angry, such blows come, and when you show pity, they cease.* (See the Ritual.)

Fifth Dialogue

The Chevalier

Well, Senator, how did you enjoy last night's entertainment?

The Senator

Very much, to tell the truth, fully as much as it is possible to be amused at spectacles of this kind. The fireworks were superb, and no one perished, at least among those of our species. As for *flies* and *birds*, I cannot answer for them any better than our friend; but I thought about them a great deal during the show, and it is this meditation that I refrained from sharing with you yesterday. The more I think about it, the more I am confirmed in the idea that the spectacles of nature are for us very probably what human acts are for animals that witness them. No creature can have other knowledge than that which constitutes its nature, and which is exclusively relative to its place in the universe. In my opinion, this is one of the numerous and invincible proofs of innate ideas, for if there were not ideas of this kind in every cognitive creature, each of them, owing its ideas to fortuitous experience, could leave its own sphere and disturb the universe; however this will never happen. The dog, the monkey, the *half-reasoning*[1] elephant will approach a fire, for example, and warm themselves with pleasure like us, but you will never teach them to put a log on the embers, for fire does not belong to them; otherwise, man's domain would be destroyed. They can see *one* very well, but never *unity*, the elements of number, but never *number*, one, two, or a thousand triangles together or one after the other, but never *triangularity*. The perpetual association of certain ideas in our understanding makes us confuse them, although they are essentially distinct. I see your two eyes and I immediately associate my perception of them

---

[1] [Alexander] Pope.

with the idea of *duality*; in fact, however, these two notions are of a totally different order, and the one does not lead to the other.

Since I am on the subject I will say more: I will never understand the morality of intelligent beings,[i] or even human unity or any other *cognitive* unity, apart from innate ideas. However let us return to animals. My dog accompanies me to some public spectacle, an execution, for example. Certainly it sees everything I see – the crowd, the sorry cortege, the judicial officials, the armed forces, the scaffold, the victim, the executioner, everything that I see. But what does it understand of all this? What it should understand *in its quality as a dog*. It will know how to distinguish me in the crowd and how to find me again if we are separated by some accident; it places itself in such a way as not to be crushed under the feet of the spectators. When the executioner raises his arm, the animal, if it is near by, will cringe for fear the blow is meant for it. If it sees blood, it will tremble, but as it would at a butcher shop. Its understanding stops there, and all the efforts of intelligent teachers, untiringly employed for centuries, can never take it beyond this point; ideas of morality, sovereignty, crime, justice, public force, etc., attached to this sad spectacle mean nothing to it. All the symbols of these ideas surround it, touch it, press in on it so to speak, but without avail, since no symbol can have meaning unless the idea it represents pre-exists. It is one of the most obvious laws of the temporal rule of Providence that each active creature acts in the sphere to which it is assigned without being able to leave that sphere. And how could good sense alone imagine the contrary? Arguing from these principles, which are incontestable, would you not say that volcanoes, waterspouts, or earthquakes are to me precisely what the execution is to my dog? I understand of these phenomena what I should understand, that is to say, everything that relates to those innate ideas that constitute my nature as man. The rest is a closed book.

The Count

There is nothing so plausible as your idea, my dear friend, or better said, I see nothing so obvious as the way in which you have envisaged the matter. Nevertheless, from another point of view, what a difference! *Your dog does not know that he does not know*, and you, intelligent man, you know it. What a sublime privilege this intimation is. Follow this idea, and you will be delighted by it. However on this point, since you have raised the question, do you know that I think I can please you greatly by showing you how bad faith extricates itself from the invincible arguments in favour of innate ideas furnished by animals? You have appreciated perfectly how the identity and invariable permanence of each class of sensitive or intelligent creatures necessarily supposes innate ideas, and you have very properly cited the fact that animals have always seen what we see without ever being able to understand what we understand. However before coming to an extremely helpful citation, I must ask you if you have ever noticed that these animals furnish another direct and decisive argument in favour of this system? In effect, the particular ideas that constitute the animal, each in his own species, are literally *innate* – that is to say absolutely independent of experience. The hen who has never seen a hawk nevertheless shows all the signs of terror the instant it sees one for the first time as a black spot in the sky; it immediately calls its chicks by uttering an extraordinary cry; the chicks coming out of their shells rush at the same instant under the wings of their mother. Finally, since this observation is invariably repeated with every species of animal, why should experience be more necessary for man for all the fundamental ideas that make him a man? This is not a frivolous objection, as you see. Listen now to how two heroes of *Aesthetics*[2] extricate themselves from it.

Locke's French translator, Coste, who appears to have been a sensible man, good as well as modest, tells us, in I don't know what note of his translation,[3] that he put the same objection to Locke one day, when it came to his attention. Feeling himself touched in a sensitive spot, the philosopher became a bit angry and replied brusquely: *I did not write my book to explain the actions of animals.* Coste, who would have had the right to respond like the Greek philosopher: *Jupiter, you are angry, therefore you are wrong*, contented himself however by telling us in a seriously pleasant tone: *The reply was very good, as the title of his book clearly demonstrates.* In effect, he had not written *on the understanding of animals.* You see, gentlemen, to what point Locke found himself reduced in his embarrassment. He took good care not to propose the objection to himself in his book, since he did not want to expose his reply. Condillac, who was not hindered by his conscience, found a very different way of dealing with the issue. I don't know whether the blind obstinacy of a pride that will not withdraw has ever produced anything so ridiculous. He says: *The animal will flee because it has seen others devoured by it*; but since he has no way of generalizing this observation, he adds, "with respect to animals who have never seen their kind devoured, one has *grounds* for believing that their mothers, from the beginning, *made them promise* to flee." *Made them promise* is perfect! However I regret that he did not say *would have counselled them.* To complete this rare explanation, he adds with all the

---

[2] Properly speaking, *the science of feeling*, from the Greek *aisthēsis*.
[3] *Essai [philosophique] sur l'entendement humain [Amsterdam* 1729], Bk. II, Chap. XI, § 5.

•

seriousness in the world: *if this explanation is rejected, one cannot see how the animal could take flight.*[4]

Excellent! So we see that if someone refuses these marvellous reasons, he can be sure that the animal will cease to flee from its enemy because Condillac *does not see* why this animal must take flight.

In any case, in whatever way he expresses himself, I will never be of his opinion. *He does not see*, he says; with his permission I believe that he *sees* perfectly, but that he would rather lie than admit it.

The Senator

Thank you very much, my dear friend, for your philosophical anecdote, which I found extremely amusing. So you are in perfect agreement with me on my way of looking at animals and on the conclusion about their relation to us that I draw from this perspective. They are, as I just told you, *surrounded, touched, and pressed upon* by all the signs of intelligence, without ever being able to improve the least of their acts. Refine this concept as much as you like – this kind of soul, this unknown principle, this *instinct*, this interior light that has been given to animals with such a prodigious variety of direction and intensity – and you will find no more than an *asymptote* of reason, capable of approaching it as closely as you like, but never of reaching it; otherwise a province of creation would have been invaded, which is obviously impossible.

For a completely similar reason, we can ourselves no doubt be *surrounded, touched, and pressed upon* by the action and agents of a superior order of which we have no knowledge other than that which pertains to our actual situation. I know all about the worth of this sublime doubt about which you have just spoken: yes, *I know that I do not know*, perhaps I even know something more. However it remains true that by the very nature of our intelligence it will never be possible for us to achieve direct knowledge on this point. Nevertheless, I make a very great use of this intimation in all my inquiries into *causes*. I have read millions of witticisms about the ignorance of the ancients *who saw spirits everywhere*: it seems to me that we are much more foolish in never seeing them anywhere. They never stop talking about *physical causes*, but what is a physical cause?

The Count

It is a *natural cause*, if we want to limit ourselves to a translation of the word; but in modern usage it is a *material cause*, which is to say a cause that is not a cause, for *matter and cause* are mutually exclusive, like *black*

---

[4]   *Essai sur l'origine des connaissances humaines*, Sect. II, chap. iv.

and *white, circle* and *square*. Matter has an effect only by movement, however, all movement being an effect, it follows that a *physical cause* is, if one wants to express oneself precisely, a NON-SENSE and even a contradiction in terms. There are and can be no *physical causes* properly speaking, because there is and can be no movement without an original mover, and every original mover is immaterial; *everywhere, what moves precedes what is moved, what leads precedes what is led, and what commands precedes what is commanded.*[ii] Matter can be and even is nothing but proof of mind. If a hundred balls are placed in a straight line and each receives successively an impulse communicated from the first, does this not presuppose a hand that provided the impulse to the first by an act of will? If the arrangement of things prevents me from seeing this hand, is it any less obvious to my intelligence? Is not the mind of a clock-maker enclosed in the drum of this clock, in which the mainspring is, as it were, charged with the instructions of an intelligence? I hear Lucretius telling me: *For nothing can touch or be touched, save body.*[iii] But these senseless words designed to frighten children, what do they matter to us? In reality, they mean that *no body can be touched without being touched!* A fine discovery, as you can see. The question is to know if there are anything but material bodies in the world, and if these bodies can be moved by anything besides bodies? However, not only can they be so moved, but originally they could not have been moved otherwise: for, since every movement can only be conceived as the result of another, one must necessarily accept either an infinite series of movements, which is to say, of effects without cause, or agree that the principle of movement cannot be found in matter; and we carry in ourselves the proof that movement begins with willing.[iv] For the rest, in a common and indispensable sense, nothing prevents us from calling *causes* effects that produce other effects; thus in the series of balls that I spoke of a moment ago, all are *causes* except the last, and all are *effects* except the first. However if we want to express ourselves with philosophical precision, it is another matter. It cannot be too often repeated that the ideas of matter and *cause* are mutually and rigorously exclusive.

On the question of the forces acting in the universe, Bacon came up with a fanciful idea that has subsequently confused a host of theorists: first he supposed material forces, and then he superimposed them one on top of the other indefinitely. And I have often been unable to prevent myself from suspecting that, in introducing these genealogical trees where everyone is a son except the first and everyone a father except the last, he made for himself on this model an *idol of the ladder*, and that he arranged causes the same way in his head, in his own way thinking that one cause was the offspring of the one that preceded it, and that with the narrowing of the genealogical tree as one went back, the true interpreter of nature would finally be led to a common ancestor. These are the ideas that this great jurist formed of nature and of the science that must explain it; but nothing is more chimerical.

I do not want to drag you into a long discussion. A single observation will suffice for both of us at the moment. It is that Bacon and his disciples have never been able to cite for us and will never be able to cite for us a single example in support of their theory. Let someone show us this supposed order of *general, more general, and most general* causes, as they are pleased to call them. Much has been discussed and much discovered since Bacon: let someone give us an example of this wonderful genealogy, let someone show us a single mystery of nature that they have explained, I do not say by a cause, but simply by a previously unknown primary effect, arrived at by going back from one to the other. Imagine the most common phenomenon, elasticity, for example, or any other you care to choose. Now I will not be difficult, I will not ask for either the grandparents or great-great-grandparents of the phenomenon; I will be content with its mother. Alas, everyone remains silent, and it is always (I mean in the material order) *proles siné matre creata* [offspring that were created without a mother]. Well, how can they be so blind as to seek causes in *nature* when nature itself is an effect? So long as we do not leave the material sphere, no man can advance more than any other in the investigation of causes. All are and must be stopped at the first step.

The genius of discovery in the natural sciences consists solely in the uncovering of unknown facts or relating unexplained phenomena to already known primary effects that we take for causes. Thus, those who discovered the circulation of the blood and the sex of plants undoubtedly advanced their sciences, but the discovery of facts has nothing in common with that of causes. Newton, for his part, immortalized himself by relating to gravity phenomena that no one had ever thought of relating to it; but the great man's footman knew as much about the cause of gravity as his master. Certain disciples, for whom he would blush if he returned to the world, have dared to say that gravitation is a *mechanical* law. Newton never uttered such a blasphemy against common sense, and it is of course in vain that they have sought to give themselves such a famous accomplice. On the contrary, he said (and certainly this is already a lot) *that he left to his readers the question of deciding if the agent that produces gravity is physical or spiritual.* Read, I pray you, his theological letters to Dr Bentley; you will be equally instructed and edified by them.ᵛ

So you see, Senator, that I strongly approve your way of envisaging this world, and if I am not absolutely mistaken, I even support it with very good arguments. For the rest, I repeat what you said, *I know that I do not know;* and this uncertainty fills me with both joy and gratitude, since I find united in it the indelible title of my greatness and a salutary preservative against all ridiculous or reckless speculation. In looking at nature from this point of view, from the greatest to the least of its productions, I continually recall (and this is enough for me) the phrase of a Lacedaemonian thinking about what prevented a stiffened corpse from standing upright however it was positioned: MY GOD, he said, *there must have been something inside.*[vi] Always and everywhere the same things must be said, for without this *something* everything is a corpse and nothing stands upright. The world thus envisaged as a simple collection of appearances, in which the least phenomenon hides a reality, is a true and wise idealism. In a very real sense, I can say that material objects are nothing like what I see; but what I see is real in relation to me, and it is enough for me to be thus led to the existence of another order in which I firmly believe without seeing. Relying on these principles, I understand perfectly that prayer is not only generally useful for warding off physical evil, but that it is the true antidote, the natural specific, for it, and that by its very nature it tends to destroy it. It does this in precisely the same way as the hidden power that comes to us from Brazil hidden in a light-coloured bark,[5] which by virtue of its very nature goes to seek the source of the fever, finds it, and attacks it with varying success, depending on circumstances and temperament; at least no one would claim that wood cures fever, which would be quite funny.

The Chevalier

As *funny* as you like, but apparently I must a *curious character*, because in my whole life I have never had any scruple about this proposition.

The Count

But if wood cures fever, why go to the trouble of looking for it in Peru? Let us go down to the garden; these birch trees will furnish us with enough for all the fevers in Russia.

The Chevalier

Be serious, I beg you. This not a question of *wood* in general, but of a *certain wood* whose particular quality is to cure fever.

The Count

Very well, but what do you mean by *quality*? In your mind, does this word mean a simple accident, and do you believe, for example, that *cinchona* cures because it is *symbolic, or heavy, or coloured*, etc.?

---

[5] [Cinchona bark contains quinine, an alkaloid used to reduce fever. Its properties were studied in the early nineteenth century by Hahnemann, the founder of homeopathy. (Darcel ed.)]

The Chevalier

You are quibbling, my friend; it goes without saying that I mean to speak of a real quality.

The Count

So then, *real quality!* What does that mean, I ask you?

The Chevalier

Oh! For my part, I ask you not to argue about words; surely you know that military common sense is offended by these sorts of quibbles.

The Count

I esteem military common sense more than you think perhaps, and I protest to you that these *quibbles* are no less odious to me than to you. But I do not believe that one is arguing about words to ask what they mean.

The Chevalier

I understand *by real quality*, then, something really subsisting, *an I don't know what* that I am not obliged to define apparently, but that nevertheless exists, like all that exists.

The Count

Wonderful, but this *something*, this *unknown* whose *quality* we are looking for, is it matter or not? If it is not matter ...

The Chevalier

Ah! I did not say that!

The Count

But if it is material, certainly you can no longer call it a *quality*; if it is not an *accident*, a *modification*, a *mode*, or whatever you might be pleased to call it, it is a substance similar in its essence to any other material substance, and this substance, which is not *wood* (otherwise all wood would cure) exists in wood, or more correctly *in this wood*, in the way that sugar, which is neither water nor tea, is contained in the infusion of the tea we are discussing. So we have done no more than recast the question, which begins again. In effect, since whatever substance that cures the fever is in the matter, I ask again: why go to Peru? Matter is even easier to find than wood; it seems to me that it is everywhere, and that everything that we see is good for curing. Then you will be forced to repeat to me about matter in general everything that you said to me about wood. You will tell me: *It is not a question of matter in general, but of this particular matter, that is to say, of the matter, in the most abstract sense, plus a quality that distinguishes it and that cures fever.*

For my part, I will attack you again by asking you what is this quality that you suppose material, and I will pursue you with the same advantage, without your good sense ever being able to find a point on which to resist me; for matter being by its nature inert and passive, and acting only by virtue of a movement it cannot give itself, it follows that it can act only through the action of a more or less remote agent, veiled by *it*, and which cannot be *it*.

So you see, my dear Chevalier, it is not simply a question of words. However, let us return to our original topic. This digression on causes leads us to an equally just and fruitful idea: it is to envisage the effects of prayer simply as a secondary cause, for from this point of view it is that and should not be distinguished from any other. So if a fashionable philosopher is surprised to see me using prayer to protect myself against lightning, for example, I will say to him: *And you, sir, why do you use lightning rods?* Or to restrict myself to something more usual, *Why do you use fire engines in fires and medicines in illnesses? Are you not thus opposing yourself to eternal laws, just like me?* "Oh, this is very different," I will be to told, "since if it is a *law*, for example, that fire burns, it is also one that water extinguishes fire." Then I will reply: *This is exactly what I say for my part, for if it is a* law *that lightning produces a certain havoc, it is also one that prayer, sprinkled in time on the* FIRE OF HEAVEN, *extinguishes or diverts it.* You can be certain, gentlemen, that there is no objection of this kind that I cannot counter to my advantage. There is no midpoint between a rigid, absolute, and universal fatalism, and the common faith of mankind in the effectiveness of prayer.

Do you recall, Chevalier, that fine man who a few days ago made fun of these two verses by Boileau:

For me who even in health is astonished by another world,
Who believes the soul immortal and that it is God who thunders.[6]

"In Boileau's time," he said, "before witches and such were brought down by so much science, they did not know that a lightning bolt was only a reinforced flash of electricity; and it would have been a grave affair if one did not see thunder as a divine arm destined to chastise crimes. However you should also know that already, in those old days, certain theorists embarrassed the believers of their time a bit by asking them why Jupiter

---

[6]   [*Satire I*, next to last two verses. (Darcel ed.)]

amused himself blasting the rocks of the Caucasus or the uninhabited forests of Germany." For my part, I embarrassed this profound theorist a bit by telling him: "But you have failed to notice, sir, that you have yourself furnished an excellent arguments to the devout of our time (for there are always some of them, despite the efforts of the wise) to continue to think like our good man Boileau; in effect, they will very simply tell you: *The lightning bolt, though it kills, was not created to kill, and what we ask of God, precisely, is that in his goodness he send his lightning bolts to rocks and deserts, which undoubtedly suffices for the accomplishment of physical laws."* You will understand that I did not want to offer a thesis to such a listener, but you see, I hope, where we are led by misconceived science, and what we must expect from a youth imbibed with such principles. What profound ignorance, and what horror of the truth! Notice, especially, this fundamental fallacy of modern pride, which always confuses the discovery or generation of an effect with the revelation of a cause. Men recognize in an unknown substance (amber) the property that it acquires through friction of attracting light bodies. They name this property *ambréité* (electricity). They do not change the name as they discover other substances with the same property; soon new observations lead them to discover the electric current. They learn how to accumulate it, to conduct it, etc. Finally, they believe they are sure that they have recognized and demonstrated the identity between this current and lightning, so that if names were imposed rationally, according to received ideas, today we would have to substitute the word *thunderism* for *electricity*. So with all this, what have they done? They have enlarged the miracle; they have done this to compare them, as it were. But what more do they know about its nature? Nothing. It even seems to become more inexplicable the more closely it is examined. Moreover, admire the beauty of this reasoning: "It is proved that electricity, such as we observe it in our laboratories, differs little from this terrible and mysterious agent that we call *lightning*, THEREFORE it is not God who thunders." Molière would have said: *Your* THEREFORE *is only a fool!* We would be better off if it were only a fool. You see the real consequences: *"Therefore* it is not God who acts through secondary causes; *therefore* their action is invariable; *therefore* our fears and prayers are equally in vain." What a monstrous string of errors! Not long ago I read in a French newspaper *that for an educated man, thunder no longer means lightning launched from on high to make men tremble, that it is a very natural and very simple natural phenomenon that passes high above our heads, and of which the nearest stars have not the least news.* If we analyze this reasoning, here is what we will find: "that if lightning came, for example, from the planet Saturn, *as if it were then nearer to God*, there would be reason to believe that he was involved in it; *but since it is formed some distance above our heads*, etc." They never stop talking about the ignorance of our ancestors, but there is nothing more ignorant than the philosophy of our century; the good sense of the second century would rightly have mocked it. The king prophet certainly did not place the phenomenon of which we are speaking in such an elevated region, since he named it, with much oriental elegance, *the sky thundered;*[7] he could have even recommended himself to modern chemists by saying that *with lightning God makes rain,*[8] but he says to us no less:

> YOUR thunder sounded in the hurricane, lightning lit up the world; the earth shook and trembled.[9]

Science and religion agree very well, as you can see. It is we who reason badly. It is certainly man's fault, for God had safeguarded him sufficiently; but pride lent its ear to the serpent, and again man put his criminal hand to the tree of knowledge. He has lost his way, and unfortunately he does not know it. Notice a fine law of Providence: since primitive times, of which I am not speaking at the moment, it has given experimental science only to Christians. The ancients certainly surpassed us by the power of their minds; this point is proved by the superiority of their languages, to an extent that seems to impose silence on all the sophisms of our modern pride. By the same reason, they surpassed us in everything they had in common with us. On the other hand, their physics amounted to almost nothing, for not only did they not attach any value to physical experiments, they even distrusted them and even suspected them slightly of impiety,[vii] and this confused sentiment was very ancient. When all of Europe had become Christian, when priests had become the universal teachers, when all the institutions of Europe had been Christianized, when theology had taken its place at the head of all teaching and the other faculties had arranged themselves around her like ladies-in-waiting around their sovereign, the natural sciences were given to it, *tantæ molis erat* ROMANAM *condere gentem!*[10] Ignorance of this great truth has misled very strong minds, not excepting Bacon, and perhaps even beginning with him.

---

[7] Psalm 77:17.

[8] Psalm 134(135):7. Another prophet took up this expression and repeated it twice. See Jeremiah 10:13 and 51:16. "Thunderclaps appear to be the combustion of oxygen and hydrogen; and so we see them followed by sudden rains." ([Antoine-François] Fourcroy, [*Philosophie chimique, ou*] *Vérités fondamentales de la chimie moderne,* [Paris 1792], p. 38)

[9] Psalm 76(77):19.

[10] [Such great toil was it to found the Roman state. Vergil]

The Senator

Since you have made me think of him, I confess that he has often amused me very much with his *desiderata*. He has the air of a man who pouts besides a cradle, complaining that the infant who is being rocked is not yet a mathematics professor or an army general.

The Count

In truth, this is very well said, and I don't even know if it would be possible to quarrel with the exactitude of your comparison, since at the beginning of the seventeenth century science was certainly not *an infant in a cradle*. Without speaking of the illustrious monk of the same name,[11] who preceded him in England by three centuries and whose knowledge could have won him the title of *scholar*, even from men of our own time, Bacon was a contemporary of Kepler, Galileo, and Descartes. Copernicus had preceded him. These four giants alone, without speaking of a hundred other less famous persons, deprive him of the right of speaking so scornfully of the state of science, which had already thrown a dazzling light on his time, and which was then all it could have been. The sciences do not develop as Bacon imagined it; they grow like everything else that grows; they are linked to man's moral state.

Although free and active, and in consequence capable of indulging in the sciences and perfecting them, like everything else that is given to him, man is nevertheless left to himself less in this field than any other. Bacon took it into his head to abuse the knowledge of his own time without ever being able to grasp it himself, and nothing in the history of the human mind is more curious than the imperturbable obstinacy with which this famous man never ceased denying the light that shone around him because his eyes were incapable of seeing it. Never was a man less acquainted with the natural sciences and the laws of nature.

Bacon has very rightly been accused of delaying the progress of chemistry by trying to make it mechanical, and I am fascinated that it is in his own country that one of the leading chemists of our time has addressed this reproach to him.[12] He did even more harm by retarding the progress of transcendental or *general* philosophy, of which he never stopped telling us, without ever suspecting what it must be. He even invented words that were false and dangerous in the sense that he gave to them, like *form*, for example, which he substituted for nature or *essence*, and which modern ignorance has not failed to claim, thus very seriously proposing to

---

[11] [Roger Bacon (1214–94).]

[12] Joseph Black, *Lectures on Chemistry*, [2 vols.] (London [1803]), 1:261.

investigate the *form* of heat, expansiveness, etc. Who knows if someone following in his footsteps will not come along someday to teach us about *the form of virtue*.

The current that carried Bacon away was not yet fully developed when he was writing; however it was already fermenting in his writings, where it boldly sketched the outlines of what we have seen come to fruition in our own time. Full of an unthinking rancour against all spiritual ideas, whose source and nature he did not himself recognize, Bacon used all his abilities to promote the physical sciences to the point of leading men to dislike all the rest. He spurned all metaphysics, all psychology, and all natural theology; and all positive theology he locked up in the Church, forbidding it to come out. He was always maligning final causes, which he called the *remora* on the ship of science, and he dared to assert straight out that inquiry into causes harmed true science, an error as glaring as it was dangerous, and yet, who could believe it, a contagious error even for well-disposed minds, to the point that one of the most fervent and most worthy disciples of the English philosopher has unhesitatingly warned us *to take good care not let ourselves be seduced by the order that we perceive in the universe*.

Bacon spared nothing to turn us away from the philosophy of Plato, which is the human preface of the Gospel, and he praised, explicated, and propagated that of Democritus, that is to say atomic philosophy, the despairing effort of materialism pushed to its limits, which sensing that matter escapes it and explains nothing, plunges itself into the infinitely small, seeking, so to speak, matter without matter, always happy even amid absurdities, so long as it does not find intelligence.[viii] In conformity with this system of philosophy, Bacon enlisted men to seek the cause of natural phenomena in the configuration of constituent atoms or molecules, the most false and crude idea ever to have defiled human understanding. This is why the eighteenth century, which never loved nor praised men except for the evil they did, made Bacon its god,[ix] while nevertheless refusing to acknowledge what was good and even excellent in him. It is a very great error to believe that he influenced the progress of science: all the true founders of science preceded him or were ignorant of him. Bacon was a barometer who announced good weather, and because he announced it, was thought to have made it. Walpole, his contemporary called him *the prophet of science*,[13] and this is all that can be conceded to him. I have seen the design of a medal struck in his honour, which has a rising sun with the legend: *Exortus uti æthereus sol* [Arising like the sun in the heavens].

---

[13] See the preface of the small English edition of *The Works of Francis Bacon*, edited by Dr [Peter] Shaw, 12 vols. (London 1802).

Nothing is more obviously false; I would rather consider a dawn with the inscription: *Nuncia solis* [messenger of the sun], and even this could be thought exaggerated, for when Bacon *arose* it was at least ten o'clock in the morning. The immense reputation that he has had in our time, as I have just said, is due only to his reprehensible sides. Notice that he was not translated into French until the end of this century, and by a man who told us naively *that he had, against his own experience, a hundred thousand reasons for not believing in God.*[x]

The Chevalier

Count, are you not afraid of being stoned for such blasphemies against one of the *great gods* of our time?

The Count

If it were my duty to be stoned, I would have to bear it patiently, but I doubt if anyone here is going to stone me. Moreover, even if it were a question of writing and publishing what I'm telling you, I would not hesitate for a moment. I would not be very afraid of the storms, so convinced am I that an author's real intentions are always felt and that the world renders justice to those. So I would be believed, I feel sure, when I would protest that I believe myself inferior in talent and knowledge to the majority of those writers you have in mind at the moment, as much as I may surpass them by the truth of the doctrines that I profess. I am even pleased to admit this first superiority since it furnishes me with the subject of a delightful meditation on the inestimable privilege of truth and on the sterility of talents that dare to separate themselves from it.

There is a beautiful book to be written, gentlemen, *on the injury inflicted on all the productions of genius, and even on the character of their authors, by the errors they have professed for three centuries!* What a subject if it were well treated! The book would be that much more useful in that it would rest entirely on the facts, and thus be nearly safe from quibbling criticism. On this point, I can cite for you a striking example, that of Newton, who presents himself to my mind as one of the leading men of science. There is only one thing lacking to him to justify completely this beautiful passage by an English poet, who called him

... Pure intelligence whom God
To mortal lent, to trace his boundless works
From law sublimely simple.[14]

---

[14] [James] Thompson, *The Seasons,* "Summer."

He lacked the ability to rise above national prejudices,[xi] for certainly if he had had one more truth in his mind he would have written one book less. So you can exalt him as much as you like and I will agree with you, provided that he keeps to his place. However when he descends from the heights of his genius to talk theological nonsense, I no longer owe him anything. In the realm of error there are not and never can be great names, ranks, or distinctions; there Newton is equal to *Villiers*.[15]

After this profession of faith, which I never desist from repeating, I live perfectly at peace with myself. I assure you that there is nothing I can accuse myself of, since I know what I owe to genius; but I also know what I owe to truth. Moreover, gentlemen, *the time has come* when all the idols must fall. Please, let us continue.

Do you find the least difficulty with the idea that prayer is a secondary cause, and that it is impossible to make against it a single objection that you could not make, for example, against medicine? *This sick person must die or must not die; therefore it is useless to pray for him.* Moreover I say: *therefore it is useless to administer remedies; therefore there is no art of medicine.* Where is the difference, I ask you? We do not want to admit that secondary causes combine their actions with a higher cause. *This sick person must die or must not die*: yes, undoubtedly, *he will die if he does not take remedies*, and he will not die *if he uses them*; this situation is, if one may express it this way, *part* of the eternal order.

No doubt God is the universal mover, but each creature is moved according to the nature it has received. You yourselves, gentlemen, if you wanted to bring here that horse that you see over there in the field, how would you do it? You would mount it, or you would lead it by its bridle, and the animal would obey, *according to its nature*, although it has all the strength it needs to resist you, and even though it could kill you with a kick. If you wanted to have that child that we see playing in the garden come to us, you would call it, or if you did not know its name, you make some sign to it; the most intelligible undoubtedly would be to show it this biscuit, and the child would come, *according to its nature*. Finally, if you needed a book from my library, you would go and get it, and the book would be moved by your hand in a purely passive way, *according to its nature*. This is a natural enough image of God's action on his creatures. He moves angels, men, animals, brute matter, in short, all created things, but each *according to its nature*; and man, having been created free, is moved freely. This law is truly *the eternal law*, and this is what we must believe in.

---

[15] [Most likely George Villiers, the 2nd Duke of Buckingham (1628–87), English politician, poet, and playwright.]

The Senator

I believe this with all my heart, just as you do; however it must be admitted that this agreement between divine action and our freedom, and the events that flow from it, is one of those questions in which human reason, even when it is perfectly convinced, is nevertheless unable to free itself from a certain doubt springing from fear, and which always assails it despite itself. This is an abyss in which it is better not to look.

The Count

My good friend, we are not free not to look. It is there before us, and one would have to be blind not to see it, which would be much worse than being afraid of it. Rather let us repeat that there is no philosophy without the art of spurning objections, otherwise even mathematics would be shaken. I admit that one's head turns a bit in contemplating certain mysteries of the intellectual world. Still, it is possible to be entirely reassured, and nature itself, wisely interrogated, guides us towards the truth. No doubt you have thought a thousand times about the way movements are combined. For example, if you run from east to west while the earth is turning from west to east, what do you want to achieve? Let us suppose you wanted to cover a verst [Russian measure, a bit longer than a kilometre] in eight minutes, running from east to west. You do it; you are there, covered with sweat; you are experiencing all the symptoms of fatigue. However what did this superior power, this *prime moving force,* which carried you along with itself, aim at? It wanted you carried back in space at an incredible speed, instead of your advancing from east to west, and this is what happened. So, like you, it has achieved what it wanted. If you play shuttle-cock on a ship at sea, is there not in the movement that carries both you and the shuttle-cock along something that impedes your action? Suppose you hit the shuttle-cock from the prow to the stern with a speed equal to that of the ship (a supposition that can be rigorously true). The two players are certainly doing *all that they want to do*; but the prime moving force is also doing *what it wants.* One of the two believed he hit the shuttle-cock, but he only stopped it; the other went forward to meet it rather than, as he believed, waiting for it and getting it on his racquet.

Would you perhaps say that, since you have not done all that you thought you were doing, you have not done all that you wanted to do? In this case, you would not have noticed that the same objection could be addressed to the superior moving force, about which it could be said that while it wanted to carry the shuttle-cock forward, yet the shuttle-cock remained immobile. Thus the argument would be equally valid against God. Since the argument that divine power can be limited by human power has precisely the same force as the converse argument, it follows that it is not applicable in either case, and the two powers act together without detriment to each other.

Much can be learned from the relationship between moving forces that, whatever their number and direction, can act on the same body simultaneously, and that all have their effect, so that the moving body at the end of a single movement produced by them will be at precisely the same point at which it would have stopped if they had all acted one after the other. The only difference to be found between the one dynamic and the other, is that in the case of bodies, the force moving them never belongs to them, while in the case of minds, wills (which are really motions) themselves unite, intersect, and collide, since they are only motions. It can even happen that a created will cancels, I would not say the *exertion*, but the result of divine action; in this sense, *God* himself has told us that God WISHES things that does not happen because man DOES NOT WISH THEM.[16] Thus the rights of man are immense, and his greatest misfortune is to be unaware of them. However his true spiritual action is prayer, by means of which, by putting himself in harmony with God, he exercises an omnipotent power, so to speak, since he directs it.

Do you want to know what this power is and to measure it, as it were? Think of what the human will can do in the sphere of evil; it can contradict God, as you have just seen. So what can this will do when it acts in harmony with him, and what are the limits of this power? Its nature is not to have any. The power of the human will in the social order somewhat impresses us, and we often say that *man can do all that he wishes*; but in the spiritual order, where effects are not so visible, ignorance on this point is only too general; and even in the material sphere we are far from reflecting enough. You could, for example, easily pull up this rosebush, but you cannot pull down an oak tree. Why not, I ask you? The earth is covered with foolish men who will quickly tell you: *Because your muscles are not strong enough*, thus taking, in all good faith, the *limit* for the *means* of power.

Man's power is limited by the nature of his physical organs, which is necessary so that he can disturb the established order only up to a certain point. You can appreciate what would happen if a man with only his own hands could overturn a building or uproot a forest. It is perfectly true that the wisdom that created man perfectible has given him the science of dynamics, that is to say the artificial means of augmenting his natural

---

[16] *Jerusalem, Jerusalem ... how often would I have gathered your children together ...* BUT YOU WOULD NOT! (Luke 13:34)

There are in the spiritual order, as in the material order, *living forces and dead forces*, and this is as it must be.

powers. But still, this gift is accompanied by a striking sign of infinite foresight: for, wishing that every possible advance be proportionate, not to the limitless desires of man, which are immense and almost always disordered, but only to his wise desires, based on his needs, this wisdom has willed that each of his powers is necessarily attended by a check that is born and grows with it, so that the power must necessarily destroy itself by the very effort it makes to expand.

For example, one cannot increase the power of a lever without a proportional increase in the difficulties of working it, which must eventually render it useless;[xii] moreover, it can be said that in general and in operations that are not strictly speaking mechanical, man cannot increase his natural forces without employing proportionately more time, space, and materials, which in the first place inconveniences him in an ever increasing way, and which prevents him from acting clandestinely – and this is something that must be carefully noted. Thus, for example, any man could blow up a house by means of explosives; but the indispensable preparations are such that the public authorities will always have the time to ask him what he is doing. Optical instruments present another striking illustration of the same law, since it is impossible to perfect one of the qualities whose combination constitutes the perfection of these instruments without weakening another. One could make a similar observation with respect to firearms. In a word, there is no exception to a law whose suspension would annihilate human society. So therefore, on all sides, and in the natural order as well as in that of art, the limits are set. You would not bend the bush I was talking to you about earlier if you went about it with a reed; this would not be because you lacked the strength, but because the reed did; and this too feeble instrument is to the rosebush what your arm is to the oak tree. By its nature the will would move mountains, but the muscles, nerves, and bones given to it for acting in the material world give way to the oak as the reed gives way to the bush.

So, in your mind, take away the law that prescribes that the human will can act materially in an immediate way only on the body that it animates (a law that is purely accidental and relative to our state of ignorance and corruption) – and the will would uproot an oak as easily as it lifts an arm. In whatever way one looks at the human will, one finds that its powers are immense. Since prayer is the *dynamic* granted to men in the spiritual order, of which the material order is only an image and kind of reflection, let us take great care not to deprive ourselves of it, for this would amount to wanting to substitute our arms for a winch or a fire engine.

The philosophy of the last century, which will appear to the eyes of posterity as one of the most shameful epochs of the human mind, forgot nothing in trying to turn us away from prayer by means of its *eternal and immutable laws*. Its favourite, I almost said its *unique*, object was the separation of man from God; and how could it have accomplished this more surely than by preventing man from praying? This whole philosophy was nothing but a veritable system of practical atheism;[17] I have given this strange malady a name: I call it *theophobia*. Look closely, and you will find it in all the philosophical books of the eighteenth century. They did not say frankly: *There is no God*, an assertion that could have led to some physical inconveniences, but they said: *"God is not there*. He is not in your ideas, which come from the senses; he is not in your thoughts, which are only *transformed sensations*; he is not in the scourges that afflict you, for these are physical phenomena like others that can be explained by known laws. He does not think of you; he has made nothing for you in particular; the world is made for the insect as for you; he does not revenge himself on you, you are too small, etc." In short, one could not mention the name of God to this philosophy without throwing it into convulsions. Even the most eminent writers of this period, remarkable for their excellent if partial views, frankly denied the creation.[xiii] How could one speak to these men of celestial punishments without throwing them into a rage? *No physical event can have a superior cause relative to man*; this was their dogma. Sometimes, perhaps, this philosophy did not articulate this dogma in general terms, but when it came to application, they constantly denied it in detail – which amounts to the same thing.

I can cite for you a remarkable example of this, which is in some ways amusing, although sad from another point of view. Nothing shocked these writers like the Flood, which was the greatest and most terrible punishment that the divinity ever imposed on man; and nevertheless nothing is better established by all the kinds of proofs capable of establishing an important fact. So what were they to do? They began by obstinately refusing to us all the water necessary for the Flood; and I recall that in my youth my fledgling faith was alarmed by their reasoning. However since it has taken their fancy to create a world by precipitation,[18] and water being rigorously necessary for this remarkable operation, the lack of water no longer embarrasses them, and they have gone so far as to grant us freely that there was an *envelope* three leagues high over the whole surface of the globe; which is very honest. Some of them have even thought of calling Moses to their assistance and forcing him, in the most tortuous ways, to give evidence in favour of their cosmogenetic dreams. Of course, for them it is

---

[17]   The theory that denies the utility of prayer is formal atheism or differs from it only in name. (Origen *On Prayer*)

[18]   It is not a question *of creating a world, but of forming geological strata*, as the author himself remarked in one of his notes preceding this comment. (See endnote xii to the Second Dialogue) (Editor's note)

well understood that divine intervention has nothing at all do with this venture, which has nothing extraordinary about it. Thus they have admitted the total submersion of the globe at the same epoch as that fixed by this great man, which appears to them sufficient seriously to declare themselves as *defenders of revelation*; but of *God*, of *crime*, of *punishment*, not a word. They have even hinted to us very gently *that there were no men on the earth at the time of the great Flood*, which is quite *Mosaic*, as you can see. This word *Flood* having about it something *theological*, which displeases them, they have suppressed it and said *catastrophe*. So, they accept the *Flood*, which they need for their futile theories, and they remove *God*, who tires them. I think this is a clear enough symptom of *theophobia*.

I honour with all my heart the numerous exceptions that console the eye of the observer and, among the very writers who have been able to sadden legitimate belief, I am pleased to make the necessary distinctions; but the general character of this philosophy is no less what I have shown it to be; and this philosophy, working tirelessly to separate man from the divinity, finally produced the deplorable generation that has accomplished or allowed everything that we are seeing.

As for us, gentlemen, we also have our *theophobia*, but ours is the good kind. If sometimes the supreme justice frightens us, let us remember this phrase from St Augustine, undoubtedly one of the most beautiful that has ever come out of a human mouth: *Do you fear God? Save yourself in his arms.*[19]

Permit me to think, Chevalier, that you are now perfectly at ease with *eternal and immutable laws*. Nothing is necessary but God, and nothing is less necessary than pain. All pain is a punishment, and every punishment (except the last) is inflicted for love as much as for justice.

The Chevalier

I am delighted that my little quibbles have won us reflections from which I will profit. However I pray you, what did you mean to say by these words, *except the last*?

The Count

Look around you, Chevalier, and you will see the actions of human justice. What is it doing when it condemns a man to less than capital punishment? It is doing two things with respect to the condemned: it is chastising him, which is the work of justice; but it also wants to correct him, which is the work of love. If justice were not able to hope that the punishment will

---

[19] VIS FUGERE A DEO? FUGE AD DEUM.

make the condemned man come to his senses, it would punish by death in almost all cases. However, when justice is finally persuaded that the criminal is incorrigible, either by the repetition or the enormity of his crimes, love withdraws, and justice pronounces an eternal punishment. Since all death is eternal, how could a dead man cease to be dead? Undoubtedly, human justice and divine justice punish only to correct, and all punishment, *except the last*, is a remedy; but the last *is death*. All the traditions of mankind can be cited in favour of this theory, and even fables proclaim its dreadful truth:

THESEUS IS IN PLACE AND WILL BE THERE FOREVER.[xiv]

This stream that only passes once;[xv] this barrel of the Danaïdes, *always* full and *always* empty;[xvi] this liver of Tityus, *always* under the beak of the vulture, which devours it *always*;[xvii] this Tantalus, *always* ready to drink this water, to seize these fruits that escape him *always*;[xviii] this stone of Sisyphus, *always* carried up or coming down;[xix] this circle, eternal symbol of eternity, inscribed on the wheel of Ixion;[xx] these are so many talking hieroglyphics, about which it is impossible to be mistaken.

So we can contemplate divine justice in our own, as in a mirror, a dull reflector of the truth, yet faithful, because it can reflect no other images than those it has received. We see there that punishment has no other purpose than the prevention of evil, and that the greater the evil and the more deeply rooted, the longer and more painful the operation. If a man has made himself completely evil, how can it be wrested out of him? What purchase does he leave for love? All true instruction, thus mixing fear with consoling ideas, warns the free being not to advance to the limit beyond which there is no limit.

The Senator

For my part, I would again like to say many things to the Chevalier, for I have not for a moment lost sight of his exclamation: *And what do we say of war?* Moreover, it seems to me that this scourge deserves to be examined separately. However, I see that these earthquakes have led us much too far. We must part. Tomorrow, gentlemen, if you judge it appropriate, I will share with you some of my ideas on war, for this is a subject about which I have meditated much.

The Chevalier

I assure you that this is a subject about which I am not very proud. However I only know that it happens that I always love to make war or to talk about it, so I will listen to you with the greatest pleasure.

The Count

For myself, I accept our friend's commitment; but I do not promise you that I will have nothing more to say tomorrow on prayer.

The Senator

In that case, I will cede the floor to you tomorrow; but I will not cede my commitment. Good-bye.

NOTES TO THE FIFTH DIALOGUE

i   This was Origen's opinion: *men,* he said, *would not be guilty if they did not carry the notions of common and innate morality written in their minds in divine letters. (Grammasi (tou) theou* [in divine letters]) *Against Celsus* I.iv,v.

   [Pierre] Charron thought the same when he addressed to conscience this very original and penetrating apostrophe: "What are you doing looking elsewhere for the law or rule of the world? Who told you or suggested to you that you do not have it with you or within you if you wanted to be silent and listen! It must be said to you as to the payer of bad faith who asked to be shown the receipt that he actually had: *Quod petis intùs habes* [You have within you what you are seeking]; you ask for what you have in your heart. All the tables of the law – the two of Moses, the dozen of the Greeks, all the good laws in the world – are only copies and extracts exhibited in judgement against you who keep the original hidden and who feigns to know only what is, stifling as much as you can this light by which you are enlightened from within, but which has never been outside and humanly published, so that which was inside all heavenly and divine has been too much scorned and forgotten." *(De la sagesse,* Bk. II, chap. 3, n° 4.)

ii   Plato *Laws* XIII. [In fact from *Epinomis* 980 e (an appendix to the *Laws* – perhaps apocryphal) and not from Bk. XIII of the *Laws.* (Darcel ed.)] One can observe in passing that Plato's comment, *that what commands precedes what is commanded,* effaces the maxim so famous in our theatres:
   The first king was a lucky soldier![1]
       The very expression Voltaire used mocked him; *for the first SOLDIER* [soldat] *was PAID* [soldé] *by a king.*

iii   Lucretius *On the Nature of Things* 1.305.
       Dr Robison, Black's learned editor, justly mocked mechanical chemists *(the most ridiculous of men), who have wanted to transport the dreams of Lucretius into their science. *Thus,* he said, *if heat is produced in some*

---

[1]   ["Le premier qui fut roi fut un soldat heureux!" Voltaire, *Mérope,* I, 3.]

chemical solutions, this is, say the mechanists, through the effect of the rubbing and clashing of the different particles that have entered into the solution; but if one mixes salt and snow, these same things and this same rubbing produces a sharp cold. (Black, *Lectures on Chemistry*, On heat, 1:126.)

iv   "Can movement have another principle than the force by which it is itself moved?" (Plato *Laws*) *And since there should be no process to infinity in the order of bodies, we shall have to come to an incorporeal first mover ... Every moving thing [comes] from an unmoving principle.* (St Thomas, *Summa Contra Gentiles*, I, 44; III, 23. [Pegis]) Plato has not been copied here, but there is a perfect concurrence.

v   Newton's letters can be read in the *Bibliothèque britannique*, February 1797, Vol. IV, n° 30. See especially the letter of 3 February 1693. Ibid., p. 192.

He had already said in his immortal work: *The reader is not to imagine that by those words* ["attraction," "impulse" or "propensity"] *I anywhere take upon me to define the kind or the manner of any action, the causes or the physical reason thereof, or that I attribute forces, in a true and physical sense, to certain centres (which are only mathematical points) when I at any time happen to speak of centres as attracting or as endowed with attractive powers.* (*Philosophiae Naturalis Principia Mathematica*, Bk. III, Definition VIII, and Scholia, Proposition XXXIX.)

[Roger] Cotes, in his celebrated preface to this work, said *that when one has arrived at the most simple cause, that it is not permitted to advance further* [p. 33]; in which he does not seem to have understood his master very well. Clarke, of whom Newton said: *Clarke alone understands me,* made a remarkable admission on this point. *Attraction,* he said, *can be the effect of an impulsion, but certainly not of a material force (impulsu NON UTIQUÈ CORPOREO)*; and in a note, he added: Attraction is certainly not a material action at a distance, but the action of some immaterial cause (CAUSAE CUJUSDAM IMMATERIALIS, etc. See [Jacques] Rohault's [*Traité de] physique*, translated into Latin by [Samuel] Clarke, [London 1796], Vol. II, Chap. xi, § 15, text and note). The whole piece is curious.[2]

Let us never abandon an important question without having listened to Plato. "*The moderns* (the moderns!), he said, *have imagined that a body could act on itself by its own properties; and they have not believed that the soul could move itself and bodies; but for us who believe quite the opposite,*

---

[2]   [The piece is indeed curious. Samuel Clarke's notes to his Latin translation of Jacques Rohault's Cartesian *Traité de physique* (first edition, 1697) amounted to a "systematic refutation of the text" from a Newtonian point of view. See Michael A. Hoskins, "Mining All Within," *Thomist* 24, nos. 2, 3, 4 (April, July, Oct. 1961): 357–61.]

we will not hesitate to look on the soul as the cause of weight." (Or if one prefers a more literal translation): *There is not any reason for us to doubt, under any aspect, that the soul has not the power to move the heavy loads.* (Plato *Laws* XIII)

It must be noted that in this citation *peripherein* [bear around] does not mean *circumferre* [carry round], but only *ferre* [carry] or *ferre secum* [carry with one]. The thing being clear on the least reflection, it suffices to notice it.

vi   *By Zeus, he said, there is need of something inside.* (Plutarch, in *Moralia, Various Sayings of Spartans to Fame Unknown* 234F.50)

vii "One must not busy oneself overmuch with causes," says Plato, "for this is not pious." (Plato *Laws* VIII.821a).

viii Being pressed a little too far by the indispensable necessity of admitting an agent outside of nature, Bacon's French translator, a thoroughly modern man, is led to console himself thus in the following passage: "All philosophers have admitted the necessity of I don't know what indefinable fluid that they have called by different names, such as *subtle matter, universal agent, spirit, car, vehicle,* electric *fluid,* magnetic *fluid,* GOD, etc." (Cited in the *Précis de la philosophie de Bacon* [by Jean André de Luc, 2 vols. (Paris 1802)], 2:242.)

ix   There have been opponents, however. We know that Hume placed Bacon beneath Galileo, which was not a great feat of justice. Kant praised Bacon with a remarkable economy. He found no epithet more brilliant than *ingenious (Sinnreich).* [Emmanuel] Kant, *Kritik der reiner Vernunft* (Leipzig 1779), pp. 12–13), and Condorcet said plainly that Bacon had no talent for the sciences, and that his methods for discovering the truth, of which he gave no examples, did nothing to change the progress of science. *Esquisse d'un tableau historique du progrès de l'esprit humain,* [Paris An III], p. 229).

x   [Luc], *Précis de la philosophie,* 2:177. For the rest, the same century that discerned unmerited honours in Bacon, did not fail to refuse him those that were legitimately due to him, or to punish him for the venerable remnants of the old faith that remained *in the air* in his mind, and that would furnish the topic for a very good book. It was the fashion, for example, and I'm not sure it has yet passed, to prefer Montaigne's essays to those of Bacon, which contained more solid, practical, and positive true knowledge than can, in my opinion, be found in any other book of this kind.

xi   *He would have been more fortunate, if just as he perceived the power of religion, so also he had understood its purity.* (Christopher Stay, Preface to *Philosophiae recentioris a Benedicto Stay ... versibus traditae,* [2 vols.] (Rome: Palearini 1755), 1:29).

xii From the known principle that the velocities at the two extremities of a lever vary reciprocally with the strength of the two forces, and length of the arms directly with the two velocities, Ferguson amused himself by calculating what would have happened if God had taken Archimedes at his word when he made his celebrated statement: *Give me a place to stand on, and I shall move the earth.* He calculated that the length of the lever from the fulcrum ought to be 12,000,000,000,000,000,000,000,000, or 12 quadrillions of miles, to raise the earth one inch, and that if the power applied moved as swiftly as a bullet, it would take 27,000,000,000,000, or 27 billion years. (James Ferguson, *Astronomy Explained upon Sir Isaac Newton's Principles*, (London 1803), chap. VII, p. 83.)

xiii Some have given the beginning of the world, such as Moses has described it for us, the name *reformation*; others have candidly admitted *that they cannot imagine its beginning*, and this philosophy is not at all dead. However, let us not despair, since the armorial bearings of a celebrated city prophesied, like Caiaphas, without knowing what it was saying: POST TENEBRAS LUX. [After the darkness, light.]

xiv *Poor Theseus sits and will sit forever.*
Vergil *Aeneid* VI.617-18.

xv "... that stream whence none return."
Ibid., 425.

xvi "... with unremitting toil seek again and again the waters, only to lose them."
Ovid *Metamorphoses* IV.462 [Trans. Frank Justus Miller, Loeb Classical Library, 1916].

xvii "... a monstrous vulture with crooked beak gnaws at his deathless liver ... nor is any respite given to the filaments that grow anew."
Vergil *Aeneid* VI.598–600 [Loeb].

xviii "The lips can catch no water, Tantalus, and the tree that overhangs ever eludes thee."
Ovid *Metamorphoses* IV.458–59 [Loeb].

xix "Thou, Sisyphus, dost either push or chase the rock that must always be rolling down the hill again."
Ibid., 459 [Loeb].

xx "There whirls Ixion on his wheel, both following himself and fleeing,
...
[Why does he] suffer unending pain?"
Ibid., 460, 466 [Loeb].

Sixth Dialogue

The Senator

I have very expressly left the floor to you, my dear friend; so it is up to you to begin.

The Count

I would not take the floor because you have abandoned it to me, for that would be a reason for me to refuse it; but I will take it uniquely not to leave a gap in our conversation. So permit me to add some reflections to those that I presented to you yesterday on a very interesting subject: it is precisely to war that I owe these ideas. Our dear Senator should not be disturbed, for he can be sure that I have no wish to follow on his tracks.

It is often said *that whether someone prays or not things will go their own way: someone prays and wins, someone else prays and is defeated, etc.* However it seems to me strictly impossible to prove the proposition: *We prayed for a good war, and the war was miserable.* I will pass over the question of the legitimacy of the war, for this is an excessively equivocal point; I will only take up the question of prayer. How can one prove *that someone has prayed?* You will say that for this it is sufficient to have rung the bells and opened the churches. However that is not quite the way things happen, gentlemen. *Nicole, the scrupulous author of some good works* said some place *that the foundation of prayer is desire.*[1] This is not true, but what is sure ...

---

[1] Not without difficulty, I unearthed this maxim in [Pierre] Nicole's *Instructions [théologiques] sur le [premier Commandement du] Décalogue*, [2 vols. (2nd ed.)(Paris 1776)], Vol. II, sect. II, chap. 1, II, V, art. iii.

The Senator

With your permission, my dear friend, *this is not true* is a bit strong; and again, with your permission, the same proposition can be read word for word in the *Maximes des saints* of Fénelon,[i] who copied or consulted Nicole very little, if I am not mistaken.

The Count

If both of them said it, I would believe myself correct in thinking that both of them were mistaken. However, I agree that appearances favour this maxim, and that several ascetic writers, ancient and modern, have expressed themselves in this sense, without intending to examine the question deeply. Yet when it comes to sounding the human heart and asking an exact account of its movement, one is soon embarrassed, and Fénelon sensed this very well, for in more than one place in his spiritual works he retracted or expressly restricted his general proposition. He affirmed, without the slightest equivocation, *that one can strive to love, that one can strive to desire, that one can strive to want to love; that one can even pray while lacking the efficient cause of this will; that the willing depends on us, but that the feeling does not*; and a thousand other things of this sort.[2] Finally, he expresses himself in one place in such an energetic and original way that if someone reads this passage they will never forget it. This is in one of his spiritual letters where he says: *If God bores you, tell him that he bores you, that you prefer the most vile amusement to his presence, that you are only at ease far from him, and tell him:* "See my misery and my ingratitude. Oh God! Take my heart, since I do not know how to give it to you; have pity on me despite myself."[ii]

Gentlemen, do you find here the maxim that desire and love are indispensable to prayer? I do not have Fénelon's precious book handy at the moment, but you can verify the passages at your leisure.

In any case, if he exaggerated a bit here and there, he admitted it; let us speak of him only to praise him and to exalt the triumph of his immortal obedience. Standing, arms raised to teach men, he may have an equal; prostrated to condemn himself, he has none.

Nicole is another sort, and I have fewer compliments for him; for this maxim that shocked me in his writings comes from the dangerous school of Port-Royal and their whole deadly system that, while awaiting grace and

---

[2] See [François de Salignac de la Mothe] Fénelon's *Oeuvres spirituelles*, [4 vols.] (Paris [1802]),2:94; letter to P. Lamy on prayer, n. 3, 4:498; 3:162; letter 195, 4:242; and Ibid., pp. 470, 472, and 476, where one can find all these sentiments expressed.

desire, tends directly to discourage man by leading him insensibly from discouragement to hardness or despair. Everything from these rebellious doctors displeases me, even the good things they have written: *I fear the Greeks even when they bring gifts.*

What is desire? Is it, as has often been said, *love of an absent good*? However if this is so, love, or at least emotional love, cannot be commanded, and therefore man cannot pray before he experiences this love, otherwise the desire would have to precede the desire, which would appear to me a bit difficult. What would happen to man, supposing that there were no real prayer without desire and without love? How could he bring himself to ask, which his duty often obliges him to do, and which his nature abhors? By itself, Nicole's proposition seems to me to annihilate the commandment *to love our enemies.*

The Senator

It seems to me that Locke solved the question by deciding *that we can raise desire in ourselves in exact proportion to the value of the good that is proposed to us.*[3]

The Count

Believe me, do not rely on Locke, who never understood anything very deeply. *Desire*, which he never defined at all, is *only a movement of the soul towards an object it desires.* This movement is a fact of the moral order as certain and as palpable as magnetism, and as general as universal gravitation in the physical order. Since man is continually agitated by two contrary forces, examination of this terrible law must be the beginning of any study of man. Neglecting this issue, Locke was able to write fifty pages on liberty without even knowing what he was talking about. This law being posed as an incontestable fact, we must note that if an object does not by its nature attract man, it is not in man's power to create the desire, since we cannot create in the object a power that is not there, and that if, on the contrary, this power exists in the object, we cannot destroy it, since man has no power over the natures of external things, which are what they are without him and independent of him. So what is the power of man reduced to? It is to work around himself and on himself to weaken or to destroy, or on the contrary, to set at liberty or make victorious the action whose influence he experiences. In the first case, which is more simple, it is to

---

[3] This, in fact, is what he said in his *Essay Concerning Human Understanding*, Bk II, § 21, 47. "By a due consideration, and examining any good proposed, it is in our power to raise our desires in a due proportion to the value of that good, whereby in its turn and place, it may come to work upon the will, and be pursued."

distance oneself, as one distances a piece of iron from the active sphere of a magnet if one wants to avoid the action of its force. Man can also willingly and by deliberate means expose himself to a contrary attraction, either by linking himself to something immovable or by placing between himself and the object something whose nature is capable of intercepting its power, just as glass prevents the transmission of electrical current; or finally, he can work on himself to make himself less or less completely seducible; this is, as you can see, much surer, and certainly possible, but also much more difficult. In the second case, he must act in a precisely opposed way; he must, according to his strength, approach the object, avoid or destroy the obstacles, and, remember especially that according to the reports of certain travellers an extreme cold can extinguish a magnetic needle's attraction for *the attracting pole.* So man must beware the *cold.*

Even reasoning according to Locke's false or incomplete ideas, it will always remain certain *that we have the power to resist desire,* a power without which there is no more liberty.[4] Moreover, if man can resist desire, and even act against desire, he can therefore pray without desire and even against desire, since prayer is an act of the will, and like any other such act subject to the general law. *Desire* is not the will, but only a passion of the will; moreover, since the force that acts on it is not invincible, it follows that, really to pray, it is necessary to will, but not *to desire,* prayer being in essence *only a movement of the will enlightened by the understanding.* What deceives us on this point is that we ordinarily ask only for what we desire, and a great number of these elect who have spoken of prayer since men have known how to pray, having almost extinguished in themselves the fatal law, no longer experienced within themselves the conflict between will and desire. Nevertheless two forces acting in the same sense are no less essentially distinguishable. So let us admire how two perhaps equally enlightened men, though very unequal in talent and merit, can arrive at the same exaggeration by beginning from totally different principles. Nicole, seeing in legitimate desire only grace, leaves nothing to the will, to give everything to that grace that distances itself from him to chastise him for the greatest crime that can be committed against it, that of attributing to it more than it wishes; and Fénelon, who was so penetrated by grace, took prayer for desire, because in his celestial heart desire had never abandoned prayer.

---

[4] *Essay,* Bk. II, chap. xxi, § 47. *This* [power] *seems to me the source of all liberty.* Why this redundancy of words and this uncertainty, instead of telling us simply if, according to him, *this power is liberty?* But Locke very rarely says what he ought to say; vagueness and irresolution necessarily reign in the way he expressed himself as well as in his thought.

The Senator

Do you think that one can desire desire?

The Count

Ah! You have raised a great question. Fénelon, who was certainly a *man of desire*, seems to have leaned towards the affirmative, if, as I think I read in his works, *one can desire to love, strive to desire, and strive to want to love*. If some metaphysicians worthy of the name want to treat this question deeply, I would propose this passage from the psalms as an epigraph: *My soul is consumed with longing for your commandments.*[5] While waiting for this dissertation to be written, I persist in saying: *this is not true*, or if this expression appears too hard to you, I would consent to say: *this is not true enough*. What you will certainly not contest (and which is what I was on the point of telling you when you interrupted me), *is that the ground of prayer is faith*, and that you can see this truth even in the temporal order. Do you think that a prince would be well disposed to pour out his favours on men who doubted his sovereignty or who blasphemed against his goodness? If there can be no *prayer* without faith, there can be no *efficacious prayer* without purity. You will understand easily enough that I do not intend this word *purity* to be understood rigorously, for what would become of us if the guilty were unable to pray? What you will understand well enough, always following the same comparison, is that to outrage a prince would be quite a poor way to solicit his favours. The guilty person has, properly speaking, only the right to pray for himself. I have never attended one of these holy ceremonies intended to avoid the scourges of heaven or to solicit its favours without asking myself with a real terror: *In the midst of these pretentious hymns and august rites, how many among this assembled crowd are there who, by their faith and by their works, have the right to pray, and who have a well-founded hope of praying efficaciously? How many are there who are really praying? This one is thinking of his business, that one of his pleasures, a third is preoccupied with the music; the least guilty perhaps is the one who yawns without knowing where he is.* So again, how many of those present are really praying, and how many merit a response?

The Chevalier

For myself, I am already sure that there is certainly at least one man at these solemn and pious occasions who is not praying ... and this is you,

---

[5]   Psalm 118(119):20.

Count, who are occupying yourself with these philosophical reflections instead of praying.

The Count

Sometimes you slay me with your *Gallic wit*; what a prodigious talent for pleasantries! It never deserts you, even in the middle of the most serious discussions. But that is how you are, you Frenchmen!

The Chevalier

Believe me, my dear friend, that we value it more than others, when we are not ill; believe me even when I say that our pleasantries are needed in the world. By its nature reason is not very penetrating, and it cannot make its way easily, so that it often must be, as it were, *armed* with a formidable epigram. The French point pricks like a needle, so that the thread can pass through. So, for example, what do you have to say to my *needle prick*?

The Count

I would not want to ask you for an accounting of all the *threads* your nation has sewn, but I can assure you that this time I willingly pardon you for your jest, the more so in that I can immediately turn the argument against you. If the simple fear of praying badly can prevent prayer, what do we think of those who do not know how to pray, who can scarcely remember praying, who do not even believe in the efficacy of prayer. The more you think about it, the more you will be convinced that there is nothing as difficult as offering up a genuine prayer.

The Senator

One necessary consequence of what you have said is that there is no composition more difficult than that of genuine written prayer, which is and can only be the faithful expression of an interior prayer. It seems to me that not enough attention is paid to this fact.

The Count

Indeed, Senator, you have hit upon one of the most essential points of true doctrine! There is nothing more true than what you have just said; and although written prayer is only an image, it can nevertheless serve us in judging the original, which is invisible. Even for mere philosophy, the material remains of prayer, such as men of every age have left us, is no small treasure – for on this evidence alone we can make three fine observations.

In the first place, every nation in the world has prayed, and always in virtue of some true or supposed revelation – that is to say, in virtue of ancient traditions. As soon as man bases himself on his reason, he ceases to pray; so that he has always confessed, without noticing it, that of himself he does not know that he must ask or how he must pray or even precisely to what he must address himself.[6] In vain therefore does the deist set out for us the most beautiful theories on the existence and attributes of God; without telling him (which is nevertheless incontestable) that he got these from his catechism, we will always have the right to say to him like *Joas*: YOU DO NOT PRAY.[7]

My second observation is that all religions are more or less fruitful in prayers; but the third observation, which is incomparably the most important, is this:

Order your hearts to be attentive and to read all these prayers: you will see the true religion as clearly as you see the sun.

The Senator

I have made this observation a thousand times in assisting at our beautiful liturgy. Such prayers could only have been produced by the truth, and in the bosom of the truth.

The Count

This is certainly my opinion. In one way or another God has spoken to all men; but there are privileged ones to whom it is permitted to say: *He has not done in like manner to any other nation,*[8] for God alone, according to the incomparable expression of the incomparable apostle, *can create in the heart of man a spirit capable of saying: MY FATHER!*[9] Moreover David had preluded this truth by crying out: *He put a new song in my mouth, a hymn to our God.*[10] If this spirit is not in the heart of man, how will he be able to pray? Or how will his impotent pen be able to write what is dictated to the one who holds it? Read the hymns of Santeuil, adopted a little too carelessly perhaps by the Paris church; they make a certain noise in the ears, but they never *pray*, because he *was alone* when he composed them. The beauty of a prayer has nothing in common with that of expression, for

---

[6] Plato having confessed explicitly, in one of the most extraordinary humanly inspired pages in the world, *that man reduced to himself does not know how to pray*, and having moreover evoked by this admission *some celestial messenger who finally came to teach this great science to men*, we can say that he spoke in the name of humankind.

[7] [Jean Racine], *Athalie*, II, 7.

[8] Psalm 147(147B):20.

[9] Galatians 4:6

[10] Psalm 39(40):4.

a prayer is like the mysterious daughter of the great king - *all her beauty is born from within*.[11] There is something here that has no name, but that one senses perfectly, and that talent can only imitate.

Since nothing is more difficult than *praying*, it is at once the height of both blindness and temerity to dare to say that one has prayed and that one has not been heard. I especially want to speak to you of nations in this case, for this is the principal object in these sorts of questions. To avoid an evil, to obtain a national good, it is certainly right that the nation *prays*. So what is a nation? What conditions are required for a nation *to pray*? Are there in each nation men who have the right *to pray* for it? And is this right a question of their interior dispositions or of their rank in the nation, or of the two circumstances taken together? We know very little of the secrets of the spiritual world, and how could we know them since no one has troubled to tell us about them. Without wanting to penetrate into these depths, I will limit myself to the general proposition *that it will never be possible to prove that a nation* has prayed *without being heard*. I believe I can be just as sure of the positive affirmation, that is to say *that every nation that* prays *is heard*. Exceptions prove nothing, even if they could be verified, and they all disappear before the simple observation *that no man can know, even when he prays perfectly, that he is not asking for something harmful to himself or the general order*. So therefore let us pray, let us pray with all our strength, and with all the dispositions that can legitimate this great act of an intelligent creature; let us especially never forget that all true prayer is efficacious in some way. All the supplications presented to the sovereign are not acted upon favourably, and not all could be, for not all are reasonable; all however contain a profession of express faith in the power, the goodness, and the justice of the sovereign, who can only be delighted to see them flowing in from all parts of his empire. Just as it is impossible to entreat the prince without, by so doing, making an act of loyal subjection, in the same way it is impossible to pray to God without putting oneself in a relation of submission, confidence, and love with him. In this way, there is in prayer, considered only in itself, a purifying virtue whose effect is usually worth more to us than what we too often ask for in our ignorance.[12] All legitimate prayer, even when it cannot be answered, nonetheless elevates us to higher regions, from whence it comes back upon us, after having undergone certain preparations, like a beneficial shower

---

[11] Psalm 44(45):14.

[12] The mere act of prayer perfects man, because it makes God present to us. How this action inspires good actions! How it prevents crimes! Experience alone teaches us this ... The wise man not only *pleases himself* in prayer, *he delights in it*. (Origen *On Prayer* nos. 8 and 20.)

that prepares us for another world. Only when we ask God *that his will be done*, that is to say, that evil disappear from the world, then only are we sure that we have not prayed in vain. We are so blind and foolish! Instead of complaining that we have not been heard, let us rather tremble for having prayed badly and for having asked for evil. The authority that orders us to pray also teaches us how and with what dispositions we must pray. To disobey the first commandment is to reduce ourselves to brutality and even to atheism; to disobey the second is to expose ourselves to yet another anathema, that *of seeing our prayer construed as a crime*.[13]

So let us not, like foolish servants,
Prescribe to heaven its gifts and favours.
Let us ask for equitable prudence,
And sincere, charitable piety;
Let us ask for grace and love;
And if we must someday
Tire patient indulgence
By other requests, let us provide ourselves in advance
With enough zeal and enough virtue
To be worthy of refusal.[14]

The Chevalier

I do not repent, my good friend, of having *frosted* you. I have gained, in the first place, the pleasure of having been scolded by you, which is always very good for me; and I have gained something even better. I was afraid, to tell the truth, of having trifled with you; for man can scarcely dispense with what he is led to do with pleasure and profit. So, I entreat you, do not refuse me a great satisfaction: you have *frosted* me in turn when I heard you speak of Locke with so much irreverence. We still have time, as you see; I will willingly sacrifice the whist game in the company of a charming companion who awaits me if you would have the goodness to tell me your considered opinion of this famous author of whom I have never heard you speak without a certain irritation that is impossible for me to understand.

The Count

My God! I can refuse you nothing, but I foresee that you would involve me in a long and cheerless dissertation, and to tell you the truth, I don't know how I can treat Locke without losing your attention or boring you, two

---

[13] Psalm 108(109):7.
[14] Jean-Baptiste Rousseau, *Épître à Rollin*, II, 4.

improprieties I would equally like to avoid. What you ask does not appear to me to be easy. Moreover I fear that I would be led too far.

The Chevalier

I confess to you that the likelihood of this misfortune appears to me low or even nil. Is it really necessary to write an epic poem to enjoy a few episodes?

The Count

Oh! You are never embarrassed by anything. As for me, I have my reasons for fearing to launch myself on this discussion. Still if you want to encourage me, begin, I beg you, by sitting down. Your restlessness worries me. I don't know what imp is always pricking you, but what is sure is that you can't stay in one place for ten minutes; more often than not my words must follow you like a shot aimed at a bird in flight. What I am going to say to you might well resemble a sermon somewhat. So you must sit down to listen to me. Well then! Now, my dear Chevalier, let us begin, with a confession. Tell me, in all conscience, have you read Locke?

The Chevalier

No, never. I have no reason to hide this from you. Only one day on campaign, one rainy day, I recall having opened him, but it was only a pose.

The Count

I do not always want to be scolding you; sometimes you hit on altogether happy expressions. In fact, Locke's book is almost never taken and opened except *as a pose*. Among serious books, there are none less read. One of the things I'm really curious about, but which can never be known, is to know how many men there are in Paris who have read *The Essay Concerning Human Understanding* from one end to the other. They often speak of it and cite it, but always second-hand; I myself had spoken of it boldly, like so many others, without having read it. In the end, however, wanting to have the right to speak about it in good conscience, that is to say with full and complete knowledge of the question, I read it patiently from the first word to the last, pen in hand;

But I was fifty when this happened

and I don't think that I have ever in my life been so bored. Moreover you know my valour for this sort of thing.

The Chevalier

Do I know it? Did I not see you reading, last year, a deadly German octavo volume on the Apocalypse? I recall seeing you, at the end of that task, full of life and health, and telling you that after such an experience *you could be compared to a cannon that had survived a double charge.*

The Count

Nevertheless I can assure you that compared to Locke's *Essay Concerning Human Understanding* the German work was a light pamphlet, a pleasant divertissement, literally; there at least one read some interesting things. There one learned, for example, *that the purple with which abominable Babylon once furnished other nations evidently signifies the red robes of the cardinals; that in Rome antique statues of false gods are displayed in the churches*, and a thousand other things of this kind, equally useful and entertaining.[15] But in the *Essay* there is nothing to console you. One must traverse this book, like the sands of Libya, without ever encountering the least *oasis*, the least green point where one can catch one's breath. There are books of which one can say: show me the fault that you find in it. As for the *Essay*, I can well say to you: *Show me the ones that you do not find.* Name the fault for me, if you will, among those you judge most capable of cheapening a book, and I can immediately, without even looking, cite an example of it. Even the preface is inexpressibly shocking. Locke says he hopes *Thou wilt as little think thy money, as I do my pains, ill bestowed.*[16] How commercial! Continue and you will see that the book is *the diversion of some of my idle and heavy hours*, that he was happy to compose the book since *He that hawks at larks and sparrows has no less sport though a much less considerable quarry than he that flies at nobler game*, and finally *that his book was begun by chance, continued by entreaty, written in incoherent parcels, often abandoned and resumed again as my humour or occasions permitted.*[17] It must be admitted that this is a singular confession on the part of an author who is going to speak to us of human understanding, the spirituality of the soul, liberty, and, finally, God.

---

[15] It appears that this reference is to the German book entitled: *Die Siegs- geschichte der christlichen Religion in einer gemeinnützigen Erklärung der Offenbarung Johannis* [by Johann Jung-Stilling], (Nuremburg 1799).

This book can be found in the libraries of a numerous enough class of men; but since it is a question here of an inconsequential citation, I thought it useless to waste my time verifying it. (Editor's note.)

[16] "Epistle to the reader." [Maistre cites a two-volume London edition published by Becroft, Straham and company in 1755.]

[17] Ibid.

If such impertinent platitudes were found in a preface by Malebranche, what a clamour there would be on the part of our bothersome *ideologues*!

Before passing to more substantive issues, gentlemen, I want you to notice how often Locke's book borders on the ridiculous through his use of the gross expressions that he loves so much and that flow from his pen with such marvellous ease. Sometimes Locke will tell you in a second or a third edition, and after having thought about it as hard as he could *that a determinate idea ... is that simple appearance which the mind has in its view.*[18] "Has in its view!" Imagine, if you can, anything more ponderous.

Sometimes he will speak to you of the memory as a box in which one holds ideas until they are needed, and which is separated from the mind, as if you could have one in something other than oneself.[19] Elsewhere he makes the memory a secretary that keeps registers.[20] In one place he presents the human intelligence to us as a dark room pierced by some windows through which the light comes in,[21] and in another place he complains about *a certain sort of men who make men* swallow *innate ideas that can no longer be doubted.*[22] Forced to pass quickly over so many different examples, I assure you that for every one my memory allows me to mention, I could add a hundred if I were to write a dissertation. The list of Locke's discoveries alone could amuse you for two days.

He is the one who discovered that *confusion ... concerns always two ideas.* So that in a thousand years, one idea, so long as it remains alone, can never be confused with another.[23]

He is the one who discovered that if men do not think of transferring to species of animals the usual names of relationships among themselves, that if, for example, they SELDOM say this bull is the grandfather of such a calf, or these two pigeons are first cousins,[24] this is because these names are useless with regard to animals while they are necessary for men to regulate inheritance in the courts or for other reasons.[25]

---

[18]   Ibid.

[19]   *Essay*, Bk. II, chap. IV, § 20.

[20]   "... before the memory begins to keep a register of time and order." Ibid, Bk. I, chap. I, § 6.

[21]   "The windows by which light is let into this dark room." Ibid., Chap. XI, § 17. To which Herder asked Locke *if the divine intelligence is also a dark room?* An excellent question posed in a very bad book. See [Johann G. von] Herder's *Gott einige gespräche uber Spinosas system.* (Gotha 1800), p. 168.

[22]   *Essay,* Bk. I, chap. IV, § 25.

[23]   Bk. II, chap. XXIX, § 11.

[24]   Bk. II, chap. XXVIII, § 2.

[25]   Ibid.

He is the one who discovered that if one does not find among modern languages national names to express the ideas of *ostracism* or *proscription*, for example, there is neither *ostracism* nor *proscription* among the peoples who speak these languages,[26] and this consideration leads him to a general theorem that throws a great light on all metaphysics of language: *It is that men speak rarely to themselves and never to others of things that have no name*: so that (note this well, please, for it is a principle) *what has no name is never mentioned in conversation.*[iii]

He is the one who discovered *that relations can change without the subject changing.* You are a father, for example, and your son dies; Locke thinks that you cease to be a father at that instant, even when your son died in America: *Caius, whom I consider to-day as a father, ceases to be so tomorrow,* ONLY (this is marvellous!) *by the death of his son, without any alteration made in himself.*[27]

The Chevalier

How charming! You know if he were still alive I would go to London just to meet him.

The Count

However I would not let you leave, my dear Chevalier, before having explained to you his doctrine of negative ideas. Locke would first have taught you *that we have negative names that stand directly for positive ideas,*[28] which you will readily believe. You will learn subsequently that a negative idea is nothing other than a positive idea, plus that of the absence of something, as he immediately demonstrates for you by the idea of silence. In effect, *what is silence? It is noise,* PLUS, *the absence of noise.*

And what is NOTHING? (This is important, for this is the most general expression of negative ideas.) Locke responds with a profundity that cannot be too highly exalted: *It is the idea of the thing*, to which one simply adds to be sure, that of *the absence of the thing.*[29]

---

[26]   Bk II, chap. XXII, § 6.

[27]   Bk. II, chap. XXV, § 5. "Caius" – college rhetoric! This Caius is peculiar enough to have shocked the refugee ear of Coste, Locke's translator. With a marvellous taste, he substituted *Titius.*

[28]   Bk. II, chap. VIII, § 5. He was led to this great truth by consideration of *shadows*, which he found as real as the sun. By confusing light with the sun's direct rays, and their absence with the absence of light, he makes us laugh.

[29]   *Negative names ... such as* insipid, silence, NIHIL ... *denote positive ideas,* v.g. taste, sound, being, *with a signification of their absence.* (Ibid.)

Even this *nothing* is nothing compared to all the fine things I would have to tell you about Locke's talent for definitions in general. I recommend this point to you as very essential, since it is one of the most amusing. Perhaps you know that Voltaire, with the frivolity that never abandoned him, told us *that Locke is the first philosopher who taught men how to define the words they use,*[30] *and who with his good sense never ceased to tell us: DEFINE*! Now this is exquisite, since we find that Locke is precisely the first philosopher who told us *not to define,*[31] and who, however, never ceased to define, and in a way surpassing all the boundaries of ridicule.

For example, would you like to know what *power* is? Locke will have the goodness to teach you *that it is the succession of simple ideas by which some are born and some perish.*[32] You are no doubt bowled over by this clarity; but I can cite even finer examples for you. In vain have all metaphysicians with one voice warned us not to define those elevated notions that themselves serve to define others. Locke's genius dominates these heights; and he is able, for example, to give us a definition of *existence* much clearer than the idea revealed in our mind by the simple enunciation of the word. He teaches us that *When ideas are in our minds,*

---

[30] As you can see, what a learned scholar! In fact, no one defined *more* or *better* than the ancients; Aristotle especially was marvellous in this genre, and his entire metaphysics is only a dictionary.

[31] See his Bk. III, chap. IV, so well commented upon by [Etienne B. de] Condillac (*Essai sur l'origine des connaisances humaines* [Amsterdam 1746], Section III, § 9 and following). One reads there, among other curious things, *that the Cartesians, not being ignorant that there are ideas clearer than all the definitions that one can give of them, did not however know the reason* for this, something that it appears easy to perceive. (§ 10.) [Here Maistre seems to be paraphrasing Locke's argument.] If Descartes, Malebranche, Lamy, Cardinal Polignac, etc., returned to life, *ô qui cachinni!* [Oh what laughter].

[32] I am not sure that Locke gave such a positive definition of power; rather he explained how this idea is formed in our mind. But the speaker is very far from recalling for us Locke's verbiage. *The mind,* he says, *being every day informed, by the senses, of the alteration of simple ideas it observes in the things without* (ideas in things!!!), *and taking notice of how one comes to an end, and ceases to be ... considers in one thing the possibility of having any of its simple ideas changed, ... AND SO comes by that idea which we call POWER.* (Bk. II, chap. XXI, § 1.) (Editor's note)

"And so, comes by that idea which we call power." (Bk II, chap. XXI, § 1.

we consider them as being actually THERE, *as well as we consider things to be actually without us; – which is, that they exist, or have existence.*[33]

We would not have believed that it was possible to rise so high if we had not immediately encountered his definition of unity. Perhaps you know how Alexander's teacher once defined it in its most general sense. *Unity,* he said, *is being*; and numerical unity, in particular, *is the beginning and the measure of all quantity.*[34] Not so bad, as you can see! Here, however, is where the progress of enlightenment is striking. Unity, says Locke, *is whatever we can consider as one thing, whether a real being or idea.* And to this definition, which would have aroused a fit of jealousy in the late *M. de la Palice*, Locke adds in all seriousness, this *suggests to the understanding the idea of unity.*[35] So here we are, well advanced, certainly, towards the origin of ideas.

His definition of solidity also has its merit. *That which ... hinders the approach of two bodies, when they are moved towards another, I call solidity.*[36] Those who have always judged Locke by his reputation, can scarcely believe their eyes or their ears when they finally judge Locke on his own merits; but I can still astonish astonishment by citing his definition of an atom for you. He says it is *a continued body under one immutable superficies.*[37]

Are you curious now to learn what Locke knew about the natural sciences? Listen well to this, I beg you. You know that when, in ordinary conversation, we compare speeds we rarely mention the spaces to be compared, seeing that speeds are commonly enough related to the same distances run. To compare, for example, the speeds of two horses, I will not tell you that one runs from here to Stelna in forty minutes and the other to Kamini-Ostroff in ten minutes, which would oblige you to get out your pencil and make an arithmetical calculation to know what I wanted to say. Rather, I will tell you that the two horses went, let us suppose, from St Petersburg to Strelna, the one in forty minutes and the other in fifty. Moreover, it is obvious in cases of this sort that, speeds being simply proportional to the times, one does not need distances to compare them. Well, gentlemen, mathematics of this sort were beyond Locke's reach. He believed that his brother humans up to his time had not perceived that

---

[33] (Bk. II, chap. VII, § 7). This philosopher forgets nothing, as we can see; after having told us: *Here is what authorizes us to say that things exist,* he adds, *or that they have existence.* After that if we do not understand him it is not his fault.

[34] Aristotle *Metaphysics* III.1, and X.1.

[35] Bk. II, chap. VII, § 7.

[36] Bk. II, chap. IV, § 1.

[37] Bk. II, chap. XXVII, § 3.

distance must be taken into consideration in comparing speeds; he tells us gravely *that whilst all men manifestly measured time by the motion of the great and visible bodies of the world, yet time should be defined by the "measure of motion": whereas it is obvious to anyone who reflects ever so little on it, that to measure motion, space is as necessary to consider as time.*[38] In truth, this is a great discovery! A thousand thanks to MASTER JOHN who has deigned to share it with us; but there is still more to come. Locke discovered too that *those who look a little farther* (such as himself, for example) *will find also the bulk of the thing moved necessary to be taken into the computation by any one who will estimate or measure motion so as to judge right of it.*[39] Did Locke want to say that *to compare* the quantity of movement *everyone who wants to look a little further must take mass into consideration*? This would be foolishness of the first order. Or on the contrary (and this seems infinitely more probable), did he want to say *that to compare speed, a man,* if he is intelligent, *understands that he must take account of the* distance covered, *and if he is* still more intelligent, *he will perceive that he must also take account of mass?* Then it seems to me that it is impossible to characterize such a proposition in the way it deserves.

So you see, gentlemen, what Locke knew of the elements of the natural sciences. Would you like to know something of his erudition? Here is a marvellous example. Nothing is better known in the history of human opinions than the dispute of the ancient philosophers on the true sources of happiness, or the *summum bonum.*[iv] Do you know how Locke understood this question? He believed that the ancient philosophers were disputing, not on the good, but on the fact; he changed a question of morals and high philosophy into a simple question of taste or caprice, and on the basis of this fine observation, he decided, with rare profundity, that *they (the philosophers of old) might have as reasonably disputed whether the best*

---

[38] [Bk. II, chap. IV, § 22.] It is essential to observe that by the word *motion* Locke here means *speed [vitesse]*. There can be no doubt about this if the whole passage is read.

[39] Bk. II, chap. XIV, § 22. It must be remarked here that the speaker honoured Locke too much in generously granting him the word *masse* [for *bulk*]. These sorts of expressions consecrated and used by science are not at all the usage of Locke, who always employs common English words, such as he found used on the streets of London. In English, he said *bulk*, an equivocal word, which is equally related to mass and to volume, and which his French translator, *Coste*, very accurately translated with the word *grosseur*, precisely as vague and common. (Editor's note.)

relish were to be found in apples, plums, or nuts.[40] You see that he is learned as well as moral and great.[v]

Now would you like to know how far Locke was dominated by the prejudices of the grossest sect and to what point Protestantism had dulled his good sense? He wanted, I don't know where in his book, to talk about the *real presence.* Why this, I have no idea; he was reformed, he could well have wanted to pass the time. Still he could at least have spoken like a man who has a head on his shoulders instead of telling us as he did: *Let the idea of infallibility be inseparably joined to any person; and these two constantly together possess the mind; and the one body in two places shall* unexamined *be* swallowed *as a certain Truth by an implicit faith whenever that imagined infallible person dictates and demands assent without inquiry.*[41] What can we say of a man who was free to read Bellarmine; of a man who was the contemporary of Petau and Bossuet; who could hear the bells of Calais from Dover; who moreover travelled in France and even lived there; who passed his life in the midst of controversies; and who seriously maintains in print that the Catholic Church believes in the real presence *on the faith* of a certain person *who has given his word of honour?* What we have here is not one of those distractions, one of those purely human errors that are in our interest to forgive one another; this is a sign of a uniquely inconceivable ignorance, which would have embarrassed the Count de Mansfeld's shop-boy in the sixteenth century; and what is incredibly funny is that Locke, with this scurrilous tone that never abandons otherwise quite knowledgeable and elegant Protestant pens when it is a question of contested dogmas, bluntly charges us with SWALLOWING *this dogma without inquiry.* Without inquiry? What a clown! So what does he take us for? Is it, perhaps, that we are not as intelligent as he? I confess to you that if I had suddenly just learned this by some revelation, I would be very surprised.

In any case, gentlemen, you can appreciate well enough that a thorough examination of a work as dull as the *Essay Concerning Human Understanding* would exceed the bounds of a conversation. At the most a conversation can point out the general spirit of the book and its most particularly

---

[40] Bk. II, chap. XXI, § 55. Coste, finding *nuts* unworthy, again allowed himself to make a change no less important than the one we noticed earlier, where he changed *Caius* to *Titius.* Instead of *nuts,* he put the word *apricots,* which is wonderful.

[41] Bk. II, chap. XXXIII, § 17. The speaker does not appear to have been aware of the fact that Coste, although a good Protestant, fearing, it seems, the laughter of the French, who could not but maintain a certain order in the world, suppressed this passage in his translation, as *too much* and *too obviously* ridiculous. *Sed manet semel editus* [But once it has been set down it remains]. (Editor's note.)

dangerous or ridiculous aspects. If you are ever called on to undertake a rigorous examination of the *Essay*, I recommend to you the chapter on liberty. La Harpe, forgetting that he had more than once said *that he understood only literature,*[42] went into ecstasies over Locke's definition of liberty. *Now here,* he said majestically, *now here is philosophy!*[43] One would have to say: *Now here is incapacity demonstrated,* for Locke makes liberty consist in the power to act, whereas this purely negative word only signifies *the absence of obstacles,* so that liberty can only mean the *unimpeded will,* which is to say, *the will.* Condillac, adding his decisive tone to the mediocrity of his master, said in his turn *that liberty is only the power of doing what one has not done or of not doing what one has done.*[vi] This pretty antithesis can no doubt dazzle a mind unaccustomed to these sorts of discussions, but for every educated or experienced man, it is evident that Condillac here takes the result or the exterior evidence of liberty, which is physical action, for liberty itself, which is entirely moral.

Liberty is the power to do. How can this be? Does it mean that a man imprisoned and enchained does not have the power, without acting, of making himself guilty of all sorts of crimes? He has only to will them. On his point, Ovid speaks like the Gospels: *Qui, quia non licuit, non facit, ille facit* [He who does not do it because it is illegal, (really) is doing it]. If then liberty is not the *power to do,* it can only be the *power to will*; but the power to will is the will itself, and to ask if the *will can will,* is to ask *if perception has the power to perceive, if reason has the power to reason,* which is to ask if a circle is a circle, a triangle a triangle, etc. – in a word to ask *if an essence is an essence.* Now if you consider that even God cannot force the will, since a *forced will* is a *contradiction in terms,* you will appreciate that the will can be moved and led only by *attraction* (an admirable word that all the philosophes together would not have known how to invent). Moreover, attraction can have no other effect on the will than that of enhancing its energy by making it want to will more, so that

---

[42] See [Jean François de La Harpe] *Lycée,* [*ou Cours de littérature ancienne et modern*], [19 vols. Paris 1799–1805], Vol. XXII, article on d'Alembert, and elsewhere.

[43] Locke gave us several definitions of liberty, for he changed them so often that his conscience or his friends could have said to him: *So what do you want to say?* But the one that yielded La Harpe's comic exclamation is the following: *Liberty is* [the idea] *of a power in any agent to do or forbear any particular action, according to the determination or thought of the mind, whereby either of them is preferred to the other.* [Locke, *Essay,* Bk. II, chap. XXI, § 8] (*Lycée,* Vol. XXIII, "Philosophie du XVIIIᵉ siècle," art. on Helvétius.) A terrible lesson on speaking about only what one knows, for I do not believe anyone has ever written anything as miserable as this definition.

attraction could no more harm liberty or the will than teaching of any kind could harm the understanding. The curse that weighs on unfortunate human nature is the double attraction:

Vim sentit geminam paretque incerta duobus.[44]

The philosopher who reflects on this terrible enigma will render justice to the Stoics, who long ago discovered a fundamental dogma of Christianity in declaring that *only the wise man is free.* Today this is no longer a paradox, but an incontestable truth of the first order. *Where the spirit of God is, there liberty is to be found.*[vii] Anyone who fails to grasp these ideas will forever turn around this principle, like Bernouilli's curve, without ever touching it. Now, would you like to know how far Locke was from the truth on this issue, as on so many others? Listen well, I beg you, for this is ineffable. He claimed *that liberty, which is one faculty, has nothing in common with the will, which is another faculty; and that it is as insignificant to ask whether man's will be free, as to ask whether his sleep be swift, or his virtue square.*[45 and viii] What do you say to that?

The Senator

This, indeed, is a bit much! Would your memory still be good enough to recall his demonstration of this fine theory, for no doubt he provided one.

The Count

It is of a kind that could never be forgotten, and that you can judge for yourself. Listen well.

You are going across a bridge: it collapses; at the moment you feel it giving way under your feet, the effort of your will, if it were free, would no doubt carry you to the opposite bank; but its effort is useless: the sacred laws of gravitation must be carried out in the world, and you must therefore fall and perish: THEREFORE *liberty has nothing in common with the will.*[46] I hope you are convinced. Moreover Locke's inexhaustible genius can provide you with another even more luminous demonstration.

---

[44] [(As a ship, driven by the wind and against the wind by the tide) She feels the double force and yields uncertainly to both. Ovid *Metamorphoses* VIII.472.]

[45] [The first half of this citation appears to be Maistre's paraphrase of Locke's argument; the second is from the *Essay*, Bk. II, chap. XXI, § 14.]

[46] [This is Maistre's paraphrase of Locke's demonstration; but his note cites Locke in English.] "A man falling into the water (a bridge breaking under him) has not herein liberty, he is not a free agent. For though he has volition, though he prefers his not falling to falling; yet the forbearance of this motion not being in his power, etc." (Bk. II, chap. XXI, § 9.)

A sleeping man is carried to his mistress's room; or, as Locke puts it with the elegant precision that distinguishes him, *into a room where is a person he longs to see and speak with.* At the moment he awakes, his will is as content as yours would be when you fell under the bridge. Moreover, it happens that his man, thus transported, cannot leave *this room where there is no one*, etc., *because someone has locked the door. So, Locke says,* THEREFORE, *liberty has nothing in common with the will.*[47]

In any case, I flatter myself that you have nothing more to desire; but to speak seriously, what do you say of a philosopher capable of writing such absurdities?[ix]

Everything that I have cited for you is only false or ridiculous, or both. Moreover Locke certainly merits other reproaches as well. What a plank in the storm he offered to materialism (which hastened to seize it) when he claimed *that thought can pertain to matter.* In truth, I believe, in principle, that this assertion was only a simple slip that escaped Locke when he was diverting himself in some *idle and heavy hours*, and I do not doubt that he would have effaced it if some friend had gently warned him, just as in a new edition he changed his whole chapter on liberty, which had been found to be too bad.[48] Unfortunately, ecclesiastics got mixed up in the matter, and Locke could not stand them; so he became obstinate and refused to retrace his steps. Read his reply to the Bishop of Worcester; you will sense there an indefinable but evident sense of poorly suppressed haughtiness, and an indefinable sense of poorly disguised acrimony, completely natural to the man who, as you know, called the episcopal body of England the *caput*

---

[47] "Again, suppose a man be carried whilst fast asleep, into a room where is a person he long to see and speak with; and be there LOCKED FAST IN [Maistre's capitals; he no doubt perceived a pun on his adversary's name], beyond his power to get out; he awakes is glad to find himself in so desirable company which he stays willing in, i.e. prefers his stay to going away (another explanation of the greatest importance [Maistre's comment]) ... yet being locked fast in, it is evident ... he has not freedom to be gone ... So that liberty is not an idea belonging to volition." Ibid., § 10.

WHICH IS WHAT MUST BE DEMONSTRATED.

[48] Locke was ashamed of it, it appears, and in overturning the whole chapter he has left us with the happy problem of knowing if his first version could have been worst than the second. (Of Power, Bk. II, chap. VII, § 71) [This appears to be an incorrect reference. Locke's chapter on power is Chapter XXI, which is a chapter that he revised extensively following the first edition of the work.]

These variations prove that Locke really did write, as he said, *to kill time*, as he would have played cards, except however, that in the latter case he would have had to know how to play.

mortuum [dead head] of the Chamber of Peers.[49] It is not that he does not have a confused sense of principles, but that with him pride and party are stronger than his conscience. He will confess as often as you like *that matter, in itself, is incapable of thought, that perception is alien to matter, and that it is impossible to imagine the contrary.*[50] He will even add *that in virtue of these principles that he has proved and even demonstrated the immateriality of supreme thinking Being, and that the same reasons that form the basis for this demonstration imply a very high degree of probability that the thinking principle in man is immaterial.*[51] With this, you might think that since the highest degree of probability can always be taken for certitude, the question is settled, but Locke does not step back. He will agree if you wish that the Omnipotent only being able to operate on itself, it is certainly necessary that it permit its own nature to be what it is; but he does not want to admit that it is not the same with created natures, which it kneads as it pleases. *In effect,* he says with a scintillating wisdom, *it is an absurd insolence to dispute God's power to* superadd[52] *a certain excellence*[53] to a certain portion *of matter in communicating to it vegetation, life, sentiment, and finally, thought.* This is, in effect, to refuse to him the power to create;[54] *for if God* has *that of superadding to a certain mass of matter a certain* excellence *that makes it a horse, why can he not*

---

[49] This same sentiment, which can be called according to its accidental intensity, *distance, antipathy, hate, aversion, etc.* is general in countries that embraced the Reformation. It is not that there are not among the ministers of the separated cult very justly admirable and esteemed men; but is very essential that they do not deceive themselves: they are never and can never be esteemed because of their office; when they are admired they are so *independently* and often *in spite of* their office.

[50] "I never say nor suppose, etc." (See his response to the Bishop of Worcester [Stillingfleet]. *Essay,* Bk. IV, chap. III, in the notes [5th edition of the *Essay].*) "Matter is EVIDENTLY in its own nature, void of sense and thought." (Ibid.)

[51] "This thinking eternal substance ... I have proved to be immaterial." (Ibid.) "I presume from what I have said about the supposition of a system of matter, thinking (which there *demonstrates* that God is immaterial) will prove it in the highest degree probable, etc." (Ibid.)

[52] *Superadd;* this is a word Locke uses frequently in this long note.

[53] "All *the excellencies* of vegetation, life, etc." (Ibid.) "Excellencies and operations." (Ibid.)

[54] "What it would be less than an *insolent absurdity* to deny his power, etc." (Ibid.) "... than to deny his power of creation." (Ibid.).

This fine reasoning applies equally to all essences; thus, for example, one could not, without an *absurd insolence* contest God's *power to create* a square triangle or some other curiosity of this kind.

superadd *to this mass another* excellence *that makes it a thinking being?*[55] I must confess that I give way under the weight of this argument. However as one must be just even to people one doesn't like, I would willingly agree that Locke can be excused to a certain point by observing that he didn't understand himself, which is something incontestable.

The Chevalier

Every surprise that does no harm is a pleasure. I cannot tell you how much you surprise me by telling me that Locke *did not understand himself.* If, by chance, you are right, you will have delighted me.

The Count

There is nothing less astonishing than your surprise, by dear friend. You have accepted the commonly accepted prejudice that considers Locke a thinker; I would also quite willingly consent to regard him as such, provided that one agrees with me (and this is what, I think, cannot be denied) that his thoughts didn't lead him very far. He *looked* a great deal, if one wishes, but he *saw* little. He always stopped with the first glance; and whenever he treated abstract ideas, his view grew dim. I can still give you a singular example that occurs to me at the moment.

Locke had said that bodies can act on other bodies only by way of contact: *Tangere enim et tangi nisi corpus nulla potest res.*[56] But when Newton published his famous *Principia*, Locke, with that weakness and precipitation of judgement which were, no matter what one says, the distinctive characteristic of his mind, hastened to say *that he had learned in the incomparable book of the judicious Mr. Newton*[57] *that God is*

---

[55] "An horse is a material animal, or an extended solid substance with sense and spontaneous motion ... to some part of matter he (God) superadd motion ... that are to be found in an elephant ... but if one ventures to go one step farther, and says God may give to matter thought, reason and volition ... there are men ready presently to limit the power of the omnipotent creator, etc." (Ibid.) One must admit that this is to do a great injury to God.

[56] *To touch and to be touched belongs only to bodies.* (Lucretius [*On the Nature of Things* I.304]) This axiom, which the school of Lucretius did so much to make famous, nevertheless means precisely: *that no body can be touched without being touched.* No more; let us restrain our admiration on the importance of this discovery.

[57] These two epithets obviously clash, for if Newton is only *judicious*, his book cannot be *incomparable*, and if the book be *incomparable*, the author must be more than *judicious*. The judicious Newton recalls too much the *joli Corneille*, born of the *joli Turenne*. [The country bumpkin ridiculed by Boileau says "A mon gré, le Corneille est joli quelquefois." *Satire* III. v. 183. (Darcel ed.)]

certainly the master to do what he wills with matter, and consequently can communicate to it the power of acting at a distance; and consequently, Locke says, he will not fail to make a retraction and to make his profession of faith in a new edition of the *Essay.*[58]

Unfortunately, the *judicious Newton* roundly declared in one of his theological letters to Dr Bentley *that such an opinion could only find lodging in the head of a fool.*[59] In perfect conscience I can apply the back of Newton's hand to Locke's cheek. On the basis of this great authority, I repeat to you with the greatest assurance that on the question of which we were just speaking Locke did not understand himself any more than he did on that of gravitation; and nothing is more evident. The question between him and the bishop had begun over the question of knowing *if a purely material being could think or not.*[60] Locke concludes that *it being impossible for us ... without revelation to discover whether Omnipotency has not given to some system of matter fitly disposed, a power to perceive and think, or else joined and fixed to matter fitly disposed a thinking immaterial substance.*[61] So you see, gentlemen, that all this is only an English comedy, *Much ado about nothing.*[62] What did this man want to say? Who ever doubted that God could unite a thinking principle to organized matter? This is what happens to materialists of any sort: in believing that they are claiming that matter thinks they are, without knowing it, claiming that matter can be united to a thinking substance, which is what no one would be tempted to dispute. However Locke, if my memory is not completely faulty, maintained the identity of these two suppositions;[63] so that one must agree that if he was less guilty he was also more ridiculous.

---

[58]   Bk. IV, chap. III, § 6, p. 149, note.

[59]   Newton was not so laconic. Here is what he said, in the same sense to tell the truth: "That gravity should be innate, inherent, and essential to matter, so that one body may act upon another at a distance through a vacuum ... is to me so great *an absurdity* that I believe no man who has in philosophical matters a *competent faculty of thinking* can ever fall into it." ["Editor's" italics] (Newton's Letters to Dr Bentley, Third letter, of 25 February 1693, in the *Bibliothèque Britannique*, February 1797, Vol. IV no. 30, p. 192.) (Editor's note.)

[60]   "That possibly we shall never be able to know whether mere material Beings thinks, or no, etc." (*Essay*, Bk. IV, chap. III, § 6) This is clear.

[61]   Bk. IV, chap. III, § 6.

[62]   This is the title of one of Shakespeare's comedies.

[63]   There is nothing so true, as we have just seen in the passage where he liberally grants the Creator the power to give the faculty of thought to matter, OR ELSE *to glue* together the two substances.

It took a subtle logician to confuse these two things!

I would also like to ask this philosopher, who has spoken so much of the senses and accorded the senses so much, and I would even have the right to do so, by what right it pleased him to decide *that the most instructive of our senses* [is] *seeing.*[64] The French language, which is a beautiful enough spiritual creation, does not agree since it possesses the sublime word *understanding* in which the whole theory of the word is written.[65] But what can we expect from a philosopher who tells us in all seriousness: *Now that languages are made.*[66] He would have to tell us *when they had been made,* and *when they had not been made.*

Would that I had the time to go into all his theories about *simple, complex, real, imaginary, adequate,* etc., ideas, some coming from the senses and others from reflection! Would that I could speak to you at my leisure about his idea of *archetypes,* a sacred word for the Platonists who placed it in the heavens, and which this imprudent Briton used without knowing what it was! Soon his venomous disciple in turn seized it and plunged it into the depths of his vulgar *aesthetics.* "Modern metaphysicians," he tells us, "have often used the term *archetypical ideas.*"[67] Undoubtedly, just as moralists have often used the word *chastity* but never, as far as I know, as a synonym for *prostitution.*

Locke is perhaps the sole known author who has taken the trouble to refute his whole book and or to declare it useless, from the beginning, by telling us, *that all our ideas come from sensation or from reflection.* But who has ever denied that some ideas come to us from the senses? What is Locke trying to teach us? The number of simple perceptions being negligible compared to the innumerable combinations of thought, it remains clear, from the first chapter of his second book, that the immense majority of our ideas do not come to us from the senses. But then from where do they come? The question is embarrassing and, in consequence, his disciples, fearing the results, no longer speak of reflection, which is very prudent.[68]

---

[64] Bk. II, chap. XXIII, § 12.

[65] I do not want to reject this compliment addressed to the French language, but it is nevertheless true that Locke here seems to have translated Descartes who said *Visus sensuum nobilissimus* [sight the most noble sense] (*Dioptrica* I [1639]). Perhaps one would not be mistaken in saying that hearing is to sight what the word is to writing. (Editor's note.)

[66] Ibid, chap. XXII, § 2.

[67] [Condillac], *Essai sur l'origine des connaissances humaines,* Sect. III, § 5. Why *modern,* since the word archetype is old and even antique! And why *often enough used* since the [French] Academy, in its entry on *archetype,* tells us that this word is *hardly* used except in the expression *world archetype.*

[68] Condillac, *Art de penser* [Vol. IV of his *Cours d'étude pour l'instruction du Prince de Parme* (Parma 1775)], Chap. VII.

Since Locke began his book without reflection and without deep knowledge of his subject, it is not surprising that he constantly went astray. First, he had put forward his thesis that all our ideas come to us from the senses or from reflection. Then, spurred on by his bishop who pressed him hard, and perhaps by his conscience, he came to agree *that general ideas* (which alone constitute an intelligent being) come neither from the senses nor reflection, but are the *inventions*, and the CREATURES *of the human mind.*[69] For, according to the doctrine of this great philosopher, a man *makes* general ideas *with* simple ideas, just as he *makes* a boat *with* planks, so that the most general ideas are only *collections*, or as Locke, who always seeks the coarsest expression, says, *companies of simple ideas.*[70]

If you would like to bring these lofty conceptions down to practice, consider, for example, the Church of St Peter in Rome. This is a passable general idea. At bottom, however, it all reduces itself to individual stones, which are the simple ideas. This is not something great, as you can see, and yet the privilege of simple ideas is immense, since Locke has also discovered that they are *all real* EXCEPT ALL. He only excepts from this small *exception* the primary qualities of bodies.[71]

Here I beg you to admire the illuminating course of Locke's argument: first he establishes that all our ideas come to us from the senses or reflection, and he seizes this occasion to tell us that *he understands by* reflection *that notice which the mind takes of its own operations.*[72] Then, torturing the truth, he confesses *that general ideas come neither from the senses nor from reflection, but are created, or* in his ridiculous phrase, INVENTED *by the human mind.* Now, as reflection has just been expressly excluded by Locke, it follows that the human mind *invents* general ideas *without reflection,* which is to say *without any knowledge or examination of its own operations.* However every idea that does not originate in the interaction of the mind with external objects, or the consideration of the mind of itself, necessarily appertains to the substance of the mind.

---

[69] "General ideas come not into the mind by sensation or reflection; but are the Creatures, or inventions of understanding." (*Essay,* Bk. II, chap. XXII, § 2 [note to the 5th edition of the *Essay,* from Locke's First Letter to Stillingfleet.])

[70] Consisting of a company of simple ideas combined. (Bk. II, chap. XXII, § 3.)

[71] "Not that they are all of them the images or the representations of what does exist; the contrary whereof, in ALL BUT the primary qualities of bodies, has been already shown." Bk. II, chap. XXX, § 2.

One can rightly be astonished by this strange expression: *All simple ideas, except the primary qualities of bodies*; but such is this philosophy, blind, materialist, gross to the point of confusing things with the ideas of things; and Locke will say equally: *All ideas, except that of quality*: or *all the qualities, except such an idea.*

[72] Bk. II, chap. I, § 4.

Therefore there are ideas that are innate or anterior to all experience; this, it seems to me, is his inevitable conclusion, which does not surprise me.

All the writers who have carried on against innate ideas have found themselves led by the simple force of truth to make admissions somewhat favourable to this theory. I do not except even Condillac, although he was perhaps the eighteenth-century philosopher most on guard against his conscience. I have no wish to compare these two men whose characters were very different, the one foolish, the other brazen. Yet what reproaches cannot one rightly level against Locke, and how can he be exonerated from having unsettled morality to overturn the theory of innate ideas without knowing what he was attacking? In the bottom of his heart he sensed that he was making himself guilty, *but*, he said excusing himself by deceiving himself, *the truth must come first.*[73] What this means is *that the truth comes before the truth.*

The most dangerous, perhaps, and the most guilty of those deadly writers who will never cease to accuse the last century in the eyes of posterity, the one who employed the most talent in the most cold-blooded way to do the most harm, Hume, also told us in one of his terrible *Essays, that the truth comes before everything else, that it is a somewhat ingenuous critic who reproaches certain philosophers for the harm that their opinions can do to morality and religion, and that such injustice can only hamper the discovery of truth.*[x] But no man, at least if he does not wish to deceive himself, will be duped by this treacherous sophism. No error can be useful, just as no truth can be harmful. What is misleading on this point, is, in the first place, that the error is confused with some element of truth that is mixed with it, which is, according to its nature, beneficial despite its association with error; and, in the second place, that the *announcement* of truth is confused with its *acceptance*. Doubtless it can be imprudent to expose the truth, but it is never injurious unless it is rejected, whereas error, knowledge of which can be useful only like knowledge of poisons, begins to do harm from the moment it gets itself accepted under the mask of its divine enemy. Therefore it is harmful *because people accept it*, whereas truth can be harmful only *because people combat it*; therefore everything that is harmful in itself is false, just as everything that is useful in itself is true. Nothing is clearer to those who understand.

Nevertheless blinded by his self-styled *respect for the truth*, which in cases like this however is only a public offence disguised under a fine name, Locke, in the first book of his sorry *Essay* ransacks history and travel literature to embarrass humanity. He cites the most shameful dogmas

---

[73] "But, after all, the greatest reverence (reverence!) is due to truth." Bk. I, chap. IV, § 24.

and customs; he forgets himself to the point of exhuming from an unknown book a story that makes us vomit; and he takes care to tell us that the book being rare, he has judged it appropriate to recite this anecdote for us in the author's own language,[74] and all this to establish *that there is no innate morality.* It is too bad that he forgot to produce a catalogue of diseases to demonstrate that there is no such thing as health.

In vain does Locke, always interiorly perturbed, seek to deceive himself in another way with the expression declaration: "that in denying an *innate law* I do not at all intend to deny a *natural law*, that is to say, a *law anterior to all positive law*."[75] This is, as you can see, a new struggle between conscience and committed position. In effect, what is this natural law? Moreover if it is neither positive nor innate, what is its foundation? Has he shown us a single argument against an innate law that is not valid as well against natural law? *The latter*, he tells us, *can be known by the light of reason alone, without the help of positive revelation.*[76] What then is this *light of reason*? Does it come from men? Then it is positive. Does it come from God? Then it is innate.

If Locke had more insight, or diligence, or good faith, instead of saying *a certain idea is not present in the mind of such and such a people, therefore it is not innate*, he would on the contrary have said *therefore it is innate for every man who possesses it;* for it is a proof that if the idea did not pre-exist the senses would never have given birth to it since the nation that is deprived of it has five senses like all the others, and he would have inquired into how and why such and such an idea could have been destroyed or distorted in the minds of this human family. However such a fruitful thought[xi] was far from a man who went so far as to claim *that a single atheist* in the world sufficed for him to justify denying that the idea of God was innate in man;[77] which is to say that a single monstrous infant born without eyes, for example, would prove that sight is not natural to man. Nothing stops Locke. Has he not boldly told us that the voice of

---

[74] "A remarkable passage to this purpose, out of the voyage of Baumgarten, which is a book not every day to be met with, I shall set down at large in the language it is published in." Bk. II, chap. II, § 9.

[75] "I would not here be mistaken, as if, because I deny an innate law, I thought there were none but positive laws." Bk. II, chap. III, § 13.

[76] "I think they equally forsake the truth, who, running into contrary extremes, either affirm an innate law, or deny that there is a law knowable by the light of nature, i.e., without the help of positive revelation." Ibid.

[77] "Whatsoever is innate must be universal in the strictest sense (an enormous error!). One exception is a sufficient proof against it." Bk. I, chap. IV, § 8, note [5th edition, from Locke's Third Letter to Stillingfleet].

conscience proves nothing in favour of innate principles, *since each one can have his own.*[78]

It is very strange that it has never been possible to make this great patriarch or any of his sad posterity understand the difference between ignorance of a law and admitted errors in the application of this law.[79] An Indian woman sacrifices her new-born infant to the goddess Gonza, and they say *therefore there is no innate moral law;* on the contrary it is still necessary to say *Therefore it is innate,* since the idea of duty is strong enough in this unfortunate mother to lead her to sacrifice to this duty the most tender and powerful feeling of the human heart. Abraham once earned immense merit by deciding to make the same sacrifice, which he rightly believed he had been ordered to do; he said precisely what the Indian woman said: *The divinity has spoken; I must close my eyes and obey.* The one, bowing before a divine authority that only wished to test him, obeyed a sacred and direct command; the other, blinded by a deplorable superstition, obeyed an imaginary command; but, for both, the fundamental idea is the same, the idea of duty carried to its highest degree. *I must do it!* This is the innate idea whose nature is independent of any error in application. Would the errors in calculation that men commit every day prove, by chance, that they have no idea of number? Now, if this idea of number were not innate, they would never be able to acquire it; they would not even be capable of being mistaken, since *to be mistaken* is to deviate from a prior and known rule. It is the same with other ideas; and, I would add, what seems to me clear in itself, that without this assumption, it becomes impossible to conceive of *man,* that is to say, *the unity of mankind,* or *the human species,* or consequently any order relative to a given class of intelligent beings.[80]

---

[78]   "Some men with the same bent of conscience prosecute what others avoid." Ibid., chap. II, § 8. Reconcile this fine theory, which permits each to have his own conscience, with *a natural law anterior to all positive law!*

[79]   With the permission of the speaker, I believe that he is mistaken. The men he has in mind *understand* very well, but they refuse to admit it. They lie to the world after having lied to themselves; they are more lacking in integrity than talent. See Condillac's works; a person of conscience who pages through them will sense there only *obligatory* bad faith. (Editor's note.)

[80]   *Our souls are created in virtue of a general decree, by which we have all the notions that are necessary for us.* ([Nicolas Malebranche], *Recherche de la vérité* [Paris 1774–5], Bk. I, chap. III, n. 2.)

This passage from Malebranche seems to place itself here very appropriately. In effect, every *cognitive* being can only be what it is, can only belong to a particular class, and can only differ from another class, through its innate ideas.

It must also be admitted that Locke's critics fare poorly when they distinguish between ideas, and take *innate* ideas to be only first-order moral beliefs, which seems to make the solution of the problem depend on the rightness of these beliefs. I do not say that they do not deserve particular attention, and this point could be the topic of a second examination, but for the philosopher who looks at the question in all its generality, there is no distinction to be made on this point, because there is no idea that is not innate or foreign to the senses by the universality from which it takes its form and by the intellectual act which *thinks* it.

All rational doctrine is founded on antecedent knowledge,[xii] for man can learn nothing except by what he knows. Since syllogism and induction always proceed from principles posed as already known,[xiii] it is necessary to acknowledge that before reaching a particular truth we already know it in part.[xiv] Take, for example, an actual or perceived triangle;[xv] of course you were ignorant of it before seeing it, yet you already knew, if not this triangle, *the* triangle or *triangularity*, and this is how from different viewpoints one can know and be ignorant of the same thing. If one rejects this theory, one inevitably falls into the insoluble dilemma of Plato's Meno, and one is forced to admit either that man can learn nothing or that everything he learns is only recollection.[xvi] If one refuses to admit these innate ideas, no proof is any longer possible, because there are no longer principles from which it can be derived.[xvii] In effect, the essence of principles is that they are anterior, evident, non-derived, indemonstrable, and *causes* in relation to the conclusion;[xviii] otherwise they would have to be demonstrated themselves, which is to say that they would cease to be principles, and it would be necessary to admit what the schools call *infinite regression*, which is impossible.[xix] Moreover notice that these principles on which proofs are founded must be not only *known* naturally, but be *better known* than the truths discovered by their means, for *anything that communicates something must necessarily possess it more fully than the subject that receives it*. For example, just as the man that we love for love of another is always less loved than the latter, in the same way every acquired truth is less clear to us than the principle that made it visible to us. The *illuminator* being by nature brighter than the *illuminated*,[xx] it is not sufficient to believe in science; it is necessary to believe in the principle of science,[xxi] whose character is to be at once both necessary and necessarily believed. For demonstration has nothing in common with the external and perceptible assertion *that denies whatever it wishes*; it derives from that more profound voice that speaks within man,[81] and that has no power to contradict the truth.[xxii] All the sciences communicate with one another by these common principles; and I beg you to notice well that by this word *common* I intend to express not what these different sciences prove, but what they use in order to prove[xxiii] – which is to say *the universal*, which is at the root of every demonstration, which exists prior to any impression or sensory process, and which is so little the result of experience that without it experience will *always* remain solitary, and could be repeated to infinity and *always* leave an abyss between it and the universal. This puppy playing with you at the moment, played in the same way yesterday and the day before. Thus it has played, and played, and played, but from its point of view, it has not played *three times*, as it has for you; for if you take away the fundamental and consequently pre-existing idea of *number* by which one experience can be related to another, *one* and *one* are nothing but *this* and *that*, never *two*.

So you see, gentlemen, how pitiful Locke is with his "experience," since the truth is only *an equation between human thought and the object known*,[82] so that if the first term of the equation is not natural, pre-existent, and immutable, the latter necessarily fluctuates, and there is no truth.

Every idea therefore being innate in relation to the universal from which it derives its form, it is moreover totally foreign to the senses by the intellectual act that affirms, for thought or (what is the same thing) speech belongs only to the mind, or better being the mind,[83] no distinction should

---

[81] *This word, conceived within God himself and by which God speaks to himself, is the uncreated Word.* (Bourdaloue, "Sermon sur la parole de Dieu," Exorde.)

Undoubtedly, and reason alone can raise itself to this point; but, and by a necessary consequence: *This word, conceived in man himself and by which man speaks to himself, is the* word created *in the image of its model*. For thought (or the human word) *is only the speech which the soul has with itself*. (Plato. See above, p. 134.)

[82] St Thomas. See endnote xl to the Second Dialogue.

[83] A being that only thinks and that has no other action than thought. ([François] Lamy, *De la connaissance de soi-même*, [2 vols. (Paris 1699)], 2nd part, 4th reflection.)

The content of the soul is not distinguishable from its faculties. (Fénelon, [*Explications des*] *Maximes des Saints* [*sur la vie intérieure*], [Brussels 1698], art. XXVIII.) [The precise text reads: "le fonds de l'âme n'est point réellement distingué de ses puissances." (The content of the soul is not really distinguishable from its powers.) Article XXIX, not Article XXVIII. The editor of the Pléiade edition of Fénelon's *Oeuvres* notes: "Fénelon was alluding not only to St Augustine (*De*

be made in this regard between the different orders of ideas. Once man says THIS IS,[xxiv] he is necessarily speaking by virtue of an internal and anterior knowledge,[xxv] for the senses have nothing in common with the truth, which the understanding alone can attain. Since what does not pertain to the senses is foreign to matter, it follows that there is in man an immaterial principle in which knowledge resides, and since the senses can only receive and transmit impressions to the mind,[84] not only is its function, which essentially is to judge, not helped by these impressions,[85] but rather it is hindered and confused by them.[86] We should therefore assume, with the greatest men, that we naturally have intellectual ideas that have not come to us by the senses,[xxvi] and that the contrary opinion offends good sense as well as religion.[87]

I read somewhere that the celebrated *Cudworth*, disputing one day with one of his friends on the origin of ideas, said to him: *Please take a book from my library, the first that comes to hand, and open it at random.* The friend picked Cicero's *De Officiis* and opened it at the beginning of the first book and read: ALTHOUGH *a year ago*, etc. – *That is enough*, replied Cudworth, *tell me how you could have acquired the idea of* ALTHOUGH *from the senses.*[88] The argument is excellent under a very simple form: man cannot speak, he cannot articulate the least element of his thought, he cannot say AND, without refuting Locke.

The Chevalier

When we began you said to me: *Speak to me in all conscience.* Permit me to address the same words to you: *Speak to me in all conscience*, have you not chosen the passages from Locke that are most susceptible to criticism? This is a seductive temptation when speaking of a man one does not like.

---

magistro XII) but undoubtedly to Descartes and Malebranche." I:1600 (Darcel ed.)]

[84] *Something immaterial by itself in which there is knowledge.* (Justin Martyr, *On the Resurrection* (fragment), Question II.)

[85] *Even if the eyes could be struck by spectres, I do not see how the mind can,* etc. (Cicero *Epistle XV.16.*)

[86] *The function of the intellect specially consists in judging; but fantasy and bodily image by no means aid judgment but rather hinder it.* (Lessius [Leonard Leys], de immortalitate animae, in *Opuscula* [Lyons 1651], lib. III, n° 53.)

[87] [Antoine] Arnauld and [Pierre] Nicole, *La Logique ou l'art de penser (Port-Royal)*, First part, chap. 1.

[88] This anecdote, which is unknown to me, is probably taken from somewhere in [Ralph] Cudworth's great work, *Systema intellectuale*, published first in English [London 1678] and subsequently translated into Latin with the notes of Laurent Mosheim. 2 vols. (Jena [1733]) and 2 vols. (Leyden [1773]). (Editor's note.)

The Count

I can assure you that the contrary is the case, and I can assure you moreover that a detailed examination of his book would furnish me a much more abundant harvest. However to refute an *in-quarto* it would require another, and who, I ask you, would read the second? When a bad book has captured men's minds, there are no other means of disabusing them than by demonstrating the general spirit that dictated it, classifying its faults, pointing out its most salient errors, and leaving the rest to the conscience of the reader. In my opinion, to render Locke's book completely irreproachable, it would suffice to change two words. It is entitled *An Essay Concerning Human Understanding*; let us simply substitute *An Essay on Locke's Understanding*, and never would a book more fully justify its title. The work is a complete portrait of the man; nothing is missing.[89] One easily recognizes here an honest man, and even a man of good sense, but one *deceived* by the sectarian spirit that led him without his perceiving it or without his even wanting to perceive it; moreover, he lacked the most indispensable philosophic learning and all depth of understanding. He is really comical when he tells us seriously that he has taken up his pen *to give men the rules by which a reasonable creature can wisely govern his actions*, adding that to attain this end *it occurred to him that it would be most useful first of all to fix the boundaries of the human mind*.[90] Never can anything so foolish have *occurred to anyone*; for, in the first place, with respect to what pertains to morals, I would much prefer the *Sermon on the Mount* to all the scholastic nonsense with which Locke has filled his book, and which is, moreover, as far as one can imagine from real morality. As to the limits of human understanding, take it as a sure thing that it is an excess of temerity to want to question them; even the expression lacks a precise meaning. However we will speak of this question some other time, since there are certainly some interesting things to be said on this issue. For the moment, it is enough to observe what Locke would first impose on himself, and then on us. He really didn't want to say anything that he said. He wanted *to contradict* and nothing more. Recall this Boindin of the *Temple of taste*:

---

[89] Jean Le Clerc once wrote under Locke's portrait:
Lockius humanae pingens penetralia mentis
Ingenium solus pinxerit *ipse suum.*
[Locke, in portraying the secrets of the human mind, only portrayed his own genius.] He was right.
[90] [Paraphrase from] Locke's "Introduction," § 7.

Crying: Gentlemen, I am this honest judge
Who is always judging, arguing, and contradicting.[91]

This is the spirit that animated Locke. Enemy of all moral authority, he wanted to oppose received ideas, which are a great authority. Above all, he wanted to oppose his church, which I have more reason than he to hate, and which I nevertheless venerate in a certain sense as the most reasonable among the unreasonable. So Locke took up his pen only *to argue and to contradict*, and his book, entirely negative, is one of the numerous productions born from the same spirit that ruined so many minds much superior to Locke's. The other striking, distinctive, and invariable character of this philosopher is his *superficiality* (permit me to coin this word for him). He understands nothing completely, he examines nothing deeply. What I would especially like you to observe is his most decisive sign of mediocrity, which is the fault by which he bypasses the most significant questions without even noticing them. I can give you a striking example that comes to my mind at the moment. He says somewhere with his truly pitiable masterly tone: *I confess myself to have one of those dull souls, that doth not perceive itself always to contemplate ideas, nor can conceive it any more necessary for the soul always to think, than for the body always to move; the perception of ideas being (as I conceive) to the soul, what motion is to the body.*[92] My Lord! I might well ask Locke's pardon for it, but I find nothing in this fine passage but a joke. So where has he seen matter in repose? I would not claim that motion is essential to matter, and I believe it quite indifferent to direction, but in the end one must know what one is saying, and when one is unable to distinguish between relative and absolute motion, one is certainly dispensed from writing on philosophy.

Following this comparison, which Locke seized upon so badly, you can see all that it would be possible to draw from it when taken up by others. *Movement is to bodies what thought is to the mind*; so why are there not absolute thoughts and relative thoughts? *Relative* when a man finds himself in relation to sensible objects and with his fellow men and can compare them to one another; *absolute* when this communication is suspended by sleep or other unusual causes, thought no longer being *carried along* by the superior motion that carries everything along. While we are sitting here in our seats quietly as far as our senses can tell, we are really flying through space at a speed that startles the imagination, since it is at least thirty versts per second, which is to say that it is nearly fifty times that of a cannon ball; and this movement is complicated moreover by that of the earth's rotation

---

[91] [Voltaire, *Le temple du goût, Oeuvres* ed. Molund, 8:563.]
[92] Bk. II, chap. I, § 10.

which at the equator is almost equal, without our being in the least conscious of these two motions. So how would it be possible to prove that it is impossible for a man to think, just as he moves with the superior motion, without knowing it? It would be easy to say: *Oh! That is very different!* But not so easy, perhaps, to prove it. In any case, every man has his pride from which it is difficult to separate him absolutely; so I will naively confess to you *that I happen to have a heavy enough soul* to believe that my comparison is not more *weighty* than Locke's.

Take this too for one of those examples that must be related to many others. There is no way to say everything. However you are free to open Locke at random: without hesitation I will bet I can show you that he never encountered a single important question that he did not treat with the same mediocrity. Since a mediocre man can thus convict him of mediocrity, judge what would happen if some superior man took the trouble to *cut him up.*

The Senator

I don't know if you are aware of a problem that you are creating for yourself without noticing, for the more you accumulate reproaches against Locke's book, the more you make inexplicable the immense reputation it enjoys.

The Count

I am not at all worried about creating a problem that is not extremely difficult to resolve. Since our young friend involved me in this discussion, I will willingly end it in favour of the truth.

Who knows better than I the full extent of the authority so unfortunately accorded to Locke, and who has ever complained about it in better faith? Ah! What a grudge I bear against this futile generation that has made him its oracle, and that we see still *locked fast in,*[93] so to say, locked in error by the authority of a vain name that it has itself created in its folly! And what a grudge I bear especially against these Frenchmen who have abandoned, forgotten, and even outraged the Christian Plato [Malebranche] born among them, and with whom Locke was not worthy to cross pens, in order to cede the sceptre of rational philosophy to this idol, *the work of their own hands,* to this false God of the eighteenth century, who knew nothing, said nothing, and who they have put on a pedestal *before the face of the Lord* on the faith of some fanatics who are even worse citizens than they are bad philosophers! These Frenchmen, thus degraded by the vile

---

[93]   [Maistre's pun on Locke's own expression.]

instructors who teach them to believe no longer in France, remind us of a millionaire sitting on a strongbox he refuses to open, and who grasps the base hand of a smiling stranger.

However this idolatry is not surprising. The fortune of books would be the subject of a good book. What Seneca said of men is perhaps more true of these monuments of their minds. *Some have reputations and others merit them.*[94] If books appear in favourable circumstances, if they flatter great passions, if they engage the proselytizing fanaticism of a numerous and active sect, or, what always happens, the favour of a powerful nation, their fortune is made. The reputation of books, if one perhaps excludes those by mathematicians,[xxvii] depends much less on their intrinsic merit than on these strange circumstances, such as the one I place first, as I have just told you, the power of the nation that produced the author. If a man such as Father Kircher,[95] for example, had been born in Paris or London, his bust would be on everyone's mantelpieces, and it would be taken for granted that he had seen or foreseen everything. So long as a book is not, if it may be put this way, *pushed* by an influential nation, it will only achieve a mediocre success. I could cite a hundred examples for you. Take these considerations, which appear to me palpably true, into account, and you will see that Locke had all possible chances in his favour. Let us speak first of his country. He was English; England has undoubtedly shone in all ages, but let us consider only the beginning of the eighteenth century. It then possessed Newton and was defeating Louis XIV. What a moment for its writers! Locke profited from this. However his inferiority is such that he would not have succeeded, at least beyond a certain point, if other circumstances had not favoured him. Sufficiently prepared by Protestantism, the human mind was beginning to shake off its own timidity, and preparing boldly to draw out all the consequences of the principles that had been posed in the sixteenth century. A dreadful sect was beginning to organize itself; it was its good luck to come upon a book written by a very honest and even *reasonable* man,[96] where all the germs of the most abject and detestable philosophy were found covered by a meritorious reputation, enveloped by wise forms, and even flanked as needed by some texts of Holy Scripture. So the evil genius could receive this present from one of the separated tribes, for in

---

[94] Seneca is rich enough in maxims for it to be unnecessary for his friends to claim more for him. The one cited here really belongs to Justus Lipsius: *quidam merentur famam, quidam habent.* (Justus Lipsius, *Epistolarum centuriae duae* [Leyden 1591], Epistle I.) (Editor's note.)

[95] [On Kircher, see Third Dialogue, footnote 13.]

[96] [Maistre's epithet undoubtedly refers to Locke's *The Reasonableness of Christianity* (1695).]

Jerusalem this perfidious amalgam would have been forestalled or denounced by a vigilant and inexorable religion. This book was therefore born where it had to be born, and came from a hand made expressly for the satisfaction of the most dangerous views. Locke enjoyed a just title to general esteem. He called himself a Christian, even if he wrote in favour of Christianity following his own bent and prejudices, and a very edifying death terminated his holy and laborious life.[97] How the conspirators must have rejoiced to see such a man posing all the principles they needed, and especially to see him favouring materialism *by delicacy of conscience*. So they pounced upon Locke's unfortunate *Essay*, and cherished it with an ardour that one can scarcely understand unless one pays particular attention. I remember that I was once shocked by seeing one of the most hardened atheists who has perhaps ever existed recommending to young people an edition of Locke abridged, that is to say *concentrated*, by an Italian writer who should have been acting in a way more in keeping with his vocation. *Read him*, he told them with enthusiasm, *read him and learn him by heart*; he would have wanted, as Madame de Sévigné said, *to give him to them with their soup*.[98]

There is a sure rule for judging books just as there is for judging men: it is enough to know *by whom they are loved and by whom they are hated*. This rule never fails, and I have already proposed it to you with respect to Bacon. As soon as you see a book made popular by the encyclopedists, translated by an atheist, and unstintingly praised by the past century's flood of philosophers, you can be sure, without further examination, that its philosophy is false and dangerous, at least in its general thrust. For the opposite reason, if you see these philosophers often embarrassed by this writer, and vexed by some of his ideas, seeking to hide these ideas and even allowing themselves to mutilate them boldly or alter his writings, again you can be sure, always without further examination, that Bacon's works present numerous and magnificent exceptions to the general reproaches that are rightly fully addressed to them. However do not think that I want to establish any comparison between these two men. Bacon, as a moral philosopher, and even as a writer in a certain sense, will always merit the admiration of connoisseurs, while the *Essay Concerning Human Understanding* is very certainly, and whether one is persuaded by it or not, as boring as anything an absolute lack of genius and style could create.

If Locke, who was a very honest man, returned to the world, he would weep bitterly to see how his errors, sharpened by French methods, have

---

[97] One can read about this in Savérien's little history of philosophers [Alexandre Savérien, *Histoire des philosophes modernes*, 8 vols. (Paris 1773)].

[98] [Letter of 4 November 1671 (Pléiade, 1:375) (Darcel ed.)]

become the shame and misfortune of an entire generation. Do you not see that God has proscribed this vile philosophy, and that it has even pleased him to make the anathema visible? Look through all the books of its devotees; you will not find there a single line whose good taste and virtue are worth remembering. This philosophy is the death of all religion, of all delicate feelings, of all sublime enthusiasm; every father of a family especially must be clearly warned that in receiving it under his roof, he is really doing all that he could do to chase out life, since no warmth can survive its glacial breath.

But let us come back to the fortune of books, which we can explain precisely like that of men. For the one as for the other, there are fortunes that are veritable curses and that owe nothing to merit. So, gentlemen, success alone proves nothing. You must especially distrust a very common and very natural prejudice, which however is completely false: that of believing that a book's great reputation supposes a very widespread and reasonable knowledge of the book. I assure you that this has nothing to do with it. The immense majority judge and can only judge on the word of a small number of men who first establish opinion. They die, and this opinion survives them. The arrival of new books leaves no more time to read the earlier ones, and soon these are only judged on the basis of a vague reputation, founded on some general characteristics or on some superficial and sometimes perfectly false analogies. Not long ago an excellent judge, but one who can however judge only on the basis of what he knows, said in Paris that the antique talent most resembling that of Bossuet was that of Demosthenes. Now these two different orators differ as much as two things of the same genre (two beautiful flowers, for example) can differ from each other. All his life he had heard it said that Demosthenes *thundered*, and Bossuet *thundered* also; therefore, etc. This is how judgements are formed. Did not La Harpe say formally *that the purpose of the entire book,* An Essay Concerning Human Understanding, *is to demonstrate rigorously that the understanding is spirit and of an essentially different nature than matter?*[99] Moreover, did he not say: *Locke, Clarke, Leibniz, Fénelon, etc.,* recognized this truth (respecting the distinction between the two substances[xxviii])? Can you wish for a clearer proof that this celebrated writer never read Locke? Can you imagine how he could have made such a (slightly comical) mistake of inscribing Locke in such good company if he had seen him exhaust all the resources of the most captious dialectic to relate thought to matter in some way?

You have heard Voltaire tell us: *Locke, with his good sense, never ceased to repeat to us: define!* But, again I ask you, would Voltaire have

---

[99] *Lycée*, Vol. XXIV. Philosophie du XVIIIᵉ siècle, Tom. III, art. "Diderot."

addressed this eulogy to the English philosopher if he had known that Locke is above all eminently ridiculous with his definitions, which are all nothing but watered down tautologies. This same Voltaire tells us also, in a sacrilegious work, *that Locke is the English Pascal.*[xxix] You will not, I hope, accuse me of a blind tenderness for *François Arouet.* I will assume that he was as frivolous, as ill-intentioned, and, especially, as bad a Frenchman as you wish, but I will never believe that a man who had so much taste and tact would have permitted himself this extravagant comparison if he had judged the matter for himself. What then! The tedious author of the *Essay Concerning Human Understanding,* whose merit in rational philosophy reduces itself to telling us, with the eloquence of an almanac, what everyone knows or what no one needs to know, and who moreover would be totally unknown to science if he had not discovered *that speed is measured by bulk*; such a man, I say, compared to Pascal! To Pascal! A great man at thirty: a physicist, a distinguished mathematician, a sublime apologist, a polemicist superior to the point of making calumny entertaining, a man whose extraordinary qualities could never be eclipsed by all imaginable mistakes. Such a comparison permits no other supposition than that Voltaire himself knew little of the *Essay Concerning Human Understanding.* Add to this the fact that French men of letters in the last century read very little, first, because they led a very wild life, second, because they wrote too much, and finally, because their pride would scarcely have permitted them to suppose that they had need of the thoughts of others. Such men had many more things to do than read Locke. I have good reasons for suspecting that generally he was not read by those who praised him, by those who cited him, or even by those who tried to explain him. It is a great error to believe that to cite a book with the strong appearance of speaking of it knowledgeably, it is necessary to have read it, at least completely and with attention. One reads the passage or the line that one needs; one reads some lines from an *index* on the faith of an *index*; and this is really all that one wants. What does the rest matter?[100] There is also an art of getting those who have read to talk; and this is how it is very possible that the book that is the most talked about is, in effect, the least known through reading. However this is enough on this reputation that is so great and so little merited. The day will come, and perhaps it is not far off, when Locke will be unanimously placed among those writers who have done the most harm to men. However, despite all the reproaches I have made against him, I have touched on only part of his errors, and

---

[100] For my part, I would not want to bet that Condillac ever read Locke completely and attentively; but if it were absolutely necessary to bet on the affirmative or the negative, I would decide for the second.

perhaps the least. After having laid the foundations of a philosophy as false as it is dangerous, his deadly mind turned towards politics with a no less deplorable result. He spoke about the origin of the laws as badly as about the origin of ideas; and on this point he again laid down principles whose consequences we are now seeing. These terrible seeds would perhaps have withered in silence in the coldness of his style, but nurtured in the hot houses of Paris, they produced the revolutionary monster that has devoured Europe.

Moreover, gentlemen, I cannot repeat often enough that the judgement that I cannot dispense myself from making against Locke's works, does not prevent me from rendering to his person or his memory all the justice that is due. He had virtues, even great virtues; and although they remind me a bit of the dancing master cited, I think, by Dr Swift, *who had* all imaginable good qualities *except that he was lame*,[101] I nevertheless profess my veneration for Locke's moral character. However I still deplore the influence of his *bad principle* on the best minds. It is this principle unfortunately that has reigned in Europe for three centuries, it is this principle that denies everything, that overturns everything, that *protests* against everything. NO is written on the brazen brow of this principle. This is the real title of Locke's book, which in turn can be considered as the preface of all eighteenth-century philosophy, which is totally negative and in consequence null. Read the *Essay*; on every page you will sense that Locke only wrote to contradict received ideas, and especially to humiliate an authority that shocked him immeasurably.ˣˣˣ He tells us his secret himself quite straightforwardly. *He bore a grudge against a certain kind of people who, affecting to be masters and teachers, and hoping to govern others more easily,* enlisted the aid of blind credulity to make the others

---

[101] One can read a curious comment on Locke in the work by Dr James Beattie cited above (*On the nature and immutability of truth.* (London 1772), pp. 16–17.) After a magnificent eulogy of this philosopher's moral character, the doctor is obliged to condemn an absolutely inexcusable doctrine, which however he excused as well as he could with a poor reason. [Beattie acknowledges that he objects to parts of Locke's philosophy because he thinks "them erroneous and dangerous," and adds: "I am convinced, that their author, if he had lived to see the inferences that have been drawn from them, would have been the first to declare them absurd, and would have expunged them from his works with indignation."] One is reminded of Boileau on Chapelain:

He has been praised for his faith, honour, honesty,
We have been taken with his candour and civility, *etc., etc.*
But it is true that, if he had taken my advice, he would not have written one verse.
[*Satire IX.*]

SWALLOW innate principles that must not be questioned.^{xxxi} In another place in his book, he examines how men arrive *at what they call their principles*; and he begins with this remarkable observation. *This, however strange it may seem, is that which every day's experience confirms ... that doctrines* (he would have done well to name them) *that have been derived from no better original than the superstition of a nurse, or the authority of an old woman, may, by length of time and consent of neighbours, grow to the dignity of* principles *in religion and morality.*[102] It is not a question here of Japan or Canada, or even less of rare and extraordinary facts: it is a question of *what every man can see every day of his life.* Nothing is less equivocal, as you can see. However Locke appears to me to have exceeded the bounds of the ridiculous when he put in the margin of this fine chapter: *Whence the theory of innate principles?*^{xxxii} He must have been *possessed* by the sickness of the eighteenth century, daughter of the sixteenth, to attribute to ecclesiastics the invention of this system, unfortunately rare enough, but certainly as well, as old as common sense.

Yet another comment on Locke's reputation, which embarrasses you. Do you think it is general? Have you counted opinions, or, what is more important, have you weighed them? If you can disentangle the voice of wisdom from amidst the clamours of the ignorant and the spirit of party, you would already know *that Locke is very little esteemed as a metaphysician in his own country;*[103] that on the fundamental point of his philosophy, *given over like so many others to verbiage and ambiguity, he was convicted of not understanding himself;*[104] *that his first book* (the basis of all the others) *was the worst;*[105] *that the second treats the operations of the soul only superficially;*[106] *that the entire work is disconnected and written by chance;*[107] *that his whole philosophy of the soul is very thin and is scarcely worth being refuted seriously;*[108] *that it contains opinions*

---

[102] Locke expresses himself to this effect in Bk. I, chap. III, § 22.

[103] *Spectateur français au XIXᵉ siècle*, Vol. I, n° 35. p. 249.

[104] [David] Hume, *Essays into Human Understanding*, (London 1758), Sect. III, p. 292. [Hume's work was first published in 1748 with the title *Philosophical Essays concerning Human Understanding*; the 1758 edition carried the title *Enquiry concerning Human Understanding*. (Darcel ed.)]

[105] "The first book which, with submission I think the worst." (Beattie, *On Truth*, II, 2, 1.) Which is to say that *all* his books are bad, but the first is the worst.

[106] Condillac, *Essai sur l'origine des connaissances humaines*. Introduction, p. 14.

[107] Ibid., p. 13. Citing Locke's own "Epistle to the Reader."

[108] Leibniz, *Works*, V:394. Epist. ad Korth. "To this philosophical conundrum (the *tabula rasa*) I confess I can give no serious answer." Beattie, *On Truth*.

as absurd as they are dangerous in their consequence;[109] *that when they are neither false nor dangerous they are only good for young people and even then only up to a certain point;*[110] *that if Locke had lived to see the inferences that have been drawn from his principles, he would have expunged them from his works with indignation.*[111]

In any case, gentlemen, no matter what we say, Locke's authority will be difficult to overturn so long as it supported by the great powers. In twenty French works of the last century I have read: *Locke* and *Newton!* Such is the privilege of great nations; it pleased the French to say: *Corneille* and *Vadé!*[112] Or even *Vadé* and *Corneille!* If euphony, which often decides many things, had the goodness to consent to it, I would be ready to believe they would have forced us to repeat with them: *Vadé* and *Corneille!*

The Chevalier

You accord us Frenchmen great power, my dear friend; I owe you a debt of thanks in the name of my country.

The Count

I do *not accord* this power, my dear chevalier, I only *recognize* it; so you owe me no thanks. Moreover, I would rather not have only compliments to address to you on this point. Nevertheless, you are a terrible power! Never, undoubtedly, has there ever been a nation easier to deceive, more difficult to undeceive, nor more powerful in deceiving others. Two particular characteristics distinguish you from all the other peoples of world: a spirit of association and a spirit of proselytism. Among you ideas are completely national and completely passionate. It seems to me that twenty-five centuries ago a prophet painted you quite naturally with one stroke of his proud brush when he said: *For every word this people speaks is a conspiracy.*[113] An electric spark, like the lightning bolt from which it derives, traversing a mass of men in communication, is a weak image of the instantaneous (I almost said exploding) invasion of a fashion, a system, or a passion among Frenchmen, who cannot live *apart.* At least if you only acted on yourselves, we could let you be; but the desire, the need, the rage to act on others is the most salient trait of your character. One could say

---

[109] Leibniz, *Works.*

[110] Ibid., Vol. V.

[111] Beattie, *On Truth*, pp. 16–17.

[112] [Jean-Joseph Vadé (1720–57) was the author of comic poems, parodies, and light comedies, some of which were enormously popular for a time.]

[113] Isaiah 8:12.

that this trait is *you*. Every people has a mission; this is yours. The least opinion that you hurl at Europe is a battering ram backed by thirty million people. Always hungry for success and influence, one could say that you live only to satisfy this need, and since a nation cannot have been given a purpose without the means to achieve it, you have been given this means in your language, by which you reign much more than by your armaments, although they too have overturned the world. The empire of this language is not a question of its present form; it is as old as the language itself. Already, in the thirteenth century, an Italian wrote the history of his country in French *because the French language is known by everyone, and is more delectable to read and to hear than any other.*[114] There are a thousand other testimonies of this kind. I remember once having read a letter of the famous architect *Christopher Wren*, wherein he was investigating the dimensions that must be given to a church. He determined them uniquely by the power of the human voice; this had to be the case, preaching having become the principle concern and almost the entire ecclesiastical worship in sects that had ceased to sacrifice. So he fixed these limits at the point beyond which the voice, for English ears, is only a noise; *but*, he adds, *a French orator could make himself understood farther, his pronunciation being more distinct and solid.*[xxxiii] What Wren said of the oral word seems to me even more true of the even more penetrating words that are captured in books. Those of the French are always heard farther, for style is an accent. May this mysterious force, so poorly explained up to now, and no less powerful for good as for evil, soon become an organ of salutary proselytism, capable of consoling humanity for all the injuries that it has done us!

While waiting, Chevalier, as long as your inconceivable nation remains infatuated with Locke, I can only hope to see him put in his place in England. His rivals having dispensed his reputation in Europe, the Anglomania that captured them and that subsequently condemned them in the last century, was extremely useful and honourable for the English who habitually profited from it. A number of English authors, such as Young, Richardson, etc., were only known and fashionable in Europe through French translations and recommendations. In Gibbon's memoirs there is a letter in which, speaking of the novel *Clarissa*, he says: *It is bad enough.* Horace Walpole, later Count of Oxford, scarcely thought more highly of it,

---

[114] Brother Martin de Canal. See Tiraboschi, *Storia della letteratura italiana*, Bk III, chap. 1, n° 4, 4:321.

from what I read somewhere in his works.[115] With the excited Diderot in France lavishing on Richardson the praises that he perhaps would not have accorded to Fénelon, the English let him have his say, and rightly so. The infatuation of the French with certain points that the English themselves, although somewhat interested, judged very differently, will someday be noticed. However, just as in the study of philosophy a contempt for Locke is the *beginning of wisdom*, the English would conduct themselves in a manner worthy of themselves, and render a valuable service to the world, if they themselves had the wisdom to break a reputation of which they have no need. A cedar of Lebanon does not impoverish itself by shedding a dead leaf; rather it beautifies itself.

If they would try to defend this artificial reputation as they would defend Gibraltar, my goodness, I would withdraw. Already having France on my hands, I would have to be much stronger than I am to make war on Great Britain. Rather than hoping for victory, let us admit, if necessary, that Locke's pedestal remains immovable. ... *e pur si muove*.[116]

But I don't know, my dear Chevalier, why I am always the one whom you attack, nor why I always let myself be led where you want. You have really worn me out with your miserable Locke. Why don't you pester our friend the Senator in the same way?

The Chevalier

Let me be, his turn will come. Moreover he is calmer than you, more phlegmatic than you. He needs more time to breathe freely; and his reasoning, I don't why, impresses me more than yours. So if it took my fancy to worry one or the other of you, I would willingly decide in your favour. I also think you have this distinction because of our community of language. Twenty times a day, I imagine you are French.

The Count

What then, my dear Chevalier, do you think that Frenchmen all have the right to weary one another?

---

[115] I have not myself paged through his works, but the letters of Madame du Deffand can make up for this to a certain extent. ([*Correspondance inédite*], Vol. II, letter cxxxii, 20 March 1772.)

[116] ["And yet it moves." Maistre again cites Galileo's legendary remark.]

The Chevalier

No more than Russians have the right to weary one another. However let us depart quickly, I beg you, for I see, by a glance at the clock, that in a moment *it will be tomorrow.*

NOTES TO THE SIXTH DIALOGUE

i   In fact, it is to be found there word for word. *One can pray*, he says, *only as much as one desires, and one desires only as much as one loves, at least with a disinterested love.* (*Maximes des Saints*, art. xix, p. 128.) Elsewhere he says: *One who does not desire prays deceitfully. Even if he passed whole days reciting prayers or exciting pious feelings in himself, he would not really pray if he did not desire what he asked for.* (*Oeuvres spirituelles*, [4 vols. (1740)], n° 111, 3:48.)

One can read in Madame de Guyon's *Discours chrétien et spirituel* the following passage: *Prayer is nothing but the love of God. ... The heart only asks through its desires; to pray, therefore, is to desire. One who does not desire from the bottom of his heart prays deceitfully. Even if he passed his entire days reciting prayers or meditating or exciting in himself pious feelings, he would not really pray if he did not desire what he asked for.* ([Paris 1790], Vol. II, disc. vii, pp. 56–57)

Here one can see how one's notes can get mixed together.

ii "But what do you say in dryness, in disgust, in coldness? You always say what you have in your heart. You say to God ... that you are bored, ... that you are longing to leave him for vile amusements ... You say to him: Oh my God! See my ingratitude," etc. etc. ([Fénelon, *Oeuvres spirituelles*], Vol. IX, letter clxxv.)

Another master of the spiritual life, a century before Fénelon, had used the same language: *One can make acts of confidence without confidence ... although we make them without desire, we need not worry about it ... and do not say that you give only lip service; for if the heart does not will it, the lips will not say a word. Having done this, remain at peace, paying no attention to your problem ...* (St Francis de Sales, [*Les Entretiens et colloques spirituelles* (Tournon 1628)] 11ᵉ Entretien.) *There are perfectly strong persons to whom our Lord never gives sweetness nor quietude, who do everything* with the superior part of their soul, *and who kill their will in the will of God* with the live strength and force of reason. (St Francis de Sales, 11ᵉ Entretien). Where is desire in this?

iii "Ideas, as ranked under names, being those that FOR THE MOST PART men reason of within themselves, and ALWAYS those which they commune about with others." (Bk. II, chap. XXIX, § 2. [Maistre's small capitals]) This passage, considered seriously, contains three enormous errors: (1) Locke expressly recognizes the *internal word*, and yet he makes it depend on the *external thought*. This the eighteenth-century extravagance; (2) he believes that man (apart from organic deficiencies) can sometimes express to himself only what he can express to others; (3) he believes that man can only express an idea that has a distinct name. But all this can only be pointed out.

iv "What is more important for man than to seek this end, this goal, this unique centre towards which he must direct all his thoughts, all his counsels, all his projects leading to the roads of wisdom? What does nature show us as the supreme good to which we must prefer nothing else? On the other hand, what does nature reject as the sum of evil? The greatest geniuses have remained divided on this question." etc. (Cicero *De Finibus* I.5.)

v "Men who call themselves *philosophers*, but who are really only professional quibblers, come to tell us *that men are happy when they live according to their desires*. Nothing is more falacious; for the height of human misery is to want what is not appropriate; and the misfortune of not attaining what one desires is certainly less than that of pursuing what we are not permitted to desire." (Cicero, cited in St Augustine *On the Trinity* XIII.5)

vi Dissertation sur la liberté, no. 12, Condillac, *Oeuvres*, [Paris 1789], III:429. Voltaire said: *Liberty is the power to do what the will requires*; but he adds in a way that is worthy of him, *by an absolute necessity*. This is the opinion Voltaire "came to in his prose as an old man, after having defended liberty poetically in his youth." (*Mercure de France*, 21 January 1809, n° 392.) Even abstracting from the fatalism, one still finds in Voltaire's definition the error of Locke and of all those who have not understood the question. In any case, there are a thousand ways to be in error, and there is only one way to be correct: *the will, in St Augustine's style, is only liberty*. ([Nicolas] Bergier, *Dictionnaire de théologie* [8 vols. (Liège 1789)], art. "Grâce.")

vii *Where the Spirit of the Lord is, there is freedom*. (2 Corinthians 3:17.) One must be just to the Stoics. This sect alone merited being called *fortissimam et sanctissimam sectam* [a couragous and saintly sect]. (Seneca *Epistle* LXXXIII.) It alone (outside Christianity) could say *that we must love God* (Ibid., XLVII.), that all philosophy reduces itself to two words: *suffer and abstain*, that we must love those who beat us and love them while they beat us. (Justus Lipsius, *Manuductionis ad Stoicam philosophiam* [Antwerp 1604], phil. i, 13.) It produced the hymn of Cleanthes and invented the word *Providence*. It could get Cicero to say: *I fear they are the only ones to merit the name philosophers*; and the Fathers of the Church to say: *that the Stoics agreed with Christianity* on several points. (Cicero, *Tusculan Disputations* IV; Jerome, *Commentary on Isaiah* C.x; St Augustine *The City of God* v.8.9.)

viii Bk. II, chap. XXI, § 14. However, according to Locke, in the same place where he retails this fine doctrine, *Volition ... is an act of the mind knowingly exerting that dominion it takes itself to have ... by employing it in, or withholding it from, any particular action; ... the power of the mind to determine its thought, to the producing, continuing, or stopping any action.* (Ibid., § 15.) From which it follows that THE POWER THAT IS THE PRINCIPLE OF THE ACTION HAS NOTHING IN COMMON WITH THE ACTION; which is very fine, and what one expects from Locke.

Elsewhere he will tell you that liberty supposes the will. (Ibid., § 9.) Again it follows that *liberty has nothing in common with that faculty, without which there could be no liberty;* which is quite curious. All this is good for the eighteenth century.

ix "Liberty is a property so essential to all spiritual beings, that not even God can deprive them of it. ... To remove liberty from a spirit would be the same thing as to annihilate it; which can only be understood to mean that the spirit itself, and not the actions of the body that the spirit decides, conforms to its will ... ; for we must carefully distinguish between the will or the act of the will and the execution it makes by means of the body. The act of the will cannot be prevented by any exterior force, not even by that of God ... But there are means of acting on a spirit that tend not to contradict it but to persuade it. By binding a man to prevent him from acting, one does not change either his will or his intention; but one could provide motives to him, etc., etc." ([Leonard] Euler, *Lettres d'Euler à une Princesse d'Allemagne sur divers sujets de physique et de philosophie* [Berne 1775], Vol. II, Bk. XCI.)

Perhaps, and even *probably,* this great man here had Locke in mind, whose philosophy never knew how to leave behind material ideas. He always speaks to us of *broken bridges,* of *locked doors* (Bk. II, chap. XXIX, § 9 and 10), of *paralysis,* of *St Vitus dance* (Ibid., § 11.), and *tortures* (Ibid., § 12.).

x Hume, in fact, said that "there is no method of reasoning more common and *yet more blameable,* alas, in philosophical dispute, to endeavour the refutation of any hypothesis, by a pretence of its dangerous consequences to religion and morality. When any opinion leads to absurdities it is certainly false, but it is *not certain* that an opinion is false because it is of dangerous consequence." (*Essays [into Human Understanding* (London 1758)], Section VIII, *Of the Liberty and Necessity,* p. 105.)

Here one can admire the morality of these philosophers! *It is not certain,* Hume tells us (for his conscience prevents him from saying more about it) and nevertheless he goes ahead, and with full deliberation risks deceiving men and injuring them. It must be admitted that the probabilism of these philosophers is more dangerous than that of theologians.

xi With the permission of the speaker, this thought certainly occurred to Locke's mind; but he repressed it by a new crime against good sense and morality by maintaining that no man has the right, by presenting himself as the rule, to regard others as corrupted in their principles; *for,* he says, this *is a very pretty method of arguing, and a short cut to infallibility.* (Bk. I, chap. III, § 20.

Certainly, he must have had a great fear of infallibility, to permit himself to be led to such extremities. To console the reader for so many sophisms, I am going to cite for him a veritable oracle pronounced by the illustrious Malebranche: *Infallibility is included in the idea of any divine society.* (*Recherche de la vérité*, Bk. III, chap. I, p. 194.) What wisdom! This is a characteristic of invincible light; it is a solar ray that penetrates the very eyelids lowered to repulse it. Locke was always led by his dominant prejudice; loyal to the principle that rejects all authority, he could not pardon those *such, who are careful (AS THEY CALL IT) to principle children well, (and few there be who have not a set of those principles for them, which they believe in), instil into the unwary, and as yet unprejudiced understanding, (for white paper receives any characters,) those doctrines they would have them retain and profess.* (Bk. I, chap. II, § 22. [the "editor's" small capitals]) We see who and what he was aiming at here, and why he has become the idol of the enemies of any *set of principles.* (Editor's note.)

xii *All teaching and learning that involves the use of reason proceeds from pre-existent knowledge.* (Aristotle *Posterior Analytics* I.i. [Trans. Hugh Tredennick, Loeb Classical Library 1960])

xiii *... logical arguments, whether syllogistic or inductive; both effect instruction by means of facts already recognized.* (Ibid.)

xiv *Before the process of relation is completed or the conclusion drawn, we should presumably say that in one sense the fact is understood ...* (Ibid.)

xv "Sensible triangle." (Aristotle *Prior Analytics* II.21 [Trans. Hugh Tredennick, Loeb Classical Library, 1938)

xvi *Unless we make this distinction, we shall be faced with the dilemma reached in the* Meno: *either one can learn nothing, or one can only learn what is already known.* (*Posterior Analytics* I.i. [Loeb])

xvii *Syllogism indeed will be possible without these conditions, but not demonstration.* (Ibid., I.ii.)

xviii *... demonstrative knowledge must proceed from premises which are true, primary, immediate, better known than, prior to, and causative of the conclusion.* (Ibid., I.ii.)

"All reasoning terminates in first principles: all evidence is ultimately intuitive." (Dr Beattie's *On Truth*, 8, chap. 2.)

xix *... for it is impossible to traverse an infinite series.* (*Posterior Analytics* I.iii. [Loeb])

xx *... it is necessary not merely to know the primary premises ... beforehand, but to know them better than the conclusion.* (Ibid., I.ii. [Loeb]) Oh desperate language!

xxi *... we hold not only that scientific knowledge is possible, but that there is a definite first principle of knowledge.* (Ibid., I.iii. [Loeb])

xxii *That which is in itself necessarily true and must be thought to be so [is not a hypothesis nor a postulate] for demonstration is concerned not with external but with internal discourse; and it is always possible to object to the former, but not always possible to do so to the latter.* (Ibid., I.x [Loeb])

xxiii *All the sciences share with one another in the use of the common principles. By "common principles" I mean what they use for the purpose of demonstration ... not what they prove.* (Ibid. I.xi [Loeb])

xxiv *With all those things which we stamp with the seal of "absolute" etc.* (Plato *Phaedo* 75d.)

xxv *A knowledge (which is) within.* (Ibid.)

xxvi *There is no judgement of truth in the senses* (St Augustine). Fénelon, who cites this passage (*Maximes des Saints*, art. xxviii.) says as well in speaking of this Father: "If an enlightened man were to assemble from St Augustine's books all the sublime truths that he scattered at random, such carefully chosen extracts would be very superior to the meditations of Descartes, although these meditations were the greatest effort among the reflections of this philosopher ... for whom I have a great esteem." (*Oeuvres spirituelles*, 1:234–5.)

xxvii I approve the speaker's *perhaps*. The reputation of a mathematician is undoubtedly the most independent of the rank his country holds among nations; however I do not believe it is absolutely independent. For example, I understand very well that Kepler and Newton are well known everywhere, but I will never believe that the latter would have shown with the same brilliance if he had been born in some corner of Germany, or that the former would not have enjoyed even more striking renown if he had been *Sir John Kepler* and had been buried beside kings under the marble of Westminster Abbey.

It would also be necessary, if it was a question of another book, to account for the power of style, which is a veritable magic. I would certainly like to know what success the *Esprit des lois* would have known if it had been written in the Latin of Suarez, or what would have been that of Suarez's book, *De legibus et legislatore*, written with Montesquieu's pen. (Editor's note)

xxviii *Lycée*, Vol. XXIII. art. "Helvétius." – It is to be regretted that a man as admirable as La Harpe was so infatuated with Locke, one knows neither why nor how, to the point of declaring to us *ex cathedrâ* that *this philosopher reasons as Racine versified*; both recalling perfection ...; *that Locke is the most powerful logician who ever existed, and that his arguments are only the corollaries of mathematics.* (Why not theorems?) *Lycée*, Vol. XXIII, art. "Helvétius," and Vol. XXIV, art. "Diderot." Leibniz is not so enthusiastic. *He is not very satisfied* with Locke; *he finds him tolerable for young people only,* and just up to a certain point, *since he rarely penetrates to the bottom of his material.* (*Epistle ad Kortoltum, Opera omnia,* [6 vols. Geneva 1768], 5:304.)

I do not want to dwell on this opposition; La Harpe's memory deserves respect. It must be noted, however, that Locke is precisely the philosopher who *reasoned* least, taking this word in its most rigorous sense. His philosophy is all negative or descriptive, and certainly the least *rational* of all.

xxix   *"Locke, the Pascal of the English who could not read Pascal ..."* (Why not? Didn't Locke know how to read in 1688?) *"However Locke, aided by his good sense, always said:* Define the terms." (Voltaire's notes on Pascal's *Pensées*, (Paris: Renouard [1803]), p. 289.)

In the Port-Royal *Logic* one can read a piece on definitions that is quite superior to all that Locke could write on this subject. (Part I, chaps. xii and xiii.) ... *However Voltaire could not read the Port-Royal Logic;* moreover, he would not derogate from the general rule adopted by him and his whole phalanx, of never praising any but foreign knowledge. He certainly paid in good coin for the foolish idolatry with which his country honoured him!

xxx   At the moment, this authority, which seems to have reflected sufficiently on all the questions that concern its origin and its powers, must seriously ask itself about the cause of this prodigious disfavour that surrounds it, and of which Europe has seen such striking testimony in the famous case that agitated the English Parliament in 1813 with respect to Catholic emancipation. It will see that the man who knows perfectly in the depths of his conscience, both Locke and his works, has the right to despise and to hate all that comes only from this man. This authority has only to attach itself to something higher and immediately it will recover the place that belongs to it. While waiting, we can console it by an attendance full of esteem and love for the disgust with which it is covered in England. This seems to be a paradox, and yet nothing is more true. *It can no longer dispense with us.*

xxxi   Locke so expressed himself in the indicated passage. ... *it was no small advantage to those who affected to be masters and teachers, to make this the principle of principles* – that principles must not be questioned. *For, having once established this tenet* – that there are innate principles, (what an overturning of all logic! what a horrible confusion of ideas!) *it put their followers upon a necessity of receiving some doctrines as such; and which was to take them off the use of their own reason and judgement.* (A Protestant song which the Protestants themselves will soon scoff at) ... *in which posture of blind credulity, they might be more easily governed by, and made useful to some sort of men who had the skill and office to principle and to guide them ... and to make [them] ... SWALLOW that for an innate principle which may serve his purpose who teacheth them.* (Bk. I, chap. IV, § 24.)

We saw earlier (see p. 356) how this expression SWALLOW was highly pleasing to Locke's fine ear.

xxxii   It was not a question of a chapter; these are the words that Locke wrote beside the 25th division of the third chapter of his first book, where we in fact read: *Whence the opinion of innate principles?* In putting all his verbs in the past tense, he seems to have wanted to direct his attacks more particularly against Catholic teaching, and as usual good sense and good faith immediately abandoned him; but looking at the matter more closely and considering his whole argument, we see that he attacked all spiritual authority. This especially is what led the Bishop of Worcester *to box* publicly with Locke, but without exciting any interest; for in the bottom of his heart:

Who could tolerate a Gracchi

While complaining about a seditious people.   (Editor's note.)

xxxiii One can read Wren's letter in the *European Magazine* 18 (August 1790): 91. It was recalled, a little while ago, in an English newspaper where we read that according to the judgement of this celebrated architect: "it is not practicable to make a simple room so capacious with pews and galleries as to hold 2,000 persons and both to hear distinctly and to see the preacher." (*The Times*, 30 November 1812, n° 8761.)

Wren decided that the voice of an English orator could not make itself understood farther than fifty feet to the front, thirty feet to the side, and twenty feet behind him; and, he said, *even this was on condition that the preacher pronounce distinctly and that he prolong his final sounds.* (*European Magazine*, Ibid.)

Seventh Dialogue

The Chevalier

This time, Senator, I hope you will keep your promise, and tell us something about war.

The Senator

I am quite ready to do so, for this is a subject on which I have meditated a great deal. I have been thinking about war ever since I began to think; this terrible subject has seized my full attention, and yet I have never gone into it deeply enough.

The first thing I am going to tell you will undoubtedly astonish you, but for me it is an incontestable truth: *"Given man with his reason, his feelings, and his affections, there is no way of explaining how war is humanly possible."* This is my well considered opinion. Somewhere La Bruyère describes this great human absurdity with all his characteristic energy.[i] It was many years ago when I read this piece, but I still recall it perfectly. He insists strongly on the folly of war; yet, the more foolish it is, the less explicable.

The Chevalier

However it seems to me that one can say quite briefly: *kings order you, and you must march.*

The Senator

Oh! Not at all, my dear Chevalier, I assure you that this is not the case. Every time that a man who is not an absolute fool presents you with a question he considers very problematic after giving it careful thought, distrust those quick answers that come to the mind of someone who has considered it only briefly or not at all. These answers are usually simplistic views lacking in consistency, which explain nothing, or which do not bear examination. Sovereigns command effectively and in a lasting way only within the circle of things acknowledged by opinion, and they are not the ones who trace the circle of opinion. In every country there are much less shocking things than war that a sovereign would never venture to command. Remember the joke that you told me one day about a nation *that has an academy of sciences, an astronomical observatory, and a faulty calendar.* More seriously, you also told me that you heard one of this nation's statesmen say *that he would not be at all sure about innovating on this last issue; and that under the last government, so distinguished by liberal ideas* (as they say today), *they never dared undertake this change.* You even asked me what I thought about it. Be that as it may, you see that there are subjects much less essential than war on which the authorities sense that they must not commit themselves; and note carefully, I beg you, that is not a question of explaining the *possibility* of war, but its *facility.*

To cut beards off and to shorten robes, Peter the Great needed all the strength of his invincible personality; but to lead innumerable legions onto the field of battle, even at a time *when he was being defeated to learn how to defeat,* he, like any other ruler, only needed to say the word. Yet there is in man, despite his immense degradation, an element of love drawing him towards his fellowmen; compassion is as natural to him as breathing. By what inconceivable magic is he always ready, at the first beat of the drum, to cast off this sacred character and to be off without resistance, often even with a certain elation (which also has its own peculiar character), to blow to pieces on the battlefield a brother who has never offended him, and who on his side advances to do the same thing to him if he can? I could conceive of a national war, but how many such wars have there been? One in a thousand years, perhaps; for the rest, among civilized nations especially, who reflect on it and know what they are doing, I confess I don't understand it at all. It could be said that *glory explains everything*; but, in the first place, glory only goes to the leaders; in the second place, this only evades the difficulty, for then I must ask precisely why this extraordinary glory is attached to war.

I have often had a vision that I would like to share with you. I imagine that a stranger to our planet comes here for some *sufficient* reason,[1] and talks to one of us about the order that reigns in this world. Among the curious things that are recounted to him, he is told that corruption and vices, about which he has been fully informed, in certain circumstances require men to die by the hand of men, and that we restrict this right to kill legally to the executioner and to the soldier. He will also be told: "The first brings death to convicted and condemned criminals, and these executions

---

[1]   [Most likely an allusion to Voltaire's *Micromégas*.]

are so rare fortunately, that one of these ministers of death suffices for each province. As for soldiers, there are never enough of them for they kill without restraint, and they always kill honest men. Of these two professional *killers*, the soldier and the executioner, the one is greatly honoured, and has always been so honoured among the peoples that up to the present have inhabited this planet to which you have come. The other, on the contrary, has just as generally been declared infamous. Can you guess on which one the condemnation falls?"

Surely this travelling spirit would not hesitate for a moment; he would accord the executioner all the praise that you could not refuse him the other day, Count, despite all our prejudices, when you spoke to us of this *gentleman*, as Voltaire would have said. "This sublime being," he would have told us, "is the cornerstone of society; since crime has become habitual on your earth, and since it can only be arrested by punishment, if you deprive the world of the executioner all order will disappear with him. Moreover, what greatness of soul, what noble disinterestedness must necessarily be assumed to exist in a man who devotes himself to functions that are undoubtedly worthy of respect, but which are so trying and contrary to your nature! For, since I have been among you, I have noticed that it distresses you to kill a chicken in cold blood. I am therefore persuaded that opinion surrounds him with all the honour that he needs and that is justly due him. As for the soldier, he is, all things considered, an agent of cruelty and injustice. How many obviously just wars have there been? How many obviously unjust! How many individual injustices, horrors, and useless atrocities! So I imagine that opinion among you has very justly poured as much shame on the head of the soldier as it has poured glory on that of the impartial executor of the judgement of sovereign justice."

You know what the situation really is, gentlemen, and how mistaken the spirit would be! In fact, the serviceman and the executioner occupy the two extremities of the social scale, but at quite the opposite ends from this fine theory. There is nothing so noble as the first, nothing so abject as the second; I would not be indulging in a play on words by saying that their functions only approach each other in diverging; they touch each other in the same way that in a circle 1° touches 360°, precisely because they cannot be farther apart.[2] The soldier is so noble that he even ennobles what public opinion regards as the most ignoble, since he can exercise the functions of an executioner without debasing himself, provided however

---

[2] It seems to me, without being able to prove it, that this happy comparison was made by the Marquis de Mirabeau, who used it somewhere in his *Ami des hommes* [Avignon 1756].

that he only executes his fellow soldiers and that he uses only his weapons for this purpose.

The Chevalier

Ah, what you have said is important, my dear friend! In any country where, for any reason whatsoever, a soldier is ordered to execute criminals who are not soldiers, in a twinkling of an eye, and without apparent reason, all the glory that surrounds the serviceman will disappear. He will still be feared, not doubt, for any man who is always armed with a good rifle merits great respect; but the indefinable aura of honour will be irretrievably lost. The officer will no longer be anything as an officer; if he is a man of birth and merit, he can still be well thought of, *despite* his rank rather than *because* of it. He would ennoble it instead of being ennobled by it; and if his rank provides a large salary, he would enjoy the consideration of wealth, but never that of nobility. As you have said, Senator, *"provided however that he only executes his fellow soldiers and that he uses only his weapons for this purpose."* Moreover we must add: *provided that it is a question of a military crime*; once it is a question of a *common* crime, it is a matter for the executioner.

The Count

In fact, this is the custom. Ordinary courts having jurisdiction over civil crimes, soldiers guilty of such crimes are sent before them. However, if it pleased the sovereign to order otherwise, I am far from thinking it certain that the character of the soldier would suffer by it. Nevertheless we are all three agreed on the other two conditions, and we do not doubt that his character would be irreversibly tarnished if he were ordered to shoot a simple civilian or to put his comrade to death by burning or hanging. For maintenance of the honour and discipline of any group or association, privileged rewards have less effect than privileged punishments. The Romans, who were at once the most sensitive and the most warlike people in antiquity, came up with a singular idea with respect to simple correction in military discipline. Believing that there could be no discipline without a stick, and nevertheless not wanting to debase either the one who strikes or the one who is struck, they thought of consecrating military beatings in a certain way. For this purpose they chose the wood that was the most useless for anything else, the vine branch, and designated it uniquely for the punishment of soldiers. The vine branch in the hand of the centurion was the sign of his authority and the instrument of non-capital corporal punishment. In general, among the Romans the military beating was a penalty acknowledged by the law.[3] However no non-military person could be struck with a vine branch, and no other wood other than that of the vine could be used to strike a soldier. I don't know why some similar idea has never occurred to a modern sovereign. If I were consulted on this matter, my thought would not go back to the vine, since servile imitations are worthless; I would propose the laurel.

The Chevalier

Your idea enchants me, the more so in that I think it quite capable of being put into execution. I assure you that I would very willingly present to His Imperial Majesty a plan for a large greenhouse, which would be established in the capital, and devoted exclusively to growing the laurel required to furnish sticks for all the junior officers in the Russian army. This greenhouse would be under the supervision of an officer in charge, a Chevalier of St George of at least second class, who would carry the title of *high inspector of the laurel greenhouse*; the plants would be cared for, worked, and cut by old veterans of unblemished reputations. The model stick, of which all others would have to be rigorous copies, would be kept in the war office in a silver-gilt case; each stick would be suspended from the junior officer's buttonhole by a ribbon of St George. And over the door of the greenhouse one would read: *This is my wood, which produces my foliage*. In truth, this nonsense would not be the least stupid. The only thing that embarrasses me a bit is that the corporals ...

The Senator

My dear young friend, any genius whatsoever, in any country there might be, would find it impossible, without stopping for breath, to produce a *Code* without a single fault, even if it were only a question of a *stick code*. So, while you allow your idea to ripen a bit, permit me to continue.

Although the military is in itself dangerous to the well being and liberty of every nation, because the motto of this profession will always be, more or less, that of Achilles, *Jura nego mihi nata* [I claim that for me no laws exist], nevertheless the nations most jealous of their liberties have never thought differently than the rest of mankind about the pre-eminence of the

---

[3] The law even gave it a mild enough name, since it called it simply the *warning with the stick*, whereas it named whipping a *punishment*, which had something dishonourable about it. *The admonition of clubs, the admonitions of rods*. (Callistratus, in lege vii, digesta de poenis. [Callistratus was third-century Roman jurist whose work was used in putting together the *Digest*.])

military profession.[4] Antiquity thought no differently than we do on this point; it is one of those on which men have always agreed and always will.[ii] So this is the problem I want to pose for you: *Explain why the most honourable thing in the world, according to the judgement of all of humanity, without exception, has always been the right to shed innocent blood innocently?* If you look at the matter closely, you will see that there is something mysterious and inexplicable in the extraordinary value that men have always attached to military glory, the more so in that, if we took into account only theory and human reasoning, we would be led to directly opposite ideas. So it is not a question of explaining the possibility of war by the glory that surrounds it, but of explaining this glory itself, which is not easy.

I would also like to share you with another idea on the same subject. We have been told a thousand and one times that, since nations are in a state of nature with respect to one another, they can only settle their differences by war. Since I am in a questioning mood, I will also ask: *why has every nation remained in a state of nature with respect to every other without ever making a single try, a single attempt, to break out of it?* According to the foolish doctrines in which we were nurtured, there was a time when men did not live in society; this imaginary state was ridiculously called the *state of nature.* They add that men, having wisely weighed the advantages of the two states, chose the one that we see ...

The Count

Allow me to interrupt you for a moment to share with you an argument that comes to my mind against this doctrine, which you have so rightly called *foolish.* The savage holds so strongly to his most brutal habits that nothing can break him of them. You have undoubtedly seen, at the head of the *Discourse on the Inequality of Conditions,* the engraving based on the true or false anecdote of the Hottentot who returns to his fellows. Rousseau little suspected that this frontispiece was a powerful argument against his book. The savage sees our arts, laws, sciences, luxuries, pleasures of every kind, and especially our superiority, from which he cannot hide and yet which would excite some desires in hearts that were capable of it; but all this does not even tempt him, and continually *he returns to his fellows.* If the savage of our own time, knowledgeable about both states and being able to compare them daily in certain countries, remains resolutely in his own, how can it be imagined that the primitive savage emerged from his by means of

---

[4] *Everywhere where men are religious, warlike, and obedient, how can they not by right be full of good hope?* (Xenophon *Hellenica* III.4.18.). In fact, these three points include everything.

deliberation to pass into another state of which he had no knowledge? Therefore society is as old as man; therefore the savage is and can only be a degraded and punished man. In truth, I see nothing as clear for unadulterated good sense.[iii]

The Senator

You are preaching to the converted, as the saying goes, but I thank you for your argument; one never has too many weapons against error. But to return to what I was just saying, if man passed from *the state of nature,* in the common usage of the term, to the state of civilization, either by deliberation or *by accident* (I am still speaking the language of the foolish), why have nations not had as much wit or luck as individuals, and how is that they have never agreed to establish a general society to bring an end to national quarrels in the same way that men have agreed to establish a national sovereign in order to bring an end to the quarrels of individuals? It is easy to ridicule *the impracticable peace of the Abbé Saint-Pierre*[5] (and I agree that it was impracticable), but I ask why this is so, why nations have been unable to raise themselves to the social state like individuals, and how it is that reasoning Europe, above all, has never attempted anything of this kind?

In particular, I would address this same question to believers with still more confidence. How is it that God, who is the author of the society of individuals, has never permitted man, his cherished creature who has received the divine attribute of perfectibility, even to attempt to elevate himself to a society of nations? Every possible argument for showing that such a society is impossible militates in the same way against a society of individuals. The argument drawn principally from the impracticable universality that would have to be given to the great sovereign holds no force, since it is false that it would have to include the whole world. Nations are sufficiently distinguished and divided by rivers, seas, mountains, and religions, and especially by languages that have a greater or lesser affinity. If even a certain number of nations agreed together to enter *the state of civilization,* this would already be a great step in favour of humanity. Other nations, you might say, would attack them. Well, so what? They would always be more peaceful among themselves and stronger than the others, which would be sufficient. Perfection is not at all necessary on this point; it would already be a great deal even to approach it. I cannot persuade myself that nothing of this sort had ever been attempted, if it were not for an occult and terrible law demanding human blood.

---

[5]   [In 1713 Saint-Pierre published a *Projet de paix perpétuelle.*]

The Count

You took it as an undeniable fact that this *civilization of nations* has never been attempted, yet in truth is has often been tried and even stubbornly – true without it being known that this is what was being attempted, which was a circumstance very favourable for its success – and it has even been close to succeeding, at least in so far as the imperfection of our nature allows. However men made mistakes: they took one thing for another, and everything failed, from all appearances, because of this occult and terrible law of which you spoke.

The Senator

I would ask you several questions if I were not afraid of losing the thread of my ideas. So please observe, I beg you, a phenomenon well worth your attention, which is that the profession of arms, as we might think or fear if we were not instructed by experience, does not in the least tend to degrade, brutalize, or harden those who follow it – on the contrary, it tends to improve them. The most honest man is usually the honest soldier, and for my part I have always been partial, as I told you before, to military good sense, which I very much prefer to the long-windedness of businessmen. In the ordinary commerce of life, military men are more likeable, easier to get along with, and often, it appears to me, more obliging than other men. In the midst of political conflicts they are generally intrepid defenders of the old maxims, and the most dazzling sophistries are usually defeated by their uprightness. They willingly occupy themselves with useful things and useful knowledge, such as political economy, for example. Perhaps the only work antiquity has left us on this topic was by a soldier, Xenophon,[6] and the first work of this kind that was produced in France was by another soldier, Marshal Vauban.[7] Among soldiers, religion is allied to honour in a remarkable way, and even when religion reproaches them gravely for their conduct, they do not refuse it the aid of their swords, if it needs them. Much is said about the *licence of camps*. No doubt it is great, but usually soldiers do not find vices in the camps; they carry them there. A moral and austere people always furnishes excellent soldiers, terrible only on the battlefield. Virtues, even piety, combine very well with military courage; far from enfeebling the warrior, these virtues exalt him. St Louis was not inconvenienced by the hairshirt beneath his armour. Even Voltaire agreed

---

[6] [Xenophon was the author of a work called *Oeconomicus* (Economics).]

[7] [In 1707 Vauban wrote *Projet d'une dîme royale*, in which he advocated a single tax as fairer than existing taxes. The work annoyed Louis XIV and was suppressed.]

in good faith that *an army ready to die in obedience to God would be invincible*.[8] You have no doubt learned from Racine's letters that when he was with Louis XIV's army in 1692, he never attended Mass in the camp without seeing some musketeer communicating with the greatest edification.[iv]

Look up in Fénelon's *Oeuvres spirituelles* the letter he wrote to an officer among his friends. Heartbroken at not being employed in the army, as he had flattered himself he should, this man had been led, probably by Fénelon, into the ways of the highest perfection: he had achieved *pure love* and *the death* [of self] *of the Mystics*. Now perhaps you would think that the tender and loving soul of the *swan of Cambrai* would find compensations for his friend in the scenes of carnage in which he no longer had to take part; that he would say: *After all, you are lucky, you are no longer seeing the horrors of war and the frightful spectacle of all the crimes that it involves.* He carefully avoids such cowardly considerations; on the contrary, he consoles him and grieves with him. He sees in this privation an overwhelming misfortune, a bitter cross, completely suitable for detaching his friend from the world.[v]

What do we say of this other officer, to whom Madame Guyon wrote that he must not worry if he sometimes had to miss Mass on working days, *especially in the army?*[vi] The writers from whom we have these anecdotes, however, lived in a passably warlike century, it seems to me. In short, nothing in this world agrees better than the religious spirit and the military spirit.

The Chevalier

I am very far from contradicting this truth. However, it must be admitted that if virtue does not harm military courage, it can at least be bypassed by the latter, since we have seen, in certain periods, legions of atheists obtain prodigious successes.

The Senator

Why not, I ask you, if these atheists are fighting other atheists? However allow me to continue. Not only does the military profession ally itself very well with morality in general, but what is quite extraordinary is that it does not in the least weaken those gentle virtues that seem to be most opposed to the profession of arms. The gentlest characters love war, desire war, and go to war with passion. At the first call, this likeable young man, brought

---

[8] It was with respect to the valiant and pious Marquis de Fénelon, killed at the Battle of Rocoux, that Voltaire made this admission. (*Histoire de Louis XV*, Vol. I, chap. XVIII.)

up with a horror of violence and blood, rushes from his father's house, his weapons at hand, and seeks on the battlefield what he calls *the enemy*, without yet knowing what *an enemy* is. Yesterday he would have been ill if he had accidentally killed his sister's canary; tomorrow you will see him climbing a pile of cadavers *to see farther*, as Charron said. The blood flowing on all sides only inspires him to shed his own and that of others; he inflames himself by degrees until he reaches *an enthusiasm for carnage*.

The Chevalier

You have not exaggerated. Before my twenty-fourth birthday I had seen *the enthusiasm of carnage* three times; I have experienced it myself, and I especially recall a terrible moment when I would have put an entire army to the sword if I had been able.

The Senator

But if, while we are speaking here, someone asked you to grab a white dove with the cold-bloodedness of a cook, then ...

The Chevalier

What! You make me sick at heart!

The Senator

This is precisely the phenomenon that I was just telling you about. The terrifying spectacle of carnage does not harden the true warrior. Amid the blood he sheds, he is humane, just as the wife is chaste in the transports of love. Once he has put his sword back in its scabbard, sacred humanity recovers its rights, and perhaps the most exalted and most generous feelings are to be found among soldiers. Remember, Chevalier, France's great century. It was a time when religion, valour, and science had been put in equilibrium, so to speak, and when the result was the beautiful character that everyone unanimously hailed as the model of European character. If the first element is taken away, the ensemble, that is to say all its beauty, disappears. What has not been noticed enough, is how necessary religion is for the whole, and the role that it plays even where frivolous observers might have thought it foreign. The divine spirit, which has particularly blessed Europe, has even mitigated the scourge of eternal justice, and *European war* will always have a special place in annals of the world. Undoubtedly Europeans killed, burned, ravaged, and even, if you wish, committed thousands of useless crimes; but nevertheless they began war in the month of May and ended it in the month of December; they slept under canvas; soldiers fought only soldiers. Whole nations were never at war, and all that was weak was sacred amidst the dreary scenes of this devastating plague.

It was a magnificent spectacle though to see all the sovereigns of Europe, restrained by I don't know what imperious moderation, never asking of their peoples, even in the moment of greatest peril, all that it would have been possible to obtain from them. They used men gently, and all of them, led by an invisible force, avoided striking killing blows against the sovereignty of the enemy: glory, honour, and eternal praise to the law of love proclaimed unceasingly at the centre of Europe. No nation triumphed over the other; antique war no longer existed except in books or among peoples *seated in the shadow of death*. Fierce wars were ended by a province, a city, often even a few villages, changing masters. Airborne shells avoided royal palaces; more than once dances and spectacles served as interludes for the combatants. The invited enemy officers came to feasts to speak laughingly of the battle that must take place the next day, and even in the horrors of the most bloody clashes, the accents of pity and the formulas of civility greeted the ears of the dying. At the first sign of action, vast hospitals came into being everywhere; medicine, surgery, and pharmacy sent their numerous experts. In the middle of them arose the genius of *St John of God*, of *St Vincent de Paul*, greater, stronger, more than human, constant as faith, active like hope, able as love. All the living victims were collected, treated, and consoled, every wound cared for by the hand of science and charity! ... A little while ago, Chevalier, you spoke of legions of *atheists* who achieved prodigious successes; I believe that if one could regiment tigers you would see even greater marvels. If you look closely at war, never will Christianity appear more sublime, more worthy of divinity, and better suited for men. Moreover, when you said *legions of atheists*, you did not mean it literally; nevertheless suppose these legions to be as bad as they could be, do you know how they could be defeated most easily? It would be by opposing to them the principle diametrically opposed to that by which they are constituted. You can be sure that *legions of atheists* could not stand against *burning legions*.

In short, gentlemen, the functions of the soldier are terrible, but of necessity they belong to a great law of the spiritual world, and we must not be astonished that all the nations of the world have agreed in seeing in this scourge something more particularly divine than others. You may believe that it is not without a great and profound reason that the title GOD OF HOSTS shines forth from all the pages of Holy Scripture.[vii] Guilty mortals, and unhappy because we are guilty, we ourselves make necessary all physical evils, but especially war. Men usually lay the blame on rulers, and nothing is more natural: Horace said playfully in this regard:

By the madness of kings peoples are punished.

J.-B. Rousseau said more seriously and more philosophically:

> It is the wrath of kings that arms the earth,
> It is the wrath of heaven that arms kings.[9]

Notice, moreover, that this law of war, already so terrible, is nevertheless only a chapter in the general law that hangs over the world.

In the vast domain of living things, there reigns an obvious violence, a kind of prescribed rage that arms all creatures to their common doom. As soon as you leave the inanimate kingdom, you find the decree of violent death written on the very frontiers of life. You feel it already in the vegetable kingdom: from the immense catalpa to the humblest herb, how many plants *die*, and how many are *killed*! As soon as you enter the animal kingdom, the law suddenly becomes frighteningly obvious. A power at once hidden and palpable shows itself continually occupied in demonstrating the principle of life by violent means. In each great division of the animal kingdom, it has chosen a certain number of animals charged with devouring the others; thus, there are insects of prey, birds of prey, fish of prey, and quadrupeds of prey. There is no instant of time when some living thing is not being devoured by another.

Above all these numerous animal species is placed man, whose destructive hand spares nothing that lives. He kills to nourish himself, he kills to clothe himself, he kills to adorn himself, he kills to attack, he kills to defend himself, he kills to instruct himself, he kills to amuse himself, he kills to kill: a superb and terrible king, he needs everything and nothing resists him. He knows how many barrels of oil he can get for himself from the head of a shark or a whale; with his sharp pins he mounts for museum display the elegant butterfly he caught in flight on the summit of Mount Blanc or Chimborazo;[10] he stuffs the crocodile and embalms the hummingbird; at his command, the rattlesnake dies in preserving fluids to show itself intact to a long line of observers. The horse carrying its master to the tiger hunt struts under the skin of this same animal. Man demands everything at the same time; he takes from the lamb its entrails to make his harp resound, from the whale its bones to stiffen the corset of the young girl, from the wolf its most murderous tooth to polish his pretty works of art, from the elephant its tusks to make a child's toy; his tables are covered with corpses. The philosopher can even discover how this permanent carnage is provided for and ordained in the great scheme of things. But will this law stop at man? Undoubtedly not. Yet who will exterminate him who

---

[9] [*Odes*, Livre IV, Ode VIII, "A la paix," *Oeuvres*, 1:312 (Geneva: Slatkine Reprints 1972 [1820]).]

[10] [Chimborazo in a volcano in the Andes of Ecuador.]

exterminates everything else? Man! It is man himself who is charged with slaughtering man.

But how can he accomplish this law, he who is a moral and merciful being, who is born to love, who weeps for others as for himself, who finds pleasure in weeping and who even invents fictions to make himself weep, and finally, to whom it has been said that *whoever sheds blood unjustly, by man shall his blood be shed.*[11] It is war that accomplishes the *decree.* Do you not hear the *earth* itself crying out and demanding blood? The blood of animals does not satisfy it, nor even that of criminals spilled by the sword of the law. If human justice struck down all criminals, there would be no war, but it can catch only a few of them, and often it even spares them, without suspecting that this cruel humanity contributes to the necessity of war, especially if at the same time, another blindness no less stupid and no less blind works to extinguish atonement in the world. The *earth* did not cry out in vain; war breaks out. Man, suddenly seized by a *divine* fury foreign to both hatred and anger, goes to the battlefield without knowing what he intends nor even what he is doing. How can this horrible enigma be explained? Nothing is more contrary to man's nature, yet nothing is less repugnant to him; he does with enthusiasm what he holds in horror. Have you never noticed that men never disobey on the field of death. They might well massacre a Nerva or a Henry IV,[12] but what the most abominable tyrant, the most insolent butcher of human flesh, will never hear is: *We no longer want to serve you.* A revolt on the battlefield, an agreement to unite to repudiate a tyrant, is an unheard-of phenomenon. Nothing can resist the force that drags men into combat; an innocent murderer, a passive instrument in a formidable hand: *he plunges head first into the abyss he has dug for himself; he bestows and receives death without suspecting that he himself prepared it.*[13]

Thus, from the maggot up to man, the universal law of the violent destruction of living things is unceasingly fulfilled. The entire earth, perpetually steeped in blood, is nothing but an immense altar on which every living thing must be immolated without end, without restraint, without respite, until the consummation of the world, until the extinction of evil, until the death of death.[14]

---

[11] Genesis 9:6.

[12] [The Roman Emperor Nerva was assassinated in 98; King Henry IV of France was assassinated in 1610.]

[13] *Infixae sunt gentes in interitu, quem fecerent.* Psalm 9:16. [A more literal translation would read: "The nations have sunk into a pit of their own making."]

[14] *And the last enemy to be destroyed will be death.* 1 Corinthians 15:26.

But the anathema must strike down man most directly and most visibly: the exterminating angel circles this unhappy globe like the sun, and allows one nation a respite only to strike down others. When crimes, and especially crimes of a certain kind, accumulate to a designated point, the angel relentlessly quickens its tireless flight. Like a rapidly turning burning torch, the immense speed of his movement allows him to be simultaneously present everywhere in his formidable orbit. He strikes all the peoples of the earth at the same time. At other times, a minister of a precise and infallible vengeance, he pursues particular nations and bathes them in blood. Do not expect them to make any effort to escape or alleviate their sentence. It is as if we saw these great criminals, enlightened by their consciences, requesting the punishment and accepting it for the sake of their atonement. So long as they have any blood left they will come to offer it, and soon a *sparse youth* will get used to telling of these devastating wars caused by the crimes of their fathers.

War is therefore divine in itself, since it is a law of the world.

War is divine through its consequences of a supernatural nature, which are as much general as particular, consequences little known because little studied, but which are nevertheless incontestable. Who could doubt the great privileges to be found in death in battle? Who could believe that the victims of this dreadful sentence have shed their blood in vain? However this is not the time to insist on matters of this kind; our century is not yet mature enough to occupy itself with these matters. Let it keep to its physics, but we must nevertheless keep our eyes fixed on the invisible world that will explain everything.

War is divine in the mysterious glory that surrounds it, and in the no less inexplicable attraction that draws us to it.

War is divine in the protection granted to its great leaders, even the most venturesome, who are rarely struck down in battle, and then only when their reputation can no longer be increased and when their mission has been fulfilled.

War is divine by the way in which it breaks out. I do not want to excuse anyone too easily, but how many of those regarded as the immediate authors of war are themselves carried along by circumstances! At the precise moment caused by men and prescribed by justice, God himself comes forward to avenge the iniquity committed against him by the inhabitants of the world. *The earth, thirsty for blood,* as we heard a few days ago,[15] *opens its mouth to receive it and to keep it in its bosom until the time when it must render its account.*[viii] So let us applaud as loudly as you wish the worthy poet who cries out:

---

[15] See p. 48 above.

To the least interest that would divide
These blazing sovereigns,
Bellona [god of war] sustains the reply,
And saltpetre always announces
Their willing murderers.

However these very secondary considerations do not at all prevent us from looking to higher things.

War is divine in its results, which absolutely escape the speculations of human reason, since they can be totally different for two different nations, even though the war appears to have affected them both equally. There are wars that degrade nations, and degrade them for centuries; others exalt them, perfect them in all sorts of ways, and even soon replace momentary losses by a visible increase in population, which is something quite extraordinary. History often shows us the spectacle of a rich and growing population in the midst of the most murderous battles. There are also vicious wars, accursed wars, that the conscience recognizes better than reasoning; nations are mortally wounded by them, both in their power and in their character; then you will see even the victor degraded, impoverished, and groaning under his sad laurels, whereas in lands of the vanquished, in a short time, you will not find an unused workshop or plough.

War is divine by the indefinable force that determines success in it. It was surely without thinking, my dear Chevalier, when you repeated the other day the celebrated maxim that *God is always on the side of the big battalions*. I will never believe that it really came from the great man to whom it has been attributed;[16] perhaps he put forward this maxim in jest, or seriously in a limited and very true sense, for God in the temporal government of his Providence does not derogate, except in the case of miracles, from the general laws that he established for all time. Thus, just as two men are stronger than one, a hundred thousand men must be more powerful and effective than fifty thousand. When we ask God for victory, we do not ask him to derogate from the general laws of the world; that would be too much. However these laws can combine in a thousand different ways, and can permit victory in ways that cannot be foreseen. Undoubtedly three men are stronger than one; this general proposition is incontestable, but an able man can profit from certain circumstances, and a single Horatius will kill three Curiatii.[17] *A body with the greater mass has the greater momentum*; this is undoubtedly true if their speeds are

---

[16] Turenne.

[17] [In Roman legend, three Horatii brothers fought three Curiatii brothers, enemies of Rome. The survivor of the first three brothers managed to slay the three enemies who had killed his brothers.]

equal, but three parts of mass and two of speed are equal to three parts of speed and two of mass. In the same way, an army of 40,000 men is physically inferior to another army of 60,000, but if the first has more courage, experience, and discipline, it will be able to defeat the second, for it is more effective with less mass. This is what we can see on every page of history. Moreover, war always supposes a certain equality between the two sides. I never read of the Republic of Ragusa declaring war on the sultans, or that of Geneva on the kings of France. There is always a certain equilibrium in the political world, and (if certain rare, precise, and limited cases are excepted) it is not up to man to upset it. This is why coalitions are so difficult. It they were not, since politics is so little governed by justice, coalitions would be assembled every day to destroy particular powers; but such projects seldom succeed, and history shows even weak powers escaping from them with astonishing ease. When a too predominate power frightens the world, men are irritated at not being able to find any way to check it, and bitter reproaches are made against the egotism and immorality of cabinets that are preventing an alliance against the common enemy. This is the cry that was heard in the heyday of Louis XIV.[ix] But in the end these complaints are ill founded. A coalition between several sovereigns, based on a pure and disinterested morality, would be a miracle. God, who owes miracles to no one, and who never works them needlessly, uses two very simple means to re-establish political equilibrium: sometimes the giant overreaches itself, and sometimes a very inferior power puts a tiny obstacle in the giant's way, something imperceptible that subsequently grows in an unaccountable way until it becomes insurmountable, just as a small branch, stuck in the current of a river, can in the end produce a blockage that diverts it.

Starting, then, from this hypothesis of at least an approximate equilibrium, which is always the case, either because the two belligerent powers are equal or because the weakest has allies, how many unforeseen circumstances can upset the balance and can abort or promote the greatest projects despite all the calculations of human prudence! Four centuries before our era, geese saved the [Roman] Capitol; nine centuries into our era, under the Emperor Arnoulf, Rome was taken by a hare.[x] I doubt whether the one or the other counted on such allies or feared such enemies. History is full of inconceivable events that disconcerted the finest speculations. Moreover, if you take a more general look at the role that moral power plays in war, you will be convinced that nowhere does the divine hand make itself felt more vividly to man. One could say that this is a *department*, if you will allow me the term, whose direction Providence has reserved to itself, and in which man is only allowed to act in an almost mechanical way, since success here depends almost entirely on what he can least control. Never is he warned more often and more vividly of his own powerlessness and of the inexorable power ruling all things than in war. *The intrepid Spartan used to sacrifice to fear* (Rousseau somewhere expressed astonishment at this, I don't know why); Alexander also sacrificed to fear before the Battle of Arbela. Certainly these people were quite right. To correct this sensible devotion, it suffices to pray to *God that he deigns not to send us fear.* Fear! Charles V made good fun of this epitaph that he read in passing: *Here lies one who never felt fear.* What man has never known fear in his life? Who has never had occasion to respect, both in himself, and in those around him and in history, the all-powerful weakness of this passion, which often seems to have more power over us the fewer the reasonable causes for it. *So let us pray,* Chevalier, *for it is to you, if you please, that this discourse is addressed,* since you have called forth these reflections. Let us pray to God with all our strength that he spares us and our friends from fear, which is within his power, and which, in an instant, can ruin the most splendid military plans.

Do not be frightened by this word *fear,* for if you take it in its strictest sense, you can say that what it expresses is rare, and that it is shameful to be afraid of it. There is a womanish fear that cries out in flight; and this sort we are permitted, even ordered, to regard as quite unacceptable, although it is not at all an unknown phenomenon. There is another much more terrible fear that descends into the most courageous heart, freezes it, and persuades it that it is defeated. This is the frightful scourge that always hangs over armies. One day I put this question to a first-class soldier whom you both know: *Tell me, General, what is a lost battle? This is something I have never understood.* After a moment's silence, he replied: *I just don't know.* Then, after another moment, he added: *It is battle one believes one has lost.* Nothing is more true. One man fighting with another is defeated when he has been killed or brought to earth and the other remains standing. This is not the way it is with two armies; the one cannot be killed while the other remains on its feet. The forces swing back and forth as do the deaths, and especially since the invention of gunpowder has introduced more equality into the means of destruction, a battle is no longer lost materially, that is to say because there are more dead on one side than the other. It was Frederick II, who understood a little about these things, who said: *To win is to advance.* But who is the one who advances? It is the one whose conscience and countenance makes the other fall back. Do you recall, Count, that young soldier of your particular acquaintance who in one of his letters painted for you *that solemn moment when, without knowing why, an army senses itself advancing, as if it were sliding down an inclined plane.* I remember that you were struck by this phrase, which was a marvellous description of the crucial moment; but this moment is not at all a matter of reflection, nor is it, and this is particularly important to notice, in any way a question of numbers. Has the soldier *who slides forward* counted the dead? Opinion is so powerful in war that it can change the nature of the same event and even give it two different names, for no other reason than its own good pleasure. One general throws himself between two enemy armies, and writes to his court: *I have split him, he is lost.* The other writes to his court: *He has put himself between two fires, he is lost.* Which of the two is mistaken? The one who allows himself to be taken by the *cold goddess.* If all the circumstances, and the numbers especially, are at least approximately equal, show me a difference between the two sides that is not purely moral. The term *turn* is also one of those expressions that opinion *turns* in war, depending on how it is understood. Everyone knows the response the Spartan woman made to her son who complained of having too short a sword: *Step forward.* If the young man had been able to make himself heard on the battlefield and cried out to his mother: *I am turned*, the noble lady would not have failed to reply: *Turn the other.* It is imagination that loses battles.[18]

It is not even by any means always on the day that they take place that it is known whether they have been won or lost; it is on the next day, or often two or three days afterward. People talk a lot about battles without knowing what they are really like. In particular, they tend to consider them as occurring at one place, whereas they cover two or three leagues of country. They ask you seriously: *How is it that you don't know what happened in this battle, since you were there?* Whereas it is precisely the opposite that would often have to be said. Does the one on the right know what is happening on the left? Does he even know what is happening two paces from him?

I can easily imagine one of these frightful scenes. On a vast field covered with all the apparatus of carnage and seeming to shudder under the feet of men and horses, in the midst of fire and whirling smoke, dazed and carried away by the din of firearms and cannon, by voices that order, roar, and die away, surrounded by the dead, the dying, and mutilated corpses, seized in turn by fear, hope, and rage, by five or six different passions, what happens to a man? What does he see? What does he know after a few hours? What can he know about himself and others? Among this crowd of warriors who have fought the whole day, there is often not a single one, not even the general, who knows who the victor is. I will restrict myself to citing modern battles, famous battles whose memory will never perish, battles that have changed the face of Europe and that were only lost because such and such a man thought they were lost; they were battles where all circumstances being equal and without a drop of blood more being shed on either side, the other general could have had a *Te Deum* sung

---

[18] *And first of all to be conquered, the eyes.* (Tacitus.)

in his own country and forced history to record the opposite of what it will say. Yet, for heaven's sake, what period has ever seen moral power play a more astonishing role in war than our own times? Is there not real magic in what we have seen the last twenty years? Undoubtedly men of this epoch can cry out: *And what age has been more fertile in miracles?*

Without leaving the topic that now occupies us, has there been in this genre a single event contrary to the most obvious calculations of probability that we have not seen occur despite all the efforts of human prudence? Have we not even seen won battles lost? In any case, gentlemen, I don't want to exaggerate anything, for you know that I have a particular hatred of exaggeration, which is the falsehood of honest men. For the little that you find of exaggeration in what I have just said, I pass sentence without dispute, so much the more willingly in that I have no need to be correct in the fullest sense of the term. In general, I believe that battles are not won or lost physically. There is nothing rigid about this proposition, which can be subject to all the restrictions you judge convenient, provided that in your turn you agree with me (and this is something that no man can deny) that moral power has an immense effect in war, which is all that I need. So let us no longer speak of *big battalions*, Chevalier, for no idea, if we restrict it in the sense that I have just explained, is more deceptive and crude.

The Count

Your country, Senator, was not saved by *big battalions*, when at the beginning of the seventeenth century Prince Pozharsky and a horse merchant named Minin delivered it from an insupportable yoke. The honest merchant promised his goods and those of his friends in assisting Pozharsky, who promised his arms and his blood; they began with a thousand men, and they succeeded.[19]

The Senator

I am charmed that your memory recalls this episode, but the history of every nation is filled with similar facts demonstrating how the power of numbers can be produced, enhanced, weakened, or nullified by a host of circumstances beyond our control. As for our *Te Deums*, so frequent and so often misplaced, I willingly abandon them to you, Chevalier. If God resembled us, they would attract his anger, but he knows what we are and treats us according to our ignorance. In any case, although there are abuses

---

[19]   [In 1612, Kuzma Minin, a Nizhi-Novgorod merchant, and Prince Dimitry Pozharsky, a nobleman, provided the leadership that defeated a Polish force encamped in Moscow.]

in this matter as in all things human, the general custom is no less sound and praiseworthy.

We must always ask God for success and always thank him for it, since nothing in the world is more immediately dependent on God than war. Since here he restricts man's natural power, and since he loves to be called *the God of war*, there are all sorts of reasons for us to redouble our entreaties when we are struck by this terrible scourge. Christian nations have still more reason to be in tacit agreement, when their armies succeed, in expressing their thankfulness to *the God of hosts* by a *Te Deum*, for I do not think it would be possible to employ a more beautiful prayer to thank him for the victories that he gives. We owe this prayer to your church, Count.

The Count

Yes, it was born in Italy, from all appearances, and the title *Ambrosian hymn* would lead us to believe that it was exclusively the work of St Ambrose. However it is commonly enough believed, simply on the basis of tradition to be sure, that the *Te Deum* was *improvised*, if we may use that term, in a transport of religious fervour in Milan by the two great and holy doctors St Ambrose and St Augustine, an opinion that appears very probable. In fact, this inimitable canticle, preserved and translated by your church and by Protestant communions, presents not the least trace of labour and reflection. It is not a *composition*, it is an *effusion*; it is burning poetry, free of all metre, it is a divine dithyramb where enthusiasm, flying on its own wings, scorns all the resources of art. I doubt whether faith, love, and thanksgiving have ever spoken a truer and more penetrating language.

The Chevalier

I remember what you said in our last dialogue about the intrinsic character of different prayers. This is a subject I have never thought about, but you have made me eager to take *a course on prayers*. This will be a topic of erudition, for all nations have prayed.

The Count

This will be a very interesting course and it will not be pure erudition. Along the way you will find a host of interesting observations, for each nation's prayer is a kind of indicator that shows us with mathematical precision the nation's moral standing. The Hebrews, for example, sometimes gave God the name *father*; even the pagans made great use of this title. However when it comes to prayer, it is something else; you will not find in all of pagan antiquity, nor even in the Old Testament, a single example of man giving God the title *father* in speaking to him in prayer.

Again, why is it that, apart from the revelation of Moses, none in antiquity knew how to express repentance in their prayers? Like us, they knew remorse, since they had a conscience; their great criminals traversed earth and sea to find expiation and victims. They incensed themselves, they immersed themselves in water and blood, but they never experienced a *contrite heart*; they never knew how to ask pardon in their prayers. Ovid, like a thousand others, could put these words in the mouth of the outraged man who pardoned the criminal: *non quia tu dignus, sed quia mitis ego;*[20] but no one in antiquity could put these words in the mouth of a criminal talking to God. We seem to translate Ovid in the liturgy of the Mass when we say: *Non œstimator meriti, sed veniœ largitor admitte;*[21] and yet we are then saying what the entire human race could never learn to say without revelation, for men knew well that they could *irritate* God or *a god*, but not that they could *offend him*. The words *crime* and *criminal* are found in all languages, but *sin* and *sinner* belong to Christian language. For a similar reason, men have always called God *father*, which expresses a relationship of creation and power, but no man on his own could say *my father*, since this is a relationship of love foreign even to Mount Sinai, and which belongs only to Calvary.

One more observation: the barbarism of the Hebrew people is one of the favourite theses of the eighteenth century: it is not permitted to acknowledge that this people possessed any science whatsoever; they did not know the least truth in physics and astronomy; for them the earth was only a *flat plate*, the heavens only a *canopy*; its language was derived from another, and none derived from it; they never achieved either philosophy, arts, or literature; never until a very late date did foreign nations have the least knowledge of the books of Moses, and it is very false to think that superior truths disseminated in the writers of pagan antiquity came from that source. Let us obligingly agree to all this; how is it then that this nation was constantly sensible, interesting, touching, and very often even sublime and delightful in its prayers? In general, the Bible includes a host of prayers from which we have made a book in our own language; but it includes, moreover, the book of books in this genre, the book par excellence, the one without rival, the Book of Psalms.

The Senator

We have already had a long conversation with the Chevalier on the Book of Psalms; on this subject I complained to him, as I complain to yourself,

---

[20] [Not that you merit it but that I need it. *Heroides* VI.148.]

[21] [Not according to our merits but according to thy great mercy. Canon of the so-called St Pius V Mass. (Darcel ed.)]

about not understanding Slavonic, for the translation of the Psalms that we possess in this language is a masterpiece.

The Count

I don't doubt it; everyone agrees on this, and besides your opinion suffices for me. However on this point you must forgive my prejudices and unalterable views. Three languages were consecrated on Calvary: Hebrew, Greek, and Latin. I would like to stick with them; two languages for private prayer, one for church – that is enough. For the rest, I honour all the efforts that have been made in this respect in all nations; but you know well that we are scarcely likely to agree.

The Chevalier

I repeat to you what I said the other day to our dear Senator when talking about the same subject: I admire David a bit as I admire Pindar, on hearsay.

The Count

What are you saying, my dear Chevalier? Pindar has nothing in common with David. The first has himself taken care to inform us *that he spoke only to the learned, and that he cared little about being understood by the mass of his contemporaries, for whom he would not be upset to require interpreters.*[22] To understand this poet perfectly it is not enough to *pronounce* him or even to *sing* him; he must be *danced*. Someday I will tell you about this quite astonishing new *Dorian measure* that is prescribed by Pindar's impetuous muse.[23] However when you have come to understand him as perfectly as one can in our times, you will be little interested. Pindar's odes are the kind of corpses from which the spirit has retired forever. What do the *horses of Hièron* or the *mules of Agèsias* matter to you? What interest do you have in the nobility of his cities or their founders, in the miracles of the gods, the exploits of his heroes, or the love affairs of his nymphs? His charm belonged to certain times and places; no effort of the imagination can bring them to life again for us. There is no more Olympus, no more Elis, no more Alpheus; someone who thought they could find the Peloponnesus in Peru would be less ridiculous than the one who looked for it in the Morea.

---

[22] *Olympian Odes* II.152–4.

[23] *Fitting to the DORIAN MEASURE the voice of festive revellers.* (*Olympian Odes* III.9 [Trans. John Sandys, Loeb Classical Library 1915].)

David, on the other hand, defies time and place because he accorded nothing to place and circumstance; he sang only of God and his immortal truths. Jerusalem has not disappeared for us: *it is everywhere we are*; and it is David especially who makes it present to us. Therefore read the Psalms and read them unceasingly; not, if you take my advice, in our modern translations, which are too far from the source, but in the Latin version adopted in our church. I know that Hebraisms, always somewhat visible through the Vulgate, can be astonishing at first glance, for the Psalms as we read them today, although not translated directly from the original, are nevertheless derived from a version that was itself very close to the Hebrew, so that the difficulty is the same. However this difficulty quickly gives way to an honest effort. *Choose a friend who*, without knowing Hebrew, can nevertheless by attentive and repeated reading penetrate the spirit of a language that is incomparably more ancient than any other whose remnants survive. It is a language whose logical laconism is more cumbersome for us than the most hardy grammatical brevity, and which accustoms us especially to grasping the almost invisible Oriental link between ideas, a bounding genius that understands nothing of European nuances. You will see that the essential merit of the Vulgate translation is to have known how to be both close enough and far enough from the Hebrew; you will see how a syllable, a word, how some indescribable assistance lightly given to a phrase, brings forth first-order beauties before our eyes. The Psalms are a veritable *gospel preparation*, for nowhere is the spirit of prayer, which is that of God, more visible, and everywhere we read there the promises of all that we possess. The primary characteristic of these hymns is that they always pray. Even when the subject of a Psalm appears accidental and quite relative to some event in the life of the prophet-king, his genius always escapes this limited circle. He always generalizes since he sees everything within the immense unity of the power that inspires him; he turns all his thoughts and all his feelings into prayers. There is not a line that does not belong to all ages and to all men. He never needs that indulgence that permits enthusiasm to be obscure, and yet nevertheless when the eagle of Cedron takes its flight towards the clouds, your eye will be able to measure beneath him *more air* than Horace once saw under the swan of Dirce.[24] Sometimes he allows himself to be penetrated by the idea of the presence of God, and the most magnificent expressions crowd his mind:

Where can I hide from your spirit?
And where can I flee from your face?

---

[24] *Many a breeze lifts Dirce's swan*, etc. (Horace [*Odes* IV.2.25])

If I take the wings of the dawn,
if I dwell in the uttermost part of the sea:
even there will your hand guide me,
and your right hand hold me.
If I ascend into heaven, you are there;
if I lie down with the dead, you are there.[25]

Sometimes his eyes turn towards nature, and his rapture teaches us how we must envision it:

For you delight me, O Lord, by your deeds,
I rejoice in the works of your hands.
How great are your works, O Lord,
how deep your thoughts!
The senseless man knows not,
nor does the fool understand these things.[26]

If he descends to particular phenomena, what an abundance of images! You see with what vigour and grace he expresses the *wedding* of the earth and its watering:

You have visited the earth and watered it,
greatly have you enriched it.
The river of God abounds with water,
You have prepared grain for them;
for thus have you prepared it.[27]
Its furrows you have prepared,
its clods you have made smooth,
with showers you have softened it,
You have blessed its sprouting seed.[28]
You have crowned the year with your kindness,
your clouds will distil abundance.[29]
The pasture lands of the desert drip,[30]
and the hills gird themselves with great joy.

---

[25] Psalm 138 (139):7, 9, 10, 8.

[26] Psalm 91 (92):5–7.

[27] Psalm 64(65):10.

[28] Ibid., 11. I can't imagine a more beautiful expression.

[29] *Nubes tuae stillabunt pinguedinem* [Thy clouds will drip fatness]. (Ibid., 12.) [This text differs from Clementine version of the Vulgate, which reads *Et campi tui replebuntur ubertate* (And your fields will be filled with fatness). Another Latin version from the Biblical Institute of Pius XII reads *Et emitae tuae pinguedinem stillant* (And your paths drip with fatness).]

[30] Ibid., 13.

The fields are clothed with your flocks,
and the valleys are covered with grain:
they cry aloud and sing.[31]

It is in the loftiest realms that he must be heard to explain the marvels of this interior worship that in his time could only have been perceived by inspiration. The divine love that embraces him lends him a prophetic character; he anticipates the centuries and he already belongs to the law of grace. Like Francis de Sales or Fénelon, he discovers in the human heart *these mysterious decrees*[32] *that lead us from strength to strength until we shall see the God of gods.*[33] He is inexhaustible when he exalts the sweetness and excellence of the divine law.

[This law] is a lantern for his uncertain feet,
a light, a star, that light for him the dark paths of life.[34]
It is truth, it is truth itself,
it carries its justification within itself;
it is sweeter than honey,
more desirable than gold and precious stones;
and those who are loyal to it,
find there unlimited recompense.[35]
He meditates on it day and night.[36]
He treasures God's oracles in his heart
so that he may not offend against Him.[37]
If you will give me a docile heart,
I will run in the way of your commands.[38]

Sometimes the feeling that oppresses him stops his breath. A word coming forth to express the prophet's thought halts on his lips and falls back to his heart; but piety will understand him when he cries out: YOUR ALTARS, O LORD OF HOSTS![39]

---

[31] Ibid., 14.
[32] *Asensiones in corde suo disposuit.* Psalm 83(84):6. [Maistre's translation seems idiosyncratic here; most translations read something like the following: "Happy the men whose strength you are! Their hearts are set upon the pilgrimage."]
[33] (Ibid., 8)
[34] Psalm 118(119):105.
[35] Psalm 18(19):10–11.
[36] Psalm 118(119):97.
[37] Ibid., 11.
[38] Ibid., 32.
[39] Psalm 83(84):4.

Other times we hear him foreshadowing all of Christianity in a few words. *Teach me*, he says, *to do your will, because you are my God.*[40] What philosopher of antiquity ever knew that virtue is nothing but obedience to God *because he is God*, and that merit depends exclusively on this obedient conduct of thought?

He knew well the terrible law of our defiled nature; he knew that men *are conceived in inequity, and rebel against the divine law from their mother's womb.*[41] As well as the great apostle he knew that *man is a slave sold to the iniquity that has him under its yoke, so that only where the Spirit of the Lord is, is there freedom.*[42] Thus he cried out with a truly Christian exactness: *Through you I am snatched from temptation, with your assistance I leap the wall.*[43] This wall of separation raised from the beginning between man and the Creator, this wall absolutely must *be cleared*, since it cannot be *overturned*, and when he says to God *Give me a sign,*[44] does he not confess, does he not teach the whole truth? On the one side, *nothing in us*, and on the other, *nothing without you*. If man boldly dares to rely on himself, vengeance is all ready: *He is delivered up to the inclinations of his heart and to the dreams of his imagination.*[45]

Certain that man of himself is incapable of prayer, David asks God to fill him *with this mysterious oil, with this divine unction that will open his lips and allow them to pronounce words of praise and elation.*[46] Since he only tells us his own experience, he lets us see the work of inspiration in him. *I felt my heart grow hot within me*, he says, *a fire blazed forth from my thoughts. Then my tongue was freed and I spoke.*[47] Compare these chaste flames of divine love, these sublime outbursts of a spirit delighted with heaven to the putrid heat of Sappho or the paid enthusiasm of Pindar. Taste alone can decide, virtue is not required.

See how the prophet deciphered the unbeliever with a single phrase: *He refused to believe, for fear of acting rightly,*[48] and how, again in a single

---

[40] Psalm 142(143):10.

[41] *In guilt was I born, and in sin my mother conceived me.* (Psalm 50(51):7) *From the womb the wicked are perverted; astray from birth have the liars gone.* (Psalm 57(58):4.)

[42] Romans 7:14 and 2 Corinthinians 3:17.

[43] Psalm 17(18):30.

[44] Psalm 85(86):17.

[45] Psalm 80(81):13.

[46] Psalm 62(63):6.

[47] Psalm 38(39):4.

[48] Psalm 35(36):4.

phrase, he gives a terrible lesson to believers when he tells them: *You who profess to love God must therefore hate evil.*[49]

This extraordinary man, enriched with such precious gifts, nevertheless made himself enormously guilty; but atonement enriched his hymns with new beauties. Never has the repentant sinner spoken a truer, more pathetic, more penetrating language. *Ready to receive all the scourges of the Lord with resignation,*[50] *he is ready to admit his iniquities.*[51] *His sin is ever before his eyes,*[52] *and his grief is with him always.*[53] In the middle of Jerusalem, in the heart of that sumptuous capital soon destined to become *by far the most famous city in the East,*[54] on the throne where he had been led by the hand of God, *he is like the pelican of the desert, like an owl among the ruins, like a bird all alone on the housetop.*[55] *He has wearied himself with groaning, night after night he waters his couch with his weeping.*[56] *The arrows of the Lord have pierced him.*[57] *For there is nothing healthy in him, his bones are broken,*[58] *There is no health in his flesh; he is stooped and bowed down profoundly; all the day he goes in mourning:*[59] *he no longer hears; he has lost his voice; all that remains to him is hope.*[60] Nothing can distract him from his sorrow, and this sorrow always turning him towards prayer like all his other feelings, his prayer has something living that can be found nowhere else. He unceasingly recalls the oracle he has pronounced against himself: *God says to the sinner: "Why do you declare my precepts with your impure mouth?"*[61] *I want praise only from the virtuous.*[62] So with the psalmist, terror is always mixed with confidence, and even in the transports of love, in the ecstasy of admiration, in the most touching effusions of unlimited thanksgiving, the sharp point of remorse makes itself felt like the thorn in a ruby bunch of roses.

---

[49]   Psalm 96(97):10. Berthier has spoken beautifully about this text. (See his translation. [*Les Psaumes traduits en français.*])

[50]   Psalm 37(38):18.

[51]   Ibid., 19.

[52]   Psalm 50(51):5.

[53]   Psalm 37(38):11, 18.

[54]   Pliny *Natural History* V.15.

[55]   Psalm 101(102):7-8.

[56]   Psalm 6:7.

[57]   Psalm 37(38):3.

[58]   Psalm 6:3.

[59]   Psalm 37(38):4,6,7.

[60]   Ibid., 16.

[61]   Psalm 49(50):16.

[62]   Psalm 32(33):1.

Finally, nothing strikes me more forcefully in these magnificent psalms than the breadth of the prophet's religious ideas; although restricted to a small point on the globe, the ideas he professed are nevertheless distinguished by a marked leaning towards universality. The temple in Jerusalem was open to all nations, and the disciple of Moses did not refuse to pray to his God with any man or for any man; full of these great and generous ideas, and, moreover, pushed by a prophetic spirit that showed him in advance *the swiftness of his word and the power of his good news,*[63] David never ceased to address the human race and to call all mankind to the truth. This call to the light, this heartfelt pledge, is always present in his sublime compositions. To express this in a thousand ways, he exhausted the language without every being able to satisfy himself. *Hear this, all you nations; give ear, all you inhabitants of time.*[64] *The Lord is good to all, and merciful to all his works.*[65] *Your kingdom is a kingdom of all ages, and endures through all ages.*[66] *Shout with joy all you lands. Let all the earth adore you and sing to you, let it sing your name. Bless our God, O nations, and declare the fame of his praise.*[67] *Say to God: How tremendous are your deeds, for your great strength your enemies fawn upon you.*[68] *Let kings of the earth and all the nations, let princes and judges of the earth, let them praise the name of the Lord because his name alone is exalted.*[69] *I am the friend of all who fear you and keep your commandments.*[70] *Kings, princes, the great and all peoples who cover the earth, praise the name of the Lord, for his name only is great.*[71] *Then the peoples gather, and the kingdoms, to serve the Lord.*[72] *Nations of the earth, applaud and sing, sing to your king! Sing, for your Lord is king of*

---

[63] *Swiftly runs his word.* (Psalm 147(147B):15). *The Lord gives the word.* (Psalm 67(68):12).

[64] *Omnes qui habitatis tempus.* Psalm 48(49):2. This beautiful phrase comes from the Hebrew. The Vulgate reads: *Qui habitatis orbem.* Alas, the two phrases time and world are synonymous.

[65] Psalm 144(145):9.

[66] Ibid., 13.

[67] Psalm 65(66):1,4,8.

[68] Psalm 66(67):3.

[69] Psalm 66(67):3.

[70] Psalm 118(119):63.

[71] Psalm 148:11–12.

[72] Psalm 101(102):23.

the world. SING WITH INTELLIGENCE.[73] *Let everything that has breath praise the Lord!*[74]

God did not disdain to satisfy this great desire. The prophetic view of the holy king, in burying itself in the far future, already saw the great explosion of the *cenacle* and the face of the earth renewed by the effusion of the divine spirit. How beautiful are his expressions, and especially how appropriate! *All the ends of the earth* SHALL REMEMBER *and shall be converted to the Lord; and all the families of the nations shall bow down in his sight.*[75]

Wise friends, let us notice here in passing how infinite goodness could *overlook forty centuries;*[76] it awaited the *remembrance* of man.[77] I will finish by recalling for you another wish of the prophet-king: *Let these things be written for a generation to come, and let a people that shall be created, praise the Lord.*[78]

His wish was fulfilled. Because he sang only of the Eternal, his hymns participated in eternity. The fiery accents imparted to his divine lyre still resound in all parts of the world after thirty centuries. The synagogue preserved the Psalms; the Church hastened to adopt them. The poetry of all Christian nations has laid hold of them, and for more than three centuries the sun has never ceased to shine on churches whose vaults resound to these sacred hymns. They are sung in Rome, Geneva, Madrid, London, Quebec, Quito, Moscow, Peking, and Botany Bay; they are whispered in Japan.

The Chevalier

Can you tell me why I cannot recall having read in the Psalms anything of what you have just told me?

---

[73] Psalm 46(47):8. [Maistre's translation somewhat expands the text. A more typical translation for this verse would read: "For God is king of all the earth, sing a hymn."]

[74] Psalm 150:5. This is the last verse of the last Psalm.

[75] Psalm 21(22):28.

[76] Acts 17:30 [Maistre paraphrases; the Jerusalem Bible reads: "God overlooked that sort of thing when men were ignorant."]

[77] *Yes, Plato, you were right.* All the verities are within us; they are US, and when man thinks to discover them, he has only to look within himself and to say YES!.

[78] Psalm 101(102):19.

The Count

Of course, my young friend, *I can tell you why*. This phenomenon belongs to the theory of innate ideas. Although there are original notions common to all men, without which they would not be men, and which are in consequence accessible, or rather natural, to all minds, it is nevertheless unnecessary for all minds to arrive at the same point. On the contrary, some ideas are somewhat dormant and others are more or less dominant in each mind; and this forms what is called its *character* or its *talent*. So it happens that when we receive some sort of spiritual food through reading, each mind appropriates to itself what particularly suits what I would call its *intellectual temperament*, and the rest escapes it. This is why we do not all read the same things when we read the same books; which is what happens especially with the other sex compared to our own, for women do not read as we do. This difference being so general, and at the same time so obvious, I invite you to reflect on it.

The Senator

The night that is catching up with us recalls for me, Count, since you are carrying on so well, that you could very well have recalled for us something that David said about the night. This is something that concerned him very much and that he talked about a great deal, and I have been expecting among all the outstanding texts that have struck you some on the night, for this is a great subject to which David often returned; and who could be surprised by this. You know very well, my good friends, that the night is dangerous for man, and that without perceiving it we all love it a little because it puts us at ease. Night is the natural accomplice constantly at the service of every vice, and this seductive indulgence means that we generally value the night much less than the day. Light intimidates vice; darkness lends it all its forces, and this is what virtue fears. Again, night is of no value for man, and, yet, and perhaps even because of this, are we not all a little idolatrous of this easy divinity? Who can pride himself on never having invoked it for evil? From the highway brigand to the salon wrongdoer, what man has never said: *Flecte, precor vultus ad mea furta tuos?*[79] Again, what man has never said: *Nox conscia novit* [The night shares your secret and knows]? The best society, the best regulated family, is the one that stays up the least; and the extreme corruption of morals always announces its presence by the extremity of abuses of this kind. Night being, therefore, by its nature, *malè suada* [a persuader of evil], a

---

[79] [Turn, I beg, your face to my thefts. Ovid *Heroides* XVIII.64. (Darcel ed.)]

bad counsellor, it follows that false religions have often consecrated their criminal rites to it, *nota bonæ secreta deæ*.[80]

The Count

With your permission, my dear friend, I would rather say that *antique corruption* consecrated the night to criminal orgies, but that *antique religion* was not wrong, or was less wrong than impotent, for I believe that nothing begins with evil. For example, antique religion put these mysteries that you have just mentioned under the care of the most severe modesty; it chased even the smallest male animal from the temple – even paintings of men; the poet whom you have just cited himself recalls this law with his mad gaiety in order to make a frightening contrast stand out better.[xi] You see that the original intentions could not have been clearer; I would add that even in the bosom of error the nocturnal prayer of the Vestal seems to have been invented to provide a balance at some point to the mysteries of the good goddess;[81] but the true cult must have distinguished itself on this point and lacked nothing. If night gives bad counsel, as you have just said, it must also be rendered justice for it also gives excellent counsel. It is a time of profound meditations and sublime delights; in order to profit from these divine effusions and in order also to counteract the deadly influence of which you spoke, Christianity in its turn has also seized the night and consecrated to it holy ceremonies that it animates with austere music and powerful canticles.[xii] Even religion, in everything that does not pertain to dogma, is subject to certain changes that our poor nature make inevitable; nevertheless down to matters of pure discipline certain things are always invariable. For example, there will always be feast-days that will call us all to the night office, and *always* there will be chosen men whose pious voices will be heard in the darkness, since legitimate praise must never be silent on the earth:

> The day recalls it to the day,
> And the night announces it to the night.[82]

The Senator

Alas! Who knows if you are not expressing a wish rather than a truth, at least at the moment! How the reign of prayer has been weakened, and what

---

[80] [well known for all the mysteries of the good goddess.] Juvenal *Satires* VI.314. [The cult of *Bona Dea*, a female liturgy, was corrupted by Clodius in Caesar's time.]

[81] [See previous note.]

[82] [Psalm 18(19):2.]

means have not been used to extinguish its voice! Has our century not asked *Of what use are those who pray?* How can prayer pierce the darkness, when it is scarcely allowed to make itself heard by day? However I don't want to go astray in these sad forebodings. You have said everything I wanted to say about the night, without however saying what David said of it, and this is what I wanted you to supply. In my turn I now ask for your permission to proceed with my principle idea. Full of ideas he owed to no man, David never ceased exhorting man *to suspend his sleep to pray;*[83] he thought that the august silence of the night lent a particular strength to holy desires. *I sought God in the night,* he said, *and I was not deceived.*[84] Elsewhere he says: *During the night I meditate within my heart, I think back, and my spirit searches diligently.*[85] In musing another time on certain dangers that must have been stronger in antiquity than in our time, he said in his victorious conscience: *O Lord, I remember your name* in the night, *and I will keep your law.*[86] Undoubtedly he believed that the influence of the night was the test of hearts, since he added: *You tested my heart, searching it in the night.*[87]

Night air is worthless for the material man; animals teach us this since they all stop their activities to sleep. Our illnesses teach us this by dealing most severely with all of us at night. Why do you inquire in the morning of your friend to ask *how he passed the night,* rather than asking in the evening *how he has passed the day?* It must be because there is something bad about the night. From this comes the necessity of sleep, which is not made for the day, and which is no less necessary for the mind as for the body, for they are both continually exposed to the action of certain powers that unceasingly attack them so that neither could *live;* so it is necessary that these harmful actions are periodically suspended and that they are both put under a protective influence during these intervals. Just as the body continues its vital functions during sleep, without the sensible principle being conscious of it, the *vital* functions of the mind continue as well, as you can convince yourself independently of all theory by a common experience, since man can learn during sleep, and know, for example, on

---

[83] ... *during the night, lift up your hands toward the sanctuary,* etc. (Psalm 133(134):2)

[84] Psalm 76(77):3.

[85] Ibid., 7.

[86] Psalm 118(119):55.

[87] Psalm 16(17):3.

waking, verses, or the tune of a song that he did not know on going to sleep.[88]

However for the analogy to be perfect, the intelligent principle must not even be conscious of what happened to it during this time, or at least that it have no memory of it, which amounts to the same thing with respect to the established order. From the universal belief that man then finds himself under a good and preserving influence, comes another belief, likewise universal, *that the time of sleep is favourable to divine communications.* This opinion, in whatever way it might be understood, is incontestably based on Holy Scripture, which presents a great number of cases of this kind. Moreover we see that false religions have always professed the same belief, for error, in turning its back on its rival nevertheless never ceases to repeat all its acts and all its doctrines, which it alters according to its character, that is to say in such a way that the model can never be misidentified nor the image taken for the reality. Middleton[89] and other writers of the same sort have used great erudition to prove that your church *imitates* a host of pagan ceremonies, a reproach that they would also address to ours if they ever thought of us. Deceived by a negative religion and by a fleshless cult, they misunderstood the eternal forms of a positive religion that can be found everywhere. In America, modern travellers have found Vestals, new fire, circumcision, baptism, confession, and finally, the *real presence*, under the *species* of *bread* and *wine.*[xiii]

Do we say that we owe these ceremonies to the Mexicans or the Peruvians? We must always take care not to conclude from conformity to subordinate derivation; for the reasoning to be legitimate, common derivation must have been previously excluded. Moreover, to return to the night and to dreams, we see that the greatest geniuses of antiquity, without distinction, never doubted the importance of dreams, and that they even went so far as to sleep in temples to receive oracles there.[90] Did not Job say that *God uses dreams to warn men,* AND REPEATETH NOT THE SELFSAME THING A SECOND TIME,[91] and did not David say, as I recalled for you a little while ago, *that God visits hearts in the night?* Did Plato not

---

[88] The speaker could have added that man possesses as well the power of waking up at almost precisely the time he prescribes for himself before going to sleep; this is a phenomenon as constant as it is inexplicable. Sleep is one of the great human mysteries. The one who would understand it would, it appears, have penetrated all the others. (Editor's note.)

[89] [Conyers Middleton (1683–1758), an English deist.]

[90] *... holds converse with the gods.* Virgil *Aeneid* VII.90–1 [Loeb].

[91] Job 33:14,15,17.

want us *to prepare for dreams by great purity of soul and body*?[92] Did not Hippocrates compose a special treatise on dreams, where he went so far as to refuse to accept as a real doctor anyone who could not interpret dreams?[xiv] It seems to me that a Latin poet, Lucretius if I am not mistaken,[93] went even farther in saying *that during sleep the gods speak to the soul and to the mind.*

Finally, Marcus Aurelius (I do not cite a weak mind here) not only regarded these nocturnal communications as an incontestable fact, but he declared moreover, in his own terms, of having received them.[xv] What do you say to that, gentlemen? Would you by chance want to maintain that all the sacred and profane science of antiquity talked nonsense? That men have never seen what they have seen, experienced what they have experienced? That the great men I have cited for you had weak minds? That ...

The Chevalier

For myself, I do not believe that I have yet acquired the right to be impertinent.

The Senator

As for me, I also believe that no one has the right to acquire this right, which, thanks to God, does not exist.

The Count

Tell me, my dear friend, why you would not collect a host of the very elevated and quite uncommon thoughts that constantly come to you when we are talking of metaphysics or religion? You could entitle this collection *Philosophic Flights*. If fact, there exists a work with the same title written in Latin; *but these are flights that could break your neck*; yours, it seems to me, could uplift man without danger.

The Chevalier

I also exhort you to do this, my dear Senator. While waiting, gentlemen, something will happen to me, thanks to you, that certainly never happened before in my life: this is to go sleep thinking of *the prophet king*. To your honour!

---

[92] ["Now Plato's advice to us is to set out for the land of dreams with bodies so prepared that no error or confusion may assail the soul."] Cicero *On Divination* I.30 [Trans. William Armstead Falconer, Loeb Classical Library, 1923].

[93] No. The verse is from Juvenal. *A pretty kind of mind and spirit for the Gods to have converse with by night!* Juvenal [*Satires*] VI.531 [Loeb]. (Editor's note.)

NOTES TO THE SEVENTH DIALOGUE

i   "If someone told you that all the cats of a great country assembled together on a plain, and after caterwauling to their hearts' content, threw themselves at one another in a rage, attacking each other tooth and claw, and that this scrimmage left some nine or ten thousand cats lying dead on the ground to infect the air for ten leagues around with their stink, would you not say: 'That is the most abominable din I have ever heard of.' And if wolves did the same thing, what howls! What butchery! And if the cats and the wolves told you that they love glory, would you not laugh heartily at the ingenuity of these poor beasts?" [Jean de] La Bruyère, [*Les Caractères ou les moeurs de ce siècle*, "Des jugements," No. 119].

ii   Lycurgus took from the Egyptians the idea of separating warriors from the rest of the people, and distinguishing merchants, artisans, and professional people, a means by which he established a veritably noble, pure, and decent republic. (Plutarch, *On Lycurgus*, Chap. VI of Amyot's translation.)

     Among us still, a family that has never borne arms, whatever other merits it has acquired in all the most honourable civil functions, will never be *veritably noble, pure, and decent*. It will always lack something.

iii   Error, during the whole past century, was a kind of religion that the philosophers professed and preached as loudly as the apostles professed and preached the truth. It is not that these philosophers had never been in good faith; on the contrary, this is what they always and obviously lacked. However, they were agreed, like the augurs of antiquity, never to laugh while watching each other, and as much as possible they put audacity in the place of persuasion. Here is a passage from Montesquieu that shows quite clearly the general spirit animating all these writers:

The laws of nature are those that derive uniquely from the constitution of our being; to know them well it is necessary to consider man before the establishment of societies: the laws of nature are those that they would have received in such a state. (*Esprit des lois*, Bk. 2.)

     Therefore, *the natural laws for the political and religious animal* (as Aristotle says) derive from a state before all civil and religious association! Whenever it is not a question of style, I am a calm enough admirer of Montesquieu; however I will never persuade myself that he was serious when he wrote what we have just read. Quite simply, I believe that he was, like so many others, reciting his *Credo* with his lips to be accepted by the brothers, and perhaps, in order not to fall out with the inquisitors of error, who do not waste their time.

iv   "I was telling you about a lieutenant in the grenadier's company who was killed. Perhaps you will not be upset to learn that they found a hairshirt on the body. He was of a singular piety, and even made his devotions the day before. It is said that there are some very disciplined people in this company.

As for myself, I hardly ever attend a Mass in the camp that is not served by some musketeer, or where someone does not communicate in the most edifying way." (Racine to Boileau, from the camp before Namur, 1692. *Oeuvres*, Geoffroi Ed., (Paris 1808), 7:275, Letter XXII.)

v "I was grieved that you were not serving; but this is a design of pure mercy to detach you from the world and to lead you to a life of pure faith, which is a death without respite." (Fénelon, *Oeuvres spirituelles*, 4:171–2, Letter CLXIX.)

vi "You do not have to be peculiar; thus you must not make a big thing about having to miss Mass on work days, *especially in the army*. Everything that pertains to your state of life is God's will for you." (Madame [Jeanne-Marie Bouvier de la Mothe] Guyon, *Lettres chrétiennes et spirituelles*, (London 1768), Letter XVI, p. 54.)

vii In his funeral oration for Turenne, Mascaron said, at the beginning of the first part: "Almost all the peoples of the earth, however different in temperament and inclination they might be, are agreed on the point of attaching the greatest degree of glory to the profession of arms. Nevertheless, if this feeling was only based on human opinion, we could regard it as an error that has captivated the minds of all. But something more real and more solid settles the matter for me; and if we are deceived in the noble idea we have created for ourselves of the glory of conquerors, great God, I almost dare to say that it is you who have deceived us! Is not the most august title that God has given to himself that of GOD OF HOSTS? etc., etc."

But who would not admire the wisdom of Homer, who, almost three thousand years ago, made his Jupiter say: *Look you now, how ready mortals are to blame the Gods. It is from us, they say, that evils come, but they even of themselves, through their own blind folly, have sorrows beyond that which is ordained.* Could we express it any better? Please pay attention to the *hyper moron* [blind folly]. (*Odyssey* 1.30–34.)

viii Isaiah 26:21; Genesis 4:11. In the Greek tragedy of Orestes, Apollo declares: "That it is not necessary to blame Helen for the Trojan War, which has cost the Greeks so dearly; that this woman's beauty was only an instrument that the gods used to bring about war between these two peoples *to cause their blood to flow, to purify the earth, defiled by the overflowing of all their crimes*." (Literally, *to PUMP OUT the stains*.) Euripides *Orestes* V.1677–80.

Few antique authors showed themselves better acquainted than Euripides with all the dogmas of antique theology. He spoke like Isaiah, and Mohammed spoke like the two of them: *If God did not raise nation against nation, the earth would be completely corrupted.* (The *Koran*, cited by Sir William Jones in his history of Thomas-Kouli-Khan. *Works*, 5:8.) *Fas est ab hoste doceri* [It is right to learn from a foe].

ix Here is what Bolingbroke wrote on the subject of the war ended by the Peace of Nimwegen in 1679: "The miserable conduct of Austria, the poverty of some princes of the Empire, and the disunion and, to speak plainly, the mercenary policy of all them; in short, the confined views, the false notions, and to speak plainly of my own country as of other nations, the iniquity of the councils of England, not only hindered the growth of this power from being stopped in time, but nursed it up into strength almost insuperable by any future confederacy." ([Henry St John, Lord Viscount] Bolingbroke, *Letters on the Study and Use of History*, (Basel [Paris] 1788), Letter VII, p. 184.)

In writing these lines, Bolingbroke little suspected that the Dutch would soon trip Louis XIV at Gertruidenberg, and that they would be the centre of a formidable coalition that would, in its turn, be broken by a second-rate power: *A glove and a glass of water.*

x The emperor Arnoulf was besieging Rome. A rabbit that had wandered into the prince's camp escaped by running toward the city; with great cries the soldiers chased it, and the besieged, who thought they were under a general assault, lost their heads and took flight or threw themselves down from the ramparts. Arnoulf, profiting from this panic terror, took the city. (Luitprand, *History*, Bk. I, Chap. 8.) Muratori put little stock in this story, although it is told to us by a contemporary author. (Muratori, *Annali d'Italia, da ann. DCCCXCVI*, [12 vols. (Milan 1744–9] 5:215.) However I believe it iss as certain as the story of the geese.

xi *... place from which every buck mouse scuttles away conscious of its virility ... and in which no picture of a male form may be exhibited except behind a veil.* (Juvenal *Satires* VI.338,341 [Loeb])

xii In order to sing your praises here,
Our zeal, Lord, precedes the day;
Thus grant that we may one day sing with your angels
The good that your love has reserved for your elect.
Rise up, adorable sun
That from eternity makes a happy day
Make your helpful clarity shine in our eyes,
And pour the fire of your love into our hearts.
Flee dreams, a dangerous company,
Dangerous enemies born of the night;
And may there flee with you the dangerous memories
Of the things you have presented to our senses.
That this day may pass without crime,
That our tongues, our hands, our eyes be innocent;
That all be chaste within us, and that a legitimate check
To the yoke of reason subjugate our senses ...
Let us sing to the author of light
Until the day when his command marks our end;
And that in blessing us our last morning

We are lost in a noon without night and without morning, etc.
(See the hymns of the Roman breviary, translated by [Louis] Racine, in the collected works of this great poet.) Anyone without a vocation who attempts something of this kind, in appearance so simple and so easy, will learn two things by taking up the pen: what prayer is, and what the talent of Racine was.

xiii Nothing is truer than this assertion. (See Carli's *Lettres américaines*, Vol. I, letters 4, 5, 6, and 9.)

In Peru, the sacrifice consisted of the *Cancu*, or consecrated bread, and the *Acu*, or sacred liqueur, of which the priests and the Inca drank a portion after the ceremonies. (Ibid., Letter 9.)

The Mexicans made an image of their idol out of corn dough, which they baked like a bread. After having carried it in procession and having brought it to the temple, the priest broke it and distributed it to his assistants. *Each one ate his piece, and believed himself sanctified after eating his God.* ([Guillaume] Raynal, *Histoire philosophique et politique [des établissements et du commerce des Européens dans les deux Indies*, (1770)], Bk. IV). Carli is wrong to cite this treatise without the least sign of disapproval. (Ibid., Letter 9.) In passing, it can be observed that the unbelievers of the last century, Voltaire, Hume, Frederick II, Raynal, were extremely amused to make us say: *That we eat our God after having made him; that a wafer becomes God, etc.* They found an infallible way to make us look ridiculous, which was to lend us their own thoughts. However this proposition, *the bread is God*, falls of itself *by its own absurdity*. (Bossuet, *Histoire des variations*, II, 3.) Thus all these clowns are free to beat the air if they want to.

xiv In this treatise Hippocrates said: *that every man who judges well the signs given in dreams will sense their extreme importance*; and he later decided, in a more general way than the speaker's memory recalled, that *the understanding of dreams is a great part of wisdom*. (Hippocrates, *De Somniis* Van Der Linden edition, chap. 2, in fin. 2:635.) I know of no other text by Hippocrates relating directly to this subject. (Editor's Note)

xv In fact, this is what one reads in one of the passages by this great person: *The gods have the goodness to give men, through dreams and oracles, the assistance they need. One of the gods' great marks of care for me is that they have, in my dreams, often taught me remedies for my illnesses, especially for my fits of giddiness and for my spitting blood, as happened to me at Caieta and at Chryse. (The Meditations of Marcus Aurelius*, Bk. I, near the end; Bk. IX, § 27.)

Eighth Dialogue

The Chevalier

Would you find it agreeable, gentlemen, if before continuing our conversations, I presented you with the minutes of the preceding sessions?

The Senator

So what is it you want to say, Chevalier?

The Chevalier

The pleasure I have been getting from our conversations gave me the idea of writing them down. Everything that we have been saying here has been deeply engraved in my memory. You know that I have a very good memory, though this is not a gift I would brag about; moreover I have not given these ideas time to slip away. Every evening before going to bed, and while they are still quite fresh in my memory, I outline on a piece of paper the principal points, that is to say the *woof* of our conversation. The next morning I set to work early and add the *warp*, applying myself especially to following the thread of the discourse and the line of ideas. You know as well that I do not lack time, for if I did we could not meet at exactly the same time every day. I even think it impossible that three independent people can do the same thing at the same hour for even two or three weeks. It is in vain that they agree, that they promise each other, that they give their word to give up other affairs; there will always be a time when some other insurmountable obstacle will come up – and often it will be only a trifle. Men cannot meet for a given end without a law or a rule that deprives them of their will; they would have to be either monks or soldiers. So I have had more time than I need, and I believe that few essential ideas have escaped me.

Moreover you will not refuse me the pleasure of listening to the reading of my work; and you understand, from the width of the margins, that I am counting on numerous corrections. I am promising myself genuine enjoyment from this common enterprise; but I confess to you that in imposing this hard task upon myself I have been thinking of others more than of myself. I know many men in the world, many young people extremely disgusted with modern doctrines. Others are drifting and ask only to settle down. I would like to communicate to them these very ideas that have occupied our evenings, persuaded that I would be very useful to some and at least agreeable to many others. Every man is a kind of *faith* for another man, and nothing delights him when he is penetrated by a belief and in the measure that he is penetrated by it, as finding it in the man he esteems. If it seems to you that my pen, aided by a happy memory and a severe revision, has rendered our conversations faithfully, I would be quite ready to commit the folly of carrying them to the printer.

The Count

I could be mistaken, but I don't think such a work would succeed.

The Chevalier

Why not, I ask you? Did you not tell me, a little while ago, *that a conversation is worth more than a book*?

The Count

Undoubtedly it is better for instruction, since it admits interruption, questioning, and explanation; but it does not follow that it is suitable for publication.

The Chevalier

Let us not confuse terms: *conversation, dialogue,* and *entretien* are not synonymous.[1] *Conversation* rambles by its very nature; it never has a prior purpose, it depends on the circumstances and admits an unlimited number of speakers. So I would agree with you, if you like, that it would not be suitable for publication, even if the thing were possible, because of a certain *pell-mell* of thoughts, the fruit of the most bizarre transitions that often lead us, in the same half hour, to speak of the existence of God and comic opera.

However the *entretien* is much more serious; it supposes a subject, and if the subject is important, it seems to me that the *entretien* is subject to the

---

[1] [See Introduction, p. xvi.]

rules of dramatic art, which does not admit a fourth speaker.[2] This is a rule of nature. If we had a fourth here, he would greatly embarrass us.

As for *dialogue*, this word represents only a fiction, for it supposes a conversation that never existed. This is a purely artificial creation, where one can write whatever one pleases; it is a composition like any other, with the parts all formed, like Minerva, in the brain of the writer. Dialogues of the *dead*, which have been exemplified by more than one pen, are as real, and even as probable, as those of the living published by other authors. So this genre is absolutely foreign to us.

Since you have both involved me in serious reading, I have read Cicero's *Tusculan Disputations*, translated into French by President Bouhier and Abbé d'Olivet.[3] This is still a work of pure imagination, and gives no idea of a real *entretien*. Cicero introduces a listener whom he designates simply by the letter A; he has a question raised by this imaginary auditor, and answers him with a regular uninterrupted dissertation. This cannot be our genre either. We are not capital letters; we are very real, very palpable human beings. We are talking to instruct and console each other. There is no subordination among us; and despite your superiority of age and knowledge, you have accorded me an equality I did not request. So I persist in thinking that if our *entretiens* were faithfully published, that is to say with all the exactitude possible ... Senator, why are you laughing?

The Senator

I am laughing because it seems to me, in effect, that without perceiving it, you are arguing powerfully against your project. How could you more clearly demonstrate the embarrassment that it would involve than by leading us into a conversation on conversations? Would you also, by chance, want to record this one?

The Chevalier

I would not fail to do so, I assure you, if I published the book; and I am persuaded that no one would be upset by it. As for the other inevitable digressions of a real *entretien*, I see more advantages than inconveniences, provided that they spring from the subject without doing violence to it. It seems to me that not all truths can stand on their own; they need to be, as it were, *flanked* by other truths. This is the origin of that very true maxim, which I read I don't know where: *that to know one thing well, one must know a bit about a thousand.* So I believe that this facility that a conversa-

---

[2] *Let not a fourth actor strive to speak.* (Horace [*Art of Poetry* 192])

[3] [*Les Tusculanes de Cicéron*, Trans. Bouhier and d'Olivet, 2 vols. (Paris 1766).]

tion has of assuring its way by propping up one proposition by others when needed, could be worthwhile if carried over into a book and be a way of lending art to negligence.

The Senator

Listen, Chevalier, I put it on your conscience, and I think our friend does the same. In any case, I'm not worried that the responsibility will cost you sleep, since it seems to me that the book cannot do much harm. What we ask in common is that no matter what, even if you do not publish it until after our deaths, you do not say in the preface: *I hope the reader will not think his money ill-bestowed*,[4] otherwise you will see us appear before you as two furious ghosts, and woe unto you!

The Chevalier

Don't worry; I don't think I will ever be surprised pillaging Locke after the fear you inculcated in me.

Whatever may happen in the future, we can, I think, see where we are today. Our conversations began with an examination of the great and eternal complaint that is always raised about the success of crime and the misfortunes of virtue. We came to the firm conclusion that nothing in the world is less ill-founded than this complaint, and that even for those who do not believe in an afterlife, the path of virtue will always be the surest way of obtaining the best chance for temporal happiness. What we said about punishments, illnesses, and remorse left not the slightest doubt on this point. I have paid special attention to these two fundamental axioms: namely, in the first place, *that no man is punished because he is just, but always because he is a man*, so that it is false to say that virtue suffers in this world, whereas it is human nature that suffers, and it always merits suffering. In the second place, *the greatest temporal happiness is not promised, and could not be promised, to the virtuous man, but to virtue*. In fact it is enough for this order to be visible and irreproachable even in this world that the greatest amount of happiness be bestowed on the greatest amount of virtue in general; and given man as he is, it is not possible for our reason even to imagine another order of things that would have any appearance of rationality and justice. As there is no such thing as a just man, none have the right to refuse to accept in good grace their share of human miseries, since all are necessarily criminal or have criminal blood – which brought us to examine in depth the whole theory of *original sin*, which unfortunately is that of human nature. We saw in savage nations a

---

[4] See p. 165 above.

feeble image of the primitive crime; and since man is nothing but an animated word, the degradation of language presented itself to us not as a sign of human degradation, but of this degradation itself, which led us in turn to several reflections on languages and the origin of speech and ideas. These points cleared up, prayer naturally presented itself to us as a supplement to all that had been said, since it is the remedy granted to man to restrain the empire of evil by perfecting himself; and if he refuses to employ this remedy, he can only blame his own vices. The great objection that we have seen a blind or guilty philosophy raise against this word *prayer* is that, seeing physical evil as nothing but the inevitable result of eternal laws of nature, it obstinately maintains that these laws are entirely immune to the action of prayer. This deadly sophism was discussed and refuted in great detail. These scourges by which we are stricken, and which we very rightly call *scourges of heaven*, appeared to us *laws of nature* in precisely the same way as punishments are *laws of society*, and consequently of a purely secondary necessity, which should stimulate rather than discourage our prayer. No doubt we could have contented ourselves by simply looking at the issue in general terms and only looking at all kinds of calamities en masse. However we allowed the conversation to wander a bit at this point, and we concerned ourselves particularly with war. I can assure you that of all our excursions, this is the one to which I am most attached, for you made me look at this scourge of war from a point of view that was totally new to me, and I intend to reflect more about this with all my might ...

The Senator

Excuse me if I interrupt, Chevalier, but before completely abandoning this interesting discussion of the sufferings of the just, I still want to submit to your examination some ideas that I think well founded and that can, in my opinion, make the temporal pains of this life appear as one of the greatest and most natural solutions to all the objections raised against divine justice on this point. The just man, as a man, is nevertheless subject to all the evils that menace humanity, and as he is so subject precisely because he is man, he has no right to complain; you have noted this, and nothing is clearer. You have also noted, what unfortunately requires no proof, that there is no such thing as a *just man*, in the strict sense of the phrase; and it follows that every man has something to expiate. Moreover, if the just man (so far as he is possible) accepts the sufferings that come to him as a man, and if divine justice in its turn accepts his acceptance, I see nothing so fortunate for him, nor so evidently just.

Moreover, I believe in my soul and conscience that if man could live in this world exempt from every kind of misfortune, that he would end up by degenerating to the point of completely forgetting all spiritual matters and even God himself. How could he, in this supposition, occupy himself with a superior order, since even in the one in which we live, the miseries that overwhelm us cannot disenchant us from the deceptive charms of this unhappy life?

The Chevalier

I don't know if I'm mistaken, but it seems to me that nothing could be so unfortunate as a man who never experienced the test of misfortune, for never would such a man be sure of himself or know his own worth. Sufferings are for the virtuous man what battles are for the soldier; they improve him and add to his merits. Does the brave man ever complain to the army about always being chosen for the most hazardous expeditions? On the contrary, he searches them out and glories in them; for him, sufferings are an occupation and death an adventure. Let the coward amuse himself by living as he likes, but let him not come and try to confuse us with his impertinences on the misfortunes of those who do not resemble him. The comparison seems to me to be perfectly fair. If the brave man thanks the general who sends him to the assault, why should he not in the same way thank God who makes him suffer? I do not know how it happens, but it is nevertheless certain that the one who suffers voluntarily gains in stature and is more highly regarded by public opinion. I have noticed with respect to religious austerities that the very vice that mocks them cannot prevent itself from offering them homage. What libertine has ever found a rich courtesan who goes to sleep at midnight on eiderdown happier than the austere Carmelite who rises at the same hour to pray for us? I am always returning to what you so rightly observed: *that there is no such thing as a just man.* Thus it is by a special act of kindness that God chastises in this world instead of chastising more severely in the next.

You should know, gentlemen, that there is nothing I believe in more firmly than purgatory. How is it that punishments are not always proportionate to crimes? I find it especially strange that these new reasoners who have denied eternal punishments do not expressly admit the existence of purgatory. For, I ask you, how can these people persuade us that Robespierre's soul springs from scaffold to God just like that of Louis XVI? Yet this opinion is not as rare as one might think. I have spent several years since my *hegira* in certain parts of Germany where the doctors of law no longer want to acknowledge either hell or purgatory. Nothing could be so absurd. Who could ever think of shooting a soldier for stealing a clay pipe from a barrack room? Yet this pipe must not be stolen with impunity; the thief must be *purged* of this theft before he can return to the line with his brave comrades.

The Senator

It must be admitted, Chevalier, that if we ever had a *theological summa* written in this style, it could not fail to win worldly success.

The Chevalier

It's not a question of style; everyone has his own. It's a question of content. Now, I say that purgatory is a dogma of good sense, and since every sin must be expiated in this world or the next, it follows that the afflictions sent to men by divine justice are a real benefit, since these punishments, when we have the wisdom to accept them, are, so to speak, *deducted* for us from those of the future life. I would add that they are a manifest pledge of love, since this anticipation or this commutation of punishment evidently excludes eternal punishment. Whoever has never suffered in this world can not be sure of anything; and the less he has suffered, the less sure he is. However I do not see what he can fear, or to express myself more precisely, what he can *allow himself* to fear, who has willingly accepted suffering.

The Count

You have reasoned perfectly, Chevalier, and I must even congratulate you for having encountered Seneca, for you have said of the Carmelites precisely what he said of the Vestals.[5] I was not aware that you knew that these famous virgins got up in the night and that they had their *matins*, literally, like our religious of the strict observance. In any case, accept this as a fact of history. The only critical observation that I will permit myself on your theology, can also, it seems to me, be addressed to Seneca: "Would you rather be Sylla than Regulus, etc.?"[6] However, be on your guard, I beg you, for there is here a slight confusion of ideas. It is not at all a question of the glory attached to the virtue that quietly supports dangers, privations, and sufferings; on this point the whole world is in agreement. It is a question of knowing why it has pleased God to make this merit necessary. You will find blasphemers and even simply shallow men disposed to tell you *that God could well have dispensed virtue from this kind of glory.* Seneca, not being able to reply as well as you (which is something I ask you to note carefully), made much of this glory, which lent itself to rhetoric, and this is what gives his treatise on Providence, otherwise so fine

---

[5] *Is it not unjust that the noblest maidens should be aroused from sleep to perform sacrifices at night, while others stained with sin enjoy soundest slumber?* (Seneca *On Providence* V.3 [Loeb].)

[6] Ibid. These are not his exact words, but the sense is rendered.

and worthy, a light colour of declamation. Even putting this consideration aside, you, Senator, have very rightly recalled that every man suffers because he is a man, and because he would be God if he did not suffer, and because those who ask for a man not subject to suffering ask for another world. Moreover you have added something no less incontestable when you said that, as no man is just, that is to say exempt from present sin (if sanctity, properly speaking, which is rare, is excepted), God is really merciful to offenders by chastising them in this world. I believe that I would have spoken of these temporary future punishments that we call *purgatorial*, if the Chevalier had not forbidden me from looking for my proofs in the next world.[7]

The Chevalier

You have not understood me completely; I only excluded from our considerations the punishments with which the perverse man is menaced in the next world. As for temporary punishments imposed on the predestined, that is something else ...

The Count

As you wish. It is certain that these future and temporary punishments furnish for all those who believe in them a direct and peremptory response to all the objections founded on the sufferings of the supposed just; and it is still true that this doctrine is so plausible that it would have occurred to good sense, quite apart from revelation.[i] In any case, I don't know if you were not in error in believing that in the country in which you *have spent* so much zeal and valour fruitlessly, but not without merit, you had heard *the doctors of the law* deny both hell and purgatory. You could well have taken the denial of the word for that of the thing. Some minister who is angered by the word purgatory, will make no difficulty in allowing us a *place of expiation* or an *intermediary state*, or perhaps even *stations*; who knows? He will do this without thinking himself in the least ridiculous. – You have nothing to say, my dear Senator? – I will continue. – One of the great causes in the sixteenth-century quarrel was precisely the issue of *purgatory*. The insurgents wanted nothing less than hell pure and simple. However when they became philosophers, they came to deny the eternity of punishments; nonetheless they allowed a *hell in time* to subsist, uniquely for the sake of good order and for fear for letting Nero and Messalina go straight to heaven beside St Louis and St Theresa. However a temporary hell is nothing but purgatory; so that after having quarrelled with us

---

[7] See p. 8 above.

because they did not want purgatory, they are quarrelling with us anew because they want only purgatory,[ii] which is quite absurd as you just said. So this is enough on this subject. I hasten to come to one of the considerations most worthy of exercising all man's intelligence, although in fact the ordinary man gives it little thought.

The righteous, by suffering voluntarily, make satisfaction not only for themselves, but for sinners by way of the substitution of merits.

This is one of the greatest and most important truths of the spiritual order, but to treat it in depth would take more time than remains to me this evening. So let us put off discussing it until tomorrow, and allow me to devote the last few moments of tonight's conversation to the development of some reflections that have come to my mind on this subject.

It is said *that the light of reason alone cannot explain the success of the wicked and the sufferings of the righteous in this world.* Which doubtless means *that there is in the order we see an injustice that does not square with the justice of God,* otherwise the objection would not make sense. Now, since this objection could be made by either an atheist or a theist, I will begin with the first supposition to avoid any kind of confusion. So let us see all that can be said by one of these persuaded and professed atheists.

In truth, I do not know if the unfortunate Hume understood himself when he said, so criminally and even, with all his genius, so foolishly, *that it was impossible to justify the character of the Divinity.*[8] To justify the character of a being that does not exist!

Again, what do they want to say? It seems to me that it all reduces itself to this argument: God IS unjust, therefore he does not exist. This is curious! This is as good as Voltaire's Spinoza who said to God: *Just between us I believe that you do not exist.*[9] The unbeliever must therefore turn around and say *that the existence of evil is an argument against the existence of God, because if God existed, this evil, which is an injustice, would not exist.* So these gentlemen know that the God who does not exist *is just by nature*! They know the attributes of an imaginary being, and they are able to tell us, if we wish, how God would be made if by chance there was one. In truth, nothing could be more completely foolish. If one were permitted

---

[8] In effect, in his own words, he said: "It is impossible for natural reason to justify the character of the Divinity." (*Essay on Liberty and Necessity,* near the end. [In fact, "Essay Concerning Liberty and Understanding," which is No. 8 of Hume's *Philosophical Essays Concerning Human Understanding* (London 1748]) He adds with a cold and revolting audacity: "To show that God is not the author of sin is something that up to now has surpassed all the forces of philosophy." (Ibid. See Beattie, *On Truth,* Pt. II, chap. ii.)

[9] See the very well known piece entitled *Les Systèmes.*

to laugh about such a sad subject, who would not laugh to hear men, who certainly have heads on their shoulders like us, argue against God using the very idea that he has given them of himself, without noticing that this idea alone proves the existence of God, since one cannot have an idea of something that does not exist?[iii] In effect, can a man represent to himself, can a painter represent to his eyes, other things than what exist? The inexhaustible imagination of Raphael could cover his famous gallery with fantastic assemblages, but each piece existed in nature. It is the same thing in the moral world; man can conceive only what is; thus the atheist, to deny God, assumes him.

Moreover, gentlemen, all this is only a kind of preface to a favourite idea that I would like to share with you. Suppose I admit the foolish supposition of a hypothetical God, and that I also admit that the laws of universe can be unjust or cruel in respect to us without their having an intelligent author: all this is nevertheless the height of nonsense, for what follows from it against the existence of God? Nothing at all. Intelligence proves itself to intelligence only by *number*. All other considerations can only relate to certain properties or qualities of the intelligent subject, which have nothing in common with the basic question of existence.

Number, gentlemen, *number*! Or order and *symmetry, for order is nothing but* arranged number, and symmetry is nothing but *order perceived and compared.*

Tell me, I ask you, if, when Nero illuminated his gardens with torches each of which enclosed and burned a living man, the alignment of these terrible flares did not prove to the spectator the existence of an ordering intelligence, just as well as the peaceful illumination put on yesterday for the name day of the mother of His Imperial Majesty?[10] If the month of July brought the plague each year, this pretty cycle would be as regular as that of the harvests. So let us begin by seeing if *number* exists in the universe, and only then inquire *if* and *why* man is treated well or badly in this world, which is another question that can be examined another time, and which has nothing in common with the first.

Number is the obvious barrier between beasts and ourselves; in the immaterial as in the physical order, the use of fire distinguishes us from them in a sharp and indelible way. God gave us number, and it is by number that he proves himself to us, as it is by number that man proves himself to his fellowman. Take away number, and you take away the arts, the sciences, speech, and, in consequence, intelligence. Bring it back, and with it reappear its two celestial daughters, harmony and beauty; *cries* become *songs*, noise receives *rhythm*, a leap becomes *dance*, force is called

---

[10] This circumstance fixes 23 July as the date of this dialogue. (Editor's note.)

dynamics, and marks become *figures*. A notable proof of this truth is that in languages (at least in the ones that I know, and I believe it is the same in the ones I do not know) the same words express both number and thought. For example, it is said that the *reason* of a great man discovered the *reason* for such and such progression; we say *direct ratio* and *inverse ratio*, *miscalculations* in politics and *miscalculations* in reckoning; even the word *calculation* seems to me to have a double meaning, and we say *I am mistaken in all my calculations* when it is not at all a question of calculation. Finally, we say both: *he is counting his money*, and *he is counting on going to see you*; only habit keeps us from seeing something extraordinary in this. The words relating to weight, measure, and equilibrium always lead to using *number* as a synonym for thought or its derivatives. Does not the word *thought* itself come from a Latin word that relates to number?[11]

Intelligence, like beauty, takes pleasure in contemplating itself; and the mirror of intelligence is number. From this arises the taste we all have for symmetry, for every intelligent being likes to place and to recognize its sign on every side, which is *order*. Why is it more pleasing to see soldiers in uniform than in civilian clothes? Why do we prefer to see them marching in line rather than straggling? Why must the trees in our gardens, the plates on our tables, be placed symmetrically to please us? Why do rhymes, meters, refrains, time, and rhythm please us in music and poetry? Could you ever imagine, for example, that there is any intrinsic beauty in rhyming couplets? This form and so many others can please us only because intelligence takes pleasure in everything that proves intelligence, and its principal sign is number. Thus it rejoices whenever it recognizes itself, and the pleasure symmetry gives us can have no other cause. Let us abstract from this pleasure and look at the thing in itself. Just as these words that I am now speaking prove to you the existence of the speaker, and if they were written, would in the same way prove it to all those who read these words arranged according to the laws of syntax, in the same way all created beings prove by their *syntax* the existence of a supreme writer who speaks to us by these signs. As a matter of fact, all these beings are the letters whose combination forms a discourse proving God, that is to say the intelligence that speaks it, for there can be no discourse without a *talking soul*, nor writing without a writer, unless one wants to maintain that the curve that I trace on paper with compasses clearly proves that an intelligence has drawn it while the same curve described by a planet proves nothing, or that an achromatic telescope clearly proves the existence of

---

[11] [The French *pensée* derives from the Latin *pendere*, which meant "to cause to hang down," or "to pay" (since money was originally paid by weight), and thus, "to weigh, consider, judge." (See *Casssell's Latin Dictionary* (1959), 431.)]

Dolland and *Ramsden*,[12] etc., but that the eye, of which the marvellous instrument I have just mentioned is only an imitation, does not in any way prove the existence of a supreme artist or an intention to prevent optical aberration! If a sailor, tossed by a storm onto an island he believes deserted, sees a geometrical figure traced on the shore, he will recognize the presence of men and give thanks to the gods. So would the same kind of figure have any less force by being written in the heavens, and is not number always the same in whatever way it presents itself to us? Look well; it is written in all parts of the universe, and especially in the human body. *Two* strikes us by the marvellous equilibrium of the two sexes, which no science can derange; it shows itself in our eyes, our ears, etc. *Thirty-two* is written in our mouth, and *twenty* divided by *four* carries its invariable *quotient* to the extremity of our four limbs. Number is deployed in the vegetable realm with a richness that astonishes by the invariable constancy in its infinite varieties. Recall, Senator, what you were telling me one day from your ample memory about the number *three* in particular: it is written in the stars, and on the earth; in the intelligence of man and in his body; in the truth, and in fable; in the Gospel, in the Talmud, in the Vedas, and in all religious ceremonies, ancient and modern, legitimate or illegitimate, aspersions, ablutions, invocations, exorcisms, charms, spells, black or white magic; in the mysteries of the cabala, theurgy, and alchemy, in all sorts of secret societies; in theology, geometry, politics, grammar, and in an infinite number of oratorical or poetic formulas that escape *unguarded* attention – in a word in everything that exists. Perhaps it will be said *that this is chance.* Come now! Some desperate madmen take it another way; they say, and I have heard this, *that this is a law of nature.* So what is this law? Is it the will of a legislator? In this case, they are saying what we are saying. Is it the purely mechanical result of certain elements set going in a certain way? Then, these elements, to produce a general and invariable order, must have been arranged and acted upon themselves, and the question comes up again, and it is found that, in place of one proof of order and the intelligence that produced it, there are two, just as if several dice thrown a great number of times all always *come up sixes*, intelligence will be proved by the invariability of the number which is the effect, and by the behind-the-scenes work of the artist who is the cause.

In a certain city all excited by the philosophic ferment, I had the occasion to make a singular observation, which is that the appearance of

---

[12] [John Dolland and Jesse Ramsden were eighteenth-century English instrument-makers who improved the performance of optical instruments by constructing achromatic object lenses that combined lenses made of different kinds of glass.]

order, of symmetry, and in consequence of number and intelligence struck certain men, whom I remember very well, too vividly for them to escape the torture of their conscience, and they invented an *ingenious* subterfuge of which they made great use. They undertook to maintain that it is impossible to recognize *intention* without knowing the *object of the intention.* You would not believe how strongly they held to this idea, which enchanted them because it dispensed them from the torment of common sense. They made the search for intentions a major affair, a kind of *arcanum*[iv] that required, according to them, profound knowledge and immense labours. I heard them say, in speaking of a great physicist who had said something of this sort: *He dared to raise the issue of final causes* (which is what they call intentions). What a great effort! Another time they warned us *to take great care not to mistake an effect for an intention*; this would be very dangerous, as you can see, for if one came to believe that God intervenes in something that goes all alone, or that he had such and such an intention while he had another, what dangerous consequences would follow from such an error! To give all possible force to the idea that I have been talking about, I have always noticed that as much as they can they affect to restrict the search for intentions to the realm of inanimate nature. That it is to say they entrench themselves in mineralogy and in what they call geology, where intentions are less visible, at least for them, and where they present moreover a much larger field for disputation and denial (which is the paradise of pride). As for the *realm of life*, from which a voice that is a little too clear *makes itself heard*, they do not like to talk about it too much. Often when, by pure malice, I spoke to them of animals, they always brought me back to molecules, atoms, gravity, terrestrial strata, etc. *What do we know*, they always said to me with the most comic modesty, *what do we know about animals? Does the germ theorist know what a germ is? Do we understand anything about the nature of organization? Have we made a single step in our knowledge of reproduction? The production of organized beings is a closed book for us.* Now the result of this great mystery is this: it is that animals being *a closed book*, one can read no intention in them.

Perhaps you find it difficult to believe that they could reason so badly, but you do them too much honour. This is what they think, or at least this is what they want understood (which is not at all the same thing). On points where it is not possible to argue well, the sectarian spirit does what it can; it rambles, it changes the subject, and it tries especially to leave things in a certain half light favourable to error. I repeat to you that when these philosophers theorize about intentions, or as they say, about *final causes* (but I don't like this word), when they control the discussion, they always talk about dead nature, carefully avoiding the vegetable and animal realms, where they clearly sense that the terrain resists their tactics. Everything eventually comes back to their great maxim that *intention* cannot be proved unless one has proved *the object of the intention*. I cannot imagine a more vulgar sophism. How is it not seen[13] that there can be no symmetry without purpose, since symmetry itself is a *purpose* of the maker of symmetry. A timepiece lost in the American forest and found by a savage demonstrates to him the hand and intelligence of a worker, just as certainly as it demonstrates them to Mr Schubbert.[14] Thus having no need of *a purpose* to draw our conclusion, we are not obliged to respond to the sophist who asks us, *what purpose?* I have a canal dug around my chateau: someone says, *it is for a fishpond*; another says, *it is for protection against thieves*; finally a third says, *it is for draining and reclaiming the land*. They can all be mistaken, but he would certainly be right who restricted himself to saying, *he had it dug for reasons known to himself*. As for the philosopher who would want to tell us: "As you are not in agreement on the intention, I have the right to see none. The canal bed is only a natural subsidence of the soil, the facing is a solidification, the railing is only the work of a volcano, no more extraordinary in its regularity than the groupings of basaltic pillars that one sees in Ireland, and moreover, etc. ..."

The Chevalier

Do you think, gentlemen, that it would be too brutal to say to him: *My good friend, the canal was designed for dunking fools*, which one could prove immediately.

The Senator

I would be opposed to this method of reasoning for the simple reason that on coming out of the water the philosopher would have the right to say: *That proves nothing.*

---

[13] They see very well, but irritated by seeing, they do not want to see. Moreover they are ashamed not to see what others see, and to receive a demonstration *ex ore infantium et lactentium* [from the mouths of babes and sucklings]. Pride revolts against the truth *that lets children draw near*. Soon *the shadows of the heart* rise up to the mind, and cataracts are formed. As for those who deny through pure pride and without conviction (the number of these is immense), they are perhaps more guilty than the first.

[14] A learned astronomer of the Academy of Science of St Petersburg, distinguished by great knowledge, and whose good manners always puts it at the disposal of every amateur who wants to profit from it.

The Count

Ah, my dear Senator, you are the one who is in error! Never has pride said, *I was wrong*, and these people less than any others. So when you have presented the most demonstrative arguments to them, they will always say: *That proves nothing*. Since the response will always be the same, why not adopt a good argument? Since the philosopher, the canal, and the chateau are all imaginary, I will continue, if you allow me.

They talk of *disorder* in the world; but what is *disorder*? Apparently it is a derogation from *order*. Therefore one cannot object to *disorder* without admitting a previous *order*, and consequently intelligence. A perfectly accurate idea of the world can be formed by seeing it under the aspect of a great natural history museum overturned by an earthquake. The door is open and broken; there are no more windows; entire cupboards have fallen over; others are still hanging by their fasteners, ready to let go. Shellfish have rolled into the mineral room, and a bird's nest rests on the head of a crocodile. Nevertheless, what idiot would doubt the original intention, or think that the building was constructed in this state? All the great parts are together; the entire thing can be seen in the least splinter of glass; the emptiness of a chest fills it; order is as visible as disorder, and the eye, in looking over the vast temple of nature, easily re-establishes everything that some dangerous agent has broken, falsified, soiled, or displaced. There is more: look closely, and you will recognize a restoring hand. Some beams are propped up; some routes have been laid out amidst the wreckage; and in the general confusion a host of *equivalents* have already taken their places and are in contact. So there are two intentions visible instead of one, that it is to say, order and its restoration. Limiting ourselves to the first idea, *disorder* necessarily supposing *order*, the one who argues disorder against the existence of God, assumes order to combat it.

So you see what this well-known argument comes down to: *Either God could prevent the evils that we see and lacked the kindness, or wanting to prevent them could not, and lacked the power*. MY GOD! What does this mean? It is neither a question of omnipotence nor omni-benevolence, but only of *existence* and *power*. I know very well that God cannot change the nature of things, but I know only an infinitesimal part of these natures, so that I am ignorant of an infinitely large number of things that God cannot do, without his ceasing because of that to be omnipotent. I do not know what is possible, I do not know what is impossible. In my lifetime, I have only studied number; I only know number, I only believe in number. It is the sign, it is the voice, it is the word of intelligence; and as it is everywhere, I see it everywhere.

However let us leave aside the atheists, who happily are not very numerous in the world,[15] and take up the question with the theist. I want to show myself just as obliging to him as to the atheist, so he will not take it amiss if I begin by asking him what an injustice is. If he does not agree with me that *it is an act that violates a law*, the word no longer has any meaning; and if he does not agree with me that *law is the will of a legislator, made manifest to his subjects to be their rule of conduct*, I will not understand the word *law* any better than the word *justice*. Now I understand very well how a human law can be *unjust* when it violates a divine, revealed, or innate law. But the legislator of the world is God. What, then, is an injustice of God with respect to man? Is there by chance some common legislator above God who prescribes to him how he must act towards man? Who will judge between him and us? If the theist believes that the idea of God does not imply a justice similar to our own, what is he complaining about? He doesn't know what he is saying. If, on the contrary, he believes God just according to our own ideas, all the while complaining about the injustices he sees in our present state, he unwittingly admits a monstrous contradiction, that is to say, *the injustice of a just God. A certain order of things is unjust; therefore it cannot take place under the role of a just God.* This argument is only an error in the mouth of an atheist, but in the mouth of the theist, it is an absurdity. Once God is admitted, and once his justice is admitted as an attribute of his divinity, the theist cannot retrace his steps without talking nonsense, and he must on the contrary say: *A certain order of things takes place under the rule of an essentially just God; therefore this order of things is just for reasons of which we are ignorant*, explaining the order of things by the attributes instead of foolishly accusing the attributes because of the order of things.

I shall even accord this imaginary theist the culpable and no less foolish proposition *that there is no way of justifying the character of the divinity*.

What practical conclusion are we to draw from this? For this is surely the important question. Allow me, I pray you, *to set up* this fine argument: *God is unjust, cruel, pitiless, God takes pleasure in the misfortunes of his creatures, therefore* – and here is where I take the grumblers into account – *therefore*, apparently, *there is no need to pray to him*. On the contrary, gentlemen, and nothing is more obvious: *therefore it is necessary to pray to him and to serve him with much more zeal and anxiety* than if his mercy

---

[15]   I do not know if there are only a few atheists in the world, but I know very well that the entire philosophy of the last century was completely *atheistic*. I even find that atheism has the advantage of being frank. It says, *I do not see Him*, while the other says, *I do not see Him there*; but it never says anything else. I find this less *honest*.

was limitless, as we think is the case. I should like to put a question to you. If you had lived under the laws of a prince, not, what I would call wicked, but only severe and touchy, never easy about his authority, and closely watchful of every movement of his subjects, I would be curious to know if you would have believed yourself able to give yourself the same liberties as under the rule of another prince of a completely opposite character, content with general liberty, always favouring individual freedom, and never ceasing to fear his own power so that no one else should fear it? Certainly not. Well, the comparison leaps to the eye and admits no reply. The more God seems terrible to us, the more we must redouble our religious fear of him, the more ardent and indefatigable our prayers must be, since nothing tells us that his goodness will make up for them. The proof of God's existence preceding that of his attributes, we know *that he is* before knowing *what he is*; and we can never know completely *what he is*. So here we are, placed in an empire whose sovereign has published once and for all the laws that rule everything. These laws in general bear the stamp of wisdom and even a striking goodness; nevertheless some of them (I assume for the moment) appear hard, even *unjust*, if you like. This being the case, I ask all the discontented, what are we to do? Leave the empire, perhaps? Impossible, it is everywhere and there is nothing outside it. Complain, take offence, write against the sovereign? This will result in being punished or put to death. There is no better course to take than that of resignation and respect, I will even say *of love,* for as we start from the supposition that the master exists and that it is absolutely necessary to *serve* him, is it not better (whatever he is) to serve him with love than without?

I will not go back over the arguments in our previous conversations with which we have refuted the complaints that have been raised against Providence, but I think I should add that there is in these complaints something false and even foolish, or, as the English say, a certain *non-sense* that strikes the eye. In fact what do these sterile or culpable complaints mean? They offer no practical consequences for anyone, no guide capable of enlightening or improving anyone. On the contrary, these complaints, which can only harm and which are useless even to the atheist since they do not touch the most basic truth and even argue against it, are even more ridiculous and dangerous in the mouth of the theist, since they can only end in depriving him of love while leaving him in fear. For my part, I know nothing so contrary to the simplest lessons of common sense.

Do you know, gentlemen, the source of this flood of insolent doctrines that unceremoniously judge God and call him to account for his decrees? They come to us from that numerous phalanx we call the *learned*, and whom we in this century have not known how to keep in their place, which is a secondary one. In the past there were very few savants, and very few of this very small number were impious; today we see nothing but *savants*;

it is a profession, a crowd, a nation, and among them the already unfortunate exception has become the rule. Everywhere they have usurped an unlimited influence, and yet, in my view, if there is one thing certain in this world, it is that is not for science to guide men. Nothing necessary is confided to it; it would be necessary to have lost one's mind to believe that God had charged academies to teach us who he is and what we owe him. It belongs to prelates, to noblemen, to great officers of the state to be the depositories and guardians of saving truths, to teach peoples what is good and what is bad, what is true and what is false in the moral and spiritual orders. The others have no right to reason about these sorts of things. They have the natural sciences to amuse them; what do they have to complain about? As for the one who speaks or writes to deprive people of a national dogma, he must be hung like a housebreaker. Rousseau himself agreed with this without dreaming of what he was asking for himself.[16] Why have we been so imprudent as to grant freedom of speech to everyone? This is what has ruined us. The philosophers (or those who have been called such) all have a certain fierce and rebellious pride that puts up with nothing; without exception they detest every distinction they do not share; there is no authority that does not displease them; there is nothing above them they do not hate. If they are allowed, they will attack everything, even God, because he is the master. See if it is not the same men who have written against kings and against the one who established them! Ah, if when the earth is finally re-established ...

The Senator

What a singular peculiarity of climate! After the warmest day, here is a wind so cold that the place is no longer habitable. I would not want an excited man to find himself on this terrace; I would not even want to have too animated a conversation. It would be enough to lose one's voice. So, until tomorrow, my good friends.

NOTES TO THE EIGHTH DIALOGUE

i The very books of the Protestants offer several testimonies favourable to this dogma. I will not refuse myself the pleasure of citing one of the most striking, and I will not have to exhume a folio edition to do it. In the *Mélanges extraits des papiers de madame Necker* [3 vols. (Paris 1798)] the editor, Monsieur Necker, with respect to the death of his *incomparable* spouse, recalled this remark by a country woman: "If that one is not received in paradise, we are all lost." And he adds, *Ah! Undoubtedly she is there in*

---

[16] *Contrat social.*

that celestial place; SHE IS THERE OR SHE WILL BE THERE, and her credit will be of service to her friends! (Observations de l'éditeur, 1:13.)

One would have to agree that this text emits a strong enough odour of Catholicism, with respect to purgatory as well as with respect to the cult of the saints; and I don't think that one could cite a more natural and more spontaneous protest of good sense against the prejudice of sect and education.

ii Dr Beattie, in speaking of the sixth book of the *Aeneid*, notes Vergil's *sublime theory of future rewards and punishments, the outlines of which he is known to have taken from the Pythagoreans and Platonists, who probably were indebted for them to some ancient tradition.* He adds *that this theory, however imperfect, is consonant enough with the hopes and fears of men, and their natural notions of virtue and vice, to render the poet's narrative alarming and interesting in a high degree.* (*On Truth*, Part III, Chap. II, pp. 221, 223.)

As a Protestant, the doctor did not allow himself to speak more frankly; however one can see how his reason accommodated itself to a system that included above all *lugentes campos* [morning fields]. Protestantism, which is self-deceived about everything, as it will soon recognize, has never been mistaken in a more *anti-logical* and more *anti-divine* way than on the matter of purgatory.

The Greeks called the dead *the sufferers.* (*hoi kekmēkotes, hoi kamontes* [those who have laboured, the sufferers]) [Samuel] Clarke, on verse 278 of the third book of the *Iliad* [Greek and Latin edition (London 1729-32)], and [Johann August] Ernesti, in his Lexicon [*De glossariorum graecorum,* Leipzig, 1773], (see under KAMNŌ [sufferer]) claims that this expression is exactly synonymous with the Latin *vitâ functus* [dead]; it seems to me that this cannot be true, especially with respect to the second form *kamontes,* since Homer's verse where this remarkable expression is found indicates, without the least doubt, life and *actual suffering.*

Kai potomoi kai gaia, kai hoi hypernethe KAMONTAS
anthrōpous tinysthon, etc.

[And you, rivers, and you, earth, and you who under the earth punish the dead.] (Homer *Iliad* III.278–79.)

iii Malebranche, after having given this fine demonstration of the existence of God by the idea that we have of him, with all the force, clarity, and elegance imaginable, adds these words so worthy of him and so worthy of our most prudent meditations: *But,* he says, *it useless enough to propose to ordinary men these demonstrations ... that might be called personal.* (Malebranche, *Recherche de la vérité,* Bk. IV, chap. II.) So everyone for whom this demonstration is made cries with all his heart: *I thank you for not being like one of those!* Here the prayer of the Pharisee is permitted and even ordered,

262 St Petersburg Dialogues

provided that in saying it *no one* thinks at all of his talents, and does not experience the least movement of hate against *one of those.*

iv One of these desperate fools, remarkable by I know not what bitter, immoderate, and repulsive pride, who would give every reader the desire to go and beat the author if he were alive, particularly distinguished himself by what he drew from this great sophism. He presented us with a theory of ends *that included works of art and those of nature* (a shoe, for example, and a planet), *and which proposed rules of analysis for discovering the design of an artist by the inspection of his work.* For example, someone just invented a stocking frame; you are bound to *discover by means of analysis the design of the artist*, and because you have not guessed that it is for *silk stockings*, there is no *purpose*, and, in consequence, no artist. *This theory is destined to replace the works where this question is poorly treated, for up to the present the majority of works written on final causes include principles so hazardous, so vague, observations so puerile and so disconnected, reflections so trivial and so declamatory, that one must not be surprised that they have disgusted so many persons with these sorts of readings.* However he very carefully refrains from naming the authors of these *puerile* and *declamatory* works, for he would have had to name all that has ever been seen of the greatest, most religious, and most loveable authors in the world, which is to say, all those who resemble himself the least.

Ninth Dialogue

The Senator

Well, Count, are you ready to take up the question you were talking about yesterday?

The Count

There is nothing, gentlemen, I will not do to satisfy you, so far as I am able. However, first permit me to point out to you that all sciences have their mysteries and at certain points the apparently most obvious theory will be found in contradiction with experience. Politics, for example, offers several proofs of this truth. In theory, is anything more absurd than hereditary monarchy? We judge it by experience, but if government had never been heard of and we had to choose one, whoever would deliberate between hereditary and elective monarchy would be taken for a fool. Yet we know by experience that the first is, all things considered, the best that can be imagined, while the second is the worst. What arguments could not be amassed to establish that sovereignty comes from the people? However they all amount to nothing. Sovereignty is always *taken*, never *given*, and a second more profound theory subsequently discovers why this must be so. Who would not say the best political constitution is that which has been debated and drafted by statesmen perfectly acquainted with the national character, and who have foreseen every circumstance? Nevertheless nothing is more false. The best constituted people is the one that has the fewest written constitutional laws, and every written constitution is WORTHLESS.

You will not have forgotten the day when Professor P... burst out so strongly against the French system of venality of offices. I do not think that there is anything more revolting at first glance, and yet it would not be difficult to demonstrate, even to the professor, the fallacy of considering venality *in itself* instead of considering it simply as a means *of rendering office hereditary;* and I had the pleasure of convincing you that hereditary magistracy was the best that could have been imagined for France.[1]

So we should not be astonished if, in other branches of knowledge, especially in metaphysics and natural theology, we encounter propositions that completely scandalize our reason, and that nevertheless are subsequently demonstrated by the most solid arguments.

Among the most important of these propositions must be ranged the one I was happy to announce to you yesterday, *that the righteous, suffering voluntarily, satisfy not only for themselves, but for the culpable, who, of themselves, could not expiate their own debts.*

Instead of talking to you myself, or if you wish, before talking to you myself about this great subject, allow me, gentlemen, to cite for you two writers who have each treated it in their own way, and who without reading each other or being known to each other, are found to be in surprising agreement.

The first is an English gentleman named [Soame] Jenyns,[2] who died in 1787, a distinguished man in every respect, who won greater honour for himself by producing a very short but quite substantial book entitled *A View of the Internal Evidence of the Christian Religion.*[i] I know no work more original nor more deeply thought out. The second is the anonymous author of *Considérations sur la France*, published for the first time in 1794.[3] He was a long time contemporary of Mr Jenyns, but without ever having heard of him or his book before the year 1803; this is something of which you can be perfectly sure. I have no doubt that you will listen with pleasure to the reading of these two pieces so peculiar by their agreement.

The Chevalier

Do you have these two works? I would read them with pleasure, the first especially, which would certainly suit me, since it is very good without being long.

The Count

---

[1]   [In 1788, Maistre had written a brief memoir defending venality. For the text, see "De la vénalité des charges dans une monarchie" in Jean-Louis Darcel, "Joseph de Maistre et la reforme de l'état en 1788," *Revue des études maistriennes*, no. 11 (1990): 62–69.]

[2]   [Maistre spelled this name as "Jennyngs."]

[3]   Count de Maistre himself. (Editor's Note) [For some inexplicable reason, Maistre here gives an incorrect date for his book. In fact, the work did not come off the presses in Neuchâtel until April 1797 – with the false imprint of London, 1797. See the Introduction to the critical edition published by Jean-Louis Darcel, (Geneva: Slatkine 1980), 44–54.]

I have neither of these two books in my possession, but you see these immense volumes lying here on my desk. There is where, for more than thirty years, I have written all the most striking things I have encountered in my reading. Sometimes I limit myself to simple references; other times I transcribe essential passages word for word; often I accompany these with notes, and often too I put down my thoughts of the moment – those *sudden illuminations* that would remain mute if their flash of lightning was not captured in writing. Carried by the revolutionary whirlwind to various countries of Europe, I have never abandoned these notebooks; and so you must believe me when I tell you of my great pleasure in paging through this great collection. Every passage awakens in me a multitude of interesting ideas and melancholy memories a thousand times more agreeable than what are usually called *pleasures*. I see there pages dated Geneva, Rome, Venice, Lausanne. I cannot come across the names of those cities without recalling those of the excellent friends whom I had there and who once consoled my exile. Some of them are no longer alive, but their memory is sacred to me. Often I come across pages written at my dictation by a well-loved child separated from me by the tempest. Alone in my solitary study, I extend my arms to her, and I believe I hear her call to me in her turn. A certain date recalls for me a time on the banks of a river suddenly frozen with ice when I ate with a French bishop a dinner that we had prepared ourselves. I was cheerful that day; I had the strength to laugh softly with the excellent man who today awaits me in a better world; but the night before I had passed at anchor in an open boat, in the midst of profound darkness, with neither fire nor light, without being able to go to bed or even to rest a moment, hearing only the sinister cries of some boatmen who never ceased menacing us, and only being able to extend a miserable mat over cherished heads to protect them from heavy snow that kept falling ...

But, good God! What have I been saying, and where have I been straying? Chevalier, you are the closest, would you please pick up Volume B of my collection, and without further ado, read first the passage from Jenyns, since it is dated first. You will find it on page 525. I put a bookmark there this morning.

The Chevalier

Yes, here it is.

"Reason cannot assure us that some sufferings of individuals are not necessary to the happiness and well-being of the whole; it cannot convince us, that they do not actually arise from this necessity, or that, for this cause, they may not be required of us, and levied like a tax for the public benefit; or that this tax may not be paid by one Being as well as another; and therefore if voluntarily offered, be justly accepted from the innocent instead of the guilty ... as we do not know the root of the disease, we cannot judge of what is, or is not, a proper and effectual remedy. It is remarkable, that, notwithstanding all the seeming absurdities of this doctrine, ... it has been universally adopted in all ages, as far as history can carry us back in all our inquiries to the earliest times; in which we find all nations, civilized and barbarous, however differing all other religious opinions, agreeing alone in the expediency of appeasing their offended Deities by sacrifices, that is, by the vicarious sufferings of men or other animals. This notion could never have been derived from reason, because it directly contradicts it; nor from ignorance, because ignorance could never have contrived so unaccountable an expedient, ... nor from the artifice of kings or priests, in order to acquire dominion over the people, because it seems not adapted to this end; and we find it implanted in the minds of the most remote savages at this day discovered, who have neither kings or priests, artifice or dominion, amongst them. It must therefore be derived from natural instinct or supernatural revelation, both which are equally the operations of divine power ... Christianity has discovered to us many important truths, with which we were before entirely unacquainted; and amongst them are these: ... that *God will accept the sufferings of Christ as an atonement for the sins of mankind* ... This truth is no less intelligible than the truth that ... *One man acquits the debt of another man.*[4] But ... why God accepts these vicarious punishments, or to what purposes they may be subservient, Christianity informs us not, because no information could enable us to comprehend these mysteries; and therefore it does not require that we should know or believe anything about them."

[The Count][5]

Now I am going to read you the other passage, taken from *Considérations sur la France.*

---

[4] It is difficult in these sorts of things to perceive anything that escaped Bellarmine. He said: *Satisfactio est compensatio pœnæ vel solutio debiti: potest autem unus ità pro alio pœnam compensare vel debitum solvere, ut ill satisfacere meritò dici possit.* Which is to say: "The compensation of a punishment or the payment of a debt is what is called *satisfaction.* Moreover, a man can compensate a punishment or pay a debt for another man, so that one can say with truth, that *satisfies.*" (Robert Bellarmine, *Controversiis christianae fidei adversus hujus temporis haeretica.* Bk. I, chap. II, [3 vols.] (Ingolstadt 1601), Vol. 3, col. 1493.)

[5] [The 1821 and subsequent editions seem to have forgotten that the floor had been given to the Chevalier; the comments that follow this citation from Maistre's own work are obviously those of the Count and not those of the Chevalier. See the Darcel edition, 462, n. k.]

"I know well that in all these considerations we are continually troubled by the wearisome sight of the innocent who perish with the guilty, but without becoming deeply involved in this most profound question, we can consider it solely in the light of the universal and age-old dogma that *the innocent suffer for the benefit of the guilty.*

"It was from this dogma, it seems to me, that the ancients derived the custom of sacrifices that was practised everywhere and that was judged useful not only for the living but also for the dead,[6] a typical custom that habit has led us to regard without astonishment, but whose roots are nonetheless difficult to discover.

"*Self-sacrifices*, so famous in antiquity, come from the same dogma. Decius[7] had *faith* that the sacrifice of his life would be accepted by the divinity and that he could use it to balance all the evils that menaced his country.[8]

"Christianity came to consecrate this dogma, which is perfectly natural to man although appearing difficult to arrive at by reason.

"Thus, there could have been in the heart of Louis XVI, in that of the saintly Elizabeth, such an impulse, such an acceptance, capable of saving France.

"Sometimes it is asked, of what use are these terrible austerities, which are also *self-sacrifices*, practised by certain religious orders? It would be precisely the same thing to ask of what use is Christianity, which rests entirely on an enlargement of this same dogma *of innocence paying for crime.*

"The authority that approves these orders chooses certain men and insulates them from the world in order to make them *conductors.*

"There is nothing but violence in the universe; but we are spoiled by a modern philosophy that tells us that *all is good*, whereas evil has tainted everything, and in a very real sense, *all is evil*, since nothing is in its place.

---

[6] They sacrificed, literally, *for the repose of souls. – But*, says Plato, *it will be said that we will be punished in hell, in our person or in that of our descendants, for the crimes we have committed in this world. To that one can respond that there are sacrifices of great efficacy for the expiation of sins, as has been said by entire cities, by poets born of the gods, and by prophets sent by the gods.* (Plato *Republic* II.)

[7] [Decius was the name of three Romans who are supposed to have sacrificed themselves to the gods to secure victories for the Roman armies in 340, 295, and 290 B.C.]

[8] *To expiate all anger of the gods ... the one had drawn all the threats and menaces of the supernal and infernal gods upon himself alone.* (Livy [*From the Founding of the City*] VIII.9 and 10 [Trans. B.A. Foster, Loeb Classical Library 1926])

The keynote of the system of our creation has been lowered, and following the rules of harmony, all the others have been lowered proportionately. *All creation groans,*[9] and tends with pain and effort towards another order of things."

I am persuaded, gentlemen, that you cannot but be astonished to see two writers perfectly unknown to each other agreeing on this point, and that you will undoubtedly be disposed to believe two instruments could not be heard so perfectly in harmony with each other if they had not been, both of them, in harmony with a superior instrument that put them in tune.

Men have never doubted that innocence can make satisfaction for crime and have believed, moreover, that there is an expiatory power in blood; so that *life*, which is blood, can redeem another *life*.

Look closely at this belief, and you will see that if God himself had not put it into the human mind, it would never have arisen. The big words *superstition* and *prejudice* explain nothing, for no error has been universal and constant. If a false opinion reigns over one people, you will not find it among its neighbour, or if sometimes it seems to spread over a great number of peoples, the passing of time will efface it.

However the belief I am talking about suffers no exceptions of time and place. Antique and modern nations, civilized or barbaric nations, scientific or backward ages, true or false religions – there has not been one single voice in disagreement in the world.

Lastly, the ideas of *sin* and *sacrifice* were so closely amalgamated in the minds of men in antiquity that the sacred language expressed both ideas with the same word. Hence that well-known Hebraism, used by St Paul, *that the Saviour was made sin for us.*[10]

To this theory of sacrifices is also attached the inexplicable custom of circumcision, practised among so many nations of antiquity, which the descendants of Isaac and Ismael perpetuate to our day with a not less inexplicable constancy, and that the explorers of the past few centuries have found in a Pacific archipelago (namely Tahiti), in Mexico, on the island of

---

[9] St Paul to the Romans, 8:19. Charles Bonnet's system of palingenesis has some similarities to St Paul's text; but this idea does not take him to that of a prior degradation. Nevertheless they agree quite well. [Charles Bonnet (1720–93) was a Swiss naturalist and philosopher whose philosophical theories combined Leibnizian and Christian metaphysics. His *Palingénésie philosophique* was published in 1769.] The divine hand's terrible blow against man necessarily produced a counter-blow on all the parts of nature.

EARTH FELT THE WOUND.

(Milton, *Paradise Lost*, IX, 783.)

This is why all creatures groan.

[10] 2 Corinthians 5:21.

Hispaniola, and in North America, up to 30° of latitude.[11] Some peoples may vary in the way they carry it out, but everywhere one finds *a painful and bloody operation* carried out on the organs of reproduction. Which is to say: *Anathema on human generation, and SALVATION BY BLOOD.*

Humanity professed these dogmas since the time of its fall, until the great victim, *raised to draw all to him,* cried out on Calvary:

ALL THINGS ARE ACCOMPLISHED.[12]

Then the veil of the temple was torn in two,[13] the great secret of the sanctuary was known, as far as it can be known in the order of things of which we form a part. We understood why man has always believed that one soul could be saved by another, and why he was always sought his regeneration through blood.

Without Christianity man does not know what he is because he finds himself isolated in the world and cannot compare himself to anything. The first service this religion renders him is to show him what he is worth by showing him what he has cost.

BEHOLD, IT IS GOD WHO HAS A GOD KILLED.[14]

Yes, let us behold it attentively, my friends who hear me! We will see everything in this sacrifice: the enormity of the crime that required such an expiation, the inconceivable greatness of the being capable of accomplishing it, and the infinite price of the victim who said, *Here I am.*[15]

Now, it can be seen, that on the one hand, this whole doctrine of antiquity was only the prophetic cry of humanity announcing salvation by blood, and that on the other hand, Christianity has come to justify this prophecy by putting the reality in place of the type, so that an innate and fundamental dogma never ceased to announce that this great sacrifice was the basis of the new revelation, and that this revelation, glittering with all the brilliance of truth, proves in its turn the divine origin of the dogma that we constantly perceive as a bright light amidst all the shadows of paganism.

---

[11] See the *Lettres américaines* of Count Gian-Rinaldo Carli-Rubbi (translated from the Italian), 2 vols. (Paris 1788), Letter IX, pp. 149 and 152.

[12] [John 19:30.]

[13] [Mark 15:38]

[14] Aeschylus *Prometheus Bound* 92. [I have given an English translation of Maistre's French. David Grene's translation of the Greek reads: "See what I, a God, suffer at the hands of Gods." (*The Complete Greek Tragedies* (Chicago 1953), Vol. I.)]

[15] *You prepared a body for me ... and then he says:* Here I am. (Psalm 39(40):7; Hebrews 10:5.)

This agreement is one of the most convincing proofs that it would be possible to imagine.

However these truths are not proved by calculation or by laws of movement. The person who has passed his life without ever having tasted things divine, the person who has narrowed his mind and dried up his heart in sterile speculations that could never make him better in this life nor prepare him for the next, such a one, I say, will reject proofs of this kind, and will not even understand them. There are truths that a man can grasp only with *the spirit of his heart*.[16] Often an upright man is shaken by seeing persons whose intelligence he esteems reject proofs that appear clear to him; this is a pure illusion. These people lack sense, and that is all there is to it. When the most capable man lacks the religious sense, not only can we not convince him, we do not even have any means of making him understand us, which only proves his misfortune. Everyone knows the story of the man born blind who discovered, by a great deal of reflection, *that bright red is very much like the sound of a trumpet*. Whether this blind man is a fool or a Saunderson,[17] what does it matter to someone who knows what bright red is?

It would require many more details to plumb the depths of this interesting subject of sacrifices; but I am afraid I would be abusing your patience and going astray. It is a question that to be treated in depth needs all the calm of a written discussion.[18] In any case, my good friends, I think that we know enough about this to deal with the sufferings of the just. This world is a military expedition, an eternal combat. No doubt all those who fought courageously in a battle are worthy of praise, but also there is no doubt that the greatest glory goes to the one who returns wounded. You have not forgotten, I'm sure, what we were told the other day by a witty man whom I love with all my heart. *I do not at all agree with Seneca*, he said, *who would not be the least surprised if God occasionally gave himself*

---

[16] MENTE CORDIS SUI. (Luke 1:51) [Maistre's translation of Luke appears idiosyncratic; most translations read "conceit of their heart."] *Mens pectoris*. (Ovid *Fasti* II.798) *Mens animi* (Plautus *Epid.* VI.I.3) [The last two references are from the manuscript of the *Soirées*. (Darcel ed.)]

[17] [Nicholas Saunderson was a blind English thinker; Diderot, in his *Lettre sur les aveugles á l'usage de ceux qui voient*, had Saunderson remark that if he, being blind, had to prove the existence of God, he would have to touch him. This invented passage, in turn, provoked an exchange of comments between Voltaire and Diderot on logical proofs for the existence of God.]

[18] See, at the end of this volume, the piece entitled "An Elucidation on Sacrifices."

the pleasure of contemplating a great man grappling with adversity.[19] *For myself, I admit to you that I cannot understand how God can amuse himself by tormenting honest people.* Perhaps he could have embarrassed Seneca with this philosophic banter, but he would scarcely embarrass us. There is no wholly *just man*, as we have so often said, but if there were a man *sufficiently just* to merit the approval of his creator, who could be surprised if God, ATTENTIVE TO HIS OWN WORK, took pleasure in perfecting him? The father of a family can laugh at a crude servant who swears or lies, but his tenderly severe hand rigorously punishes these faults in an only son for whom he would willingly sacrifice his own life. If tenderness forgives nothing, it is because there no longer is anything to forgive. In putting a good man to grapple with misfortune, God purifies him for his past faults, puts him on guard against future faults, and matures him for heaven. Undoubtedly *he takes pleasure* in seeing him escape the inevitable justice that waits him in the next world. Is there a greater joy for love than the submission that disarms it? Moreover, when one reflects that these sufferings are not only useful for the just but that they can by religious acceptance be turned to the profit of the guilty, and that in suffering they really *sacrifice* for all men, one will agree that in fact it is impossible to imagine a sight more worthy of the divinity.

One more word on the sufferings of the *just.* Do you by chance believe that the viper is venomous only at the moment it strikes and that the man afflicted with a hidden illness is truly epileptic only at the moment of an attack?

The Senator

Where do you want to take us, my dear friend?

The Count

I will not make a long circuit, as you will see. The man who knows men only by their actions calls them *wicked* only when he sees them committing a crime. However one might as well believe that the viper's venom is engendered at the moment it strikes. The event does not create wickedness, it manifests it.[20] God, who sees all things, God, who knows our most intimate inclinations and thoughts better than men who only know one

---

[19] *For my part, I do not wonder if sometimes the gods are moved by the desire to behold great men wrestle with some calamity ... Here is a spectacle worthy of the regard of God as he contemplates his works ... A brave man matched against ill fortune!* (Seneca *On Providence* II.7–8 [Loeb].)

[20] Every educated man will recognize here some of Plutarch's ideas. *On the Delays of Divine Vengeance, [Moralia]*)

another through sense experience, employs punishment as a remedy, and strikes this man who appears healthy to us to extirpate the disease before the seizure. It often happens that in our blind impatience we complain of the slowness of Providence in the punishment of crimes, and yet by a singular contradiction we also accuse it when its beneficent swiftness represses vicious inclinations before they have produced crimes.

Sometimes God spares a known sinner because the punishment would be useless, while he chastises the hidden sinner because this chastisement will save a man. Thus the wise doctor avoids tiring an incurable patient with useless medicines and operations. *"Let him be,"* he says while withdrawing, *"keep him amused, and give him everything he asks for."* If the nature of things allowed him to see clearly in the body of an apparently healthy man the germ of an illness that will kill him tomorrow or in ten years, would he not advise him to submit to the most distasteful remedies and to the most painful operations? If the coward preferred death to the pain, would not the doctor, whose eye and hand we are supposing to be equally infallible, advise his friends to tie him down and save him for his family in spite of himself? Those surgical instruments whose sight makes us faint – the saw, the trepan, the forceps, the lithotrite, etc. – were certainly not invented by some evil enemy of humanity. Well, these instruments for the cure of physical ills are in man's hand what physical ills are in God's hand for the extirpation of real ills.[21] Can a dislocated or fractured limb be restored without pain? Can a wound or an internal illness be cured without abstinence, without privations of all kind, without a more or less tedious regime? In the whole of pharmacology, how many medicines are there that do not revolt our senses? Are sufferings, even those caused directly by illnesses, anything other than the effort of life to defend itself? In the sensible order as in the higher order, the law is the same and as old as evil: THE REMEDY FOR DISORDER WILL BE PAIN.

The Chevalier

When I have edited this conversation, I want to read it to our mutual friend whom you mentioned to me a little while ago; I am persuaded that he will

---

[21] One can say of sufferings precisely what the prince of Christian orators said of work: "We are sinners, and Scripture says, *We have all been conceived in iniquity* ... God therefore sends pain to man as a punishment for his disobedience and rebellion, and this punishment is, at the same time, in its relation to us, a satisfaction and a preservative. A satisfaction to expiate for sins committed, and a preservative to prevent us from committing them; a satisfaction because we have been liars, and a preservative so that we will cease to be such." (Bourdaloue, *Sermon sur l'oisiveté.*)

find your reasons good, which will give you great pleasure since you love him so much. If I am not mistaken, he will even believe that you have added to the arguments of Seneca, who must nevertheless have been a great genius, since everyone cites him. I recall the first version I could have known in a little book entitled *The Christian Seneca*, which contained only this philosopher's words. He must have been a man of great ability to have been accorded this honour. So I had a great veneration for him, when La Harpe came and disrupted all my ideas with an entire volume in his *Lycée* series, quite filled with cutting citations against Seneca. However I must admit that I still tend to agree with the valet in the comedy:

This Seneca, sir, was a very great man!

The Count

You have done very well, Chevalier, not to change your opinion. I know by heart everything that can be said against Seneca, but there are also many things to be said in his favour. You need only notice that the greatest fault for which he is reproached, his style, turns out to be to the profit of his readers. Undoubtedly it is too elaborate, too prolix; undoubtedly he aims too much at singularity; but with his original turns of phrase, with his unexpected barbs, he penetrates minds deeply,

Moreover everything he says leaves a long memory.

I know no other author (except perhaps Tacitus) that one remembers more easily. For getting to the heart of things, he has invaluable pieces; his letters are a treasure of morality and good philosophy. There are some of his letters that Bourdaloue or Massillon could have recited from the pulpit with some slight changes. His *natural questions*[22] are without contradiction that most precious thing that antiquity has left us of this kind. He did a beautiful treatise on *Providence*, which was not yet known in Rome in the time of Cicero. I will not insist on citing him on many questions that had not been treated or even occurred to his predecessors. However, despite his merit, which is very great, he would allow me to agree, without pride, that I could add to his arguments. For in this I would have no other merit than to have profited from the greatest assistance; and I also believe, to tell the truth, that he is superior to those who preceded him for the same reason, and that if he had not been bound by the prejudices of his time, country, and class, he would have been able to tell us just about everything I have told you, for everything leads me to think that he had a deep enough knowledge of our dogmas.

---

[22] [*Quaestiones Naturales (Investigations in Natural Philosophy)*]

The Senator

Do you perhaps believe in the Christianity of Seneca or in his correspondence with St Paul?

The Count

I am very far from supporting either the one or the other as facts, but I believe that these beliefs have a real root, and I am as sure that Seneca heard St Paul as I am that you are hearing me this moment. Born and living in the light, we know nothing of its effects on men who have never seen it. When the Portuguese brought Christianity to the Indies, the Japanese, who are the most intelligent people of Asia, were so struck by this new doctrine of whose fame they were as yet very imperfectly informed, that they sent two members of their principal academies to Goa to inform themselves about this new religion. Soon Japanese ambassadors came to the Viceroy of the Indies to ask for Christian preachers – so that in passing we can say that there was never anything more peaceful, more legal, and more free than the introduction of Christianity to Japan,[ii] which is something profoundly ignored by many of people who take it upon themselves to talk of the matter. Yet the Greeks and the Romans of the time of Augustus were certainly quite different men from the Japanese of the sixteenth century.[23] We do not reflect enough on the effect that Christianity must have had on many of the good minds of this period. The Roman governor of Caesarea, *who had very precise information about this doctrine*, and who, quite frightened, said to St Paul: *"That is enough for the present, go your way,"*[24] and the men of the Areopagus, who said to him, *"We will hear you again on these matters,"*[25] rendered, without knowing it, fine praise for his preaching. When Agrippa, after having heard St Paul, said to him: *In a short while you would persuade me to become a Christian*, the apostle replied to him: *"I would to God that, whether it be long or short, not only you but also all who hear me today might become such as I am, EXCEPT FOR THESE BONDS,"* and he showed them his chains.[26] Though these pages are eighteen centuries old, and though I have

---

[23] In their knowledge of science, perhaps, but as for their character, good sense, and natural intelligence, I am not so sure. St Francis Xavier, the European who knew the Japanese best, had the highest opinion of them. *This is,* he said, *a nation that is prudent, ingenious, submissive to reason, and very avid for instruction.* (St Francis Xavier, *Epistolae* (Wratislavia 1734), 166.) He often spoke of them in this way. (Editor's note.)

[24] Acts 24:22,25.

[25] Acts 17:32.

[26] Acts 26:29.

read this wonderful reply a hundred times, *I still believe I am reading it for the first time*, so noble, gentle, ingenious, and penetrating does it appear to me! I cannot tell you how touched I am by it. The heart of d'Alembert, although shrunken by pride and by an icy philosophy, could not hold out against this discourse.[27] Judge the effect it must have produced on his listeners. Remember that these men of antiquity were made like us. This king Agrippa, this queen Bernice, these proconsuls Sergius and Gallio (of whom the first became a Christian), these governors Felix and Faustus, this tribune Lysias, and all their kind, had parents, friends, and correspondents. They spoke, they wrote. What we read today was repeated by a thousand mouths, and the news made a greater impression because the doctrine was announced by miracles that were undeniable, even for our days for anyone who judges dispassionately. St Paul preached a year and half at Corinth and two years at Ephesus;[28] everything that happened in these great cities was immediately known in Rome. Finally the great apostle arrived in Rome itself where *for two full years he remained, welcoming all who came to him, and preaching with all boldness and without hindrance.*[29] Do you think that such preaching could have escaped the attention of Seneca, who was then sixty years old? When later on, prosecuted at least twice before the tribunals for the doctrine he taught, Paul defended himself and was acquitted,[30] do you think that these events would not have made his preaching more celebrated and more powerful? All those who have the least knowledge of antiquity know that Christianity, in its early days, was for the Christians an *initiation*, and for the others a *system*, a philosophic or theurgic *sect*. Everyone knows how avid they then were for new opinions; it is not even permitted to imagine that Seneca would have had no knowledge of St Paul's preaching, and the demonstration can be had by reading his works in which he speaks of God and of man in an entirely new way. Alongside the passage in his letters where he says that *God must be honoured and loved*, in the margin of the copy I use, an unknown hand once wrote: *Deum amari vix alii auctores dixerunt.*[31] The expression is at least very rare and very remarkable.

---

[27] Here perhaps there could have been a slight error of memory, for I do not know where d'Alembert spoke of this discourse. If I am not mistaken, he only praised the one that this same apostle gave at the Areopagus, and that had such an admirable effect. (Editor's note.)

[28] Acts 17:11, 19:10.

[29] Acts 28:30,31.

[30] 2 Timothy 4:16.

[31] *Elsewhere one will scarcely read that God is loved.* If there exists something of this kind, one will find it in Plato. St Augustine did him this honour. (*The City of God*, VIII, 5 and 6. See Seneca, *Epistle 47*.)

Pascal has very appropriately observed *that no other religion but our own asks that God be loved;* on this I recall that Voltaire, in the shameful commentary that he added to the thoughts of this famous man, objected *that Marcus Aurelius* CONTINUALLY *spoke of loving God.*[iii] Why didn't this fine scholar deign to cite the passages for us? Nothing would have been easier, since, according to him, they abounded. However let us return to Seneca. Elsewhere he said, *My Gods,*[32] and even, *our God and our father;*[33] he said emphatically: *That the will of God be done.*[34] Some are unimpressed by these expressions, but look for anything similar in the philosophers that preceded him, and look for them especially in Cicero who dealt with precisely the same subjects. You will not, I hope, require other citations from my memory right now, but read the works of Seneca, and you will sense the truth of what I have had the honour of telling you. I flatter myself that when you come upon certain passages that I have only a vague memory of, where he speaks of the unbelievable heroism of certain men who have braved the most horrible torments with a fearlessness that appears to surpass all the strength of humanity, you will scarcely doubt that he had the Christians in mind.[iv]

Moreover, without being decisive, the tradition on the Christianity of Seneca and his relations with St Paul is nevertheless something more than nothing, especially if one adds to it other presumptions.

Finally, Christianity was scarcely born before taking root in the world's capital. The apostles had preached in Rome twenty-five years before the reign of Nero. St Peter had met there with Philo; similar conferences would necessarily have produced great results. When we hear of Judaism in Rome under the first emperors, and especially among the Romans themselves, very often it is a question of Christians; nothing was easier than to confuse them. We know that the Christians, at least a large enough number among them, long believed themselves bound to the observation of certain points of the Mosaic law, such as abstinence from blood. Well before the fourth century, we also see Christians martyred in Persia for having refused to violate legal observances. So it is not surprising that they were often confused, and in fact you will see Christians enveloped like the Jews in the persecutions that the latter attracted to themselves by their revolt against the Emperor Adrian. It would be necessary to have a very fine eye and a very accurate view, and one would have to look very closely to distinguish the two religions in the writings of the authors of the first two centuries. For example, whom did Plutarch want to speak about when, in his treatise on

---

[32] *Epistle 93* [.10].

[33] *Epistle 110* [.20].

[34] *Let man be pleased with whatever has pleased God. Epistle 74* [.20].

superstition, he cried out: *Oh Greeks, what have the barbarians done to you?* And immediately following when he spoke of *sabbaths*, of *prostrations*, of shameful squatting, etc.?[v] Read the entire passage, and you will not know if it is a question of a Sunday or a sabbath, or if you are contemplating a Judaic wake or the first rudiments of a canonical penance. For a long time I saw there Judaism pure and simple; today I lean towards the contrary opinion. I would cite for you on this matter the verse of Rutilius, *if I remembered*, as Madame de Sévigné said. I refer to his travels; you will read there the bitter complaints he made *about this Jewish superstition that has taken over the whole world*.[vi] He begrudged Pompei and Titus for have conquered this miserable Judea that has poisoned the whole world: now who could believe that it is a question here of Judaism? Is it not, on the contrary, Christianity that has taken over the world and that is pushing back equally both Judaism and paganism? Here the facts speak; there is nothing to dispute.

For the rest, gentlemen, I will readily assume that you would agree completely with Montaigne, and that a sure means to make you hate probable things would be *to plant* them for you as proved. So believe what you will on this particular question; but tell me, I beg you, do you think that Judaism alone was not sufficient to influence the moral and religious system of a man as sharp as Seneca, and who knew this religion quite well?[vii] Let the poets speak who only saw the surface of things, and who believed that they had said everything when they called the Jews *verpos* [circumcised] and *recutitos* [circumcised], and anything you wish. Undoubtedly the great anathema was already upon them. However could not one, then as now, admire the writing while despising the persons? By means of the Septuagint version, Seneca could have read the Bible as easily as ourselves. What must he have thought when he compared poetic mythologies to the first verses of Genesis, or when he related the flood of Ovid to that of Moses? What a great source of reflection! All antique philosophy pales before the single book of *Wisdom*. No man who is intelligent and free of prejudices will read the Psalms without being struck with admiration and transported into a new world. Even with respect to persons, there are great distinctions to be made. Philo and Josephus were apparently quite accomplished men, and they could undoubtedly have been instructed by them. In general, there was in this nation, even in the most ancient times and long before their involvement with the Greeks, much more instruction than has commonly been believed, for reasons that it would not be difficult to determine. Where did they get their calendar, for example, one of the most accurate, and perhaps the most accurate of antiquity? Newton, in his chronology, did not disdain rendering it full justice,[viii] and he held that we can admire it even in our own times, since we see it marching in rank with those of other nations, without errors or embarrassment of any kind. One can see, by the example of Daniel, how the able men of that nation were considered by Babylon, which was certainly very knowledgeable. The famous Rabbi, *Moses Maimonides*, some of whose works I have looked at in translation, tells us that at the end of the great captivity a very large number of Jews did not want to return to their homes, that they established themselves in Babylon, that there they enjoyed the greatest measure of liberty, the greatest consideration, and that the guardianship of the most secret archives at Ecbatana were confided to men of that nation.[ix]

The other day in paging through my little Elzevirs[35] that you see there arranged in a circle on my rotating bookstand, I fell by chance on the Hebrew republic of *Pierre Cunæus*. It recalled for me a very curious anecdote about Aristotle, who conversed in Asia with a Jew, after which the most distinguished scholars of Greece appeared to him to be barbarians of some kind.[x]

The translation of its sacred books into what had become the world language,[xi] the dispersion of Jews in the different parts of the world, and the natural curiosity of men for everything that is new and extraordinary, made the Mosaic law known everywhere, so it could thus become an introduction to Christianity. For a long time Jews had served in the armies of several princes, who willingly employed them because of their recognized valour and unequalled loyalty. Alexander, especially, counted on them greatly and showed them the greatest respect. His successors on the throne of Egypt imitated him on this point and constantly gave to Jews the greatest marks of confidence. Lagus put the strongest fortresses of Egypt under their care, and to maintain the cities he had conquered in Libya found nothing better than sending Jewish colonies there. One of his Ptolemy successors wanted to procure for himself a dignified translation of their sacred books. [Ptolemy] Evergetes, after having conquered Syria, came to offer his thanksgiving in Jerusalem: he offered GOD a great number of victims and presented rich presents to the temple. Philometor and Cleopatra confided the government of the realm and the command of the army to two men of this nation.[36] In a word, everything justifies the discourse of Tobias to his brothers: *God has therefore scattered you among the Gentiles, who know*

---

[35] [The Elzevirs, a family of Dutch publishers who flourished in the seventeenth century, were particularly famous for their fine editions of classical and French authors. A passionate bibliophile, Maistre collected and cherished Elzevir editions. See Darcel, "Les bibliothèques de Joseph de Maistre 1768–1821."]

[36] Josephus *Against Apion* II.2.

not him, that you may declare his wonderful works, and make them know that there is no other almighty God besides him.[37]

According to the old ideas that admitted a crowd of divinities and especially of national gods, the God of Israel was, for the Greeks, for the Romans, and even for all the other nations, a new divinity added to others, which was nothing shocking. As there always is in the truth a secret action stronger than every prejudice, the new God, everywhere he showed himself, must necessarily have made a great impression on many minds. I will quickly cite for you some examples, and I could cite many others for you as well. The court of the Roman emperors had a great respect for the temple in Jerusalem. Caius Agrippa having traversed Judea *without having made his devotions there* (will you pardon me this expression?), his relative the Emperor Augustus was extremely irritated by this; and what was certainly singular is that a terrible scarcity that afflicted Rome at this time was regarded by public opinion as a punishment for this failure. As a kind of reparation, or as a spontaneous gesture still more honourable for him, Augustus ordered a daily sacrifice at the altar in Jerusalem at his own expense. Livia, his wife, had considerable gifts presented there. This was a fashion at court, and it developed to the point that all the nations, even those least friendly to the Jew, feared to offend him for fear of displeasing the master; and any man who would have dared touch the sacred book of the Jews or the money they sent to Jerusalem would have been considered and punished as having committed sacrilege. The good sense of Augustus must undoubtedly have been struck by way in which the Jews conceived the divinity. Through a singular blindness, Tacitus, in a celebrated text, praised this doctrine extravagantly while believing it blameworthy;[xii] but nothing has made such an impression on me as the astonishing wisdom of Tiberius on the subject of the Jews. Sejanus, who detested them, had wanted to throw on them suspicion for a plot, which would have cost them dearly. Tiberius paid no attention to this, *for,* this intelligent prince said, *this nation, by principle, will never lift a hand against a sovereign.* These Jews, who have been represented as a rabid and intolerant people, were, however, in certain respects the most tolerant of all, to the point that one sometimes has difficulty understanding how the exclusive possessors of the truth could have shown themselves so accommodating to foreign religions. We know the quite *liberal* way that Elisha resolved the case of conscience posed by a captain of the Syrian guard.[38] If the prophet had been a Jesuit, no doubt Pascal would have pilloried him in his *Provincial Letters.* Philo, if I'm not mistaken, observed somewhere that the Jewish high priest, alone

---

[37] Tobias 13:4.
[38] 4 Kings 5:19.

in the world, prayed for the nations and foreign powers.[39] In fact, I do not believe there is another example of this in antiquity. The temple of Jerusalem was surrounded by a portico meant for foreigners who came there to pray freely. A crowd of these *Gentiles* had confidence in this God (*whatever he was*) that was adored on the Mount of Sion. No one interfered with them or asked them to account for their national beliefs, and again we see them in the Gospel, coming, on the solemn day of Easter, to adore in Jerusalem, without the least mark of disapprobation or surprise on the part of the sacred historian.

The human mind having been sufficiently prepared or informed by this noble cult, Christianity appeared; and almost from the moment of its birth it was known and preached in Rome. This is enough for me to be correct in affirming that the superiority of Seneca over his predecessors, and by way of parenthesis I could say as much of Plutarch, on all the questions that really interest man can only be attributed to the more or less perfect knowledge that he had of Mosaic and Christian dogmas. The truth is made for our intelligence, just as the light is made for our eyes; both insinuate themselves in us without effort and without instruction any time they are free to act. From the moment Christianity appeared in the world, it made a perceptible change in the writings of philosophers, even the hostile or indifferent. All these writings have, if I may express it this way, *a colour* that works did not have before this great epoch. So therefore if human reason wants to show us its power, it looks for its evidence before our era, it is not above *beating its nurse*, it cites for us what it has received from revelation to prove to us that we do not need it. Please let me recall for you an indelible characteristic of that *all-purpose fool* (as Buffon called him) who had so much influence on a century quite worthy of listening to him. In his *Emile*, Rousseau tells us proudly: *It is in vain that the necessity of a revelation has been maintained, since God has said everything to our eyes, to our conscience, and to our judgement: God wants to be adored* IN SPIRIT AND IN TRUTH, *and the rest is only a procedural matter.*[40] There, gentlemen, you have what they call reasoning! *To adore God in mind and in truth!* This is a trifle, undoubtedly! It only required God to teach it to us.

When we were young our *nurse* asked us: *Why did God put us into the world?* We answered: *To know him, to love him, and to serve him in this life, and thus to merit his rewards in the next.* You see how this answer, which is comprehensible to the youngest child, is nevertheless so admirable, so amazing, so incontestably above everything that human knowledge has

---

[39] Baruch 1:11 – In doing this they were obeying a divine precept. Jeremias 29:7.

[40] *Emile*, [4 vols.] (The Hague 1762), 3:135.

ever been able to imagine, that the divine seal is as visible on this line of the elementary catechism as on the canticle of Mary or on the most penetrating oracles of the SERMON ON THE MOUNT.

So we must not be the least surprised if this divine doctrine, more or less known to Seneca, produced in his writings a great deal of evidence that cannot be too much noticed. I hope that this little discussion, which we have so to say found on our way, has not bored you.

As for La Harpe, whom I had completely forgotten, what can I tell you? In favour of his talents, his noble resolution, his sincere repentance, and his invariable perseverance, let us be thankful for all that he said about things that he did not understand or that revealed in him some slumbering passion. *May he rest in peace!* And we as well, gentlemen; let us *rest in peace*. We have done too much today, for it is two in the morning. Nevertheless we have done nothing to be sorry for. Not all the evenings of this great city are as innocent nor in their consequences as happy as ours. *So let us rest in peace!* May this tranquil sleep, preceded and produced by useful work and innocent pleasures, be the image and the wage of that unending repose, which is only granted in the same way for a succession of days passed like the hours that have just unfolded for us!

NOTES TO THE NINTH DIALOGUE

i This book was translated into French under the title *Vue de l'évidence de la religion chrétienne, considérée en elle-même*, by M. Jenyns, (Paris 1769). The translator, M. [Pierre] Letourneur, permitted himself to mutilate and alter the work without notice, which, I believe, must never be done. One will read with more profit the translation with notes by the Abbé Feller, (Liege 1779). It is inferior with respect to style, but that is not the question. Le Tourneur's version is remarkable for this epigraph, made for the century: *You have ALMOST persuaded me to be Christian.* (Acts 26:29)

ii Nothing is more true; it suffices to cite the letters of St Francis Xavier. He wrote from Malaca, 20 June 1549: "I am departing (for Japan) with Cosma, Turiani, and Jean Fernand; we are accompanied by three Japanese Christians, subjects of rare probity. ... The Japanese had reached a deliberate decision to send ambassadors to the Viceroy of the Indies in order to obtain priests who can instruct them in the Christian religion." And on 3 November of the same year, he wrote from Congoximo in Japan, where he had arrived on 5 August: "Two bonzes and other Japanese in great number had gone to Goa to be instructed there in the faith." (St Francis Xavier, *Epistolae*, 160 and 208.)

iii See *Les Pensées de Pascal*, Reynouard ed., 2 vols. (Paris 1803), 2:328. This passage from Voltaire contains as many blunders as words. For without speaking of *continually*, which is quite ridiculous, *to speak of loving God* is not at all the same as *to ask God to love him*; and this is what Pascal said. Next, Marcus Aurelius and Epictetus were not *religions*. Pascal did not say (what he could have said however): *No man outside* our religion, etc. He said, and this is quite different: *No other religion than ours*, etc. What does it matter if such or such man was able to say a few poor words on the *love of God*? It is not a question of *talking* about it. It is a question of *having* it, and of inspiring it by virtue of a general institution reaching all minds. Moreover, this is what Christianity did, and this is what philosophy never did, and will never be able to do. It can never be repeated often enough: philosophy does nothing for man's heart. *Circùm præcordia ludit.* It plays around the heart; it never enters it.

iv In *Epistle 78*, Seneca writes: "Worse than these are the stake, the rack, the red-hot plates, the instrument that reopens wounds while the wounds themselves are still swollen and that drives their imprint still deeper. Nevertheless there have been men who have not uttered a moan amid these tortures. 'More yet!' says the torturer; but the victim has not begged for release. 'More yet!' the victim has smiled, and heartily, too." And elsewhere: "'What then?'" is the query; "if the sword is brandished over your brave man's neck, if he is pierced in this place and in that continually, if he sees his entrails in his lap, if he is tortured again after being kept waiting in order that he may thus feel the torture more keenly, and *if the blood flows afresh out of bowels where it has but lately ceased to flow*, has he no fear? Shall you say that he has felt no pain either? Yes, he has felt pain; for no human virtue can rid itself of feelings. But he has no fear; unconquered he looks down from a *lofty height* upon his sufferings." (*Epistle 85*.)

Of whom therefore did Seneca want to speak about? Before the martyrs were there examples of such atrocities on the one hand and of such courage on the other? Seneca had seen Nero's martyrs; Lactantius, who saw those of Diocletian, described their sufferings, and we have very good reasons for believing what he wrote about them; he had in mind the passages from Seneca that have just been read. Two phrases especially relate to each other remarkably.

If the blood flows afresh out of bowels where it has but lately ceased to flow. (Seneca *Epistle 85* [§ 29. Loeb].)

The only thing they avoid is that the men die after torture. They take great care with the tortured ones that their limbs be revived for torture on another occasion and fresh blood is readied for punishment. (Lactantius, *Divine Institutions*, Bk. V, chap. ii.)

v Among the Hebrews, and no doubt among other Oriental nations as well, the man mourning the loss of a cherished object or some other great misfortune, stayed seated, and this is why *to sit* and *to weep* are often synonymous in Holy Scripture. Take this passage from the Psalms, for example, (totally garbled in our unfortunate translations): *To sit up late into the night, you who eat the bread of hard toil.* (Psalm 126(127):2), which means: "Console yourself, after having cried, you who eat the bread of sorrow." A host of other texts attests to the same custom, which was not foreign to the Romans. However Ovid said, when speaking of this with respect to Lucretius:

She sat with hair dishevelled, like a mother who must attend the funeral pyre of her son.

(*Fasti* II.813–14. [Trans. James George Frazer, Loeb Classical Library 1951])

He is surely not to be understood as describing the ordinary attitude of a seated woman; and when the children of Israel seated themselves in the temple to cry there for their crimes or their misfortunes (Judges 20:26, etc.) they surely were not seated comfortably on chairs. It appears certain that, in these circumstances, they sat on the floor or squatted; and it is this posture of a man seated on his legs to which Plutarch makes allusion by the expression he uses, and which cannot be easily rendered in our language. *Seated ignobly* would be the proper expression, if the word *seated* had not lost, like the word *session*, its original meaning.

However to be exact it must be observed that a difference in punctuation could alter Plutarch's phrase, so that the epithet *ignobly* would fall on the word *prostration* instead of referring to squatting. The Latin translator chose the sense adopted by the memory of the speaker. The principal observation retains its full force in any case. (Editor's note.)

vi   I don't think anyone will be upset to read here the verse by Rutilius:

Atque utinam nunquam Judæa subact fuisset

Pompeii bellis imperioque Titi!

Latiùs excisæ pestis contagia serpunt,

Victoresque suos natio victa premit.

[Rutilius Namatianus *The Return* 395–98. (Darcel ed.)]

Which is to say: "Would that Judea had never succumbed to the wars of Pompei and the rule of Titus! The poisons that they imparted were spread further by the conquest, and the vanquished nation overwhelms its conquerors." In fact it seems that these words, cited especially in the fifth century, were applied to the Christians, and they are taken in this sense by the learned Huet in his *Demonstratio evangelica* (Proposition III, § 21.) However a very able interpreter of Holy Scripture, and one who explains it to us with a wealth of erudition that sometimes approaches ostentation, takes the contrary view, and believes that in the passage from Rutilius it is only a question of the Jews. ([Alfonso] Niccolai, S.J., *Dissertazioni e lezioni di Sacra Scrittura* (Florence 1756), first dissertation, 1:138.) So difficult is it to see clearly on this point and to distinguish the two religions exactly in the writings of pagan authors.

vii He knew it so well that he noted its principal character, in a work that we no longer have, but of which St Augustine has preserved this fragment.

"There are," says Seneca, "among the Jews, men who know the purposes of their mysteries, but the crowd does not know why it does what it does." (Seneca, as cited by St Augustine *City of God* VII.11.) Moreover did not St Augustine himself say: *that few people understand these mysteries, although many celebrate them.* (Ibid., X.16.) Origen is more detailed and more explicit. *Is there anything more beautiful,* he says, *than to see the Jews instructed from their cradle about the immortality of the soul, and the penalties and rewards of the next life? These things are, however, only represented under a mythical cover to* children and to ADULT-CHILDREN. *But for those who seek the word and want to penetrate to the meaning of these mysteries, this mythology is, if one may put it this way, in truth a* metamorphosis. (Origen *Against Celsus* Bk. V, n° 42) Moreover, this is no less remarkable: *Christian doctrines on the resurrection of the dead, on the judgement of God, and on the punishments and rewards of the next life are not new; they are the ancient doctrines of Judaism.* (Ibid., Bk. II, n° 1, 4.)

Eusebius, cited by the celebrated Huet, uses exactly the same language. In his own words, he said: "that the multitude among the Hebrews had been subjected to the letter of the law, deprived of any explanation, but that educated minds, freed from this servitude, had been directed towards the study of a certain divine philosophy, high above that of the vulgar, and towards interpretation according to allegorical senses." (*Demonstratio evangelica*, Vol. II, Prop. IX, c. 171, n° 8.)

This tradition (or *reception*) is the true and respectable Cabala, of which the modern is only an illegitimate and counterfeit daughter.

viii I did not know that Newton had spoken of the Hebrew calendar in his chronology; but he did say a bit about it in his other book, about which it has been rightly said: *Many have spoken of it, but few have known it well*; this is in his commentary on the Apocalypse, where he said laconically (but this is an oracle): *Judæi usi non sunt vitioso cyclo* [The Jews did not use a vicious circle]. (Isaac Newton, *Ad Danielis profetae vaticinia, opus postumum*, Suderman's Latin translation, (Amsterdam 1737), Ch. ii, p. 113.) Scaliger, an excellent judge on this topic, decided *that there is nothing more exact, nothing more perfect* than the calculation of the Jewish year; he even referred modern calculators to the Jewish school, and unceremoniously advised them *to instruct themselves in this school or to keep quiet.* ([Joseph Juste] Scaliger, *Opus de emendatione temporum* (Geneva 1629), Bk. VIII, p. 656.) Elsewhere he tells us: *These things are very ingenious ... nobody who is at all skilled in these matters will deny that this method of lunar calculation is very keen and very elegant.* (Ibid., Bk. VII, p. 640.) (Editor's note)

ix Whatever esteem is due this justly celebrated rabbi (Moses Maimonides), I would like, however, on the particular fact of the archives of Ecabana, to identify the authorities on which he relies, which I am not able to do at the moment. As for the immense establishment of the Jews beyond the Euphrates, where they constituted a real power, there is not the least doubt of this fact. (See Philo's *Embassy to Gaius, Inter opera græc. et lat.*, (Geneva 1613), p. 792, litt. B.)

x In fact Cunæus said: "A man of such great learning and knowledge that *beside him all the Greeks who were present looked like bare trees and logs.*" ([Petrus Cunæus, *La Respublica hebraicum*], Elzevir ed. (1632), Bk. I, chap. iv, p. 26.) Here, however, this author, otherwise learned and exact, if he is not deceived by his memory, permits himself a slight hyperbole. Aristotle praised this Jew as an amiable, hospitable, virtuous man, *especially chaste*, learned and eloquent. He adds, *that he has learned much from conversation with him*, but he in no way compares him in a way humiliating for the Greeks. So I do not know where Cunæus got his *trunci* and his *stipites*. In any case, the speaker appears not to know that it is not Aristotle who speaks here, but rather Clearchus, his disciple, who makes Aristotle speak in a dialogue that he composed. (See the fragment of Clearchus in the book of Josephus *Against Apion*, Bk. I, chap. viii, translation by Arnaud d'Andilly.) (Editor's note.) [The reference to Bk. I, chap. viii of Josephus should be to chap. xxii.176–82. See Darcel ed.]

xi A long time before the Septuagint, there was a Greek translation of part of the Bible. See the preface at the head of the Bible of Beyerlinck. [Laurens Beyerlinck, editor, *Biblica sacra latine*, 3 vols. (Antwerp 1556)]; [Nicolas] Fréret, *Défence de la chronologie* [Paris 1758], p. 264, [Philippe-Louis Gérard], *Leçons de l'histoire*, [2 vols. (Paris 1786)], 1:616; and [Jean-François] Baltus, *Défense des [SS.] Pères [accusez de platonisme, etc.*], (Paris 1711), Chap. xx, pp. 614 ff.

On this matter, one can be dispensed from proofs, for the *official* translation ordered by Ptolemy necessarily presupposes that the book was then, not only *known*, but celebrated. In effect, *one cannot desire what one does not know*. What prince would ever order the translation of a book or such a book without having determined that there is a universal demand for it, based in its turn on a great interest excited by this book!

xii *"The Jews conceive of one god only, and that with the mind alone ... that supreme and eternal being is to them incapable of representation and without end."* This is the same man who will say of the *same* cult and in the *same* chapter: *the ways (of the Jews) are preposterous and mean.* (Tacitus *The Histories* v.5. [Trans. Clifford H. Moore, Loeb Classical Library 1951]) To render justice to what is hated is a feat almost always beyond the greatest minds.

Perhaps it would be rewarding to read Philo for the details of certain extremely interesting circumstances, touched on briefly in a dialogue that is worth recalling. Speaking to a prince like Caligula, and citing for him the

acts and opinions of the imperial family, Philo was surely not tempted to lie
or even to exaggerate. He said:

"Agrippa, your maternal grandmother, having gone to Jerusalem during the
reign of Herod, was enchanted by the religion of the Jews, and could no
longer be silent about this. ... The emperor Augustus ordered that, from his
own revenues and according to the legitimate forms, there be offered each
day TO THE VERY HIGH GOD, on the altar at Jerusalem, a bull and lambs in
holocaust, although he knew very well that the temple contained no show,
either public or hidden. But this great prince, whom no one surpassed in
philosophic spirit, sensed well the necessity that exists in the world for an
altar dedicated to the invisible God, and that it is to this God that all men
can address their prayers in order to obtain the communication of a happy
hope and the joy of perfect goods ...

"Julia, your great grandmother, gave magnificent presents to the temple
in vases and cups of gold, and although the feminine mind detaches itself
from images with difficulty, and cannot conceive things entirely foreign to
the senses, Julia, as superior to her sex by education as by other advantages
of nature, came to the point of preferring to contemplate intelligible things
rather than sensible, and to appreciate that the latter are only the shadows of
the first." N.B. By this name *Julia*, one must understand *Livia*, the wife of
Augustus, who had passed by adoption into the family of Jules, and who in
effect was the great grandmother of Caligula.

Moreover, and in the same discourse to the terrible Caligula, Philo says
expressly: *That the emperor Augustus* not only admired *but* adored *this
custom of not employing any images to represent materially an invisible
nature.*

Ethaymaze kai prosekyei, x, t, l.
[be admired and adored, etc.]
(Philo *Embassy to Gaius*)

Tenth Dialogue

The Senator

Tell us, Chevalier, did you dream of sacrifices last night?

The Chevalier

Yes, undoubtedly, I dreamed; and since this is absolutely new country for me, I only saw things in a confused way. It seems to me, however, that the subject would be very much worth exploring, and if I believe that interior feeling that we were talking about the other day in our last dialogue, our common friend would really have opened a rich mine that only remains to be explored.

The Senator

This is precisely what I would like our dialogue to be about this evening. It appears to me, Count, that you have put the principle of sacrifices beyond any attack, and that you have drawn from it a host of useful consequences. I believe, moreover, that the theory of *substitution* is so natural to man that it can be regarded as an *innate* truth in the full meaning of the term, since it is absolutely impossible for us to have learned it. But do you think that it is equally impossible to *discover* or at least to *glimpse* the reason for this universal dogma?

The more one examines the world, the more one feels oneself led to believe that evil originates in a certain inexplicable division and that the return to good depends on an opposite force that unceasingly pushes us towards a certain unity just as inexplicable.[1] This community of merits, this

---

[1]   The human race in the flesh could, in this supposition, address God with the same words used by St Augustine in speaking of himself: "I was broken into pieces the moment I separated myself from your unity to lose myself in a host of things;

substitution that you have so well proved, can come only from this unity that we do not understand. Reflecting on the general beliefs and natural instincts of men, one is struck by this tendency that they have to unite things that nature seems to have separated totally. They are very disposed, for example, to regard a people, a town, a corporation, and above all, a family as a single moral being having good and bad qualities, capable of winning praise or blame, and consequently open to punishment or rewards. From this predisposition stems the *prejudice*, or, to speak more precisely, the *dogma* of nobility, so universal and so deeply rooted among men. If you submit this belief to the examination of reason, it will not pass the test, for if we consult reason alone, there is no distinction more foreign to us than that which we owe our ancestors; yet there is none more esteemed, nor even more willingly recognized except in factious times, and even then the attacks made on it are still an indirect homage and a formal recognition of its greatness by those who would want to destroy it.

If common opinion believes glory hereditary, so too is blame, and for the same reason. It is sometimes asked, without too much thought, why the shame of a crime or a punishment must fall on the descendants of the criminal; and yet those who put the question then brag about the merits of their ancestors: it is an obvious contradiction.

The Chevalier

I had never noticed this analogy.

The Senator

Yet it is striking. One of your ancestors, Chevalier, was killed in Egypt in the company of St Louis (I take great pleasure in recalling this for you); another perished at the Battle of Marignan fighting to capture an enemy flag; finally, your grandfather lost an arm at Fontenoy. No doubt you do not hear of this distinction as something foreign to you, and you will not disavow me if I affirm that you would rather renounce life than the glory that comes to you through these great acts. However, if your thirteenth-century ancestor had surrendered St Louis to the Saracens instead of dying at his side, and if we believed only our poor reason, we would think that you would have shared this infamy for the same reason and with the same justice that has transmitted to you a distinction as personal as the crime. There is no middle ground, Chevalier: you have to accept the shame in good grace, if it falls to you, or renounce the glory. Moreover there is no doubt about opinion on this point. The only one who does not believe in

---

you deigned to reassemble the pieces of myself." (St Augustine *Confessions* II.1.2.)

hereditary dishonour is the one who suffers it, and his judgement is obviously worthless. As for those who, for the simple pleasure of being witty or contradicting received ideas, speak, or even write books against what they call the *chance* or *prejudice* of birth, propose to them, if they have a name or only honour, to associate themselves by marriage to a family tarnished in earlier times, and you will see how they answer you.

As for those who have neither a name nor honour, as they will also speak for themselves, one must let them have their say.

Could not this theory shine some light on the inconceivable mystery of the punishment of sons for the crimes of their fathers? At first glance, nothing is so shocking as hereditary malediction; yet why not, since benediction is the same? Notice that these ideas do not pertain to the Bible only, as is often imagined. This fortunate or unfortunate heredity belongs to all times and to all countries; it belongs to paganism as well as to Judaism or Christianity, to the infancy as well as to the old age of nations; the idea is found in theologians, philosophers, poets, in the theatre, and in the Church.

The arguments that reason furnishes against this theory resemble those of Zeno against the possibility of movement.[2] One knows how to reply, but one is carried along. The family is no doubt composed of individuals who, according to reason, have nothing in common; but according to instinct and universal persuasion, every family is *one*.

It is in sovereign families, especially, that this unity shines forth; the sovereign changes his name and face, but he is always, as they say in Spain, MYSELF THE KING. You Frenchmen, Chevalier, have two fine maxims, truer perhaps than you think: one of civil law, *The dead distrain the living*; and the other of public law, *The king does not die*. Therefore, when it is a question of judging him, the king should never be treated as a separate entity.

We are sometimes astonished to see an *innocent* monarch perish miserably in one of those political catastrophes so frequent in the world. You must not think that I want to stifle compassion in men's hearts and you know how recent crimes have wrung my own; nevertheless, sticking to strict reasoning, what can be said? Every culprit can be *innocent* and even *saintly* on the day of his punishment. There are crimes that are only consummated and characterized as such after a long period of time; there are others that consist of a host of acts more or less excusable if taken separately, but whose repetition in the end becomes highly criminal. In

---

[2] [Zeno (Zenon) of Elea was a Greek philosopher who used a series of brilliant paradoxes to defend Parmenides' belief that motion and change are illusory.]

cases of this sort, it is obvious that the punishment cannot precede completion of the crime.

Even in instantaneous crimes, punishments are always suspended, and this must be the case. This again is one of those so frequent occasions where human justice serves as an interpreter of that of which ours is only an image and a derivation.

An oversight, a frivolous act, a contravention of some police regulation, can be reprimanded on the spot; but when it is a question of a crime properly speaking, the culprit is never punished the moment he becomes one. Under the rule of Muslim law, authority punishes, even with death, the man it thinks deserves it, at the very moment and place it seizes him; these brusque executions, which have not lacked blind admirers, are nevertheless one of the numerous proofs of the brutalization and reprobation of these peoples. Among us, things are totally different. The culprit must be arrested, he must be charged, he must defend himself; above all he must settle his conscience and his affairs; preparations must be made for his punishment; and finally, to take everything into account, there must be a certain time left to take him to the place of punishment, which is assigned. The scaffold is an *altar*; therefore it can neither be set up nor moved except by authority. These delays, honourable in their very excesses, which do not lack blind detractors, are no less a proof of our superiority.

If then it happens that, during the indispensable interval that must occur between the crime and its punishment, sovereignty changes hands, what does it matter to justice? It must take its ordinary course. Quite apart from the unity I am considering at the moment, nothing is more just, humanly speaking; for nowhere can a natural heir be dispensed from paying the debts of his inheritance, unless he *renounces* it. The sovereign is responsible for all the acts of sovereignty. All its debts, all its treaties, all its crimes constrain him. If, by some disorderly act, he plants a bad seed today whose natural growth will bring about a catastrophe in a hundred years, the blow will justly strike the crown *in a hundred years*. To escape the blow, the king would have to refuse the crown. It is never THIS king, it is THE king who is innocent or guilty. Plato, I don't know where, in the *Gorgias* perhaps, said a shocking thing I would scarcely dare to have thought;[3] but if his proposition is understood in the sense that I am now presenting to you, he could well be right. Centuries can pass between the meritorious act and the reward, as between the crime and the punishment. The king can be born and can die only once; he lasts as long as the monarchy. If he becomes guilty, he is treated with weight and measure; he is, according to

---

[3] *The governor of a city would never be unjustly slain by the city of which he is governor.* (Plato, *Gorgias* [519b])

circumstances, warned, menaced, humiliated, suspended, imprisoned, judged, or sacrificed.

After having examined man, let us examine his most marvellous characteristic, speech. Again we find the same mystery, that is to say an inexplicable division and a tendency towards an equally inexplicable unity. The two greatest epochs in the spiritual world are without doubt that of *Babel*, when languages split up, and that of *Pentecost*, where they made a marvellous effort to reunite; on this point one can even observe, in passing, that these two most extraordinary events in human history are, at the same time, the two of which we are most certain. To contest them is to lack both reason and honesty.

So it is that everything having been divided, everything desires reunion. Led by this feeling, men never cease to attest to it in a thousand ways. They have wished, for example, that the word *union* signifies *tenderness*, and that this word *tenderness* itself only signifies a disposition to union. All their signs of *attachment* (another word created by the same feeling) are material unions. They touch each other's hands, they embrace. The mouth being the organ of speech, which is itself the organ and expression of intelligence, all men have believed that in the coming together of two mouths there is something sacred that announces the union of two souls. Vice lays hold of everything and uses everything. But I am only looking at the principle.

Religion has carried the *kiss of peace* to the altar with great knowledge of cause; I even recall having encountered somewhere in paging through the Church Fathers, passages where they complain that crime dares to make use of the excesses of a holy and mysterious sign.[i] But whether it satisfies shamelessness, whether it frightens modesty, or whether it laughs on the lips of a spouse or a mother, from whence comes its generality and its power?

Our mutual unity results from our unity in God, so celebrated by philosophy itself. Malebranche's theory of *vision in God* is only a superb commentary on the well known words of St Paul, *It is in him that we live, move, and have our being.*[4] The pantheism of the Stoics, and that of Spinoza, is a corruption of this great idea; but it is always the same principle, it is always this tendency towards unity. The first time that I read in the great work of this admirable Malebranche, so neglected by his unjust and blind country, *That God is the place of spirits as space is the place of bodies,*[ii] I was dazzled by this flash of genius and ready to prostrate myself before it. Men have said few things as beautiful.

---

[4] [Acts 17:28.]

One day I had the whim to page through the works of Madame Guyon, simply because she was recommended to me by the best of my friends, François of Cambrai.[5] I came across a passage on the *Song of Songs* where this celebrated woman compared human intelligences to the currents of water that circulate in all parts of the ocean and that move about unceasingly only to return again. The comparison is pursued quite convincingly; but you know that bits of prose do not remain in one's memory. Happily I can replace it by reciting for you two inexpressibly beautiful verses of Metastasio,[6] who translated Madame Guyon, at least what he had come across as by a miracle.

L'ondo dal mar divisa
Bagna la valle e il monte:
Va passaggiera in diume;
Va prigioniera in fonte:
Mormora sempre e geme
Finche non torni al mar;
Al mar dove ella nacque,
Dove acquistò gli umori,
Dove da' lunghi errori
Spera di riposar.[7]

---

[5] [François de Salignac de la Mothe-Fénelon, bishop of Cambrai.]

[6] *The Muses' comrade, whose joy was ever in song and lyre and in the stringing of notes upon cords.* (Vergil *Aeneid* IX.775–76.)

[7] [The wave divided from the sea / bathes the valley and the mountain; goes temporarily into the river; goes prisoner to the spring; Always painfully murmurs / until it returns to the sea. To the sea where it was born, where it acquired its moods, where it hopes to rest / (away) from long errors.] [Pietro] Metastasio, *Artas*, III, i. Here is the passage from Madame Guyon indicated in the dialogue: "God being our last end, the soul can unceasingly flow into him as into its end and centre, and there be mixed in and transformed without ever having to come out again. Thus it is that a river, which is a flow of water coming into the sea and quite distinct from the sea, finds itself outside its origin, worked by various motions as it approaches the sea until it finally falls into it, loses itself, and blends itself with it, so that it is lost there and mixed in with it before coming out, and can no longer be distinguished from it." (*Commentaire sur le Cantique des cantiques*, (1687), chap. I, v., i.)

Madame Guyon's famous friend [Fénelon] also expressed the same idea in his *Télémaque. Reason*, he said, *is like a great ocean of light; our minds are like little streams that come out of it and return to it without being lost.* (Bk. IV) One senses in these two pieces two *melded* souls.

But all these waters cannot come together in the ocean without being mixed together, at least in a certain way that I do not understand at all. Sometimes I should like to spring beyond the narrow limits of this world, I should like to anticipate the day of revelations, and plunge myself into infinity. When the twofold law of man's nature will be effaced and his two centres will be merged, he will be ONE, for no longer experiencing internal combat within himself, how could the idea of duality still occur to him? But if we consider men in their relations with one another, what will become of them when evil is annihilated and passion and self interest no longer exist? What will become of the SELF when all thoughts, like all desires, are common, when every mind will see itself as others see it? Who can comprehend, who can imagine this heavenly Jerusalem, where all the inhabitants, pervaded by the same spirit, will be mutually joined and reflect happiness on one another?[8] An infinite number of luminous spectres of the same dimension, if they come together at exactly the same place, are no longer an infinite number of luminous spectres, they are one infinitely luminous spectre. However I am taking good care not to deal with the *personality* without which immortality is nothing; nevertheless I cannot help being struck how everything in the world leads us back to this mysterious unity.

St Paul invented a word that has passed into every Christian language; it is *to edify*, which is quite astonishing at first glance, for what is there in common between the construction of an edifice and the good example one gives one's neighbour?

The root of this expression in soon discovered. Vice separates men, just as virtue unites them. There is no act against order that is not born of a particular interest contrary to the general order; there is no pure act that does not sacrifice a particular interest to the general interest, that is to say that does not tend to create a unified and steady will in place of a multitude of divergent and culpable wills. So St Paul begins with this fundamental idea that we are all *the edifice of God, and this edifice that we must raise is the body of the Saviour.*[9] He used this idea in many ways. He wanted us to *edify* one another, that is to say he wanted each man to take his place freely as a stone in the spiritual edifice, and to work with all his strength to call others to the same task, so that every man *edifies and is edified.* Above all, he provided us with the well-known saying, *Knowledge puffs up, but charity edifies,*[10] an admirable phrase and strikingly true, for knowl-

---

[8] *Jerusalem which is built as a city, all its parts harmoniously united.* [Psalm 121(122):3]

[9] 1 Corinthians 3:9–11.

[10] 1 Corinthians 8:1

edge left to itself divides rather than unites, and all its works are only appearances, while virtue really *edifies* and indeed cannot act without *edifying*. St Paul had read in the sublime testament of his master that men are one and severally like God,[11] so that all *are brought to fulfilment and perfected in unity*,[12] for until then the work is unfinished. Moreover how could there not be a certain unity (be it what you will and call it what you will) among us, since *a single man ruined us by a single act*?[iii] Here I am by no means, as they say, arguing in a circle by proving unity by the origin of evil and the origin of evil by unity: not at all, for evil is only too well proved by its own existence; it is everywhere and especially within ourselves. But of all the suppositions one can imagine to explain its origin, none satisfies good sense, the enemy of quibbling, as well as this belief, which presents it as the hereditary consequence of a fundamental transgression, and which has the support of the mass of human traditions.

The fall of man can thus be numbered among the proofs of human unity and can help us understand how, by the law of analogy that rules all divine things, *salvation likewise came* from a single man.[13]

You were saying the other day, Count, that there is no Christian dogma that is not based on some tradition as universal and ancient as man, or on some innate feeling that pertains to us by our very existence. Nothing is more true. Have you never reflected on the importance men have always attached to meals taken in common. *The table*, says an old Greek proverb, *is the intermediary of friendship*. There are no treaties, no accords, no festivals, no ceremonies of any kind, even gloomy ones, without meals. Why is an invitation to a man who would dine just as well at home considered a favour? Why is it more honourable to be seated at the table of a prince than to be seated elsewhere near him? You can descend from the palace of a European monarch to the hut of a savage, you can pass from the highest civilization to the simplest society; you can look at every rank, every condition, every kind of character, and everywhere you will find meals treated as a kind of religion, as a system of respect, of benevolence, of etiquette, often of politics, a system that has its laws, its observances, and its very remarkable refinements. Men have not found a more expressive sign of union than that of assembling to take common nourishment. This sign has appeared to exalt union to the point of unity.

---

[11] "That they may be one even as we are" (John 17:11), so "that all may be one, even as you in me and I in you, that they also may be ONE in you." (Ibid, 21) "And the glory you have given me, I have given them, that they may be ONE, even as we are ONE." (Ibid, 22.)

[12] "I in them and you in me, that they may be perfected in unity." (Ibid., 23.)

[13] Romans 5:17–19.

This feeling being universal, religion has chosen it to make it the basis of its principal mystery. Just as every meal, according to universal instinct, was also a *communion*,[14] religion in its turn wanted its *communion* to be a *meal*. For spiritual life as for bodily life, nourishment in necessary. The same material organ serves both. At this banquet, all men become ONE by satisfying themselves with a nourishment that is one and that is all in all. The ancient fathers, to make this transformation into unity somewhat more apparent, willingly drew comparisons from the *wheat* and the *grape*, which are the materials of the mystery. For just as the many grains of wheat or the many grapes make one bread and one drink, so do this bread and wine that are given to us at the holy table break the ME and absorb us in their inconceivable unity.[iv]

There are many examples of this natural feeling, legitimated and consecrated by religion, and that can be regarded as the almost effaced traces of a primitive state. Following this train of thought, Count, do you think it absolutely impossible to form some idea of this joint responsibility between men (if you will permit me this phrase from jurisprudence), from which comes this substitution of merits that explains everything?

The Count

It would be impossible for me, my respectable friend, to express to you, even in a very imperfect way, the pleasure your discourse has given me. Nevertheless I confess to you with a frankness you fully deserve that this pleasure is mixed with a certain fright. The flight you take can too easily lead you astray, all the more so in that you do not have, like me, a beacon that you could always look to from any distance. Is it not recklessness to want to understand things so far above us? Men are always tempted by singular ideas that flatter their pride; it is so pleasant to walk along extraordinary paths that no human foot has trodden! But what do we gain by this? Does it make man better? This is the important point. I would also ask: does it make man wiser? Why should we place our trust in these fine theories if they cannot lead us very far or in the right direction? It is not that I refuse to acknowledge some very profound insights in everything that you have just told us, but, again, do we not run two great dangers, that of being led astray in a dangerous way, and that of losing precious time in vain speculations that we could have used in studies, and perhaps even in useful discoveries?

---

[14] *As a symbol of communion and participation in sacrifices, because the table is sacred in itself, and the suppers are nothing other than sacrifices.* ([Pirolis], *Antichità di Ercolano,* (Naples 1779), tav. ix, 7:42.)

The Senator

The case is precisely the contrary, my dear Count. Nothing is more useful than these studies that have as their object the intellectual world; this is precisely the great route to discoveries. Everything that can be known in rational philosophy can be found in a passage from St Paul; this is it:

THIS WORLD IS A SYSTEM OF INVISIBLE THINGS VISIBLY MANIFESTED.*

The world, Charles Bonnet once said, *would therefore be only an assemblage of appearances!*[15]

This is undoubtedly true, at least in a certain sense, for there is a kind of idealism that is very reasonable. Perhaps it would be difficult to discover any well-known system that did not include something true.

If you consider that everything has been made *by* and *for* intelligence; that all movement is an effect, so that properly speaking the *cause* of a movement cannot be a movement;[16] that these words *cause* and *matter* are as mutually exclusive as *circle* and *triangle*; and that everything that we see in this world is related to another world that we do not see;[17] then you will sense that, in effect, we live *in the midst of a system of invisible things visibly manifested.*

Scan the circle of sciences, and you will see that they are all based on a mystery. The mathematician feels his way along, calculating on the basis of imaginary quantities, although his operations are quite accurate. He understands even less the principles of infinitesimal calculus, one of the most powerful tools that God has confided to man. He is astonished to draw infallible results from a principle that shocks good sense, and we have seen academies asking the scholarly world for the explanation of these apparent contradictions. Gravitational astronomy says *that it is in no way embarrassed in not knowing the cause of* universal attraction *provided it can demonstrate that this force exists;* but, deep down, it is very much embarrassed by it. The *germ theorist,* who has just demolished the romantic theories of the *epigenesist,* must stop and think on seeing a mule's ear; all his science is shaken and his sight troubles him. The physicist who has

---

[15] *All nature therefore appears to us as only a great and magnificent spectacle of appearances.* (Bonnet, *La Palingénésie philosophique,* Part XIII, chap. ii.)

[16] St Thomas said: *Every moving thing [comes] from an unmoving principle. Summa Contra Gentiles,* I, 44, n° 2, and 47, n° 6. Malebranche repeated the same idea: God alone, he said, *is at the same time the mover and immobile.* (*Recherche de la vérité,* Append., p. 520.) But this is a maxim of antique philosophy.

[17] This whole world is only made for the eternal century where nothing will occur; everything we see is only the symbol and the sign of invisible things. ... God acts in time only for eternity. (Massillon, *Sermon sur les afflictions,* Third part.)

tried the experiment of Hales[vi] will ask himself what plant is, what wood is, and finally, what matter is, not daring to mock the alchemists. However nothing is more interesting than what is happening in the science of chemistry in our time. Pay close attention to the progress of its experiments, and you will see where its adepts are being led. I sincerely respect their work, but I very much fear that posterity will profit from it without gratitude, and look upon these chemists themselves as blind men who arrived without knowing it at a country whose existence they denied.

There is therefore no law of nature that does not *have behind it* (allow me to use this ridiculous phrase) a spiritual law of which the first is only a visible expression; and this is why any material explanation of causality will never satisfy a good mind. As soon as one leaves the domain of material and sensory experience to enter that of rational philosophy, one must leave matter behind and explain everything by metaphysics. I mean true metaphysics, and not that which has been cultivated so ardently during the last century by men who are seriously called *metaphysicians*! Funny metaphysicians, who spent their lives proving that there is no such thing as metaphysics; famous monsters in whom genius was *brutalized*!

So it is very certain, my worthy friend, that one cannot succeed except by *these extraordinary routes* that you fear so much. Still if I do not succeed, either because I lack the ability or because authority has raised obstacles along my way, is it not already an important point to know that I am on the right road? All the inventors, all the men of originality, have been religious men, and even fanatically so. Perverted by irreligious scepticism, the human mind resembles fallow land that produces nothing or is covered with wild plants useless to man. Then even its natural fertility is an evil, since these plants harden the soil by tangling and intertwining their roots, and form a barrier between earth and sky. Let us break up this accursed crust, destroy these fatally hardy weeds, call on all the abilities of man; let us push in the ploughshare, let us dig deeply for the powers of the earth to put them in contact with the powers of heaven.

Here, gentlemen, is the natural image of human intelligence open or closed to divine knowledge.

Even the natural sciences are subject to the general law. Genius scarcely relies on syllogisms. Its pace is free, its path derived from inspiration; we see its success, but no one has seen its progress.[18] For example, is there

---

[18] *Divina cognitio non est inquisitiva ... non per ratiocinationem causata, sed immaterialis cognitio rerum absque discursu.* [Divine knowledge is not by enquiry – it is not caused by reasoning, but it is an intuitive knowledge of things, without restless motion.] (St Thomas, *Summa Contra Gentiles*, I, 92.) In effect, knowledge being an intuition, the more it has this character in man, the more it approaches its

anyone who can be compared to Kepler in astronomy? Is Newton himself anything but a sublime commentator on this great man, who alone could write his name in the skies? For the laws of the universe are Kepler's *laws*.[vii] In his third law, especially, there is something so extraordinary, something so independent of any preliminary knowledge, that we cannot help recognizing it as the result of a real inspiration. Moreover, he only arrived at this immortal discovery by following unknown mystical ideas of numerical and celestial harmonies, which accorded very well with his profoundly religious character, but which are, for cold reason, only pure dreams. If someone had submitted these ideas to the scrutiny of a philosopher on guard against any kind of superstition, such as Bacon, for example, who loved astronomy and physics as the *first men* of Italy loved women, he would not have failed to see in them *idols of the cave* or *idols of the tribe*, etc.[19]

But Bacon, who *had substituted the method of induction for that of the syllogism*, as they said in a century that exhausted every kind of delirium, not only remained ignorant of the discoveries of his immortal contemporary, but obstinately maintained the system of Ptolemy, despite the work of Copernicus, and he called this obstinacy *a noble consistency*.[20]

And in Roger Bacon's own country, he believed, even after Galileo's discoveries, that ground lenses must be concave, and that the adjustment of a lens to find its true focal point increased the heat of solar rays.[viii]

It is impossible that you have not been amused sometimes by mechanical explanations of magnetism, and especially by Descartes' atoms formed into *corkscrews*;[21] but surely you have not read what Gilbert had to say about this, since these old books are no longer read. I do not mean to say that he was right, but I would willingly bet my life, and even my honour, that nothing will ever be discovered in this profound mystery of life except by following Gilbert's ideas, or others of the same kind,[ix] just as the general movement of the tides will never be explained in a satisfactory way

---

model. [Maistre's "citation" from Aquinas is probably second-hand from some theology manual. Aquinas makes the argument in Bk I., chap. 57 (rather than chap. 97) of the *Summa Contra Gentiles*, but the text Maistre cites does not appear in Aquinas, a point that may be confirmed by checking the concordance in Robertus Rusa's *Index Thomisticus* (1980).]

[19] Those who know Bacon's philosophy will understand this jargon; it would take too long to explain it to others.

[20] *And so will hold, as the heavenly bodies do, a noble constancy. (The Works of Sir Francis Bacon, Thema cœli, 9:252.)*

[21] *Cartesii principia philosophica* (Amsterdam: Blaen 1685), Part IV, n° 133, p. 186.

(supposing that it is explained) without following Seneca's approach,[22] that is to say by methods totally different from our material experiments and mechanical laws.

The more the sciences relate to man, such as medicine for example, the less can they dispense with religion. If you wish, read irreligious doctors as scholars or as writers, if they have the merit of style, but never call one of them to your bedside.[x] Let us leave aside, if you will, the metaphysical reason, which however is very important; but let us never forget the precept of Celsus, who at one point tells us to seek out whenever possible *the caring doctor*;[23] so above all let us look for the one who has sworn to love all men, and let us likewise flee the one who, in theory, must love no one.

Even mathematics is subject to this law, although it is a tool rather than a science since its only value is in leading us to knowledge of another sort. Compare the mathematicians of the seventeenth century with those of the following century. Ours were *able calculators*; they wielded the instruments delivered into their hands with marvellous dexterity that cannot be too much admired. These instruments, however, were invented in the century of faith[xi] and religious factions even, which had an admirable talent for creating great personalities and great talents. To advance along a route and to discover it are two different things.

The most original eighteenth-century mathematician, so far as I can judge, the most fertile, and the one whose work will turn out to be most profitable to man (a point that must never be forgotten) by its application to optics and to nautical art, was Leonard Euler, whose tender piety was known to everyone, and to me especially, who has been able to admire him at first hand for a long time.

So let no one cry out *illuminism* or *mysticism*. The words mean nothing, and yet it is with this nothing that genius is intimidated and the route to discoveries barred. Certain contemporary philosophers have taken it into their heads to speak of *causes*, but when will it be understood that there can be no *causes* in the material order and that they must all be sought in another sphere?

Now, if this is the rule, even in the natural sciences, why, in sciences of a supernatural order, should we not, without the least scruple, devote ourselves to research that we can also call *supernatural*? I am astonished,

---

[22] *Investigations in Natural Philosophy* III.10.12.15.

[23] *Although their knowledge is equal, still you would know that a doctor is a more useful friend than a stranger.* (Aulus Cornelius Celsus *Of Medicine* Preface, Bk I.73)

Count, to find in you prejudices from which the independence of your mind could easily have enabled you to escape.

The Count

I assure you, my dear Senator, that there may well have been a misunderstanding, as happens in most discussions. I never intended to deny that religion was the mother of science – God preserve me from such an idea. Theory and experience unite to proclaim this truth. The sceptre of science belongs to Europe only because it is Christian. It has attained this high point of civilization and knowledge because it began with theology, because its universities were first schools of theology, and because all the sciences, *grafted* onto this divine *subject*, manifested their divine sap by an immense vegetation. The indispensable necessity of this lengthy preparation of the European genius is a capital truth that has totally escaped modern thinkers. Bacon himself, whom you have rightly nipped, was as mistaken about this as lesser people. He is really quite amusing when he treats this subject, and especially when he carries on against scholasticism and theology. It must be agreed that this famous man appears to have completely ignored the preparations necessary if science is not to be a great evil. Teach young people physics and chemistry before they have been imbued with religion and morals, or send a new nation academicians before sending missionaries, and you will see the result.

I believe it can even be proved conclusively that there is in science, if it is not entirely subordinated to the national dogmas, some hidden quality that tends to degrade man and above all make him a useless or bad citizen. This principle, if it were well developed, could furnish a clear and decisive solution to the great problem of the utility of the sciences, a problem that Rousseau in the middle of the last century greatly confused with his wrong-headedness and his half-formed ideas.[24]

---

[24] The study of the natural sciences has its excess like anything else, and that is where we are now. It is not, and it must not be, the principal goal of intelligence, and it would be the height of folly to expose ourselves to a lack of *men* in order to have more *physicists*. Seneca put it very well when he said: *Philosopher, begin by studying yourself before you study the world.* (*Epistle 65* [Loeb].) But these words of Bossuet are even more striking, because they come from a higher source: "Men suffer from different kinds of vanity: those thought to be the most reasonable are proud of their gifts of intelligence; ... in truth, they are worthy of being distinguished from others, and they constitute one of the most beautiful adornments of the world; but who can put up with them when as soon as they feel a bit talented ... they tire every ear ... and think they have the right to be heard without end, and to have the last word on everything? *Oh correctness in life! Oh equality in morals! Oh measure in passions! Rich and veritable adornments of a reasonable nature,*

Why are scholars usually bad statesmen, and generally inept in administration?

How does it happen, on the contrary, that priests (I say PRIESTS) are naturally statesmen? In other words, why does the sacerdotal order produce proportionately more statesmen than all the other orders of society? Why especially does it produce more of these *natural* statesmen, if I can use the phrase, who launch themselves into government, and succeed without preparation, such as, for example, those whom Charles V and his son employed a great deal, and who astonished us by their role in history?

Why has the noblest, strongest, and most powerful of monarchies been literally *made* by BISHOPS (as Gibbon admitted) *as a hive is made by bees*?

I could go on and on about this great subject; but, my dear Senator, for the very benefit of this religion and the honour due it, let us remember that it commands nothing to us so strongly as simplicity and obedience. Who knows our clay better than God? I dare say that what we ought to be ignorant of is more important for us than what we ought to know. If he has placed certain objects beyond the limits of our vision, it is no doubt because it would be dangerous for us to perceive them distinctly. With all my heart I adopt and admire your comparison of the earth open or closed to the influences of the sky; however take care not to draw a false conclusion from an obvious principle. That religion, and even piety, is the best preparation for the human mind, that religion disposes the mind, as far as individual ability permits, to every kind of knowledge, and that it sets the mind on the route to discoveries, is an incontestable truth for every man who has even moistened his lips at the cup of true philosophy. But what conclusion do we draw from this truth? *That we must make every effort to penetrate the mysteries of this religion?* Not at all; permit me to tell you that this is an obvious sophism. The legitimate conclusion is that we must subordinate all our learning to religion, believe firmly that we study by praying, and above all, when we occupy ourselves with rational philosophy, never forget that every metaphysical proposition that does not issue from a Christian dogma is and can be nothing but a culpable extravagance. In practice, this is sufficient for us; of what importance is all the rest?

I have followed with very great interest all you have told us about this incomprehensible unity, the necessary basis of *substitution*, which would explain all things if they could be explained. I applaud your learning and the way you know how to pull things together: yet what advantage does this give you over me? I believe in substitution just like you, as I believe in the existence of Peking just as much as the missionary with whom we dined the other day who had just returned from there. When you penetrate

---

when will we learn how to appreciate you?"(Sermon sur l'honneur.)

the meaning of this dogma, you will lose the merit of faith, not only without profit but moreover with a very great danger to yourself, for in this case you will not be able to answer for your thoughts. Do you recall what we read together, some time ago, in a book by Saint-Martin? *That the unwary chemist runs the risk of adoring his own work.* This is not an idle warning: did not Malebranche say that *a false belief about the efficacy of secondary causes could lead to idolatry?* It is the same idea. Not long ago we lost a common friend eminent in science and sanctity. You know well that when he conducted certain chemical experiments, always for himself alone, he believed he had to surround himself with religious precautions. It is said that the chemistry of gases dates only from our own time, but there has been, there is, and undoubtedly there will always be a chemistry that is too *gaseous.* The ignorant laugh at these sorts of things because they understand nothing; so much the better for them. The more intelligence knows, the guiltier it can be. We often speak with a silly astonishment about the absurdity of idolatry, but I can well assure you that if we had the learning that misled the first idolaters, we would all be idolaters, or at least God would scarcely be able to count as his own *twelve thousand men in each tribe.*[25] We always start from the banal hypothesis that man has gradually raised himself from barbarism to science and civilization. This is the favourite dream, this is the fundamental mistake, or as the scholastics would say, this is the *protopseudodox* [original error] of our century. If the philosophers of this unfortunate age, who with the horrible perversity we know is theirs are still obstinate despite the warnings they have received, had also possessed some of the learning that must necessarily have belonged to the first men, woe onto the world! They would have brought some transcendent disaster upon humanity. See what they have done and what they have brought upon us, despite their profound stupidity in the spiritual sciences.

I am therefore as opposed as I can be to all curious research that goes beyond man's temporal sphere. *Religion is the spice that prevents science from becoming tainted*: this is Bacon's excellent advice, and, for once, I have no desire to criticise him. However since he worked expressly to separate the *spice* from science, I am a bit tempted to believe that he did not reflect enough on his own maxim.

Again notice that religion is the greatest vehicle of science. No doubt it cannot create talent where none exists. Wherever it finds it, however, it exalts it beyond measure, especially the talent of making discoveries, whereas irreligion always restrains and often stifles it. What more do we want? We are not allowed to pry into the secrets of the apparatus that has

---

[25] [Apocalypse 7:3–5]

been given to us for fathoming secrets. It would be too easy to break it, or, and this is perhaps worse, to distort it. I thank God for my ignorance even more than for my knowledge, for my knowledge is my own, as least in part, and in consequence I cannot be sure it is good, while my ignorance, on the contrary, at least that of which I am speaking, is from him, and so I have all possible confidence in it. I am not at all tempted to try to scale the salutary wall with which the divine wisdom has surrounded us; on this side I am sure to be on the grounds of truth. But who can assure me that on the other (to make the least unfavourable assumption) I shall not find myself in the realm of superstition?

The Chevalier

Between two superior powers who are fighting, a third, although very weak, can well propose itself as a mediator, provided that it is acceptable to them and that it acts in good faith.

It seems to me, Senator, that you have given a little too much latitude to your religious ideas. You say that the explanation of causes must always be sought outside the material world, and you cite Kepler, who reached his famous discoveries by I know not what kind of system of celestial harmony of which I understand nothing; but I do not see in all this a shadow of religion. One could well be a musician and work out chords without being pious. It seems to me that Kepler could very well have discovered his laws without believing in God.

The Senator

You have replied to yourself, Chevalier, by pronouncing these words, *outside the material world*. I never said that each discovery must come directly out of a dogma like a chicken out of an egg; I said that there are no causes in matter and that consequently they should not be sought in matter. Now, my dear friend, it is only religious men who can and want to go beyond it. The others believe only in matter, and get angry if someone even mentions another order of things. Our century must have a mechanistic astronomy, a mechanistic chemistry, a mechanistic gravity, a mechanistic morality, a mechanistic language, mechanistic remedies to cure mechanistic illnesses, and who knows what else – is not everything mechanistic? Now only the religious spirit can cure this illness. We talked of Kepler, but Kepler would never have taken the route he followed so well if he had not been eminently religious. I would want no other proof of his character than the title he gave to his work on the true date of Christ's birth.[26] I doubt whether an astronomer in our time in London or Paris would choose a similar title.

So you see, my dear chevalier, I have not mixed things up as you first thought.

The Chevalier

All right, I am not able to best you in argument, but there is one point on which I would still like to quarrel with you. Our friend has said that your taste for explanations of an extraordinary kind could perhaps lead you and others into very grave dangers, and that they have the serious disadvantage of being prejudicial to useful studies. To this you replied that precisely the opposite was true and that nothing favours the advancement of the sciences and discoveries of every kind as this turn of mind that always carries us outside the material world. This is another point on which I do not think I am able enough to argue with you, but what seems obvious to me is that you passed by the first objection in silence, and yet it is serious one. I agree that mystical and extraordinary ideas can sometimes lead to important discoveries, but the drawbacks that can result from them must be put in the other side of the balance. Let us agree, for example, that they can inspire a Kepler; but if they must also produce ten thousand fools who disturb and even corrupt the world, I would certainly be inclined to sacrifice the great man.

So, if you would please excuse my impertinence, I think that you have gone a bit too far, and it would not be a bad thing for you to be a bit more suspicious of your *spiritual impulses:* at least, I would never have said as much, as far as I can judge the matter. However as the duty of a mediator is to deny and to concede something to both sides, I must also tell you, Count, that you appear to me to push timidity to excess. I have seen much of the world, and, in truth, I have found nothing better; but I cannot easily understand how faith leads you to fear superstition. Quite the opposite should happen, it seems to me; moreover I am surprised that you would bear so much ill-will against this superstition, which does not seem to me such a bad thing. At bottom, what is superstition? Abbé Girard, in an excellent book whose title however is in direct opposition with the

---

[26] One of the works of this famous astronomer is known by the title: *De vero anno quo [aeternus] Dei Filius humanam naturam [in utero benedictae Virginis Mariae] assumpsit.* Joh. Keppleri commentatiuncula, [Frankfurt 1614]. Perhaps a learned Protestant would not express himself this way in our time.

contents,[27] teaches me that languages do not contain synonyms. So superstition is neither *error* nor *fanaticism*, nor any other monster of this kind under another name. So I repeat, what is superstition? Does not *super* mean *beyond*? So, superstition is something *beyond* legitimate belief. In truth, it is nothing to get excited about. I have often noticed that in this world that *what suffices is not sufficient*. Do not take this as a play on words, for the one who wants to do precisely what it permitted will soon do what is not. We are never sure of our moral qualities except when we have known how to exalt them a bit. In the political world, the constitutional powers established in free nations only subsist by being in conflict with each other. If someone comes to push you over, it is not sufficient to stand your ground; you must hit him yourself and push him back if you can. To jump a ditch, you must always fix your eyes well beyond the bank or fall in. In short this is a general rule; it would be very peculiar if religion were an exception to it. I do not believe that a man, and still less a nation, can believe precisely what it necessary. He will always believe a little more or a little less. I imagine, my good friends, that honour could not displease you. Yet what is honour? It is the *superstition of virtue*, or it is nothing. In love, in friendship, in loyalty, in good faith, etc., superstition is pleasing, even valuable, and often necessary; why should it not be the same with respect to piety? I am led to believe that the outcries against *the excesses of the thing* originate with the enemies of *the thing*. Reason is no doubt good, but it is not necessary for everything to be ruled by reason. Listen to this little tale, I beg you; perhaps it is a history.

Two sisters have a father who is at war. They are sleeping in the same room; it is cold and the weather is bad. They are talking of the troubles and dangers that surround their father. *Perhaps*, says the one, *he is bivouacking right now, perhaps he is sleeping on the ground with neither fire nor blanket; who knows if this is not the moment the enemy has chosen ... ah!*

She gets out of her bed, and in her night-dress runs to the dresser, picks up the portrait of her father, puts it under her pillow, and places her head over her beloved jewel. *Dear papa, I will take care of you. But, my poor sister*, says the other, *I think you are confused. Do you think that by catching a cold you can save our father, and that he could be safer because you have your head upon his portrait? Take care not to break it; and, please, go to sleep.*

Certainly she is right and everything she has said is true; but if you were to marry one or the other of these two sisters, tell me, my critical philosophers, would you choose the logical one or the *superstitious* one?

---

[27] [Gabriel Girard, *Les Synonymes françois, leurs différentes. Significations et le Choix qu'il en faut faire pour parler correctement* (Paris 1736).]

To get back to the topic, I believe that superstition is *an advance fortification* of religion that must not be destroyed, for it would not be good to allow men to come unimpeded to the foot of the wall to measure its height and plant ladders. You will cite errors as an objection; but first, do you not think that abuses of something divine have in themselves certain natural limits, and that the disadvantages of these abuses could ever equal the danger of disturbing belief? To follow my comparison, I would add that if an advanced fortification is too far forward, this is also a great *misuse*, for it would be useful only to the enemy, who would use it to take cover and to attack the town. So must one give up using advanced fortifications? With this great fear of *misuse*, one would end up by no longer daring to move.

However there are ridiculous abuses and there are criminal abuses, which is a distinction that intrigues me. This is a point that I have not been able to figure out. I have known men completely devoted to these peculiar ideas you have just been telling us about, and who are good men, I assure you, the most honest and most likeable men that it would be possible to know. In this regard, I would like to tell you a little story that cannot fail to amuse you.

You know where and with whom I spent the winter of 1806. Among the persons to be found there, one of your old friends, Count, was one of the delights of our society. This was the old commander M..., whom you once saw much of in Lyon, and who had just completed a long and virtuous career. He had just completed his seventieth year, when we saw him get angry for the first time in his life. Among the books sent to us from a neighbouring city to occupy our long evenings, one day we found the posthumously published work, put out by some little-known house in Geneva, of someone who had spent his life searching for the mechanical cause of gravity, and who, flattering himself that he had found it, modestly cried out EUREKA, and who was nevertheless astonished by *the glacial welcome given his system.*[28] At his death he had charged his executors to publish this rare discovery, along with several morsels of a pestilential metaphysics, for the good of humanity. You can well understand that he was promptly obeyed, and that this book, which had fallen to the good commander, put him in an altogether entertaining rage.

"The *wise* author[29] of this book," he told us, "has discovered that the cause of gravity must be found outside the world, seeing that there is no

---

[28] See p. 307 of the book in question. ([George-Louis Le Sage, *Opuscule de ... sur les causes finales*, published with *Notice sur la vie et des écrits de G.-L. le Sage*, Rédigée d'après ses notes par Pierre Prevost] Geneva 1805).

[29] [*"Le sage auteur."* Obviously a pun on the name of the author, Le Sage.]

mechanism within the world capable of executing what we see. Perhaps you will ask me what is a region *outside the world*? The author does not say it, but it must be quite far away. Whatever the case, *in this country outside the world there was once* (one knows neither how nor why, for neither he nor his friends have any idea of any beginning), *there was once a sufficient quantity of atoms in reserve. These atoms were made like cages, whose bars are several million times as long as their width.*[xii] They are called other-worldly *atoms, on account of their origin, or* gravitational *atoms, on account of their functions. Moreover, what happened is that one day God took as many of these atoms as he could in his hands and cast them with all his might into our world, and this why our globe turns. But it must be carefully noted that this projection of atoms took place* once and for all,[30] *for since then there have been no examples of God interfering with gravity.*

"Look what has happened to us! Look what can be said to us, for they dare to say anything to those who can listen to anything. In our reading today we resemble those impure insects that can live only in the mire; we disdain everything that instructed and charmed our ancestors, and for us a book is always good, provided that it be bad."

Up to this point we could all agree with this excellent old man; but we were devastated when he added:

"Have you never noticed, among the innumerable things they have said, especially in this time of balloons, about the flight of birds and about the attempts that our heavy species has made at various times to imitate these wonderful mechanisms, that it has never occurred to any philosopher to ask if birds could not have led us to some particular reflections on weight? However if men would recall that all antiquity was agreed in recognizing something divine in birds,[xiii] that it always questioned them about the future, that, following a bizarre tradition, it had consecrated certain birds to its principle divinities, that the Egyptian priests, according to Clement of Alexandria, would, during their time of legal purification, eat only the flesh of fowl, *because birds are the lightest of all animals*,[31] and that, according to Plato in his book of laws, *the most agreeable offering it is possible to make to the gods is a bird.*[32] Moreover if they had considered the host of

---

[30] This is the author's phrase.

[31] If this citation is accurate, which I cannot verify at the moment, it is unnecessary to observe that this phrase must be taken in the common meaning of *light meat*. (Editor's note.)

[32] Citations from memory are rarely perfectly accurate. Plato, at this place in his work, does not say that *the bird* (singular) *is the most pleasing offering*, he says that "the most divine (*Theiotata (de) dōra* [gifts]) are the birds *and the figures that a painter can execute in a day*." (*Laws* 956a–b) The second item would have to be put among those where the good pleasure of the greatest philosopher of antiquity

supernatural events where birds intervened, and especially the noteworthy honour given to doves, I do not doubt that they would have been led to question whether the common law of gravity affected living birds to the same degree as the rest of brute or organized matter.

"However, to take a higher point of view, if instead of reading Lucretius, which he received at thirteen from a murderous father,[xiv] the blind pride that I have just cited for you had read the lives of the saints, he would have been able to conceive some correct ideas on the route that must be followed to discover the cause of weight; he would have seen that among the incontestable miracles worked by these elect or that were worked on their persons, and of which impudent scepticism will never disturb the certitude, there are none more incontestable nor more frequent than that of material ecstasy. Read, for example, the lives and the canonization procedures of St Francis Xavier, St Phillip Neri, St Theresa [of Avila],[xv] etc., and you will see if it is possible to remain in doubt. Will you contest the facts told by this last saint herself, whose genius and candour equals her sanctity? One would think one was hearing St Paul describe the gifts of the primitive Church and prescribing the rules to manifest them usefully, with a naturalness, a calm, and a detachment a thousand times more persuasive than the most solemn sermons.

"Young people, and especially studious young people, and again especially those who have had the good fortune of escaping certain dangers, are quite subject to imagining during their sleep they can raise themselves into the air and that they can move about there at will. A man of much wit and of excellent character, whom I once saw much of but whom I can no longer see, told me one day that he had been visited with dreams of this sort so often in his youth that he had come to suspect that weight was not natural to man. For my part, I can assure you that this illusion was sometimes so strong that I would wake up for several seconds before being undeceived.

"But there is something even greater than all this. When the divine author of our religion had accomplished all that he still had to do on earth after his death, when he had given to his disciples the three gifts he will never take away from them – understanding,[33] mission,[34] and indefectibility[35] – then *all things being consummated* in a new sense, and in the presence of his disciples who had just touched him and eaten with him, the God-Man *ceased to have weight* and lost himself in the clouds.

---

was enigmatic or even bizarre, without being able to say why. (Editor's note.)

[33]   Luke 24:45.
[34]   Mark 16:15–16.
[35]   Matthew 28:20.

"All this is very different from *gravitational atoms*. However, there is no other way of knowing, or at least of questioning what gravity is."

At these words, we were disconcerted by a burst of laughter coming from a corner of the room. Perhaps you might think that the commander got angry, but he did not; he remained silent, but we saw on his face a profound expression of sadness mixed with terror. I cannot tell you how interesting I found this. The one who laughed, whose name you can no doubt guess, believed himself obliged to offer excuses, which were made and received in good grace. The evening ended peacefully.

That night, when my four curtains separated me by a *double boundary* from men, light, and affairs, this whole discourse returned to my mind. *So, I told myself, what harm can come from this worthy man believing that sanctity and the impulses of an ardent piety have the power of suspending the laws of gravity for man, and that one can draw from this belief certain legitimate conclusions about the nature of this law? Certainly nothing is more innocent.*

Then I recalled certain persons of my acquaintance who appeared to me to have arrived by the same way at a very different result. It is for these that some have coined the word *illuminist*, which is always taken in a bad sense. There is certainly something true in this movement of the universal conscience that condemns these men and their doctrines. Moreover, I have known several of very equivocal character, of a problematic enough honesty, and remarkable especially for their rather obvious hatred for sacerdotal orders and hierarchy. So what should we think? I went to sleep with this doubt, and I come across it again amongst you. I am undecided between the two systems that you have proposed. The one appears to me to deprive men of the greatest advantages, but at least it lets them sleep soundly; the other warms their hearts and disposes their minds to the noblest and best efforts, but there is something about it that is upsetting to good sense and even to something higher. Could we not find a rule that could put me at ease, and allow me to make up my mind?

The Count

My dear Chevalier, you are like a man thrown into the water who would ask for a drink. The rule you are asking for exists; it presses in on you, it surrounds you, it is universal. I am going to prove to you in a few words that without this rule it is impossible for a man to walk firmly at an equal distance between illuminism and scepticism; and for that ...

The Senator

We will listen to you another day.

The Count

Ah! You have the deciding vote. All right! We will not talk about it any more today. Nevertheless, Chevalier, I owe you my thanks and my congratulations for your charming apology for superstition. As you talked, I saw the disappearance of those hideous traits and those long ears with which paintings have never failed to decorate her, and when you finished, she seemed to me almost a pretty woman. When you are our age, alas, we will no longer hear you, but others will listen to you and you will pass on to them the culture you have gained from us. For we are the ones, if you will, who have given the first turn of the spade to this good earth. Moreover, gentlemen, we have not come together to dispute, but to discuss. This table, although it only bears some tea and some books, is also *a procuress of friendship*, as the proverb our friend just cited would have it. So we won't argue any more. I would only like to propose to you an idea that could, it seems to me, serve well as a peace treaty between us. It has always appeared to me that there are in higher metaphysics, as there formerly were in arithmetic, rules of *false position*. This is how I regard all these opinions that go beyond express revelation, and that are used to explain such and such a point of this revelation in a more or less plausible way. If you like, let us take as an example the theory of the pre-existence of souls, which has been used to explain original sin. Immediately you will see everything that can be said against the successive creation of souls and the use that can be made of pre-existence to provide a host of interesting explanations. Nevertheless I expressly declare to you that I do not claim to adopt this system as a truth; but I say (and here is my rule of *false position*), "If I, as a weak mortal, have been able to find a by no means absurd solution that accounts reasonably well for an embarrassing problem, how can I doubt that, if this theory is not true, there is another solution of which I know nothing, and which God has thought appropriate to refuse to our curiosity?" I say as much of the ingenious hypothesis of the renowned Leibniz, which he based on the crime of Tarquin, and which he developed with so much wisdom in his *Théodicée*; I say as much of a hundred other theories and yours in particular, my worthy friend. Provided they are not regarded as proved, that they are proposed modestly, and that they are only propounded to set the mind at rest, as I have just told you, and that above all they lead neither to pride nor contempt for authority, it seems to me that criticism should be silent in the context of these precautions. We grope along in all the sciences; why should metaphysics, the most obscure of all, be an exception? However, I always come back to saying that if ever you indulge too much in this kind of transcendental inquiry you will experience at least a certain disquiet, which clearly shows the merit of faith and docility. Do you not find that we have already been in the clouds quite a long time? Have we become better as a result? I rather doubt it. It is time to come down to earth. I must confess that I am very fond of practical ideas, and especially of those striking analogies to be found between Christian dogmas and these universal doctrines that the human race has always professed without it being possible to assign them any human origin. After the voyage we have just made sailing in the highest regions of metaphysics, I would like to propose to you something less sublime. For example, let us talk of *indulgences*.

The Senator

The transition is a little abrupt!

The Count

What do you call *abrupt*, my dear friend? It is neither abrupt nor insensitive, for it is not really a transition. We have never gone astray a moment, and we are not now changing the topic of our discourse. Have we not examined, in general terms, the great question of the sufferings of the just in this world; and have we not clearly recognized that all the objections based on this claimed injustice were obvious sophisms. This first consideration brought us to that of *substitution*, which is the great mystery of the world. I did not refuse, Senator, to stop a moment with you on the edge of this abyss, where you took a very penetrating look. However in reflecting on this great subject, we were well advised to think that this great mystery, which explains everything, had need of being explained itself. It is a fact, it is a belief as natural to man as seeing or breathing, and this belief throws the greatest light on the ways of Providence in the governance of the moral world. Now I want to make you see this universal dogma in the Church's doctrine on a point that excited so much excitement in the sixteenth century, and that was the first pretext for one of the greatest crimes men have ever committed against God. However there is no Protestant father of a family who has not granted indulgences in his own home, who has not pardoned a punishable child, *through the intercession*, or *through the merits* of another child with whom he is content. There is not a Protestant ruler who has not signed fifty *indulgences* during his reign, in providing a position, or in remitting or committing a punishment, etc., *through the merits* of father, brothers, sons, parents, or ancestors. This principle is so general and so natural that it is always being displayed in the least decrees of human justice. You have laughed a thousand times at the foolish scales that Homer placed in the hands of his Jupiter, apparently to make him appear ridiculous. Christianity shows us quite another set of scales. On one side are all the crimes, on the other all the satisfactions; on one side the good works of all mankind, the sacrifices and the tears of the innocent accumulating endlessly to be weighed against the evil that since the beginning of things has poured its poisonous waters into the other basin. In the end the side of salvation must prevail, and to hasten this universal work, until whose coming *all creation groans in pain*,[36] it suffices that man wishes it. Not only his own merits, but the satisfactions of others are imputed to him by eternal justice, provided that he wishes it, and that he makes himself worthy of this *substitution*. Our separated brothers have argued with us over this principle, as if the *redemption* that they adore with us was something other than *a great indulgence accorded to humanity through the infinite merits of innocence par excellence, freely immolated for us!* Let us make a very important observation on this point: man, who is the son of truth, is so well made for truth that he can only be deceived by corrupted or poorly interpreted truth. They said: *The Man-God paid for us; therefore we have no need of other merits*; but one must say: *Therefore the merits of the innocent can be of use to the guilty.* As redemption is only a *great indulgence*, an indulgence, in its turn, is only a *reduced redemption*. Undoubtedly, the disproportion is immense, but the principle is the same, and the analogy incontestable. Is not a *general indulgence* useless for someone who does not want to profit from it and annuls it for himself by the bad use he has made of his freedom? It is the same with respect to a *particular redemption*. It could be said that error has, in advance, put itself on guard against this obvious analogy by contesting the merits of personal good works. However, the astounding greatness of man is such that he has the power to resist God and to turn down his grace; it is so great that the sovereign lord, the *king of virtues*, treats man WITH RESPECT.[37] God only acts for him and with him, he does not force his will (this expression does not even make sense); it is necessary that the will acquiesce, it is necessary that, by a humble and courageous co-operation, man appropriate this satisfaction to himself – otherwise it will always remain foreign to him. *He must no doubt pray as if he could do nothing, but he also must act as it he could do everything.*[38] Nothing is bestowed without his efforts, whether he draws on his own merits, or whether he appropriates the works of another.

You see how each Christian doctrine attaches itself to fundamental laws of the spiritual world; it is also quite important to notice that there is not one that does not tend to purify man and to exalt him.

What a superb picture is offered by this immense city with three orders of spirits always in contact with each other! The world that *fights* gives one hand to the world that *suffers*, and with its other hand grasps that of the

---

[36] Romans 8:22.
[37] *Cum magnâ reverentiâ.* [with great favour.] (Wisdom 12:18.)
[38] Louis Racine, the Preface to his poem about grace.

world that *triumphs*. The actions of grace, prayer, satisfaction, assistance, inspiration, faith, hope, and love circulate from one to the other like beneficial waters. Nothing is isolated, and spirits, like the strips of a magnetized beam, enjoy their own strengths and those of all the others.

Again, what a beautiful law that has set down two indispensable conditions for every *indulgence* or *secondary redemption*: superabundant merit on the one side, prescribed good works and purity of conscience on the other! Without the meritorious work, without *the state of grace*, there would be no remission through the merits of the innocent. What noble emulation for the virtuous! What a warning and what encouragement for the guilty!

"You are thinking," the Apostle of the Indies once said to his neophytes, "you are thinking of your brothers who are suffering in the other world; you have the religious ambition to relieve them. But think first of yourselves; God does not listen to the one who presents himself to him with a defiled conscience. *Before trying to save souls from the pains of purgatory, begin by saving your own from hell.*"[39]

There is no more noble nor more useful belief, and every legislator must try to establish it in his land, without even informing himself if it is well founded; but I do not believe that it would be possible to produce a single universally useful opinion that was not true.

So, the blind and the rebels can argue as much as they want against the principle of *indulgences*. We will let them have their say, but it is the principle of *substitution*: it is the faith of the world.

I hope, gentlemen, that in these last two dialogues we have added much to the mass of ideas that we had assembled in our first dialogues on the great question that concerns us. Pure reason furnished us solutions capable by themselves of making Providence triumph, if *one dare judge it*.[40] However, Christianity has come to present us a new idea, all the more powerful in that it rests on a universal idea as old as the world, and that only needed to be rectified and sanctioned by revelation. So when the guilty ask us *why the innocent suffer in his world*, we are not lacking in responses, as you have seen, but we can choose one that is more direct and perhaps more convincing than all the others. We can reply: *Innocence suffers for you, if you wish it.*

---

[39] *And certainly it is right that when he is about to free the soul of another from purgatory, he should first free his own (soul) from hell.* Letter from St Francis Xavier to St Ignatius, Goa, 21 October 1542. (*Epistolae,* p. 16.)

[40] *And right in your judgement.* (Psalm 50(51):6.)

NOTES OF THE TENTH DIALOGUE

i It is impossible to know what texts the speaker had in mind, nor even if he recalled very clearly any particular one. I can cite on this point only two passages: one from Clement of Alexandria, the other from St John Chrysostom. The first says *that there is nothing more criminal than to put a mysterious sign of this nature to the service of vice.* (*Pedagogy* III,xi)

The second is less laconic. "It has been given to us to light in us the fire of charity, so that in this way we may love one another like brothers, like fathers and children love one another ... Thus souls advance towards one another to be united ... But I can add some other things on this subject ... *You understand me, you who have been admitted to the mysteries* ... And you who dare pronounce insulting or obscene words, think of the mouth you are profaning and tremble ... When the apostle said to the faithful: *Greet one another with a holy kiss.* [2 Corinthians 13:12] ... This was in order to unite and merge their souls." *Per oscula inter se copulavit [By kisses he joined them].* (St John Chrysostom, *Homily xxx, on 1 Corinthinians, Opera omnia,* ed. by Bernard Montfaucon, 13 vols. (Paris 1732) 10:650–51.)

One can also cite Pliny the Elder. "There is a kind of religious sanctity attached to certain parts of the body. The back of the hand, for example, is presented to be kissed ...; when we kiss the eyes, we seem to penetrate right to the soul and to touch it." (*Natural History* [XI.54.146]) (Editor's note.)

ii *Recherche de la vérité.* In any case, this system of *vision in God* is clearly expressed by St Thomas, who would have been, had he lived four centuries later, Malebranche or Bossuet, or perhaps both. *Videntes Deum, omnia simul vident in ipso.* [Those who see God see all things in him at once.] (St Thomas, *Summa Contra Gentiles,* III, 59.) So they see in the breast of the one *who fills all, who contains all, and who understands all.* (Ecclesiasticus 1:7.) St Augustine also comes very close to the same idea when he calls God with so much elegance and no less justice: SINUM COGITATIONIS MEÆ [the generative centre of my thoughts] (*Confessions* XIII.xi.) Father Berthier, following the same ideas, said: "All your creatures, the work of your hands, although very worthy of you since they are finite, are always in you, and you are always in them. The sky and the earth do not contain you, but you contain them in your immensity. *You are the place of everything that exists, and you are only in yourself. (Réflexions spirituelles,* 3:28.) This system is necessarily true in some sense; as to the conclusions that one would like to draw from it, this is the not the place to be occupied with them.

iii "All men are to grow up in all things in him who is the head, Christ. For from him the whole body (being closely joined and knit together through every joint of the system through the functioning in due measure of each single part) derives its increase to the building up of itself in love." (Ephesians 4:15-16.)

And this great unity is so much the goal of all divine action with respect to us, *that the one who accomplishes everything in us will only find himself completed when this will be accomplished*. (Ibid., 1:23.)

And then, that is to say at the end of things, *God will be all in all*. (1 Corinthians 15:28.)

This is how St Paul comments on his master; and Origen, in his turn, commenting on St Paul, asks himself the meaning of the words, *God will be all in all*, and answers: "I believe that they mean that God will also be *all in each*, that is to say that for each intelligent being, being perfectly purified, *all its thoughts will be God*; it will only be able to see and understand God; it will possess God, and God will be the principle and measure of all the movements of its intelligence; thus God will be *all in all*; for the distinction between good and evil will disappear, since God, in whom evil cannot subsist, will be *all in all*; thus at the end of things we will be led back to the point from which we started ..., when death and evil will be destroyed, then God will really be ALL IN ALL." (*On First Principles* III.vi.)

iv   One could cite several passages in this sense; one from St Augustine can suffice: "My brothers," he said in one of his sermons, "if you are the body and the members of the Saviour, it is your own mystery that you receive. When the words are pronounced: *Here is the body of Jesus Christ*, you respond: *Amen*; you are thus responding to what you are (*ad id quod estis respondetis*), and this response is a confession of faith ... Let us listen to the Apostle who tells us: *Although many, we are one body, all who partake of the one bread*. (1 Corinthians 10:17.) Remember that the bread is not made of a single grain, but of many. The exorcism, which precedes Baptism, *ground* you under the millstone; the water of Baptism fermented you, and when you received the fire of the Holy Spirit, you were so to say *baked* by this fire ... It is the same with the wine. Remember, my brothers how it is made. Many grapes hang from the branch, but the liquid pressed from these grapes is a confusion in unity. Thus the Lord Jesus Christ established in his table the mystery of peace and of our unity." (St Augustine, *Sermons, Opera*, Ed. by the Benedictines of St Maur, 14 vols. (Paris 1679–1700), Vol. V., part 1; 1103, col. p. 2, litt. D.E.F.)

v   (Hebrews 11:5) The Vulgate translated: *Ut ex invisibilibus visibilia fierent* [That visible things should be made out of invisible]. Erasmus in his translation dedicated to Leo X: *Ut ex his quæ non apparabant ea quæ videntur fierent* [That those things which are seen should be made for those things which did not appear]. Le Gros: *Tout ce qui est visible est formé d'une matière ténébreuse*. The Mons Version: *Tout ce qui est visible a été formé, n'y ayant rien auparavant que d'invisible*. Sacy like the Mons Version (he worked with Arnauld). Osterwald's Protestant translation: *De sorte que les choses qui se voient n'ont pas été faites des choses qui apparoissent*. That of David Martin, (Geneva 1707) (Synodal Bible): *En sorte que les qui se voient* n'ont point *été faites des choses qui apparoissent.* The English translation accepted by the Anglican Church: *So that things which are seen were not made of things which do appear.* The Slavonic translation, whose author is unknown, but which is very old since it has been attributed, although falsely, to St Jerome: *Vo ege ot neyavliaemich vidimym byti* (which completely returns to the Vulgate). Luther's German translation: *Dass alles was man sihet aus nichts worden ist.* [The Douay translation: *So thus things visible were made out of things invisible.*]

St John Chrysostom understood this text like the Vulgate, whose sense is only a little developed in the dialogue. *That things came from things which do not appear.* (Homily XXII, on the Epistle to the Hebrews, chap. 11.)

vi I believe I must observe in passing, since this is little enough known, that this famous experiment of Hales on plants, which did not remove the least weight from the soil that nourished them, can be found word for word in the book called *Actus Petri, seu Recognitiones.* The famous [William] Whiston, who made much of this book, and who translated it from the Greek, inserted this entire passage in his book entitled: *Astronomical Principles of Religion [natural and revealed].* (London 1725), 187. On this book *Recognitiones*, attributed to St Clement, a disciple of St Peter, written in the second century and interpolated in the third, see Joannes Millius, *Prolegomena in N.T. græcum,* [Oxoni 1707], 1, n° 277, and Rufinus's work, *De adulteratione librorum Origenis,* inter opp. Origen, 2 vols. (Bâle: Episcopius 1771), 1:778.

vii It is more than probable that Kepler would never have thought of the famous law that immortalized him if it had not emerged of itself from his harmonic system of the heavens, founded ... on I know not what pythagorean perfections of numbers, figures, and consonances, a mysterious system with which he occupied himself from his earliest youth until the end of his days, to which he related all his works, of which it was the soul, and to which we owe the greatest part of his observations and his writings. ([J.J. Portous de] Mairon, *Dissertation sur la glace* (Paris 1749), préf., p. 11.)

viii The gathering together of the rays of the sun augments the heat, as it proved by burning glasses, *which are thinner in the middle than towards the edges,* "thus differing from eye glasses, *as I think.* In order to use one, one first places the burning glass, *so far as I can recall,* between the sun and the body that one wants to ignite; then one raises it towards the sun, which makes the angle of the cone more acute. But I am persuaded that, if it had been first placed at the distance where one places it after having raised it, it would not have had the same strength, and nevertheless the angle would not have been less acute." (*Inquisitio legitima de calore et frigore.* 2:181.) Elsewhere Bacon comes back to the topic and tells us: "That if one first places a burning glass at a palm's distance, for example, it will not burn as well as if, after having placed it at half the distance, one withdrew it slowly and gradually to the first distance. *Nevertheless the cone and the conver-*

gence remain the same; it is the movement that augments the heat." (Ibid., *Novum Organum*, Bk. II, n° 28, 8:101.) Nothing beats that. In its genre, this represents the highest point of ignorance.

ix Not only have I not read, I have not even been able to obtain this book by William Gilbert, of which Bacon speaks so often (*Commentarii de magnete*). However, I can supply enough of it to suffice for my purpose by citing the following passage from Gassendi's physics, abridged by [François] Bernier ([*Abrégé de philosophie de Gassendi*, (Paris 1674)], ch. xvi, 1:170–1): "I am persuaded that the earth is nothing but a great magnet, and the magnet ... is nothing but a small earth that derives from the veritable and legitimate substance of the earth. If, after having observed that a shoot that one has planted puts out roots, that it grows, that it puts out branches, etc., one would have no difficulty in being assured that this shoot had been cut from an olive tree (for example) or the veritable substance of the olive tree; in the same way, after having put a magnet in equilibrium and having observed that not only does it have poles, an axis, an equator, parallels, meridians, and all the other things that pertain to the earth as a body, but that it also bears a conformation with the earth itself by turning its poles towards the poles of the earth and its other parts towards similar parts of the earth, why can one not be assured that the magnet has been cut from the earth or from the veritable substance of the earth?"

x I find among my papers the following observation, which strongly supports this thesis. I took it from an anonymous précis concerning Dr Cheyne, an English doctor, that appeared in Vol. 20 (November 1791, p. 356) of the *Magasin européen*:

"It must be said to the glory of professors of medicine, that the greatest innovators in this science and the most celebrated practitioners were no less renowned for their piety than for their knowledge; and really one must not be surprised that men called by their professions to scrutinize the most hidden secrets of nature, are the men most imbued with the wisdom and goodness of its author. ... This science has produced in England perhaps the greatest *constellation* of men famous for their genius, wit, and science than any other branch of knowledge."

We can also cite the illustrious Morgagni. He often repeated *that his knowledge in medicine and anatomy had made his faith immune from temptation.* One day he exclaimed: *Oh! If I could just love this great God as I know him!* (See *Elogio del dottore Giambattista Morgagni, Efemeridi di Roma*, 13 July 1772, n° 24.)

xi The word *century* here must not be taken literally, for the modern era of inventions in the mathematical sciences extends from the triumvirate of Cavalieri, Father Grégoire de Saint Vincent, and Viette [François Viète], at the end of the sixteenth century, to Jacques and Jean Bernouilli, at the beginning of the eighteenth century, and it is very true that this epoch was that *of the faith and of religious factions.* A man of the last century, who appears to have had no equal in the variety and the extent of his knowledge, and of talents free of any harmful qualities, Father Boskowich,[1] thought in 1755, not only that there was *then* nothing to oppose to the *giants* of the period that had just ended, and that all the sciences were on the point of declining, and he proved it by a fine curve. (See Roger Joseph Boskowich, S.J., *Vaticinium quoddam geometricum,* in the supplement to Benedetto Stay, *Philosophiae recentioris ... versibus traditae,* [2 vols. (Rome 1755)] 1:408.) It does not behove me to comment on these *Récréations mathématiques,* but I think that, in general and taking account of some exceptions that can easily be brought back to the rule, *the close alliance of religious genius and inventive genius* will always be apparent to every good mind.

xii   "This excess of the length of the bars on their width must be expressed as being *at least* in the order of the number 10 raised to the 27th power. As to the width, it is constantly the same, with no exception, and smaller than an inch of a quantity that is 10 elevated to the 13th power." Here there is neither more, nor less, nor pretty close; the count is round.

xiii   Aristophanes, in his comedy *The Birds,* made allusion to this ancient tradition:

Love hatched us, commingling in Tartarus wide,

with Chaos, the murky, the darkling,

And brought above, as the firstlings of love, .

and first to the light we ascended.

There was never a race of Immortals at all

till Love had the universe blended.

(V. 699–702 [Trans. Benjamin Bickley-Rogers, Loeb Classical Library, 1924])

xiv   Ibid. [Le Sage, *Opuscule de ... sur les causes finales*], 23. At one point he calls Lucretius *my master in physics.* He does not doubt that he has found the solution *to the greatest problem physicists have ever considered, and that the majority have always regarded as absolutely insoluble or as inaccessible to the human mind* (244). However he takes care not to give way to pride: *The only thing that he has more of than other men is the good fortune of having been led, even as a student,* to the good source, *and to have used it* (150). And to honour his master, he says in announcing to his friends the death of a Scot: *That the poor man has only gone* QUO NON NATA JACENT [where the unborn lie] (219). At least no one can gainsay his candour.

---

[1]   [Roger Joseph Boskowich (as his Serbo-Croatian name, Rudger Josip Bošković, is usually rendered) was a distinguished Jesuit scientist who lived from 1711 to 1787. He is credited with developing the first coherent atomic theory in his work *Theoria Philosophiae Naturalis* (1758).]

xv   I thought it my duty to find and cite here the narrative in which St Theresa
describes this extraordinary state:

"The state of ecstasy is one that can very seldom be resisted. ... It often
occurs without its being thought about ..., with an impetuosity so prompt and
so strong that we find ourselves suddenly elevated to the clouds in which the
divine eagle hides us under the shadow of his wings. ... Sometimes I resist
a little, but afterward I find myself so weary and tired that it seems to me
my body is broken. ... This a struggle that one has waged against a powerful
giant. ... At other times it is impossible for me to resist such a violent
movement: *I feel myself raised up soul and head, and finally my whole body,
so that it no longer touches the ground.* Just such an extraordinary thing
happened to me one day when I was kneeling in the choir, in the middle of
all the nuns, ready to communicate; I used my authority as their superior to
forbid them from speaking of it. An other time, etc."

(*Oeuvres et vie de sainte Thérèse, écrite par elle-même et par l'ordre de
ses supérieures.* Translated by Arnaud d'Andilly, (Paris 1680), cap. XX, p.
104.) See as well, *Les vies de Saints,* translated from the English of [Alban]
Butler, 12 vols. [Paris 1764]: life of St Thomas, 4:572, and that of St Philip
Neri, 4:541 ff; and the *Vie de saint François Xavier* by Father [Dominique]
Bouhours [Paris 1682], 2:572. Also, *Prediche di Francesco Masotti, della
compagnia di Gesù,* (Venice 1769), 330.

Eleventh Dialogue

The Chevalier

Although you are not very fond of these voyages in the clouds, my dear Count, I would nevertheless like to take you there again. You cut me off the other day by comparing me *to a man plunged into water and asking for a drink*. This was very well said, I assure you, but your epigram did nothing to allay my doubts. In our day man no longer seems able to live within the old sphere of human faculties. He wishes to pass beyond it; he is as restless as an eagle angry at the bars of his cage. See what he is attempting in the natural sciences! See too the new alliance he has created and that he promotes with such success between physical theories and the arts. As it works wonders in the sciences, how can you keep this general spirit of the age from extending itself to questions of the spiritual order? Why should it not be allowed to direct its attentions towards the subject that is most important for man, provided that it knows how to restrain itself within the boundaries of a prudent and respectful moderation?

The Count

In the first place, Chevalier, I do not think it would be demanding too much if I asked that the human mind, free on every other subject with this one exception, denied itself all rash inquiry into this topic. In the second place, this moderation of which you speak and which is such a fine thing in theory, is really impossible in practice; at least, it is so rare that it must pass for impossible. Now, you will acknowledge that when a certain inquiry is unnecessary, and that when it is capable of producing countless evils, it is a duty to abstain from it. This is what has always made all these spiritual impulses of the illuminists suspect, and even, I confess, odious to me, and I would a thousand times prefer ...

The Senator

You are certainly afraid of the illuminists, my dear friend! However I do not think that I, on my part, am asking too much if I humbly ask that words be defined, and that someone finally have the extreme goodness to tell us what an illuminist is, so that we know who and what we are talking about. This is always useful in a discussion. This name, illuminists, is given these guilty men in Germany who have dared in our time to conceive and even to organize, by the most criminal association, the frightful project of stamping out Christianity and sovereignty in Europe. The same name is given to the virtuous disciples of Saint-Martin, who not only profess Christianity, but work only to raise themselves to the most sublime heights of this divine law. You must admit, gentlemen, that never have men fallen into a greater confusion of ideas. I even confess that in society I am unable to listen calmly to fools of both sexes crying out against illuminism at the least word that passes their understanding, with a frivolity and ignorance that pushes the most practised patience to the limit. But you, my dear *Roman* friend, you, who are such a strong defender of authority, tell me frankly. Can you read the Scriptures without finding there a host of passages that oppress your intelligence and that invite it to indulge in attempts at prudent *exegesis*? Have not you like others been told, *Search the Scriptures*? Tell me in good conscience, I pray, do you understand the first chapter of Genesis? Do you understand the Apocalypse and the Song of Songs? Does Ecclesiastes cause you no difficulty? When you read in Genesis that the moment our first ancestors became aware of their nakedness, *God made them garments of skin*, do you take this literally? Do you think the All-powerful spent his time killing animals, skinning them, curing their pelts, finally creating needles and thread to complete these new clothes? Do you believe that the guilty ones of Babel, to put their minds at rest, really undertook to raise a tower whose weather-vane merely reached the moon (I am not saying much, as you see!); and *when the stars fall on the earth*, will you not be at a loss to situate them? Since it is a question of heaven and stars, what have you to say of the way this word *heaven* is often used by the sacred writers! When you read that *God created the* heaven *and the earth; that the* heaven *is for him*, but that he gave *the earth to the children of men; that the Saviour ascended to* heaven *and that he descended to hell*, etc., how do you understand these expressions. And when you read *that the Son is seated at the right hand of the Father*, and that *St Stephen in dying saw him in that situation*, doesn't your mind experience a certain discomfort and a kind of hidden wish that other words had occurred to the sacred writer? A thousand expressions of this kind will prove to you that it pleased God, sometimes to let men speak at will according to the reigning ideas of such and such an epoch, and sometimes to hide high mysteries not made for all eyes under apparently simple and at times vulgar forms. Now, given these two assumptions, what harm is there in mining these depths of grace and divine goodness just as we mine the earth for gold or diamonds? More than ever, gentlemen, we must devote ourselves to these lofty speculations, for we must hold ourselves ready for an immense event in the divine order, towards which we are moving with an increased speed that must strike every observer. There is no more religion on earth, and humanity cannot remain in this state. Moreover, formidable prophets are announcing that *the time has come*. Several theologians, some Catholic even, believed that facts of the first order and not so remote were announced in St John's revelation; and although Protestant theologians have usually dug only sad dreams out of that book, in which they have only seen what they wanted to see, nevertheless, after having paid this poor tribute to sectarian fanaticism, I see that certain writers of this party have already adopted the principle *that several prophecies contained in the Apocalypse are related to modern times*. One of these writers has even gone so far as to say that the event has already begun, and that the French nation must be the great instrument of the greatest of revolutions.[i] There is perhaps not one truly religious man in Europe (I speak of the educated class) who is not at this time awaiting something extraordinary. Now, tell me, gentlemen, do you believe that this agreement among all men can be scorned? That there is nothing in this general cry announcing great things?

Go back to past centuries, take yourselves back to the birth of the Saviour. At that time, did not a lofty and mysterious voice, coming from the East, write: *The Orient is on the point of triumphing; the conqueror will come from Judea; a divine infant is given to us, he is going to appear, he descends from the highest heaven, he will bring back the golden age upon the earth?* You know the rest. These ideas were spread everywhere; and as they were perfectly suited to poetry, the greatest Latin poet laid hold of them and clothed them with the most brilliant colours in his *Pollio*,[1] which was then translated into beautiful enough Greek verse and read in this language to the Council of Nicea on the orders of the Emperor Constantine.[ii] Certainly, it was worthy of Providence to command that this cry of humanity be retained forever in the immortal verses of Vergil. Yet the incurable incredulity of our century, instead of seeing in this piece what it really contains, that is to say an ineffable monument to the prophetic spirit

---

[1] [Alternate title for Vergil's *Eclogues* or *Bucolics*; a man by the name of Pollio is thought to have been the poet's first patron. Maistre's reference is to Vergil's *Eclogue IV*, the Messianic *Eclogue*, which describes a new era of peace to be ushered in by the birth of a child. In the Middle Ages this poem was thought to refer to the birth of Christ.]

then at work in the world, amuses itself by learnedly proving to us that Vergil was not a prophet, which is to say that a flute is not a musical instrument, and that there is nothing extraordinary in this poet's fourth eclogue. You will not find a new edition or translation of Vergil that does not contain some noble effort of reasoning or erudition aimed at confusing something that is perfectly clear. Materialism, which defiles the philosophy of our time, prevents it from seeing that the doctrine of spirits, and in particular that of the prophetic spirit, is quite plausible in itself, and the best supported by the most universal and most imposing tradition that ever was. Do you think that the ancients were all agreed in believing that the divinatory or prophetic power was an innate privilege of man?[2] That is not possible. Never has a being and, with greater reason, never has an entire class of beings, been known to display generally and invariably an inclination contrary to its nature. Moreover, since man's eternal sickness is to penetrate the future, this is a certain proof that he has rights on that future and that he has means to attain it, at least in certain circumstances.

The oracles of antiquity had their origins in this interior movement of man that alerts him to his nature and his rights. In the last century the ponderous erudition of Van Dale[3] and the pretty phrases of Fontenelle were vainly employed to establish the nullity of these oracles. But whatever the case, man would never have had recourse to oracles, could never have imagined them, if he had not begun with an original idea in virtue of which he regarded them as possible, and even as existing.[iii] Man is subject to time, and nevertheless, he is by nature a stranger to time; it is so foreign to him that even the idea of eternal happiness, joined to that of time, tires him and frightens him. When he reflects on it, he feels himself overwhelmed by the idea of a continuing bliss without end. I would say that *he is afraid of being bored*, if this expression was not out of place in dealing with such a serious subject; but this leads me to an observation that perhaps you will find of some value.

Enjoying the privilege of leaving time, his ideas being no longer bound by ordinary duration, the prophet feels confused by virtue of a certain analogy, and being mixed up necessarily introduces great confusion into his

---

[2] *Our elders contend that there is sometimes naturally in men a divining force ... nor are there lacking those who, among the more recent writers of our age, provide the elders with their agreement in this matter, etc.*

See Sam. Bochart, Epist. ad dom. de Segrais, Blondel, Reinesius, Fabricius and others as well cited in the dissertation of Mr. Barth. Christ. Richard, *De Româ ante Romulum conditâ* (in *Thesaurus dissertationum*, ed. by Johann Christoph Martini, [7 vols. (Nuremberg 1763–7)]).

[3] [See below, "Elucidation on Sacrifices," Chap. 1, n. 49.]

he Saviour himself was subject to this state when, willingly
himself to the prophetic spirit, analogous ideas of great
arated in time led him to mix up the destruction of Jerusalem
he world. Thus it was that David, led by his own sufferings to
meditate on *the persecution of the just*, suddenly left his own time, and
cried out, as if present in the future: *they have pierced my hands and my
feet, they have numbered all my bones; they have divided my garments
amongst them; they have cast lots for my vesture.* (Psalm 21(22):17–19).
Another no less remarkable example of this prophetic lapse is found in the
magnificent Psalm 71;[4] David, in taking up his pen, was thinking only of
Solomon; but soon the idea of the type became confused in his mind with
that of the model, and by the time he has reached the fifth verse he has
already cried out: *He will live as long as the stars*; and enthusiasm
increasing from minute to minute, he brings forth a superb piece, unique in
warmth, quickness, and poetic movement.

One could add other reflections drawn from judicial astrology, oracles,
and divinations of all kinds, of which the abuse has undoubtedly dishonoured the human mind, but which however has an authentic root like all
other general beliefs. The prophetic spirit is natural to man, and will never
cease to act in the world. Man, by always and everywhere trying to
penetrate the future, declares that he was not made for time, for time is *a
forced thing that only asks to end.* This is why in our dreams we never
have any idea of time, and why the sleeping state has always been judged
favourable for divine communications. While waiting for this great enigma
to be explained to us, let us celebrate in time the one who said to nature:
Time will be for you, eternity will be for me;[5] let us celebrate his mysterious greatness, *now and forever, and in all the centuries of centuries, and
in all eternity*[6] *and forever and ever,*[7] and iv *and when all things having*

---

[4] In the Vulgate, the last verse of this psalm reads: *Defecerunt laudes filii
Jesse.* Le Gros translates: *Ici finissent les louanges de David.*

The French Protestant translation says: *Ici se terminent les requêtes de David*;
and the English translation reads: *The prayers of David are ended.* M. Genoude
extricates himself from his platitudes with marvellous ease by saying: *Ici finit le
premier recueil que David avait fait de ses Psaumes.* For myself, I would be
tempted to write fearlessly: *Ici David, oppressé par l'inspiration, jeta la plume*
[Here, David, oppressed by inspiration, threw down his pen.], and this verse would
be no more than a note by David's editors, or perhaps his own. [In fact, recent
editions of the Vulgate drop this "verse."]

[5] [Antoine-Léonard] Thomas, *Ode sur le temps,* [in *Oeuvres diverses* (Lyons
1763)].

[6] Daniel 12:3.

[7] Exodus 15:18.

been consummated, an angel will cry in the midst of vanishing space:
THERE IS NO MORE TIME![8]

If you then ask me what is this *prophetic spirit* that I have just mentioned, I would answer that never have *great events occurred in the world that had not been predicted in some way.* Machiavelli is the first man to my knowledge to have advanced this proposition,ʸ but if you reflect on it yourselves, you will find the assertion of this *pious* writer justified by all history. The last example you have of this is the French Revolution, which was predicted from all sides in the most incontestable way. However to come back to the point where I began, do you think that Vergil's century lacked bright wits who laughed at *the great year, the century of gold, the chaste Lucina, the holy mother, and the mysterious child?* Nevertheless it was all true:

The child from the skies was ready to descend.

You can see in several writings, notably in the note Pope joined to his verse translation of *Pollio*, that this piece could have passed for a verse of Isaiah. Why would you expect it to be different today? The world is waiting. How can we scorn this general persuasion, and by what right do we condemn men who, warned by these divine signs, devote themselves to holy studies?

Would you like another proof of what is being prepared? Look for it in the sciences: consider well the progress of chemistry, and even of astronomy, and you will see where they are taking us. Would you believe, for example, if you were not alerted to it, that Newton is bringing us back to Pythagoras, and that soon it will be demonstrated that the heavenly bodies are moved precisely like the human body, by intelligences that are united to them, without our knowing how? Yet this is what is on the point of being verified, so that soon there will be no way of disputing the matter. Undoubtedly this doctrine could seem paradoxical, and even ridiculous, because it is directly opposed to prevailing opinion, but wait until the natural affinity of religion and science are brought together in the head of a single man of genius. The appearance of such a man cannot be far off, and perhaps he exists even now. He will be famous, and will end the eighteenth century, which still endures today, for intellectual centuries do not conform to the calendar like *centuries* properly speaking. Then opinions that seem bizarre or nonsensical to us today will be axioms impossible to doubt. Then men will talk of our present *stupidity* as we talk of the superstition of the Middle Ages. Already even, the force of things has

---

[8] Then the angel will swear by Him who lives forever and ever ... THERE WILL BE NO MORE TIME. Apocalypse 10:6.

constrained several scholars to make concessions that bring them back to talking about the *spirit*. Others, being unable to avoid sensing this silent tendency of a powerful opinion, take precautions against it that make more of an impression on authentic observers, perhaps, than would direct resistance. This is the source of their careful attention to employing only material expressions. In their writings they speak of nothing but *mechanical* laws, *mechanical principles*, *physical* astronomy, etc. It is not that they do not sense how little material theories satisfy the intelligence, for if one thing is evident to the unprejudiced human mind it is that physical laws alone do not explain the movements of the solar system;[vi] but it is precisely because they sense this that they put words on guard, so to say, against the truth. They don't want to admit it, but they are only held back by commitment and human respect. European scientists are presently a species of conjurers or initiates, or whatever you would like to call them, who make of science a kind of monopoly and who absolutely will not have anyone know *more* or *other* than themselves. Nevertheless this science will be continually despised by an *enlightened* posterity, who will justly accuse today's devotees with having been unable to draw from the truths God had confided to them those conclusions most valuable to man. Then all science will appear differently. The spirit, for so long dethroned and forgotten, will take its former place. It will be shown that all the ancient traditions are true, that all of paganism is nothing but a system of corrupted and displaced truths, which only need *cleaning*, so to speak, and restoring to their place, to shine forth all their light. In a word, all ideas will be changed, and then from all sides a crowd of elect will cry out in concert: COME, LORD, COME! Why do you blame those men who have projected themselves into this majestic future and who glory in having predicted it? Like the poets who, even in our time of weakness and decrepitude, still show some pale flashes of the prophetic spirit that manifests itself in poets by their ability to intuit languages and to speak them purely before they are formed, so spiritual men sometimes experience moments of enthusiasm and inspiration that transport them into the future and permit them to sense developments that time will eventually bring to fruition.

Recall too, Count, the compliment you addressed to me on my erudition on the subject of the number *three*. In fact this number is to be found everywhere, in the physical world as in the moral, and in divine things. God spoke to men the first time on Mount Sinai, and this revelation, for reasons that we do not know, was restricted to the strict limits of a single people and a single country. After fifteen centuries, a second revelation was addressed to all men without distinction, and this is the one we enjoy. But the universality of its action still had to be greatly restricted by the circumstances of time and place. Fifteen more centuries passed before the discovery of America; its vast regions contained a crowd of savage hordes so alien to the great blessing of revelation that we could be led to think that they had been excluded from it by some original and inexplicable curse. The great Lama alone has more subjects than the pope; Bengal has sixty million inhabitants, China two hundred million, Japan twenty-five or thirty million. Think also of the vast archipelagos of the Pacific, which today form a fifth part of the world. Your missionaries have undoubtedly made marvellous efforts to announce the gospel in some of these far regions, but you know with what success. How many myriads of men that the *good news* has never touched! Has not the scimitar of the sons of Ishmael almost entirely chased Christianity from Africa and Asia? Finally, in our Europe, what a spectacle is offered to religious eyes! Christianity has been radically destroyed in all the countries subjected to the foolish reform of the sixteenth century, and even in Catholic countries it seems to exist in name only. I do not claim to put my church above yours; we are not here to argue. Alas! I know as well as you what it lacks, but I ask you, my good friends, to examine yourselves with the same sincerity. What hate on the one side, and on the other, what prodigious indifference among you for religion and for everything connected with it! What an outburst of all the Catholic powers against the chief of your religion! To what extremities has not the general invasion by your princes reduced the priestly order among you! The public opinion that inspires them or imitates them turns entirely against this order. It is a conspiracy, it is a kind of madness, and for myself I do not doubt that the pope would rather negotiate ecclesiastical affairs with England than with certain Catholic governments that I could name. What will be the result of the storm that is beginning to break out again at the moment? Perhaps millions of Catholics will pass under sceptres that are heterodox for you and even for us. If this happens, I hope you are too enlightened to count on what they call *tolerance*, for you know that Catholicism is never *tolerated* in the full sense of the word. When they permit you to hear mass and do not shoot your priests, they call this *tolerance*; however this is not entirely to your advantage. Moreover, examine yourselves without prejudice, and you will appreciate that you are losing your power, you no longer have that *consciousness of strength* that Homer wrote about so often when he wanted to make us aware of the heights of courage. You have no more heroes. You no longer dare anything, and they dare everything against you. Contemplate this dismal picture; join the elect in their wait, and you will see if the illuminists are wrong to see a third explosion of all powerful goodness as more or less near. I would never stop if I wanted to assemble for you all the proofs that are coming together to justify this great expectation. Again, do not blame these people who occupy themselves with it and who see, in revelation itself, the reasons for foreseeing a revelation of revelation. Call these men illuminists if you wish; I will be in complete agreement with you, provided that you use the name seriously.

You, my dear count, who are so severe an apostle of unity and authority, you surely have not forgotten what you told us at the beginning of these dialogues about all the extraordinary events of the times. Everything announces, and your own observations even demonstrate, *that we are moving swiftly towards some unknown kind of unity.* So, you cannot without contradicting yourself condemn those who, as you say, *welcome this unity from afar,* and who, according to their abilities, try to penetrate mysteries no doubt difficult, but at the same time so consoling for us.

Do not say that everything has been said, that all has been revealed, and that we are not permitted to hope for anything new. No doubt we lack nothing necessary for salvation, but with respect to divine knowledge we lack a great deal. As for future manifestations, I have a thousand reasons to wait for them, as you see, while you do not have one to prove the contrary to me. Was not the Hebrew who fulfilled the law secure in conscience? I could cite for you, if required, I don't know how many Biblical passages that promise to Judaic sacrifice and to the throne of David a duration as long as the sun. *Until the event,* the Jew who took this literally was entirely right to believe in the temporal reign of the Messiah; nevertheless he was deceived, as we have since seen. However do we ourselves know what we are waiting for? *God will be with us until the end of time, the gates of hell will not prevail against the Church, etc.* Very well! Does it follow, I ask you, that God has forbidden himself all new manifestations, that he is not permitted to tell us anything beyond what we already know? It must be admitted that this would be a very strange way of reasoning.

Before ending, I want to draw your attention to two remarkable circumstances of our time. I want to speak first of the present state of Protestantism, which is everywhere declaring itself Socinian; this is what can be called its *last end, so often predicted for its founders.* This is European Mohammedanism, the inevitable consequence of the Reformation. Undoubtedly this word *Mohammedanism* sounds surprising to you at first; however nothing is more simple. Abbadie, one of the first doctors of the Protestant church, as you know consecrated an entire volume of his admirable work *On the Truth of the Christian Religion* to proving the divinity of the Saviour. Moreover, in this volume, with great knowledge of cause, he argued that if Jesus Christ is not God, Mohammed must undeniably be considered as the apostle and benefactor of the human race, since he would have uprooted the most guilty idolatry. Sir William Jones remarked somewhere *that Mohammedanism is a Christian sect,* which is unquestionable and not enough known. The same idea occurred to Leibniz, and before him, to pastor Jurieu.[9] Since Islam admits the unity of God and the divine mission of Jesus Christ, in whom however it sees only an excellent creature, why should it not belong to Christianity as much as Arianism, which professes the same doctrine? There is more: one could, I believe, take from the Koran a profession of faith that would greatly embarrass the delicate conscience of Protestant ministers if they had to sign it. Protestantism having therefore established Socinianism almost generally everywhere it reigns, it may be considered to have wiped out Christianity in the same proportion.

Does it seem to you that this state of things can last, and that this great apostasy not be at the same time the cause and the portent of a memorable judgement?

The other circumstance I want you to notice, and which is much more important than might appear at first glance, is the Bible Society. On this point, Count, I could say to you, in the style of Cicero, *novi tuos sonitus* [I know your sounds].[10] You bear quite a grudge against the Bible Society, and I will freely admit that you have given me some very good arguments against this inconceivable institution. If you like even, I will add that, despite my stand as a Russian, I much defer to your church on this matter; since the whole world admits that with respect to proselytism you are such strong workers that in more than one place you have been able to frighten governments, I did not see why they do not defer to you on the propagation of Christianity, which you Catholics understand so well. I will not argue with you about all this, provided that you allow me to revere, as much as I ought to, certain members and especially certain protectors of this society, whose noble and holy intentions we may not question.

Moreover, I believe I have found an aspect of this institution that has not been noticed, and that I would like you to judge. Hear me out, I beg you.

When an Egyptian king (we don't know which one or in what period) had the Bible translated into Greek, he thought to satisfy his own curiosity, benevolence, or policy; and unquestionably true Israelites were extremely

---

[9] "The Mohammedans, whatever can be said to the contrary, are certainly *a sect of Christians*, if the men who followed the impious heresy of Arius merited the name *Christians*." (*A Description of Asia*, in *The Works of Sir William Jones*, 5:388.)

It must be admitted that the Socinians are very near the Mohammedans. (Leibniz, *Oeuvres philosophiques*, [Amsterdam 1765], 5:481. and *Esprit et pensées du Leibniz*, [2 vols. (Paris, 1803)] 2:84.)

The Mohammedans are, as Jurieu says, a sect of Christianity. ([Pierre] Nicole, *Unité de l'Eglise*, [Paris 1687], Bk. III, Ch. 2, p. 341.) So one can add the testimony of Nicole to the three already cited.

[10] *Nosti meos sonitus* [I know my sounds]. (Cicero, *Epistles to Atticus* [I.14])

displeased to see this venerable law thrown before all nations, as it were, and no longer speaking exclusively the sacred idiom that had transmitted it in complete integrity from Moses to Eleazar.[11]

Then Christianity appeared, and by putting the Sacred Scriptures into the universal language the translators of the Bible had laboured for it, so that the Apostles and their first successors found the work done. The Septuagint version was suddenly found in every pulpit, with translations into all the living languages of the time based on its text.

At the moment something similar is happening in a different form. I know that Rome cannot stand the Bible Society, which it regards as one of the most powerful mechanisms ever put in play against Christianity. However, it is becoming too alarmed; even if the Bible Society doesn't know what it is doing, it will nonetheless be doing something for the future in precisely the same way as the makers of the Septuagint, who certainly little suspected the appearance of Christianity and the fortune it would owe to their translation. A new effusion of the Holy Spirit henceforth being among the most reasonably waited events, the preachers of this new gift must be able to cite Holy Scripture to all peoples. Apostles are not translators; they have many other occupations. Nevertheless the Bible Society, a blind instrument of Providence, is preparing these different versions that the true envoys will one day explain in virtue of a legitimate mission (new or original doesn't matter), *which will chase doubt from the city of God*;[12] and so it will happen that the terrible enemies of unity will help to establish it.

The Count

My dear friend, I am delighted that your brilliant explanations lead me to explain myself in my turn so that I can at least convince you that I have not had the great misfortune of talking about what I do not know.

So first you want someone *to have the extreme kindness* of explaining to you *what an illuminist is*. I do not deny that this name has often been abused and that it has been made to mean whatever someone wished; but if, on one side, we must scorn certain too commonly held opinions, we must not, on the other side, discount the vague but general disapproval attached to certain names. If this name illuminist implied nothing reprehen-

---

[11] [There were a number of Old Testament figures who bore this name, as well as some well known Rabbis in post-biblical times; it seems impossible to determine which of these persons Maistre had in mind.]

[12] *Fides dubitationem eliminat è civitate Dei.* [Faith eliminates doubt from the city of God]. [Pierre-Daniel] Huet, *De imbecillitate mentis humanæ,* [Paris 1738], Bk. III, n° 15.)

sible, one could not easily understand how opinion, constantly deceived, could not hear it pronounced without joining to it the idea of a ridiculous exaltation or something worse. However since you are formally requesting me to tell you what an illuminist is, few men, perhaps, are better able to satisfy you than I am.

In the first place, I do not say that all illuminists are Freemasons; I only say that all those I have known, in France especially, were. Their fundamental dogma is that Christianity, such as we know it today, is only a veritable *blue lodge* made for the common people; but that it depends on *the man of desire* to raise himself step by step to sublime knowledge such as that possessed by the first Christians, who were really initiates. This is what certain Germans call *transcendental Christianity.* This doctrine is a mixture of Platonism, Origenism, and hermetic philosophy on a Christian base.

Supernatural knowledge is the great goal of their works and their hopes; they do not doubt that it is possible for men to put themselves in communication with the spiritual world, to have commerce with the spirits, and thus to discover the rarest mysteries.

Their invariable custom is to give extraordinary names to things that are well known under consecrated names. Thus, a *man* for them is a *minor*, and his birth, *emancipation*. Original sin is called the *positive crime*; the acts of divine power or of his agents in the world are called *benedictions*, and the pains inflicted on the guilty, *pâtiments* [state of bearing suffering]. Often I myself have held them in *pâtiments* when I tried to argue with them that all they said that was true was only the catechism covered with strange words.

I have had the occasion, more than thirty years ago in a great city in France, to satisfy myself that a certain class of these *illuminists* had higher grades unknown to the initiates admitted to their ordinary assemblies, and that they even had a cult and priests to whom they gave the Hebrew name of *cohen.*

It is not that they cannot have or that they did not really have in their works true, reasonable, and touching things, but that these things are bought at too high a price because they are mixed with the false and the dangerous, and especially because of their aversion for all authority and sacerdotal hierarchy. This characteristic is general among them; I have never met a perfect exception among the numerous devotees I have known.

The best educated, the wisest, and the most elegant of modern theosophists, Saint-Martin, whose works were the code among the men of whom I speak, nevertheless shared in this general characteristic. He died without wanting to receive a priest, and his works present the clearest proof that he did not believe in the legitimacy of the Christian priesthood.[13]

While protesting that he had never doubted the sincerity of La Harpe's conversion (and what honest man could doubt it), he nevertheless adds *that this famous literary author did not appear to him to have been guided by true principles.*[14]

Above all, you must read the preface that he wrote for his translation of the book *Description of the Three Principles of Divine Being,* written in German by Jacob Böhme. It is there, that after having justified to a certain extent the insults against Catholic priests vomited out by this fanatic, he accuses our priesthood as a body of having been mistaken in its goal,[15] which is to say, in other words, that God did not know how to establish in his religion a priesthood such that it would have been able to fulfil his divine wishes. Certainly this is a great fault; for this attempt having failed, there remains little hope. However I will go my way, gentlemen, as if the All-Powerful had succeeded, and while the *pious disciples* of Saint-Martin, *directed,* according to the doctrine of their master, *by the true principles,* try to traverse the waters of the flood, I will sleep in peace in this ship that has been sailing happily among the reefs and storms for eighteen hundred years.

I hope, my dear Senator, that you will not accuse me of speaking of the illuminists without knowing them. I have seen much of them; I copied their writings in my own hand. These men, among whom I had friends, often edified me, often amused me, and often ... But there are certain things I do not want to recall. On the contrary I look to see only the favourable sides. I have told you more than once that this sect can be useful in countries separated from the Church, because it maintains religious feeling, accustoms the mind to dogma, preserves it from the deleterious effects of the Reformation that has no other limits, and prepares it for reunion. I even recall with the greatest satisfaction that, among the Protestant illuminists

---

[13] In fact, Saint-Martin died 13 October 1804 without wanting to receive a priest. (*Mercure de France,* 18 March 1809, N° 408, 499 ff.)

[14] The paper cited by the speaker does not put matters in quite these terms. It is less laconic and explains Saint-Martin's ideas a little better. "While proclaiming," says the journalist, "the sincerity of La Harpe's conversion, he added however *that he did not believe it guided by truly enlightened ways.*" (Ibid.) (Editor's note.)

[15] In the preface of the translation in question, Saint-Martin expresses himself in the following way: "The display of all the wonders and all the enlightenment of which the heart and spirit of man have such a pressing need *should have belonged to this priesthood.*" ([2 vols.], (Paris 1802), 3.) This passage, in fact, needs no commentary. It amounts to saying that there is no priesthood, and that the Gospel does not suffice *for the heart and spirit of man.*

that I have known in a great enough number, I have never met a certain bitterness that must be expressed by a particular name because it resembles no other feeling of this kind; on the contrary I have found among them only goodness, sweetness, and even a piety that is peculiar to them. I hope it is not in vain that they have drunk of the spirit of St Francis de Sales, Fénelon, and St Theresa. Even Madame Guyon, whom they know by heart, will not have been useless to them. Nevertheless, despite these advantages, or rather despite these compensations, *illuminism* is no less mortal for our church than for your own, in that it totally annihilates authority, which is still the base of our system.

I admit to you, gentlemen, that I understand nothing of a system that only wants to believe in miracles, and that absolutely requires its priests to perform them, on pain of being declared null. Blaïr has made a fine speech on these well known words of St Paul: "We see *things* now as in a mirror and under obscure images."[16] He proves wonderfully that if we had knowledge of what was happening in the other world, the order of this world would be troubled and soon annihilated, for man, informed as to what awaits him, would no longer have the desire nor the strength to act. Think only of the brevity of our lives. Less than thirty years on average is what we are granted; who can believe that such a being is destined to converse with the angels? If priests were involved in communications, revelations, and manifestations, etc., the extraordinary would soon become our ordinary state. This would be a great prodigy; but those who want miracles would come to want them everyday. The true miracles are good actions despite our character and our passions. The young man who masters his eyes and his desires in the presence of a beautiful woman is a greater thaumaturge than Moses, and what priest would not recommend prodigies of this sort. The simplicity of the Gospel often hides great profundity. One reads there: *If they see miracles, they do not believe.* You know very well, my old friend, that certain men, if they happened to find what they were seeking, are quite capable of becoming guilty rather than perfecting themselves. So what do we really lack, since we are free to do good? And what is lacking to priests, since they have received the power to proclaim the law and to forgive transgressions?

That there are mysteries in the Bible is beyond doubt, but to tell the truth, it matters little to me. I am very little concerned with knowing what a *coat of skins* is. Do you know more about it than I do, you who have worked to discover it? Would we be any better if we did know it? Again,

---

[16] 1 Corinthians 13:12. [Blaïr is most probably Hugh Blair, an Anglican bishop and rhetorician; Maistre's library included a French translation of Blair's sermons. (See Darcel "Les Bibliothèques de Joseph de Maistre, 1768–1821," 75.)]

look as much as you please; however take care that you do no go too far, and that you do not deceive yourself by giving reign to your imagination. It has been well said, as you recall: *Search the Scriptures*, but how and why? Read the text, *Search the Scriptures, and you will see that they bear witness to me.*[17] Thus it is a question of an already certain fact, and not of this interminable research into a future that does not belong to us. As for the other text, *the stars will fall*, or better, *they will be falling or failing*, the evangelist immediately adds that *the powers of the sky will be overturned*, expressions that are only a rigorous translation of the preceding one. I must admit that the falling stars that you see on beautiful summer stars scarcely embarrass my intelligence more. Now we see ...

The Chevalier

Please, not until I have a little quarrel with our good friend on a proposition that he let slip. He told us in his own words: *you have no more heroes*. This is what I cannot accept. Let other nations defend themselves as best they can, but I will not cede my nation's honour. French priests and knights are related, and one like the other is *without fear and without reproach*. We must be just, gentlemen; I believe that with respect to the glory of priestly fearlessness, the Revolution offered scenes that yield nothing to anything ecclesiastical history can offer in this genre. The Massacre of the Carmelites, that of Quiberon, and a hundred other events will always be remembered.

The Senator

Do not scold me, my dear chevalier; you know, and your friend also knows, that I honour the glorious actions that have made the French clergy famous during this terrible period that has just occurred. When I said *You have no more heroes*, I spoke in general terms, and without excluding noble exceptions. I only meant to indicate a certain universal weakening that you feel as well as I. However I do not want to insist, and I give you the floor, Count.

The Count

I will take it then, since that is what you both want. You are waiting for a great event. You know that on that point I agree with you completely, and I explained myself to you about this clearly enough in one of our first conversations. I thank you for your reflections on this great subject, and I thank you in particular for your simple, natural, and ingenious explication

---

[17]   John 5:39.

of Vergil's *Pollio*, which seems to me completely *acceptable* before the tribunal of common sense.

I thank you no less for what you have said about the Bible Society. You are the first thinker who has been able to reconcile me even a bit with an institution that is based entirely on a capital error, for it is not the *reading*, but the teaching of Holy Scripture that is useful. The quiet dove, first swallowing and then half-pulverizing the seeds that it subsequently distributes to its brood, is the natural image of the Church explaining to the faithful this written word, which it has placed at their disposal. Read without notes and without explanation, Holy Scripture is a poison. The Bible Society is a Protestant creation, and as such, you must condemn it as much as I; moreover, my dear friend, can you deny that it contains, not only a crowd of the indifferent, but even Socinians, complete deists, and even, I must say, mortal enemies of Christianity? ... You do not answer... A better reply could not be found... One must certainly admit that these people are singular propagators of the faith! Can you deny as well the concerns of the Anglican Church, although it has not yet expressed them formally? Can you ignore the fact that the *secret intentions* of this society have been discussed with fright in a number of works written by Anglican doctors? If the Anglican Church, which includes such great lights, has kept silent up to now, this is because it finds itself placed in the painful dilemma of either approving a society that attacks its fundamental beliefs, or of abjuring the foolish and yet fundamental dogma of Protestantism, *private interpretation*. There are other objections as well to be made against the Bible Society, and most weighty is the one you have raised, Senator: *with respect to proselytism, what displeases Rome is worth nothing*. Let us wait for the results, which will decide the question. They never stop talking about the number of *editions*; let them speak to us a bit about the number of *conversions*. In any case, you know how much I honour the good faith to be found in the Society, and how much I venerate especially the great names of some of its protectors! This respect is such that I often surprise myself by arguing against myself on the subject that occupies us at the moment to see if there might be some way to compromise with intractable logic. So you can judge why I welcome your delightful and completely new point of view, which has made me see the prophetic long-term effects of an enterprise, which separated from this comforting spirit, tries religion instead of gladdens it ...

Cætera desiderantur

NOTES TO THE ELEVENTH DIALOGUE

i The following passage, which will not be read without interest, is from a German book entitled: *Die Siegesgeschichte der christlichen Religion in einer gemeinnützigen Erklärung der Offenbarung Johannis* (Nuremberg 1799). The anonymous author is well known in Germany, but not known at all in France, at least as far as I know.[1] His work is worth reading by all those who have the patience. Amidst the flood of a frightening fanaticism, *erat quod tollere velles* [there was something you would want to remove]. So here is the passage, which is quite analogous to what the speaker was just saying: "The angel who cries: *Babylon has fallen,* is *Jacob Böhme.* No one has prophesied more clearly than he on what he calls *the era of the lilies* (LILIENZEIT)." All the chapters of his book cry out: "Babylon has fallen! Its prostitution has fallen; *the time of the lilies has arrived.*" (Ibid., Chap. XIV, v, viii, p. 421.)

"King Louis XVI matured in his long captivity and he had become *a perfect bouquet.* When he mounted the scaffold, he lifted his eyes to heaven and said like his redeemer: *Lord, forgive my people.* Tell me, my dear reader, if a man can speak like this without being penetrated (*durchgedrungen*) by the spirit of Jesus Christ! Following him, millions of innocents were harvested and gathered *into the granary* by this dreadful revolution. The harvest began on the French field, and from there it will be extended to all the Lord's field in Christendom. So hold yourself in readiness, watch, and pray. (429) This nation (France) was the first of everything in Europe; it is not surprising that the first was also ripe in every sense. The two angel harvesters began with it, and when the harvest is ready in all of Christendom, then the Lord will appear and put an end to all harvesting and pressing on the earth." (Ibid., 431.)

I cannot say why Protestant doctors generally have such a great taste for the end of the world. Bengel, who wrote almost sixty years ago, by counting the years of the *beast* since the year 1130 with the most learned calculations, found that the world must be annihilated precisely in the year 1796. (Ibid., 433.)

The anonymous author whom I am citing tells us in a quite peremptory way: "It is no longer a question of building palaces or buying land for posterity; *we have no more time for all that.* (Ibid., 433.)

Every time, since the birth of their sect, when there has been a little too much noise in the world, they have always believed it was going to end. Already, in the sixteenth century, a Reformed German jurist, dedicating a book of jurisprudence to the Elector of Bavaria, seriously excused himself

---

[1] [The author's name was, in fact, Johann Jung-Stilling.]

in the preface for having undertaken a profane work *in a time when the end of the world felt visibly present.* This piece is worth citing in the original language; a translation cannot do it justice.

In hoc imminente rerum humanarum occasu, circumactâque jam fermè præcipitantis ævi periodo, frustrà tantum laboris impenditur in his politicis studiis paulò post desituris... Quum vel universa mundi machina suis jam fessa fractaque laboribus, et effecta senio, ac hominum flagitiis velut morbis confecta lethalibus ad eamdem* apolygrōsin, si unquam aliàs, certe nunc imprimis quadam* apochoradochia *feratur et anhelet. Accedit miserrima, quæ præ oculis est Reip. fortuna, et inenarrabiles* ōdines *Ecclesiæ hoc in extremo sæculorum agone durissimis angoribus et sævissimis doloribus laceratæ.* [In this imminent downfall of humanity, since now the period of the falling age is almost here, in vain is so much trouble expended on these political studies which a little later will come to an end. Since the universal machine of the world is, as it were, wearied and broken by its toils and worn out by age and brought to its end by the evil deeds of men as much as by fatal diseases, it is brought to the same dissolution if at any time certainly and it is borne by a set (?) of eager expectations and gasps with longing. There is also the wretched fortune of the state which is before our eyes and the unspeakable labour pains of the Church in this last agony of the ages, pains which have been torn (harassed) with the severest anguish and the wildest grief.] (Mathieu Van Wesenbeke, *Paratila in Pandectas juris civilis,* [Basel 1566], Preface.)

ii   There is nothing more curious than what the celebrated Heyne[2] wrote about the *Pollio.* He cites in good faith a crowd of ancient and contemporary authors who have seen something extraordinary in the piece, but nevertheless this does not prevent him from saying: *I see nothing more vain and more useless than this opinion.*[3] But what *opinion?* It is question of a *fact.* If someone believed that Vergil had been directly inspired, that is what could be called an *opinion,* which can be mocked if they wish; but that is not what is at issue. Do they want to deny that at the birth of the Saviour the world was not awaiting some great event? Undoubtedly no, this is not possible; and the learned commentator himself agrees that *never was the rage for prophecies stronger than at that time,*[4] *and that, among these prophecies, there was one that promised an immense felicity.* He adds that Vergil *made good use of these oracles.*[5] It is in vain that Heyne changes the question by

---

2   [Christian Gottlob Heyne edited a number of classical authors.]
3   Heyne, on the *Fourth Eclogue,* in his edition of Vergil. (London 1793), 1:72.
4   Ibid., 73.
5   Ibid., 74.

repeating for us banal reflections *on Roman scorn* for Judaic superstitions;[6] for, without asking him what he understands by Judaic superstitions, those who have read these conversations attentively will have been convinced that in Rome the religious system of the Jews was lacking neither connoisseurs, nor admirers, nor declared partisans, even among the upper classes. Again, we learn from Heyne that *Herod was the particular friend and host of Pollio, and that Nicolas of Damascus, a very able man who handled Herod's business affairs and who was a favourite of Augustus, could well have instructed this prince about Judaic opinions.* So, it is not necessary to think that the Romans were so alien to the history and belief of the Hebrews - but again that is not the question. Did they then believe *that a great event was going to bloom? That the East would carry it out? That men coming from Judea would overcome the world?* Was there talk on every side *of an august woman, of a miraculous child ready to descend from heaven to restore a golden age on earth,* etc.? Yes, there is no way to contest these facts; Tacitus and Suetonius testify to them. *All the earth thought it felt the approach of a happy revolution; the prediction of a conqueror who would have to subject the world to this power, embellished by poetic imagination, heated minds to the point of enthusiasm; warned by the oracles of paganism, all eyes were turned towards the East where they awaited this liberator. Jerusalem awoke to these flattering rumours, etc.*[7]

It is in vain that obstinate irreligion interrogates all the Roman genealogies trying to make them reveal the name of the child celebrated in the *Pollio*. If this child were found, it would only prove that Vergil, to pay court to some great personage of his time, applied the prophecies of the East to a new-born infant. But this child does not exist, and no matter what the efforts of the commentators, they will never be able to name anyone to whom Vergil's verses can be referred without violence. Dr Lowth especially (*De sacrâ poesi Hebræorum*) leaves nothing to be desired on this interesting point.[8]

So what is the question? And what are they arguing about? Heyne has had successors who have much outbid him. So let us pity these men who rage against the truth (I name none of them), who, without faith or conscience, change what is a very clear question to look for difficulties where there are none, and who amuse themselves by learnedly refuting what we do not say to console themselves for not being able to refute what we do say.

---

[6] Ibid., 73.

[7] *Sermons du R. P. [Jean-François] Elisée* [4 vols. (Paris 1785)].

[8] [Robert Lowth, *De sacra poesi haebraeorum proelectiones academicae* (Oxonii 1753).]

iii Nothing is so well known as Plutarch's treatise *On the Cessation of Oracles*.[9] Lucan's verses do not appear to be so well known, and yet they deserve to be. There are things that must be left to the reflections of the reader accustomed to making truths a *starting point*.

"But the Delphian oracle became dumb, when kings feared the future and stopped the mouth of the Gods; and no divine gift is more sorely missed by our age. ... Scared at last the maiden took refuge by the tripods ... bidding her human nature to come forth and leave her heart at his disposal." (Lucan *Pharsalia* V.110,161,167–8 [Trans. J.D. Duff, Loeb Classical Library 1928])

Then on the prophetic spirit in general he adds:

"She is not permitted to reveal as much as she is suffered to know. All time is gathered up together; all the centuries crowd her breast and torture it; the endless chain of events is revealed; all the future struggles to the light." (Ibid., 176–80)

iv Forever and ever.
(Exodus 15:18 and Micah 4:5)

Beyond time and ages,
Beyond eternity.
(Racine, *Esther*, last verse.)

An able French critic does not much like this expression: "We cannot imagine," he says, "how something can be beyond eternity. This expression is not immune from criticism if it is not authorized by Scripture: *Dominus regnabit in æternum et ultrà.* (Geoffroi,[10] on the text of Racine just cited.)

But Bourdaloue is of another opinion: "Forever and ever," he says, "[is a] *divine and mysterious expression.*" ("Troisième sermon sur la purification de la Vierge," third part.) And the good Madame de Guyon also says: *In the centuries of centuries AND BEYOND. (Discours chrétien*, XLVI, n° I.)

v In fact, Machiavelli's piece on prophecies merits great attention. "*Donde ei se nasca io non sò*, etc."; which is to say: "I do not know why, but it is a fact attested by all ancient and modern history that never has a great catastrophe happened to a city or a province that had not been predicted by some divines or announced by revelations, prodigies, or other heavenly signs. It is strongly to be wished that the cause of this phenomenon be discussed by men instructed in natural and supernatural things, an advantage I lack. It

---

[9] [To be found in Plutarch's *Moralia.*]
[10] [Probably Julien-Louis Geoffroy (1743–1814), a French journalist and drama critic.]

could be that our atmosphere being, as certain philosophers have believed,[11] inhabited by a crowd of spirits who foresee things by the very laws of their nature, these intelligences, who have pity on men, warn them by these sorts of signs so that they may put themselves on guard. Whatever the reason, the fact is certain, and always after these announcements, we see the occurrence of new and extraordinary things." (Machiavelli, *Discourses on Livy*, I, 56.)

Among a thousand proofs of this truth, the history of America offers a remarkable one: "If the first and most respectable Spanish historians are to be believed, there was among the Americans an almost universal belief that some great calamity menaced them and that it would be brought to them by a race of formidable conquerors coming from the East to devastate their country, etc." ([William] Robertson, *Histoire de l'Amérique*, Bk. V, p. 39.)

Moreover, the same historian reports Montezuma's speech to the great men of his empire: "He recalled for them the traditions and the prophecies that had long announced the arrival of a people *of the same race as themselves, and who must take possession of the supreme power.*" (Ibid., p. 128, on the year 1520.)

Montezuma's opinion of the Spanish can be read on p. 103, on the year 1519. Reading the celebrated Solis [Antoine de Solis y Ribadeneyra, *Conquista de México*] leaves no doubt on this point.

Chinese traditions use absolutely the same language. These remarkable words can be read in the *Tao Te Ching*: *When one family approaches the throne by its virtues and another is ready to descend in punishment for its crimes, the perfect man will be informed of it by foreshadowing signs.* (*Mémoires [concernant l'histoire, les sciences, les art, les mœurs, les usages, etc.] des Chinois*, [by the missionaries of Peking], 1:482.

The missionaries have added the following note to the text:

"The opinion that prodigies and phenomena announce great catastrophes, changes of dynasties, and revolutions in government is general among the learned. The *T'ien* [Heaven], they say, according to the *Tao Te Ching* and other ancient books, never strikes great blows against an entire nation without inviting it to repentance by evident signs of its anger." (Ibid.)

We have seen that the greatest event in the world was universally awaited. In our time, the French Revolution has furnished the most striking example of this prophetic spirit that constantly announces great catastrophes. From the famous letter dedicated by Nostradamus to the king of France (which dates

---

[11] It was a Pythagorean dogma, *that the air is full of living things.* (Diogenes Laertes, *Lives of the Philosophers*, "Pythagoras.") Plutarch says that *there are great and powerful natures in the air that reside there wicked and poorly known.* (Plutarch, *On Isis and Osiris*, chap. XXIV, Amyot translation.) Before Plutarch, St Paul had consecrated the same belief. (Ephesians 2:2.)

from the sixteenth century) to Father Beauregard's famous sermon, from verses by an anonymous author for the facade of the Church of St Genevieve to M. Delisle's song, I do not believe that any great event has been announced more clearly and from so many sources. I could accumulate a mass of citations; I am suppressing them because they are well enough known and because they would make this note too long.

Cicero, looking at the question of why we are informed in our dreams of several future events (antiquity never had any doubts on this point) tells us that according to the Greek philosopher Posidonius there are three reasons: 1) the human mind, by virtue of its relationship to the divine nature, foresees many things without any exterior assistance; 2) the air is full of immortal spirits who know things and who make them known to us; and 3) the gods reveal them to us directly.[12] Abstracting from the third explanation, which for us is included in the second, we find here the pure doctrine of Pythagoras and St Paul.

vi To these ideas, I will here permit myself to add others that I offer only as simple doubts, for we are only permitted to be dogmatic when we have the right not to doubt. Moreover, this right belongs to us only in the things that have been the principal object of our studies. Not being a mathematician, I will express, with reserve and without pretensions, doubts that are not always to be scorned, since it is not up to science to render its account to metaphysics and to answer its questions.

The word *gravitation* [*attraction*] is obviously a bad choice for describing the system of gravitation. It would be necessary to find a term that expresses the combination of two forces, for I have as much and even more right to call a Newtonian *tangential* [one who believes in centrifugal force] as *attractional* [one who believes in the attraction of gravity]. If only gravitation existed, all the matter of the universe would only be an inert and immobile mass. The tangential force that they use to explain cosmic movements is only a word put in place of a thing. This question is not one of those that it is impossible to penetrate, reserve in this matter being an error. It is not that a host of books had not told us: *that it is superfluous to involve ourselves in research of this kind; that first causes are unapproachable; that it suffices for our feeble intelligence to interrogate experience and to know the facts,* etc. However we must not be duped by this self-styled modesty. Every time that a scholar of the last century adopts a humble tone and seems to fear deciding, we can be sure that he sees a truth he wants to hide. Here it is not a question of a mystery that imposes silence on us; on the contrary, we have all kinds of knowledge that requires a solution to the problem. We know that *all movement is an effect*; and we know moreover

---

[12] Cicero *On Divination* I.

that the origin of all movement can only be found in the mind, or as the ancients so often cited in this work said: *that the principle of all movement must be sought in the immobile.* Those who have said that *movement is essential to matter* have, first of all, committed a great crime, that of speaking against their conscience, for I do not believe that any sensible man could not be persuaded of the contrary, which makes them absolutely inexcusable. Moreover, one can legitimately suspect that they do not know what they are affirming. In fact, someone who affirms in an abstract way that movement is essential to matter affirms nothing at all, since there is no movement that is abstract and real; every movement is a particular movement that produces an effect. So it is not a question of knowing *if movement is essential to matter,* but if the movement, or its result or the totality of movements it must produce, for example, a mineral, a plant, etc., are essential to matter; if the idea of matter *necessarily* carries with it that of *an* emerald, *a* nightingale, *a* rosebush, or even of this emerald, of this rosebush, of this individual nightingale, etc. – which becomes excessively ridiculous. In nature there is no blind movement or *turbulence*; all movement has a purpose and is a result of destruction or of organization, so that one cannot argue that movement is essential without affirming at the same time the essential *results.* Moreover, movement being found so obviously and necessarily joined to intention, it follows that in supposing movement essential to matter, one admits the *necessarily essential intention*; which is to say that one comes back to *mind* by the very argument that wants to get rid of it.

When the Newtonian system appeared in the world, it pleased contemporaries less by its truth, which is still disputed, than by the support that it seemed to give to opinions that will forever distinguish this fatal century. *Cotes,* in the famous preface he put at the head of the book of *Principles,* was quick to assert *that attraction was essential to matter*; but the author of the system was the first to disavow his illustrious student. He declared publicly that he had never meant to support that proposition, and even added *that he had never seen Cotes' preface.*[13]

---

[13] The thing appears incredible, and yet nothing is more true, unless we suppose, which is not permitted, that Newton had been imposed upon; for in his theological letters to Dr Bentley he says expressly, in speaking of Cotes' preface, "that he had never read it or even seen it. (*Newton* non vidit.)" It is of this *Cotes,* carried off in the prime of life, that Newton addressed this superb funeral oration: *If* Cotes had lived, we would have known something! [Newton, in a letter to Dr Bentley of 17 January 1692/93, wrote: "You sometimes speak of gravity as essential and inherent to matter. Pray do not ascribe that notion to me, for the cause of gravity is what I do not pretend to know and therefore would take more time to consider it." In *Newton's Philosophy of Nature,* ed. by H.S. Thayer (New York:

In the very preface to his famous book, Newton declared solemnly and repeatedly *that his system had nothing to do with physics; that he did not intend to attribute any power to centres, in a word, that he did not intend to leave the circle of mathematics* (although it seems difficult enough to understand this kind of abstraction).

The Newtonians, by never ceasing to talk of *celestial physics*, seem to put themselves in direct opposition to their master, who had always excluded all ideas of physics from his system, which always appears to me very remarkable.

This other striking contradiction among the Newtonians also comes from this source; for they never cease saying that gravitation is not a system but a fact, and when it comes to practice, it is certainly a *system* they defend. They speak *of two forces* as something real, and truly, if gravitation were not a system it would be nothing, since it would all be reduced to fact or to observation.

Lately again (1819), the Royal Academy of Paris asked *if, on the basis of theory alone, lunar tables could be furnished as perfect as those that had been constructed by observation.*

So there is still a doubt on this point, and simple good sense, quite apart from profound calculations, would be tempted to believe that attraction is only *observation represented by formulas*; however this is not what I affirm, for I do not intend to abandon the reserved tone that I have declared I will rigorously maintain.

However there are certain things that are independent of all calculations. It is certain, for example, that the Newtonians must not be listened to when they say *that they are not obliged to name the force that moves the stars, and that this force is a fact.* I repeat, preserve us from modern philosophy every time it bows respectfully and says: *I dare not proceed;* this is a certain sign that it sees before it a truth that it fears. The movement of the stars is no more a mystery than any other movement; all movement being born of an antecedent movement until one arrives at a will, the star can only be moved by a mechanical impulse, if it is among secondary movements, or by a will, if it is considered as an original movement. So, the Newtonians are obliged to tell us what the material motor is that they have entrusted with conducting the stars in the vacuum. In fact, they have called to their help some unknown *ether* or marvellous fluid to maintain the honour of the mechanism, and the excess of this kind of human nonsense can be seen in the works of Lesage of Geneva.[14] Such systems are not even worth a

---

Hafner 1953), 53.]

[14] [The reference is probably to George Louis Le Sage's *Opuscule de ... sur les causes finales.*]

refutation. However they are valuable from a certain point of view in that they show the despair of these sorts of philosophers, who surely would know how to support their opinions with some tolerable supposition, if it existed.

So here we are necessarily led to the immaterial cause, and it is no longer a question of knowing if we must admit a secondary cause or go immediately to the primary cause; but in either case, what becomes of *the forces* and their combination, and the whole mechanical system? The stars rotate because an intelligence makes them turn. Is someone wants to represent these movements by numbers, they can do it, I suppose; but nothing is more indifferent to the existence of the necessary principle.

If I turn around on a plain, and if distant observers say *that I am acted on by two forces*, etc., they are certainly welcome, and their calculations will be incontestable. The fact is, however, that *I turn because I want to turn.*

Here it is also necessary to remember what Newton said on the indispensable distinction between physical or simply theoretical possibilities and metaphysics.[15]

Can one, they ask, *imagine ten thousand needles standing on polished ice?* No doubt, if it is only a question of a simple theory. It suffices only to suppose them all standing perfectly straight; why would they fall to one side more than the other? However if we enter the real physical world, we know nothing is more impossible to imagine.

It is absolutely the same with respect to the system of the world; can this immense machine be ruled by blind forces? On paper, no doubt it could, with algebraic formulas and figures; but in reality, not at all. We are led back *to the needles.* Without an operating and co-operating intelligence, order is no longer possible. In a word, the physical system is physically impossible.

So, it only remains for us to choose, as I said, between the original intelligence and created intelligence.

Between these two suppositions, it does not take very long to decide; reason and antique traditions, which have been neglected very much too much in our century, would have soon decided for us.

In following these ideas, we will understand why Sabaism was the most ancient of idolatries; why they attributed to each planet a divinity who presided over it and seemed to amalgamate itself in it by giving it its name; why the moon, the satellite of the earth (something perfectly unknown to men in primitive times), why this planet, differing from the others, was presided over, according to them, by a divinity who belonged to earth as

---

[15]   Again, see his theological letters to Dr Bentley.

well as *to hells;*[16] why they believed there was so much metal on the planets, each of them giving its name and its symbol to one of the metals;[17] why Job testified to the Lord that he had never brought his hand to his mouth while looking at the stars;[18] why the prophets so often employed the expression armies of the skies;[19] why Origen says *that the sun itself and the moon and stars pray to the supreme God through his only Son ...,* that they would prefer to see us address our prayers directly to God, rather than *to take the power of answering our prayer away from God;*[20] and why Bossuet complained of the blindness and the rudeness of these men *who never want to understand* the patron geniuses of nations and the motors of all parts of the world.

To this imposing mass of evidence must be added the whole theory of judicial astronomy, which, like idolatry, has no doubt dishonoured the human mind, but which, also like idolatry, encloses truths of the first order, which we have since abandoned as useless or dangerous, or which we can no longer recognise under new forms.

Therefore everything leads us back to the incontestable truth that the system of the world is inexplicable and impossible by mechanical means. To know how this truth can be squared with mathematical theories is what I cannot decide, fearing above all to step out of my own circle of knowledge;

---

[16]   *Tergeminamque Hecaten tria virginis ora Dianæ.* [And therefore Hecate and the three faces of the maiden Diane.] (Vergil *Aeneid* IV.v.511)

[17]   There was once seven planets and seven metals; it is singular that in our times the numbers of both have grown in the same proportion, since we now know twenty-eight planets or satellites and twenty-eight metals. (*Journal de physique, Travaux et progrès dans les sciences naturelles pendant l'année 1809,* cited in the *Journal de Paris* of 4 April 1810, pp. 672–73, n° 4.)

What is no less singular is that there are as many demi-planets as there are demi-metals, for the asteroids are demi-planets.

There also always remain seven planets *according to human usage,* just as there are seven metals.

[18]   Job 31:26–28.

[19]   *The host of heaven adores you.* (Nehemiah 9:6) *All the hosts of heaven.* (Isaiah 34:4) *The host of heaven.* (Jeremiah 8:2) [They] *adored all the host of heaven.* (4 Kings 17:16)

[20]   *Our power of prayer.* (Origen *Against Celsus* V.11.) "Celsus assumes that we think the sun, the moon, and the stars are of no account, whereas we confess *that they also wait the manifestation of the children of God, who are now subjected to the vanity of material things, by reason of him who made them subject.* (Romans 8:19ff) If among the innumerable things we say about these stars, Celsus had only heard: *Praise him, O you stars and moon!* or better, *praise him, heaven of heavens!* (Psalm 148:3) he would not have accused us of saying that the vast bodies that mightily praise God are of no account." (Origen Ibid. V.13.)

but the truth that I have expressed being incontestable, and no truth being able to be in contradiction with another, it is up to the theorists in question to get themselves out of the difficulty. *Ipsi viderint [Let them see it themselves]*.

The first time that the religious spirit seizes a great mathematician, there will very surely be a revolution in astronomical theories.

I do not know if I am mistaken, but this kind of despotism, which is the distinctive characteristic of modern thinkers, is suited only to retard science. At the moment the whole thing depends on prodigious calculations by a very small number of men. They have only to agree to impose silence on the crowd. Their theories have become a kind of religion; the least doubt is a sacrilege.

The English translator of Bacon's complete works, Dr Shaw, said, in one of those notes I am no longer able to find but whose authenticity I swear: *that the Copernican system still has plenty of difficulties.*

Certainly he had to be very courageous to enunciate such a doubt. The translator is completely unknown to me as a person, and I do not even know if he is still alive; it is impossible to evaluate his reasons, which he did not judge appropriate to let us know, but with respect to courage, this is heroic.

Unfortunately, this courage is not common, and I can only doubt that there are in many heads (German especially) thoughts of this kind that dare not be expressed.

For myself, I limit myself to asking that, on the basis of this incontestable truth, *that all movement presupposes a mover, and that the mover is of absolute necessity prior to the moved*,[21] a philosophical review of the astronomical system be undertaken.

This seems to me to be a modest request, and I do not see that anyone has a right to get angry about it.

Still less would anyone be angry, I hope, if I give an example of the doubts raised in my mind by mechanical theories; I will choose my example from elementary ideas about the shape of the earth.

They all tell us, in beginning our instructions on this matter, that our planet is flattened at the poles and on the contrary raised at the equator, so that the two axes are unequal in a proportion that must be investigated.

---

[21] *Will the primary source of all their motions be anything else than the movement of that which has moved itself?* (Plato *Laws* X.895A [Loeb]) – This power is intelligence, and this intelligence is God; and it is necessary that it be prior to physical nature, which receives from it its movement, for how can the *kinœn* [moving thing] not be before the *kinoymenon* [thing moved]?

See also Aristotle, *Physics* III.I.23. *Quòd cœlum moveatur ex aliquâ intellectuali substantiâ* [Because the heavens are moved by some intellectual principle].

They tell us that there are two ways to satisfy oneself about this, experiment or geodesic measurements, and theory.

The theory rests on the physical truth that if a sphere turns on its axis, it will be raised at its equator as result of centrifugal force and will take the form of a flattened spheroid.

And in the physics laboratory we are shown a sphere of hot leather, turning on its axis by means of a crank, and as a result of the rotation taking the indicated shape.

We all say: *that is clear enough!*

But see how, in this age of reason, decisive arguments can be raised against this *decisive* demonstration.

In the first place, the earth is certainly not hot leather; its *interior* is a closed book. As for the exterior and the envelope of mean depth that God has delivered to us, we see water and earth, the immense mountains that are born in an unknown depth and that we can regard as the bones of the earth. If this supposedly immobile mass were suddenly to receive a diurnal movement, the home of men and animals would be destroyed by the waters that would accumulate at the equator: *therefore the earth, when it began to turn, can only have been what it is now*, etc.

In the second place, the physicists I have in mind do not admit *creation* properly speaking. This word alone angers them, and several of them have made their profession of faith in this regard. So beginning with this hypothesis, how can they say *that the earth has been raised at the equator by a movement that never had a beginning*? This supposition will always be found impossible it one thinks about it.

That is not all. Suppose, in the third place, and even leaving aside the question of the eternity of matter, that the world at least had a beginning; these mechanists would have to tell us by what revelation we are taught that, when the earth began to rotate, it was soft and round – two little suppositions that are worth being examined. If the world had to be round (let us suppose this for a moment) then it would have been elliptical before rotation and then elongated on its axis by the movement of rotation precisely as required for it to become perfectly round.

Thus everything is reduced to geodesic measures, and so-called theory is worthless.

In closing, let us observe that several parts of science, notably those in question at the moment, rest on infinitely delicate observations, and that all delicate observation requires a delicate conscience. The most rigorous probity is the premier quality of every observer ...

Sketch of a Final Dialogue[1]

The Count

At the beginning of these dialogues, my dear friends, we thought we could only be separated by death; and now Providence, at the blink of an eye, has again overturned the world. Duties change with political circumstances, and you, my dear Chevalier, are the first to be called. Go, go again, under flags of honour, show your honourable scars to your masters, and offer them the blood that remains to you; go, with the courage of the martyrs and with no other hope than that which animated them. For we must be under no illusion that there is any longer any hope in the world for loyalty. In great revolutions, pure victims do not die with the first blow; they are struck twice: such is your destiny. Depart, I will await your fate; and mine, which must be like yours, will not be unknown to you.

What! Soon we will no longer see each other, my dear Senator! You see my tears; they prove to you that you will always be in my memory. The days when your letters will inform me that you are still alive, that is to say that you love me, will be like feast-days for me. Would that I could show you the same thing! To my last breath I will never cease to remember Russia, and to offer my best wishes for it. Naturalized by the welcome I met in the midst of its inhabitants, I will willingly listen to my memories when they try to prove to me that I am Russian. Your happiness will never cease to be in my thoughts. What will become of you in the midst of the general confusion of minds? How will so many diverse elements be combined among you in such a short time? Blind faith, rude ceremonies, philosophic doctrines, the spirit of liberty, passive obedience, wooden huts and palaces, luxurious refinements and rude savagery, what must become

---

[1] [First published in the 1851 edition of Maistre's *Lettres et Opuscules inédits* (Vaton: Paris.)]

349 Sketch of a Final Dialogue

of such discordant elements put in movement by this taste for novelty that perhaps forms the most salient characteristic of your character, and which, unceasingly launching you towards new objects, disgusts you with what you possess? You only enjoy the house you have just bought. From laws to ribbons, everything submits to the tireless wheel of change. However, consider the nations that inhabit the earth; it is the contrary system that leads them to fame. The tenacious English prove it to you; its sovereigns are still honoured to bear the titles they received from the pope, the sword they were granted by the same hand is carried before them on the day of their coronation, so that in the future there will be nothing to change. In their almanacs, the name of *the court confessor* may still be read, so difficult is it to separate them from their ancient institutions. Finally, what people has surpassed them in strength, unity, and national glory? Do you want to be as great as you are powerful? Follow these examples, oppose unceasingly this spirit of novelty and change, even in the smallest things; decorate your walls with the reeking tapestries of your ancestors; cover your tables with their heavy silver. You say: "My father died in this house, I must sell it." Anathema on this foolish sophism! On the contrary, say: "He died here, so I can no longer sell it." Place your coat of arms executed in bronze on your door, and may the tenth generation tread the threshold that has witnessed the passing of the ashes of its ancestors. Forget your planks, nails, and vile plaster. God made you lords of granite and iron; use these gifts and build only for eternity. We look for monuments among you; it is said that you do not like them. Perhaps you will say that you are young; but do you think then that the pyramids of Egypt were modern. If you make nothing for time, what can it do for you? As for the sciences, they will develop if they want to; are you made for them? That remains to be seen. In any case, what does it matter to you? The Romans, so great in literature, heard nothing of the sciences properly speaking, yet they made a decent figure in the world. Like them, and like all the nations of the world, you began with poetry, and your beautiful language is ready for anything. Let your talents ripen without impatience, confident that it will happen to you as it happened to other nations. Your men of war and men of state, those who have made you what you are, preceded the era of science among you, as elsewhere. Galitzin, a true Russian minister of a true Russian emperor; Dolgorouky, who knew how to tame the lion without weakening it; Strogonoff, who put Siberia into the arms of your masters; the Romanzovs, the Repnins, the Souvarovs, the Soltikovs, who carried the glory of your arms to the heights – none of them belonged to any academy. It would be better to have no academies than to fill them with foreigners. Your time, if it is to come, will come naturally and effortlessly. The flame burns in all Europe; if you are combustible, how could it not seize you? While waiting, Roman glory awaits you in letters. My good wishes are nothing, my dear Senator, but as long as I tread this earth, I will never cease to offer them to you.

ELUCIDATION ON SACRIFICES

CHAPTER ONE

On Sacrifices in General

I cannot approve the impious maxim:

It was human fear that first engendered the gods.[1]

On the contrary, I am happy to observe that men, by giving God names expressing greatness, power, and goodness, by calling him *Lord, Master, Father*, etc., show clearly enough that the idea of divinity cannot have been born of fear. We can also observe that music, poetry, dance, in a word all the pleasing arts, have been called upon in religious ceremonies, and that the idea of rejoicing was always so intimately joined to that of *feast-day* that the latter everywhere became synonymous with the first.

Moreover, far be it from me to believe that for humanity the idea of God could have had a beginning, or, in other words, that it could be younger than man himself.

However, I must admit, after having been assured of the orthodoxy of the idea, that history shows us that man has always been convinced of this terrible truth, *that he lives under the hand of an angry power and that this power can be appeased only by sacrifices.*

At first sight, it is not very easy to reconcile such apparently contradictory ideas, but if we reflect on them carefully, we can very well understand how they agree, and why the feeling of terror has always existed side by side with that of joy, without the one ever being able to annihilate the other.

"The gods are good, and we are indebted to them for all the good things we enjoy; we owe them praise and thanksgiving. But the gods are just and we are guilty; we must expiate our sins; and the most powerful means of accomplishing this is *sacrifice*."[2]

Such was antique belief and such, under different forms, is still the belief of the whole world. Primitive men, from whom humanity has received its fundamental opinions, believed themselves culpable. All common institutions were based on this dogma, so that men of every century have never ceased to confess an original and universal degradation, and to say like us, although in a less explicit way: *our mothers conceived us in sin*; for there is no Christian dogma that does not have its root in man's inner nature and in a tradition as old as humanity.

However, the root of this debasement, or of the *reification* of man, if I may be permitted to put it this way, resides in *sensibility, in life, in short in the soul*, so carefully distinguished by the ancients from *the spirit* or intelligence.

Animals received only a *soul*; we have been given both *soul and spirit*.[3]

Antiquity did not believe that there could not be any sort of link or contact between *the spirit and the body*;[4] for them the *soul*, or sensibility, was a kind of proportional means or intermediary power in which the *spirit* resided, as the spirit itself resided in the body.

Visualizing the *soul* under the image of an eye, according to the ingenious comparison of Lucretius, the *spirit* was the pupil of this eye.[5] Elsewhere he calls it *the soul of the soul*.[6] Plato, following Homer, names it *the heart of the soul*,[7] an expression Philo later repeated.[8]

In Homer, when Jupiter was deciding to make a hero victorious, the god pondered the thing *in his spirit*;[9] he is *one*: he can only struggle within himself.

When, in a difficult situation, a man knows his duty and does it without hesitation, he has seen the thing like a god, *in his spirit*.[10]

If, after long hesitating between his duty and passion, this man sees himself on the point of committing an inexcusable crime, he has deliberated *in his soul and in his spirit*.[11]

Sometimes the *spirit* masters the *soul*, and makes it want to blush for its weakness: *courage my soul*, it says to it, *a worse thing even than this you once endured*.[12]

Another poet made this struggle the subject of a conversation, quite pleasant in form. *Oh my soul*, he says, *I cannot agree with all you desire; do you think that you are the only one to want what you want*.[13]

Plato asks, *what do we want to say when we say that a man has conquered himself, that he has shown himself stronger than himself*, etc.? We obviously affirm that he is, at one and the same time, stronger and weaker than himself, for if *he* is the one who is weaker, *he* is also the one who is stronger, since we are affirming both about the same subject. The will supposes *one* that would not know how to be in contradiction with itself, since the body cannot be animated at the same time by two real and opposed movements;[14] for no subject can simultaneously unite two contraries.[15] Hippocrates put it excellently when he said: *If man were one, he would never be sick*;[16] and the reason for this is simple: *for*, he adds, *we cannot conceive a cause for sickness in a being that is one*.[17]

So when Cicero writes *that when we order ourselves to do something, this means that reason must command passion,*[18] either he means that passion is a *person,* or he does not know what he means.

No doubt Pascal had Plato's ideas in mind when he said: *This duplicity in man is so obvious that there have been those who thought we have two souls; a single individual appeared to them incapable of such sudden variations.*[19]

With all the respect due such a writer, we can however agree that he does not appear to have seen to the bottom of things, for it is not only a question of knowing *how a single individual is capable of such variations so suddenly,* but rather of explaining how a single individual can combine simultaneous oppositions. How he can at the same time love both good and evil, love and hate the same object, want and not want, etc.; how can a body move itself towards two poles at the same time; in a word, to sum up, how can a simple subject not be simple?

The idea of two distinct powers is very *ancient,* even in the Church. "Those who have adopted it," said Origen, "do not think that the words of the apostle *the flesh lusts against the spirit* (Galatians 5:17) should be taken to mean *the flesh* properly speaking, but to *this soul,* which is really *the soul of the flesh:* for, they say, we have two souls, the one good and heavenly, the other inferior and terrestrial: it is of the latter that it has been said *that its works are manifest* (Ibid. 19), and we believe that this soul of the flesh resides in the blood."[20]

In any case, Origen, who in his opinions was both the boldest and the most modest of men, did not persist on this question. *The reader,* he said, *will think what he wants about this.* However, it is obvious that he did not have any other explanation for these two diametrically opposed movements within a single individual.

In effect, what is this power that opposes *the man,* or, to put it better, his conscience? What is this power that is not *he, or all of him?* Is it material, like stone or wood? In this case, it neither thinks nor feels, and consequently cannot have the power of troubling the spirit in its operations. I listen with respect and terror to all the threats made *by the flesh,* but I ask to know what it is.

Descartes, who doubted nothing, was in no way embarrassed by this duplicity in man. According to him, there are no superior and inferior parts in us, as is commonly believed. The soul of man is one, and this substance is both *reasonable and feeling.* What deceives us on this matter, he says, *is that the volitions produced by the soul and by the vital spirits sent by the body excite contrary impulses in the pineal gland.*[21]

Antoine Arnauld is even less amusing: he proposes it as an inconceivable and yet incontestable mystery "that the body, which, being only matter, is not a subject capable of sin, can however communicate with the soul that which it does not and cannot have; and that, from the union of these two things exempt from sin, there results a totality which is capable of sin, and which is *very justly* the object of God's anger."[22]

It appears that this tough sectarian scarcely philosophized about the idea *of the body*, since he thus willingly embarrassed himself, and by giving us nonsense for a mystery, he showed either inattention or ill-will by taking a mystery for nonsense.

A modern physiologist thought he had the right to declare expressly that the vital principle is one *being*: "What they call *power or faculty*, the immediate cause of all our movements and all our feelings, this principle is ONE: it is absolutely independent of the thinking soul, and even of the body, according to all appearances:[23] no cause nor mechanical law is admissible in the phenomena of the living body."[24]

Fundamentally, it appears that on this point Holy Scripture is in complete agreement with ancient and modern philosophy, since it teaches us "that man is double in his ways,[25] and that the word of God is a living sword that pierces to the division between the soul and the spirit and discerns the thoughts of the heart."[26]

St Augustine, confessing to God the dominion that old visions brought back by dreams still had over his soul, cried out with most pleasing simplicity: Then, Lord, am I MYSELF?[27]

No, undoubtedly, he was not HIMSELF, and no one knew this better than St Augustine himself, who tells us in the same passage: *Such a difference there is between MYSELF and MYSELF*;[28] he who distinguished so well the two powers in man when he cried out again, addressing himself to God: *Oh, thou mystical bread of my soul, spouse of my intelligence! How is it I could not love you?*[29]

Milton put some beautiful verses into the mouth of Satan, who roared at his degradation.[30] By analogy and truth, man could also deliver the same speech.

From where did the idea come of representing angels around the objects of our religion by groups of winged heads?[31]

I am aware that the doctrine of *two souls* was condemned in ancient times, but I do not know if it was by a competent tribunal: besides, it suffices to understand it. That man is a being resulting from the union of two *souls*, that is to say of two intelligent principles of the same nature, of which one is good and the other bad, this is, I believe, the opinion that should have been condemned, and that I also condemn with all my heart. That intelligence is the same thing as sensation, or that this element, which is also called the *vital principle*, and which is *life*, can be something material, something completely devoid of understanding and consciousness, this is what I will never believe, at least until I am warned that I am mistaken by the only power with a legitimate authority over human belief.

In this case, I will not hesitate a moment, and whereas I now have only the *certitude* of being right, then I would have the *faith* to be wrong. If I professed other opinions, I would directly contradict the principles that have dictated the work I am publishing and that are no less sacred to me.

Whatever side is taken on the question of human duality, it is on *animal power*, on *life*, on the *soul* (for all these words mean the same thing in the ancient language) that the universally acknowledged malediction falls.

The Egyptians, proclaimed by learned antiquity to be *the only trustees of divine secrets*,[32] were fully persuaded of this truth, and they renewed it daily by public profession; for when they embalmed bodies, after having washed the intestines, the soft parts, in a word all the organs of animal functions in palm oil, they placed them in a kind of casket, which they raised towards heaven, with one of the attendants saying this prayer in the name of the dead:

"Sun, sovereign master from whom I hold my life, deign to receive me near you. I have practised faithfully the religion of my fathers; I have always honoured those to whom I owe this body; I have never disowned a debt; I have never committed murder. *If I have committed any other mistakes, it was not I who did them, but these things.*"[33] Immediately *afterwards, these things* were thrown into the river *as the cause of all the sins that the man had committed*,[34] after which they proceeded with the embalming.

Moreover, it is certain that in this ceremony the Egyptians can be regarded as veritable precursors of the revelation that pronounced anathema *on the flesh*, which declared it the enemy of intelligence, that is to say of God, and which tells us expressly *that those who are born of blood or of the will of the flesh will never become children of God.*[35]

So, since man was guilty through his *sensible principle*, through *his flesh*, through *his life*, the curse fell on blood, for blood was the principle of life, or rather blood was life.[36] It is something quite singular that these old Eastern traditions, which had long been forgotten, have been revived in our day, and upheld by the greatest physiologists.

A long time ago, in Italy, Chevalier Rosa said *that the vital principle resides in the blood*.[37] He carried out many excellent experiments on this subject, and said curious things on the knowledge of the ancients in this regard. However, I can cite a better known authority,[38] that of the famous *Hunter*, the greatest anatomist of the last century, who revitalized and stimulated interest in the Eastern dogma of the vitality of the blood.

"Our ideas of life have been so much connected with organic bodies," he said, "... that it requires a new bend of mind to make it conceive that these circumstances are not inseparable. ... organization and life do not depend on each other.[39] An organ is a peculiar confirmation of matter ... to answer some purpose, the operation of which is mechanical; but, mere organization can do nothing, even in mechanics, it must still have something corresponding to a living principle, namely some *power* ...

"If we reflect very attentively on the nature of blood, we are easily led to the hypothesis that presupposes it to be living. We can not even imagine that it was possible to fashion another when we consider that there is no part of an animal that is not formed by blood, that we grow out of it, and that, if it does not have life prior to this operation, it must at least acquire it in the act of formation, since we cannot dispense ourselves from believing in the existence of life in the members or different parts as soon as they are formed."[40]

It appears that this opinion of the famous Hunter has won renown in England. Here is what we read in the *Asiatic Researches*:

"This is an opinion at least as old as Pliny, that the blood is living fluid; but it was reserved to the famous physiologist John Hunter to put this opinion among the truths that it is no longer possible to dispute."[41]

The vitality of blood, or rather the identity of blood and life, being posed as a fact that antiquity never doubted and that has been renewed in our days, it was also an opinion as old as the world *that heaven, provoked against* flesh and blood, *could only be appeased by blood*; and no nation had any doubt that there was an expiatory power in the shedding of blood. Moreover, neither reason nor folly could have invented this idea, or even less got it generally adopted. It has its root in the very depths of human nature; and history, on this point, does not present a single contrary example.[42] The entire theory rests on the dogma of substitution. It is believed (as it has been believed and will always be believed) *that the innocent can pay for the guilty*; from which it is concluded that life being guilty, *a less valuable life can be offered and accepted for another*. So one offers the blood of animals; and this *soul*, offered for another *soul*, the ancients called *antipsychon, vicariam animam*; as we say *soul for soul* or *substitute soul*.[43]

With this dogma of substitution, the learned *Goguet*[44] explained very well the legal prostitution well known in antiquity, and so ridiculously denied by Voltaire. The ancients, persuaded that an angry or maleficent divinity wished to violate the chastity of their wives, thought of delivering voluntary victims to him, thus hoping *that Venus, completely attached to her prey*, would not trouble legitimate unions – like a ferocious animal to which one throws a lamb to turn it away from a man.[45]

It must be noticed that in sacrifices properly speaking, animals that are carnivorous or stupid or foreign to man, like wild beasts, snakes, fish, birds of prey, etc., were never immolated.[46] The choice was always made from animals that are the most valuable because of their utility, the gentlest, the most innocent, those nearest to man because of their instincts and habits. Not being able to immolate men to save men, the most *human* victims in the animal kingdom were chosen, if I may express it that way. The victim was always burned entirely or in part to attest that the natural punishment for sin is fire, and that the *substitute flesh* was burned in place of *the guilty flesh.*[47]

Nothing was better known in antiquity than the cult of Mithra with its *sacrifices of bulls* and its *sacrifices of animals.* These sorts of sacrifices were supposed to achieve a perfect purification, effacing all sins and procuring a veritable spiritual rebirth for man. A pit was dug into which the person to be initiated was put; placed above was a kind of plank pierced with a great number of tiny openings, on which the victim was immolated. The blood flowed onto the *penitent* as a kind of rain, which he received on all parts of his body,[48] and it was believed that this strange baptism wrought a spiritual regeneration. Many bas-reliefs and inscriptions[49] recall this ceremony and the universal dogma that led to its creation.

Nothing is more striking in the whole law of Moses than the constant posture of contradicting pagan ceremonies and of separating the Hebrew people from all others by particular rites; but on the question of sacrifices, he abandoned his general system. He conformed to the fundamental rite *of the nations*, and not only did he conform to it, he reinforced it at the risk of giving the national character a harshness it did not need. There is not one of the ceremonies prescribed by this famous legislator, and especially, there is not a purification, that does not require blood.

The roots of so extraordinary and so general a belief must go very deep. If there was nothing real or mysterious about it, why would God himself have retained it in the Mosaic law? Where could the ancients have found this idea of spiritual rebirth through blood? Moreover, why, *always* and *everywhere*, have men chosen to honour the Divinity, to obtain its favours, and to turn away its wrath by means of a ceremony that reason in no way suggests and that feeling rejects? We must have recourse to some secret and very powerful cause.

NOTES TO CHAPTER ONE

1 *Primus in orbe deos fecit timor* [First, fear in the world made the gods]. This passage, whose true author is unknown, is to be found among the fragments of Petronius. That is where it belongs.

2 It was not only to appease evil spirits, it was not only in times of great calamities that sacrifices were offered; sacrifice was always the foundation of every kind of religion, without distinction of place, time, opinions, or circumstances.

3 *God inserted in man a spirit and a soul.* (Josephus, *Antiquities of the Jews*, Bk. I, chap. I, No. 2.)
In the beginning our common maker gave only life;
to us he gave souls as well.
Juvenal *Satires* XV.148.49 [Loeb].

4 *Moreover, God discovered that it was wrong that mind should be attached to anything without life; accordingly he enclosed intelligence in mind, and soul in body.* (*Timaeus* inter frag. Cicer., Plato, in *Timaeus, Opera*, [Bipont. ed.] T. IX, p. 312, A.B., p. 386, ii.)

5 *Even as when the eye is lacerated all around, if the pupil remains unhurt ...* (Lucretius, *On the Nature of Things*) III.409 ff. [Trans. W.H.D. Rouse, Loeb Classical Library 1924])

6 *And further the soul itself is all soul.* (Ibid.)

7 In the *Theaetetus.* N.B. Sometimes the Latins abused the word *animus*, but always in a way that left the reader in no doubt. Cicero, for example, uses it as a synonym for *anima* and opposes it to *mens*. And Vergil, in the same sense, said: *Mentem animumque.* (*Aeneid* VI.II, etc.) Juvenal, on the contrary opposes it as a synonym of *mens*, to the word *anima*, etc.

8 Philo, *On the Creation*, cited by Justus Lipsius, *Physiologia stoicorum* [Antwerp 1604], III, disser. xvi.

9 *Iliad* II.3.

10 Ibid., I.333.

11 Ibid., I.193.

12 (*Odyssey* XX.18.) Plato cited this verse in the *Phaedo*, and he saw there *one power conversing with another.*

13 *I cannot, my Soul, provide you with pleasing things,*
Endure; you are not the only one who loves fair things.
(Theognis, *Gnomology to Cyrnus*.)

14 Plato, *The Republic.*

15 *For nothing (of the things that are) at the same time receives the opposite (things).* (Aristotle, *Categories*)

16 *I say that if man knew one thing, namely when he was to suffer.* (Hippocrates, *Of Human Nature, Opera*, Van der Linden edition, chap. 2, p. 265.)

17 *For he would not know from what (cause) he would feel pain.* [Ibid.] This enlightened maxim is of no less worth in the moral order.

18 *When then we are directed to be masters of ourselves, the meaning of the direction is that reason should be a curb on recklessness.* (*Tusculan Disputations* II.21 [Loeb].) Everywhere where resistance is required, there is an *action*; everywhere there is action there is a *substance*; and no one will ever understand how a pincers can grab itself.

19 *Pensées*, III, 13. In the passage from Plato just cited, we can see that he had just told the singular story of a certain Leontius, *who positively wanted to see the corpses he positively did not want to see*; what was happening on this occasion was between *his soul* and *himself*, and the insults he believed he had to address to his own eyes. (*The Republic*)

20 Origen *On First Principles* III.4.
21 *De passionibus*, art. XLVII, *Cartesii opp.* [Amsterdam 1785], 22. I have nothing to say about this explanation: men such as Descartes merit honour as much as deadly usurpers of fame do not. I only ask that careful attention be paid to the basis of this thought, which very clearly reduces itself to this: *what is commonly believed is that there is a contradiction within man, which is a contradiction within man.*
22 *Perpétuité de la foi* [*de l'Eglise catholique touchant l'Eucharistie*], [1669], tom III, liv. XI, c. vi.
23 It seems that these words, *according to all appearances*, are again, as I have said elsewhere, a pure tribute to our century: for how can that which is ONE and which can be called *principle*, not be distinguished from matter?
24 Barthez, *Nouveaux éléments de la science de l'homme.*
25 James 1:8.
26 Hebrews 4:12. Note that he does *not* say between *the spirit* and *the body*.
27 Am I then not I, Lord my God? (*Confessions* X.XXX.1.)
28 Ibid.
29 Ibid. I.XIII.2.
30 O foul descent! That I who erst contended
With Gods to sit the high'st, am now constrain'd
Into a beast and mix'd with bestial slime
This essence to incarnate and imbrute,
That to the height of deity aspir'd.
(*Paradise Lost*, IX, 163–7.)
31 Unfortunately, too many people know the passage in Voltaire's works where he called these figures *chubby angels*. There is not a single flower in the garden of intelligence that this caterpillar did not soil.
32 *Only the Egyptians have knowledge of divine things.* (Macrobius *Saturnalia* I.12.) We can say that here this writer was speaking in the name of all antiquity.
33 *But through these things.* (Porphyry *On Abstinence from Animal Food* IV.10)
34 Plutarch (*On the Eating of Flesh* II.996E) cited by Larcher in his valuable translation of Herodotus, Bk. II, no. 95. In any case, I do not know why this great Hellenist translated *dia tayta* as *it is for these things*, instead of *it is by these things*.
There is a singular resemblance between this prayer of the Egyptian priests and the one the Church uses at the bedside of the sick: "Although he sinned, yet he always believed; he carried the zeal of God in his breast; he never ceased to adore the God who created him, etc."
35 John 1:12–13. [Maistre's paraphrase of these two verses.] When David said: *Spiritum rectum innova in visceribus meis* [Renew a right spirit in my innermost being], this was not a vague expression or a manner of speaking; he was enunciating a precise and fundamental dogma.
36 But flesh with its life – *that is, its blood* – you shall not eat. (Genesis 9:4–5) Because the life of the flesh is in the blood, *this is why* I have given it to you that you may make atonement with it upon the altar, and the blood may be for an expiation of the soul. (Leviticus 17:11) Beware of this, that you eat

not the blood [of animals], *for their blood is their life;* and therefore you must not eat the flesh *which is their life;* but you shall pour it upon the earth as water. (Deuteronomy, 12:23–24) etc., etc.

37 A fine analysis of this system will be found in the works of Count *Gian-Rinaldo Carli-Rubbi,* (Milan 1790), 30 vols., Vol. IX.

38 I did not say more DECISIVE, for his writings are no longer available to me, and I was never able to compare them. Moreover, even if *Rosa* had said everything, what does it matter? The honour of priority for the system of the vitality of the blood would not be accorded to him. His country has neither fleets, nor armies, nor colonies; so much the worse for him.

39 A truth of the first order and the greatest obviousness.

40 See John Hunter's *Treatise on the Blood, Inflammation, and Gun-shot Wounds* (London 1794).

41 See William Boag's memoir *on the venom of snakes,* in the *Recherches Asiatiques,* 6:108.

In his opinion on the vitality of the blood, Pliny may be seen as something of a latecomer; here, in any case, is what he said on this subject: *Two large veins ... distribute life to all the limbs by means of other smaller ones ... a great portion of life is in it (blood?).* (Pliny *Natural History* XII.69-70, Harduini ed., 364–65, 583.)
Hence the majority of the ancients said that the blood is the seat of life. (Harduini's note. Ibid., 583.)

42 It was a uniform opinion that prevailed everywhere, that remission could only be obtained by blood, and that someone must die for the good of the other. Bryant, *New System,* 2:455.)
The Talmudists decided moreover that sins could only be effaced by blood. (Huet, *Demonstratio evangelica,* Prop. IX, cap. 145.)
Thus the doctrine of salvation by blood is found everywhere. It braves time and space; it is indestructible, and yet it derives from no prior reason nor any assignable error.

43 [Bernard] Lami [or Lamy], *Apparatus Biblicius,* [Amsterdam, 1709], I, 7.
Take, I pray you, a heart for a heart, entrails for entrails.
This life we give you for a better life.
(Ovid *Fasti* VI.161. [Loeb])

44 [Probably Antoine Yves Goguet, author of *De l'origine des loix, des arts, et des sciences* (Paris 1758).]

45 See John Leland, *Nouvelle démonstration évangélique,* 4 vols. (Liège 1768), part I, chap. vii, 1:352.

46 With some few exceptions stemming from other principles.

47 Just as foul humours in the body produce *the fire of fever,* which purifies or consumes them without burning them, so the vices produce in souls the *fever of fire,* which purifies or burns them without consuming them. (See Origen *On First Principles* II.10.)

48 Prudentius has handed down to us a detailed description of this disgusting ceremony. "Then through the many ways afforded by the thousand chinks it passes in a shower, dripping a foul rain, and the priest in the pit below catches it, holding his filthy head to meet every drop and getting his whole

body covered with corruption. Laying his head back he even puts his cheeks in the way, placing his ears under it, exposing his lips and nostrils, bathing his very eyes in the stream, not even keeping his mouth from it but wetting his tongue, until the whole of him drinks in the dark gore." [*Crowns of Martyrdom* X.1031–40. (Trans. H.J. Thompson, Loeb Classical Library 1949)]

49 Gruter conserved a very singular one of these for us, which Van Dale cited following the passage from Prudentius:

DIS MAGNIS

MATRI DEUM ET ATTIDI

SEXTUS AGESILAUS AESIDIUS . . .

. . . . . . TAUROBOLIO

CRIOBOLIOQUE IN AETERNUM

RENATUS ARAM SACRAVIT

[Sextus Agesilaus Aesidius having been reborn dedicated this altar forever to the great gods, the mother of the gods and Attis with a taurololium (bull sacrifice) and criobolium (animal sacrifice).] (Antoine Van Dale, *Dissertationes de oraculis æthnicorum* (Amsterdam 1683), 223.)

CHAPTER TWO

Of Human Sacrifices

The doctrine of substitution being universally received, there could be no doubt about the efficacy of sacrifices being proportional to the importance of victims; and this double belief, right in its roots but corrupted by the force that corrupts everything, gave birth to the horrible superstition of human sacrifices, a practice found everywhere. In vain did reason tell men that they had no rights over their fellows; they even testified to this themselves by offering the blood of animals to atone for that of men. In vain did gentle humanity and natural compassion lend new force to the arguments of reason. In the face of this impelling dogma, reason remained as powerless as feeling.

One would like to be able to contradict history when it shows us this abominable custom practised throughout the world. However, to the shame of humanity, there is nothing more incontestable; and the very fictions of poetry bear witness to this universal prejudice.

> Hardly has the blood flown, reddening the earth,
> Than the gods loose thunder on the shrine.
> The winds furrow the air auspiciously,
> And the sea answers with a muffled roar.
> The shore far off resounds, whitening with foam.
> Unlit by hand, the pyre bursts into flame.
> The heaven's open. And the lightning's flash
> Spreads sacred awe that reassures us all.[1]

What! The blood of an innocent girl was necessary for the departure of a fleet or the success of a war! Again, where could men have got this opinion? What truth did they corrupt to arrive at such a terrible error? It is clearly established, I think, that it all stems from the dogma of substitution, whose truth is incontestable, and even innate in man (for how could he have acquired it?), but which he abused in a deplorable manner: for man, to speak exactly, cannot take up error. I can only be ignorant of or abuse the truth, that is to say, extend it by a false induction to a case to which it does not apply.

Two sophisms, it seems, led men astray; first the prominence of the subjects to be freed from anathema. They said: *To save an army, a city, even a great sovereign, what is one man?* The particular character of the two kinds of human victims already pledged under civil and political law was also considered; and they said, *What is the life of a criminal or an enemy?*

It is very likely that the first human victims were criminals condemned by the laws, for every nation believed what the Druids believed, according to Caesar: *that the punishment of criminals was something very pleasing to the Divinity.*[2] The ancients believed that every capital crime committed in the state *bound* the nation, and that the criminal was *sacred* and bound to the gods until, by the shedding of his blood, he was *un-bound*, both himself and the nation.[3]

We see here why the word *sacred* (SACER was taken in the Latin language in both a good and a bad sense), why this same word in the Greek language (*HOSIOS*) meant both what is holy and what is profane; why the word *anathema* means at the same time what is offered to God as a gift, and what is delivered to his vengeance; and finally, why in Greek as in Latin it is said that a man or a thing has been *desacralized* (expiated) to express the idea that someone has been cleansed of a stain they contracted. This word *desacralize* (*asposioun, expiare*) seems contrary to the analogy; the uninstructed ear would require *resacralization* or *re-sanctification*, but it is only an error in appearance, and the expression is very accurate. To *sacralize*, in the language of antiquity, means that which is *delivered to the Divinity*, no matter what the reason, and that which is found *bound*, so that punishment *desacralizes, expiates,* or *unbinds*, just like religious *ab-solution.*

When the Laws of the Twelve Tables[4] pronounced the death penalty they said: SACER ESTO (*that he be sacred*)! Which is to say *dedicated*, or to express it more accurately, *consecrated*, for the criminal was only, rigorously speaking, *dedicated* by execution.

When the Church prays *for dedicated women* (*pro* devoto *femineo sexu*), which is to say *for religious* who are really *dedicated* in a very true sense,[5] it is the same idea. On the one side there is crime, on the other side innocence, but both are *sacred.*

In Plato's dialogue called the *Euthyphro*, a man on the point of being brought before the courts on a horrible charge, since it was a question of having denounced his father, excuses himself by saying: "that one is soiled both by committing a crime and by allowing one to be committed, and [by saying] that he positively wanted the prosecution of his charge *in order* to absolve *both himself and the criminal at the same time.*"

This passage is an excellent expression of the system of the ancients, which, from a certain point of view, does honour to their good sense.

Unfortunately, once men were convinced of the principle that *the efficacy of sacrifices was proportional to the prominence of the victims*, it was only one step from the criminal to the enemy. Every *enemy* was a *criminal*, and equally unfortunately, every *foreigner* was an *enemy* when they needed victims. This horrible public law is only too well known, which is why HOSTIS[6] in Latin means first of all both *enemy* and *foreigner*. The most elegant of Latin writers was pleased to recall this synonym.[7] I also point out that Homer, at one place in the *Iliad*, renders the idea of enemy by that of *alien*,[8] and that his commentator warns us to pay attention to this expression.

It appears that this fatal reasoning explains completely the universality of so detestable a practice, that it explains it very well, I insist, in *human terms*, for I do not intend to deny (and how could good sense, however slightly informed, deny it?) the effect of evil, which has corrupted everything.

This effect would have no power at all over man, if it were only an isolated error. It would not even be possible, since error is nothing. Apart from any prior idea, the man who would have proposed sacrificing another to propitiate the gods would have been put to death himself or locked up as a madman. Thus it is always necessary to start out with a truth to teach an error. We will see this especially if we mediate on paganism, which sparkles with truths, but all distorted and out of place in such a way that I agree completely with the theosoph of our time who tells us that *idolatry was a putrefaction*. If we look closely we will see that among the most foolish, indecent, and atrocious opinions, among the most monstrous practices and those that have most dishonoured mankind, there is not one that we cannot *deliver from evil* (since we have been given the knowledge to ask for this gift) by showing in them the residue of truth, which is divine.

It was therefore from the incontestable truths of the degradation of man and his original *materialization*, from the necessity of reparation, from the reversibility of merits, and from the substitution of expiatory sufferings, that men were led to the dreadful error of human sacrifices.

France! You have been living in the forests too long.

"All Gaul, assailed by a grave illness or subject to the dangers of war,[9] sacrificed men or promised to sacrifice them, believing that this was the only way the gods could be appeased, and that the life of one man could only be bought by that of another. These sacrifices, carried out by the Druids, had been turned into public and legal institutions, and when they lacked criminals, it was the innocent who were tortured. Some of them filled certain colossal statues of their gods with living men; they covered them with pliant branches and set them on fire; and thus the men perished in the flames."[10] These sacrifices continued among the Gauls, as elsewhere, until Christianity was established among them; for nowhere did they cease without Christianity, never was their hold broken before its appearance.

It came to the point of believing that a head *could only be redeemed* at the cost of a head.[11] This is not all: as every truth is to be found and must be found in paganism, but, as I have just said, in a state of *putrefaction*, the Catholic theory of *prayer*, consoling and incontestable, shows itself in the midst of antique shadows under the form of a bloody superstition. Just as every real sacrifice, every meritorious action, every mortification, every act of voluntary suffering can be *offered up* for the dead, polytheism, brutally misled by some vague and corrupted reminiscences, spilled human blood *to appease the dead*. Prisoners were slaughtered around tombs. If prisoners were lacking, gladiators came to shed their blood, and this cruel extravagance became a profession, so that gladiators of this kind had a name (*Bustiarii*), which could be translated as *pyremen* [*Buchériens*], because they were destined to shed their blood around funeral pyres. Finally, if the blood of these unfortunates and that of prisoners as well was lacking, women came, despite the Twelve Tables,[12] to slash their cheeks *to give the pyres at least the appearance of sacrifices, and to satisfy the infernal gods, as Varro says, by showing them blood.*[13]

Is it necessary to cite the Tyrians, the Phoenicians, and Canaanites? Must we recall that the Athenians, in their best period, practised these sacrifices every year? That Rome, in urgent danger, sacrificed Gauls?[14] So who could remain ignorant of these things? It would be no less useless to recall the custom of sacrificing enemies and even officers and servants on the tombs of kings and great captains.

When we came to America at the end of the fifteenth century, we found the same belief there, but in a much more ferocious form. Up to twenty thousand human victims per year had to be brought to the Mexican priests, and to acquire them war had to be declared on some people; but in case of need the Mexicans sacrificed their own children. The sacrificing priest opened the chest of the victim and quickly tore out the still beating heart. The high priest squeezed the blood out of it and made it flow over the idol's mouth, and all the priests ate the flesh of the victims!

.... ô Pater orbis!
Undè nefas tantum? ....[15]

Solis has preserved for us a monument to the horrible good faith of these people by transmitting to us Magiscatzin's discourse to Cortez during this famous Spaniard's stay at Tlascala. *They did not*, he told him, believe it *a true sacrifice unless a man died for the salvation of the people*.[16]

In Peru, fathers even sacrificed their own children.[17] In short, this furore, and even that of cannibalism, has circled the globe and dishonoured two continents.[18]

Even today, despite the influence of our arms and knowledge, have we been able to root out the deadly prejudice of human sacrifice from India?

What does the antique law of this country, the gospel of Indostan, say? *The sacrifice of a man gladdens the divinity for three thousand years*.[19]

I know that in times somewhat posterior to the law, humanity, sometimes stronger than prejudice, allowed the substitution of a figure of a man formed of butter or paste for the human victim. However actual human sacrifices lasted several centuries, and that of wives on the death of their husbands still subsists.

This strange sacrifice is called the *Pitrimedha-Yaga*:[20] the prayer that the woman recites before throwing herself into the flames is called the *Sancalpa*. Before throwing herself there, she invokes the gods, the elements, her soul, and *her conscience*; she cries out *and you, my conscience!*[21] *Witness that I am going to follow my spouse*, and embracing his corpse amidst the flames, cries out *satya! satya! satya!* (this word means *truth*).

It is the daughter or nearest relative who lights the funeral pyre.[22] These horrors took place in a country where it is still a horrible crime to kill a cow, and where the superstitious brahmin dares not kill the vermin who bite him.

In 1803, the government of Bengal, wanting to establish the number of wives led by this barbarous custom to the funeral pyres of their husbands, found out that it was at least thirty thousand a year.[23]

In the month of April 1802, the two wives of Ameer-Jung, the regent of Tanjore, still burned themselves on the body of their husband. The details of this sacrifice were horrifying: all that the most powerful maternal and filial tenderness, and all that a government that did not want to use its authority could do, were used in vain to prevent this atrocity. The two women were immovable.[24]

In some provinces of this vast continent, and among the lower classes of the people, commonly enough vows are made to kill oneself voluntarily if such and such a gift is obtained from the local idol. Those who have made these vows and obtained what they want, throw themselves from a place called *Calabhairava*, situated in the mountains between the *Tapti* and *Nermada* rivers. The annual fair that is held there commonly witnesses eight or ten of these sacrifices ordered by superstition.[25]

Every time that an Indian woman delivered twins, she had to sacrifice one of them to the goddess *Gonza* by throwing it into the Ganges; some women are still sacrificed to this goddess from time to time.[26]

In this India, so praised, "the law permits the son to throw his old father, who is no longer able to work and earn his living, into the water. The young widow is obliged to burn herself on the pyre of her husband; human sacrifices are ordered to appease the spirit of destruction, and the woman who had been sterile for a long time offers to her god the child she has just brought into the world by exposing it to birds of prey or ferocious beasts, or by letting it be carried away by the waters of the Ganges. *The majority of these cruelties were still solemnly committed in the presence of Europeans on the last Indostani feast given on the island of Sangor, in the month of December 1801.*"[27]

Perhaps one will be tempted to say: *How can the English, absolute masters of these countries, see all these horrors without putting things in order? Perhaps they cry over these pyres, but why don't they put them out? Severe orders, rigorous measures, and terrible executions have been used by this government, but why always to strengthen or defend power, and never to suppress these horrible customs? One could say that the chill of philosophy extinguished in their hearts that thirst for order that accomplishes the greatest changes despite the greatest obstacles, or that the despotism of free nations, the most terrible of all, despises its slaves too much to trouble itself with making them better.*

First, it seems to me that we can make a supposition that is more honourable, and on that ground alone more likely: *That it is absolutely impossible to conquer the obstinate prejudice of the Indians on this point, and that in wanting to abolish these atrocious customs by authority, one would only end up jeopardizing authority, without benefit to humanity.*[28]

I see, moreover, a great problem to resolve: are these atrocious sacrifices that so rightly revolt us not *good* or at least *necessary* in India? By means of this terrible institution, the life of the spouse finds itself under the incorruptible guard of his wives and all those interested in them. In a country of revolutions, vengeance, vile and dark crimes, what would happen if wives had nothing to lose by the deaths of their husbands, and if they thought they had the right to acquire another? Do we even believe that these customs could have been established by purely human means? All antique legislation despised women, degraded them, embarrassed them, and more or less mistreated them.

The law of Manu says of women: *Their fathers protect them in childhood; their husbands protect them in youth; their sons protect them in age; a woman is never fit for independence. ... Through their passion for men, their mutable temper, their want of settled affection, and their perverse nature (let them be guarded in this world ever so well), they soon become alienated from their husbands.*[29]

Plato wanted the laws not to lose sight of women even for an instant: "for," he said, "if this article is poorly ordered, they are no longer half of humanity, they are more than half, and *as many times more than half than they have less of virtue than we have.*"[30]

Who does not know the incredible slavery of women in Athens, where they were subjected to endless tutelage; where, on the death of a father who left only a married daughter, the nearest relative with the same name had the right to take her away from her husband and make her his wife; and where a husband could will his wife, like a piece of his property, to any individual it pleased him to choose as his successor, etc.?[31]

Who is not familiar with the harshness of Roman law towards women? One could say that, with respect to the *second sex*, the founders of nations had all belonged to the school of Hippocrates, who believed it bad in its very essence. *The woman*, he said, *is perverse by nature; her inclination must be repressed daily, or otherwise it will sprout in all directions like the branches of a tree. If her husband is absent, her relatives will not suffice to guard her; it requires a friend whose zeal is not blinded by affection.*[32]

In a word, all legislation has taken more or less severe precautions against women; in our time they are still slaves under the Koran and beasts of burden among the savages. Only the Gospel has been able to raise them to the level of men by making them better; it alone has been able to proclaim *the rights of women* after having given birth to them, and given birth to them by establishing them in the woman's heart, the most active and powerful instrument for good as well as for evil. Extinguish the influence of the divine law in a Christian country, or even weaken it to a certain point, by allowing the freedom that is its consequence for women to subsist, and soon you will see this noble and touching freedom degenerate into shameful licence. They will become the deadly instruments of a universal corruption that will attack the vital parts of the state in a short time. It will fall into decay, and its gangrenous decrepitude will be at once its shame and horror.

A Turk or a Persian attending a European ball thinks he is dreaming; he understands nothing of these women,

> Companions of a spouse and queens in all places,
> Free without dishonour, faithful without constraint,
> And never fearing to display their virtues.

What they ignore is the law that makes this commotion and mixture possible. Even what deviates from it owes it its liberty. If there could be variation on this point, I would say that women are more indebted than we are to Christianity. The antipathy that it has for slavery (which will always be gently and unfailingly extinguished wherever it acts freely) applies especially to them; knowing too well how easy it is to inspire vice, it at least wants no one to have the right to command it.[33]

Finally, no legislator must forget this maxim: *Before effacing the Gospel, one must lock up the women,* or weigh them down with terrible laws, such as those of India. The *meekness* of the Hindus has often been commemorated, but do not be deceived. Outside the law that said, BLESSED ARE THE MEEK!, there are no *meek* men. They can be weak, timid, cowardly, but never meek. The coward can be cruel; he is so often enough; the meek man never is. India furnishes a fine example. Without talking about the superstitious atrocities I have just cited, what land on the earth has seen more cruelties?

We who blanch with horror at the very idea of human sacrifices and cannibalism, how can we be both blind enough and ungrateful enough not to recognize that we owe these feelings only to the *law of love* that watched over our cradle? A famous nation, which had attained the highest degree of civilization and refinement, dared not long ago, in a fit of delirium of which history gives no other example, formally to suspend this law. What did we see? In a blink of the eye, the customs of the Iroquois and the Algonquin; the holy laws of humanity trod under foot; innocent blood covering the scaffolds that covered France; men curling and powdering bloody heads, and the very mouths of women stained with human blood.

Here is the *natural* man! It is not that he does not bear within him the indestructible seeds of truth and virtue: his birthrights are imprescriptible; but without divine fertilization, these seeds will never germinate or they will produce only dubious or unhealthy fruit.

It is time to draw from the most incontestable historical facts a conclusion that is no less incontestable. We know by an experiment of forty centuries, which is long enough, *that wherever the true God is not known and served by virtue of an express revelation, man will always sacrifice men, and often eat them.*

Lucretius, after having told us of the sacrifice of Iphigenia (as an authentic history, of course, since that is what he needed), exclaimed in a triumphant air: *How many evils can religion spawn!*

Alas, he saw only the abuses, just like all his successors, who are infinitely less excusable than he. He was unaware that the abuse of human sacrifices, however outrageous it was, would fade in comparison to the evils produced by absolute impiety. He was unaware, or did not want to see, that there is not and cannot be a completely false religion; that the religion of all well-governed nations, such as existed at the time he was writing, was no less the cement of the political structure, and that Epicurean dogmas were about to undermine religion, and by the same token undermine the old Roman constitution in order to substitute for it an atrocious and endless tyranny.

As for us, happy possessors of the truth, let us not commit the crime of misunderstanding it. God may well have wanted to *dissemble for forty centuries*,[34] but since the new centuries have begun for man, this crime no longer has an excuse. In reflecting on the evils produced by false religions, let us bless, let us with rapture embrace the true religion, which has explained and justified the religious instinct of humanity, which has freed this universal feeling from the errors and crimes that have dishonoured it, and which has *renewed the face of the earth*. how many evils can be corrected by religion!

This is about all that can said on the subject of sacrifices, if I am not mistaken, without advancing too far, and especially of the human sacrifices that have dishonoured the whole human family. In ending this chapter, I do not think it would be useless to show how modern philosophy has considered the same subject.

The common idea that first comes to mind, and that apparently precedes reflection, is that of a homage or a kind of *present* made to the Divinity. *The gods are our benefactors* (datores bonorum), *it is quite simple to offer them the first fruits of these goods that we have from them*; from this source come antique libations and the opening of meals with the offering of first fruits.[35]

Heyne, in explaining this verse of Homer, *Of the meal he threw the first fruits into the flame*,[36] found in this custom the origin of sacrifice; he says, "The ancients offered part of their nourishment to the gods (the flesh of animals must be thought of as comprising *the sacrifice*)," and he adds, "*envisaged in this way, it is not offensive*."[37] These last words, it may be observed in passing, prove that this able man confusedly saw in the general idea of sacrifice something more profound than a simple offering, and this other point of view *offended* him.

It is not simply a question of a *present*, an *offering*, or *first fruits*, in a word, of a simple act of homage and of recognition rendered, if it may be expressed this way, to the divine *sovereign*; for in this supposition men would have looked in the butcher's shop for the flesh they had to offer on the altars; they would have limited themselves to repeating in public, with suitable pomp, this same ceremony that opened their domestic meals.

It is a question of *blood*, it is a question of *immolation* properly speaking; it is a question of explaining how men in all times and in all places could agree in believing that there was, not in the offering of flesh (this must be noted carefully), but in the *shedding of blood*, an expiating virtue useful to man. That is the problem, and at first glance it remains unyielding.[38]

Not only were sacrifices not a simple extension of *aparques*, or of the offering of first fruits burned at the beginning of the meal, but these *aparques* themselves were quite obviously only a kind of *diminished sacrifices*, just as we can bring into our houses certain religious ceremonies executed with public pomp in our churches. Everyone will agree with this as soon as they take the trouble to reflect about it a bit.

Hume, in his odious *Natural History of Religion*, adopted this same idea from Heyne, and embittered it in his own way: "A sacrifice," he says, "is conceived as a present; and any present is delivered to the deity by destroying it and rendering it useless to men; by burning whatever is solid, pouring out the liquid, and killing the animate. For want of a better way of doing him service, we do ourselves injury; and fancy that we thereby express, at least, the heartiness of our good will and adoration. Thus our mercenary devotion deceives ourselves, and imagines it deceives the deity."[39]

But all this acrimony explains nothing; it even makes the problem more difficult. Voltaire did not fail to exert himself on this subject as well; taking only the general idea of sacrifice as a *given*, he dealt in particular with human sacrifices.

"In the temples," he said, "we see only vices, spits, kitchen knives, long iron forks, *spoons*, or *ladles*,[40] great jars for storing grease, and everything that can inspire contempt and horror. Nothing contributes more to perpetuation of this harshness and to this atrocity of customs, which finally led men to sacrifice other men and even their own children. But the sacrifices of the Inquisition of which we have spoken so much were a hundred times more abominable; we have substituted executioners for butchers."[41]

Voltaire undoubtedly never put a foot in an antique temple; even engravings of this sort of building must have been unknown to him if he thought that the temple, properly speaking, presented the spectacle of a butcher shop and kitchen. Moreover, he did not notice that these grills, these spits, these long forks, these spoons or ladles, and other instruments just as terrible, are as in fashion today as they once were, without any mothers of families, or even butcher's wives or cooks, being the least bit tempted to put their children on the spit or to throw them in the pot. Everyone senses that this kind of harshness that results from the habit of spilling the blood of animals, and that can at most facilitate such or such particular crime, will never lead to the systematic immolation of man. Moreover, can one read without astonishment this word FINALLY employed by Voltaire, as if human sacrifices were only the tardy result of animal sacrifices, previously used for centuries? Nothing is more false. *Always* and *everywhere* where the true God was not known and adored, men were sacrificed; the most ancient monuments of history attest to it, and even fable adds its testimony, which, with great differences, must never be rejected. Now to explain this great phenomenon, it does not at all suffice to have recourse to *kitchen knives and great forks.*

The piece on the Inquisition, which ends Voltaire's note, seems to have been written in a fit of madness. So then! The legal execution of a small number of men, ordered by a legitimate tribunal in virtue of a previously solemnly promulgated law whose consequences each victim was perfectly free to avoid, this execution is a *hundred times more abominable* than the horrible crime of a mother and a father putting their child on the flaming arms of Moloch! What atrocious madness! What negligence of all reason, justice, and modesty! Anti-religious rage has carried him to the point that at the end of this fine tirade he no longer knew exactly what he is saying. *We have,* he says, *substituted executioners for butchers.* So he thinks he has only been talking about animal sacrifices, and he has forgotten the phrase he has just written about the sacrifices of men; otherwise, what is the meaning of this opposition of *butchers* to executioners? Were the priests of antiquity, who slaughtered their fellows *with a sacred iron,* any less *executioners* than the modern judges who send men to death by virtue of a law?

However, let us come back to the main subject. There is nothing weaker, as we see, than the reason offered by Voltaire to explain the origin of human sacrifices. That simple conscience called good sense suffices to demonstrate that there is in this explanation not the least shadow of sagacity, nor of real knowledge of man and antiquity.

Finally, let us listen to Condillac, and see how he sets about explaining the origin of human sacrifice to his supposed PUPIL who, for the good of a people, never wants to allow himself *to be raised.*

"*They will not be content,*" he says, "*with addressing their prayers and vows to the gods; they believe it their duty to offer things they imagine to be agreeable to them ... fruits, animals, and* MEN *...*"[42]

I will be careful not to say that this is a passage worthy of a child, for there is not, thank God, any child bad enough to write it. What shocking levity! What scorn for our unfortunate species! What accusatory rancour against the most natural and most sacred instinct! It is impossible for me to express how much my conscience and feelings are revolted by this Condillac; this is one of the most hateful traits of this hateful writer.

NOTES TO THE SECOND CHAPTER

1 [Racine, *Ephigenia,* Act 5, Scene 6. Tr. John Cairncross (Baltimore, Maryland: Penguin Books 1963).]

2 *Commentaries on the Gallic War* vi.16.

3 These words *bind* and *unbind* are so natural, that they are found taken up and fixed forever in our theological language.

4 [The first written laws of Rome, drawn up by the ten officers known as *decemvirs*, in 451 and 452 B.C.]

5 A French journalist, joking about this text *Pro devoto femineo sexu*, did not fail to say that *the Church awarded women the title of being the DEVOUT SEX* (*Journal de l'Empire*, 26 February 1812). We should not quarrel with these jokers who are learning Latin, for soon they will know something. However it would be good if they learned it before taking on the Roman Church, which knows it tolerably well.

6 (Eustathius, *Commentarii ad Homerii Iliadem*) The Latin word HOSTIS is the same as the word HÔTE (*hoste* [guest]) in French; both are also found in the German *hast*, although they are less visible there. The *hostis* being an *enemy* or a *foreigner* therefore, and under this double relationship subject to sacrifice, the sacrificed man, or, following the analogy, the sacrificed animal, will be called *host*. We know how this word has been denatured and ennobled in our Christian languages.

7 *I soror, atque* hostem *supplex affare superbum* [Go, sister, and in supplication address the haughty foe]. (Vergil *Aeneid* IV.424.) Ubi Servius: – *Nonnulli juxtà veteres* hostem *pro* hospite *dictum accipiunt* [Some besides the ancients agree that *hostem* was said in place of *hospite*]. (Forcellini in *hostis*.)

8 *Some alien.* (*Iliad* V.214.)

9 But war was the natural state of this country. *And before Caesar's coming this would happen well-nigh every year, in the sense that they would either be making wanton attacks themselves or repelling such.* (*Commentaries on the Gallic War* vi.15. [Trans. A.G. Way, Loeb Classical Library 1955])

10 Ibid., vi.16.

11 *For that oracle ordained that offering should be made "for heads with heads," and for some time the ritual required the sacrifice of boys to the goddess Mania, the mother of Lares, to insure the safety of the family.* (Macrobius *Saturnalia* I.7.)

12 *Women are not to shave their cheeks.* Twelfth Table.

13 *In order that the statue be restored to the pyre, or as Varro says, that satisfaction be given to the dead by display of blood.* (Joannes Rosinus, *Antiquitatum Romanorum Corpus Absolutissimum, cum notis. Th. Demsteri à Murreck*, (Amsterdam: Blaen 1685), 5:442.)

14 For the Gauls were, for the Romans, the HOSTIS, and in consequence the natural HOSTIS. *With other peoples*, says Cicero, *we fought for glory, but with the Gauls, for salvation. – As soon as Rome was threatened, the laws and customs of our ancestors demanded that the enrolment knew no more exceptions.* In effect, even the slaves marched. (Cicero *Pro Fonteio*.)

15 [O father of the world / Whence such a great wrong?]

16 Solis y Ribadeneyra, *Conquista de México*, Bk. III, chap. 3.

17 An accurate description of these atrocities will be found in the *American Letters* of Count Carli-Rubbi, and in the notes of the fanatical translator who, unfortunately, defiled this interesting research by all the excesses of modern impiety. (See *Lettres américaines*, by Count Gian Rinaldo Carli, translated from the Italian by M. Le Comte, Letter 8, p. 116, and Letter 27, pp. 407 ff.) In reflecting on these very learned notes, I am tempted to believe that the translation, begun by a pure hand, has been ruined in the new edition by a very different hand. This is a modern and well known manoeuvre.

18 Carli's French editor asks himself *why*, and gives this learned reply: *Because common people have always been deceived by opinion.* (Letter 13, 1:456.) A fine and profound solution!

19 See the *Rudhiradhyaya,* or the *bloody chapter,* translated from the *Calica-Puran* by M. Blaquière. *Asiatic Researches, The Works of Sir William Jones,* 2:1058.

20 This custom, which requires women to accept death or burning on the tombs of their husbands, is not peculiar to India. It was also to be found in Northern nations. (Herodotus, Bk. V, chap. 1, § 11.) See [Gabriel] Brotier on Tacitus, *Germania* c. xix, note 6. And in America. (Carli, *Lettres américaines,* Vol. I, Letter 10.)

21 *The conscience.* Who knows the worth of this persuasion before the tribunal of the infallible judge *who is good to all men and sheds his mercy on all his creatures,* like his rain on all his plants? (Psalm 144(145):9)

22 *Asiatic Researches,* 7:222.

23 Extracts from English papers translated in the *Gazette de France,* 19 June 1804, n° 2369. – *Annales littéraires et morales,* (Paris 1804), 2:145. – M. Colebrook, of the Society of Calcutta, to be sure, assures us in his *Asiatic Researches* (*Works of Sir William Jones,* Supplement, 2:722), *that the number of martyrs to this superstition has never been very considerable, and that examples have become rare.* But first of all, this word *rare* is not very precise; and moreover I observe that this prejudice being incontestable and reigning over a population of more than sixty millions, it seems that it must necessarily produce a very great number of these atrocious sacrifices.

24 See the *Asiatic Annual Register,* 1802.

25 *Asiatic Researches,* 7:267.

26 *Gazette de France,* as cited.

27 See *Essays by the Students of Fort William in Bengal.*

28 It would nevertheless be unjust not to observe that in the parts of India subject to Catholic rule, the burning of widows has disappeared. Such is the hidden and admirable force of the true *law of grace.* But England, which allows the burning of thousands of innocent women under what is certainly a very kind and very humane empire, still very seriously reproaches Portugal for the orders of its Inquisition, which is to say for some drops of very guilty blood shed *legally* from time to time. EJICE PRIMÒ TRABEM, etc. [First cast out the beam from your own eye, etc. Matthew 7:5]

29 *The Laws of Manu,* son of Brahma, translated by Sir William Jones, *Works,* Chap. XI, n° 3, 3:335 and 337.

30 Plato *The Laws* VI.781B. *For it is not merely, as one might suppose, a matter affecting one-half of our whole task – this matter of neglecting to regulate women,) – but in as far as females are inferior in goodness to males, just so far it affects more than the half.* [Loeb]

31 The mother of Demosthenes had been so bequeathed, and the formula of this disposition has been preserved for us in his discourse against Stephanus. (See the Commentaries on the arguments of Isœus by Sir William Jones in his *Works*, 3:210–11.)

32 Hippocrates, *Of Human Nature, Opera,* Van der Linden edition, 2:911. *For it has by nature the element of intemperance in it.*

33 It must also be observed that if Christianity protects women, they, in their turn, have the privilege of protecting the protective law to a point that is well worth noting. One would even be tempted to believe that this influence involves a secret affinity, some *natural* law. We see salvation commencing with a woman announced since the beginning of things; in the whole gospel story, women play a very remarkable role; and in all the celebrated conquests of Christianity over individuals as well as nations, we always see women appear. This must be, since ... But I fear that this note is becoming too long.

34 Acts 17:30. *Et tempora quidem hujus ignorantiæ despiciens Deus,* etc. [Vulgate] *yreridōn.* Arnauld, in the Mons New Testament, translates: *Dieu étant en colère contre ces temps d'ignorance,* etc., and in a note at the bottom of the page writes: *autrement – Dieu ayant laissé passer et comme dissimulé; et,* literally, *méprise ces temps,* etc. – In effect, it is all quite *otherwise.* [The Douay version of Acts 17:30 reads: "The time of this ignorance God, has, it is true, overlooked."]

35 This part of their nourishment, which was separated and burned in honour of the gods, the Greeks named *Aparque (aparchē),* and the very action of offering these sorts of first fruits was expressed by a verb (*aparchesthai*) *aparquer* or *to begin* (par excellence).

36 *Iliad* XI.220; *Odyssey* XIV.436,446.

37 *It is clear that this religious ritual created a method of sacrifice; for after it had arisen they adopted it for domestic feasts, since a part cut from the food to be eaten was to be thrown on the fire and offered to the gods. This is the real origin and there is no reason why this religious custom should be displeasing.* (Heyne, Note to his edition of the *Iliad.*)

This explanation by Heyne does not surprise me, for in general the Protestant school does not like ideas that go beyond the material circle; it distrusts them without distinction and seems to condemn them en masse as vain and superstitious. I have no difficulty confessing that its doctrine can be useful to ourselves, never to the truth as nourishment, but sometimes as a remedy. In this case, nevertheless, I certainly believe it false, and I am astonished that Bergier adopted it. (*Traité historique et dogmatique de la vraie religion,* II:303–04, VI:296–97, after Porphyry *On Abstinence from Animal Food* II, cited Ibid.) This learned apologist *saw* very well; it only seems that he did not *look.*

38 The Persians, according to Strabo's report, divided the flesh of the victims among themselves, *without setting apart a portion for the gods. For, they say God requires only the soul of the victim, and nothing else.* Strabo, Bk. XV, chap. 13, p. 695, cited in Cudworth's dissertation, *de verâ notione cænæ Domini,* cap. I, n° vii, at the end of his famous book, *Systema intellectuale universum.* This curious text directly refutes Heyne's ideas, and will be found completely in agreement with Hebraic theories, according to which *the shedding of blood constitutes the essence of sacrifice.* (Ibid., cap. II, n° iv.)

39 Hume "The Natural History of Religion," in *Essays and Treatises on Several Subjects,* (London 1758), Sect. IX, p. 511.

We can notice in this passage, considered as a general formula, one of the most striking characteristics of impiety; this is its contempt for man. The daughter of pride, the mother of pride, always drunk with pride, it breathes only pride, yet impiety never ceases to outrage human nature, to degrade it, to envisage whatever man has done and thought, to envisage it, I say, in the manner most humiliating for him, the manner best suited to debase him and drive him to despair; and thus it is without noticing it, that it most clearly exhibits its character so opposed to religion, which always uses humility to raise men to God.

40 A superb observation! And especially to the point.

41 See note xii to his decrepit tragedy, *Minos.*

42 Condillac, *Oeuvres,* [23 vols. (Paris An VI–1798)], *Histoire ancienne,* tom. I, chap. xii, 98–99.

CHAPTER THREE

The Christian Theory
of Sacrifices

What truth cannot be found in paganism?

It is quite true that in it there are several *gods* and several *lords*, as many in heaven as on earth,[1] and that we must aspire to the friendship and the favour of these *gods*.[2]

But it is also true that there is one single Jupiter, who is the supreme god, the god who is the first,[3] who is very great;[4] *the best nature* that surpasses all other natures, even divine;[5] *the what that is* which has nothing above him;[6] the god not only *God*, but WHOLLY GOD;[7] the motor of the universe;[8] the father, the king, *the emperor*;[9] the god of gods and men;[10] the all-powerful father.[11]

It is also quite true that *Jupiter* was only properly adored with *Pallas* and *Juno*, the cult of the three powers being by its nature indivisible.[12]

It is quite true *that if we reason wisely about God, ruler of all things present and to come, and on the Lord, father of the ruler and cause, we will know clearly as well as it is given to the most fortunately gifted to know.*[13]

It is quite true that Plato, who made the preceding comment, could only be corrected with respect when he says as well: *That the great king being in the middle of things, since he is the author of all good, the second king is however in the middle of secondary things, and the third in the middle of tertiary,*[14] *all of which could not be spelt out in a clearer way, so that the writing having been lost by some event on sea or land, anyone who finds it will understand nothing.*[15]

It is quite true that *Minerva* came forth from the brain of *Jupiter*.[16] It is quite true that *Venus* originally came forth *from the water*;[17] and that she returned there at the time of the flood during which *all things were sea and the shores of the sea were gone,*[18] and that she went to sleep there in the depths of the waters;[19] if we add that she subsequently came forth again in the form of a dove, which became famous in all the East,[20] this is not a great error.

It is quite true that each man has his *conducting* and *initiating spirit*, which guides him through the mysteries of life.[21]

It is quite true that *Hercules* could only climb *Olympus* and there marry *Hebe* after everything *human* in him had been consumed by fire on Mount Oeta.[22]

It is quite true that *Neptune* commanded the *winds* and the *sea*, and that he made them fear him.[23]

It is quite true that *the gods* nourish themselves on *nectar* and ambrosia.[24]

It is quite true that *heroes* who have merited well of humanity, *founders* especially, and legislators, have the right to be declared *gods* by legitimate power.[25]

It is quite true that when a man is ill, it is necessary to try gently *to enchant* the illness by *powerful words*, without however neglecting any means of material medicine.[26]

It is quite true that medicine and *divination* are very closely related.[27]

It is quite true that *the gods* sometimes came to sit at the table of just men, and that at other times they came to earth to seek out the crimes of these men.[28]

It is quite true that nations and cities have *patrons*, and that, in general, *Jupiter* accomplishes very many things in this world through the ministry of *spirits*.[29]

It is quite true that the very elements, which are empires, are presided over, like empires, by certain *divinities*.[30]

It is quite true that the *princes of the peoples* are called to counsel by the God of Abraham, because the *powerful* gods *of the earth* are much more important than it was thought.[31]

But it is also true that "there is none among the *gods* equal to you, O *Lord*, there is no work like unto your work."[32]

"For who in the clouds will be compared to the Lord, *who is like the LORD among the sons of God?*"[33] And "who alone does wondrous things?"[34]

How then can we fail to recognize that paganism could not be mistaken about an idea as universal and fundamental as that of sacrifices, that is to say on *redemption by blood*? Humanity could not guess how much blood it needed. Left to himself, what man could suspect the immensity of the fall and the immensity of the restoring love? Yet every people, by admitting this fall more or less clearly, has also admitted the need and the nature of the remedy.

This has been the constant belief of all men. In practice it has been modified according to the characteristics of peoples and religions, but the principle appears always. In particular, all nations agree on the marvellous efficacy of the voluntary sacrifice of innocence dedicating itself to God as a propitiatory victim. Men have always attached a boundless value to this submission of the just who accept sufferings; it is this motive that leads Seneca, after having delivered his famous saying: *Ecce par Deo dignum! vir fortis cum malâ fortunâ compositus,*[35] to add immediately: UTIQUE SI ET PROVOCAVIT.[36]

When King Louis XVI's ferocious jailers, when he was a prisoner in the Temple, refused him a razor, the faithful servant who has given us the interesting story of his long and frightful captivity told him: *Sire, present yourself to the National Convention with a long beard, so the people will see how you are being treated.* The king answered: I MUST NOT SEEK TO AROUSE INTEREST IN MY FATE.[37]

So what must have been happening in this heart, so pure, so submissive, so prepared? The august martyr seemed to fear escaping the sacrifice or making the victim less perfect. What acceptance! And what must this acceptance have been worth!

On this point we could invoke experience to support theory and tradition, for the happiest changes that have happened among the nations have usually been bought by bloody catastrophes of which innocence was the victim. The blood of Lucretia chased out the Tarquins, and that of Virginia chased out the *Decemvirs.* When two parties clash in a revolution, if we see precious victims fall on one side, we can bet that this side will end up winning, despite all appearances to the contrary.

If the history of families was as well known as that of nations, it would furnish a crowd of observations of the same kind. We might very well discover, for example, that the most lasting families are those that have lost the most individuals to war. An ancient would have said: "For earth, for hell, the victims sufficed."[38] Better informed men could say: *The just man who gives his life in sacrifice, will see a lasting posterity.*[39]

Again, war, an inexhaustible subject for reflection, will display the same truth under a different face, the annals of all peoples having with one cry shown us how this terrible scourge always chastises with a violence rigorously proportional to the vices of nations, so that when there is an *overflowing of crimes,* there is always an *overflowing of blood. Sine sanguine non fit remissio.*[40]

Redemption, as was said in the *Dialogues,* is a universal idea. Always and everywhere men have believed that the innocent could pay for the guilty (*utique se et provocaverit*); but Christianity has corrected this idea as well as a thousand others that, even in their negative state, had rendered in advance the clearest testimony to it. Under the empire of this divine law, the just man (who never believes himself to be such) nevertheless tries to come up to his model through suffering. He examines himself, he purifies himself, he works on himself with efforts that seem to surpass humanity, to obtain finally the grace of being able *to return what has not been stolen.*[41]

Christianity, in certifying the dogma, does not explain it, at least publicly, and we see that the secret roots of this theory very much occupied the first *initiates* of Christianity.

Origen especially must be heard on this interesting subject about which he meditated a great deal. It was his well known theory "that the blood shed on Calvary was not only useful to men, but to the angels, the stars, and all other created beings;"[42] this will not appear surprising to anyone who recalls that St Paul said: *For it has pleased God ... that through him he should reconcile to himself all things, whether on the earth or in the heavens, making peace through the blood of the cross.*"[43] And if all creatures *groan,*[44] according to the doctrine of this apostle, why should not all be *consoled?* Origen's great and holy adversary [St Jerome] is a witness that at the beginning of the fifth century of the Church it was still a received opinion *that redemption belonged to heaven as much as to earth,*[45] and St [John] Chrysostom did not doubt that the same sacrifice, continued until the end of time and celebrated daily by legitimate ministers, operated in the same way *for the whole universe.*[46]

It is in this immense scope that Origen envisaged the effect of the great sacrifice. "But this theory," he said, "belongs to celestial mysteries, which is what the apostle himself declared to us when he told us: *that it was necessary, therefore, that the copies of the heavenly realities should be cleansed by these things; but the heavenly realities* themselves *require better sacrifices than these.* Contemplate the expiation *of the whole world,* that is to say of the heavenly regions, terrestrial and inferior, and see how many victims would be needed! ... But the *lamb* alone could take upon himself the sins of the whole world, etc."[47]

In any case, although Origen was a *great author*, a *great man, and one of the most sublime theologians*[48] who ever adorned the Church, I do not however intend to defend every line of his writings; it is enough for me to sing with the Roman Church:

And the earth, the sea, the stars themselves;
All creatures, finally, are washed by this blood.[49]

This is why I am so astonished by the strange scruples of certain theologians who deny themselves the hypothesis of a plurality of worlds for fear that it would overturn the dogma of the redemption;[50] which is to say, according to them, that we must believe that man, travelling in space on his sad planet, miserably *cramped* between *Mars* and *Venus,*[51] is the sole intelligent being in the system, and that the other planets are only globes *without life and without beauty,*[52] which the creator, like a ball player, launched into space for his amusement apparently. No, never has a meaner thought occurred to the human spirit! Democritus once said in a famous conversation: *Oh my dear friend! Take good care that in your mind you do not speak disparagingly of nature, which is so abundant.*[53] We would certainly be inexcusable if we did not profit from this advice, we who live in the bosom of the light, and who can contemplate in the clarity of supreme intelligence the place of this vain phantom of *nature.* Let us not miserably shrink the infinite Being by imposing ridiculous boundaries on his power and love. Is there anything more certain than the proposition that *everything has been made* by and for *intelligence?* Can a planetary system be anything else than a system of intelligences, and each planet in particular be anything else than a home for one of these families? So what is there in common between matter and God? *Does the dust know him?*[54] If the inhabitants of the other planets are not guilty like us, they have no need of the same remedy; and if, on the contrary, the same remedy is necessary for them, these theologians that I just mentioned, do they therefore fear that the power of the sacrifice that saved us cannot reach the moon? Origen's glance is much more penetrating and more *comprehensive,* when he says: *The altar was in Jerusalem, but the blood of the victim bathed the universe.*[55]

However he did not think it permissible to publish all that he knew on this point: "In order to speak," he said, "of this victim of the law of grace offered by Christ, and in order to understand a truth that surpasses human intelligence, it would require nothing less than a *perfect* man, trained in judging good and evil, who had the right to speak by a pure movement of the truth: we preach wisdom to the *perfect.*[56] The one of whom St John said: *Here is the lamb of God who takes away the sins of the world ...* served for expiation, according to certain mysterious laws of the universe, having willingly submitted to death by virtue of the love he has for men, and bought us one day through the blood from the hands of the one who seduced us, and to whom we had been *sold by sin.*"[57]

From this general redemption, accomplished by this great sacrifice, Origen goes on to these particular redemptions that could be called *diminished,* but that always derive from the same principle. "From other victims," he says, "nearer to these ... I want to speak of generous martyrs who have also given their blood: *but where is the wise man to understand these marvels, and who has the intelligence to penetrate them?*[58] It would require profound research to form even a very imperfect idea of the law in virtue of which these sorts of victims purify those for whom they are offered.[59] A vain pretence of cruelty would want to attach itself to the Being to which one offers them for the salvation of men; but an elevated and vigorous mind knows how to repel the objections that can be raised against Providence, *without nevertheless revealing the last secrets:*[60] for the judgements of God are very profound; it is certainly difficult to explain them, and a number of weak souls have found them an occasion of falling. But finally since it is taken as a constant among the nations that a great number of men voluntarily deliver themselves to death for the salvation of all, in the case, for example of pestilential epidemics,[61] and that the efficacy of these sacrifices had been recognized on the faith even of Scriptures by this faithful Clement, to whom St Paul rendered such a beautiful witness (Philippians 4:13); it is necessary that the one who would be tempted to blaspheme mysteries that pass the ordinary extent of the human mind decide to recognize in the martyrs *something similar*.

"The one who kills ... a poisonous animal undoubtedly merits well of those who could have been harmed if it had not been killed ...; let us believe that something similar happens through the death of the most holy martyrs ..., that they destroy powerful malefactors ..., and that they procure marvellous assistance for a great number of men, in virtue of a certain force that cannot be named."[62]

The two redemptions therefore do not differ in nature, but only in excellence and results, according to the merit and power of the agents. I will recall in this regard what had been said in the *Dialogues* on the subject of divine intelligence and human intelligence. They can only differ like similar figures that are always such no matter what the differences in dimension.

In conclusion, let us contemplate the most beautiful of analogies. Guilty men can only be absolved by the blood of victims: this blood therefore being the link of reconciliation, the error of the ancients was to imagine that *the gods* would come anywhere blood flowed on the altars;[63] this is what our first doctors even refused not to believe by believing in their turn *that the angels come everywhere there flows the true blood of the true victim.*[64]

By a continuation of the same ideas on the nature and efficacy of sacrifices, the ancients still saw something mysterious *in the communion of the body and blood of the victims.* According to them, it brought with it the complement of sacrifice, that of religious unity, so that, for a long time, the Christians refused to eat sacrificed meats, *for fear of being in communion.*[65]

Nevertheless, this universal idea of *Communion by blood*, although vitiated in application, was nevertheless just and prophetic in its root, like all that from which it derived.

It entered into the incomprehensible designs of all-powerful love to perpetuate until the end of the world, and by means far above our weak intelligence, this same sacrifice, offered materially only once for the salvation of humankind. *The flesh* having separated man from heaven, God took on flesh to unite himself to man by what had separated him from it; but this was still too little for an immense goodness attacking an immense degradation. This flesh divinised and perpetually sacrificed is presented to man under the exterior form of his privileged nourishment; *and the one who refuses to eat of it will not live.*[66] Like the word, which in the material order is only a series of circular waves excited in the air, and similar in every way imaginable to those we perceive on the surface of water struck at a point, so this word, I say, yet arrives in all its mysterious integrity, to every ear touched in every point of this excited fluid, of the same corporeal nature[67] of the one who calls himself *word*, radiating from the centre of the All-Powerful, who is everywhere, and who enters wholly entire into each mouth, and who multiplies himself to infinity without dividing himself. More rapid than lightning, more active than thunder, this *theandric* blood penetrates *the guilty entrails* to devour the defilements within them.[68] It goes to the unknown boundaries of these two irreconcilably united powers[69] where the *intentions of the heart*[70] strike the intelligence and trouble it. By a truly divine affinity, it lays hands on the elements of man, and transforms them without destroying them. "Undoubtedly, we have a right to be astonished that man can raise himself to God. But here is another prodigy! It is God who descends to man. This is not yet enough: to become an even more intimate part of his cherished creature, *he enters into man*, who becomes truly a temple inhabited by the Divinity."[71] This is an inconceivable marvel, undoubtedly, but at the same time an infinitely plausible one, which satisfies reason by crushing it. There is not in the whole spiritual world a more magnificent analogy, a more striking proportioning of intentions and means, of effect and cause, of evil and its remedy. There is nothing that demonstrates in a way more worthy of God what the human race has always confessed, even before it learned it: its radical degradation, the substitution of the merits of the innocent paying for the guilty and SALVATION BY BLOOD.

NOTES TO CHAPTER THREE

1 *For even if there are what are called gods, whether in heaven or on earth (for indeed there are many gods, and many lords), yet ... etc. etc.* (1 Corinthians 8:5; 2 Thessalonians 2:4)

2 St Augustine *City of God* VIII.25.

3 *For carrying out the worship of the deity, God first is enough for us.* (Arnobius *The Case Against the Pagans* III)

4 *Deo qui est maximus.* (Inscription on an antique lamp in the Museum of Passeri. [Pirolis], *Antichità di Ercolano*, VIII:264.

5 *Nature (is) better.* (Ovid *Metamorphoses* I.21) *Where is divine power, where are the gods?* (Ovid *Heroides* XII.119) *By Zeus and the gods.* (Demosthenes *On the Crown*) *The gods and the divine spirit will know.* (Demosthenes *On the Embassy* 68)

6   *The highest (is) god, whatever that "highest" is.* (Pliny *Natural History* II.4.)
7   *Chief, and especially of the gods.* (Lactantius, ethn. ad Stat. Theb., IV, 516, cited in the *Bibliotheca latina* of [Johann A.] Fabricus, [Hamburg 1697].
8   *Rector orbis terrarum.* (Seneca, cited in Lactantius *Divine Institutions* I.4)
9   *Ruler of gods and men.* (Plautus, *The Rope*, Prologue, verse 11.)
10 *God of all the gods.* (Seneca, see above.). *Zeus is god of the gods. Jupiter, son of the gods.* (Plato *Critias*). *God of gods.* (Psalm 83(84):8). *Our Lord is above all gods.* (Psalm 134(135):5). *The great God ... above all the gods.* (Psalm 94(95):3). *God over all.* (Plato, Origen, passim.)
11 *Pater omnipotens.* (Vergil *Aeneid* I.65; X.2, etc.)
12 *Jupiter is not usually worshipped without the close association of wife and daughter.* (Lactantius *Divine Institutions.*)
13 Plato, *Epistle 6.* – In effect, how could one know one without the other? (Tertullian, *On the Testimony of the Soul*, chap. i.)
14 *Related to the king of all are all things, and for his sake they are, and of all things fair he is the Cause. And related to the Second and the Second things and related to the Third the third.* Plato, *Epistle 2,* and in Eusebius *Præparatio Evangelica* XI.

Anyone who is curious to know what has been said about this text will want to consult Origen *On First Principles* I.3 n. 5, – See [René-Paul] Huet's edition of Origen [Cologne 1685], lib. II, chap. 2, n. 27, 28; and La Rue's notes, pp. 63 and 135. – *Clemens Alexandrinus*, 5:598, Paris edition. – *Athenagorae Legatio pro Christianis*, Oxoniæ, ex theatr. Seldon, 1706, *curis* Dechair, p. 93, n. XXI, in not. It is quite peculiar that neither Huet nor his learned commentator cited the passage of Plato, of which Origen's is a remarkable commentary. Here is this last text such as Photius preserved it for us in the original (Cod. VIII): *the Father embraces all that exists; the Son is limited to intelligent beings only, and the Spirit to the elect alone.*

15 *I must speak to you in riddles so that whatever fate the writings of land or sea may suffer, who reads it may not know.* (Plato, *Epistle 2*)
16 [Fénelon], [*Aventures de*] *Télémaque*, Bk. VIII. *Il chanta d'abord*, etc. [He sang first, etc.]
17 In memory of this birth, the ancients had established a ceremony in order to witness in perpetuity *that from water comes the growth of all organized things.* See the scholiast on the hundred and forty-fifth verse of Pindar's fourth *Pythic Ode.* According to the antique doctrine of the *Vedas*, Brahma *(who is the spirit of God) was carried on the waters* in a lotus leaf at the beginning of things, and the sensible power takes its origin in water. (William Jones, in his *Researches Asiatiques, Dissertation sur les dieux de la Grèce et d'Italie*, Vol. I.) – M. Colebroke, ibid., 8:403. – Modern physics is in agreement. See Black's *Lectures on Chemistry*, 1:245. – *Lettres physiques et morales*, etc., by [Jean André] de Luc, [The Hague 1778], 1:112, etc.
18 Ovid *Metamorphoses.*
19 See the dissertation on the Caucasus Mountains by F.R. Wilford in the *Researches Asiatiques*, 7:522–23.

20 Thus we will not be surprised that men were agreed in recognizing the dove as *the bird of Venus*; nothing is false in paganism, but everything is corrupted.

21 *Good guide to the mysteries of life.* (Menander in Plutarch *On Tranquillity of Mind.*) *These spirits live on earth by Jupiter's command in order to be the beneficent guardians of unfortunate mortals* (Hesiod); but without ceasing nevertheless to see the one who sent them. (Matthew 18:10.) *When* therefore *we have closed the door and brought darkness into our apartments, let us remember never to say* (that it is night and) *we are alone, for GOD AND OUR ANGELS are with us, and to see us they have no need of light. (Arrian's Discourses of Epictetus,* I.14.) Bacon, in a fairly suspect work, places among the number of *paradoxes* or *apparent* contradictions of Christianity: *that we ask nothing of the angels and we thank them for nothing, all the while believing that we owe them much. (Christian Paradoxes,* etc., *Works,* 2:494.) This contradiction, which is not wholly *apparent,* is not be found in *all* of Christianity.

22 *Meanwhile whatever the flames could destroy, Mulciber had and consumed, and no shape of Hercules that could be recognized remained, not was there anything left which his mother gave. He kept traces only of his father ...* (Ovid *Metamorphoses* IX.262 ff. [Loeb])

23 "From the two opposing corners of heaven he called the winds to him. How is it then, he said to them, that you could have been entrusted with what you are, enough for you to dare to trouble the earth and the seas, and to raise up enormous waves, without remembering my power? For the price of such audacity, I owe you ...; but above all the waters must be calmed; another time you will not defy me with impunity. Leave without delay. Go tell your master that the empire of the seas does not belong to him; fate has put the formidable trident in my hands. Aeolus lived in the palace of the winds, in the midst of high rocks; that he moves about in his retreats! That he reigns in these vast prisons! He speaks, and already the tempest has ceased; Neptune scatters the towering clouds, makes the sun break through, and drives his light chariot on the flat surface of the waters." (Vergil *Aeneid* I.131 ff.)

Then he rebuked the winds and said to the sea: BE STILL ... and suddenly there came a great calm. (Mark 4:39, Luke 8:24, Matthew 8:26.)

Here we see the difference between truth and fable: the first makes God *speak*; the second makes him *hold forth*; but it is always, as we will see below, something *differently alike.*

24 "I am the angel Raphael ... I seemed indeed to eat and to drink with you, but I use an invisible meat and drink, which cannot be seen by men." (Tobias 12:15, 19)

25 The *deification* of a sovereign in pagan antiquity and the *canonization* of a *hero* of Christianity in the Church, following the expression already used, differ only as negative and positive actions. On the one side are error and corruption, on the other truth and holiness, but everything stems from the same principles, for error, again, can only be corrupted truth, that is to say a thought proceeding from a more or less degraded intelligent principle,

which yet acts according to its nature, or if you will, following its innate or natural ideas. *Is not almost the whole of heaven filled with gods of mortal origins?* (Cicero *Tusculan Disputations* I.13. [Loeb]) - Yes, certainly! This is its destiny. The thing is no longer subject to doubt or joking. But why would there be a distinction for *heroes*?

As for those who would obstinately see here as elsewhere only calculated imitations, there is nothing more to say to them; let us await the awakening!

26 *(He loosed and delivered diverse of them from diverse pains), tending some of them with kindly incantations, giving to others a soothing potion, or, haply, swathing their limbs with simples [or amulets?], or restoring others by the knife.* (Pindar *Pythic Odes* III.91–95. [Trans. John Sandys, Loeb Classical Libralry 1915])

Locus classicus de medicinâ. (Heyne, ad loc. v. *Pindari carm,* (Gottingæ 1798), 1:241.)

Perhaps it would be permitted, without lacking respect for the memory of such a learned man, to observe that he seems to have been mistaken in seeing *amulets* in verses 94 and 95, for it appears that Pindar, in this passage, was simply speaking of applications, of compresses, and, in a word, of *tonics*; but I scarcely dare to be right against Heyne.

27 *Medicine and prophecy are very closely akin.* (Hippocrates, *Epist. ad Philop., Opera,* Van der Linden Edition, 2:896) "For without the help of Aesculapius, who received his secrets from his father, men would never have been able to invent remedies." (Ibid., p. 966.) Medicine placed its first inventors in the sky, and even today everyone asks for remedies from oracles. (Pliny *Natural History* XXIX.1.) We must not be astonished at this since "the most High has created the physician, for all healing is from God. ... The Most High has created medicines out of the earth, ... and has given knowledge to men; by these he shall cure and shall allay their pains. ... Pray to the Lord; ... turn away from sin and cleanse your heart ... give place to the physician, for the Lord created him." (Ecclesiasticus 38:1–12)

28 No more of talk where God or angel guest
With man, as with his friend, familiar used
To sit indulgent, and with him partake
Rural repast, permitting him the while
Venial discourse unblamed: ...
(Milton, *Paradise Lost,* I, 1-5.)–

This is an elegant paraphrase of Hesiod, who was himself cited by Origen as rendering witness to the truth. (*Against Celsus*)

For then both immortal gods and mortal men sat and dined together. (Ovid *Metamorphoses* I.210 ff, and see Genesis 18 and 19)

29 *For it is well known that every city is under the protection of some deity,* etc. (Macrobius *Saturnalia* III.9) *In the same way as the pagans of old had guardian deities of their kingdoms, provinces and citizens (the guardians by which their empire had stood) so the Roman Church has its guardian saints,* etc. (Henry More, *Opera theologica,* [London 1675], 665.)

Exodus 13; Daniel 10:13, 20–1; Apocalypse 8:3, 14:18, 16:5. Huet, *Demonstratio evangelica,* prop. VII, n° 9. St Augustine *City of God* VII.30.

St Augustine said that God exercised his jurisdiction over the gentiles through the ministry of angels, and this opinion is founded on several texts of Scripture. (Berthier, *Les Psaumes traduits en français avec des notes et réflexions*, Psalm 114, 4, 5:363.) – "but those who, by a coarse imagination (*in fact, there is nothing coarser*), always think to take away from God all that he gives to his angels and his saints ..., will they ever take Scripture in the right sense?" (Bossuet, *Préface sur l'explication de l'Apocalypse*, n° xxvii.) See the *Pensées de Leibniz sur la religion et la morale* [ed. J.-A. Emery, 2 vols. (Paris 1803)], 2:54 and 66.

30 When I see in the prophets, in the Apocalypse, and even in the Gospel, *this angel of the Persians, this angel of the Greeks, this angel of the Jews, the angel of the little children who takes care of them ...; the angel of the waters, the angel of fire*, etc., I recognize in these words a kind of mediation by holy angels: I even see the foundation that could have given the pagans the occasion to distribute their gods in the elements and in realms to preside there: *for every error is founded on a truth which they abuse* (Bossuet, ibid.) *and of which it is only a vicious imitation*. (Massillon, *Vérité de la religion*, 1st point.)

31 *When Saturn's son from his high throne saw this he groaned and recalling the revels of the infamous feast he conceived a mighty wrath worthy of the soul of Jove and summoned a council of the gods. Naught delayed their answer to the summons ... On either side the palaces of the gods of higher rank are thronged with guests through folding doors, ... So when the gods had taken their seats amid the marble council chamber, the king himself seated high above the rest ...* (Ovid *Metamorphoses* II.163 ff. [Loeb]).

 The princes of the peoples are gathered together with the people of the God of Abraham. For the illustrious of the earth are of God: he is greatly exalted. (Psalm 46(47):10.)

32 Psalm 85(86):8.

33 Psalm 88(89):7.

34 Psalm 71(72):18.

35 *See the great man grapple with the wretch! These two wrestlers are worthy of God's attention.* (Seneca *On Providence* 11. [Loeb])

36 *At least a great man provoked the combat.* (Ibid.)

37 Jean Cléry, *Journal de ce qui s'est passé à la tour du Temple pendant la captivité de Louis XVI, Roi de France*, (London 1793), 175.

38 "They were accepted by the gods beneath." (Juvenal *Satires* VIII.257. [Loeb])

39 *... because he has done no iniquity ... If he shall lay down his life for sin, he shall see a long-lived seed.* (Isaiah, 53:9–10.)

40 *Without the shedding of blood there is no forgiveness.* (Hebrews 9:22.)

41 *Shall I return that which I took not away?* (Psalm 68(69):5.)

42 Huet's edition of Origen, lib. ii, cap. ii, quæst. 3, n° 20, tom. IV, p. 149.

43 Colossians 1:19–20 and Ephesians 1:10. – [William] Paley, in his *Horæ Paulinæ* (London 1790, p. 212) observes that these two texts are very remarkable, seeing that this joining of divine and human things is "a very singular sentiment and found no where else but in these two epistles." If the

phrase (*no where else*) relates to the canonical epistles, the assertion is incorrect, since this *very singular sentiment* is found expressly in Hebrews 9:23. If the phrase is taken in the broadest sense, Paley is even more mistaken.

44   Romans 8:22. ["For we know that all creation groans and travails in pain until now."]

45   *THEY ARE SAID (to believe) that the cross of the Saviour brought peace not only to those things which are on earth but also those which were in heaven.* (St Jerome, Epist. LIX, ad Avitum, c.i.v.22.)

46   We sacrifice for the good of the earth, the sea, and the whole universe. (St [John] Chrysostom, *Homily LXX, Commentaries on St John the Apostle*) And St Francis de Sales having said "that Jesus Christ suffered principally for men, *and partly for angels*," we see (without looking closely at what he wanted to say) that he did not limit the effect of the redemption to the boundaries of our planet. (See *Les lettres de saint François de Sales* [Paris 1713], Bk. V, pp. 38–39.)

47   Origen, *Homily XXIX*, on Numbers.

48   Bossuet, See the Preface to his edition of the Apocalypse [Paris 1689], n^{os} xxxvii, xxix.

49   *Hymn for Lauds for Passion Sunday.*

50   A remarkable example of this can be found in the notes with which the famous Cardinal Gerdil thought he had to honour the last poem of his colleague, Cardinal de Bernis.

51   "For he placed us between Venus and Mars, and shut us in (ah! too wretched!) unjust places." (Boskowich, *De Solis ac lunae defectibus* [London 1760] lib. i.)

52   Genesis 1:2

53   See Hippocrates's *Letter to Damagates, Opera,* Van der Linden edition, 2:918–19.) Here it is not a question of the authenticity of these letters.

54   *Shall dust praise you or declare your faithfulness?* (Psalm 29(30):10)

55   Origen, *Homily I*, on Leviticus, n° 3.

56   1 Corinthians 2:6.

57   Romans 8:14. – Origen, *Commentary on St. John*, chs. xxxii and xxxvi.

58   Hosea 14:10.

59   *The martyrs dispense the forgiveness of sins; their martyrdom, in the example of that of Jesus Christ, is a baptism by which the sins of many are expiated; and we can in some way be bought by the precious blood of the martyrs as by the precious blood of Jesus Christ.* (Bossuet, *Méditation* [*sur la rémission des péchez*] *pour le temps du jubilé* [Paris 1696]. V° Point; after this same Origen in *Exhortation to Martyrdom*.)

60   *For they are not to be uttered in public and are beyond human nature.* (Ibid.)

61   If we scan the spectrum of the human mind from Origen to La Fontaine, we will see how natural these ideas are to man.

   History tells us that in such accidents
   Similar sacrifices are made.
   (*Animaux malades de la peste.*)

391 The Christian Theory of Sacrifices

62 Origen *Exhortation to Martyrdom.*
63 Porphyry, *On Abstinence from Animal Food, Bk II*, in [John] Leland's
    Nouvelle démonstration évangelique, Vol. I, chap. v, § 7. (St Augustine *City
    of God* X.11, Origen *Against Celsus* III.)
64 St John Chrysostom, *Homily III, on Ephesians, orat. de Nat. Chr., Hom III,
    de Incomp. Nat. Dei.* – [Arnauld], *Perpétuité de la foi*, tom. I, liv. ii, c. 7, n°
    1. All these doctors spoke of the *reality* of sacrifice, but none of them more
    really than St Augustine when he said *that the Jew, converted to Christian-
    ity, drank the same blood that had been shed* (on Calvary). Augustine, *Serm.
    LXXVII.*
65 *For all those who participate in the same victim are of one body.* (1
    Corinthians 10:17.)
66 John 6:54.
67 *Same sacred body.* (Origen *Against Celsus* Bk. VIII. n° 33, cited in
    [Arnauld], *Perpétuité de la foi*, tom. II, liv. vii, chap. 1)
68 *Let it adhere to my inward parts ... so that there may remain in me no stain
    of evil.* (Liturgy of the Mass.)
69 *Even to the division of soul and spirit.* (Hebrews 4:12.)
70 Ibid.
71 *Do you wonder that men go to god? God comes to men; nay, more properly,
    HE COMES IN MEN.* (Seneca, *Epistle 74.*) *In every good man dwells a god (IT
    IS NOT CERTAIN WHICH GOD).* (Id., *Epistle 41*).
    What a beautiful movement of human instinct, which looks for what faith
    possesses!
    INTUS CHRISTUS INEST ET INOBSERVABILE NUMEN. [Christ is within and an
    invisible divine power.]
    (Vida, *Hymn. in Euchar.*)
    QUIS DEUS CERTUM EST. [Which God (it is) is certain.]

Index

Boerhave, Hermann, 71n71
Böhme, Jacob, 332, 336ni
Boileau, Nicolas, 138, 176
n57, 193n101
Boindin, 186
Bolingbroke, Henry St.
John, Viscount, 241nix
Bonald, Louis de, 66n66,
67n68
Bonnet, Charles, 83, 84n2,
268n9, 296
Books, fortunes of, 191
Bošković (see Boskowich)
Boskowich, Roger Joseph,
318nxi, 390n51
Bossuet, Jacques-Begnigne,
22, 31nx, 57, 59, 65n65,
80nxxxiii, 171, 191, 300
n24, 314nii, 345nvi, 389
nn29, 30, 390nn48, 59
Bougeant, Guillaume-
Hyacinthe, 39n11
Bouhier, J., 245
Bouhours, Dominique,
319nxv
Bourdaloue, Louis, 23n22,
80nxxxiii, 94, 106n2, 184
n81, 272n21, 273, 339niv
Brahma, 17, 18
Bray, Chevalier François
Gabriel de, xv
Bryant, Jacob, 42n18, 74
nxiv, 80nxxxiv, 362n42
Buckley, Michael J., xxvi
Buffon, Georges-Louis,
280
Burke, Edmond, xiii, 69
n70

Cabala, 284nvii
Cabinis, Pierre, 60, 60n55
Caesar, 365, 375n9
Calas affair, 20
Calcutta Academy, 42
Calica-Puran, 376n19
Caligula, 285nxii
Callistratus, 209n3
Canal, Martin de, 196n14
Cannibalism, 371
Cantiques spirituels (Ra-
cine), 88n11

Capital punishment, 149
Captives (Plautus), 94n19,
103niii
Caractères (La Bruyère),
239ni
Carli-Rubbi, Giovanni-
Rinaldo, 41n15, 73nxii,
242nxiii, 269n11, 362n37,
376nn17, 20
Carmelites, massacre of,
334
Case Against the Pagans
(Arnobius), 385n3
Catéchisme philosophique
(Feller), 70niii
Categories (Aristotle),
360n15
Catholic emancipation,
203nxxx
Catholic Way of Life
(Augustine), 59n52
Catholicism, state of, 327
Cato, 128nviii
Cattolicismo e civiltà
moderna (Omodeo), xxvi
n42
Causes: natural, 133;
nature of, 296; physical,
133–4; search for, 302
Caylus, 41n17, 74nxiv
Celsus, 299, 299n23
Chapelain, 193n101
Characteristics (Shafts-
bury), 103niv
Charlemagne, 92
Charles Emanuel IV, xiv
Charles V, 221
Charron, Pierre, 47, 151ni,
214
China illlustrata (Kircher),
114n13
Chinese language, 50
Christian dogmas, roots in
human nature, 356
Christian Gospel, and the
treatment of women, 370
Christian Paradoxes
(Bacon), 387n21
"Christianisme de J. de
Maistre" (Soltner), xvin44
Christianity: character of,

122; and doctrine of sacrifices, 266; and the ending
of human sacrifices, 367;
and idea of redemption,
381; as initiation, 275;
introduction to Japan,
274; introduction to
Rome; 276, 280; and pun-
ishment, 289; and the
Reformation, 327; and
role of women, 370; and
science, 122; and self-sacrifices, 267; and war, 214
Christians, confused with
Jews, 276–77
Chrysostom, St John, 314
ni, 316nv, 382, 391n64
Cicero, 11, 36n2, 37, 37n7,
49, 59, 59n53, 72nvi, 77
nxxvii, 88, 103ni, 103nii,
128nvi, 185, 185n85, 199
nniv, v, vii, 238n92, 245,
273, 276, 329, 355, 360
n7, 375n14, 388n25
Cinchona, 136
Cinchona bark, 136n5
Cioran, E.M., xxiii
Circumcision, 269
City of God (Augustine),
199nvii, 275n31, 284nvii,
385n2, 388n29, 391n63
Clarissa (Richardson),
127niv, 196
Clarke, Samuel, 53n40, 152
nv, 152n2, 191, 261nii
Clement of Alexandria,
307, 314ni
Clement, St, 316nvi
Cleopatra, 278
Cléry, Jean, 389n37
Coalitions, fragility of, 220
Cohen, illuminist grade,
331
Colebrook, 376n23, 386n17
Commentaire sur le Can-
tique des cantiques
(Guyon), 292n7
Commentaries on St. John
the Apostle (Chrysostom),
390n46
Commentaries on the Gal-

Shaftesbury, Anthony
  Ashley Cooper, 4th Earl
  of, 103niv
Shakespeare, William, xxi,
  56n45, 177n62
Shaw, Peter, 142n13, 346
  nvi
*Siegesgeschichte der christ-
  lichen Religion* (Jung-
  Stilling), 165n15, 336ni
Sin, and sacrifice, 268
Sleep: character of, 236;
  and divine communica-
  tions, 237; a human mys-
  tery, 236
Society of nations, impos-
  sibility of, 211
Socinianism, 329
Socinians, 335
Socrates, 59n53
"Soirées de J. de Maistre"
  (Vallin), xxvn24
Soirées de Rothaval
  (Nolhac), xxvin40
Soldier: agent of injustice,
  207; nobility of, 207; role
  of, 206, 208; terrible
  functions of, 215
Soldiers, character of, 214
Solis y Ribadeneyra, Anto-
  nio, 45n23, 340nv, 375
  n16
Soltner, Jean-Louis, xxi
Solzhenitsyn, Alexander,
  xxiii
Soul, distinguished from
  spirit, 354, 356
Souls, doctrine of two, 356
Sovereignty, 263
Spectacle of nature, 130
Speculations, dangers of,
  297
Speech: mystery of, 291;
  origins of, 65
Spinoza, Baruch, 251, 291
St Petersburg, 3
St Petersburg Dialogues
  (Maistre): character of, ix,
  xviii; composition of,
  xvi; identity of partici-
  pants, xvii; influence of,

xxii–xxiii; interpretation
  of, ix; literary form of, x;
  power of, xx; subtitle of,
  xviii; topics treated in, x
State of nature, 44–45;
  among nations, 210–11
Stay, Christopher, 153nxi
Steiner, George, ix, x, xxi,
  xxiii, xxivn6, xxvn36,
  xxvin53
Stillingfleet (Bishop of
  Worcester), 174, 179,
  181n77, 204nxxxii
Stoics, 118n18, 173, 199
  nvii, 291
*Storia della letteratura
  italiana* (Tiraboschi),
  73nxi, 196n114
Stourdza, Alexander, xxiv
  nn15, 20
Strabo, 378n38
*Studien sur literarischen
  Technik J. de Maistre*
  (Finger), xxvn30
Suarez, Francisco, 202
  nxxvii
Substitution: doctrine of,
  301, 312–14, 358, 364,
  366, 385; of merits, 295;
  theory of, 287
Suetonius, 338nii
Suffering: as punishment,
  84, 246; test for the just,
  248
Sufferings: of the innocent,
  314; of the just, 250, 264,
  270–71; utility of, 271–72
Suger, Abbot, 92
Summa Contra Gentiles
  (Aquinas), 62n61, 81
  nxxxviii, 152niv, 296n16,
  297n18, 314nii
Summa Theologiae
  (Aquinas), 14n8, 127nii
Superstition, 8, 268, 310;
  nature of, 305–6; and
  religion, 306
Swedenborg, Emanuel, xvii
Swift, Jonathan, 193
Symmetry, and intelli-
  gence, 252–53

Synonymes français
  (Girard), 305n27
Systema intellectuale (Cud-
  worth), 185n88, 378n38

Tacitus, 77nxxxvii, 97n23,
  222n18, 273, 279, 285
  nxii, 338nii
Tactique (Voltaire), 108n5
Talmud, 254
Tamara, Senator, xvi–xvii
Tasso, Torquata, 36
Te Deums, 223–24
Télémaque (Fénelon), 57,
  292n7, 386n16
Temple du goût (Voltaire),
  187n91
Terence, 77nxxxvii, 91n14
Tertullian, 386n13
Tetragrammaton, 28nii
Theaetetus (Plato), 65n65,
  127ni, 360n7
Theocrites, 78nxxxix, 79
  nxxx
Théodicée (Leibniz). 310
Theodicy, theme in *St
  Petersburg Dialogues*, xix
Theognis, 360n13
Theogony (Hesiod), 41n15,
  74nxvi
Theologicorum Dogmatum
  (Petau), 127niii
Theology: and European
  science, 300; and science,
  140
Theophobia, 148–9
*Theoria Philosophiae Natu-
  ralis* (Boskowich), 318n1
Theresa, St, 250, 308, 319
  nxv, 333
Thomas à Kempis, 24n24
Thomas, Antoine-Léonard,
  324n5
Thomassin, Louis, 55
Thompson, James, 143n14
Thought, essence of, 64
Three, reflections on the
  number, 326
Throne and Altar (Lebrun),
  xxvin43
Tiberius, 92n17, 96, 279